AMERICA'S MOST
HATED WOMAN

AMERICA'S MOST
HATED WOMAN

THE LIFE AND

GRUESOME DEATH

OF MADALYN MURRAY O'HAIR

ANN ROWE SEAMAN

continuum

NEW YORK • LONDON

2005

The Continuum International Publishing Group Inc
15 East 26 Street, New York, NY 10010

The Continuum International Publishing Group Ltd
The Tower Building, 11 York Road, London SE1 7NX

www.continuumbooks.com

Printed in the United States of America

Library of Congress Cataloging-in-Publication Data

Seaman, Ann Rowe.
   America's most hated woman : the life and gruesome death of Madalyn Murray O'Hair / Ann Rowe Seaman.
     p.   cm.
   ISBN 0-8264-1644-6 (hardcover : alk. paper)
   1. O'Hair, Madalyn Murray. 2. Atheists – United States – Biography. I. Title.
BL2790.O38S43 2005
211'.8'092 – dc22
                                                          2004022066

To my husband, Gary,
who suggested the topic;
to my family;
and to the U.S. Constitution

Contents

Part Two
THE MIDDLE

Part Three
THE END

The photo section follows page 218

Chapter 1 ~ Waterloo

AUSTIN, TEXAS, March 23, 2001. The sky was gray and drizzling, but the rain had stopped at the funeral home by quarter to nine. Bill Murray hadn't spoken to his three family members for more than 20 years, but he wanted to give them a decent burial.

The ceremony was kept secret from the public; for once in the deceased's lives, there were no news trucks. Only a handful of people stood at graveside — two lawmen, two FBI agents, Bill Murray and his mother's biographer, and a preacher. No prayers were said. "Baptists don't pray for the dead," Bill told the news media later. "They either accepted Christ before they died or they didn't."

He had had his mother cremated, in accordance with her oft-expressed wish. Her urn sat at the head of the burial vault, as was appropriate, for she had ruled the other two inside it with an iron hand. She was Madalyn Murray O'Hair, 76, the strident, brilliant, profane founder of American Atheists, a self-made millionaire, and the Most Hated Woman in America — a sobriquet she relished.

The remains of the other two in the vault were Madalyn's children, Jon Garth Murray, 40, and Robin Murray-O'Hair, 30.

None of the mourners but Bill had ever met Madalyn, but they all remembered when they had first heard her name. It was Madalyn Murray back then, that atheist woman from up North, who got prayer taken out of the public schools with a noisy Supreme Court lawsuit in 1963. Not long after, she moved to Austin. High school kids would drive by her house on Shoal Creek Boulevard and stare. She had gone on to file suit after suit, to get the government to tax the churches, to keep the astronauts from praying in space, to get the words "under God" out of the Pledge of Allegiance. She said God was sadistic and brutal, that believers were delusional, ignorant, groveling worms, and that the Constitution was not written by Christians. She said most American women were stupid cows, interested only in laundry detergent, or words to that effect. She was associated with the Vietnam War protests, Communism, and feminism. Some present at her grave remembered how in high school on November 22, 1963, the principal couldn't lead a prayer for their slain President.

It had taken five years to find the three bodies and bring their killers to justice. This was their second burial. The first had been a shallow, mass grave on a South Texas ranch. The bodies had been sawed up, doused with gasoline, and burned.

Gerald Carruth, the prosecutor who had searched for the missing family for nearly four years, remembered watching their excavation from that earlier grave a few months back, hoping it was really them this time. The one thing that wouldn't have decayed, he figured, was the hip-replacement joint Madalyn had gotten in 1988.

A shovelful of dirt was lifted, and there was the stainless-steel appliance, "shining in the sun like a trailer hitch."

In the shallow grave along with the three bodies was a fourth skull and a fourth pair of hands.

Ten months earlier, May 15, 2000, 201 prospective jurors packed the courtroom of U.S. District Court Judge Sam Sparks on West 8th Street in Austin, a few blocks from the Capitol. The room was also jammed with spectators and reporters awaiting the unfolding of a four-year mystery.

Judge Sparks charmed the jury pool and put them at ease. He resembled a jowly Jimmy Stewart, with direct, unblinking eyes. His turf was the huge Western District of Texas. He'd seen terrible depravity from the bench, and had heard in chambers some of the horrors of this case — murder, rape, the beheading of one who got in the way.

He wanted this trial to take no more than three weeks because the jurors had families, summer was coming up, swimming lessons, vacations, camp. The room seemed filled with people who had these busy lives. But some of them must have had lives closer to that of the trapped man sitting at the defense table, who had spent so many of his days in little cement rooms behind bars, where anyone could walk by and stare at him any hour of the day or night.

He was Gary Paul Karr, charged not with murder, but with "conspiring" to kidnap the Murray-O'Hair family and using force, violence, and fear to rob them of close to a million dollars in cash and possessions — activities which led to their deaths, said the prosecutors. They were trying Karr with no bodies, no witnesses to any murders, and no murder weapon.

The indictment didn't say who he conspired with, but the newspapers spoke of little else: David Waters, an ex-employee of Madalyn's, a charmer with a genius IQ and a dark past. In fact, said *San Antonio Express-News* reporter John MacCormack, Karr's trial was "a trial of David Waters in absentia."

MacCormack drove up to Austin from San Antonio nearly every day to cover the three-week trial, the climax of his dozens of stories on the Murray-O'Hairs and his uncovering of the crimes behind their disappearance. Before MacCormack's labors, the Austin police seemed indifferent that three prominent people had abruptly gone missing, though it was being covered by news media all over the world. Such was Madalyn's popularity in her adopted city.

It hadn't started out that way, in 1965 when she arrived in Austin. Like so many others, she fell in love with the town, picked in 1838 by Mirabeau Buonaparte Lamar, President of the Republic of Texas, as a likely capital. It was then a tiny settlement called Waterloo on the north bank of the Colorado River. Watered by spring-fed creeks, Austin was laid out between two of the prettiest, Waller on the east and Shoal on the west, with Congress Avenue up the middle, leading to the Capitol. The cross streets were named for the abundant native trees, and south of the river was beautiful Barton Springs, the spring-fed public swimming pool that, in its setting in Zilker Park, became the symbol of Austin's natural beauty.

By the time Madalyn arrived, Austin's character was stamped by independent spirits — both conservative Christians and iconoclasts — church-state separationists, and liberals who had informed the Texan character from the earliest days of the Republic. When she arrived, the "university of the first class" mandated by the Republic in 1839 — the University of Texas System — was already the incubator for the large high-tech and research consortiums that would dominate Austin's economy by the time she died.

A burgeoning hippie counterculture greeted Madalyn's arrival. Defined by youth, idealism, marijuana, peyote, cheap beer, and psychedelic drugs, it had transformed itself by the millennium into a powerful environmental preservation force, a fraternity of top-flight writers, artists, and entrepreneurs, and an eclectic music scene that made Austin an entertainment mecca for the world. Austin birthed the psychedelic music era that resonated in San Francisco's Avalon Ballroom and Fillmore Auditorium in the 1970s, and today the city's love of creatures of the night — from the huge colony of Mexican freetail bats that lived under the river bridges to that plated, night-hunting digging machine called the armadillo — included the many clubs and bars of Sixth Street, a few blocks from Sam Sparks' courtroom. There, thousands milled nightly, listening to blues, rock, folk, country, progressive, bluegrass, and party music, and drinking $4 bottles of designer beer instead of 50-cent quarts of Grand Prize.

Madalyn would call Austin home for almost exactly 30 years, until the day there was a fatal knock on the door of her American Atheist General Headquarters.

Part One

The Beginning

Chapter 2 ~ Madalyn Evalyn

MADALYN'S MOTHER, Lena Christina Scholle, was the daughter of hardworking German immigrants from the Pittsburgh glassworkers' suburb of Tarentum. One of ten children, Lena was farmed out at age ten to a rich family as an upstairs maid. She got up at six and made the beds before school, came home and tidied up after 15 or 20 people, and at week's end, took her one dollar's pay home to her mother. It was 1901.

Lena was always hungry. In the mansion, the family ate first, then the cook, then the servants. Child servants got the scraps. She used to watch with envy the pampered twin girls of another rich Tarentum family. They had long blond hair, dressed in lace and ruffles, and got driven around in a fringed surrey pulled by two ponies. Their names were Madalyn and Evalyn.

Lena made it through eighth grade. She later left to work as a domestic for several wealthy families in the seaside resort of Asbury Park, New Jersey. Tall and wiry, with a roguish smile, she fell in love with a jewel merchant's son.

She wandered back to Pittsburgh, and in the summer of 1912, met an ambitious farm boy from tiny Knox Township, Pennsylvania. Barrel-chested, with bright, slitted blue eyes, John Irvin Mays had style, dressing all in white and driving a fancy car when he could get one. After a night of carousing, the two impulsively decided to marry, though they barely knew each other.

Lena was 22, and had cast her lot with a 19-year-old carpenter and sometime milkman who worked 14-hour days for a little over a dollar. She tried to back out, moving in with her parents. Her married sister Marie, a telegraph operator, got her a job. But Mother Scholle wouldn't let her disgraced daughter be seen with the family or even sitting on the front porch. Lena moved in with Marie, and soon reconciled with John Mays.

Marie dabbled in the black arts and was suspected of having aborted three of her own babies with witchcraft. When her husband died suddenly and she married John Mays' brother David, tongues clucked wildly, and the two couples left Tarentum for Pittsburgh. There, John was introduced to the steelworking trade by a Jewish businessman named Sammy Passman, with whom he and Lena lived for a time.

Lena became pregnant, and on November 20, 1916, in the Pittsburgh suburb of Crafton, she gave birth to John Irvin Mays Jr. — "Irv" — near midnight. The 25-year-old mother was in a dangerous, excruciating labor for 48 hours. It had been "drummed into her head," she said, that "sex is sin and woman shall bring forth in misery," and this seemed to confirm it. She vowed to have no more children.

The vow lasted less than two years, and Lena tried everything to abort her second child — hot baths, chamomile, ergot. She turned to witchcraft in earnest with another sister, Annie. She ate a jar of mustard to start her pains. She climbed a ladder to the roof and jumped off.

In the spring of 1919, the Mayses were living above a bakery on a busy commercial strip in the Beechview area of Pittsburgh. One day, Lena threw herself down the steep, narrow stairs. Crumpled against the door, she couldn't get her breath; she made a fist and pounded it into her chest.

Soon after, she started labor, and just as she feared, the ordeal was worse than with Irv. After 72 hours, the doctor told John Mays he could save one of them, but probably not both. John replied that either they both should live or both die. "You SOB!" his wife screamed.

But the doctor was wrong; they both lived. At 9 a.m. on April 13, 1919, Palm Sunday, a 7.5-pound girl was born, blue, under a dark caul that the doctor had to remove so she could breathe. Lena was stressed to the point of shock. Nevertheless, gazing at the daughter who had defied her will and claimed her own fate, Lena hoped it would be a good one. She named the child Madalyn Evalyn, after the rich twins from Tarentum.

Let there be wealth.

The baby had a deformed chest, with a depression the size of her tiny fist, and her rib cage was misshapen. The former was actually a fairly common genetic defect, *pectus excavatum,* and was diagnosed immediately, but secretly Lena believed she'd caused it. The doctor and her parents talked about surgery to correct Madalyn's ribs and spine, and later in childhood, they were broken and reset.

Her birthday was the same as Thomas Jefferson's in 1743, and Madalyn would invoke his name like a charm during her life's work of trying to pry apart her homeland's Siamese twins of Church and State.

She loved "Pup," as she called her father, but their bond was blighted by a complex power struggle. When she was little, he called her "Sissy-Babe" and, according to her son Bill, recruited her to help hide his bootleg whiskey from the revenuers; her job was to lie on the back seat of his car and pretend to sleep so the lawmen wouldn't look for the reservoir of moonshine underneath. Later, in a backhanded tribute to his manipulative child, Pup dubbed her "the Spider," after a cunning, two-faced character in the Street & Smith pulp magazines he liked to read. They lived under the same roof and quarreled bitterly until the day he died.

Lena and Pup quarreled bitterly, too; Madalyn remembered watching the fights and feeling her mind grow calm. She learned early the value of being in control when others were not. It so marked her that she eventually sought out or created chaotic conditions so she could feel in control.

The Mayses moved frequently around the Pittsburgh area, living at addresses in Beechview, Brookline, and Mt. Lebanon. By the time Madalyn was seven or eight, they moved to a small brick home with a catalpa tree on steep, cobblestoned Gallion Street. Pup's widowed sister-in-law, Ada Mays, a typist, lived with them, as did his nephew Walter, a worker for the new Internal Revenue Service.

Madalyn had some happy memories of childhood — Fourth of July fireworks by one of Pittsburgh's three rivers, Easter egg hunts, parades. She learned to read early from Irv's schoolbooks, and loved the public library and the smell of books. And she loved Christmas, trimming the tree with Irv and helping Lena cook the feast, filling the house with music, presents, liquor, and cousins — both parents came from large families. Lena had acquired a taste and the skills for lavish entertainment in her girlhood, and she made yuletide a release from trouble and evil. Her whole life, Madalyn would love Christmas.

But the family's rise to the top of Gallion Hill was short-lived. In the late 1920s Pup and Sammy Passman split. Passman was blamed, and forever after, the Mayses called him Sammy the Shyster. Madalyn later branded numerous Jewish men she crossed — mostly lawyers — Sammy the Shyster.

Pup started his own construction business, but was broke by 1929, and the Mayses were on the move for the next four years. They lived with relatives in Pennsylvania and Ohio, including Akron and Cleveland; in Madison, Ohio, Pup and one of Lena's sisters reportedly opened a roadhouse that doubled as a sometime brothel. Madalyn missed a year of school because of all the moving.

The Depression was a time when fiery, itinerant preaching and bootlegging were cottage industries in America. Pup did both, running moonshine from West Virginia to Pennsylvania. In Akron, he added a bit of lay preaching to the subsistence carpentry that was barely keeping the family afloat.

"They'd work and then they'd quit workin'," said Madalyn's cousin Homer Lacy. "He was always into some kinda little business, nothing big. He's a Mays!"

Pup's widowed mother, Alice McHenry Mays, lived near Altoona, Pennsylvania, and the family moved there when Madalyn was 11 or 12. She was already a handful, and ran away from home at 13. But her grandmother, "old Al," loved and understood the girl. She sewed her granddaughter matching outfits, and shared her love of reading — Alice once got so absorbed in a book that she failed to notice that the kitchen had caught fire. When she died in 1936, Madalyn was devastated. It was her first traumatic loss, and she never forgot her intense grief. "My whole world shifted," she remembered in late life.

By 13, Madalyn was the dominant cousin in her extended family, and felt firmly that she was smarter and faster at everything. "Madalyn was conceited," cousin Homer Lacy said, "always a big shot." The other cousins didn't like her. "She wanted it *all*. She was knowin' everything. She was the top one . . . very smart. Was she bossy? She was *all* boss!" Still, he liked her, and they remained close throughout life.

Part of her arrogance came because she really could run circles around other children, especially Irv. Instead of getting the traditional worship due an older brother, Irv found his little sister intensely competitive.

Lena's dreams of glitter and class, of the jeweler's son, the rich little girls, and the soirées of the past gave way to hard work and good housekeeping. She taught Madalyn to iron, scrub, cook, launder, and clean. She joined discussion groups and committees — "always helping out and joining in stuff — had a big mouth, alla time a-hollerin'," was the way Homer Lacy remembered Lena — but her marital disappointment curdled early into emasculation, Bill Murray concluded. In fact, he said, the tendency might have been there from the start. Pup's mother was a domineering woman, and Pup had begun running away from home as a young child.

"The cousins and things [Madalyn] had up in Pennsylvania, *all* of the heads of households were women, and the kind of men that came through there, the father, the children, were ex-convicts and [such]. We never went to visit a ... relative but that the head of the household wasn't a woman. And this was in an era where that *didn't happen.* There was no such thing in the '50s.

"My grandfather ran away [from Lena] *many* times ... and [Irv] was completely dominated and controlled exactly the way my brother was [by Madalyn]." Irv had rheumatic fever in puberty, and was in a wheelchair for two years. But even before the illness, Lena had never allowed "Little Irvie" to attend gym at school, insisting he was too delicate.

One day, Pup had had enough. "You're gonna get up out of that goddamned wheelchair!" he told his sickly son. Lena shrieked protest.

"You get up out of that goddamned wheelchair up on those goddamned legs and *walk!*" Pup took the chair and threw it out of reach.

Irv got up and walked.

It was a dramatic assertion of their masculinity, but by adolescence, said Bill, "My grandmother had Irv 100% convinced that all women were whores except her. 'All they want is to rob you, take advantage of you — all of them except me, I'm the *only* woman who isn't like that.'"

Lena continued dabbling in the occult. "Virtually every Saturday night there was fortune telling in our house," said Bill. "She summoned up demons, she would burn hair — give me the hair of your enemy ... I'll put a curse on them."

There was a family tradition that Lena's grandfather had escorted Aleister Crowley on his 1914 visit to the U.S. Her family, the Scholles, Bill said, were also "involved with the darkest days of the union, getting votes by breaking people's knees with a baseball bat."

(Madalyn later confided that one of Lena's brothers went to prison in Pennsylvania for blowing up a mine after a failed attempt to organize a union. But during the Depression, Lena's youngest brother, August Scholle, rose to prominence as a labor leader. In 1935 he was elected president of his local union, and he later moved to Michigan and became an associate of both Henry Ford and Walter Reuther. He was elected a delegate to the Democratic National Convention several times.)

Yet even as Lena sought her children's fate in tea leaves and delved into the popular mysticism movements of her day, the other entrée to society was church. She took the children regularly, had them baptized, and taught them a bedtime prayer in her native German. Madalyn loved church, the "gleaming wood and nice, clean smells . . . starched little girls' dresses . . . everybody was on their best behavior." She liked preparing her Sunday school lessons, and getting little paste-on stickers for finishing. But Lena was ashamed that they didn't have enough money for a tithe.

One bored weekend, Madalyn claimed years later, she read the Bible through. When she realized what was actually in there — the cruelty and immorality — she peeked at her parents in the kitchen, and reflected with dismay that they actually believed this stuff. Visiting her grandparents a short time later, she was sent to get the mail, a mile or so walk. It was snowing, and when it stopped, the sun came out and she was snow-blinded. She thought she'd been struck blind because of her bad thoughts about God. Her reaction was not fear, but anger at a God who would so harshly punish a little girl. That was her official story of the seeds of her atheism.

Chapter 3 ~ Rossford, Ohio

BY 1931 MADALYN'S UNCLE August Scholle had a job as a crane operator in the young glassworking town of Rossford, Ohio, across the Maumee River from Toledo. Several of his brothers and his parents moved there from Tarentum. In the spring of 1933, Madalyn graduated from Bettes Corners School in Akron, and by fall, the Mayses were lodging temporarily in Rossford with Lena's brother Louis Scholle. It was a humiliation for Lena to take charity from her family.

Rossford was only 36 years old, a quintessential company town, drawing Catholic immigrants — Pavlicas, Tarkiewiczs, Stvartoks, Golbinecs — with the Libbey-Owens-Ford Glass Company funding their housing, libraries, and schools.

"So many people from Central Europe," said Madalyn's classmate Naomi Twining, "not forward-thinking at all . . . they were peasants, from a peasant background, and persecuted the Protestants." Protestant children were bullied by the Polish and Ukrainian Catholic kids, who called them "the English."

"It was a Town and Gown place," Twining said. You knew on which side of the tracks you belonged. Rossford was loaded with churches, but for ballast, it had 13 saloons. "Back in the old days," said a lifelong resident, "they used to come out from Toledo on the streetcar to watch 'em fight."

But it was also where some of Madalyn's ideas of government paternalism were forged, for stories abounded of how founder Captain Edward Ford would visit his sick workers and pay their grocery and medical bills, fund civic events, and build parks.

Pup found work as a laborer at L-O-F, and the Mayses moved to the Dixie Terraces, company row housing strung along the famous Dixie Highway through town. Madalyn, 14, was enrolled as a freshman at Rossford High, and Irv, nearly 17, a junior.

Rossford took seriously the job of a well-rounded education, and Madalyn's stout work ethic from Lena was reinforced at school, an imposing new Art Deco building — a far cry from the prison-like buildings her granddaughter's generation would fall heir to. It was academically rigorous, with many of the teachers holding masters' degrees. Christmas holiday was mostly a chance to study for January finals. This rigor was underpinned by religion — a school chapel program every week, sophisticated Christmas and Easter pageants. Good Friday was a school holiday, with Easter baskets provided to all by L-O-F.

"Little Irvie," as his sister mockingly called him even into adulthood, neither joined sports nor participated in any clubs or associations. With his long face and robust jaw, Irv had a peculiar kind of intelligence; he had no social grace at all, said Bill, but "You could give him a string of numbers ten deep and he could add them up just by glancing at it. You could ask him what's 534 times 631 and he could — *boom* — answer."

He and Madalyn walked home from school each day on opposite sides of muddy, unpaved Dixie Highway, quarreling loudly back and forth. Irv was tall and husky, "like her," remembered a classmate, "and he had black hair. They'd *fight* all the way home . . . They fought about anything and everything." In their arguments, nothing was off limits as to propriety; they made the most intimate personal attacks on each other's dignity and privacy, name-calling and accusing. No grudge was ever forgotten.

Madalyn was 5′ 7″, taller than her peers, and wore flat heels to diminish her height. She had learned to sew her own simple dresses in 7th grade in Ohio, with prim jabot or Peter Pan collars. She had long, elegant arms and legs, and wore her thick hair shoulder length and side-parted, with a deep wave at the temple. Though she had her father's husky shoulders and narrow eyes, and Lena's boxy jaw, she had a pretty cupid's-bow mouth and full, straight teeth.

She was witty, said Mary Jane Davenport, a fellow student; "She was *smart*. She told me she was going to design one of the big roads like we have now, the freeways. Her thoughts were of what she was going to do in the future . . . She always had bigger things in her mind."

She loved history and was outspoken in class. "She wanted to be president of the United States, wanted to be famous," said Arnold Frautschi, a classmate.

But the Mayses were outsiders, without many friends. Lena's brothers in Rossford had bought decent homes, while she and Pup lived in the Terraces and later in a rented cottage in nearby Northwood. "Their house was very austere, no decorative things at all," remembered classmate Betty Jane Ligget. "They didn't seem to have much. I didn't see any books . . . I would have noticed that. No books."

Pup soon left L-O-F. Madalyn's classmates recalled him being a rather mysterious character. "The mother and dad never seemed to be home for some reason or other," said Ligget. "The kids went home alone." No one knew how Pup made a living. "Rum runner, I heard that rumor . . . He was never home. They were *very much* loners . . . very secretive." Pup had aliases — John Ivan and John I. Martsoff. Neither he nor Lena was good with money; Lena had never written a check for a bill, and their life before Rossford was marked by crises from the department store tabs she ran up, bill collectors at the door, and repo men they dodged. By high school Madalyn was doing most of the family budgeting and making major purchasing decisions.

Madalyn never dated, or went to dances or games. Nobody recalled her ever attending church. Her best friend was Jeanette Zemanski, "a big, tall girl who rode her bicycle around all over town and never got married," said Davenport.

She got a crush on Jack Conn, a judge's son who was a year ahead of her, echoing her mother's unrequited crush on the jeweler's son. Conn was the "top boy" in his class all through high school — Class president, National Honor Society, Student Council. Madalyn joined several groups he was in — the newspaper staff, French Club, and Girl Reserves, sister club to the boys' Hi-Ys. But she knew he was out of her league.

(Writing about him in late life, she recalled "a miniature of Pup . . . blue eyes, wavy black hair." Interestingly, and consistent with the fluid sense of reality Madalyn would later exhibit, Jack Conn did not resemble Pup at all. He had brown eyes, straight hair, and a baby face.)

Madalyn performed well in school and skipped her sophomore year. She was coming into a distinctly political identity. She hung out at Brooks Drug Store, across from the Terraces. Izzy Brooks, a Jewish immigrant from Poland, held court with the area politicos. "You could have gone into the store at any hour of any day, and heard some kind of real exciting discussion — politics, cultural things, history," said his daughter, Ruth Palmer. "We always had the radio tuned to Saturday opera and Sunday afternoon symphonies."

Madalyn hungrily absorbed the discussions, the classical music. She associated them with the intellectual elite, to which Lena had taught her to aspire. "There was a good deal of conversation in my home," she said later, "that we had to have the best." Her mother romanticized the Chautauquas that died out in the 1920s, and "a thing called Elocution that swept all over the East in which people got in groups . . . and read poetry . . . I've got to say my father read, but I don't know what in the hell he read. I haven't the faintest idea."

The Brookses remembered Madalyn well. She was "really, really adamant about her beliefs," said Palmer, "that the government and society were not giving people like her a chance . . . people with ideas that don't fit the so-called norm."

She began reading the newspapers, feeling connected to a bigger, more exciting world. She fiercely wanted to join the Spanish Civil War, to volunteer as "an ambulance driver or something," she said later. "I was caught up in the tragedy of Spain. I just wanted to help the people of Spain."

"She was interested in what was going on down at the city," said Arnold Frautschi. "She talked a lot in civics class. It had to be political or she wasn't interested in it." She spoke of unionizing women, of equal pay for equal work.

"I don't remember any time in my life when I was not politicized," she said at 50. She remembered her parents talking about the despised "Hog Hoover" and how he should deal with the Depression, and about the official family hatred of William Howard Taft for his purported statement that "any working man, if he wasn't a pig," should be able to live on a dollar a day. She felt pressure to become a leader like Uncle Gus, and was in a constant state of upset and impotence over her inability to *do* something about the world's ills.

Her parents attended a group she remembered as the Rossford Roosevelt Recovery League, and Madalyn sometimes waited tables at their meetings, listening to them trying to organize pressure groups. One jobless member heaved a brick through the window of the Rossford A&P, and walked off with food, and no one dared arrest him.

"He was the town hero…a modern Robin Hood," Madalyn said later.

Around her 16th birthday, a rolling wall of dust boiled across 97 million acres of the Great Plains, blasting windmills and grain elevators and scouring the villages raw. The price of wheat had plummeted with the stock market, and now the crops perished with the drought and the "black northers" that continued until the end of the decade. The government started buying and killing cattle.

The Dust Bowl made a deep impression on Madalyn. By her 17th year, when the Social Security Act was passed (with the promise that citizens' numbers would *never* be used for identification) she had developed a firm faith in government's responsibility to rectify situations like that of the Robin Hood of Rossford. She promptly got a Social Security card — relishing later that her number contained 666, mark of the beast.

In May, 1936, barely 17, she graduated, wearing a dress with military epaulets, her hair sculpted into dramatic waves. That summer was to be her last in Rossford, and she remembered it wistfully — gazebo quartets and local band concerts with people dancing in the park, fireworks by the river on the Fourth. Living in Baltimore years later, she would go out of her way to drive past a certain gazebo in a downtown park that reminded her of Rossford.

Arnold Frautschi summed up those most stable years of her youth. You could see hints of her future, he said. "Remember Kennedy's statement about do whatever you have to for your government? Well, that didn't go down so good with her, or any of her cohorts who wanted to tax the rich, you know, and put some of that in their pocket."

Chapter 4 ~ Love and War

I N THE FALL OF 1936, Madalyn enrolled in the University of Toledo on a National Youth Administration scholarship, which she had to pay back by working at the school. She entered in pre-med, taking five courses. It was "understood," she later said, that Irv was going to be a lawyer and she a doctor, but she couldn't make herself dissect a frog. Irv had graduated the year before, and also entered the University of Toledo.

The family left at the end of her freshman year, in May 1937, as Pup wanted another try at the construction business in Pittsburgh. He started a small subcontracting business. Madalyn ran both the household and business accounts, handling payroll and bookkeeping. She enrolled in civil engineering classes at the University of Pittsburgh at Pup's behest, though Irv was the one Pup reported as his business partner. She also worked as a clerk at the telephone company.

Pittsburgh was "bustling... an upcoming city, a dirty, raw city, with a whole life centered on steel," Madalyn recalled, and Lena loved being back. After moving several times, they rented a nice house on top of a hill on Oneida Street, where Lena acquired a grandfather clock and a piano. She was an avid reader of *Good Housekeeping* magazine, the popular arbiter of taste for women. It solved ordinary problems like dishpan hands and underarm odor, but Lena also liked losing herself in the problems of the wealthy, like how to brighten up your summer cottage, and in the novellas about nurses falling for doctors, and shipwrecks in the Caribbean, that took away the Depression.

The magazine ads and stories showed an undercurrent of new values for women. They were shown driving automobiles, grabbing the check at dinner, smoking cigarettes. The new working-class women like Madalyn devoured secrets of being a lady (learn to charm men and not startle them, never wear too much jewelry or too-long nails); how to be stylish (eschew lugubrious talk of disease and disaster, learn to decorate with needlepoint); and how to clean and clean (Halo, Camay, Windex, Super Suds, Arrid, Lavoris, Ipana, Lux, Sani-Flush, Lysol, Rinso...). And, was it luck or just good sense that women had found Kotex?

But Madalyn was not a typical working-class woman. Though the ads and stories aroused in her a yearning to belong, she simply couldn't make herself cater to men and worry about "startling" them. She didn't linger on campus with the other students. She was so bored that at 19, unknown to her parents, she tried to talk a cousin from Chicago into running off and joining the army with her. (In fact, at 17, just after the family's return to Pittsburgh, she ran away with a truck driver, making "Missing Girl" headlines.)

As in high school, she didn't date. She was ashamed of the depression in her chest and her misaligned ribs. She never wore a low-neck dress — or belts, because of the lump at her waist. Changing clothes in high school gym class was agony. She would turn her back, cross her arms over her chest. She would take a bath with a slip on because she couldn't bear to look at her body. She never wore a bathing suit or a sweater. Even without the body shame, though, she knew she wasn't in the mainstream. You didn't see ads or stories about her kind of woman in *Good Housekeeping* — bright, aggressive, rowdy women who loved a good argument.

In the back of the magazine were dozens of small ads she and Lena grazed — for Eastern prep schools, finishing schools, academies, and conservatories. Highland

Hall, Miss Beard's School, Valley Forge Academy, Cedar Crest, Knox School. The kind of education the rich gave their children.

Like her mother, Madalyn married at 22. John Henry Roths worked for Pup, and was a year younger than Madalyn. On October 9, 1941, the couple eloped to Cumberland, Maryland, and were wed by a Methodist minister.

The marriage was an impulse, like Lena's had been. Madalyn was a virgin, and ashamed of it, she said later. She wanted to go ahead and lose her virginity and see what it was like.

She was shocked at the crassness of it. Her new husband expected her to just open her legs as soon as they got the nuptials out of the way. She wouldn't do it. Instead of "I love you," she told her cousin, "he said, 'Jesus Christ! You've *got* to get your legs apart!'" It was a bad start, but there was a lesson in it for Madalyn: the mystique and sacredness of sex were vaporized. Like everything else, it was just a commodity. But she understood that it was a very, very powerful one.

Roths moved in with his new in-laws, to a home in Pittsburgh's Mt. Lebanon area, but neither marriage nor business was going well on December 7, 1941, when, on a streetcar entering one of the Port Authority tunnels, Madalyn heard the news about Pearl Harbor.

She'd heard the military wouldn't take anyone who wasn't physically perfect, but she entered the Women's Auxiliary Army Corps with no problem on January 22, 1943, looking splendid and willowy in her uniform. That same month, she filed for divorce. Roths joined the Marines.

Madalyn's 150 IQ qualified her for officer training, and by May, she was a Second Lieutenant in the Women's Army Corps, and a cryptographic officer for the Signal Corps.

Before she shipped out to Algiers, she visited Pup, who'd had gallstone surgery but couldn't get out of the hospital until his bill was paid. Madalyn wrote the hospital a check, but then went to the bank and stopped payment. Shortly after arriving in Algiers, she was called in by her commanding officer. She was accused of committing "larceny by trick" and threatened with court-martial. She managed to convince her superiors that the $80 deception was not worth losing a trained officer. They allowed her to wire the money to Lena, and she was abruptly transferred to Italy.

She never got over that incident, storming about it even decades later. Someone had had to rat her out to her superiors for the hospital to find her. Pup would never have told; he'd taught her that stop-payment trick himself. It must have been either her mother or "Little Irvie," she told her cousin. She nursed that grudge her whole life, for she enjoyed outsmarting people and getting out of scrapes, and the only way to defeat her was either trickery or betrayal. She would navigate hundreds of close calls in her life, and develop an addiction to brinkmanship and even danger.

In Algiers, she had a denouement. "The higher officers from chicken colonels on up had women," whom Madalyn was ordered to train on the switchboard. That rankled, but when they were put into WAC uniforms, she got the other WACs to refuse to work until the French women were got rid of. It led to an argument in her unit about whether people had the right to strike during wartime. When Madalyn argued that morality itself was subjective, one of the other officers said, "You're nothing but an atheist!" She rather liked the distinction; no one else was accused of it.

One of her jobs in the army was to write detailed descriptions of battles that hadn't been fought yet — down to the time of day they marched down a specific street — and put the victory out on the newswires. "Hell, they didn't take those [towns] for two weeks and later sometimes . . . just all of this was a pack of lies. But those things went out over the teletype regularly." The ability of those in power to manipulate the media, and to lie and get away with it, impressed her.

Her three years in the military broadened Madalyn. She got to visit Paris and Rome, and a passion for travel was born, a never-ending quest to recapture those heady days. It "was probably the most exciting time that I ever had . . . I was still provincial until I got to Europe." In France, she had another denouement, seeing flowers painted on the toilet seats. She realized that these people weren't ashamed of bowel movements or private functions like she was. She saw children running naked on the beaches, and realized that this was natural. These people didn't entertain body shame like hers.

If France released her from guilt about bowel movements and nudity, Italy changed her idea of what a whore was. Her fellow soldiers brought women "into our mess halls and into the restaurants, and the hotels where we were assigned . . . because they were going to take and lay them that night and the thing they could do was give them some food before they did this."

She watched the women stuff extra food into pockets and purses and scarves. "And you knew gawd-damn well they were taking that home to their kids." And, she thought, given these circumstances, she'd be a whore too.

Another death-knell of her provinciality was being an officer. She was among monied, educated people who were now her peers, not distant power figures echoing through the prep-school ads in the back of Good Housekeeping. It was one of the few settings where she was unable to immediately show dominance, and she allowed herself to be swept along — especially by one William Joseph Murray Jr. of Long Island. He was an officer in the Eighth Army Air Corps, "the son of a large and wealthy Roman Catholic family" and one of 13 siblings, she said.

He was tall, handsome, dashing — and married, with children. But the time spent listening to opera and classical music at Brooks Drug Store and learning to play Lena's piano now stood her in good stead, for she felt cultured. Murray's brothers, Matt and Morgan, infantry officers who met her on a stay in Paris, liked her. Her uncle Gus Scholle was traveling to Yunan, China, representing the CIO War Relief Committee, and Madalyn arranged to have him contacted by one of the Murray brothers in a way that showed she had important connections.

Madalyn's wit, cunning, and ribald sense of humor, sharpened by barracks life, took Murray's breath away. She was charming and generous, yet fearless; she never backed down from a fight. He wrote her years later,

> ... in our first year you were ... everything I wanted ... [You] gave me your complete love and solace, your understanding and your comfort ... The chance to hold my head high in combat and to win a few of America's Honors was due to the *courage* and *spirit* you helped me to use ...

Her restless questioning of authority was accepted in the brash climate of war. Among the ancient ruins and great architecture of Europe, in an intense brew of danger and romance, she was liberated from the hooks set in her flesh by family, class, and culture. There was a sense of license. Promiscuity was rampant in the army. She started her affair with William Murray Jr. in November 1944. He was shortly transferred to Germany, and Madalyn told an FBI agent years later that, on the day before her 26th birthday in 1945, she and Murray "pledged to each other that [we] were to be man and wife in order to create a common law marriage."

But it was August 24, 1945, that would "always be a *very* special day" for him, Murray wrote her afterward. He had a two-week leave, and he chose to spend it with Madalyn in France. Exactly nine months later, she gave birth to his son.

Chapter 5 ～ Master William Mays

MADALYN REMEMBERED LAUGHINGLY how the replacement depots were all named after cigarettes — Camp Lucky Strike, Camp Chesterfield — and when Germany and France collapsed, they started filling up with people waiting to be sent to the Far East. No one, she said, had a clue about the atom bomb.

Asked years later what she was looking forward to after getting out of the army, she couldn't remember wanting to get out. But in September 1945, Japan surrendered, and there she was, going home like everyone else — except she was pregnant. That ended any chance of an army career; mothers weren't allowed.

She was shipped home by boat, arriving on U.S. *terra firma* November 7. Her parents and Irv had moved back to Ohio, first renting a house in the small town of Mansfield, and then a farm on Trimble Road at nearby Hayesville, partly with money she sent home.

It was hard to face Pup with her thickening waistline. He had begun to study and take comfort in the Bible, and spirituality played a role in weaning him away from his hard-drinking ways shortly before Madalyn returned. It soon became clear that William Murray was not going to divorce his wife, and Pup came down hard on his daughter. They pulled out weapons sharpened since before she'd run off with the trucker. He hammered on her for her even rottener morals gotten overseas, and her fouler mouth. She fired back that the money she'd sent home had got squandered on drink. But she was cut to the quick by his disapproval.

In the army, Madalyn had come to openly question organized religion. Now, when William Murray wouldn't marry her, she blamed his Catholicism. She was carrying his child. She was a unique woman who stimulated his mind, while his wife was a cud-chewing Catholic baby machine. Her arguments with Pup served only to fuel her contempt for religion.

"My grandfather *feared* God," said Bill. "I remember him shouting at my mother, 'Madalyn, one of these days God is going to get you for what you do!'" One night after a vicious session with him, in anemic imitation of Lena — who for some reason had repeatedly told Madalyn of her attempts to tear her from the womb — Madalyn infuriated him by going out in a lightning storm and cursing God, daring Him to strike her and her unborn child dead if He was so almighty.

But despite the fights, the excitement began to build of a new life in the family. In January of 1946, Madalyn applied for a Veterans' Administration loan to buy the farmhouse, barn, and milk cow. Hayesville was a sweet little hamlet that petered out into two-lane roads with little stone bridges, fields of corn and pumpkins, and stock tanks.

Madalyn loved nature and gardening, and she planted azaleas and spirea, whose clusters of tiny white flowers always touched her. She loved seeing the trees spurt their fiery fall colors, and the dust-devils of orange and red and yellow leaves swirling in the wind of the first icy norther. They planted cherry trees and strawberries, and in the spring, peonies.

On May 25, 1946, she gave birth in Mansfield. The certificate read William Irvin Mays, after the baby's father and grandfather, but a year later, Madalyn withdrew the homage to Pup and amended it to William Joseph Murray III. But it was several more years before she used the surname Murray, either for herself or Bill.

Not even her army experience could equal the thrill of pregnancy and mother-hood. Madalyn had high hopes and plans for her baby; before he was a year old, she started a classical library for him. Once a month, a book came in the mail for "Master William Mays" — *Robinson Crusoe, Pinocchio, Gulliver's Travels, Idylls of the King.*

When Bill was three months old, she entered Ashland College while Lena cared for the baby. She took small jobs but had trouble holding them; Bill later wrote drolly that it was because her intelligence and wit were so threatening to others. But it was hard to go from an officer who had seen Paris and Rome to a clerk in Ohio, where people's curiosity about the baby's father set her teeth on edge.

When Bill was two, Madalyn got a job in the advertising department at nearby Wooster Rubber Company, and opened a college fund for him at Farmers Bank in Ashland. The deposits were small — mostly 10 or 12 dollars; once she even deposited 26 cents. But she was determined he would be educated.

In 1946, a 14-year-old West Virginia-born girl named Betty Ann Plumley sat with a friend on her mother's front porch in Peoria, Illinois. A handsome sailor-boy in his early 20s walked past, eyeing her. He looked just like the movie star Gilbert Roland.

"*Hey!*" She pointed at him. "I'm gonna marry you!"

His name was George Waters, and less than a year later, on March 24, 1947, Betty gave birth to his son.

David Roland Waters, she named the baby, though his father slipped away. He was the first of her five sons.

David was beautiful, with black hair and eyes. He would turn out striking, a magnet for women, loaded with brains and charm, bold in nature, fun-loving, articulate. A lady-killer.

He was born less than a year after Bill Murray. But his 15-year-old mother had no thought of a library of great books or a legacy of intellect, wealth, and service for David. She was just trying to get by, maybe have a little fun.

At Ashland College, Madalyn concentrated on history. It was being made in Detroit, where the Board of Education was considering a 40,000-signature petition of Wayne County mothers to require daily recitation of the Ten Commandments and the Lord's Prayer in the public schools, to "reduce juvenile delinquency."

Arthur Cromwell, a board member of the National Liberal League (NLL) in New York and a staunch advocate of church-state separation, helped draft a protest against the Detroit petition. Mumbling magical words wasn't going to make our country great — you had to teach children ethics. "What is a child to understand by a daily repetition of 'thou shalt not commit adultery'?" His group cited a recent spate of murders by churchgoing youth.

The NLL was also watching a case in Iowa where the parochial schools had petitioned to use public school buses. They were taxpayers, and had a right to them. That ruling would go against the churches.

These skirmishes were representative of many around the country that set the stage for Madalyn's blastoff to fame in the early 1960s. But Cromwell had a special interest in them. His daughter, Vashti McCollum, had a groundbreaking case before the U.S. Supreme Court. In fact, in 14 short years, Madalyn would win Cromwell's support for a time, before her falling-out with his daughter.

McCollum had filed her suit the year before Bill was born. Her son Jim was being pressured to take an hour of regular religious instruction in his public grammar school in Champaign, Illinois every week. The McCollums weren't churchgoers. When Jim was made to sit in the hall in the detention chair, he came home crying. The school was unresponsive to the McCollums' efforts to find a compromise.

"I thought, If he can't take it, I can't take it," wrote McCollum, and filed suit to end religious instruction in the city's schools. It reached the Supreme Court, which ruled in 1948 for McCollum, saying that the First Amendment ("Congress shall make no law respecting an establishment of religion, or prohibiting the free exercise thereof") erected a wall of separation that forbade religious groups to use public classrooms to push their beliefs.

(The "wall of separation" language, quoted by Justice Hugo Black from an 1802 letter Thomas Jefferson wrote to a group of Connecticut Baptists, became, with the *McCollum* decision and one called *Everson v. Board of Education* the year before, the foundation stone for an unrelenting judicial push toward a more secular society. "Wall of separation" was picked up and used so frequently and uncritically in discussions, newspaper reports, books, and articles that it slipped unnoticed from metaphor to constitutional doctrine, with judges and advocates soon warning of cracks in the wall, speaking of how high and impregnable it must be, and lamenting breaches of it. Soon it was axiomatic that the First Amendment dealt directly with church-state separation, though Jefferson himself repeatedly asserted that the amendment's role was to *restrict* government. His "wall," said later analysts alarmed at the term's co-opting of constitutional principles, was between state and federal governments, not churches and any government. It wasn't meant to snuff out religion's influence or expression in the public commons. In fact, Jefferson was living in France when the First Amendment was proposed, drafted, and passed.)

The *McCollum* decision caused a national uproar. That fall, the 14 Catholic bishops of the U.S. met in Washington, pushing to reverse Supreme Court rulings that would "ban God from public life" and warning against the "legalistic tyranny of the omnipotent state." They said secularism was corrosive, eating into America's religious foundation. They said the First Amendment simply means that government won't establish a state religion. Nobody was forcing young Jim McCollum to attend the classes. They said the *McCollum* case would eliminate all cooperation between churches and government. If the government was to suddenly become secular, against centuries of tradition, it should at least follow a full public discussion, rather than being dictated by a handful of ideologues on the bench.

These arguments were persuasive, including the notion that American educational ideals were underpinned by Christian values. But when the bishops concluded that "Christ must be the Master in the classrooms and lecture halls and the director of our research projects," they seemed to be counting the days until science and evolution were forbidden in the classroom.

By the early 1950s, despite the *McCollum* ruling, confusion reigned. In 1952, the U.S. Supreme Court seemed to agree that the separation issue was between the states and the federal government, not the "state" and the churches, because it declined to outlaw the Bible reading mandated in New Jersey's schools. That gave a green light to the other 34 states that allowed or required such readings. A month later, the Court upheld a New York state law allowing kids to leave school for off-campus religious studies. "We are a religious people," said the Court, and our institutions "presuppose a supreme being." This is the best of our traditions, it said.

The Catholic bishops of the U.S. agreed, urging that religion was critical to good citizenship, and the state had a *duty* to help by not secularizing the nation's schools. That duty included federal aid for buses and textbooks for parochial school students — aid now stalled in legislative committees. These would be tomorrow's government employees, after all. Government wasn't secular — even foreign aid owed its impetus to the religion that inspired the charitable impulse. And the working man's rights relied on the religious conscience of the nation.

But a meeting of 30 Protestant groups from across the world said parochial schools should not get government aid. The way to get more religion in government was for religious people to run for office. A German bishop said only Christianity could conquer Communism, and another said Christians were partly responsible for the spread of Communism because they had put their faith in "money, schemes, and weapons" rather than God.

Incoming secretary of state John Foster Dulles warned at the meeting that there was something wrong with American life; we needed a spiritual revival, lest Communism replace the "ennobling purpose" that underpinned freedom.

But even as they spoke, those Christian underpinnings were turning out to not be exactly what their advocates thought. Near the Red Sea, archaeologists continued their work of several years on ruins they'd at first thought were a Roman fort, but now appeared to be an Essene monastery. They'd already found scrolls containing versions of the Old Testament with descriptions of rites such as baptism and communion, that Christians said were uniquely theirs.

Some of the scholars' work was decried as heresy. The unraveling was begun, but Madalyn was not yet interested.

Chapter 6 ~ "I'm an outsider"

By CHRISTMAS 1948, Madalyn had managed to scrape over $100 into Bill's college account. But Pup took off in 1949 for Texas to join a cousin in the oil fields. Madalyn left her job with Wooster Rubber Company in January, and took a receptionist job with the Social Security Administration in Mansfield until her semester at Ashland College was done. Then she, Irv, and Lena loaded up two cars and left for Houston to find Pup.

Bill was three. "My very first actual memory of my mother is an argument between her and my uncle driving from Ohio to Texas," he said. "Irv was out of gas. It was the wee hours of the morning. The argument was because Irv had not filled the tank, but instead put in an even number of dollars — the number thing!"

Madalyn left Bill with her parents and returned to Ohio to attend Ohio Northern University College of Law. In the spring, she returned to muggy Houston and entered South Texas College of Law, working as a probation officer for Harris County. Pup was now selling real estate, and the family rented a house where Bill put a small

American flag up on the front lawn. "Irv got upset . . . He said this was part of the Confederacy, they'll come get us."

The family stayed in Texas three years, and Madalyn received an LLB degree on July 30, 1952. She was supposed to be the doctor and Irv the lawyer, but at least one family dream got fulfilled. It was a huge triumph over her parents' limited educations, even though she never got a license to practice. (Bill said it was because she'd failed the bar. She always maintained it was because she couldn't bring herself to utter the "so help me God" required to get licensed.)

In 1952, Pup once again left the family behind, this time for a business venture with a sister-in-law's family in Baltimore. They packed up and followed him. The business deal petered out as Pup became ill from work injuries and a weak heart, and he retired, drawing a small income from Social Security. His nephew Homer Lacy, now well-off, helped the Mayses finance a modest row house in Baltimore, and gave Irv a job.

It was a three-bedroom unit at 1526 Winford Road, in a white, working-class neighborhood across from Northwood Elementary, where Bill started school. Madalyn wanted a library, and she and Pup built shelves all along the walls in the basement. Irv began his own library — a massive pornography collection kept under lock and key in his bedroom. He got a night job at the Bendix Corporation, and Madalyn began looking for a job.

On January 5, 1953, Madalyn started a diary, a "tabulation of personal, national and other events." She would faithfully write in it for more than 42 years. Her first words were about money; they needed decent clothing and a tithe, so the family could go to church.

"Bill has no overcoat or hat; Dad and Irvie have no hats . . . We had always said, Mother and I, that we never had at one time hat, shoes, dress, and a permanent . . . and it appears that we never will."

She didn't view church as a spiritual path; it was a social commodity, listed along with other commodities she couldn't afford — piano and dance lessons for Bill, patio furniture, a new car.

They settled into a routine of starchy meals, daily quarrels, and a television that ran at full volume from daybreak until sign-off. Mornings Bill would be awakened by loud disagreements; he recalled the almost-nightly dinner rituals in which Pup would sit silent while Madalyn commented until she threw down the right gauntlet. Then, after half an hour of vicious combat about what caused the Depression or the wars and who had the wealth and why things were unfair, he would make some dismissive comment about her character and leave the room, dripping with dignity, while she hurled impotent insults at his back.

"She constantly tried to emasculate [Grandfather]. He had to believe *exactly* like her," said Bill. "She tried to get me to kill him . . . she said it would be so peaceful without him around, that he was the cause of most of our problems . . . For a few months, my mother managed to twist me enough that I hated my grandfather. I believed everything was his fault. I don't remember how I reversed myself from that."

The most vicious arguments "were about my mother's personal behavior. They were about her coming home drunk in the middle of the night. You know, relationships with married men, about her not taking care of her children, and leaving them to my grandmother to raise. [They] were these horrible, dysfunctional family type arguments, screaming and name-calling."

In later life, Madalyn often wrote that she loved Pup. She wrote of him with affection, and "talked" to him in her diaries. But she also despised his lineage. "Uncouth, dirty, vulgar," she called them all. "None of the Mays side made it. Jesus Christ, we are cattle." She later called Pup a slave driver, Nazi, and racist. As for her mother, "None of the Scholles got going but Gus," but "I owe her a debt not repayable for how she has reared [Bill]," wrote Madalyn in 1952. "We love him so. He is a beautiful child — so beautiful and well behaved it raises a fear in me. This can't have happened to me."

Madalyn privately marveled at how her mother stuck by Pup and devoted herself to the family, how their life revolved around her. Lena kept order and cleanliness and a comforting routine of regular meals — "German heart cloggers," a friend called them, but nourishing and regular. She and Madalyn had a cozy evening ritual: after washing up the supper dishes, they sat at the table, chatting and drinking hot tea spiked with what Bill thought was wine, and Madalyn later said was Southern Comfort. The boy was the only male included in this custom; Irv was not invited, and Pup, now a nondrinker, sat in the living room glued to the TV.

Madalyn was lonely, and despaired that men her age preferred not women but girls, with their "bouncing pep and vitality, the giggle, and the awe of the male" — attributes she lacked. But she knew those attributes were currency, and without some form of it, she would never form a union and break away from her parents. "I need to unlock again my emotions. I need to love," she told her diary. "I have been pent up and hard and cynical too long. I need to be a woman — soft and yielding."

She was seeing Bill's father, in a struggle to define their relationship. He wrote a profuse apology to Madalyn for ignoring her after their son was born. But his refusal to make her part of his life was a deep wound. She began using the name Murray, and took her ex-lover to court to prove paternity. But his surname and Bill's child support were the only two prizes she would wring from her fateful brush with William J. Murray Jr.'s lofty world.

She applied for a job with the Welfare Department, but her former employer in Houston wrote "a condemning note" refusing to recommend her. In December 1952, she got a job in the engineering department at Glenn L. Martin Aircraft in Baltimore, a large manufacturer of bombers and transport planes. The job, doing drafting work, required security clearance up to "Secret" by the Navy. But she hated it from the start. Her fellow employees were narrow and ignorant, and she felt none of the brotherhood of the workplace. The math required for her job was beyond her.

She hated the row houses where they lived; "nests of bees," she called them, "Identical homes with identical people in identical lives." The units were all faced with red brick, each with a tiny front and back yard and common walls. "Life-hating puppets," she called her neighbors, "who plod without hope, or love, or meaning..." And yet, she wrote, "...truly I long to be part of society."

She was bored, her mind spinning like a disengaged gear wheel. "What good," she wrote, was "a restless, seething brain when it only works to kick up foam?"

She volunteered for duty in the Officers Reserve Corps, but the army required that her mother legally adopt Bill, so she withdrew.

"I have no hope for a future," she wrote after only weeks at Martin. Her boss later told the FBI that he "did not consider [Madalyn] a satisfactory employee, and would under no circumstances re-employ her or recommend her for employment. [She was] hired only because of the extreme shortage of help... Her associates were of questionable character, and the Probation Department had many reasons to question her loyalty. She was given to gossip, and could not take supervision, in addition to being an avowed atheist."

Nevertheless, by August of 1953, she was promoted to trainee engineer, and to junior architectural engineer in March of 1954.

Around that time, she met Michael Fiorillo, a Martin engineer who could help with some of the math in her job. She began an affair with him. He was another Catholic.

"He folded me into his arms and naturally and completely kissed me like I have wanted to be kissed for 20 years," the 34-year-old told her diary. "I was so absolutely pleased and surprised. I almost got kittenish."

She called him a "Damn Dago," but he made her feel like a woman; "I felt *handled* by him." She liked his hands, his "liquid" way of moving, and his love was an emotional and physical balm. She lost weight and started menstruating regularly again; strife, worry, and unhappiness had upset her cycles.

As with the other men she brought around, Pup didn't approve of Mike Fiorillo, daring to present himself at their home and confusing young Bill, who was already showing signs of emotional distress. There was something tragic about Bill, Madalyn wrote. He had a block about reading, he was sickly, hooked on the television. She tried to remedy it, to give him values and something to strive for, but Bill only remembered it as pressure to be a trophy child; he was given complicated birthday toys he was too young to master — an elaborate erector set at six, a microscope at seven.

When Madalyn found out she was pregnant, she knew immediately what she'd done. As she told a historian 16 years later, "I had to get out of there [Martin Aircraft]. I got out by getting pregnant." She quit in July 1954.

One night, a worse-than-normal fight in the kitchen intruded on Bill's television watching. He ran in to see his mother hurling plates at Pup. One hit Irv, cutting his wrist. When she seized a knife and charged them, the men disabled her and took it away. Pup had made cutting remarks about her swelling belly and loose morals until she could take no more.

Later, in misery, she castigated herself in her diary. Naturally, Fiorillo wasn't going to marry her — in fact, she didn't even try this time. She didn't respect him. Pup was right, she *was* irresponsible. Getting pregnant and quitting her job, and a month later she was listed with Retail Merchants Collection for unpaid debts — and yet, didn't Pup love Bill, another product of her immorality? During her unhappy pregnancy, her frustration boiled over. Once, on a ferry ride with Bill to a hearing on her paternity suit, "I was misbehaving," said Bill, "and she picked me up and held me out over the water and threatened to throw me in. It had enough of an impact that I developed a fairly morbid fear of drowning. I had trouble driving over a bridge."

Years later, she confided to one of her attorneys that she was deeply ashamed of the illegitimacy of her children. Divorce was shocking enough in the 1950s, but a "bastard" was a white-trash scandal. And she'd done it twice. But she never let Pup know how deeply his judgment had taken root in her. The two of them were always in slit-eyed, bawling combat for the high ground.

On November 16, 1954, she gave birth. "My little Dago cries and storms and screws his little face up in an ugly wrinkled apple and gets sour milk odor to him," she wrote, "but no one but me had better say anything about him or try to do anything to him . . . "

She named him Jon Garth Murray. The name Garth was a whimsy, according to Bill, and Murray was to spare her child the stigma of a different surname. Jon was an overture to her father, but Bill found it hard to credit his mother with sentiments untainted by malice when it came to Pup.

"She picked that name [Jon] because of [Pup], but left out the *h*. You see, she's going to honor him by giving him the name John, but not honor him *enough* to spell it properly." Indeed, she never called the child by any name but Garth.

In 1915, the year Lena reconciled with her husband, Freethinkers of America was formed. Joseph Lewis, the driving force behind it and an early advocate of athe-ism, would be one of Madalyn's mentors for awhile. He helped incorporate the organization in 1925 and start the Freethought Press Association.

The freethought movement in America had roots back to the Renaissance, when thinkers and artists began questioning the repression of the Catholic Church and the superstition to which it owed its success. By the end of the Renaissance, freethought had sent tendrils throughout Europe, in groups like the Ranters, a short-lived organi-zation in mid-17th century England that had ideals in common with the Quakers. (Like later secular humanists, the Ranters did not believe in sin, and thus had no

need for a risen Savior to absorb it. Nature, not a book of words, was the sacred expression of God. The Ranters believed people had an "indwelling spirit" that knew
how to be whole and good.)

The flowering of science during the Enlightenment fueled the maturation of reason and independent thought over blind obeisance to supernatural forces from
which morality had always been assumed to flow. Good behavior, freethinkers
said, didn't require dangerous, unquestioning obedience to religious dogma; society's need for morality and ethics was made perfectly clear through rationality
and logic. Though many freethinkers kept ties with Christianity via deism, some
broke completely with all religion. In France, Voltaire broke with Christianity; the
Encyclopedists, led by Diderot and informed by Voltaire, rejected all religion.

The oldest of several atheist organizations in the U.S. was the American Association for the Advancement of Atheism, founded in 1925 by Charles Lee Smith,
an attorney persuaded by the lives and works of people like Voltaire, Bertrand
Russell, 19th and 20th century British freethought and atheist reformers Charles
Bradlaugh, Annie Besant, and Chapman Cohen, and the great American rationalist orator Robert Green Ingersoll, among many others. Smith had written for the
Truth Seeker, an old independent freethought journal published in New York, for several years before founding the AAAA, and he entered a life of activism, debating
prominent Christian ministers and opposing anti-evolution laws in various states.
He purchased the journal, and later formed the Truth Seeker Corporation. He would
become a backer of Madalyn, and his organizations would become entangled in her
ultimate fate.

The freethought movement in America also spawned the Friendship Liberal
League, the National Liberal League, the American Rationalist Association, American Secular Union, Ethical Culturists, and others, whose aims were to further
moral, intellectual, and ethical life outside of religion. Lectures, debates, concerts,
and programs were its initial format, but politics was not far behind, and Madalyn
would be prominent in its expression.

After Garth was born, she saw an ad for *Progressive World* and sent for a copy. It
was the publication of a New Jersey atheist group, one of the few in the country,
the United Secularists of America. Its president had served as the Governor of
California during the war, refusing to say "so help me God" at his swearing-in. She
also got interested in the *Truth Seeker*, with its liberal positions on gender equality
and labor reform, and its emphasis on science and reason as emancipators of the
human race.

Those two ideals, atheism and freethought, would be where Madalyn found her
political destiny. By February of 1955, she'd decided on her ground. The twice-
unwed mother knew she was never going to join the *Good Housekeeping* ranks of
five-minute fudge, neighborhood coffee klatches, and Junior in letter sweater and
Sis in ponytail joining hands around the Christmas tree with Mom and Dad. She
was sick of the "moral code inculcated in school, church... Everyone is playing

a horrible game...one must lie and cheat and steal and dissemble to belong to society."

She lived, she wrote, "by raw rules that disgust, revolt, and injure," and she'd keep doing it. "I will be ostracized, by my own volition, from society henceforth."

In the spring, she made a concerted effort to stop drifting. She tried to get her job back at Martin Aircraft, and refinanced her loans, telling the credit bureau she was divorced from William Murray. In April 1955, she hired on as a caseworker at the Children and Family Aid Society of Baltimore County. She tried to weave it in with her legal training; the social and legal systems should work more in tandem, she felt, and tried to influence judges and agency heads to reform them.

But her restless idealism found no ready place in the thriving 1950s. She only marked herself as a troublemaker. By November, an acquaintance was complaining to the FBI that Madalyn had had Socialist Labor Party literature sent to her after the two had chatted and Madalyn mentioned she'd become a Socialist. The acquaintance wanted the FBI to know she was not a Com-symp.

Madalyn hooked up with others who were unhappy with American society. The Socialist cause was the best civilian life could offer to replace the camaraderie of the army. "Fighting for a cause and fighting for the good thing" — that was what she wanted from life.

She met Bob Lee, a bright, engaging Fuller Brush salesman and member of the Communist Party U.S.A. Under his influence, she became involved in liberal and leftist causes, volunteering the family's basement for several Socialist groups to meet. Her new companions were filled with a sense of mission. They identified with "the workers"; they believed America the most ruthless, exploitative system in history. America needed a classless society, with collective ownership of all industry.

Once again Madalyn found she was smarter than many of the people she encountered, and thought more critically. "And then I started to talk and I've never shut up."

It was a liberal shibboleth that if you got smart people to study the world's problems, and you got intelligent, educated people to come up with solutions, then the social ills of the world could be eliminated one by one. That idealism swirled through government, universities, and the military — especially among the officers. They could see the vision of Socialism, the righting of wrong through revolution, and they sympathized with a lot of the ideals of Communism, with the dismantling of the ruling class. And both the intelligence branches of government and the Communist party recruited through the higher education system.

"With the army indoctrination at the time, a lot of people came back from the war leftist-leaning," said Bill, "because we said that the Communists are our friends and the Nazis are our enemies."

The army exposed Madalyn to leftist views, and the Officers Corps to money. Bill's father took her to expensive places that impressed her. Her high regard for education was cemented in the Officers Corps.

Finding most leftist groups small-minded and pedantic, she investigated the Socialist Workers Party — SWP, founded in 1938 by Trotskyites who had been expelled from the U.S. Communist Party. A man she identified as Izzy Bisquith, the SWP's regional director, recruited her to form a Socialist Labor Party cell, which met in her basement. When she joined the SLP in July 1956, she wrote an acquaintance, "I have been labeled a 'traitor' to the American way."

"I can see my role," she wrote in 1957. "...I'm an outsider. What better is there to be? I'm a dissenter. I think I see the outline of our future here in America and me in a barbed wire enclosure with my ilk as a political renegade." When the Soviet Union launched Sputnik, the world's first artificial satellite, in October 1957, Madalyn wrote, "I am aglow with joy...and have enough pride in it that one would think they were my own accomplishments." Angry at American historians for not lauding the Russian Revolution more, she lamented, "I have been duped...I swallowed their garbage whole. I see now the daily papers reflecting a distortion — I have been long years coming of age."

Her legal training and love of history were assets, and she found she was a fluid, magnetic speaker. She enjoyed lecturing on Marxism, and began to be invited to speak at meetings around Baltimore. "She was really focused, there was no nonsense," said an attendee. "She was very different from other women I'd met...she was the star, just by listening to her." But it was less the ideology that attracted people and more the lifting of spirits and energy that always happened around her. No one was ever bored by her.

She participated in protests and marches, sometimes taking the kids, and coordinated some against the hated House Committee on Un-American Activities, mis-acronymed HUAC. She wanted prison and foster-care reform, desegregation, stronger unions, the U.S. out of Korea, and a ban on above-ground atomic testing after radioactive Strontium 90 was found in babies' teeth.

She picketed the segregated White Tower restaurants in her area, and lobbied against blacks' exclusion from certain public parks. She participated in "the Route 40 fight," getting restaurants on the highway to serve black diplomats traveling from the United Nations to Washington. "Even in their African costumes [they'd] have to go in and ask for food in the little brown bag and take it out to their car and eat," she recalled.

Her integration activities reportedly landed her a grant from the National Institute of Mental Health to enroll in Howard University's Graduate School of Social Work in the fall of 1957, as "either the first or the second [white woman]" to attend.

Her aim was a master's degree in psychiatric social work. She'd done extensive research into "bastardy" and planned to specialize in the problems of illegitimacy. But she soon became critical of both her fellow students and the faculty. None of her professors had "brains enough to recognize a good [thesis]." Her stay at Howard ended with an attack on what she saw as raw hypocrisy.

"You've no idea the racism among Negroes," she told two Baylor University historians in 1971. After working with her team in the ghetto, "on the way back in the car they'd say, 'Those gawd-damn niggers, they're giving us a black eye...'" She told her supervisor off for tolerating it, and claimed she was kicked out of Howard in February 1959 with a bad evaluation.

She wondered if she had a compulsion to fail. "Here I am," she wrote, "on the edge of 40, with no references...with a law degree and I can't practice — with all this social work background and no degree now — with two kids and no husband...with judgments galore — with a mortgaged house and a mortgaged car. Has anyone anywhere been such a glorious failure?"

She got a job as a claims examiner for Social Security in the spring of 1959, and dreamed of moving to a Chinese commune or joining the Spanish underground. She felt misplaced in America, and contemplated suicide, as she had many times in the past. "I'm trapped and I know it."

Bill had been given sleeping quarters in the basement after Garth's crib replaced his bed in their grandparents' room, and he became the mascot of his mother's activist groups, listening to their discussions into the night from his bed. He learned, he wrote later, that rich people got that way not by working, but by exploiting people who did. He learned that Jews ran all the big businesses, and that freedom was an illusion as long as we tolerated the obscene gap between rich and poor. He helped with envelope-stuffing and flyer distribution to "help the poor."

To no one's surprise, Pup heatedly opposed Bill's recruitment to the Cause, hammering at his daughter that the system she hated, which exploited workers, had that GI Bill check in the mailbox when she needed tuition or a home, and the VA payment would be lying next to her Social Security check in the mailbox when she retired. (And in fact, very shortly, Madalyn would be on unemployment and in the VA hospital with a hysterectomy.)

Bill recalled a couple of attempts she made to become independent. Once she moved in with a lover named Ricardo, leaving the kids with her parents. Pup seethed, and she sent for the boys. Bill wasn't sure if the lover was still around when it all broke down.

"I had got out of the bath. I picked up a towel, and it stunk. I took it to my mother, and said, 'this towel stinks.'" She smelled it, and slumped. "Her whole countenance dropped. And she said, 'I think we're just going to have to move back.' I mean — the towel's dirty! Wash it! She didn't have the capacity to deal with the small things." She and the boys moved back to Winford in the late summer of 1959.

The fights resumed, with Pup throwing it up to her that Lena, not she, had always been the real caretaker of Bill and Garth. Though she hid it from Pup, this barb always hit its mark. She felt a failure as Bill's mother. "Bill is," she agonized, "failing absolutely utterly. He cannot retain. He cannot learn, he cannot read. He cannot translate thought into words . . . I've engaged in an ugly brutal battle with the school because of it, but . . . If they can teach an 80 IQ, why can't Bill learn? . . . I grieve almost as if for a lost cause."

More than once she lost her temper, berated him as stupid like all males, and seized his homework to do herself. She tried cutting him off from athletics, even claiming he had rheumatic fever like Irv.

"Mother was constantly sending notes to school to excuse me from physical education," Bill said. "A couple of coaches had seen this kind of thing before, and they tried to get around her." As with Irv and the wheelchair, Pup intervened. Bill got on a Pony League team, and Irv took him to his games. "My uncle was a baseball nut . . . I could hear him yelling up in the stands."

Pup's intervention was lukewarm compared to the wheelchair episode, but the lesson was not lost on Bill. He knew his grandfather was proud of his athletic endeavors, proud that he was working on an FCC license for ham radio. "He taught me how to work with wood tools, how to build things. He taught me the masculine arts." He let Bill in on some family dirty laundry the women would rather hide, like how one of his roadhouse customers back during the Depression had been the local sheriff and his mistress, a secret successfully kept from Mrs. Sheriff.

"And I learned restraint from him, how to walk away." After a particularly nasty fight one evening, Pup "made up his mind he was never going to eat with [Madalyn] again . . . he never again sat with us. If Garth had had a few more years with my grandfather, I believe he would have been able to break away and leave, too."

But in a way it was Garth, more than Pup, who ran interference for Bill, for Madalyn was already transferring the burden of her dreams. Before he was three, she wrote in her diary, "I have a mystic assurance of this: Garth will have as much effect on the world as Jesus Christ, Freud or Marx have had on the total Western historical development."

"I never had this feeling with Bill."

Chapter 7 ~ A Discreet Inquiry

I N 1960, MADALYN BEGAN TALKING of defecting to the USSR. She already subscribed to *Soviet Life* magazine, two Communist newspapers, and a monthly from the People's Republic of China. Bob Lee, now her lover, urged her to stay in the U.S. and try to change things from within.

Her defection fever was fed by distress and unhappiness at home. Her sons quarreled constantly, just as she and Irv had done, and it depressed her. It was jealousy: "We all love Garth more . . . Bill knows this instinctively . . . and he hates Garth . . . hits him and twists his arms," she wrote. "This isn't a relationship. It's a dogfight . . . Tonight I cried and cried, but even then feeling nothing."

She lived in an utterly conformist, utterly controlled environment, where a property owners' association dictated what awnings, screen doors, and plantings you could have. She hated her job. She toyed with the idea of writing detective stories like the ones Pup loved in the Street & Smith magazines of her childhood.

Madalyn's unease corresponded to a great rumble underneath the placid surface of the Fifties. American life was on the verge of a great upheaval. Anti-war and civil rights demonstrations, the hippie movement, love-ins, and the psychedelic drug explosion were on the horizon. Rebellion was in the air on campuses throughout the nation. The conservative Young Americans for Freedom clashed with the Students for a Democratic Society. Drugs and music were emerging as the venues for an anti-establishment convulsion of the nation's youth — a convulsion that struck a passionate chord in the wounded outcast Madalyn felt herself to be. Though she was too old to writhe to Big Bopper or Elvis, the outlaw rising in the veins of rock and roll spoke to her spirit far more than the bland tunes of Dinah Washington and Perry Como — "Call Me Irresponsible," "Catch a Falling Star" — that they were eclipsing.

In early 1960, Madalyn mailed a letter to the Soviet embassy in Washington.

> I desire to make a discreet inquiry of you. It is my desire to make application for citizenship in the Union of Soviet Socialist Republics, and I further desire to go to that country to live and work. How is this to be effectuated?

She described herself as an attorney working for the U.S. government, an atheist who could no longer tolerate her homeland.

"I have certain convictions regarding eqality [sic] for women, for races, for minority groups, which are unacceptable by the nation." She enclosed a self-addressed envelope. Could they get this "culminated" and have her in Moscow by June?

A month passed with no reply, and she sat down again on her 41st birthday. "I am not just a crank letter writer. I am not a psychotic." She was healthy and responsible and so were her kids; she had made an extensive study of Russia — "her culture, her economics, her politics, her religion. I want my children to have the opportunity to grow and be educated in a Communist society."

She finally received a reply: she couldn't be considered because she knew no one in the USSR to sponsor her.

In spring 1960, after a year at her job with the Social Security Administration, Madalyn was given notice. They said she'd falsified her employment application, lied about her diploma and transcript, and failed "to take care of my financial obligations." They asked if she gambled, and told her they had rules against hiring deadbeats.

She did have debts (Bill remembered constables showing up about that time and hauling away $500 worth of repossessed furniture as the neighbors gawked), but she was certain her firing was for her political activism. She briefly took a job unionizing fellow SSA employees, and attempted the same at Fort Meade Army Base. She felt this kind of thing was in her blood; her uncle Gus Scholle was now president of the Michigan AFL-CIO. But the army wouldn't even let her hold union meetings at Fort Meade, and when her union refused to help, she was furious.

"I quit the [union] . . . I said to my family and friends, if . . . they can do this over my unionizing, . . . the United States government can take America and shove it up their ass — I'm leaving." The FBI got wind of her plans and interviewed her shortly before she left. What had been promised her by the Soviets? they asked; she'd been telling people an apartment was waiting for her. She denied that, but "expressed bitter resentment" against her government and called Vice President Nixon, who had risen to prominence from HUAC, a fascist. The U.S. had too many restrictions, she said, and was "too fascistic and too Catholic." And the FBI was the "thought control police."

So on August 24, 1960, Madalyn packed up the boys and boarded the *Queen Elizabeth* for France, where, Bill said, she thought Soviet citizenship would happen faster.

She had prepared a letter to the State Department renouncing her American citizenship and "telling them exactly what they could do with [it]," and left it with Lena to mail. After seeing them off, Lena went home, consulted her tarot cards, and concluded they'd be back soon. She put the letter away.

Numerous clumsy visits to the Soviet embassy in Paris, involving sign language and exasperating linguistic impasses, finally culminated in an unequivocal No. It was delicately conveyed that whatever assets Madalyn felt she had back home, all they saw was a woman who couldn't speak Russian and brought to the table two fatherless boys who would need welfare. Echoing Bob Lee, one embassy official suggested she might be of more use to the revolution back in the U.S.

In late September, she and the kids flew back to Baltimore. Someone who saw her at an airport restaurant said she was "extremely bitter, and . . . practically in tears, loudly proclaimed her disappointment at having to return to the U.S. . . . "

Back at Winford, she collected unemployment of $39 a week for 39 weeks, and then finagled another 13 weeks on a technicality, of which she was quite proud.

During the years of Madalyn's belated coming-of-age, a polarity was forming in postwar America that would be the perfect arena for her interests and talents — law, politics, religion, money, and fame.

The *McCollum* case had seemed dispositive about religion in school, but resistance and confusion reigned. For example, the Ten Commandments were outlawed in two Long Island towns after Jewish groups objected to them. But in New Jersey, the state supreme court ruled that the Old Testament and the Lord's Prayer were nonsectarian. One day, a complaint came in about a lunchtime elementary school prayer in a small New Jersey school district ("God is great, God is good, and we thank him for this food. By his hand we all are fed, thank thee for our daily bread."). The prayer was stopped, but a petition to restore it followed immediately.

The New Jersey attorney general ruled that particular prayer out, because it solicited divine intervention — but now that the Lord's Prayer and Old Testament were nonsectarian by law in New Jersey, they could be substituted.

That was opposed, and a moment of silence at lunch was proposed as a compromise. It was ruled illegal — *unless* the kids all agreed not to silently say grace to themselves during that moment. What was the point of that? asked both sides. A moment of silence where you agreed to think about anything but God?

The proponents of lunchtime grace also pointed out that in 1954, the *government* had inserted the words "under God" into the Pledge of Allegiance, which the kids *had* to say. Wasn't this inconsistent, if not nutty? Kids had to say "God" in the Pledge, but were forbidden to utter or even think it at lunch?

Some states' resistance to an ever more liberal U.S. Supreme Court showed in 1958's Jenner-Butler Bill. Apart from the fierce tug-of-war over the states' rights to express their majorities' wishes in public worship, the bill coded a spreading fear that Communism had infiltrated so many universities and high government niches that it had diseased the High Court itself. The bill allowed Congress to strip the court of power to hear certain cases dealing with subversion. It barely failed, and starkly reflected a widespread mistrust of the Supreme Court, and the fear that it was protecting Communists. The attempt to strip the schools of any whiff of God seemed almost certainly part of a greater Communist scheme to weaken the foundations of American-style democracy.

The debate divided among liberal Christians and Jews and conservative Christians. "Leave religion to the churches," said a rabbi at a widely reported meeting of churchmen near Christmas 1959, at a time when children were rehearsing for Christmas pageants all over the nation. But carols and crèches didn't constitute worship, countered the Christians, and even if they hinted at it, America was not a secular nation. Christianity was part of western culture. It should be enough to show tolerance for minority views. To excise all traces of religion would produce "atheistic humanism" — which, they said, amounted simply to another religion — if it wasn't a euphemism for Communism itself.

Humanism weighed in via the Friendship Liberal League, which said it didn't matter if Christianity was part of our culture, the Constitution mandated that church and state be separated. Religion had secured many privileges for itself over the decades, and diverted public funds to itself. The League wanted to abolish church tax exemptions, exemptions of clergy from military duty and from testifying in court, price breaks for clergy on common carriers, Blue Laws, public funding of military or civil chaplains, religious emblems on U.S. property, and the restoration of "E Pluribus Unum" (Out of Many, One) on all coins, bills, postage stamps, and other public property, instead of the new motto, "In God We Trust." (The phrase was made official by Congress in 1956, and began appearing on paper currency in 1957, but had been stamped on coins since the late 1870s.)

They wanted teachers and other public servants prohibited from wearing religious garb or insignia at work. Buses should not be available to parochial school pupils. They wanted no religious ceremonials at government functions, including oaths to God in court or elsewhere. Religious instruction should not be part of any convict's penalty. They wanted repeal of immigration laws giving special consideration to religion, and anything they deemed "religious propaganda" struck from the Congressional Record. They wanted schools to "[teach] natural science without consideration of alleged supernatural revelations."

While Madalyn was away in France, the presidential campaign of Senator John F. Kennedy revolved around his Catholicism; he vehemently repeated that he supported the constitutional provision for church-state separation, and would not change under any circumstances. He was reacting to a tempest created by an article in the Vatican newspaper, *L'Osservatore Romano*, which said that sometimes "politics touches the altar" and that the bishops have a right at such times to expect "dutiful discipline" from any Catholic. "The church hierarchy alone," it said, "has the right to judge whether in a certain . . . political situation the higher principles of religious and moral order are . . . compromised."

That prompted churches to collect contributions for anti-Kennedy literature, lest America start "taking orders from the Pope." The IRS warned that any church using contributions that way could lose its tax exemption.

Madalyn's absence with the kids in France was explained to the neighbors as an educational vacation. In late September 1960, Bill returned to Woodbourne Junior High. Madalyn, walking him down the hall for late enrollment, heard the classrooms swelling with a chant — the Lord's Prayer.

There are two versions of what happened next. Madalyn said Bill was disturbed about the prayers, asking if they were constitutional. Once he made it clear he wanted to fight this battle, she had to do it, or be a hypocrite.

Bill's version was that his mother strode to the front office to object to the prayer, and blurted profanity, shocking the young male clerk. In the car, she berated Bill for not telling her this kind of thing had been taking place all along. She told him America had to be changed, instructed him to start keeping a log of religious practices at school, and took up the issue with her Socialist friends.

On October 10, 1960, Madalyn wrote Woodbourne principal Dorothy Duval (whom she dubbed the "Buxom Bitch" for her cleavage) and the superintendent of schools, Dr. George B. Brain. She asked that Bill be excused during Bible reading, prayer, and the Pledge. And she wanted to give him private history lessons.

With no idea they were making history themselves, the authorities told her no — Bill had to stay there and be respectful for five minutes. And he could not substitute private history lessons. No one had ever complained about *The Story of Nations* in its 35 years in the public schools, though it presented Biblical stories as real events.

She kept Bill home two weeks in protest. The school warned he'd be charged with truancy and then ignored his absence.

Madalyn wrote a passionate letter to the *Baltimore Sun*, invoking the rights of atheists and pointing to the church-state separation guaranteed in the First and Fourteenth amendments to the U.S. Constitution.

On October 26, the education reporter from the *Sun*, Stephen Nordlinger, called. Instead of printing her letter, he wanted an interview. Madalyn was ecstatic.

"We were interested in her relationship with the school system, but she was thinking about nothing else so much as scoring a lot of points against the establishment," recalled Nordlinger.

Bill was tall, with his father's dignified good looks. He was self-possessed, and "seemed like a nice, well-spoken kid." He was articulate, and when he got to talk, he did his mother proud. But Madalyn, said Nordlinger, did all the talking. "She was running the show. Very definitely . . . very domineering."

On October 27, 1960, the *Sun* published the interview, with the angle that this was the first challenge to the 1905 school board rule of prayer and/or Bible reading. Madalyn declared she would go on a hunger strike in jail rather than let her son return to school. "My son is not going to bow down to any concept of what an average American is," she said, revealing an agenda perhaps more linked to her personal vow to be an outsider than to assaults on the Constitution.

The article brought forth Fred Weisgal, chairman of the American Civil Liberties Union's legal panel for Maryland and Washington. Weisgal said Bill should return to school immediately, check in with his homeroom teacher, and then attempt to step outside class during the Bible reading. If they expelled him for it, a lawsuit would be filed.

By that afternoon, the state school authorities had involved the attorney general. In the evening, the Murray-Mays family watched themselves being covered all over the local and national television news.

The phone started to ring off the hook. Madalyn had found her Cause at last.

Years later, Bill attributed his mother's atheism to anger, not intellectual conviction. "She felt two men had wronged her. Madalyn Murray was mad at men, and she was mad at God, who was male." It was God, via the Judeo-Christian ethic, who laid guilt and shame on her, with Pup and the schools and church and society as His agents. It was the Catholic Church that wouldn't let her marry. That was what fueled her attack on school prayer.

Others later wondered if there were more to it than shame and revenge. How did she get the money for a month in France when she'd lost her job, skipped out on debts, and had her furniture repossessed? Was she funded by the Communists?

She had seemed to come back from France with a new sense of purpose, and plunged back into her Socialist political groups with new vigor. She wrote the Soviet embassy about the prayer activity, and started shopping for support for a suit against the school. She took up again with Bob Lee, who told her that the Communist Party U.S.A. might help with her lawsuit. Her activities brought open accusations that she was a Communist, a charge she hotly denied her entire life.

Freedom of Information Act documents revealed that she never actually joined the Communist Party. However, the meetings in her basement made her a target of COINTELPRO, J. Edgar Hoover's crack counterintelligence program, and its reports indicated she was profoundly sympathetic to the Communist cause.

Madalyn later said the Party's interest in her case had always been an "enigma" to her, that she really didn't recognize that it was Communist influence fueling all the protest movements, and that she'd never taken money from CPUSA. But she engaged attorney Harold Buchman, a Bob Lee referral who had represented the Maryland Communist Party, to file her first petition. He dropped out, some said because Madalyn took $5,000 from anti-Semite Charles Smith, editor of *Truth Seeker* magazine. (Smith himself recommended the American Lawyers Guild — which Madalyn later acknowledged was Communist-infiltrated, "full of Marxists," and on the attorney general's "watch" list.)

At a meeting in August 1961, George Meyers, chairman of the Communist Party of Maryland-DC, instructed Baltimore members to set up a committee to oppose the Smith and McCarran Acts, which made it a crime to say or write anything that would lead to refusal of military duty or overthrow of the government. Several Party members had been jailed under the acts. The chairman of this committee, Meyers directed, "should be non-Party but close to the Communist Party"; it was "politically correct to have a non-CP member as head of the group in order that a larger mass following would develop." They chose Madalyn.

She began holding meetings immediately, planning press releases, telegrams to the President, and rallies. The group was called the Maryland Committee for Democratic Rights. Meyers commented that she would do a good job for the Party, which "must not leave her out in left field."

Madalyn contributed monthly to the Party, and later opened the New Era Book Shop, also funded by the Party. In fact, Meyers said that Madalyn did want to join, but he couldn't trust her. A Party district board member said she could be dangerous — she was too outspoken and wanted to simply announce the Communist Party's agenda to the American people and show them how Socialism was better. "She believed in open advocacy of revolution and the sooner the better," he said. And as early as 1961, Gus Hall, General Secretary of CPUSA, was saying that the Party "was afraid of [Madalyn] and that sooner or later she would take over the leadership locally." Indeed, by early 1962, Meyers was angry that Madalyn was not being "controlled" and the Party officer overseeing her was "letting her do everything she wanted."

Madalyn firmly denied it all. Though her three dogs were named Marx, Engels, and Tsar, the only thing she ever got from the Communist Party, she said later, was "how to completely dominate a meeting, how to misuse Robert's Rules...I can go in any place right now, and turn it into a shambles."

Communism had strong emotional attractions for Madalyn. It offered entrée into a world of artists, intellectuals, and politicos that made her feel closer to the northeastern elite. She was willing to believe the social gains being reported from Cuba — schools and hospitals going up, prostitution and crime eradicated — but "Fidelismo" and its American cousins, the civil rights and anti-war movements, were youth-driven, and though Madalyn was nearing forty, she identified strongly with that.

The American youth movement was exciting to her; the Cuban Revolution seemed almost like a second chance at the Spanish Civil War, or at the brief romance she'd found in her own wartime service. It was as if part of her was fixed at adolescence, when she found she could control things at home by being louder, better, and more dominant than the others. There was something strikingly adolescent about her anger at Pup, and even her second pregnancy seemed partly a rebellion against his moral authority.

Even in the midst of postwar prosperity and opportunity, the Mayses had remained huddled together, Madalyn and Irv loath to break out and form their own households. (In fact, Bill wrote in his autobiography, *My Life Without God*, it didn't fully sink in that Madalyn was his mother until about second grade, when she suddenly noticed he was calling her by name, and made him change to "Mother.")

But the leftist movements of the 1960s seemed to give Madalyn a focus for sex and rebellion and politics and romance. She remained fixated on sex her whole life, though there were few clues why. She hinted to a confidante that she had been sexually molested as a child; she ran off with a truck driver at 13; she wrote that it had been hammered into her that masturbation was a grave evil. But whatever caused it, the obsession never dwindled, and inappropriate and crude references to sex and masturbation became one of her trademarks. "She thought that youth, and sexuality, and vulgarity all went together," said Bill.

For him, the topic was an uncomfortable harvest of her liberation. "She would go out and watch porno movies in Baltimore and come home and talk about it. Talk to her mother about them." He remembered one such conversation when he was about 13. "I was sitting in the room and my brother was sitting in the room. She started gyrating" her pelvis, and Lena said, "Madalyn, stop that, you shouldn't be doing that with the children in the room."

Chapter 8 ~ *"Your petitioners are atheists"*

ON FRIDAY, OCTOBER 28, 1960, Bill returned to school, trailed by reporters and photographers. The principal tried to thwart a showdown by keeping him in the office all week, but he finally found a way to sneak into his homeroom. As the teacher began to read the prayer, he spoke a protest and left. He'd done his duty; the papers printed it. He was stalked, insulted, and attacked by fellow students outside of school.

Things happened rapidly; the attorney general ruled the prayer constitutional, but anyone could be excused who objected — Madalyn's original request, which the school now greatly regretted not granting.

But it was too little too late, ACLU attorney Fred Weisgal told the school board: whether you were excused or not, this was religious ceremony and had no place in the schools. They would file suit to remove it.

He wanted to join it with an almost identical suit the ACLU was already involved in, *School District of Abington Township, Pennsylvania v. Schempp*. The Schempps' three children were compelled by Pennsylvania law to listen to Bible verses over the loudspeaker each day. They'd won all their suits to ban the practice, and the school district continued to appeal until it reached the Supreme Court.

Madalyn wanted her name first on the combined suits' caption page, so it would be the citation name throughout history. Hers had an earlier docket number than the Schempps'. When Weisgal told her it was alphabetical — *Abington Township* would come before *Murray* — she blew up, and their relationship ended with Weisgal saying, "Madalyn, go fuck yourself!"

She replaced him with Leonard Kerpelman, a Baltimore native with a taste for unpopular civil liberties causes. The genial 36-year-old had just forced reform of the local jury system, after discovering that jurors were not randomly selected from voter lists but cherry-picked using their addresses.

He specialized in getting along with difficult people. He found his new client "always in a stressed condition, unattractive, overweight, slovenly looking, didn't care about how she dressed . . . angry at the whole society. But her daily living habit was to go around being angry anyway.

"But at the same time, she was also . . . 'hail fellow, well met,' and you would have a wonderful time traveling around with her. She was very intelligent . . . witty, very caustic, which can be funny . . . and a lot of very pleasant discussion [took place].

"She was in an *awful* relationship with her father, and awful relationship with her brother — either one or both of them, I think, were alcoholics — it was just *family fighting*, all the time. I don't know why they all lived together . . . she would tell me things about how she hated them, and how they were always doing this or that to her, which they weren't . . . She said many insulting things about her mother, I don't know why. Her mother was . . . a *nice* person, a *wonderful* woman. And Madalyn used to kick her around. And her father. And her brother. Not physically. But she was awful to get along with."

But he was delighted; he'd get to argue a high-profile case after Weisgal had cleared some of the jungle in the similar cases. And it was personal: "I went to the public schools, and when I was old enough to begin to understand, I would scratch my head and say, why are they talking about Jesus Christ? It was very distressing to a Jewish kid. And they used to do that *every day*."

Madalyn's case had to ripen in state court before it could be joined with the Schempps' case and brought to the Supreme Court. Styled *Murray v. Curlett* (Curlett was the school board president), it got national attention on its own, as it boldly stated, "your petitioners are Atheists." Atheists were equated with Communists. Madalyn had helped draft the petition, which spoke for the hidden Americans who weren't Communists at all, but didn't want prayer imposed on their children, who thought hospitals should be built instead of churches, that disease, war, and poverty weren't going to go away as long as we relied on some God instead of each other.

The publicity brought tons of mail — and money — to Winford Road. "Every misfit in America," wrote Bill later, "was sending my mother letters of praise with a check enclosed."

There may have been a lot of misfit money in the mail, but there was also an outpouring of relief and hope coded into the checks and bills. The Murray-Mays family was about to find out what Americans who didn't believe in God often suffered in their communities, and in what fear and persecution many of them lived. Many of the letters were anonymous; checks and money orders were sometimes signed "Thomas Paine."

Christmas 1960 was like always, according to Bill — sacred music and Christmas carols filling the house from Thanksgiving on, and a wonderfully decorated tree with an angel on top.

Madalyn was in a full-blown war with the school, claiming teachers gave Bill the silent treatment, lied that he hadn't turned in homework when he had, gave him extra work, and allowed him to be beaten up during gym class. "Madalyn Murray . . . would bypass the principal's office and head straight for her son's classroom," said a teacher, "where she would scream at the teacher and pound her desk."

The school denied it. Bill was arrogant, they said, and playing his mother. They'd given Madalyn plenty of notice that he was not attending class, turning in his homework, making up tests, or returning library books.

But there was no question Bill was getting beaten up and harassed, and it infuriated Madalyn. She filed a second suit, seeking an injunction against Woodbourne for mistreating Bill.

At the same time, she was turning Bill's suffering to good use. Freethought publications all over the country recounted his ordeals, and urged their readers to send her money. Virgil McClain, editor of an Indiana news sheet called the *Ripsaw* — "Rips Away the Bark of Superstition and Cuts to the Truth" — published a letter from Bill describing how "good Christians . . . [had] kicked, punched, tripped, [and] spat upon" him.

James Hervey Johnson, soon to take over the *Truth Seeker* from Charles Smith, sent a special mailing angrily describing the injustices done to Bill, and the venerable *Liberal*, the freethought publication of the Friendship Liberal League of Philadelphia, printed a strong appeal, saying the Schempps had the ACLU behind them, but

"Mrs. Murray...has battled on her own...Her case must be won!...Contribute as generously as you can and do it now!"

Lou Alt, publisher of the *Free Humanist,* decided to give his subscription list to Madalyn for her new monthly *Newsletter On The Murray Case* (soon changed to the *Murray Newsletter*). Later, he invited her to Philadelphia, promising to turn over his entire stock of atheist books and even his magazine, if she won. In New York, Joseph Lewis, the prolific writer, magazine editor, and atheist activist who founded Freethinkers of America, urged his readers to support her.

A major donor was 77-year-old Carl Brown of Stockton, Kansas. Brown was a college graduate, world traveler, former state legislator, and "admitted nudist atheist" who owned more than 1,000 acres in Kansas. He gave Madalyn 160 of them, plus $5,000 cash. Stockton would be the new home of an atheist headquarters, university, and radio station, and perhaps even an atheist nudist colony. Brown also gave Bill and Garth stock in a life insurance company to provide for their futures.

One welcome comrade was Arthur Cromwell, father of Vashti McCollum, into whose shadow Madalyn felt she was frequently nudged. Cromwell was an atheist and had backed his daughter in her 1948 Supreme Court battle. "If my dad was only like you!" Madalyn wrote Cromwell in late 1960. "My father is my worst enemy...Your daughter is a fortunate woman." Cromwell encouraged Madalyn, called her "my dear," praised her and Bill, and commiserated with her over the venality of the ACLU and the "pussy-footing" American Humanist Association, though his daughter was prominent in the latter. Madalyn wrote Vashti for help and received a cool response.

Madalyn quickly realized the value of mailing lists for fundraising, and asked editors for names of people who had sent letters of support about her, to send them thank you notes. This was the beginning of a lifelong pattern of accusations back and forth of mailing-list theft with one organization after another, for lists were jealously guarded. There were only so many atheist/freethought dollars to go around.

She planned to make a living selling books and launching a proper magazine, but she saw that what really fired donors up were two things: lawsuits — they would give if they thought some corrective was in the pipeline — and persecution. Her newsletter detailed Bill's bruises and trials, their vandalized cars. Their home was stoned and egged, people spat in their faces, trampled their flowers, stole their cat, and sent vicious hate mail. The police were constantly at their door. The media mischaracterized them. The neighbors scorned them. Garth came home crying, saying the kids hated him. The IRS audited her.

All of this was firmly in the realm of truth. But when she complained that Bill was not allowed to take gym, she didn't reveal that it was actually she who had pulled him out. She said he couldn't use the library, but didn't mention his privileges were suspended because of unpaid fines. She said he was barred from recess, but didn't explain it was at her request. She said the media was whipping people up to violence, but she was also whipping the media up.

One thing she'd learned writing those fake battle reports for the army was the power of manipulating information. There, the purpose was to maintain homefront morale, or confuse the enemy. Now, she was the one who determined what the homefront was, and who was the enemy.

On April 28, 1961, Judge Gilbert Prendergast scaldingly dismissed Madalyn's suit in the Superior Court of Baltimore, refusing to "subordinate all pupils to the atheist ideas of Mrs. Madalyn Murray and her son." If they had their way, they'd outlaw reference to the Declaration of Independence, because it mentioned *divine* Providence and *sacred* honor. As to the religious liberty of atheists being jeopardized, "Just how the religious liberty of a person who has no religion can be endangered is by no means made clear."

While the Murrays "clamor for religious freedom," he said, "their ultimate objective is religious suppression."

Madalyn and Kerpelman took it to the Maryland Court of Appeals, the state's highest court.

During the next few months, the atheist, legal, freethought, and religious communities watched closely a similar case called *Engel v. Vitale,* popularly known as the New York Regents Prayer case.

New York State's public schools were supervised by a Board of Regents, whose "Statement on Moral and Spiritual Training in the Schools" mandated that a daily prayer be recited by students. It was simple and nondenominational: "Almighty God, we acknowledge our dependence upon Thee, and we beg Thy blessings upon us, our parents, our teachers and our Country." That was unconstitutional, said opponents.

The Regents case was argued in the Supreme Court the week of April 2, 1962, and no matter what the outcome, it was guaranteed to change America. Madalyn knew it would determine the fate of her case.

And hers was headed for the Supreme Court, because, on April 6, the Maryland high court ruled against her, saying that none of Baltimore's religious exercises at school violated the Constitution.

Madalyn called the loss a hands-down victory: "Only the loser can appeal to the Supreme Court," she wrote her followers on the letterhead of her new nonprofit corporation, the Maryland Committee for Separation of Church and State. "We could not have got a better decision."

She had competition in the church-state separation sweepstakes; a notary named Roy Torcaso had already won a 1961 Supreme Court case over a Maryland requirement that he state a belief in God to practice. He was trolling for other cases. Joseph Lewis, a publisher and writer who helped found Freethinkers of America when Madalyn was a child, was fundraising to block the building of a chapel at Idlewild Airport, and remove "under God" from the Pledge of Allegiance. He used Madalyn's case to remind readers that he had waged this sort of battle for over 40 years.

She needed to distinguish herself to donors to get their dollars, and she reminded them that she'd been fired for her atheism, while her co-litigants' Unitarianism protected them.

She knew how to talk to her audience, knew there was a core of loneliness and suffering in her atheist followers, outsiders in their communities for the most part. One, Abigail Martin, recalled her childhood as the daughter of a Calvinist minister. One night in bed, at age seven, "It came to me that I was not good enough to go to heaven, so I was going to hell. I cried and screamed. Mother came in, but she couldn't comfort me."

When she got older, she would stare at herself in the mirror, sweeping her gaze slowly from head to toe, and hiss under her breath, "you're so useless, disgusting, worthless." She made a list of reasons why it would be better if she were dead.

She married an atheist, and finally shared her diary with him. "He saw this and said, 'This woman needs help.' He got me books to read, and took me to the Unitarian church. He took me to the doctor for panic pills. He *hated* religion from the bottom of his heart."

People like Martin felt warmth and friendship emanating from Madalyn. Years later, she told Martin that in Scotland, she visited the house where John Knox lived, and "felt a chill." Martin agreed. "Nobody ever told us this John Calvin *burned* a guy in the square because they disagreed on some little point!"

A sense of belonging, of being part of a sea-change in American culture, flowed to Madalyn's readers like mother's milk. She had a chummy, warm way of writing, making them feel like insiders. She credited them for being intelligent and informed. She praised them "as one fighter to another" for speaking out and using their real names on their letters and checks. She encouraged them to come out like her, as an atheist, out from behind the labels of humanist and freethinker and materialist. Together they would lay the groundwork for the secularization of American society. She cultivated two images with skill: the winner worth investing in and the per-secuted heroine worthy of rescue. She warned that the situation in Baltimore was "explosive," and violence expected when her case was heard. "She's Fighting Our Battle," one freethought editorial bannered.

"The more I see of Atheists, all I can say to all of you is: *Where have you been all my life? You are wonderful*," she told them. She signed the newsletters "Madalyn and the boys," and reported how the kids and Lena licked stamps and Bill ran the mimeograph machine. It was an instinctive personalizing of the Cause, and very effective. Money came in, and volunteers showed up at the door.

Madalyn was about to find that, as with the high-profile media evangelists that would emerge in the next two decades, there would always be people watching how she spent the money. She noticed an annoying ratio: the misers who sent five dollars often included pages of detailed instructions on how to proceed with the case.

From the beginning, Bill said, she had a risky habit of using donations as her personal income. She fattened Bill's college fund, and had formal oil portraits done of herself and the boys. She was criticized later for using donations to pay her mortgage and car loans. But was she supposed to do all this living under a bridge and panhandling? Or while supporting a family with a full-time job?

One day, she got a visit from a Californian named Kirby Hensley, who had started his own church. He had an idea: Madalyn could go on the church circuit as a visiting minister, and give "subtly destructive" sermons designed to sow strife and disagreement. You could do it just by using the Bible, he told her. If you set it up as a lecture and Q&A, you could even get people into fist fights.

She rolled her eyes, but later, she would become very interested in Kirby Hensley, and his Universal Life Church.

Bill graduated in June, and his agony at Woodbourne ended. Despite his grades, he was accepted that fall to the best private school in the city, Baltimore Polytech. His torment stopped. Nobody cared that he was a godless atheist.

"It was even kind of macho to be an atheist," remembered a contemporary 40 years later. "You got associated with scientists...It was almost a Masonic association. Now, no one cares."

Chapter 9 ~ A Huge Amount of Confusion

THE RULING on the Regents Prayer case came in June 1962, and caused a great furor, on whose crest Madalyn's ship would rise. The little prayer violated the Constitution, said the Supreme Court.

It drew immediate charges of Communism and atheism. How on earth could prayer be unconstitutional? How had the First Amendment been breached? Had Congress made a law establishing a religion? There were calls for constitutional amendments to legalize school prayer, to elect Supreme Court justices, to allow Congress to overrule them. The storm over the Regents Prayer decision foreshadowed exactly what would happen with Madalyn's case a year later.

Nelson Rockefeller, governor of New York, urged a moment of silence. Former President Hoover was appalled. Former President Eisenhower pointed out that the Declaration of Independence itself asserts that our rights are grounded in a Creator. President Kennedy urged citizens to view the decision as a challenge to cultivate religious devotion at home. The ACLU, which played an active role in the Regents case, alerted its affiliates to watch for violations across the land.

The decision, seen as a rigid interpretation of church-state separation, stopped pending legislation in its tracks and threw existing legislation into doubt, complained members of Congress. A resolution was put forth that the House be allowed to continue to open with prayer, and another passed immediately — to print and distribute thousands of extra copies of a brochure describing the Capitol's Prayer Room, with its window depicting Washington praying and its quotation from the Book of Psalms.

Supporters pointed out that prayer was not being barred in school, nor the mention of God forbidden (though those would not be far behind). Only "official" prayer — government-directed prayer — was out. People could still pray voluntarily. Be honest, they said, were the exercises really just an uplifting way to start the day, or a sign that people had started looking to the state to provide spiritual training instead of doing it themselves?

Justice Hugo Black, who wrote the majority opinion, said there would be no bar to things like singing "God Bless America" or quoting the Declaration of Independence. As for Christmas pageants, no school could require them, but students could voluntarily participate. It was simply not the business of government, he wrote, to compose official prayers for any group of Americans to recite. That kind of thing was "one of the reasons that caused many of our early colonists to leave England and seek religious freedom in America."

(Not true, argued both historians and churchmen; the Mayflower Compact was sworn "in the presence of God"; early proto-constitutions stated that all rights came from God; and the colonies had many laws far more religious than composing official prayers. Some required that public servants believe in the Bible's divinity, that lawgivers be Protestants, or that citizens be fined for working on Sunday. The states of Massachusetts, New Hampshire, and Connecticut all levied taxes to support religious establishments; the First Continental Congress appropriated funds to provide Bibles to the people. The Massachusetts constitution provided for "the support and maintenance of public Protestant teachers of piety, religion and morality, in all cases where such provision shall not be made voluntarily." Half a dozen presidents used federal money to support priests and build churches to bring the Gospel to the Indians, to take advantage of the already existing evangelistic outreaches and strengthen treaties.)

And church leaders pointed out that the Court, in trying to keep from establishing a religion, had in fact established one — humanism. It was predicted that secularism, materialism, and atheism would become the official, government-and-court mandated "religion" of the public schools and courts, no less tyrannical than the government control over free and independent worship the First Amendment had sought to avoid.

Others pled that the regents' bland chant didn't constitute prayer at all, and was meaningless as to "establishing" a religion — it wasn't even Christian; it didn't mention Jesus Christ. It was utterly harmless. And in any case, the First Amendment didn't prohibit the establishment of religion in the states. It only forbade a national religious establishment. There was no mandate that the federal government "of the people" was forbidden to be a friend to the overwhelmingly Christian values of those people. In fact, the framers passed a national day of Prayer and Thanksgiving the day after they adopted the First Amendment, exhorting the people to observe it "with religious solemnity" and "devout acknowledgments of Almighty God for His great goodness." Clearly they believed religious faith had a fundamental place in the political order.

And wasn't it funny, critics said, that the most vociferous opponents of school prayer were those who think there's no God to hear them anyway? And what kind of message were we sending to millions of people living under authoritarian, Communist regimes, who looked to us for hope and inspiration? The decision "broke the hearts" of those people, said Boston's Cardinal Cushing. Religion, in fact was "the only thing Communism fear[ed]."

Within a few days of the decision, the Supreme Court was buried in letters and telegrams — the largest outpouring in its history. What about the rights of the majority? Why aren't *they* protected? And exactly how did prayer injure people or deprive them of their rights? And wasn't atheism one of the bulwarks of Communism? What about *anti*-religious instruction? Wasn't that what evolution was? This decision was setting up America for destruction from within. This was beginning to smell like sedition.

And we notice you liberal justices didn't refuse to take the oath when you were ready to be covered with honor and big lifetime salaries. You solemnly swore with your hand on the Bible to uphold the Constitution. Where were your convictions then? Where are your convictions every day, when the court opens with "God save the United States and this honorable court!"? Why haven't you mentioned Congress opening its daily sessions with prayer by tax-supported chaplains?

There were many letters lamenting the godless justices who could turn their backs this way — it was only through God's grace that we had this beautiful country and our Constitution. We need to pray for these judges.

Justice Potter Stewart, the lone dissenter, said America had an unarguable spiritual heritage, and the decision would rob children of it. It was hardly establishing an official religion to let people say a prayer who wanted to.

The letters praising the decision said the nation was full of parochial schools and churches for people who felt the need to pray out loud — since they apparently wanted to ignore Jesus' admonishment to "enter into thy closet and when thou hast shut thy door, pray to thy Father which is in secret." America made generous provision for the religious through tax exemptions; let them pray in their tax-subsidized churches, not the schools. There was a right to freedom *from* religion, too. "Parents . . . who are genuinely concerned about this matter can surely have a word of prayer with Junior before shoving him out of the front door to school."

God shouldn't need a thumbs-up from the government to be present in a classroom. By banning official prayers, the law protected the freedoms of dissenters and the sanctity of personal prayers alike.

As for children being allowed to leave the room or stay seated, or not participate, what kid is going to mark himself that way? And why should they be asked to? Too, as every elementary school teacher knew, many Jewish, Muslim, Buddhist, and Hindu kids already felt distressed and excluded by the prayers and Christmas pageants at school.

Maybe we were founded on a Judeo-Christian *ethic*, but that doesn't make us an exclusively Christian country. And even if we were, it doesn't belong in school. Remember the days when the Protestants and Catholics were fighting over which Bible to use in class? Soon we'd be back to the Vashti McCollum era, with churches elbowing nonconformist children out into the hall and taking an hour of each tax-funded week to proselytize. Would a theocracy be many generations behind? President Madison himself had warned of "the danger of encroachment by Ecclesiastical Bodies," of which the Salem witch trials gave ample foretaste.

There was a huge amount of confusion over the next months; the Massachusetts education commissioner declared that Bible *reading* was legal; the Supreme Court had only outlawed *recitation*. Are they going to put us in jail for singing "America the Beautiful — God Shed His Grace on Thee"? The national anthem stanza that says "And this be our motto: 'In God is our trust' "?

When school opened in the fall, school districts across the nation, defiant or unsure, opened with the reading of the Lord's Prayer and Bible verses.

When her own Supreme Court decision came down a year later, in June of 1963, the nation was still in upheaval over the Regents case, and ripe to be polarized by a strong personality like Madalyn's. The agent of much of this polarity on which she thrived was the 16-year tenure of Chief Justice Earl Warren.

When Warren came to Washington in the fall of 1953, Joseph McCarthy was at his peak of power, and the Supreme Court was the quietest of the three branches of government. That would change. The Warren court unseated Congress as the final authority both on interpretation of the Constitution and in compelling the states to conform. It brought about profound transformations in politics, social policies, and criminal law. Its first great strike was 1954's *Brown v. Board of Education* ruling that "separate but equal" education was a fiction. The decision ignited the smoldering civil rights movement, and desegregation transformed the country, spreading from schools to parks, water fountains, restrooms, theaters, economic opportunity, higher education — *Brown* was critical to the long-overdue corrections soon made to discriminatory laws ranging from school funding to miscegenation.

The Warren court's consistent decisions in favor of individual rights — reapportionment that expanded popular voice in the government; revolutionary changes in criminal law that increased both the protections for people accused of crimes and the tools of law enforcement to search; wider guarantees of free speech, and limits on Congress to pry into the ideas people hold — even Communism — marked the end of the court's tradition of judicial restraint. Warren's conviction that the elective branches of government should not be allowed to smother individual liberties, especially those of citizens with unpopular views, was utterly sincere. He was famous for asking prosecutors, "But were you *fair?*"

Warren's positions led to accusations of Communism. The same day Madalyn's decision was announced, the Court overturned the contempt of Congress conviction of Edward Yellin, who had refused on First Amendment grounds to tell HUAC about Communist party activities in the steel industry. When Warren delivered the 5–4 decision, letters poured in to editors all over the country: Earl Warren and his fellow Commies are sending this democracy to hell in a handbasket. As head of the commission investigating the Kennedy assassination, he was accused of covering up for the Castro government.

The prayer cases seemed particularly suspicious to those who suspected the High Court was full of Com-symps. There was nothing urgent about those cases. Why did the Court agree to hear them in the first place? They yielded decisions massively disruptive of fundamental structures, like education and the family, or religion as part of bringing up children in the public commons. Over and over, the justices' votes worked to shift power to the State.

The critics of judicial activism felt this shift most acutely in the post-Warren *Roe v. Wade*. As the prayer cases had undercut respect and piety in the schools, the intellectual and psychological incubators for our children, *Roe* weakened the very organizing institution of American society — the family itself. It took women out of the context of family when it came to decisions about reproduction. Did that not echo Russia and China, who had decided that strong family structure was bad for the State, because you couldn't organize production properly? Children were left in communes with professional caregivers, and the women went to work. And of course, out went the church, too, especially the charismatic formats that bound people through emotion and worship, and in came cradle-to-grave dependence — the village; it takes a village. And of course, to pay for it they had to break up private wealth and establish financial systems manipulated only by the State. And now it had bled to the U.S.; *Roe* was the very picture of a proto-Communism building block, not through direct state ownership, but by giving the only say about reproductive rights to the female, making her now the only unit the family-hating State needed to control.

Critics saw *Roe* as part of an ever greater vestment of power in centralized institutions. And this, they said, had to be at least an unconscious agenda of a Supreme Court that would bless federal abortion clinics as the way society should deal with its children.

Even publishers like Fred Woodworth of Arizona, whose anarchist writings Madalyn greatly admired and later solicited for her magazine, would ask about the Supreme Court: wouldn't you think the lawmakers would eventually say, "okay, we have enough laws now, we can quit"? But no, there were more and more laws, and thus more lawbreakers. And more lawyers: an unintended consequence of the

Warren court's initiation of expanded legal rights — *Miranda*, the appellate process, court-appointed attorneys, tenants' rights, and others — was an increasingly litigious society. Every Supreme Court decision seemed to create a new flood of niches, new rules and regulations removed from individual choice and put into a codified state system. They had to be enforced, and violators accused and defended in court.

(Woodworth was an anarchist, but he was expressing a theory of empire, that coherent structures — religious, cultural, and economic exchange networks — can only support so much friction before people would rather revolt than submit to oppressive taxes or outrages just to farm their crops or sell their goods. That is when the empire's coherent structures break down. The Soviet Union Madalyn revered would become a historic example, falling apart from its own weight, from trying to plan everything from Moscow. It was still intact during Madalyn's rise to fame, but she never believed the warnings that the urge to centralize and rationalize all of society was an ultimately regressive, not progressive, policy, and doomed to corruption and failure. She certainly never worried that fatal stress and collapse might similarly loom as an unintended consequence of American freethinkers' longstanding attempts to make rational the nooks and crannies of society.)

Madalyn saw a way to make a living from the ideological door opened by the changing legal system. Taxpayers would now pay not only to protect defendants, but for people to *initiate* legal action, the tab either charged directly to the state or indirectly, in tax-free donations to charitable organizations. She had already set about to form several. With the prying apart of church and state in the prayer cases, she felt empowered to launch a Constitutional battle to take away the churches' other powers, starting with property tax exemptions. And if the lawyerization of America was a parasitic blob that would grow huge and kill the host, Madalyn didn't care. It was her window of opportunity, and she went through it.

Chapter 10 ~ *The Most Hated Woman in America*

IN THE SUMMER OF 1962, Madalyn added another organization, Other Americans, Inc., to the Maryland Committee for Separation of Church and State. It was a vehicle to receive Kansan Carl Brown's bequests. She also opened the New Era Book Shop, but resigned six weeks later. Both entities were part of a jumble of personal and professional agendas; between 1962 and 1964, Madalyn produced a crazy quilt of organizations, projects, and publications, most of them short-lived.

A high school biology teacher in Delaware, Garry DeYoung, contacted her in 1962. Inspired by her, he had let it be known at work that he and his family were atheists. Immediately, his wife, Mary, a supremely competent elementary school teacher and mother of their large brood, was found "unfit . . . to teach children of a tender age." The DeYoungs decided to challenge the Delaware law keeping Bible reading and prayers in the schools, basing their case on Madalyn's. Garry traveled to Baltimore to get her advice and guidance.

Madalyn rapidly calculated how to harness the energies of fellow activists, but she didn't share power. She would quickly run off would-be colleagues who didn't understand that. But when she met DeYoung — tall, good-looking, virile, a fellow veteran, full of ideas and energy equal to her own — she made an exception.

He was a *mensch* who shared her vision and passions. He'd led the kind of hands-on, authentic life that was being idealized and romanticized by the budding hippie commune movement. The DeYoungs had lived on an 80-acre farm in Minnesota, restoring by hand a shell of a house to withstand 30-below winters, keeping a milk cow, growing their own produce. All the while, they published *The Crucible,* an atheist magazine of ideas. Both were good writers, and their kids, who ultimately numbered nine, learned to write, run the press, garden, sew, do carpentry, cook. The DeYoungs were living a dream Madalyn had had her whole life, of a large family, laboring together, close to nature, fighting a good fight. It was a dream from Lena's head, passed to Madalyn's as if through a membrane they shared.

DeYoung was the involved father she'd always wanted both for herself and her kids, instead of the runaway men at whom she raged. DeYoung listened to her as Pup never had, believed as she did, engaged and absorbed her mind, and was on her side.

She helped with his lawsuit, and they schemed together. "The only thing that would bring in money," she said, "is if we filed another case . . . It would bring . . . more than was needed for the legal fees so that we could start to build an organization." Atheists needed a project, with a goal, or they wouldn't give money.

"I felt that it was necessary to pick out a very important church-state separation issue, [to] hit the churches in their pocketbooks." She and DeYoung decided to attack the churches' property tax exemption. But they also needed a symbolic suit, something inflammatory to keep in the headlines, but easily launched and expendable. For that, they would attack the Pledge of Allegiance.

Madalyn wrote the Baltimore Board of Education that she wanted "under God" removed. It was "offensive to our individual liberties and our freedom of conscience," she wrote. "We are atheists." No, Garth and Bill couldn't be excused; that wasn't the point. The practice was unconstitutional.

They agreed DeYoung would return to Baltimore when school was out and help get the organization launched by taking the printing and other matters off her hands so she could concentrate on the cases. She was more than able — she was writing parts of her own Supreme Court brief with Kerpelman.

A few days after the Regents decision, Madalyn sat down and wrote Walter Hoops, a well-connected member of the rationalist and freethinker community of St. Louis. He and fellow activist Eldon Scholl had helped found the *American Rationalist* magazine in the early 1950s, and supported Camp Solidarity, a Socialist workers' summer camp.

Hoops had given Madalyn much publicity, directed donations her way, and invited her to speak at the American Rationalist Federation convention in St. Louis in August 1962. The St. Louis German Freie Gemeinde had come across with funds. She was being considered for Rationalist of the Year, a $5,000 award, and her talk would be featured in the next issue of the *Liberal* magazine.

She enclosed her monthly newsletter, which contained more of the truth-twisting she'd had success with before. She'd had to sell a piano, Oldsmobile, fur coat, and dinette back in June 1960, she said, to pay for her lawsuit (it wasn't conceived until October; she was preparing to defect to the USSR in June). She inflated her education, saying her South Texas College of Law degree was from "a graduate law school." She claimed to be a "fellow" with the National Institute of Mental Health.

"I do insist on being characterized as an atheist," she wrote Hoops, though her mother was Lutheran, her father "a good Presbyterian." (She sometimes said both parents were Presbyterian, and sometimes that Lena was raised Catholic.) "I come from good middle class, white, protestant, conservative stock — am 14 or 15th generation American, an old (Eastern) family."

Hoops picked up on her class anxiety. He'd already detected a flair for overstatement.

At the American Rationalist Federation convention in August 1962, Madalyn spoke on Materialism, invoking the martyrs of progressive thinking whose brilliance had been savaged by religion — Giordano Bruno, Galileo, Voltaire. She described how this persecution had mutated into today's forms: being cut out of jobs, pressure on one's children, political discrediting and rabble-rousing by the media, blocked opportunity, discrimination, loneliness, even divorce. Atheists and doubters were third-class citizens.

Everyone was impressed with her. "A beautiful presentation of a positive and fighting approach," wrote Arthur Cromwell. "We are not dealing with fairies and water-nymphs, but hard cold fisted gangsters [who] would plunge America into a world war ... to safeguard their church policies." The stale air of the freethought movement, dominated by older men with fixed, conservative ideas, stirred with excitement. She crackled with authority, and many reported on her courage — Garry DeYoung accompanied her to a speaking engagement in the South with Ku Klux Klan members in the audience. Suddenly, a screaming man charged the stage. Madalyn showed no fear, but calmly got up and walked backstage until he was subdued. In Baltimore, her car was shot at. Someone threw a cinder block through her office window as she worked late one night. She got death threats and hate mail, but they didn't deter her.

In a later article calling her "the most hated woman in America," *Life* magazine said Madalyn was built like a peasant, and her name was "anathema to millions." But to younger and far-flung activists, she was a populist, vastly different from the entrenched freethinkers who dominated the movement from their snobby urban comfort zones.

Ripsaw editor Virgil McClain spoke with her about moving to Baltimore from Indiana and joining forces. He gave her his entire August issue to raise money from his subscribers.

After her talk, she took a vacation with the boys, and found a pile of mail and money awaiting her on her return.

Chapter 11 ~ *"You got your wish, Spider"*

SHORTLY AFTER THE BOYS were installed back in school in the fall of 1962, Madalyn was hauled into court for her barking dogs. She said it was a lie by her neighbors because she was an atheist.

"Aw, baloney!" said their through-the-wall neighbor, Grace Bamberger. "She kept the dogs on...the porch and they'd bark all night. And she kept chickens in the yard — we had maggots crawling up into our windows. We had to call the health department! Yeah!"

As the homeowner, Pup was listed on the warrant, which upset him so much he had a heart attack. Madalyn's activities had brought vandals, newsmen, and police to their doorstep — and now court summonses. She had received hate mail that shook him to the core.

"I'm gonna put a gun up your ass and blow the crap out between your eyes."

She received a photo, smeared with feces, of herself and Lena coming out of court, and a page with the word "kill" cut and pasted all over it.

"Somebody is going to put a bullet through your fat ass, you scum, you masculine Lesbian bitch!" They said Bill looked like a queer, that she was a slut and a bitch that had given birth to a bastard. She was told that leprosy, cancer, and blindness were too good for her. Nicer writers called her a "big crude brawling peasant" and said she would die of her own poison. They said she should go to Russia, that she was wicked and a Communist.

She received a long poem: "I dreamed that Mrs. Murray died, and no one but the Devil cried." It went on about how there was no service at her gravesite (a prophecy that turned out to be true).

A bizarre radio report that Madalyn had been burned to death in a car wreck had almost caused Pup an earlier heart attack.

Neighbors interviewed by the FBI described Madalyn as "a constant agitator in the neighborhood" who had "expressed disloyalty to the United States. [Her] father, mother and brother live in constant fear of her and the parents have expressed their opinion that [she] is mentally unbalanced."

"The parents, the Mayses, were nice people," said Mrs. Bamberger. "They were upset by the way she was doing. Mr. Mays, oh, he used to tell my father, 'This girl is gettin' into so much trouble!'" Her parents confided in the family doctor, who also suggested Madalyn needed psychiatric help.

To the doctor, minister, and neighbors, Lena presented the face of convention along with her husband, bemoaning her wayward daughter. She kept silent when Madalyn berated her for political ignorance or abused her in front of visitors. Garry DeYoung remembered, "Lena was a typical grandmotherly type, very nice, didn't like all this conflict. She was full of platitudes — 'there's two sides to every story, Garry.'"

Yet Lena hovered over the basement committee meetings, chatting and serving refreshments, and they all loved her. She was gracious and charming, and loved entertaining, while Pup stared dourly at the television, oozing disapproval.

Mrs. Bamberger liked Lena, and when she saw her welcoming guests that everyone said were Pinko anarchists, she settled the contradiction with a popular Cold War explanation: Madalyn "brainwashed her mother. And the kids." They never closed their windows, and "she used to yell at her son a lot . . . He'd holler, 'Leave me alone!' Billy — she brainwashed him. And she always used to have a glass of wine in her hand, and her mother, too. Out on the front porch. I *guess* it was wine. Maybe it was vodka! Yeah!"

Lena's role as omega female was her bond with this restless daughter, who reached for something beyond a bloodless, conventional existence, just as Lena had done in her own youth. Madalyn wouldn't fritter away her God-given promise as Pup had done. She'd make something of the family name, like Gus Scholle had.

Though she comforted and stood by Pup as a wife should, Lena supported her daughter. They commiserated over their humble circumstances, brought off magical Christmases together; Lena even welcomed her daughter's recounting of *Deep Throat* one night after Madalyn had seen it in town. In the evenings, mother and daughter savored the progress of the prayer case over their tea and Southern Comfort. Lena helped with the printing and mailing of newsletters, in addition to running the household and caring for the children to free Madalyn for the Cause.

The barking-dog incident was an early flowering of the style that attracted and bewildered Madalyn's followers. In her newsletter, she wove it into a web of persecution that, as usual, drew on the truth — and was a classic model of her need to create an environment in which she felt in control.

The snarled tale began months before, when she'd pressed charges against some Woodbourne boys for assaulting Bill. The judge dropped the charges, by Madalyn's account, because the boys were Christians. When she drew the same judge for the dog incident, she refused to enter his court, saying he was biased. He had her arrested, threatened to have the dogs killed, and set a punitive bail. When her lawyer insisted he recuse himself, he surprised them by agreeing. But the replacement judge, in ignorance, had her arrested for refusing to answer the original summons.

Informed of the error, he quickly corrected it, but that didn't make headlines in Madalyn's newsletter. What did was the persecution, the false arrest, the biased judge. It raised money. Some readers began to suspect that, though she was gutsy and all her actions could be justified, her affairs were frequently so snarled that it seemed she might be creating the chaos. She would defy a court order on some basis which she gambled would later be ruled valid, and in the meantime set in motion related actions whose outcome would conflict with that of the original defiance, whether she won or lost. And, win or lose, she could make a credible case for discrimination or harassment.

She seemed to thrive on these tortured imbroglios, which some dismissed as attention-seeking. But she had learned that an outright strategy of confusion and chaos often serves well the person at the center of the web.

Pup's heart attack seemed to sober Madalyn. "Grandfather had a serious operation [where] they took veins out of his leg, and after that she stopped her rhetoric about him," said Bill. But Pup would not live to see his daughter's greatest triumph.

He saw the first phase, on October 8, 1962, when the Supreme Court agreed to review the combined Murray and Schempp cases — a huge triumph that brought dollars in the mail. Three months later, father and daughter argued one morning. Pup's heart surgery was not long behind him, and before she drove off to see a donor, she hissed that she wished he'd drop dead of a heart attack.

When she returned, Lena greeted her. "You got your wish, Spider." Pup, 69, had collapsed in the supermarket and died.

Bill remembered his mother reacting with such callousness that at first he thought she'd killed him herself.

"She wanted to spend the absolute minimum on the burial; she told *me* to make the funeral arrangements. What was I, 16? I called the undertaker and I told him, well, we had to have a cheap funeral, and then she went up there and said, 'he doesn't know what he's talking about' and spent thousands of dollars after she had told me to do it."

It was Lena who was behind Madalyn's change of heart. She demanded that her husband of more than 50 years be embalmed, that he have a decent casket, that he be allowed to lie in a funeral home, and that his service be properly observed with printed notices and a service by a minister. It seemed to shatter Madalyn's hard wall of anger at him, and release a flood of guilt and remorse.

She sat in the funeral home for three days, talking aloud to Pup. She couldn't stop crying, Bill said. After he was buried, she sat at the grave for hours in the rain. Lena and Irv consulted an attorney about having her committed.

Bill was confused. "The relationship was so incredibly bizarre. Constant outward hatred for that man, and then when he died . . . she sat on his grave and cried for hours."

But it hardened her even more against religion. She blamed the hate mail; she later said she'd like to publish it all someday under the title "Letters From Christians."

There was little question Madalyn was devastated by her father's death, but she was soon writing her followers that the movement had killed him, that not a single visitor showed up at the funeral home. That broke her heart, she wrote. There weren't even enough men to act as pallbearers.

However, these emotional blandishments didn't work on everyone.

"I wonder if you have noticed unusual things concerning the Murrays," wrote Eldon Scholl, Walter Hoops' colleague, a month after Pup's death. A "lack of financial report on her court case" was his main concern; and he was dismayed that Madalyn apparently planned to use any overage in donations to start new activities like an atheist radio station, magazine, and retirement home. She had the wrong idea about the freethought movement if that was what she planned — he anticipated some kind of "action" against her for "making a bid for something more than honest freethought activity."

It was just the kind of niggardly, constipated thinking that infuriated Madalyn when she found out. What business was it of his, the kind of movement she wanted to build? He seemed to be saying he'd try to cut her off at the knees if she departed from *his* idea of "honest freethought activity," that a retirement home or magazine for atheists couldn't possibly fit that description. She would soon fall out with troglodytes like she considered Scholl, Hoops, and their ilk to be.

In fact, soon after Pup's death, Madalyn wrote Walter Hoops an astonishingly hostile letter. A onetime supporter of hers, Lee Meriwether, had been given the Rationalist of the Year award she was expecting to get. He'd done nothing for freethought, and shame on Hoops, she wrote, for *selling* him the award just because Meriwether promised to donate the $5,000 back to the American Rationalist Federation after he died. "I can't believe that you groveled that much for $5,000."

"You know where I stand and I know where you stand," she concluded. "I accept your offer to be associate editor of the [American] *Rationalist.*"

He immediately withdrew the offer. "After your case has been decided, we shall tell our readers what you are doing to the freethought movement of this country."

Furious, Madalyn replied that nobody ever heard of Hoops anyway. "Print anything you like . . . When you have finished we will see the big splash you make in your little pond."

And she was right.

On February 26 and 27, 1963, *Murray v. Curlett* was argued in the U.S. Supreme Court, and *Abington Township v. Schempp* on February 27 and 28.

Madalyn and the boys stayed for the whole show, and when they got home, she reported, they found a broken window, snapped-off azalea bushes, and Bill's ham radio antenna bent to the ground. Garth came home crying, saying everyone at school hated him, they snatched his cap and lunch box, pushed him, and called him names. Some boys threatened Garth and Bill at a drugstore; Bill swore out a warrant, but the judge dismissed the case, as there was no law against verbal abuse or swinging a rosary under Bill's nose. However, Madalyn said, she did succeed in getting a patrol car parked in front of the house all night. And the FBI launched a search for a letter writer who mailed repeated, detailed death threats.

With delight, Madalyn recounted how her opposition took a pounding from the justices. Her attorney, Len Kerpelman, received the most flack from Justice Potter Stewart, the only dissenter in the Regents' Prayer case. When his challenges made Kerpelman stammer — asking exactly where in the First Amendment this "wall of separation" was that he kept citing — and he got Kerpelman to admit that the overwhelming majority of parents wanted their children to participate in the prayer, the other justices broke in and rescued Kerpelman with questions that set up his desired answers.

"With the setup in the Supreme Court at that time, yes, I was just a figurehead," Kerpelman said later. "I felt that very much when I made the argument. It was a good argument, but they knew a lot more about what they were doing than I did."

Madalyn didn't report it, but the crux of the argument was reached when Justice William O. Douglas said that if the majority wanted a "religious leaven" worked into its affairs, it should be the people, not the government, who did it. The schools' lawyers replied that that was exactly the case here; the people *had* worked a religious leaven into their affairs, and the *government* was trying to work it back out.

Not long after the arguments in DC, the Maryland legislature tried to pass a bill requiring a moment of silence in school each morning. The bill scolded the Supreme Court for "taking away the right of a free people to give some brief and nonsectarian acknowledgment of . . . their God."

Madalyn told her readers she found it shocking and scandalous that the legislature would reprimand the Supreme Court, as if it were some kind of secular sacrilege to criticize those nine men — though she had no reverence for them, or any authority.

Meanwhile, support was coming in from the wilderness: a Texas mother protested when her children were made to report on Mondays whether they had attended church the day before; a tax-the-church movement arose in Michigan; a teacher in New Jersey had his class say the Pledge the pre-1954 way; an Ohio high school district banned baccalaureate exercises (this was later overturned by angry parents).

Mailed along with Madalyn's February 1963 newsletter was a profile of the new organization Eldon Scholl had fretted about: Other Americans, Inc. It was subsuming the Maryland Committee for Separation of Church and State, and the venerable Freethought Society of America was moving from Philadelphia to Baltimore, where Madalyn would become editor of its magazine, the *Free Humanist*.

Her ambition was soaring: Other Americans would build local chapters and hold national conventions and have a seven-year plan; it would build its own university, administrative campus, printing plant, radio station, summer camp for kids, swimming pool, home for the aged — the urban renewal projects sweeping the country were creating a windfall of land for the Catholic Church to gobble up; why shouldn't atheists have some of it? She would file test cases, sell books and products, start a glossy, militant magazine, run ads in every freethought journal in the country. She reported pledges already coming in for her dream. Would they support this? Would they pay monthly dues? Subscribe to the magazine? Volunteer? And send names of others she could write to?

She wrote them to expect trouble when the decision came down. Tapes, films, and interviews were already being prepared for the big day, and lecture tours planned for the months after; 16-year-old Bill would be speaking, too.

As for her, she wrote, she was struggling personally. The boys need clothes, they needed groceries and rent, postage and ink and envelopes. "I cringe" at asking for money, but couldn't they please keep the family going for another month or so? "Our morale sags from time to time. We are all too human, too."

She enclosed an "architect's drawing" (in her own hand, from her drafting days at Martin Aircraft) of the atheist Administration Center and Retired Freethinker Cottages in the woods to be built on the "fine real estate" in Stockton, Kansas, donated by Carl Brown.

Cynics said she was targeting rich, lonely oldsters with her repeated references to a home for the aged. Kerpelman affirmed, "She was always carefully constructing a sucker list . . . there seemed to be more than an occasional . . . old guy with a lot of money, with chaotic ideas in his head about anarchy . . . these people are *way out* in their beliefs. And their *intensity,* I mean, when they hook onto something, they're like bulldogs, they have one *idea* for their whole life, and everything revolves around that. Well, she had a knack for finding well-off people who were like that."

By the end of April, a retired stonemason, Gustav Broukal, had bought her a press for her brochures, stationery, booklets, flyers, and the new magazine, *American Atheist.* She was tireless, writing hundreds of letters a month, taking speaking engagements, and putting out large mailings.

On her 44th birthday in April 1963, *Life* magazine published a letter from her that would become widely quoted: atheists "find God to be sadistic, brutal, and a representation of hatred, vengeance. We find the Lord's Prayer to be that muttered by worms groveling for meager existence in a traumatic, paranoid world."

It revealed, said Bill, "Mother's talent to infuriate people with acid-coated words." It was the prelude to a courtship that would last all her life, in which she drew to herself the hate, fear, and poison of her culture that would shake nickels and dollars out of the pockets of the disenfranchised and the idealistic.

Chapter 12 ~ June 17, 1963

O N JUNE 17, 1963, the United States Supreme Court delivered its 8–1 decision in the Murray-Schempp case. They won: the required Bible reading and recitation of the Lord's Prayer were unconstitutional. The public was reassured that nothing in the decision would bar the study of religion "when presented objectively as part of a secular program of education." The government, it said, had to "maintain strict neutrality, neither aiding nor opposing religion."

The reaction was a replay of the Regents decision, with two differences. First, this decision was expected, and the editorials were more grave, as opponents pondered the slippery slope onto which they felt the High Court was nudging the nation.

The other difference was Madalyn Murray. She simply made wonderful copy, willing and able to blowtorch anyone who dared dialogue with her. She was also charming and erudite, funny, articulate, and well-informed. And when she wasn't well-informed, she made things up — and by the time someone had gone to the trouble to check it out, it was stale news with no forum.

Reporters snapped pictures and grabbed tart quotes from a jubilant Madalyn, coifed and turned out in new clothes, coat, and hat. She invited them into her home, with its floral carpet, modern lamps, and a chess set, emblem of braininess, on the coffee table. With Ellory Schempp, Bill's counterpart, quietly off at Brown University studying physics, there was little competition to block the warming light of attention shed on Madalyn.

She described herself as a scholar, psychiatric caseworker, and militant peacenik. She had demonstrated at the White House over the Bay of Pigs. She had an autographed photo of Yuri Gagarin on her wall. She'd "turn every church into a hospital, a sanitarium, or a school... leave it to God and it won't get done." She was "a troublemaker at heart [who] does not give a damn what people think." And "It is criminal," she told reporters, "to foist your own beliefs on your children."

She didn't correct reporters who assumed her sons had the same father, and that she was divorced from him. They always mentioned her divorcée status, with its whiff of scandal, no matter how out of context it was.

Donations flooded in. "The mailman just brought *bags* of mail," said Bill. "She got more cash in that first 30 days than she'd ever made in her life. I'm talking about tens of thousands of dollars.

"Here you have somebody that was struggling away at a hundred-dollar-a-week income... And she opens up an envelope and there's a thousand dollar check in it. And she opens up another envelope and there's a $10,000 check in it. Opens up — a $20 bill, there's cash pouring in, that she doesn't have to report to the IRS.

"Up to that time at Winford Road... everybody who had money was made fun of, we bought that little bitty Nash, she thought the Russians had it right, it was a waste of money to make different cars." But when the suit was won, "She was stunned, she was amazed, I mean she was *awash* in money."

"I think that when somebody that's poor finally gets a taste of money, . . . it becomes like a drug . . . you want more and more and more and more. And I think that's what happened to her. The guy that was born with money is driving a Lincoln Navigator, and the guy that's nouveau riche has to have a Rolls-Royce. And there's never enough for the nouveau riche guy."

The camera flashes also caught something else — an expression of pleasure — that would show up in decades of photos of Madalyn. It was as if this were secretly what she lived for, these moments of blinding, undivided attention.

In July 1963, to media fanfare, Madalyn filed incorporation papers for Other Americans, Inc. She announced that OA would "advance the philosophy of materialism" through tax-the-church lawsuits planned for 15 states next fall.

She kicked off her campaign with a trip to Stockton, Kansas, site of the planned atheist compound, trailed by media. The primping and styling for the cameras were gone, indulged only for the immediate aftermath of the Supreme Court victory, and she now permitted herself to be photographed barelegged and unshaved, in shapeless sack dresses she whipped up herself to save money. Her hair went from glossy waves to an unkempt mop nailed back with bobby pins. She didn't care that she was fat, that her purse didn't match her shoes, that her only makeup was lipstick if she remembered to apply it. She allowed the papers to show her real and earthly, without pretense, for she had nothing to hide or camouflage.

She, Lena, and the boys arrived in Stockton to find area papers lined up. Carl Brown presented her to the *Stockton Sentinel* publisher. "Oh!" she said, "you run the newspaper, right?" The older gentleman nodded.

"I'm going to sue your ass off."

She spent several days there, describing the atheist compound she wanted — housing the "Ingersoll Pavilion" and "Darwin Pavilion." She accepted a deed to the first half of the Promised Land — 80 acres and a residence — and pronounced the dusty field and ancient house, cluttered with books and gewgaws, "nice." Bill and Garth, she told reporters, just loved north central Kansas.

Some residents were excited. This would be Stockton's biggest distinction since the 1890s, when it was hailed as the smallest town in the country to have electric lights. Maybe the new atheist compound would boost the economy.

The property owner across the road did threaten to stink them out with a pig farm, and a feeble petition emerged briefly. Someone told the FBI that the land was being used to train civil rights workers in the use of firearms. But, "ain't a dang thing anybody can do about it — they got a right to believe whatever they want," was about as militant as the Kansans got.

One threat might have sent a secret shudder through Madalyn — most locals said they would just ignore her. Stockton schools didn't even require any Bible reading in the first place; the nearest offender was 40 miles away in the Hays school district, where some of the teachers doubled as nuns. Madalyn made a stab at it, saying she'd enroll Garth in that district and file a federal suit. Whatever, said the laconic Hays superintendent. Long as she was ready to commute from her compound — he wouldn't enroll Garth unless he lived in the district.

And then it was over. The atheist colony idea died; Madalyn lost the land in later years, but she never revealed exactly how.

Chapter 13 ~ In Government We Trust

O N OCTOBER 16, 1963, Madalyn hired Leonard Kerpelman to file the *piece de resistance* tax suit that would keep the national eye on her and create a huge hullabaloo in Baltimore. Under the name of her newly formed Freethought Society, she sued to eliminate the city's church tax exemptions. Her suit, filed in circuit court, was based on a section of the Maryland Declaration of Rights which said that no citizen was required to pay to maintain a house of worship.

To have standing, she had to be a property owner. Lena owned Winford now; to help her daughter, she put half in the boys' names, and the two women filed jointly, Lena as owner and Madalyn as trustee for the minors.

The papers were on fire with the news, and public reaction was outrage and worry, especially from the Catholic Archdiocese of Baltimore. Churchgoers would have to pay an extra $3 million a year to keep their institutions afloat if the suit succeeded. It was calculated to add another $75 million to the tax base, but it might be much more, since the tax assessor didn't bother working out the market value of church property.

Needless to say, the archdiocese immediately contested the suit. Madalyn didn't care about adding tax dollars to the city coffers, it said; she simply wanted to destroy religion. Taxes were simply her weapon of choice. The government, it said, actually had a duty to accommodate the free exercise of religion through tax breaks, because this was what the people wanted, this *was* the people's idea of church-state separation. Taxing would be the state exercising power over religious expression. A tax exemption was *not* the same as a tax subsidy. And, a Constitutional crisis might ensue if Madalyn won. Under Maryland law, for example, her atheist university could be tax-exempt. That would give nonbelief a legal advantage over belief. That was unconstitutional.

Some joked that, in assuming the government would fork over the windfall and everyone's property taxes would drop, Madalyn was displaying more faith in government than many Christians had in God.

The Supreme Court had historically declined jurisdiction over such cases, but Kerpelman was relying on the Court's liberal trajectory to depart from tradition.

The Friendship Liberal League, with whom Madalyn had been trying to build a coalition, wrote her that it disagreed with her strategy — the suit should be filed in district, not circuit, court. They didn't want procedural errors — if she lost in the lower courts on merits like venue, it could set legal precedents that would paralyze future efforts. It wasn't like she was the first person to think of this. Why hadn't she collected more of the wisdom on it?

She decided they were a bunch of old fools, bumping into each other and fussing over protocol while the country continued to roll over the Constitution. They didn't realize that their time at the helm was done, that they should move over for new leadership, or that the country was in a militant new era that called for action.

She was right; the country was in a militant new era. Two events came together to define it: the civil rights movement and growing American involvement in Vietnam.

Americans at first assumed Vietnam was a "good war" like World Wars I and II, this time against Communism. Some 1965 polls showed an approval rating for U.S. military involvement as high as 80%. But within a couple of short years, those figures plummeted. Citizens increasingly questioned why we were there. No one knew how we'd gotten involved in the first place.

The genesis was convoluted, but of special interest to Madalyn, as it involved Catholics and Communists. France had exploited its Indochina colonies for nearly a century before its surrender to Germany in 1940. It then lost Vietnam to Japan, and, after being given it back at the postwar Potsdam Conference, lost it again in 1954 to Communist Ho Chi Minh in the massive French surrender at Dien Bien Phu. The U.S. was already paying over 75% of France's war costs against Ho, hoping its old ally, which had spread Catholicism throughout Indochina, might help block the growing tide of Communism in Asia. But the 1954 Geneva Accords removed France from Vietnam and divided the country at the 17th parallel, with the north ceded to Ho's Communists, and instructions to hold elections to reunify.

The U.S. had a chance to bow out then. But fearing a Communist election victory, it instead put its muscle behind a South Vietnamese Catholic, Ngo Dinh Diem, who had firm support both from then-senator John F. Kennedy and Vice President Richard Nixon. Within months of his 1961 inauguration, Kennedy, the first Catholic president, sent 400 Green Beret "Special Advisors" to Saigon; soon (contrary to what he told the American people), they were involved in combat operations. By the end of the year, it was costing a million dollars a day to prop up South Vietnam's army, and, Catholic or not, Diem headed a brutal regime that ended with his assassination just three weeks before Kennedy's.

By that time, the U.S. was spending hundreds of millions in the belief that all of Southeast Asia would go Communist if Vietnam did (indeed, China would soon be massing troops along the border, and testing its first atomic bomb). But to the taxpayers at home, there was nothing clear-cut about exactly what the objective was in Vietnam, or how we would achieve it. We had simply backed into this war. As casualties grew, doubts got more and more vocal.

The early anti-war protesters were mainly white, middle-class, and educated, suspicious of the government. But by the late 1960s, they were from all ethnic and socio-economic groups, demanding answers. The demographics mirrored the civil rights movement, and the aftermath of sweeping changes wrought by the Warren court fueled the unrest. Coalitions formed among civil rights and anti-war activists, and the "issue" groups they spawned, from women's rights and the environment to Yippies and Weathermen and Black Panthers. Martin Luther King Jr. said the draft tapped a disproportionate number of blacks. It drained money from President Johnson's Great Society programs. It was immoral; let Vietnam run its own affairs. It was illegal; the 1964 Gulf of Tonkin Resolution giving President Johnson the power to wage it was illegal.

Draft evaders multiplied more than a hundredfold between 1965 and 1969; the number of deserters soared. Tens of thousands fled the U.S. to avoid conscription, while others went to prison or filed as conscientious objectors. Frustration turned to rage as the "living room war" brought images of Buddhist priests burning themselves to death in protest of our presence, our own soldiers butchered, children burned with napalm, people we were liberating screaming for us to get out. It birthed an era of hard-hitting investigative journalism, as reporters unearthed government lies, exaggerations of body counts, and other manipulations that were standard fare in the "good wars."

And there were the images of America's own streets, the breakdown of civility and authority as protesters grew more militant. Nuns and priests broke into a Maryland draft office and poured blood over the conscription records. Law-abiding youth burned their draft cards. Police at rallies were taunted and called pigs and fascists; unruly crowds shoving, screaming obscenities, and throwing bottles and rocks were clubbed with nightsticks and tear-gassed as they ran through the streets. The protesters carried Viet Cong flags. They accused their government of infiltrating their meetings, tapping their phones, planting provocateurs. They started underground anarchist presses.

Conservative parents watched their children metamorphose into long-haired, unwashed, draft-dodging, drugged-out dropout flower children with incoherent ideas about free love, who worshipped that Commie traitor Jane Fonda for going to Hanoi and betraying her own country. When the 1968 Democratic National Convention in Chicago was disrupted by student-led riots, the Silent Majority backlash was galvanized. Bumper stickers supported the police, and exhorted ingrates to Love America or Leave It. President Nixon dubbed these law-abiders, uneasy with society's dramatic changes and furious at the disrespect for authority during wartime, the Silent Majority, and called for their support.

Nineteen sixty-eight was one of the century's most divisive, bloody, and traumatic years. The Tet Offensive left horrific American casualties; massive riots erupted in the cities of America and Europe and culminated in the assassinations of Dr. King and Bobby Kennedy. American soldiers massacred civilians in the village of My Lai. "Americans don't think of themselves as doing that," said a military wife-turned-pacifist. "But we did." When National Guardsmen killed four students at a Kent State University anti-war demonstration in 1970, campuses shut down all over the country as fellow students poured out their rage against their government, rioting, taking over administration buildings, demanding that defense contractors and researchers be ordered off campus, sabotaging banks because they were symbols of the capitalist system that fueled war.

Everything military came to be hated. Returning veterans found themselves spat on, ostracized, and called baby-killers. Some reclaimed normal lives, some became super-patriots, some became anti-war and lobbied Congress, and some ended up in ruins, living under bridges.

Into this matrix, Madalyn introduced the Baltimore school board to her Pledge of Allegiance issue on April 11, 1964. Kerpelman and the media were with her, and the attendance was large.

As she expected, the board said it had no authority to remove the phrase "under God." Dr. Brain told the meeting that this had raised more emotional hackles than anything Madalyn had done yet. An enormous influx of mail had come in from all over the world. A group called Freedom of Prayer had collected nearly 2,700 signatures in only hours, opposing any change.

But with national media coverage, public support for Madalyn's challenge was also immediate. In Albany, a group of students refused to salute the flag or say the Pledge. The state education department had to hire a lawyer, who told the school board president that if she was going to let the kids get away with refusing the required "citizen instruction," what was to stop them from refusing to take American History? One of the boys said he believed in world government, and wouldn't salute any flag until there was one that flew over the entire world.

Madalyn could see the impact she was having. Her talk roughly coincided with the Judiciary Committee's public hearings on the 144 resolutions to amend the Constitution that had been presented in the less than two years since the Regents Prayer case. On April 24, Madalyn went to U.S. District Court and filed suit to challenge Maryland's newly adopted "moment of silence" law. She was elected to the board of the American Humanist Association, serving alongside Vashti McCollum.

Sometime during all this activity, a minister showed up at Winford. In 1926, he had founded the Gospel Tract Society in Independence, Missouri, with nothing but $11 and the Lord's mandate, and he now had a very successful printing and publishing enterprise with a large budget. Could he just have a few moments of Madalyn's time? He wanted to explain about Jesus, about the blessings that could come when you did the Lord's work.

"Sure, come on in." As Bill watched from a living room chair, she let him inside and then started up the stairs, beckoning him to follow. "You can tell me all about Jesus, but first let's go up and f---. Then after we're through f---ing we can talk about Jesus. Or maybe we can talk about Jesus *while* we're f---ing."

She had long ago learned that stunning her foes with obscene or hostile language would provoke them to anger and emotion, whose inherent rationality was then easily attacked. But it didn't work that way with the Reverend Lester Buttram. Instead, it bound him to her. He would dog her tracks the rest of his life, and have a profound effect on her family.

Chapter 14 ~ "Get that bitch!"

BY THE TIME BILL GRADUATED high school in 1964, Madalyn, tending a hundred different fires and dealing with volunteers and sometime employees, decided to get embroiled in something that would undermine everything she'd worked for.

About a year before, Bill had met a student at all-girls Western High. In conservative, Catholic Baltimore, Susan Abramovitz felt like a halfbreed. Her father, an anesthesiologist, was an orthodox Jew and her mother a Gentile.

The Abramovitzes lived in a large house in a well-heeled area of Baltimore, with a cook and laundress and two Volkswagen buses for carting their seven kids around. Dr. Abramovitz was a sober man, rather distant from his children. "Nice enough, but very serious," said an acquaintance. "No cutting up with *him*."

His wife, Jeanne, was a lively woman, easy to talk to, fun-loving and busy, who kept up a secret rebellion against her adopted religion by regularly sneaking over to a restaurant in Towson to eat bacon. But her daughter Susan, a slender, bespectacled redhead who was president of the United Nations Club at school, was shy. And "If Susan is at a gathering," Jeanne told a friend, "she'll be drawn to the oddball of the crowd. Like a magnet."

Madalyn later claimed that Susan's faith required her to cover her head, obsequiously serve the males, and bathe after school because "she might have been touched by a Gentile in the streetcar." Whether that was true or not, there was little question the girl was primed for rebellion, and was attracted to the exotic world of notoriety, outsider camaraderie, and intellectual ideology that Bill Murray inhabited.

Madalyn bought an office building at 2502 North Calvert, and Susan attended parties there teeming with activists, intellectuals, college students, and elders, all aglow in the excitement of revolution. Bill had confidently taken over the printing of Madalyn's newsletter, though he was a novice on the expensive new press, and his performance was as sporadic as would be expected for a 17-year-old. Half the time Madalyn had to farm out the printing because he'd let ink dry on the rollers.

Unlike Susan's proto-Soccer Mom, Madalyn was a star, an outlaw, filing her high-profile suits and giving lectures; her home was a beehive, her life crowded with volunteers, lawyers, reporters, hangers-on, and officers in her organizations.

Bill had stopped volunteering for the Cause, and Madalyn was now paying him. She bought him a 1963 Oldsmobile Cutlass when he was a junior in high school. But Bill began pulling away from his upbringing just as Susan was hers.

"Was there a point where I believed all this leftist gobbledygook? Yes, it was shoved at me 24 hours a day. We would be eating cereal and my mother would say there was rat shit in there, because our government allowed it, allowed the capitalists to get away with it because they paid them off, but the Communists don't allow rat feces in their grain. They're better, they're pure, they're good, and the capitalists are rotten to the core. But at some point, I went from believing to enduring."

Susan's father was dead-set against the courtship. Bill believed it was because he wasn't a Jew, but the source of the doctor's disapproval hardly mattered. It did its job, driving the kids into each other's arms. But one day in March 1964, Bill came back from a meeting of his ham radio club to find Susan in his basement room, unpacking her suitcases. Madalyn said the girl had shown up at the door with "a black eye and a swollen nose and a piece chipped off her tooth and swollen mouth and bruised breasts. . . ."

"She told us that her father had beaten her with his fists and had kicked her" because she didn't want to serve the food or something at a Jewish ritual. "I needed this like I needed a hole in the head. But there she sat." She couldn't in good conscience send the girl home.

Bill had planned on letting *l'affair Susan* die a natural death and entering the University of Maryland in the fall. He later denied the body bruises and chipped tooth. He did admit that her father once hit her in the face so hard it broke a bone in his hand. But his mother, he said, was exaggerating the initial injuries to cover her real motive. "She thought she could use Susan to control me. But the reality was, I was not controllable." He was too much like his grandfather.

Susan briefly moved back home. One day, Jeanne Abramovitz called repeatedly, demanding to know where she and Bill were. Nobody heard from them all night, and then, about ten the next morning, the phone rang. It was Susan, said Madalyn. "She said, 'Madalyn Murray? I want you to know that I have been up here in Canada fucking your son.' And she said it *just like that*."

Madalyn said her first thought was, 20 years in jail. Bill had taken a minor across state and national borders and committed statutory rape — a girl's consent didn't count in Maryland. "I . . . aged forty or fifty years in the next three or four minutes." She asked for Bill. He told her they were in Niagara Falls. Had they got married? No. Had they registered as man and wife? Yes. She went out and wired enough money to get them home, and didn't answer the phone the rest of the day.

That was Madalyn's version. Bill vehemently denied the telephone call. "A teenage girl would call her and say, 'We're up here having sex'? Does this make sense? You know what this is? This is for her to prove, after the fact, that she was controlling the situation. If she could control my sexual relationships, then she could control me."

The next day, they arrived back at Winford. Madalyn took Susan to the American Jewish Family and Children's Agency and asked them to intervene. But they could work only with the parents, and the Abramovitzes wouldn't speak with Madalyn.

Angry, Madalyn went to court and filed an abuse complaint against Dr. Abramovitz. She said Susan requested it, that she had sought refuge with her. She signed a school form declaring herself *in loco parentis* for Susan.

Her volunteers, lawyers, and assistants, though they liked Bill, said he was self-importantly advising Susan of her constitutional rights. Susan was now refusing to return home unless she got the following concessions: a car, a college education, no pressure about any kind of religious training, and permission to come and go as she pleased and keep whatever company she wanted. Her parents finally got her to agree to live with relatives. But Madalyn wouldn't turn the girl over without a court order. That would serve little purpose but to tweak a rich Jewish doctor she knew scorned her.

The day after he turned 18, Bill read in the paper that he had been sued in criminal court under a rarely used law against causing a minor to be without proper guardianship. He was also charged with illegally taking Susan out of Maryland.

A hearing was set for June 1, but the Abramovitz lawyers never served the Murrays with formal notice. Here was another opportunity for chaos. Lawyer Madalyn believed the Abramovitzes' complaint should have been filed in juvenile, not criminal court, so there was a procedural error. Moreover, since she and Bill were never given formal notice, she ignored the hearing, knowing full well that she and the kids would probably be found in contempt (they were). She then filed a countersuit for neglect, requesting psychiatric exams for both Abramovitzes and asking that all their children be put in foster homes.

This maneuvering would tie up staggering amounts of time, energy, and money, and change the course of Madalyn's life.

On the hearing date, the courtroom was so packed that people were turned away. Judge James Cullen signed a restraining order directing Bill and Madalyn to keep away from Susan. He placed her in the custody of her aunt and uncle, but Susan wasn't to be found.

As the scandal blazed up in the papers, Susan told Bill she'd missed her period.

A wedding, reasoned Madalyn, would be the perfect end run, mooting the Abramovitzes' court order and the charges, since Susan would by law become a ward of her husband. Maryland law allowed underage girls to marry if they were pregnant.

Madalyn called on a 26-year-old army microbiologist at Ft. Detrick named Lemoin Cree, who was deeply involved in her church tax suit. The young couple was whisked off to the Crees' home in Frederick, Maryland, and the Crees paid their $45 marriage fee. Then the kids went off for a honeymoon, in violation of the restraining order and courtesy of Madalyn's donors, with the police looking for them.

In the *Murray Newsletter*, Madalyn used this imbroglio to both raise money and hide her mistakes. The court system of Baltimore, she said, had trumped up the charges to derail her church tax suit, which had grown fat with intervenors, *amici*, and revelations of how much property the churches actually owned. The papers were now saying billions were at stake if Madalyn's case was successful, for the Fourteenth Amendment's equal protection clause would insure that it applied to all the states.

Doubtless her foes were figuring how to use her troubles against her, but in actuality, Kerpelman had been telling Madalyn for three months that she was playing with dynamite by letting Susan stay there, and had urged her to get the girl into the YWCA. He was exasperated with her personal messes; instead of working on the church tax lawsuit, he was spending his time on dogs, chickens, and teenagers. There was an important hearing on the tax suit the day Bill and Susan were married, in fact.

It was at this busy and troubled time that *Ripsaw* publisher Virgil McClain and his wife sold their home in Indiana and took Madalyn up on an offer made months before, of lodging at her rambling Calvert Street office and an opportunity to work in the exciting new atheist movement. She badly needed a reliable printer, and McClain agreed to combine *Ripsaw* with Madalyn's *Free Humanist*. He was excited about the move. He'd brought his own personal stock of new books to get sales going — and his all-important mailing list.

But the McClains found their promised living quarters filled with printing and ham radio equipment. A promised parking spot had been fenced off so Tsar could guard the building, though he preferred sleeping inside with the cat. Believing it was temporary, they plunged into the work, renting their own apartment and attacking the backed-up book orders. But the office was unworkable. Madalyn sometimes locked certain rooms, including the one with the phone. The printing equipment was idle 95% of the time, either because of dirty rollers, no one having bought supplies, locked doors, or other disorganization. Madalyn constantly complained about money, though she and Bill both drove new Oldsmobiles, and McClain found himself buying gas when they traveled, and printing materials at his own cost.

Madalyn kept liquor at the office, and sometimes had drunken, emotional outbursts. Some days she went through the building locking every door, and others she would have a breakdown and storm off for the day without even closing the front door. One of her tantrums drove the cat off; it never returned.

Garry DeYoung had seen her moods, too; one day she was burning trash behind her bookstore, and the owner of the neighboring beauty shop came over and politely asked if she might put off burning until later in the day, when the wind shifted.

"[Madalyn] lit out after that woman with a string of vulgarities... telling her to mind her own f---ing business, that she had the legal right to burn that garbage, that the trash barrel was within the fifty feet requirement from a structure, that if she didn't like it, she could call the f---ing cops." Then she added scraps of linoleum to the fire, generating foul black smoke.

One night the McClains rode with Madalyn to Philadelphia to hear her speak at Temple University. She drove at breakneck speed, all the while explaining her theory of why it took so much energy to have an orgasm.

The next day, they told Madalyn they were leaving. She didn't seem upset; in fact, she began singing. The McClains joined the growing cadre of her detractors. They accused her of stealing the Schempps' thunder — the outcome would have been the same if she'd never joined the suit. She just drowned them out and grabbed all the money and glory for herself.

It would be an oft-repeated criticism over the years, but, as her defenders noted, it was loud-mouthed Madalyn Murray who put in people's faces, and Madalyn Murray O'Hair who kept it there for the next 30 years, that in ways large and small, religion was violating the Constitution and marbling itself into the government. Despite the *McCollum* and Regents and *Murray-Schempp* cases, towns in Iowa and Texas and Missouri and New Jersey and every state kept right on doing exactly what they wanted in the public schools, no matter what the lawgivers in Washington said. They just rolled over the Constitution — until this brassy fighter came along and rolled back. And who else was going to do it? Who else was going to put that kind of energy into it? She worked 16 hours a day. So what if she had an Oldsmobile? So what if she got drunk and threw a fit now and then?

When Bill and Susan returned from their honeymoon on June 20, 1964, all hell broke loose. According to Bill, almost as soon as they got back to Winford, patrol cars and neighbors gathered out front.

"They wanted that doctor's daughter," said neighbor Grace Bamberger. "I told 'em [Madalyn] was hidin' Billy and his girlfriend in the cellar."

They didn't have a warrant, and Madalyn refused to let them in. As they moved off to confer, Madalyn and Susan suddenly darted out the door and raced for the car, and Bill blocked a policeman while the women made their escape. Madalyn dropped Susan at another location and returned to find police in her house and her mother lying on the sofa. Kicking and screaming, she was arrested along with Bill and Lena.

Madalyn was charged with kicking an officer and threatening two more with a tear gas pen. Bill was charged with hitting two officers to keep them from arresting Susan. Lena was charged with hitting an officer. A hearing was set for next day.

Lemoin Cree, who saw the melée, said the cops were subduing Bill as his mother drove off, when Lena came up and slapped one of them on the head. He scowled at her. She passed out. The cops carried her inside as Madalyn came tearing back in the car. "Get out of my house!" she screamed. When they tried to subdue her, "She became very wild," said Cree. They were quite rough with her, though Cree didn't see them hit her, and they used abusive language. There were 16–20 police, and a crowd of about 100 neighbors.

Madalyn's version had the police beating the door down, neighbors screaming, "Get that bitch!," the police clubbing her shoulders and arms, pummeling her, dragging her to the door as she grabbed the screen and porch rail, punching her in the face, and pushing her face in the dirt with a foot on her neck. (To *Playboy* magazine later, she gave a more dramatic and bloody version: her fingernails were ripped completely off, she was rolled on the ground to the car and clubbed all the way, she tripped four officers like clowns, her hands turned black from the tight cuffs, she saw boot marks on Bill's face, crotch, and chest, Lena was out cold for three hours, someone lacerated Tsar's face, and the police tried to sneak into her house that night to steal a tape recording of the fracas.)

Kerpelman got them all out about 11 p.m., and they went home — carting along Mae Mallory, who had been working in the Cause, and a woman reporter from the Associated Press. They sat up into the wee hours discussing whether Madalyn should leave Baltimore. Assault and battery against the police was strong medicine. She criticized Kerpelman for not filing illegal entry and assault countercharges against the police.

They didn't have visas for Cuba, to join Robert Williams. Boston? No, the Catholics were so strong there. New York? No, Cardinal Spellman. Los Angeles? No, Cardinal McIntyre. Mae Mallory suggested Hawaii, because it was Buddhist, she said, and she'd heard you couldn't be extradited from there.

The next day, June 21, 1964, the fight was covered in papers across the land, and a hearing was held in Municipal Court for the three generations of Mays-Murrays. They requested jury trials and waived preliminary hearings on what finally totaled 11 charges.

The hearing was "turbulent," reported the newspapers, with Madalyn and Bill standing out in the hall "shout[ing] profanities" at police witnesses and officers of the court as they walked into the courtroom. Inside, the family refused to take the collective oath. Though Kerpelman told Judge Joseph G. Finnerty that Bill and Susan were married, Mrs. Bill Murray was immediately arrested on contempt charges from her June 2 failure to appear in court. She was later released on $5,000 bail.

Bill, wearing khaki shorts and sandals, stood quietly during the hearing. But near the end, he suddenly dropped to the floor and wrapped his legs around a table leg, yelling that he wouldn't "go back to that cell and be worked over again." (Though Madalyn's tale of boot marks was untrue, Bill had indeed been beaten in jail.) He was carried out by six cops as he yelled, "You Christian, you Christian, you Catholic!" Contempt and disorderly conduct were promptly added to his tab. With Susan's fee, bail for all of them totaled $8,750.

Madalyn's mind was made up. She got Irv, Lena, Bill, Susan, Garth, the dogs, and herself all tickets to Hawaii with Bill's college fund.

June 22, 1964, was the day Madalyn's church tax suit was to start; she was granted a continuance. It was also her last night in Baltimore. She got drunk and told Mae Mallory that if she couldn't beat all the charges against her, she was going to defect to Cuba to join Robert Williams.

On Tuesday, June 23, 1964, the family fled, leaving Mallory in charge of their home, and the Calvert Street office in the care of Lemoin Cree, though Madalyn took a copy of the mailing list. Cree was to publish the new *American Atheist* magazine and hold down the fort until things could be sorted out.

Before she left, Madalyn gazed at her house one last time. (Shortly, in an interview, she would transform the despised, faceless row house into a "nice brick Colonial.") She showed her reporter friend her bruised arms and wrists. "We are fleeing for our lives," she said. "That may sound corny, but it's true." She was going to ask Hawaii's governor for religious asylum.

The family flew to San Francisco under Lena's maiden name. Bill was zombie-depressed, his mother in a corresponding state of euphoria. They arrived in Honolulu in a flurry of national publicity; even a story about their lost baggage made the local front page.

Madalyn was in for a surprise; only a third of the state was Buddhist. The rest were mostly Catholics, including the governor. Nonetheless, Honolulu churches reached out to the atheists, offering lodging; a children's group raised $22.50 for the family, saying they were their brother's keeper, and a minister denounced the attacks on the Murrays in Maryland, asking Madalyn to address his congregation. She declined. A teenage girl, under the same illusion as the Reverend Lester Buttram, offered to drive the family around, adding, "With a little bit of kindness, maybe they will begin to love Jesus as I do." Madalyn found the gestures cloying. There were always parasites around, leeching off the attention she generated. These "Christers" were transparent with their saccharine gestures.

However, she and her entourage did end up at a Unitarian church. They rented a station wagon, bought five mattresses, and spread out their belongings in a large room above the sanctuary, "the sun room," Madalyn called it. She, Susan, and Bill sat with a city map and newspapers and searched for an apartment.

Convinced that they were being shown only dirty, bug-infested properties, she turned to an old ally. "The Communist Party is terribly powerful in Hawaii," Madalyn avowed later, and someone affiliated with the Party helped secure a big, rambling house in the Punchbowl area at 1060 Spencer Street. Anyone else would pay $400, but for them — "$150, simply because we were who we were."

Immediately, Maryland tax officials raised doubt as to whether Madalyn now had standing to pursue her church tax suit, since she'd abandoned her property. Nonsense, said Kerpelman; she didn't have to be present, she just had to still be a taxpayer. But her suit challenging Maryland's new "moment of silence" law went on hold, as she no longer had children in school in Baltimore.

On June 25, contempt citations were issued in Baltimore for Bill and Madalyn for ignoring the restraining order to stay away from Susan. It was a hostile, ridiculous gesture, said Madalyn — Susan was now Mrs. Bill Murray. If they tried to extradite her to face these now-moot charges, she would fight it to the Supreme Court. The next day, the grand jury handed down an 11-count indictment against Madalyn. She hired prominent Honolulu attorney Hyman Greenstein to fight extradition.

She was genuinely afraid to go back. Bill's beating in jail was real. Her hate mail was real. The neighbors' animosity was real; as Mrs. Bamberger later snickered, "When they were building that [recreation center] there across the street, they told us, 'Bring her over here and we'll put her in the foundation . . . said 'we're pourin' the concrete, put her *right here!'*'" There was certainly no reason the police shouldn't have had an arrest warrant for Susan, and whether it was from police brutality, as she said, or an existing condition, she got treated for neck pain at the army's Tripler Hospital shortly after arriving in Hawaii. Moreover, a couple of nights after the fracas at Winford, someone broke into the Calvert Street office and rifled through her files. A witness told Kerpelman the intruder was driving a city car. "He was a city inspector . . . we identified him . . . and the state's attorney refused to do anything!" It seemed clear that Madalyn had reason to be paranoid.

But there was also a legitimate concern about "Billy and Sue." Marriage didn't magically erase the Abramovitzes' claim that their daughter was brainwashed or coerced. She was not yet 18.

And coercion seemed realistic; Bill and Susan fought all the time, and a few weeks after their arrival in Honolulu, Susan was seen trying to board a plane back to Baltimore while Bill talked her out of it.

Madalyn pleaded with her son to present a united front in public.

"You have to stay with her. You have to pretend there is a marriage," she told him. But he didn't want to. "He ran away from Susan twice a week, I would go with Susan to help her to find him and I tried to keep the marriage together. I was on Susan's side constantly against my son . . . He was very, very angry with me."

He was indeed angry, that she'd taken Susan in in the first place. "Had not it been for my mother's intervention," he said years later, "it would have ended. There would probably not even have been a child. The relationship was basically coming to a conclusion when my mother intervened." It was almost as if she had set him up to rewrite her own story. With her connivance, another Bill Murray had made a child, and, unlike the Catholic Bill Murray, this one was going to marry the mother.

While pressuring Bill and Susan to behave like a conventional married couple, though, Madalyn gave a bawdy interview to *Playboy*. It made no sense, she said, to repress our sex drive for six or eight years beyond puberty. Look at nature, at cows, flowers. They do it when they're ready, and it should be the same for kids. Just teach them about birth control and VD and then "[let them] go at it." There should be no judgment or rules, and certainly no license to couple, any more than you should be licensed to eat or defecate.

Most men, she said, were shallow cretins who wanted young, submissive, empty-headed, big-titted chicks. They were intimidated by mature, intelligent, educated, confident women such as herself.

"It's going to take a pretty big man to tame this shrew. I need somebody who can at least stand up to me and slug it out, toe to toe...a man who would lay me, and when he was done, I'd say: 'Oh brother, I've been *laid.*'" He would be her intellectual equal, "whole and wholesome [with] as much zest for living as I have." He'd tear into a steak but love ballet. He'd have culture, and money to support her in the way she wanted, and when she was done with him, he should be willing to say, fine, *ciao.* These men were so scarce, she said.

But in less than a year, she would find one.

Madalyn fired a steady stream of requests to Kerpelman to do whatever it took to keep the church tax case on track, and it started July 1, 1964. Kerpelman argued that the exemptions amounted to state-supported religion, which violated the First Amendment and the Maryland Declaration of Rights. When it was his turn, the city attorney blew past the merits of the case to Madalyn's sensational flight, and asked that the trial be postponed until she was brought back to testify.

Judge Wilson Barnes said no. He gave Kerpelman, the city, the state, and the churches who had intervened until September to file briefs.

Meanwhile, only a week after arriving in Hawaii, Madalyn found that her organization had been taken over by the people she left in charge, headed by Lemoin Cree. He'd called an emergency board meeting, and they'd resolved to offer Madalyn $10,000 a year to be chairman and step down as president and editor. Shocked, she refused. They voted her out, installed their own officers, and took over all the assets, including the Calvert Street building, press, files, and equipment.

The Freethought Society letterhead now listed Cree, not Madalyn, as president; he also became president of Other Americans. The *Free Humanist* had become the *American Atheist* magazine in January, and Cree started putting out issues asking readers to support the new regime, and requesting donations to erase the disgrace and pandemonium Madalyn had caused.

Madalyn read in her own magazine Kerpelman's effusive praise of Lemoin Cree as a witness in the church tax case. Cree's testimony was "splendid and brilliant," and he skillfully disarmed the state's and archdiocese's lawyers. Cree and his wife, Maria, were now co-plaintiffs with Madalyn's Freethought Society.

She was furious. It should have been her there in court, giving splendid and brilliant testimony and humiliating churchmen, her being praised, her publishing *American Atheist* magazine. Even worse, after he finished testifying, Cree went to the bank and told them that he was the only one authorized to sign checks for Other Americans. Madalyn had tried that very day to withdraw funds, and been blocked. The bank asked the circuit court to settle who owned the money. (It was a bad day all around; Maryland governor Millard Tawes signed extradition papers for her and Bill, and she was arraigned that day in Baltimore, *in absentia,* on the 11-count grand jury indictment handed down June 26.)

She immediately put out an issue of her old *Murray Newsletter* from Honolulu. Cree and the new ersatz board were undercover church operatives who had fooled her and gotten her confidence, she wrote; she found out when she sent a "true friend" — Mae Mallory — in to check what was happening. Mallory found that the board was working in tandem with the city and state governments to derail the church tax suit. Madalyn begged her readers not to send any more checks to Lemoin Cree, and not believe a word he was saying. The organization would be restarted from Honolulu. She was trying to get her printing equipment out of the grip of the religionists who had tricked her.

She demanded that Kerpelman remove the Crees from the church tax suit. When he refused, she fired him, replacing him with Joe Wase, who, according to Cree later, had only four cases to his credit. This snarled her suit, as Kerpelman was representing other entities besides Madalyn in the suit.

When her Honolulu newsletter came out, Cree wrote members that it was full of lies, and was illegally mailed to "our members." He notified the post office that Madalyn had stolen the organizations' mailing list and was fraudulently using it from Hawaii. He reminded readers that the Freethought Society of America was *not* Madalyn's property — the members and subscribers and donors and Lou Alt's lifetime of work built it.

But Cree misjudged his audience. What Madalyn's followers were smitten by was her air of leadership and authority — "command presence," one member called it. However sagacious Cree might have appeared to Kerpelman, he didn't have what Madalyn had, and her defenders came forward. *Progressive World* ran an August editorial, "Madalyn Murray, Valiant American," and printed her July 2 newsletter *in toto.* Harvey Lehrum of Oakland was sending SOSs to the freethought community on her behalf, urging people to send her money in Honolulu and pressure the Hawaii governor to refuse extradition.

Cousin Homer Lacy and his wife, Leona, rushed to Baltimore to help with the Winford House. Madalyn had asked them to get it rented, but in the short time she had been gone, her enemies had apparently rolled over Mae Mallory. "The house was destroyed, they trashed it" said Leona. "There were rows and rows of books, all gone."

Hyman Greenstein had grown up in one of Chicago's tough neighborhoods, but Hawaii had been good to him. A liberal who liked constitutional and unpopular causes, he was a well-known figure, driving a white sports car, always wearing a white suit and green bow tie, and smoking a white pipe.

He already had 50 trials pending, but he was considering taking over Madalyn's church tax suit in Maryland. The string of high-priced lawyers lined up against her was proof of her momentum, and it would go to the Supreme Court if it held together. But her personal problems threatened it: she could be required to appear personally as a witness, and if she set foot in Maryland, she'd be arrested. If she didn't, her case would be dismissed. The bail bondsman was already suing to get the Winford house. If he succeeded, she would no longer have standing as a plaintiff. Lena was nervous; that house was her only investment.

Lemoin Cree had branded as gullible anyone who thought Madalyn was really afraid for her life in Maryland, but Greenstein, Kerpelman, and Joe Wase all disagreed. The way the police, court, and political systems worked in Maryland, there was no way she could get a fair trial there. Under the state's 16th-century common-law codes, even a misdemeanor sentence had no ceiling; it was totally at the judge's discretion.

And they were out to get Madalyn, spending thousands to extradite her. On July 22, 1964, a month after they fled the city, she and Bill were sentenced for contempt of court *in absentia* in Baltimore, even though both the contempt charge and their extradition were under appeal. Two empty chairs stood in for the defendants (charges against Lena were dropped). Bill was given six months in jail, and Madalyn a year plus a $500 fine.

She had made herself so visibly hateable, with her foul mouth and unthinkable assaults on the sacred, it seemed clear Maryland wanted to punish her. She was even more of a heroine in her supporters' eyes.

Greenstein appealed, saying the indictments were flat illegal, because Maryland didn't permit atheists to testify or be jurors — therefore the Murrays couldn't even testify on their own behalf. That was clearly unconstitutional. The Hawaii judge agreed, but said it was up to them to test it in the Maryland courts. He released Madalyn and Bill into Greenstein's custody, on the condition that he would be responsible for getting them into court.

That made Greenstein a little nervous. If they lost the next appeal and she fled again, judicial action could be taken against *him.*

And in fact, Madalyn was already applying for new passports for herself, Susan, Lena, Bill, and Garth. Irv didn't want to move again, and that was fine with Madalyn; she'd always considered him a burden. She designated that Gus Scholle, not Irv, be notified in the event of her death.

Chapter 15 ~ Training School for Boys

Peoria, Illinois, started as a French and Indian settlement, and became an important frontier outpost for the military and trading, reached by stagecoach and steamboat at its perch on the bluffs and plains sloping down to the Illinois River. It later became a rail and manufacturing center, and an important vaudeville stop; the answer to the famous query, "How will it play in Peoria?" determined if a live act or stage show would be successful in the rest of the country. It was judged the most American of towns.

But when David Waters was growing up there, said his son Darren Martin years later, "there was a lot of massage parlors, and prostitution, and a lot of taverns...Peoria was the number one distiller in the United States. Pabst, Hiram Walker. That was the history of Peoria."

Its warehouse district on the river was crowded with breweries and distilleries, their smell steeped into the pavement and bricks of the businesses — cordage and twine, scrap metal, tires, truck parts, feeds, and into the stockyards and tracks dating from the days when things were shipped by river and rail. Even after urban renewal gashed out many of the old buildings in the 1970s, anywhere near the river you could still smell the faintly poison ghosts of hops, grain, and yeast from generations past.

David Waters roamed Peoria's alleys and dives from a young age, with older boys whose last names he didn't know, playing with knives and weapons, breaking into cars and homes, stealing whiskey. His mother, Betty, was repeatedly in trouble for offenses ranging from prostitution to theft, and home was a place where strangers came and went.

"The closest thing David Waters had to a father was Dean Hunt," a man who was in and out of Betty's life, said a relative. But Hunt had no authority over David. The boy, who started out bright and sweet-natured, had been operating on his own at least since age three, when his 18-year-old mother gave birth to a second son she named Stephen Douglas Plumley. As with David's father, Stevie's proved elusive, and in the turbulence of their young world, David took over the protection of his little brother.

Stevie had *petit mal* epileptic seizures, and David would hold him, and help him through them. As they grew up, he noticed Stevie had a relentlessly logical mind. "He would say exactly what he thought, would call people on these small things," remembered Waters years later. "If something they said was inconsistent, or if they told a white lie...He'd call them on it. People don't like that, and I tried to explain to him that he didn't have to correct everything that was wrong or didn't make sense. It's a small thing, just let it go. But he was never able to do it."

Stevie was also sweet, with a mild temperament. "It hurt him, his whole life it hurt him, that people saw him as an oddball. He didn't have grand seizures — It wasn't like he made a spectacle of himself or anything," David said.

When David was about five, he and Stevie were taken away from Betty for neglect, and went to a foster home. After they returned, no one could control David. He constantly ran away. It got worse in 1953, when he was six, and Betty gave birth to a third son, whose legal name was Ronald Waters, but whom she insisted on calling Jeff Hunt. (The story was that she was woozy when the nurse came with the birth certificate, and forgot that she'd intended to name him after Dean Hunt and the movie star Jeff Chandler.) David seemed overwhelmed by this new brother. He once pushed Jeff into an inferno of burning leaves; the toddler was seriously burned.

When David was eight, a fourth brother, Rodney, was born, and given up for adoption. David was still protective of Stevie, but now he was abusive as well, beating him to keep him from doing bad things — though beatings had no effect on David himself. His maternal grandmother, Ila Hayes, was "the only person who was truly nice to him," said a family acquaintance. "She provided the only really stable and loving and protecting environment, and she died a horrible cancer death."

Grandma Hayes wanted to take him in, but she became too ill. She left David a coin collection, and he later said a family member who had helped care for Grandma Hayes took it as his reward and sold it. "No one was ever a decent person around David," said a friend.

At one point, a counselor told Betty he'd try to pull some strings and get David into a private school. He had a very high IQ, in the genius range. Yeah, right, said his mother, and who's gonna pay for all this?

By 12, he'd been labeled a habitual runaway, and was sent off to reform school — the Illinois State Training School for Boys in St. Charles.

"St. Charles was a really bad place for kids back then," said a Peorian who befriended Waters when they were teens. "My brother went there...we always thought they sterilized him there." Another native called it "the place where 12-year-olds are raped and taught to hate."

He wasn't missed at home. "They left him in jail, in juvy, you know, rather than coming and getting him like on Christmas or something," said a friend. "They left him there, and I'm sure just like, step by step by step, you know, the rage probably grew."

"I missed home so much I thought my heart would break," David remembered later. But he passed his 13th birthday alone in St. Charles, and "eventually, I became acclimated to my new environment. It was not for the faint of heart."

If the idea was to break him at St. Charles, it didn't work; "I came out even more of a nonconformist." He continued to get into trouble — theft, truancy, curfew and parole violations, and general delinquency — and was transferred back there numerous times over the next two years.

But one important aspect of his character was set at St. Charles: "I would never again fear authority figures or any retributive measures they might have at their disposal."

By 15, he was transferred to the Illinois Industrial School for Boys at Sheridan. After a short stint, he was sent back to public high school. He met a tall, lanky girl named Evelyn "Cookie" Nelson. They often met at a downtown cafe called the Colonial Cove.

"I went to Woodruff, he went to Richwoods, but we used to hang out. Different people from all over Peoria. And we'd just sit around and all of us'd order a big ol' thing of french fries, and a Coke, and play music."

"The Cove" was a little shotgun place "maybe 30–40 feet wide, kinda long," said Sheriff Jim Durst of neighboring Woodford County, who knew the place well, as did everyone in law enforcement. It was the kind of place where juveniles openly passed around pints of whiskey, and adult waitresses passed along gang gossip.

David was the quintessential Bad Boy, with a turned-up collar and ducktails and a habit of skipping school. He smoked, drank, stole, and fooled with guns. He had all the girls he wanted. "He was a snappy dresser, looked *good*," said Cookie. He was like a brother to her, and over the years, always took care to keep her away from his worst deeds and rough life.

David's leadership qualities — and his cold-blooded nerve — were unquestioned by anyone. As a teenager, he started adding more serious trouble — burglary, grand theft — to his résumé. In May of 1964, he was arrested at 2 a.m. after his "borrowed" car shot out of an alley, ran three stop signs and two red lights, and sparked a high-speed chase through Peoria. Stopped from the other direction, he jumped out and tried to escape on foot. He got a year's probation and a fine. A couple of weeks later, he was picked up for curfew violation, traveling with two 24-year-olds who carried stolen IDs and a host of stolen checks, some already made out and forged.

"He chased and beat his teen brother Stevie repeatedly for hanging around and hustling gay men," said a longtime acquaintance, "which he did also," and made them suffer for their weakness. That was the best he could do to protect Stevie any more. "He was a hood," an ex-girlfriend said. "'He was just a bad guy. He carried guns, and worked for like pimps and stuff around Peoria."

He was about to graduate from "hood," but there were a few more stunts to pull first. On August 31, 1964, he was arrested downtown with another boy, drunk and kicking a third kid. He had a pint of booze under his shirt. When the three were put in the prowler, they started fighting again, and tried to grab the officer's billy club. David spent 20 days in the slammer. Upon his release, he impregnated a pretty, dark-haired girl.

A month later, a woman in Peoria's bluffside mansion district heard predawn sounds and called police. They found David and two other boys hiding on the second-floor porch with a batch of stolen items. Two more boys waiting in a get-away car escaped. It was a pattern — David always seemed to be leading a group of boys.

On November 6, police got a call from the cashier at the Colonial Cove. David and three other boys had beaten up a fifth kid, sending him to the hospital. A week later, three youths entered Clark's Service Station and asked for change. When the attendant opened the cash drawer, they overpowered him, took his glasses, and robbed the till. He picked David out of a lineup.

Bad as this all was, the 17-year-old was only a month from disaster.

Chapter 16 ~ The Switzerland of Mexico

IN SEPTEMBER 1964, while David Waters was breaking and entering, problems with
Bill were hitting the papers in Honolulu. He really wanted to break away from
Madalyn, but at 18 was too immature and angry to do it cleanly. His mother involved
him in projects too lucrative to pass up, which were often also crazily interesting.
(One such venture drummed up paying customers for a series of séances with a
Seattle psychic. It was billed as "controlled experiments," but privately Madalyn was
virtually convinced that the man had contacted three of Lena's sisters, including
witches Annie and Marie.)

Bill just wanted to get back to the mainland and disappear in some big city.
He and Susan moved out of the house on Spencer. Away from his mother, Bill
denounced her publicly, accusing her of "muckraking" in the new Honolulu-based
magazine she'd launched, A Voice of Reason. She advocated legalized prostitution
and praised Communists, he said.

Then Lemoin Cree told the Baltimore papers that Bill had called him and offered
to sell a stolen key to a lock box in Baltimore. It contained important papers Madalyn
had withheld from the board, he said. The papers also said he had stolen Madalyn's
Freethought Society mailing list and records while Lena, 73, tried to stop him.

Madalyn papered over the fissures, telling reporters that Bill was under psychiatric
care. The strain and burdens of the atheist Cause had nearly broken him.

Susan weighed in with her own interview, saying Madalyn had slandered her
and Bill, interfered with their attempts to get jobs, and tried to keep Bill under
her thumb. She confirmed Bill was seeing a psychiatrist, Dr. Linus Pauling Jr., but
he'd said that "any problems Bill has are caused by his mother." (Bill said Madalyn
was paying him $50 a visit to see Pauling, hoping to convince a judge that the
extradition stress had made him ill, and the effort should be abandoned.) Susan
had enrolled at the University of Hawaii and gotten a job teaching Hebrew. She
planned to live with an aunt in Florida—hopefully with Bill, once he got out from
under his legal troubles.

Madalyn was losing control of her family and fighting to regain her movement.
She reincorporated the Freethought Society of America in Honolulu in September 1964, with herself as president, Lena as vice president, Hyman Greenstein as
secretary-treasurer, and Irv as a director. She also formed a new entity, the International Freethought Society, as a substitute legal-action arm until Lemoin Cree
could be ousted.

But the American Humanist Association wanted her off its board. Besides the circus surrounding her flight to Hawaii and the disarray of her professional affairs, she
had hotheadedly accused president Vashti McCollum of impropriety with money.
"You are extremely irresponsible and [have] an absolute genius for making enemies
of those who wish to assist you," scolded Corliss Lamont, the philanthropist, author,

and AHA activist. Her AHA colleagues were also disgustedly circulating a September 1964 article in the *Realist*, in which Madalyn used foul language and imagery. ("Dear Reader, I can see you wet your lips and cross your legs to pinch your balls a little tighter in expectation" of a promised "tale of sadism"; she also wanted to "kick every 'respectable' college professor in the crotch" for some perceived failure to give enough respect to Mae Mallory.) Her old champion, Vashti's father Arthur Cromwell, drifted away.

She didn't care. She had other irons in the fire. First, on behalf of both her old and new Freethought Society entities, she filed a complaint with the Federal Communications Commission, charging that 15 Oahu radio stations had violated the FCC's Fairness Doctrine by refusing her free air time to counter the free time religious programs got. Next, she had Greenstein file another Pledge suit on Garth's behalf. (Garth said he liked school, and Madalyn admitted he'd suffered no persecution. "There's a real aloha spirit here," she said, and she wanted to stay.)

But she was losing her grip on her all-important church tax suit, and was angry that Kerpelman was still involved, and being contacted by others who wanted in. The suit was being opposed by huge church entities, and instead of being at the center if it, she was stranded off in Honolulu.

On February 24, 1965, Susan, 18, gave birth to a healthy daughter. The name Robin came to the young parents when they saw her bright red hair. They picked Eileen, the middle name, for teenagers' reasons, as Bill remembered it — because Ann, the name they wanted, would have given her the initials RAM.

The birth forged a fragile rapprochement between Madalyn and Bill, but Madalyn became increasingly restless and anxious about the looming extradition. Shortly after Robin's birth, a circuit court refused to reverse the extradition order, and the Hawaii Supreme Court would probably uphold it. Hawaii officials moved to block her passport applications.

"I can't let them cage me like an animal," she told her family. They were just getting the mailings and magazine back on their feet, and money coming there instead of to Lemoin Cree. Lena and Irv could hold down the fort in Honolulu, while she fled to Mexico. Soon, the escapees boiled down to just Madalyn and Bill. Garth, Susan, and the baby would stay behind.

It was unclear why only Bill was going with her — she said it was because they were the only two still under indictment, but according to Bill, it was her ever-gnawing need to isolate and control him. Finding himself an unwilling husband and father, he didn't resist the offer of an escape.

Around Memorial Day, 1965, Lena once again hugged her daughter goodbye as she left to find a better place to live than America. She begged Madalyn to tell her where she was going.

Madalyn refused, but she knew exactly where she was going. In 1963, the *Murray Newsletter* had extolled Blake College, an American school in Valle de Bravo, some

100 miles from Mexico City. Back in Baltimore she had even begun a $50,000 campaign to build an atheist-funded facility for Blake in the U.S., which she planned to run. Blake's founder was Raymond Peat, a biologist who had taught experimental, nonpedantic college classes in Ohio. Blake was aimed at smart kids who wanted to skip undergraduate drudgery and go directly to graduate school. "After they had studied freely under the direction of half a dozen masters," said Madalyn, "they would take a [test] to see if they had gained a college education." If they passed, Peat would give them a degree and a transcript for 120 hours.

Peat's floating faculties of "masters" were comprised of radical thinkers and activists like Madalyn. He had invited her long ago; this was a good time to take him up on it. He had some "well known names," according to Madalyn, lined up to teach his 20 or so students that fall, including humanistic psychology pioneer Abraham Maslow.

And Mexico had something else besides Blake College. There was a community of expatriates there from the blacklist days of the McCarthy and HUAC probes. She hoped to receive political asylum from the Mexican government; from there, a dissident could get into Cuba.

She would never see Lena again, and it would be 11 years before Irv set eyes on his sister.

"[W]e were] supposed to fly over to San Francisco," Madalyn said, "and [Peat's] girlfriend would pick us up there . . . her mother worked in an army camp and had been obtaining phony identifications for . . . some time." Madalyn and Bill, traveling as Mary Ann and Patrick O'Connor, got O'Connor birth certificates, driver's licenses, a draft card, "everything, as beautiful as they could be."

The girl's mother bought the fugitives a $300 car. In Mexico, they traveled "over some of the most wild beautiful scenery! . . . We ate the most ghastly foods . . . These people with this strangely rich, fluid language that I didn't understand at all . . . The whole thing was, was just a beautiful, beautiful adventure. I enjoyed every minute of it."

When they got to Valle de Bravo, she understood why it was called "the Switzerland of Mexico" — a mountain resort village of tiled roofs and cascading flowers, settled in Spanish colonial times.

Peat greeted his newly arrived master. A few days later, they were sitting on the porch "when this man came in on a horse," Madalyn said, "a beautiful brown horse, a real tall, skinny guy." He was balding, but wore a dashing hat. Peat invited him to sit down and have a beer. His name was Richard O'Hair. Madalyn was smitten almost immediately.

Before long, she found occasion to visit O'Hair's house, a "very Indian . . . triangular shaped" abode in the Otumba, the Indian quarter, where it was dangerous for white women to go alone, she said.

Hanging on a wall was a sword with a phrase inscribed in Spanish, "The bite of this snake is not easily cured." There was a large chess set on the table in front of an open fireplace. His saddle hung on a hook, and Madalyn found "the whole place just very, very nice, very masculine."

A big parrot flew in and perched on his shoulder. O'Hair offered her and another guest a drink, left the room, and came back "with these little delicate...brandy glasses...He could tell good tales...Richard swept me off my feet [in] a matter of two or three hours. He had a red handlebar mustache and red hair and...a Lincolnesque quality...We sat before an open fireplace with the trees burning and snapping and talked and fell in love...I felt like I was 13 years old."

She already associated Mexico with revolutionaries, creative people, rebels, heroes, Cuba. Richard embodied all of that. He had the kind of masculine boldness she loved. He had run off to join the Marines at 16. He'd studied business, and then enrolled in the Chicago Academy of Fine Arts; his walls were covered with his own paintings. He was articulate and educated, from a comfortable background in Chicago, complete with a summer home on a lake. He'd lived in Mexico for a decade. He packed a gun.

He had a dramatic scar running from his skull through his eyebrow — the result, Madalyn and others said, of an operation to install a metal plate in his head. It was understood that this was a war wound (however, a friend said the plate dated from his youth, possibly from a motorcycle accident).

To Madalyn, he'd lived the romantic life of a soldier of fortune, and she was swept away by his stories. He was rumored to be CIA; "he had a grand reputation as an international spy...everybody in the village knew...and Blake College knew all about it."

Back in 1935, while teenaged Madalyn dreamed of driving an ambulance in the Spanish Civil War, O'Hair, 21, moved to New York and learned some of the skills of private detection. By 1942 he'd moved to Detroit and taken a job as a millwright worker at a firm called Federal Mogul, which made landing-craft propellers for the army.

Federal Mogul, said a friend of O'Hair's from that time, was being infiltrated by Communists, to sabotage the military. "The unions, all of them, were being schooled by head honchos for the Communists." They targeted the trade unions because they provided access to political power, which led to Congress and the judiciary. "In some areas, the unions were like 50% fellow travelers." O'Hair was recruited by the FBI to spy on his union.

"The Commie party was Hoover's pet peeve," O'Hair's friend said. "Dick's reports were going to Sullivan, Hoover's top guy." O'Hair joined the Party in early 1943, at a Detroit dance hall called the Graystone Ballroom. He got on the press committee, distributing the Daily Worker in a Greek neighborhood, and the membership committee, recruiting. In 1944, he moved up to the local executive committee. He reported to the FBI under the names Richard St. John and Alfred St. John. Officially a fireman, he moved from Federal Mogul to the railroads, Père Marquette and Grand Trunk Western.

In 1946, according to the FBI, he was jettisoned because he tried to get a Detroit newspaper to do a story on Communism. He thought it would help the FBI.

"Dick...was a little bit careless," his friend admitted. "But he did a good job for the Bureau." He left Detroit abruptly in 1947, but in early 1952, at 38, he sat before Madalyn's hated House Un-American Activities Committee, in a trim mustache and snappy suit, and fingered at least 60 Communists by name.

After his HUAC testimony, O'Hair returned to New York State. He and two partners, one an FBI agent, formed the Committee for Americanism, aimed at exposing Communist operatives in New York State.

"This was...out in Endicott at the shoe factory, it was the fur and leather workers," said a partner. "And General Electric in Schenectady had the same problem" — fellow travelers that needed to be "laid away" — exposed. "The government doesn't want 'em and the Communists don't want 'em. It's like being excommunicated. They *hate* being exposed, it's one of the worst things that can happen to 'em." They began to weed out the Communists for a fee, but G.E. feared a strike, and the Committee for Americanism was soon abandoned.

O'Hair returned to conventional private investigator assignments. One client suspected her husband was cheating, and O'Hair confirmed it. He comforted his client, Helen Bisher, and they married in August 1953. They had two children in quick succession, but O'Hair kept it so secret that his undercover friends didn't even know he was married.

"Dick had a lot of women, and it wasn't something I talked to him about. We mainly talked about the bad Communists and the good FBI."

Helen Bisher was his second wife. Raised a Catholic, he'd been wed as a teen in Chicago and fathered two sons. His first in-laws, said his daughter, Vicki O'Hair Reed, "were well off, and when Richard left her, they paid for an annulment. And we used to laugh about [it]...usually you use an annulment when something hasn't been consummated!"

Marriage and fatherhood the second time around were no better. "He would stay in the basement and sleep all day," said Reed, "and at night he'd go in the basement and build things."

Just after his 42nd birthday, in June of 1955, "he just picked up and literally disappeared. Kinda like going to the grocery store for a carton of milk? And he never came back." Helen, who was late in her second pregnancy when he left, was granted a divorce *in absentia*. She heard nothing of him until his marriage to the notorious atheist, Madalyn Murray, hit all the papers.

A fellow FBI informant said O'Hair knew Madalyn was coming to "Valle" well before she arrived, and arranged to meet her. "His agenda was to marry her and find out what in hell she was up to, and let [the FBI] know. [He wanted] to find out her Communist connections . . . He didn't fall in love with her. He was a good patriot." O'Hair continued offering information to authorities well into his marriage to Madalyn, he said.

She didn't know about his HUAC testimony. According to a friend, he managed to keep that from her for years.

Nineteen-year-old Bill Murray liked O'Hair. He had the impression he was a smuggler. "He was an old Irish alcoholic; he could drink, eat, and live well in Mexico on his military pension. He was a very, very typical alcoholic . . . Why did he marry her? Maybe a free lunch opportunity, keep the bottle full."

O'Hair may have hoped to get back in the FBI's good graces by cultivating Madalyn, but he came to respect and love her. And if his initial mission was to seduce her, he succeeded.

While she was falling in love with Richard O'Hair, Madalyn was staying in the news. A Soviet magazine ran an article excoriating America and Baltimore for its treatment of the Murrays, opining that the treatment was because of the church tax suit. Her request for free radio air time was rejected by the FCC. The Fairness Doctrine only applied if there was a lot of controversy, and "freethought" wasn't controversial. She smoldered; they were just using the fact that the complainant was called the Freethought Society to evade justice.

But Madalyn couldn't be reached for comment. No one knew where she was, including her attorney, Hyman Greenstein. Irv denied knowing anything. He was busy keeping the movement afloat, sending A *Voice of Reason* to about 2,500 supporters of church-state separation.

Finally, in mid-July, Madalyn called Greenstein. Upset, he ordered her and Bill back immediately for their upcoming extradition hearing. She promised to return, but he didn't believe her, and made some calls to wash his hands of the Murrays. Sure enough, they were nowhere in sight on August 18, when the Hawaii Supreme Court ruled that they could be extradited to Maryland.

"[They] embarrassed me and abused the trust . . . placed in them," Greenstein said, and strongly urged Bill, wherever he was, to just go to Maryland and face the assault charges. He was too young to be running like this. Madalyn, he added, had not paid a dime of his fee.

Soon Madalyn's Mexican idyll was spoiled by the surprise arrival of Susan and Robin. Madalyn immediately sent for Garth, and an informer friend of Richard's warned Bill to get his wife and baby out of there. The situation was about to blow up, he said.

Bill took his advice. He was right; Madalyn's tenure at Blake soon ended in flames.

Madalyn's account was as follows. Only five "masters" came that summer. Abraham Maslow wasn't among them. Gustav Likan and his wife, Barbara, arrived shortly after Madalyn. Likan was a Croat, an artist with a lush, vivid style who had been commissioned by Eva Peron to paint murals in Argentina's schools. He'd also taught at the Chicago Academy of Fine Arts, Richard's alma mater. They agreed that Peat was well connected, the little campus idyllic, and his accelerated university a great idea.

"Except for one thing," said Madalyn. "Everybody was on drugs. I mean *everybody* was on drugs."

She noticed that the kids "were dreamy... [I] hadn't ever been involved with dope before... They were way, way out on those mushrooms, marijuana. They had every single possible thing."

Some of the kids "were terribly bright and from excellent families. There was one little doctor's son down there who had tested out with a 200 IQ... Well, they never cracked a book. They never cracked a book."

She and Gus Likan "more or less tried to coerce the kids into some sort of self discipline," setting up a library period and "[trying] to get them to give themselves instructions in self-psychology by reading some psychology... and then sitting down and discussing it, some theory." But it never got off the ground.

One night, she joined the kids, passing around a hashish joint in the kitchen. "I just sat there and watched... and those kids had completely blown their minds on that stuff... It had immobilized them and stopped their thought processes." She herself just got a "nice buzzy sensation, [but] this kid with a 200 IQ was under his bed, whining, whining." Then "Sherrill" started laughing hysterically; she'd fed the dog bennies, and he was disoriented, whimpering and crouching. That cruelty set Madalyn off. She loved dogs.

She told Barbara Likan they had to shut the place down. She couldn't watch the kids destroy themselves; and they were "bringing... disgrace on the whole American community in this culture."

The Likans simply left. Madalyn went to see Richard, watching his parrot stroke its neck up and down his ear while she told him she'd uncovered a drug ring. He listened, and said he'd be in touch.

Madalyn hoped, said Bill later, to barter the information for political asylum, and she mapped the drug caches and recorded who was using what and where they got it. But instead of asylum, she was given deportation. Several stories were floated: that she'd been arrested in a political demonstration and her fake passport discovered; that Mexican authorities were in on the drug ring, and didn't appreciate her blowing it; that Richard O'Hair had turned her in. And her explanation — that Raymond Peat had reported her as a fugitive because she exposed his drug ring. (A reporter was told that she only reported the drug situation after she'd tried to take over the school and been thwarted by Peat. Indeed, by her own calculations to Baylor historian Thomas Charlton later, Peat was bringing in as much as $50,000 a year with little effort.)

She and Garth were dumped in Houston on September 14. She checked into the William Penn Hotel under the name Mrs. Annie Williams of Pittsburgh, and called Richard. "He says, 'Oh, come on back down. They don't mean anything. Just get on the plane and come back down.'"

It took three days by bus, and in that time, Blake College was raided by federal drug agents and closed down. Madalyn arrived back in town a celebrity, she said; everyone was grateful to her. She requested political asylum, saying she was driven from her homeland by her own government because of her church tax suit.

"They should be pinning medals on me," she said. Instead, "I will probably have to remain in Mexico for the rest of my life." But she loved it. "Nobody bothers us; nobody's interested...in our past." And, "I've found at last what I was looking for. A man. I mean a real man."

She and Richard announced wedding plans, and moved in together. But the Maryland state's attorney said that if the bail bondsman didn't break up the wedding and bring her back, he would.

On September 23, 1965, there was a knock on her door. Richard opened it to armed officers, speaking Spanish. He turned and told Madalyn she was under arrest. Deportees were not allowed back without special permission. She would face prison if she tried to return again.

She and Garth were put on a plane, and the boy, upset, vomited all the way to San Antonio. It was night when Madalyn piloted him through customs and hailed a cab, only to be arrested on a fugitive warrant from Maryland. She refused to give her name. Garth said his was "John David." She spent the night in jail, while he was taken to a children's shelter. Reporters and photographers swarmed. For once, Madalyn was not beaming.

"She left Blake College an empty shell," said an observer.

Chapter 17 ~ Rebels without a Cause

"**D**AVE WAS IN HIS TEENS, and he'd gotten in some trouble," said a family member of Waters' late-1964 crime spree. "They were gonna put him in like a juvenile prison again. And Dean [Hunt] was friends with the sheriff of Peoria County, and he pulled some strings, and got Dave released on probation — you know. He was seeing Betty, and as a favor to her.

"And [Dean] says he always looks back on that with regret, that if he'd'a let Dave go away for the theft, it coulda all been different, maybe."

It almost was. Right after Dean Hunt pulled those strings, David walked into a Marine recruiting station. He scored so well on the test that they told him he'd be recommended for officer candidate school. All he had to do was get his guardian down there to sign for him, since he was four months shy of his 18th birthday.

"Well, my mother is not an early riser," he said years later with the sour grin he reserved for Betty. "She had to get down to the [recruiting office] before 5 p.m., that's all she had to do. But she just *couldn't make it*. And about two weeks after that, I got into some very serious trouble."

It was the afternoon of December 13, 1964. A boy named Jack Lowe came into the Colonial Cove. A waitress told him that some boys, Carl Welchman and David Waters, were saying they were going to kill him. He believed it; for three days, a couple of different cars had been following him, and a week before, someone had shot at him.

That night, 16-year-old David Gibbs, a Manual High School dropout who wore Buddy Holly glasses and had just been laid off his job, said goodbye to his mother. She knew where he was going — seeing his girlfriend and dropping his older sister off at the movies. His mother trusted him. He was a good kid, if a little lost at the moment. It was cold, and she noticed his attire — plaid shirt, undershirt, jeans, and boots. He wore the heavy chain "ID" bracelet his sister had given him. They were all the rage.

David Waters, 17, and Robert Duane Taylor, barely 16, were in the Cove that night, passing around a stolen bottle of Kessler with Carl Welchman, 17. They left with some other kids for Plato Pool Hall; by 11, the three were back at the Cove with more stolen whiskey and some ether Waters had boosted from Methodist Hospital. Taylor had gotten in a fight that required stitches in his arm.

They hooked up with David Gibbs and 19-year-old Jerry Peddicord, and started driving toward the outskirts of town.

Gibbs didn't know his car was part of a drive-by shooting plan until Waters asked to borrow it. They'd drop Gibbs off somewhere in the country, he said, and he would walk home and report the car stolen at 1 a.m. By that time, the Jack Lowe shooting would be done.

Gibbs said no, and then realized they were already out in the country, with only open fields and a far-flung farmhouse or two. Taylor hit him in the mouth and Welchman in the back. They pulled him into the back seat, and Waters got behind the wheel and drove while the others beat Gibbs. Then Waters stopped the car and said they were all in on it, and had to each hit him. They pulled him out onto the road, wrenched a fence post free, and passed it around, hitting him with it.

When he was unconscious, they peeled off in his car, first driving over his legs. Bloody pieces of his shirt and undershirt lay on the side of the road.

Peddicord got out on the highway and hitched home. The other three drove the car to a high bluff on Fondulac Drive, where you could stand between two trees and see the entire city of Peoria, twinkling under the cold night sky. They mashed the accelerator and, Rebel-without-a-Cause-style, jumped away as the car shot over the edge and crashed into the parking lot of the Carlton Russell Tire Company below. Its hood, doors, fenders, and upholstery were still smeared with blood and hair. David Gibbs' glasses were wedged into the back seat.

At 8 a.m. on December 14, Woodford County Sheriff Jim Durst picked up the ringing phone, and hurried out to Upper Spring Bay Road south of the Louis Kohl home.

A body had been spotted by two men on their way to work. It had been dragged across the road. Recognizing parts of a steering column, Durst radioed to pick up a stolen or wrecked '52 or '53 Chevy.

A call came back shortly. They had such a car, and were looking for the owner, David William Gibbs. They'd contacted his worried mother. By radio and phone, she asked them to describe the clothing on the body they'd found. Gravely, Durst complied.

He and the Peoria police quickly teamed up. They found out that, at about 3 a.m., three boys had shown up at a filling station, spattered with blood. One of the attendants recognized Robert Taylor, who was bloodier than the others. What happened to *you*, he asked, and Taylor said he'd been in a fight with a colored boy over in Peoria. They went into the bathroom to wash up. Welchman, wearing a trenchcoat, just stared at himself in the mirror. They asked for a ride and were dropped off in town.

Meanwhile, Jerry Peddicord had told his mother everything, and called the police. Before lunch, they picked up Taylor and Waters together near the Cove. Welchman spotted them from inside the Cove and slipped out. They came for him at home at 1:30 in the morning. "His mother was just as nice a lady as could be," said Durst. "She said, 'Oh, Jim, let me go in there first, he's lying there in bed with his dog and a shotgun.'" Durst said no way was he going to let her go in there. He stepped in, removed the shotgun from next to the bed, woke up the suspect, and arrested him.

Durst couldn't stomach taking Gibbs' mother in to identify the body. He asked his wife, Irene, a secretary at the jail, to do it. The boy lay on the autopsy table, grit and asphalt ground into his blood-crusted torso. His eyes and lips were hugely swollen and discolored, his face covered with deep lacerations to the bone. The death blow — unless he'd died of shock first — almost covered the back of his head. His right knee and left ankle had been battered. His spleen was torn.

His mother wheeled and left, and the sister had to make the identification. She recognized the ID bracelet she'd given him. She recognized his shredded shirt.

The four young killers were led to their preliminary hearing on December 15, 1964, handcuffed together, collars turned up, cigarettes dangling from their lips. They were sullen in the courtroom, but when flashbulbs started going off as they left, two of them broke away and spit at and kicked the reporters.

The vicious murder made the Chicago papers. The boys all had the same court-appointed lawyer, who obtained a change of venue to Taylorville in Christian County, 100 miles away.

Their statements revealed a bond between Welchman and Waters. Welchman shifted blame from Waters to Peddicord (whose parents soon hired their own lawyer). He said Waters only hit Gibbs once, and didn't want to drive the car over Gibbs' head like Peddicord suggested. And Waters later wanted to hitch a ride back and get Gibbs. It turned out Gibbs had told them to go ahead and take the car, but they beat him to death anyway.

They spent three months in the Woodford County Jail before the trial. Once Peddicord turned up with a badly bruised face and loosened teeth. Another day, Taylor smashed the bench in his cell, waving a piece with nails sticking out, saying he was going to hit Sheriff Durst with it. After Welchman managed to start a fire, he was carried, kicking and screaming, to the "hole"; deputies had to tear-gas him with "Re-pell." After he was taken away, Waters and Taylor began yelling that Durst was a "rotten mother-fucker, bald-headed son of a bitch, a dirty rotten bastard, a prick, a cocksucker." The tension became high, as Mrs. Durst's kitchen was not far from the cells and her two teenagers could hear the language. Waters threatened that if Durst tried to "squirt any of that gas in my face" he'd beat him on the head with a table leg and he'd end up like Gibbs.

Bobby Taylor's mother brought him home-cooked food, but David was used to being alone in detention. One day, however, his long-lost biological father, George Waters, showed up. Sheriff Durst knew Waters, who lived in nearby Secor, and liked him. He was a handsome motorcycle aficionado with two or three families around the Peoria area. But David had only laid eyes on him once or twice. "And when he came . . . up to the jail to see him," said a relative, "Dave spit directly into his face. Spit right in his face."

The boys eventually pled guilty and waived trial. On March 25, 1965, the day after Waters' 18th birthday, they were sentenced. They said they were sorry, had no idea they'd killed Gibbs. The parents asked for leniency; their sons would never have done it except for the booze and ether, and they would go straight if given the chance. Betty admitted she'd been "impatient" with David growing up, and for some reason, he'd just built up a wall around himself lately.

They were sentenced to 30–60 years. The judge said he'd decided not to electrocute them only because it had been a youthful gang situation, and they were drunk and high.

The prosecutor said they were animals and should get a 60-year minimum. As it was, they'd be eligible for parole in a little over eight.

Chapter 18 ~ Extraordinary Freedom in Texas

S AN ANTONIO REPORTERS showed up at the police station on Saturday, September 25, 1965, to get a look at the newly arrested, notorious atheist and her 10-year-old. A few days earlier, Bill had begun serving his six-month contempt sentence in Baltimore, and the two stories appeared in papers all over the country.

Bill's willingness to face the music had given him some much-needed psychological distance from his mother. Within days, the state's attorney dropped the assault
charges against the 19-year-old, saying he was a pawn of Madalyn — against whom
they decidedly would *not* drop charges.

From Valle de Bravo, Richard told reporters that Madalyn was "the most truthful,
honest, and one of the finest women I have ever known...I love Madalyn Murray
very much, and still hope to marry her."

Contrary to what Madalyn would later allege, the civil liberties community rallied
to her aid. Maury Maverick Jr., a state legislator and attorney from one of the first
families of San Antonio, called his friend Bill DeWolfe, a Unitarian minister who
was president of the local ACLU chapter.

"You see the headlines? We've got a case."

Maverick, a Marine veteran, was an outspoken Joseph McCarthy opponent and
champion of free speech. He had successfully guided cases through the U.S. Supreme
Court and was a true Texas original — iconoclastic and freethinking.

Maverick filed a writ of habeas corpus and got Madalyn released on bond. "The
funny thing was," DeWolfe laughed, "the first thing she said when we got her out
of jail was, 'Thank God you're here.' "

Maverick told Madalyn they'd go up to Austin and appeal directly to Governor
John Connally; he'd argue personally against extradition. He sat astonished as she
said she didn't know if she could bring herself to even speak to the man. He was
one of the poorest governors in the country, he was not a man of stature, and she
didn't know if she could keep quiet about it.

Maverick told her she could not insult the man at the same time she was asking
him for something. Further, her tasteless interview in *Playboy* was just out, and
probably wouldn't help her chances of getting asylum in the Lone Star State.

She managed to stifle her distaste for Governor Connally enough to stomach the
trip to Austin. The minute she set foot there, she knew it was home.

She began seeing endearing things about Texas. First, some Baptists told her they
could use women like her in their state. "If those damn...fish-eaters come down
here and try to get me, they'd just shoot it out." She liked that — "Texans got their
backs up that this was a *woman* being pushed around." That was totally new; in her
experience, only submissive women got protected by men.

Texas was a community property state, and private homesteads couldn't be fore-
closed — extremely progressive. The 300 families who settled the state under a
Spanish land grant in the 1820s had to promise that they either were now or would
become Catholics, but when Texas joined the United States in 1845, it had attracted
a large group of educated, abolitionist German freethinkers and independent spirits.
Its new constitution barred ministers of the Gospel from serving in the legislature.

Madalyn also liked the "actual intercourse in common society" in Texas. "You're
still fiercely independent down here," she told someone a few years after she'd
settled in Austin. "People ask me...'How can you live in Texas?' It's reactionary,

Bible belt, etc. No. I don't see that at all." Texans were conservative, but the iconoclastic kind. "We have extraordinary freedom yet, in Texas . . . there's still that deference to . . . human individuality, to human freedom . . . [a] kind of 'I don't give a damn' attitude."

In fact, she said, if the intellectual and cultural bastions of the East were "sunk in the sea tomorrow, we would be a better nation. The madness of our culture — manipulative advertising, war, intellectual and cultural tyranny — those don't come out of . . . Texas . . . They come from New York, DC, Philadelphia."

The lines ruling race, station, money, education, and gender were brittle where she came from. In Austin, they were in soft focus. After many years in row housing, Austin's economic heterogeneity gave her a "good feeling. . . . Somebody with a little French chateau right next to an English residence, a $3,000 house . . . and up the street . . . a $20,000 house, and nobody seems to care . . . Where back East, my gawd, they can't vary by $500 on a street." The endless miles of identical dwellings that Madalyn hated, with trim, awnings, and plantings decided by committee, were utterly absent from Austin's oak-and-sycamore shaded streets.

Nobody judged you for what you drove. "I see cars 5, 10, 15, 20 years old and nobody cares." Oil millionaire H. L. Hunt reportedly drove a battered old station wagon that ran like a charm. People weren't uptight about fancy clothes, either; she liked it that her plain, economical muumuus were no big deal in Austin.

"I think Texas is a good state," she said after a decade there. "I'm quite pleased with it. We had very, very little harassment as compared to Maryland, I wouldn't say 5% . . . Romance, contentment, there's a great deal of it in Texas, too. This is a very pleasant place to be."

Maury Maverick's brother-in-law, Sam Houston Clinton, was a prominent jurist and leader of the Austin ACLU, and one of the rare men Madalyn seemed to simply respect without having to challenge him. In fact, Richard jealously dubbed him her "boyfriend."

When she first arrived in Austin, Clinton found her an Austin attorney who loaded her up with groceries and took her out to his fishing cabin at Bastrop, a beautiful, wild area on the Colorado River east of the city. She stayed until her extradition hearing the first week in October.

Maverick and Clinton had secured a promise that Madalyn wouldn't be arrested afterward. She pled for asylum, filing a statement with the secretary of state that Maryland only wanted to derail her church tax suit.

The publicity brought money. One wire from Florida came with a note saying she had a hell of a nerve, living it up in jail while there was a government to attend to, now get off her ass and get her organization back together. She was encouraged by the faith they had in her.

Madalyn was invited to speak to a crowd of several thousand University of Texas students. In fact, she was in great demand all during the fall of 1965, giving lectures and interviews off the notoriety from her deportation, the extradition threat and her church tax suit (though now snarled), O'Hair's marriage proposal, Bill's laudable actions, and the *Playboy* interview. She was even able to command appearance fees. There were plenty of snipers — the *St. Louis Post-Dispatch* photographer caught her picking her nose — but things were looking up.

Then, on October 11, with eerie synchronicity, two events occurred. First, her plea for asylum failed; Governor Connally ordered her back to Maryland. But that same day, a decision in Maryland's high court, *Schowgurow v. Maryland,* made it moot.

It was similar to the case Hyman Greenstein had been planning to file before he dropped Madalyn. Schowgurow was a Buddhist convicted of murdering his wife. He said he hadn't gotten a fair trial from the start because Maryland required a God-belief oath to serve on a jury. The grand jurors who indicted him all took the oath. So he had not gotten a jury of his peers.

The high court agreed. The belief requirement was ruled unconstitutional. But what staggered the legal community and sprung Madalyn was that the court made the decision retroactive. Hundreds of indictments and convictions gotten under grand juries that had sworn the oath were overturned, including Madalyn's and Bill's.

On October 26, 1965, Schowgurow walked out of prison, and the assault charges against Madalyn were dropped the same day, followed shortly by the contempt charges and extradition requests.

Richard O'Hair had arrived in Austin a week earlier. He and Madalyn married October 18, with Sam Houston Clinton as best man, and his secretary, Claire Jones, "bridesmaid." The press was kept out and the vows secret. Richard wore cowboy boots and needed a shave, and admitted looking "[more] like a vaquero" than a bridegroom. Madalyn wore borrowed, too-large shoes with toilet paper stuffed in the toes, and interrupted the justice of the peace so many times with legal corrections that, she laughed later, "Richard finally said, 'Madalyn, will you keep quiet long enough for us to get married?'"

That night they called Lena in Hawaii. She congratulated them, but Irv wouldn't speak to his sister, yelling something about her "selling out to a Mexican."

They also called Richard's 76-year-old mother in Indiana, and got a frigid reception.

"Richard was raised a very, very, very devout Catholic," said his daughter, "and when he left us and disappeared, it was a pretty bad little sin. But *when he married Madalyn* . . . [his mother] sent him a card where she disowned him."

By November, Madalyn had fallen in love with a three-bedroom house at 4203 Shoal Creek Boulevard, across the street from one of the most beautiful of Austin's charming waterways. The living room had parquetry floors; the kitchen knotty-pine cabinets like a mountain cabin.

"The day I walked into Shoal Creek, I knew I was home," she told an interviewer. With donations and Richard's pension, they bought it for $16,000. She sewed gingham curtains. She acquired a piano, and a classic wingback leather "study" chair. She hired a maid named Charity, whose sisters Faith and Hope sometimes took her duty.

She and Richard started a little domestic ritual: "After watching [me] pop a couple of pills every morning" to ease the pain from a pinched nerve, "He said, 'I'm going to show you what a real painkiller is,'" and made her a martini. She started having one at 10 a.m. and another at 2 p.m.

She sent for Garth, who had been shipped off to relatives in Ohio after the arrest in San Antonio.

He made friends with a neighbor kid named Mike W_____. They had a clubhouse in the woods and played in the creek and went to each other's houses. Mike was a churchgoing Christian, but Madalyn let that alone; he was the only friend Garth had ever had. Mike vaguely knew who Madalyn was. He noticed that she was often out of town or at the O'Hairs' other little house on Sinclair, and Garth was left with Richard, who was sour and gruff. He'd never liked kids, even his own. Mike was told that the metal plate in Richard's head was the cause of his ill temper. Garth told him Richard would hit Madalyn, and they blamed it on the plate.

To Mike, Garth was honest and open, a nice boy, but dominated by his mother. When he wanted to join the Boy Scouts, Madalyn nixed it — the Scouts were religious. It was one of the few times Garth stood up to her, and she relented. On campouts, he and Mike talked some about religion. Garth was respectful of Mike's Christianity, and when Mike underwent a "second baptism" experience as a teen and committed his life to Christ, it didn't make any difference to their friendship — though some of the UT students hanging around the atheist movement were "aghast."

Sometimes Mike felt Madalyn didn't want him around, but she never said an unkind word to him, and he found her "a very warm person" in private. When his father suddenly died, she left her work and came into Garth's room to give the boy her condolences. He later felt that her calculated "Most Hated" public image hurt her. The Madalyn he knew wasn't like that.

Madalyn and Richard set about trying to rebuild the movement. They bought another little house at 4102 Sinclair, a few blocks away, for work. Richard became president of SOS, Inc. — the Society of Separationists, the new "action arm" she was founding to replace Other Americans. They set up shop in one of the Shoal Creek bedrooms, planning to eventually move all printing, mailing, and office activities to Sinclair, as soon as Madalyn could get her press, mailing equipment, and files back. She was now ready for Irv to turn A Voice of Reason back over to her.

As Garth started school in Austin, Bill walked out of jail a free man, ready to make a break from his mother. And he did it with boldness; returning to Honolulu and Spencer Street, he began working with Irv, untangling who owned the mailing lists for which organizations, and who controlled them. He told the newspapers he wanted to create a new image for the church-state separation movement. He would keep the donations and organizations in Hawaii. He and Irv fired Madalyn as president of the Freethought Society she'd formed there, and replaced her with Irv.

Furious, Madalyn tried to have the mailing address changed to divert contributions to Texas. Bill blocked it. The money, he said, belonged to the corporation, not her. Madalyn called on the Honolulu police to stop her family from soliciting money. She warned the printer there to stop printing A *Voice of Reason,* and asked the post office to stop delivering her mail to Irv. The post office, unsure what to do, held the mail for ten days, until Bill persuaded them to release it to him.

Bill asked the Austin postal inspectors to stop his mother from using the Freethought Society's name in her correspondence. The Society's legal address was 1060 Spencer, not someplace in Austin, Texas. Irv was paying its rent, not Madalyn. Irv began cultivating Walter Hoops and other of Madalyn's enemies, assuring them that she had no control.

In Baltimore, Lemoin Cree washed his hands of it all, leaving confusion among members, donors, and subscribers about who headed the Freethought Society of America there, and the International Freethought Society in Honolulu. It was a mess — who had charge of the church tax lawsuit? What role did Other Americans (whose charter was soon revoked) have? And where were the donations supposed to go: Baltimore, Hawaii, Texas? Both Freethought Societies were still in operation. Madalyn was putting out a new missive from Austin called the *Tax-The-Church Newsletter.* Bill and Irv were putting out a new missive from Honolulu called the *Mays-Murray Newsletter.*

Then the worst blow came. Lena announced that Madalyn no longer had standing as a property owner in Maryland to pursue her church tax suit (a decision was coming up in the Maryland appeals court in February 1966). Her family would pursue it themselves from Hawaii. Madalyn did not own Winford; she was only a trustee for her minor boys. Bill was no longer a minor, and clearly Madalyn was using Garth's interest as a front. She could return to Maryland if she really cared about the lawsuit, but chose to stay in Texas.

Madalyn was stunned. "Little Irvie" was obviously being manipulated by Bill and probably Susan, who Madalyn considered as bold and ambitious as Bill. But Lena had always backed her play. It was a terrible betrayal, and Madalyn turned her back on her mother forever. If she seemed ungrateful that Lena put up the house in the first place, and raised the boys, and cared for Garth while she was in Mexico, and helped keep the organization going so donations would continue, and cared for both Susan and Robin, Madalyn didn't see it that way. There wouldn't be any organizations or newsletters or donations or lawsuits or roof over anyone's head but for her. And plenty of her paychecks had gone to support the family at Winford so there would be money for the mortgage.

She'd had no choice about fleeing. Until the *Schowgurow* decision, it was that or jail. Now she was ready to take over and steer another landmark lawsuit to the Supreme Court. She wasn't splitting her organization with two teenagers and Irv.

But one day, Bill told Irv he was sick of it all, done with the organizations, the newsletter, the printing, done with him, Lena, Susan, Robin, sick of his whole family and their infighting. He packed and left.

In early January 1966, Irv awoke to find the office broken into, the files, records, and mailing list stolen. The police deemed it an inside job. That afternoon, Irv got a call from Richard O'Hair in Austin. Bill was offering to sell some files and records to Madalyn.

Irv didn't know if this was true, or if Madalyn was trying to frame Bill, and had engineered the break-in herself; among the missing items was a valid Cuban visa for her. Irv had seen his sister plan a similar caper in Honolulu with two "punks." Sitting at the dining-room table, she drew them a map of her office building in Baltimore and instructed them on how to break in, what to take, and where to find it. When the culprit was arrested in Nebraska, he reportedly had on him a letter from Madalyn telling him that if the theft didn't come off, to burn the building down.

Soon, Bill turned up in San Francisco with a new girlfriend, Julie Matthews. Once more, Robin and Susan were left behind with the Mayses. Then the real reason for Lena's action surfaced. She was diagnosed with cancer. The doctors were considering amputating her leg.

Chapter 19 ~ Mothers and Daughters

O N JANUARY 18, 1966, oral arguments took place on Madalyn's church tax suit in the court of appeals in Annapolis. Shortly afterward, speaking to a crowd of students, she announced she would probably run for Texas governor or senator in the next state election. And "As soon as I become comfortably ensconced in Austin," she said, she would file a church tax suit against the houses of worship in her adopted city.

A month later, on Valentine's Day, the Maryland high court ruled against Madalyn. Of the $2 billion in taxable Baltimore property, $78 million was indeed exempted as religious property. But so was that of about 60 other charitable groups — and charity was a major outreach of churches. Plaintiff Freethought Society of America could have gotten a religious tax exemption too, the court said. Besides, churches attracted people to a community and increased the tax base. One of the judges, Reuben Oppenheimer, said churches did good and helped integration. Plus, states were free to decide who to tax.

Madalyn appealed, once again headed for the U.S. Supreme Court with a high-profile lawsuit, scheduled for review in June. At Howard University, her old alma mater, 250 people listened as she pounded it home: millions and millions of dollars were siphoned away from taxpayers by the churches. They owned 20–25% of the taxable property in the U.S., and hid their wealth with dummy ownership. They were into oil, banking, media, supermarkets, hotels, steel mills, wineries, agriculture, manufacturing, universities.

The Baptist church, she said, could "register Negro voters in this country... in six weeks" if it wanted to do something good for humanity. But its tax exemption depended on staying out of politics. Nor would any denomination come out against the immoral, destructive, illegal war in Vietnam. Why? Because they held investments in companies that manufactured arms. She claimed that the Society of Jesus, a Catholic order, owned Bank of America, that the Mormons controlled Union Pacific Railroad. She was putting it all into a book called *Let Us Prey*

Home in Austin between appearances in late spring, Madalyn gave herself a late 47th birthday present. She sued two Baltimore newspapers, two wire services, Maryland Governor Millard Tawes, each member of the grand jury that voted to extradite her, Judge James Cullen, who had ordered her and Bill to stay away from Susan, each of the policemen who arrested her for assault, Susan's family, their lawyer, the Baltimore postmaster, Leonard Kerpelman, Lemoin Cree, the Baltimore office of the Associated Press, and the Sunpapers Corporation, for all the grief and hassle that started in March 1964 when Susan showed up at her door.

In the complaint was coded her deep rage and betrayal: not only had the papers deliberately omitted her efforts to get Susan into a shelter, they made her look like a mad dog. Yes, she had a big mouth and didn't pull her punches. But because of the arrogant presumptions of these *Jews*, she said, and the courts who despised her separationist activity and acted through the police, and the papers who slanted everything to sell more copies, she had come to be justifiably afraid for her life and her sons' lives. Because she acted on that fear, she was illegally ousted from her hard-won organizations; her home was ravaged and her library stolen, and the state of Maryland had gone to clearly punitive extremes to drag her back. It would take $9.25 million to ease her pain.

By summer 1966, she told her newsletter readers, she'd made 87 appearances. Television, radio, speeches, campuses — she'd flown 35,000 miles, traveling to Illinois, New York, Washington, Virginia, Missouri, California, Massachusetts, Kansas, Ohio, and Canada. She was on television for six hours over two nights in Boston; Cardinal Cushing called the station to say he was monitoring every word. At Harvard, she took on a minister, a Catholic scholar, and two law professors, by herself. In Chicago she faced a Jesuit scholar, a rabbi, and a Methodist minister.

Her adversaries used the debates to flog their new books, while she was not permitted to give out SOS's address, because that would be advertising. And when letters came into the stations, she said, they were too lazy to forward them to her. And there was only Dick back home to do the ads, maintain equipment, mail things out, keep the books, answer the phone, deal with correspondence, and schedule her appearances. She made an ardent appeal for money to buy air time, and it came.

She also raised money on the Dirksen Amendment, the latest of a nonstop spate of attempts to protect the Constitution from the judiciary. Never again, said the amendment's sponsors, should nine men be allowed to tamper with the fabric of American democracy itself.

With the theft of the printing supplies and mailing list, Irv was whipped. He couldn't raise money for a lawyer to keep his hand in on the church tax suit, or even pay the bills. He and Lena went on welfare, with only one more card to play — Winford.

On May 30, 1966, Lena announced that unless Madalyn made a reasonable offer on the house, she was going to sell it. It would put the church tax suit, on its way to the Supreme Court, in jeopardy, but she owed hospital bills and debts, some of them incurred by Madalyn before she fled to Mexico. They were subsisting on food stamps.

"I don't want to live here as a deadbeat," she said. She had notified Madalyn's New York attorney of her intentions two weeks ago.

She got an angry reply from Madalyn, who was in New York at the time. (So was Bill; he and Madalyn had reconciled once more. For the next decade, he would be in an excruciating on-again, off-again relationship with his mother.) Madalyn vowed to fight her mother in every court in the land and tie up the property. She wrote the old lady, who was still helping care for Susan and baby Robin, "I would rather see the house eaten up in legal costs than see you get a penny that does not belong to you." Lena, 75, was undergoing daily hospital treatments, paid for by welfare.

In October 1966, the Supreme Court declined to review the church tax suit. After the decision was announced, Lena was cut off from her treatments and welfare payments. Someone had told the authorities she'd gotten money from the sale of her furniture. She appealed to Kerpelman for help, and in March 1967, her benefits were restored.

But Lena didn't need them. Two weeks later, on April 3, 1967, she died.

Neither Madalyn nor Bill contacted Irv. With no money to ship the body to Baltimore to place it next to Pup, he laid his mother to rest April 6 in Hawaiian Memorial Park, paid for by the welfare department.

Jill Lunderville, an admirer of Madalyn's, had just arrived in Hawaii, and saw Lena's obituary. She sent a condolence card to Irv and invited him to dinner some evening at her little apartment.

Instead of phoning to set the date, he simply appeared at her door one day unannounced, "big, heavyset...and hungry." She hurriedly prepared the promised meal.

She would never forget Irv. "The best way to explain it is, you have a clock, and the mainspring gets wound and wound and wound, it could explode at any minute. He hated the world, he hated Madalyn, he hated everything. And the more he ate, the louder he got. I ended up closing the doors and windows. I thought, 'what have I got myself into?' I've never seen anybody quite that angry."

He said Madalyn was "a liar, a crook, she didn't care about any of her people, she just wanted to get the money." His anger at Madalyn kept orbiting around an incident back in Baltimore. "They'd rip open the envelopes and there'd be cash in there, he would pocket it. Madalyn found out and fired him." She obviously rehired him, but the Mayses had a gift for grudges.

Some months after Lena's death, Irv wrote his sister, proposing a reconciliation. He was bothered that she hadn't attended their mother's funeral. His letter was simply filed away by a volunteer, who thought it "poignant and sad."

As it turned out, the Winford sale was in court more than four years, and the lawyers did get most of it. And just as the old-guard freethought establishment had feared, the Supreme Court's refusal to review the church tax suit put a chill on other such suits. But Madalyn wasn't dismayed. She would just file another one.

Bill and Susan had divorced in October 1966 shortly after the Supreme Court threw out Madalyn's church tax suit. They agreed that Bill would take Robin until Susan finished college. She had separate papers drawn up stating that Robin could not go to Texas, nor ever be put in Madalyn's care. But they were never executed, and after a few weeks of fatherhood in San Francisco, Bill called Madalyn for help. Garth confided to his friend Mike W_____ that Madalyn had been worried about the baby for a long time. After Bill left Hawaii, Madalyn kept track of Susan's whereabouts. She claimed the child had been found living with strangers, subsisting on "beer and sweet rolls." She'd tried to get custody, and Susan had the letter drawn up forbidding Robin to go to Texas.

Robin was now a lively toddler, with bright, laughing eyes and burnished curls. Madalyn embraced her, and had a photographer take family portraits of herself, Garth, and the angelic 21-month-old. Madalyn promised Richard it was only until Bill and Julie found an apartment that allowed kids, but it wasn't to work out that way.

Garth, 12, had braces and the whisper of a man's mustache. And indeed he was to become a man that year, stepping into Bill's shoes to care for Robin. Madalyn's cause was now firmly back in her control, and she was constantly traveling and speaking to bring in needed cash.

With his new surrogate-parent duties, Garth had grown up rapidly in the past two months from the child Garry DeYoung remembered at Winford as a "totally spoiled brat."

"Len Kerpelman and Madalyn and I would be sitting in the living room talking about *serious* matters," recalled DeYoung, "and Garth would be totally disrupting the conversation." Once Kerpelman said, "please control the kid" when Garth was blatting in their faces with a toy machine gun. Madalyn turned purple. "You're not gonna tell *me* how to run my kid!" As a result, "Garth didn't feel he had any social responsibility, he had no social graces," said DeYoung. "His feeling was, 'I don't have to kowtow to anybody!'" Certainly not to Richard, who thought he was a hopeless mama's boy. He still had a marked, baby-talk speech impediment, and Madalyn indulged him with a generous allowance as she had Bill.

But spoiling was Madalyn's way of compensating Garth for being robbed of a childhood, spent among adults. And it was still being usurped daily. He worked as hard as Madalyn herself, for his age, helping with mailing and filing and collating, going to school, and caring for Robin.

Christmas 1966 found Madalyn with the things she'd always wanted — a snug little home, her Cause, a Real Man, her dogs and some rabbits (plus Richard's two pet birds and coop full of pigeons), and two adored children. Robin called Richard "Bobo," and his heart softened a little, though he still disliked kids. He began calling his wife "Grandma."

Madalyn loved creating holiday magic — the tree loaded with ornaments and tinsel, cookies, wrapped presents, and a magnificent feast for guests — volunteers, reporters, visiting members from out of town — who frequently filled her home at Christmas. She had many admirers; people traveled to Austin to knock on her door, and almost anywhere she traveled, she could find someone to help with taxis, lodging, and meals. She constantly had overnight guests in her small home.

After Christmas, Bill wrote. Susan didn't want Robin back, he said. And Julie didn't feel confident raising another woman's child until she had experienced her own.

Madalyn was crazy about the little girl; she'd always wanted a daughter. She had more than enough negligence evidence to pry Robin away from both parents, and had written a vow to fight however hard it took to keep her granddaughter out of a "Jewish foster home." By January 18, 1967, a document was in place, drafted by Sam Houston Clinton, for Susan's consent that Robin be adopted by the O'Hairs. Robin settled into family life at Shoal Creek, and, after several years of stonewalling and power plays by her parents, the adoption went through.

Chapter 20 ~ Poor Richard and Devil O'Hair

LESTER BUTTRAM, the minister Madalyn had shocked so badly back in Baltimore, had managed to hook her into a bantering correspondence. He'd say he was praying for her, and she would reply that he'd better lay off — she was getting more members all the time. If she didn't write for awhile, he'd say it was because she was afraid he would convert her. She'd ask for some of his "dirt on the RCC."

He had a standing invitation to visit, and she had a tendency to drop everything to reply to his letters. It baffled Richard and made him jealous. He didn't understand why she spent so much time on this marginal little man.

Something in Madalyn's outsider posture suggested to Buttram what Walter Hoops had seen: an underlying anxiety to be accepted. Her boasting betrayed insecurity — she told him Richard was the son of millionaires, "a man of affluence and background" who was descended from Abraham Lincoln.

Buttram grew up poor, and by 19 was teaching in a rural Missouri school. There he crossed a rough bootlegger who didn't like his kids hearing the morning prayers — which were mandated by law — and beat Buttram up when he wouldn't stop them. Buttram responded by enticing four of the man's children to a revival, where they became Christians. He'd cracked tougher nuts than Madalyn, he felt.

He played her, apologizing that she had been mistreated by so-called Christians. He said her letters proved she was kind and tolerant, not the anti-Christ she'd been made out. He asked permission before using her first name.

He knew she loved a fight, that she wanted to be rich. He knew she romanticized about being at the center of a big, loving family, all working in the Cause (he had such a family, four sons and four "adopted orphan girls"; he and his wife had never even quarreled, he told Madalyn). He knew she wanted a place in history, a big publishing enterprise, a university, and a life of travel.

So he wrote her about his visits to the West Indies, Europe, the Holy Land. His sophisticated printing plant was being upgraded again, which meant more tracts, more Bibles, and more income, while Richard struggled inexpertly with a gummy little press in a back bedroom. He was going to carry on negating atheism's gains, Buttram told her. He was going to send out millions and millions of tracts and Bibles all over the planet. She had inspired him, he said, more than anything else in his 40 years as an evangelist.

It was exactly the kind of bait she couldn't resist.

"My grandfather was actually quite fond of Madalyn Murray," a grandson said years later. "He thought he was the one who was going to bring her to the Lord.

"She tolerated him, you know, like a cat? — when the dog's going after it, will just lie there and switch its tail?"

Madalyn was partly intrigued by Lester Buttram because she could see how sophisticated the evangelists were about exploiting technology. Not only did they have state-of-the-art printing and bulk-mailing operations, they were streaming into radio and television. She could see the immense potential of this exposure, and the Christians were seizing it. She spent most of November 1967 on a speaking tour in Ohio, Illinois, and Pennsylvania, and each appearance kept generating others. She was the first guest on an exciting new television talk show out of Dayton that included live audience participation and callers. The host was an innovator named Phil Donahue.

Her appearance was electric. Dolled up in a fur hat and nice wool suit, she was perfect for the new format — confident, reasonable, and entertainingly blunt. For now, she went easy on the well-groomed, bewildered Christians who stood up to ask questions like, "If there's no God, then where did *you* come from?," patiently explaining the elements of evolution and reproduction. Later she wouldn't be so gentle in answering that question.

She returned home to piles of mail. It was so easy to see what television could do, she could taste it — she and Jimmy Swaggart, Jerry Falwell, Pat Robertson, Oral Roberts, and many other evangelists. In 1961 Pat Robertson went on the air in Virginia Beach, Virginia, and the year of Madalyn's marriage, introduced two baby-faced young puppeteers named Jim and Tammy Bakker. By the end of the decade, his Christian Broadcasting Network was syndicating the Bakkers' *700 Club*, and quietly acquiring radio and television stations across the country. Oral Roberts' 10-year-old television ministry out of Tulsa was employing hundreds and pulling in millions of dollars.

These preachers had started out humbly, in radio, and Madalyn decided to launch a radio broadcast, and move into television after she'd built a base. But atheist donors weren't as plentiful as Christians, and air time was expensive. In an attempt to get free time, Madalyn filed another suit against the FCC, similar to her 1965 suit against the 15 Oahu radio stations. Before, she'd been denied because atheism wasn't controversial enough to trigger the Fairness Doctrine. This time she came at it from a different angle, seeking to keep the FCC from enforcing the Fairness Doctrine in a way that "systematically denied [her] the use of airwaves."

Richard got excited, and took over the legwork for the FCC suit, a lifesaver given Madalyn's grueling speaking schedule. There were over 6,000 radio stations in America, and he was requesting equal time on all of them. He and Madalyn asked members in every state to sponsor a certain number of broadcasts a week.

They had hopes that the Fairness Doctrine would be triggered by *Madalyn*, a documentary film by UT graduate student Robert Elkins. When it aired on PBS stations around the country, several insisted on a disclaimer, saying some of Madalyn's assertions in it were untrue or distorted. A Pennsylvania station manager reportedly called it a "non-stop unchallenged monologue," and refused to air it. He didn't call Billy Graham's drivel that, she retorted.

"Come on, Madalyn," said an editorial, "Get yourself a radio station and sell your stuff just like the pastors do. Then you'll...find out that when people don't like what you're preaching, they just turn you off."

She did. Richard researched topics for the American Atheist Radio Series, which debuted June 3, 1968. Her voice was deep and masculine, and she had learned to enunciate with Shirley Chisholm-like authority and deliberation, erasing all traces of the tough towns from which her people had sprung. She was unable to buy air time in many places, but KTBC in Austin, owned by the Lyndon Johnson family, did sell her a weekly slot — followed by 15 minutes of gospel paid for by an Austin furniture store owner.

Around this time, the city of Austin unwittingly gave Madalyn another boost. She suspected it was a certain "Christer" city councilman who was after her when Richard got a notice that he was violating a zoning ordinance. Someone had found out that the houses on Sinclair and Shoal Creek, both residences, were being used for Society of Separationists activities.

Hitting the law library, Madalyn found one enterprise that could pass the city's review in her neighborhood — a church. She called Kirby Hensley, the self-ordained California minister who had visited her in Baltimore, and suggested she go on the evangelical circuit. Could he ordain her in his church? He happily air-mailed a charter and some credentials. Texas couldn't challenge it — it had to accept a California church if California had. Thus was born Poor Richard's Universal Life Church of Austin, Texas.

When the city said her church had to have been in existence before the zoning violation, Hensley obliged with certificates of the requisite date, saying Madalyn had been a bishop and Richard a prophet in his California church. Madalyn called a press conference and said this had been in the works a long time, and they were finally making it public.

To her triumphant hearing, she wore all black with a white cleric's collar, and took some witnesses willing to swear they attended services in her facility. The livid councilman charged her and Richard again, this time with more specificity, but the city attorney declined to go through the charade again. The publicity was fantastic.

By the end of 1969, Poor Richard's Universal Life Church was a tax-exempt entity. Richard and Madalyn took vows of poverty, and turned over all property and income to it. Members could now deduct up to 30% of their taxable income if all their donations were to churches, hospitals, and educational institutions, Madalyn wrote her members, and she was hurrying to establish the latter. Poor Richard's didn't have to pay taxes on interest income, dividends, royalties, rent, or capital gains. It could own hotels, publishing houses, mines, public utilities, ranches, radio stations — any kind of business it wanted, and neither pay taxes nor report income. You could give appreciated stocks to Poor Richard's and deduct them at their current value, for instance. It was a "unique opportunity for giving," Madalyn wrote, echoing televangelists throughout the land.

Better do your homework, suggested an official of the Southern Baptist Convention — churches pay the same taxes on their business holdings as anyone else. Only church property used for church purposes was exempt. She might be in for trouble if she lured businesses into lease-back agreements on her wrongheaded assumptions.

The Austin paper ran a story on the new "religion for atheists." The wire services distributed it and when *Time* magazine called, Richard emphasized the educational thrust of the endeavor, the first such national one in the U.S. But they had a little fun, too, making Neanderthal Man the church's patron saint. The church was housed at Sinclair, and received so much mail it had to be picked up in a leather bag from the post office. Letters were often addressed to "Devil O'Hair" or "Thing."

The California attorney general was contesting Kirby Hensley's ordination mill, but was treading carefully; Hensley was ready and eager to go to the Supreme Court on grounds that the Constitution barred government from interfering with one's religion.

In drafting the charter, Madalyn said, "We've drawn from the Mormons, the Christian Scientists. We've drawn from everybody. If they try to attack us they'll be attacking their own tenets." Her mission was to acquire property and wealth commensurate with the Catholic Church's.

The Canadian Broadcasting Corporation traveled to Austin to film the church's first planned devotional service at the university student union, but campus officials nixed it. There was a little 1963 rule against that kind of thing, they said.

Madalyn's travel and speaking schedule was packed, and Richard filled in, coordinating her trips and putting out the newsletter. With Richard setting type, the publication changed names regularly. Sometimes it was *Poor Richard's Reports* (or *Report*), sometimes *Poor Richard's Newsletter,* sometimes *SOS* or *Society of Separationists Newsletter.* Sometimes it was called *Tax-the-Church,* and sometimes just *Newsletter.*

According to Bill, the inconsistency was because his stepfather started the day with vodka, and kept it up until bedtime. But Richard's reporting voice was warm and adult compared to Madalyn's often manic, exclamatory style. She thought nothing of expressing her bitterness or despair in the publications, and he tried to get her to separate her emotions from the mission. She habitually exaggerated her hardship and persecution to pull guilt strings, but she also felt people backed winners, so her communiqués were often a schizophrenic mixture of martyrdom, moxie, and truth.

However ill-tempered Richard was in private, in print he was good with the reins, and she knew it. He kept focused on SOS's mission of education and information. Atheists were actually not very well informed about their unbelief, he wrote. They needed an Atheist Center, to sustain their feelings and arguments with history, facts, and fellowship. From this seed would come the dreamed-of atheist university, a prototype for the teaching of critical thinking which would redirect American education.

Toward that end, they'd started rebuilding the library, with books stacked in every room. Freethought materials were suppressed and destroyed, and he and Madalyn were making an organized effort to preserve them. They wanted to buy a ranch in Texas with a house and visitors' quarters, with room for the library — and later, the university.

The fledgling Charles E. Stevens American Atheist Library and Archives, CE-SAALA, had been born about the same time as Robin, when, in a shaky hand, an octogenarian admirer from California wrote a check to Madalyn Murray for a thousand dollars. Charles E. Stevens was a stonemason, living humbly off his Spanish Civil War veteran's pension. Over several months, he would send her every dollar of his life savings — a total of $8,000.

He wrote Madalyn that he'd been too poor for most of his life to afford books, but he dreamed of contributing to a library such as she was building, filled with works on atheism and freethought shunned by mainstream libraries. Genuinely touched by his humility and lonely gentlemanliness, she wrote him warm letters in return, and vowed to name her library after him. And though she later claimed that Irv stole the Stevens money while she was in Mexico, it was a promise she kept. Over the next 30 years, she built the library into an asset estimated at several million dollars. It got its official name in 1969, and though she chronically lied about everything from the size of her organizations' memberships to her number of subscribers, income, achievements, education, and troubles, she did right by the library.

Though their marriage was strained by work, alcoholism, and their difficult personalities, Richard was protective of Madalyn. He tried to get her to take breaks, just go fishing with him, the hell with the Cause. She could never do it. When she suddenly gained 40 pounds and became dizzy and exhausted with diabetes, he wrote, "Between appearances I managed to force her into a doctor's office. I have to hit her on the head once in awhile to make her obey orders and get some rest." She was just worn out, he explained — 160 appearances in less than a year, 30,000 miles of travel, 30 taped radio programs, letters to answer, mass mailings, book orders.

And in addition, she had two kids to raise. "She would be ironing for the family till late at night while I made supper," wrote Richard.

"Richard says it's something I manufacture inside," she told an interviewer, "like too much adrenaline or something, but if we could bottle it . . ."

When she was feeling good, she was funny, affectionate, almost cute. She had a warm, no-holds-barred laugh, and if you were "in" with her, it was all the way in. And she made you want to be in with her. She told the admiring college students that it didn't matter if you made mistakes, just keep trying. *Do* something, don't worry about failing. To them she was no nut, whatever their parents might say.

She even had a soft, little-girl look of idealism that was somewhat sensual. She'd look up to the ceiling, trying to find the right words, trying to tell the truth about her thoughts. She used a little flirty voice to soothe bilious Richard, who, as often as he felt tender toward her, attacked her, accusing her of going in a thousand directions at once, wasting time on trivia, and wanting to be a man.

She liked being guided by him, even though she reflexively pushed back. Once, in Los Angeles on business, she got to meet "refugees" and see some grainy footage of the Spanish Civil War, that romance of her youth. When she told Richard about it, he immediately asked if she gave them money. Yes, she said, and he called her a god-damned fool. "That war ended 35 years ago! Anyone involved in it should have gotten a job by now!"

She admitted he was right, she did feel like a fool. "He taught me . . . no matter what happens to you, you can rebound. There's no reason to stay down . . . the only thing that can actually get you is death."

It was clear Richard admired and was moved by her, working so hard on the Cause, making sure little Robin had her cookies and milk in the afternoon, hooking a rug for the living room, sewing one of her cheap dresses, training volunteers, cooking, getting the kids to the doctor and orthodontist.

But he was mysteriously perverse, jealous, and vindictive. Once he told a reporter, "She'll be saying, just as sweet, 'I'm your little cactus flower . . . Why, I can't even lift that Kleenex out of the box.' And she's probably just finished bending steel pipes in the kitchen."

He resented the camaraderie she raised with the leftist students. One, a newcomer to Texas named James Freudiger, knew printing. "Someone from Students for a Democratic Society brought her around one evening with a proposition," he remembered. "She would give us a printing press to use for the movement if we would do her printing." An escapade ensued in which the students helped spirit an AB Dick press out of a garage late at night into Freudiger's garage. Madalyn had it picked up the next day for repairs, and they never saw her again.

"Of course we all felt used and humiliated . . . I suppose that was the last time I ever trusted anyone just because they were a notorious lefty!"

Some of the SDSers were connected with the Sparticist League, a Trotskyite group that proliferated around campuses, stoking the Proletarian Revolution. Unknown to Madalyn, Richard reported this and the press caper to authorities; it was added to a growing FBI file on her.

Chapter 21 ~ Houston, We've Got a Problem

MADALYN HAD STARTED city and state chapters of SOS to keep her name and Cause spread over the country, and associated with the roiling controversy and confusion over church-state separation. In October 1968, SOS's Oklahoma director, Kent Meyer, requested that Oklahoma City take down a huge, lit cross in the state fairgrounds. The state constitution said no public money or property would ever be used to support any aspect of religion.

There was a huge outcry, and Madalyn's name was the one in lights. Letters ranged from "what does it hurt" to "this time she's gone too far" to "let's get a petition — we've given in too many times."

Lester Buttram wrote — was she "brave enough" to dialogue with him on this? He knew she liked publicity, he said, and if she got on his side, what a powerhouse she could be. She could turn the world upside down, with the talent and brains she had. This was done rather skillfully, in a hayseed sort of way, as if he was unaware that he was appealing to her hunger for attention.

And indeed, she replied with an invitation to call if he was in her area. She called him a "reasonable man, and some day you will have a clear and compelling picture of religion and will want to join us."

Richard pulled out what hair he had, that she would actually think she could convert Buttram. But she sincerely did feel there was hope, when she met a rational, intelligent Christian, that they could be made to see things her way. She was also dabbling with another devout Christian, Jane Sauter of Baltimore, who wrote regularly. But Sauter exemplified to Madalyn the unreachable Christian, the kind who blindly forked over so many millions to charlatan ministers. She accused Sauter of harboring secret doubts about her religion, and fell into the puerile battle tactics of her growing-up years.

"You sure as hell don't believe in anything then, do you — except fucking, from the size of the family you have [the Sauters had six children] . . . Can it, Jane. I don't want your prayers, your nutty letters, or your sexual guilts visited upon me. I am healthy in my head, and in bed with my man — you are not. I can't help you; only a psychiatrist can."

Another time, she sent Sauter a complimentary copy of her booklet, *Why I Am An Atheist*, addressed to "Jane Sauter, religious nut." Inside, it was inscribed, "Keep the faith, baby, but keep it to yourself."

If Buttram and Sauter thought the Oklahoma cross was a big deal, they had only to wait until Christmas.

On December 24, 1968, three Apollo 8 astronauts orbited the moon, a stupendous achievement. Before James Lovell, Frank Borman, and William Anders took off, the Gideon Society gave them each a Bible. Sixty-nine miles above the moon, beaming back to earth the first pictures of the lunar surface, Commander Borman began reading. "In the beginning . . ."

He read about the earth being without form and darkness upon its face, and so on, until Lovell took over, reading about God separating light from darkness, and back and forth, until they completed the passage. Then Borman prayed to God for vision, faith, knowledge, and world peace.

From Houston, Madalyn called it "tragic" that such a triumph of science had to be dragged to its knees to grovel under the pressures of organized religion. And unconstitutional. She would fight this.

Letters poured into NASA. If anybody had a right to pray, it was those brave men! This "Jezebel, Lady Macbeth, Lot's wife, Mary Queen of Scots, all wrapped into one foul mouthed female atheist" was simply set on crippling the church, taxing or bullying it out of any ability to manifest godliness in American life.

That *woman* again! Why do the papers give her so much space? Why can't they just ignore her? She has a right to her opinion, but why does she have a right to have it trumpeted across the nation? Why do the bigmouths always get in the news? The majority of us were *moved* by the astronauts' scriptural broadcasts. Why is this *one woman* allowed to cause so much trouble?

Pretty soon we won't be able to tell a child red is red, because he has his *rights*, and he might want to call red yellow! "Why is she so afraid of prayer," asked a writer, and what was she going to do if the President thanked God for something in public?

Lester Buttram wrote: how unhappy she must be that she and the Communists had lost this battle with "three wise men" from a space capsule. At this threat to taint her with Communism, Richard loudly urged her to withdraw her invitation to Buttram to visit. Stop wasting precious time and energy on these nuts! he scolded.

Madalyn broke the doctor's orders to rest and flew to Michigan, Houston, Atlanta, various places in Texas, Pennsylvania, Cincinnati, and Florida in just a few weeks to speak after the moon orbit. Her junket was capped with a triumphant invitation to speak at a packed symposium at the University of Florida along with a distinguished slate: William O. Douglas, Strom Thurmond, Melvin Belli, Julian Bond, and others.

Madalyn spoke of myth and materialism, of her suits against the FCC and IRS, and her protest to the Post Office when it issued a "Pray for Peace" stamp in 1960. But the students really started yelling and applauding when she came out for legalized abortion and free pills, and set about to define obscenity. "I've had my tit in the wringer since I was 14 over this sex thing, and I don't see why I need a license from a church to fuck!" They went wild.

It even flushed out two monied Florida atheists who began a flow of hundreds of thousands of dollars to her over the years. August Scholle was going to be proud. Homer Lacy was going to be proud. Even Pup would have been proud.

Her February newsletter called Florida a "historical first" — an atheist on a speaking platform with members of the nation's leadership. Rubbing elbows at dinner and cocktails, "I could hardly believe it when [former Senator] Wayne Morse recognized me on sight." She had been "publicly hugged" by none other than Melvin Belli. The sweetness of this, after all the years of marginality, exhausting work, and hate mail, came through with great pathos.

On July 20, 1969, when Apollo 11 astronauts stepped onto the surface of the moon, there were no prayers. President Nixon spoke to them at the Sea of Tranquility from the Oval Office about peace on earth. It was a triumph for Madalyn, but starvation for the Cause.

However, the spacemen placed a disk on the moon with a prayer from Pope Paul VI engraved on it, and among the United Nations flags taken to be brought back as souvenirs was the Vatican flag. Madalyn filed suit to enjoin NASA from "directing or permitting religious activities, or ceremonies" in the space program. Not only was it unconstitutional, the Pope's Christian prayer discriminated against other religions, and nonbelievers.

She filed an eight-page complaint in Judge Jack Roberts' U.S. District Court in Austin, but asked for a special tribunal because Roberts had "a Christian, sectarian bias."

Americans United for Separation of Church and State, a Washington-based watchdog group formed in 1947 to oppose religion in schools and on public property, announced it would intervene. Madalyn was going too far; the Supreme Court never barred people's expression of their religious beliefs, not in classrooms, space, or anywhere else. It barred *coerced* religious exercises, not voluntary ones. The astronauts were doing what they wanted; they weren't under orders. Madalyn had nothing to say when the Russian astronauts were reported saying they *hadn't* seen God.

In an irresistible irony, NASA's director was named Thomas Paine.

With this momentum, in September 1969, Madalyn announced she was going to sue the Austin, Dallas, and Houston school districts in federal court over various prayer infractions. At least one school in Austin was sneaking in prayers. She was also suing schools in Pennsylvania and New Jersey; in the latter, a high school principal had read part of the Congressional Record to students gathered in the gym. The part he read had a prayer in it.

She created such a firestorm that, in next November's U.S. Senate race, Texan Lloyd Bentsen, a conservative Republican, defeated longtime liberal incumbent Ralph Yarborough, who had supported the Supreme Court's decision in Madalyn's 1963 suit. Bentsen's winning strategy included a slogan: "What's The Matter With Prayer?"

Madalyn was shortly invited to appear on a panel of the National Academy of Television Arts and Sciences in New York, along with some heavyweight media bosses, including FCC commissioner Robert E. Lee and Louis Nizer, author of the preface to the Warren Commission Report on the Kennedy assassination.

Even with her grueling, health-breaking schedule, she took time to write Lester Buttram another curious pedigree of Richard — he was a distinguished spy, constantly in demand for his expertise; his first wife's family were railroad magnates. She gave Buttram her home phone number.

Richard may not have understood Madalyn's psychological attachments to Buttram, but he knew how competitive his wife was. Buttram's Gospel Tract Society dwarfed her efforts; he had 18 full-time staffers and a monthly budget of $18,000. He spent $69,000 a year for postage alone. Madalyn *knew* she was smarter and better educated than Buttram, with far more charisma. How to explain the discrepancy in the power and wealth they each wielded? It was a bone she had to gnaw.

Chapter 22 ~ To Mother, With Love

BILL HAD MARRIED Julie Matthews in early 1968, and a year later, at 22, he enlisted in the army. It unleashed a dammed-up flood of emotion and confidences from Madalyn. She trusted him now; he was like her, like his father. She wrote him letter after chatty letter about family history, sharing her days as if they were back at Winford, drinking their whiskey-tea in the kitchen after supper. He seemed relieved, too; he sent a large color photo of himself in uniform, inscribed, "To my Mother with love." In September 1969, he arrived in Austin on a 10-day leave. Julie joined him, and Madalyn happily posed herself and her offspring on the sofa for photographs.

But the harmony vanished when she discovered he'd washed out of helicopter pilot training. She chewed him out; he retorted that he hadn't failed — her NASA suit had marked him for persecution, just as with his teachers in high school. He accused her of only caring because the support checks for Robin would be smaller now that he'd been busted to private.

"I really wanted to kill her and leave the country," he wrote later. "I decided instead to just leave the country." He got on a bus for Canada, leaving Julie behind. Madalyn, expecting him to make Austin his home base now, had put Julie to work for SOS.

Soon he was AWOL, and on the Austin police pickup list. The news hit the papers two days after the first NASA hearing, and was an incredible disgrace for Madalyn. The word "deserter" was used in headlines all over the country.

She needed to spin the story. She said Bill was in Montreal, working as an antiwar activist with a pacifist group which was raided and bombed last week, and she was worried whether he was alive. Privately, Garth told Mike W_____, she was afraid he'd commit suicide.

Far from contemplating suicide, Bill was running drugs and stolen property back and forth across the Canadian border and having the time of his life.

Madalyn and Richard fought bitterly about it. Richard said Bill should come home and face the music, while Madalyn furiously defended him. "He's been through so much as my son," she grieved. "He's treated as a Communist and a spy everywhere."

(She could never stand even a breath of criticism of her children. Recently she'd taken Robin, four, to eat at Mr. Steak on Burnet Road. When the waitress took their order, she said pleasantly, "I think your granddaughter may be playing with my tip money" from the last customer. Instantly enraged, Madalyn rose and began shouting as the other customers laid down their forks to watch. "You have wrongfully accused us of theft!" The incident ended with police escorting Madalyn out.)

The honeymoon was long over, but the fight over Bill was the beginning of the end of what had been a genuine love affair. A few weeks later, Madalyn filed aggravated assault charges against Richard. They had had another huge row about

Bill. It ended with Richard striking her, bruising her face visibly. She told authorities he'd done it before.

The papers loved it; "Poor Richard," said the *Dallas Morning News*, "is now out on a $300 bond." Unkindly, the article quoted a drunken paean Madalyn had recently made on her radio broadcast, to Richard's "short-fingered powerful hands [that could] fell men with one judo-chop... [and] ripple the pages of a book of poems..." (It was the kind of thing she did when drinking, which she often indulged in on her show, during telephone interviews, and while writing.)

Reporters lurking around Shoal Creek caught Madalyn roaring off to see a divorce lawyer as Richard lifted a laundry basket full of clothing from his pickup, where Madalyn had dumped it. Drinking gin as he brought it back in, he explained that "Grandma" was a bit mercurial. "To her, every mountain is a battle — a crusade." She simply had to have "some temper tantrums," he explained. "They're a release for her."

She dropped the assault charges, and a month later Bill was discharged and took a job in Austin with Braniff Airlines.

In the summer, Bill left for a position with Braniff in New York. Once settled in, he flew Robin and Garth up for some sightseeing. Garth was already tall, and hulking after the Mayses — at 15 he was 5'10" and weighed 175. For several years he had been paying bills and shopping for the family, writing checks for clothes, groceries, and dress material. (Madalyn's taste in fabric ran to broken-glass patterns — sharp-edged fragments, pieces, and chips.) He was obedient, hardworking, a good son who spent his spare time stuffing envelopes and doing clerical work for the Cause. Madalyn rewarded him with a hardship driver's license, and by his 15th birthday, he had wheels. It was clear to Bill that "Garf," as Robin called him, was also doing most of the child care.

He had no friends but Mike, who was the only schoolmate to call him Garth — to the outside world, he was Jon. "He was considered a weirdo and non-conformist," said a schoolmate at Lamar Junior High. "I always saw Jon as ... obviously intelligent but warped by that domineering mother." His speech impediment had not abated.

Looking at his brother, Bill was reminded that when Garth was a baby, he had banged his head repeatedly against the headboard of his crib to get attention. "I was the only one who ever got that kid out of the crib. It wasn't until years later, when I saw how animals act in cages, that I realized — he reminded me of a trapped animal."

That summer Garth asked, was there some way he could get away from Austin and move to New York, too?

June 30, 1970, Peoria and Joliet, Illinois. David Waters' mother, Betty, now calling herself Waters again instead of Hunt, was picked up by police and booked, wearing a cheap, platinum-blond wig and professional hooker makeup that gave her a hard, painted look. It was her armor for the streets, but it couldn't obliterate the fun-loving little grin that came through in the mug shots. "I really liked Betty," said a girlfriend of her son Jeff later; she was funny, with lots of personality. "At Thanksgiving, she would put out this huge spread," and the jokes flew all day.

But at this juncture in her life, David was in prison in Joliet, 19-year-old Stevie Plumley was an addict, and 16-year-old Jeff Hunt/Ron Waters was the family healer, a role well established for him by then. Rodney, now 15, had long ago been adopted out. Larry Hunt, the last of Betty's sons, was five. She was pregnant with him when she stood up and asked the judge in the Gibbs murder case to go easy on David.

Someone had sent David photos of his newborn half-brother in prison in Joliet. In fact, he received many photos, mostly from teenaged girls in his 1964 high school class. Many had messages on the back, and addresses. Over the last five years, girls from other high schools had also sent him photos, and he had quite a collection.

Dear David, I don't know if you remember me . . .

To a real nut.

Beverly, Deb, Beth, Kathy, Rosie, Sharon, Melba, Lynda, Shirley, Janice. There were even photos of older women, in their 20s, with addresses; some were in negligees. Peculiarly, he was sent one of his mother vamping in a swimsuit.

He didn't display that one. In prison, he already had to deal with guys coming up and saying, "I had sex with your Mom," or "your Mom was turning tricks down on Adams."

"What's he gonna do, defend her honor?" asked a friend. "No. Of course he's just gonna act like, 'she doesn't mean anything to me, anyway.'"

But privately, he hated that his mother was a prostitute, and he hated her curled blond wig that looked like a hardened version of when he was a little boy and she was a teenager, and had bleached her hair blond. But the wig was so stiff you could tell it was just a cheap slapped-on tool of her trade. The cops made her take it off for her mug shots, showing her luxuriant brown hair with the handsome hairline like David's. Without her makeup, she looked maternal, vulnerable.

He mourned the Marines, convinced he would not be here if his mother had just gotten out of bed and gone down and signed that form. Feeling patriotic, he said years later, he volunteered for something called the Malaria Project, in which healthy subjects were injected with malaria-infected blood and studied for vector factors, strains, and so on. Some of the blood, he said, turned out to be infected with the yet-unknown hepatitis C virus.

His photo collection grew to include his brothers and beloved grandmother, numerous photos of babies and birth announcements, and photos of pets. He loved dogs; they'd always been there, been with him through everything. Dean Hunt always had dogs. The other thing that could touch him was little children. "I love kids. They are the true innocents of the world."

But, said a girlfriend, "he always told me that *nobody* visited him [in prison]. I think he said like maybe Stevie came once."

Even at that young age, though, people wrote him with what seemed like a kind of respect. A little fear, maybe.

Chapter 23 ~ Dr. O'Hair

MADALYN WAS HOOKED ON VACATIONS by the time Robin was old enough to travel. Before school started in the fall of 1970, Madalyn and the children took a trip to the Southwest to see the ruins of Casa Grande and Mesa Verde. Madalyn took it in hungrily, studying the kivas under the clouds. They visited Natural Bridge Caverns in the hills southwest of Austin, and unwound in the motel swimming pools. Richard stayed home, shorn of the desire for the pleasure he'd once urged her to take, to get away from it all with him.

Madalyn's NASA appeal was rejected by the Fifth Circuit Court of Appeals in New Orleans. The judges said she had "no ascertainable legal interest" in the issues raised. Earlier in the year, on her 51st birthday, the crew of Apollo 13 was four-fifths of the way to the moon when a tank of liquid oxygen burst, seriously crippling the spacecraft. It splashed down safely four days later, but the tenseness of the situation and the crew's bravery, played out before the world, made Madalyn's maneuvers look particularly heinous to many, and perhaps influenced the Fifth Circuit judges.

Madalyn also had a suit before the Fifth Circuit claiming that the oath "so help me God" cut atheists out of the judicial system. That argument "approaches absurdity," said the judges. Madalyn said she'd appeal both cases to the Supreme Court.

The NASA and judicial oath matters were tangled in Madalyn's trademark way. The NASA case had started out in Federal District Court in Texas, where three things were wrong. First, a 1948 law required federal judges to be sworn in with a belief in God, so all were presumed to have one. Second, all the federal courts opened with "God Save the Nation and this Honorable Court!" — as unconstitutional as the Pledge, said Madalyn. Third, all the attorneys and officers of the court, and all jurors and witnesses, had to swear to tell the truth So Help Them God. (And it hadn't come up yet, but it soon would, that the Texas Constitution itself had a requirement that you had to believe in God to hold office, be an officer of the court, serve on a jury, be a witness, and so on.)

So, Madalyn explained to her readers, "in order to file the NASA case . . . we had to challenge these court practices also." Naturally, those challenges logically extended to every case she filed over the years, and their disposition was always in various stages of consideration, delay, and appeal. Therefore, all Madalyn's subsequent cases, and parts of pending cases, were thrown into limbo until various appeals and decisions came down, some of which, when applied to a new case, contradicted themselves, each other, or other decisions. By the time some real legal troubles started for Madalyn in the late 1970s, her Rube Goldberg legal apparatus had become so complicated that no one was sure where anything stood.

By the end of 1970, Madalyn came out with an account of the 1963 suit titled *An Atheist Epic: Bill Murray, the Bible, and the Baltimore Board of Education*. It was published by American Atheist Press. (Madalyn also had a confusing gaggle of names for her publishing arm — Gustav Broukal Freethought Press, Society of Separationists Press, American Atheist Press, and others.) Later, a critic would call the book "nothing but crude propaganda about on the level of a Soviet biography of Stalin written in 1938," but Madalyn was proud of it. It was her heartfelt vision of how things were, or should have been.

On March 8, 1971, the U.S. Supreme Court "tersely dismissed" Madalyn's NASA appeal. But she had other irons in the fire; she was watching a bill in the Texas legislature that could aid parochial schools, and she announced a short-lived campaign for Place 4 on the Austin City Council; she could raise money on that. Always in need of it, she launched "Project Midas," asking for gold jewelry, coins, and tooth fillings.

In the fall of 1971, Madalyn enrolled Robin in first grade at Rosedale Elementary — just as the Wylie Amendment, another proposal to amend the Constitution to permit school prayer, was headed for the U.S. House of Representatives. After a few days at school, Robin, knowing it was important news, came home and reported that she was pledging allegiance to the flag every morning Under God.

Madalyn spoke to the teacher, who, predictably, replied that everyone had to say the Pledge. Madalyn went to the principal. She simply couldn't have this, it was unconstitutional. Couldn't they send Robin out with the milk money or something? No, they replied, and they didn't seem scared of a lawsuit. In Austin, there was no policy on prayers or Bible reading. Each school could do what it wanted.

In the end, Madalyn couldn't put her tender little "Robbie" through what Bill and Garth had endured. She decided to just tell Robin that they were making a mistake and shouldn't make her say "under God." However, she launched a volley of protest against the latest prayer bill in Washington, the oath of office, the Christianization of outer space, the Pledge, the national motto on money, crèches on public medians. She unearthed other Austin school kids who didn't want to say "under God." She helped a Detroit agnostic who found that a group of his union brethren used their meeting hall once a month for Christian fellowship. She went after a Vermont school that allowed a summer ecumenical camp on its grounds, a government booklet that said our rights under the Declaration of Independence were assumed to flow from God, a church raising money to build a school on an Indian reservation. Corpus Christi, Texas was thinking of mounting a large statue of Jesus in its harbor. Madalyn tried to block it, but made no mention of plans to change the name of the city itself.

She traveled and spoke tirelessly on these subjects, for which some accused her of trivializing the greater mission. But the trickle-down effect on the general public couldn't be overestimated. She was burrowing into the public awareness and laying the groundwork for a secular society.

It was around this time that Madalyn began calling herself "Dr. O'Hair." She wanted into the Establishment, particularly the University of Texas. She had already told a group of students a year before that she was filing a new church tax suit, and was planning to petition UT to add a course in atheism. When she found out that UT's religion classes were usually held at churches, she wrote the president, demanding that they be dropped. However, if the university wanted to create a chair for atheism studies, she'd drop her objection.

They flicked her away.

Madalyn got access to registration information about students' religious preferences. She created the CESAALA Literary Society, got it registered as a student organization, and started holding lectures on Monday evenings at the student union, inviting all the students who'd marked "none" in the religious preference box on their registration cards.

To make a case that she should be allowed to teach atheism courses for credit, she needed credentials, i.e., a doctor of theology. "This is where you must come in now, Garry," she wrote Garry DeYoung, now American Atheists' director in Minnesota. He had founded the Minnesota Institute of Philosophy, a "seminary" of his new American Atheist Church, Inc. He was also putting together a freethought library.

"You must now send me a transcript of credits showing that I have concluded studies which would give the doctorate. I would say that this should show completion of 60 hours, wouldn't you?"

Madalyn attached a list of the lectures she was offering at the student union. "You can make 60 hours out of this," she wrote, but told him to lard her transcript with lots of Old and New Testament, Life of Jesus, and Women of the Bible, "so that I can be a Bible expert." The carrot she dangled for this work was that, once she set the precedent at UT, he could do the same at the University of Minnesota with his Institute. She would also put him on the board of directors of her American Atheist University, which she promised would be up and running within a year. And she was putting him on the board of a soon-to-be-formed entity, the Fahnestock Foundation.

He should also "send" a doctoral degree to Avro Manhattan, a British author of books on church-state separation, and one to David Tribe, a publisher in England, and one to GORA — Goparaju Ramachandra Rao — the Indian social reformer, because he planned to host the first World Atheist Meet in Vijayawada this year. (GORA was an educated Brahmin who had influenced Gandhi toward compassionate atheism in the years preceding his 1948 assassination. He had founded the Atheist Centre in 1940 and settled it in Vijayawada in 1947.)

Madalyn also instructed DeYoung on a suit she planned to cut him in on. President Nixon had established a chapel in the White House East Room, where Billy Graham and others led services on Sunday. Graham was White House pastor. Madalyn planned to put a stop to it, and needed Garry to write for information on the cost of these services as a "dumb citizen" — they'd never send it to her. She wanted to file one suit against Nixon in Texas and one in Minnesota — Graham's headquarters were in Minneapolis — hoping for conflicting opinions so it would have to go to the U.S. Supreme Court.

DeYoung did award Madalyn a doctorate, her course work being a year's worth of her radio talks, published in book form in 1969 and entitled *What On Earth Is An Atheist.* Each talk required research, and the resulting book included bibliographies and references DeYoung considered as valid as any course work at an accredited university. American Atheist Press published half a dozen such volumes of her radio talks over the years.

Madalyn and DeYoung were developing a curious tug-of-war relationship. He had skills, energy, and some ineffable male thing she needed and was no longer getting from Richard. She had money, clout, and the ability to get publicity he needed. But they seemed to be continually invading each other's territory, if not rankly competing. Besides wanting the name "American Atheist Church" for herself (he grudgingly changed his church's name to the Minnesota Church of Philosophical Materialism), Madalyn already had a library well underway, and saw his planned one as competition. Like Madalyn, he was planning a run for governor.

And she wasn't pleased that DeYoung had scooped her on the atheist university idea. Not waiting for money to build edifices, he'd patterned his Institute after Göttingen University in Germany, where some classes were held in professors' homes. Within a year, Madalyn was running ads in the Austin paper offering eight "fall classes" at CESAALA, her library, though they could not be used as college credit anywhere except perhaps DeYoung's Minnesota Institute of Philosophy. It was a start, she felt.

It was Gordon Stein, in an article in *The American Rationalist,* who stated that DeYoung was selling degrees, and Madalyn's was bogus. Stein, an experienced editor and bibliographer with a master's degree in library science and doctorate in physiology, had been corresponding with Madalyn for years, and once had high hopes for her church tax activities. He had urged her to knock back the vitriol in her public appearances and back off of the atheist label, as it was tainted with Communism — the kind of counsel that didn't set well with Madalyn. When she made a deal with Arno Press, a New York publisher, to be advisory editor of a 25-book collection called *The Atheist Viewpoint,* Stein offered to correct some of her errors. She exploded, making another important enemy. He wrote to Arno Press complaining about her ignorance. It was only the beginning of the trouble he'd cause.

"That rat, that son of a bitch," said DeYoung of Stein, still angry years later. "I wanted *true* freedom from religion, I wanted a school *not* licensed by the church-sucking-up-to-the-state."

DeYoung's Institute eventually conferred 30 PhDs. All of them bogus, said Stein.

Christmas 1971 was as usual in the O'Hair home — festive and warm, overflowing with food, drink, decorations, Christmas music, and guests. It was especially wonderful for Madalyn because Bill had left New York and come home, at least for awhile. Robin made red and green paper chains to string along the wall. The tree was loaded with old-fashioned glass balls, snowflakes, and angels. Garth finished it off with icicles until it glittered.

Cute Robin, dressed in Christmas plaid, posed on the sofa with a dozen of her favorite stuffed animals. Grandma had brushed her hair glossy. In her diary, Madalyn wrote passionately of Robin, her great capacity for love, her precocious wit, her sensitivity and intelligence. She was a darling child, a treasure.

Chapter 24 ~ Money and Power

MADALYN HAD LONG UNDERSTOOD that her followers were lonely, isolated, and in need of community, and she wanted to organize a yearly convention. A 1972 effort fell apart, but a dozen or so people showed up anyway, and ended up in a wonderful weekend of work and camaraderie. They moved the library from Sinclair into its own building — a small house at 4203 Medical Parkway, only a few blocks from her home. It was a great bonding weekend, convincing Madalyn that she *had* to provide a community for atheists.

She always began the new year ambitious. She knew she was a leader and wanted to start living like one. She could change America, she told her diary. It was just a matter of hard work.

"I can take on any 10 men, hands down...I want money and power and I'm going to get it." By age 55, she wanted a $60,000 home, nice furniture, Cadillacs for everyone, "a mink coat and svelte clothes...In 1974, I will run for governor of Texas, and in 1976 for President of the United States."

She started 1972 by filing a suit against the IRS for holding up her nonprofit 501 (c)(3) application for the Stevens Library. Her January newsletter listed 36 other projects, depicting Society Of Separationists as carpet-bombing a host of insidious church-state problems that bred like roaches across the land.

She wrote indignantly that she wasn't getting enough money to do it all. "Now, how-in-the-hell can you expect us to be in any kind of significant competition with religion," she scolded members, with the peanuts you throw us?

And please, she asked, put her into your will, and send her a copy! An elderly man who'd promised $250,000 just died intestate, and that money was now lost to hostile family and courts.

Madalyn still packed audiences in, especially at colleges, where the Campus Crusade for Christers waved signs and cat-called. She didn't like getting booed and cursed and threatened, she wrote her readers, but she had no choice; she needed the speaker fees. How else was she going to file suits, fight the IRS to get her landmark tax exemptions for atheist concerns?

The Moody Bible Institute of Chicago was putting out books and teaching aids for public schools aimed at undercutting science, Madalyn wrote. It was a sneak attack; they didn't directly oppose evolution and thermodynamics and biology, but implied their source was divine. She was traveling to Colorado for a week of debates on the situation in May, armed with information from scientists. If she didn't get out there and trumpet like a bull elephant over this kind of thing, who would? It would just pass quietly and we'd all wake up one day finding rosaries handed out with our kids' biology texts.

Madalyn genuinely expected her followers to enable her to compete with the Catholic Church. She was sincerely exasperated when they didn't. But her diatribes worked. Although her enemy list grew, there was a cadre who felt angry along with her. Some felt terrible that they couldn't give more money, and resolved to just do without to donate. Some who had plenty gave in large spurts from time to time, feeling they were at least funding someone who would put up a fight, even if they didn't agree with every scrap she picked. They were investing in consciousness-raising.

In the spring of 1972, she got her tax-exempt status for CESAALA, and proceeded with plans for a foundation that she would control. Leroy Fahnestock was a wealthy Miamian she was cultivating (she'd taken Bill to Florida to charm him, and Bill delivered; he had charisma equal to hers). He had given money to Joseph Lewis and his Freethinkers of America in the 1960s. She had spoken to Fahnestock about starting an atheist Ford Foundation, and was told he "wouldn't object" to one named after him. He wanted not just Madalyn's organization, but all the nontheist groups, to benefit. How to get control of it?

She drafted a letter to several people, including Paul Kurtz, editor of *The Humanist*, the magazine of the American Humanist Association (AHA) in Buffalo, and Walter Kennon of the United Secularists of America, which published *Progressive World*. It was simply time, she wrote, for them to band together. Let's draw up an instrument, and she'd take it to Mr. F. She was already having her lawyer draw up foundation papers naming AHA, *Progressive World*, CESAALA, and Fahnestock as members. The board would consist of six people, including her and Paul Kurtz.

Almost $1 million in stocks and bonds was at stake. She was running for a position on the board of AHA, she told Garry DeYoung, and felt sure she would win, so she would have three avenues of control: AHA, herself, and DeYoung, to whom she had promised a seat on the board.

DeYoung was organizing a convention of his Minnesota Institute of Philosophy in St. Paul, where Madalyn was to speak, and she fired a set of military-like commands at him. Contact local churches and book her, and collect air fare from each of them. Find her lodging, raise a speaker fee. Call every media outlet, get her half-a-dozen talk shows, and get her union-scale fees for each appearance. Contact every college in the area, get her air fare from each one of them, too. And hurry up with the Nixon info — if they filed their suits by October 12, they'd be in demand as speakers by the 22nd during his convention. Oh, and get the Bible chair thing going "in every one of those colleges and universities in your area" by the time she got there.

This staggering load of assignments, written only five weeks before DeYoung's convention, bore the signs of something later dubbed "conflict addiction." Madalyn was increasingly setting up impossible, self-contradicting goals, and then cursing people for not meeting them — though DeYoung largely did. The frantic anxiety these situations created reinforced some things she'd always believed about herself: that she was better at everything than most people, and this was what made her an outsider, without the comfort of peers. That she yearned for friendships and partners, and that she truly needed the competent help she was getting a reputation for driving away, made no difference; she never suspected that she herself was the engineer of her loneliness, which was relieved only by her children.

Two weeks after her list went to DeYoung, a plum fell into Madalyn's lap. Billy Graham appeared on the Johnny Carson show and claimed she'd written him a letter full of four-letter words. She immediately wrote him, Carson, the FCC, and the media, calling Graham an "out and out liar" and demanding the equal time she and Richard had been unable to pry out of the FCC.

She was allowed a rebuttal, and appeared on the Carson show October 12 — perfect timing for her suit against the White House chapel and her talk at DeYoung's convention — right on Graham's home turf.

Sure enough, the convention and the Billy Graham fracas were covered in the media. Madalyn said she'd sue Graham if he didn't apologize, though she considered four-letter words "a fine art form," and peppered her convention talk with enough of them to be sure Graham got the message in his home town.

The Graham squabble produced loads of hate mail: "It is natural for women to hate God — the whole human race was plunged into the valley of sin, death and separation from God by woman . . . a baby factory for to bring more devil workers into the world."

"Why God doesn't strike you dead is beyond me. If someone doesn't bomb that blasted atheist library I hope something else happens to it."

"Do you ever listen to Billy Graham?" asked one forlorn writer. "Doesn't he kindle any form of Christian love within you?"

In one letter, someone mysteriously enclosed a bird's wing. "I could just see them," said Madalyn, "twisting it off, and saying, 'This won't hurt you, it's for Jesus.'"

Part Two

The Middle

Chapter 25 ~ Give Me a Child the First Seven Years

A SURVEY AT THE END OF 1972 showed that Richard Nixon and Billy Graham were the first and second most admired men in America. They were teamed in what unhappy liberal theologians, according to religion writer Louis Cassels, dubbed "civil religion" — a conviction that a certain brand of Protestant piety equaled patriotism.

Civil religion suffused Nixon's welfare reform plan, which he deemed an "intelligent modern application of the Puritan ethic," and liberals called "work or else." Civil religion projected that America's international postures were always moral, not venal or imperialistic, and accounted for the angry and growing split between Nixon-type patriots and those who accused America of conducting a corrupt and immoral war in Vietnam. Madalyn had already spoken on her radio show about churches holding more than $200 million worth of investments in companies like Lockheed and Honeywell that held military contracts.

And what happened when these Christian leaders felt comfortable chatting with God instead of the legislature? Well, she noted, take last November, when Philippine President Ferdinand Marcos had consulted God before declaring martial law.

"I asked for a sign," Marcos reportedly said. "He gave me several ... I was being led and guided by some strange and greater mind above me ... " He never revealed what the "signs" were, but wasn't it interesting, said Madalyn, that no one in our government was criticizing this? Could it have something to do with our huge naval and air bases in the Philippines?

Nixon's "intelligent modern application" of welfare, Madalyn claimed, had another side Graham and Nixon weren't so eager to have known. Starting this year, members of religious orders who'd taken poverty vows could apply for Social Security; and even if they didn't want the money, their superiors could apply for them. Presumably the money could then be tithed. Before Christmas, the state of Texas granted welfare assistance to 30 elderly Houston nuns.

Early the next year, Madalyn asked for support for her planned suit against Billy Graham, to fight this kind of "creeping theocracy." Almost on cue, Graham proposed at a White House prayer service that the Ten Commandments be read every day, in every classroom in America. (Graham had earlier sent a telegram to Congress noting that "when we took prayer out of the schools, sex, permissiveness, rebellion, drugs, and even crime came in." Whew! joked Madalyn's circle — seems school prayer was keeping a tsunami of debauchery at bay.) Madalyn called a press conference the same day and vowed a suit to prohibit religious services in the White House.

It was proof that constant vigilance was needed, Madalyn passionately wrote, even for seemingly petty encroachments of religion into civil life. Clearly, as Vashti McCollum had seen back in the 1940s when her young son came home from school with a poster of the Resurrection for his bedroom wall, the churches would keep pushing the envelope. They weren't interested in teaching morality or fairness or decency — they were using the schools to indoctrinate. "Give me a child the first

seven years and I'll give you the man," said the Jesuits. That's what they wanted —
to nudge in during those early years.

Over and over since June 17, 1963, attempts had been made to violate the spirit
of *Murray v. Curlett* and *Abington Township v. Schempp*. Time and again constitutional amendments were offered to preserve voluntary Bible reading and prayer in
schools. Different kinds of prayer, kids who wanted to pray five minutes before the
bell, school boards adopting verses from Star Spangled Banner and America the
Beautiful that mentioned God, and outright devotionals at morning assemblies, at
football games.

This was too expensive and insidious to fight frontally, with lawsuits. Madalyn
wanted to file discrimination complaints using the Civil Rights Act of 1964, which
said no entity that got federal money could discriminate as to color, race, religion,
or national origin. All the public schools got federal money. The ones that tried to
bring God into the building were discriminating against atheists, and should have
their aid yanked.

Madalyn wanted to get a convention off the ground in Florida, and get the rich
retirees there to put her in their wills. She wanted to take her movement to Europe.
She wanted to finish her latest book and go on a national tour; get land for her
university and get it funded and tax exempt; launch a television series; get UT to
offer atheist classes for credit; "critically wound the AHA, Rationalists, and any
other group which detracts from the main battle"; move into a new home; launch
"several good cases [where] people can identify with us even while they are hating
us"; and learn Sanskrit. That was her "to do" list for 1973.

The Sanskrit had to do with Garth. Madalyn felt guilty about him. The youth-
centered counterculture that defined his generation had peaked without him, in
a questioning of Western society, politics, and conventional religious authority.
Garth's restless peers were talking excitedly of J. Krishnamurti, Rilke, Swami Yoga-
nanda, Ram Dass, Carlos Castaneda, Herman Hesse, and Bubba Free John, massing
at the hippie trailhead in Amsterdam for the dharma-bum path to Istanbul, Mar-
rakesh, Katmandu, Calcutta. Their anti-war fervor had matured into a search for
answers to what separated humans and caused such suffering. They flocked to
Dharamsala, Tibet's capital in exile, to hear the Dalai Lama's message of global harmony and the Coming Together of the People. Seeking ways to heal the earth and all
its spirits, they found eastern gurus, studied yoga, metaphysics, transcendental meditation. They pursued peace, compassion, wisdom, empowerment, self-realization,
the Divine Feminine Principle. It was a beautiful thing to Madalyn, and she had
had a role in setting it off, even though she was born a generation too soon to fully
be part of it.

And Garth had missed it all. It had to be put aside for the Cause. Madalyn had
felt so betrayed by Richard that she'd just kicked him out of the organization, and
then "dragged Garth into it." It was wrong, but she was so alone, she wrote, so
desperate. Now he wanted to go to India.

Madalyn tried to pull together a snarled, complex personal/business agenda that involved Bill getting discounted Braniff tickets for two planeloads of members, and Garry DeYoung "sending" a doctorate to GORA, to ensure her participation in GORA's upcoming World Atheist Conference in Vijayawada, but the complicated plan fell apart; no one went to India. The closest Garth came to the revolution was getting suspended from school for refusing to cut his hair. But even that was co-opted by Madalyn, who told school authorities he'd taken a "Nazarite oath in the tradition of Samson" and making him cut it would violate his First Amendment rights. It was part of a cultural tidal wave; soon the schools were dealing with message T-shirts, girls in pants. After several Supreme Court cases begun in the 1960s Warren Court, the freedoms of speech, association, assembly, and petition guaranteed by the First Amendment transmogrified into a monolithic freedom of "expression."

Madalyn blamed Richard for draining her energy and robbing her of focus. "Richard is as cordial as a wet raccoon to people when I am not here," she warned Garry DeYoung. His daughter Katrina, who visited in 1974, found Richard un-friendly and nasty. "He insults everyone and everything he sees," the teenager wrote in her journal.

Madalyn still loved "the old son-of-a-bitch," but, she wrote Garry DeYoung un-happily, "I am not a leader: I am a referee . . . My son and my husband cordially hate each other [and] decided to engage in a family brawl" in front of GORA's son, who was a houseguest. She was embarrassed and disheartened. It was more important to them to hate each other, she said, "than it is to hate the fucking churches."

The death knell for their marriage was, as she saw it, Richard's relentless hostility toward Garth. Starting at UT in the fall of 1973, Garth had made a tepid move toward independence, taking a job at Arby's Roast Beef for a couple of months. But he was soon lured back to working for American Atheists and SOS by a generous salary and a new car.

Richard disapproved of such bribery and complained that Garth was spoiled. Garth wasn't extravagant, but he had come to enjoy buying what he wanted — books, clothes, subscriptions to Mad magazine and Record Club of America. He liked eating at restaurants like the Oyster Bar, one of his and Madalyn's favorites, and having his own bedroom instead of the dormitory/cafeteria life of his classmates.

Madalyn had also asked Garry DeYoung to write the draft board, saying he knew Garth to be a lifelong conscientious objector. Richard spat his disapproval at this maneuver to keep her baby out of harm's way in Vietnam. Garth retaliated by storming around and fighting with Richard, and by indulging in hopelessness and fatalism, which set Madalyn's teeth on edge.

She fretted that he had never dated. She wanted more grandchildren, and a DeYoung-O'Hair dynasty was a delicious thought, but Garth simply had no time. He had taken over Madalyn's appearance coordination from Richard, and in ad-dition, the 18-year-old was paying the taxes, buying Robin's clothes, working on the newsletter, forming a campus atheist group and trying to drum up attendees for Madalyn's talks, buying gifts and ordering flowers for employees and volunteers, repairing things around the house, purchasing the family liquor and groceries, getting the dogs groomed, helping Robin with her homework, taking the cars to be repaired, dropping off film, picking up the cleaning, and attending UT full time, summers included, so he could hurry up and graduate and start full-time on the Cause.

Besides Garth's womanless isolation, Madalyn brooded over Bill's sudden mass of problems. All he and Julie did was fight. He had affairs. He was drinking heavily. He was profoundly in debt. By late in the year, he'd been fired from his job at Braniff, sold all his possessions, and gone back to Hawaii, with plans to move to Guam.

"I have sat and watched him make one horrible mistake after another," Madalyn wrote, "and I have helped him till I can't stomach to do it further. When do they learn?"

If her sons were troublesome, eight-year-old Robin was an ever-giving comfort. She had "an unbelievable sense of humor and gift for tact" and took on every task assigned her with a willing spirit. Madalyn had her working on enunciation, determined to ward off another speech-impeded child. She was studying viola. Though she was shy and lonely, friendless in the family way, she was the glue that held them together in this time of marital coldness and unhappy sons. Before year's end, Madalyn managed a trip with the child to the Texas coast, and a visit to a theme park, Candy Cane City.

Chapter 26 ~ We Are the Leaders

ESTRANGED FROM HER MAN, Madalyn turned to Garry DeYoung in a flood of rambling letters in which she poured out her biggest, most outlandish dreams. She wrote him constantly, sometimes several times a day, offering to team up with him, her letters bristling with the dominance she liked to display over men who had emotional influence on her. She lectured DeYoung, instructed him, and laid out his path in flourishing detail.

Early in 1972, he had been fired from his job for his atheism, won it back in a lawsuit with Madalyn's guidance, and was on leave while his win was appealed. Madalyn told him how to act when he got back to work, how to handle his greedy attorney. Don't "bluster," she admonished, and don't charge off in all directions. She used to be like Garry, but no longer. That's why she was in such a good place today, with $70,000 worth of equipment — offset press, plate makers, collator, stuffers, and folders. This year she planned to pay $100,000 cash for a building and put a big, bold American Atheists sign on it to be seen by all. She was tax exempt, had a reduced-rate mail permit, and they all had new cars — Dick a Thunderbird, she a

Maverick, Garth a Plymouth Belvedere. Plus the brand-new Ford panel truck paid for with $6,000 cash.

DeYoung had garnered enough votes to get on the Republican primary ballot for governor of Minnesota, but he'd never get the nomination, she wrote him, because he didn't look prosperous.

"You look poor, Garry. Your home looks poor. Your car looks poor ... Your wife ... looks like the country mouse — poor."

"Mary needs some $89.50 quiet wool dresses for work — and matching calf bag and shoes. She needs a cashmere coat, and a personalized coutiere [sic] hair style." He was a handsome man; he needed "a couple new suits, Brooks Brothers." And he needed to have his shoes reheeled, and get an extra pair. He needed a "den" in his home so he could entertain important political figures.

As for herself, Madalyn chatted, "I am going to get a mink coat and some $300 to $500 dresses for my appearances, with matching calf shoes, gloves, purse at about $100 to $300 each ... If I don't look like I need money, I will get money." Garry needed people and money, and when he got them, there would be no stopping the two of them.

Early next year, she was going to "announce for Governor of Texas *from behind a mink coat,* and really scare hell out of them." She begged him to stop dissipating his energies with his own hopeless run for governor, and work with her instead on the long-term goals they shared.

She offered to hire him and all his sons and sons-in-law. "Give me perhaps 3 more years and work with me on it and we can swing it. We need an empire of 5 or 6 or 10 generations like the Rockefellers." She wanted an atheist university more prestigious than Harvard or Yale, a place in Canada where they could teach atheist kids how to farm.

She invited him to come down and sleep on the sofa, see if he could help bring in any money down in Texas. "Mary can make it with the kids for the time being." She'd fly him down to privately present him the Thomas Jefferson Atheist of the Year Award for "courage, tenacity, scholarship and dedication" to Jeffersonian principles. The award carried a $1,500 stipend.

And he should bring 15-year-old Katrina. She'd pay her way, too. Rich people have cotillions and balls, she said, where they put their kids together. Atheists can't even get a summer camp together.

"*We are the leaders.* We are the ones who count ... Garry, in reality, [the] 'big names' can't smell where we shit for either courage, tenacity, perseverance or whatever ... I want every future child in America to say that real freedom began with *the* American Atheists. I want to be cast in history with Abraham Lincoln ... And I am willing to work my ass off."

One day, she wrote a bizarre account of a discovery she'd made that was "as important as Galileo, as the wheel." It would impact mankind more than Freud or

Aristotle. It would "set my name down in the scientific community for all times." It would keep the whole free enterprise system going, it was the answer to all political corruption. She was writing a book on it, and wanted Garry's help with research — but it was so secret she couldn't risk even telling him what it was. She had told only Margaret Mead, who replied with a "scathing letter of denunciation."

All she could reveal were some of the mechanics: recruit 50 young people, one from the largest city in each state. Put them into a crash six-month training program, army-style. She had calculated room and board, development of instruction materials, salaries of professors to teach "ideology," and so on.

"We should have our cadre trained for perhaps a mere $1,000,000." Then get each state to fund the program for a year until it got on its feet.

Whoever came up with this seed money "gets the country and its future. This is why I want a finger in the pie...I can take over the entire United States in a three year period." She wanted Nelson Rockefeller to back it, but to even reveal it to Rockefeller, she required seven guarantees:

- It must be called the O'Hair Plan;

- A governorship for Bill, she didn't care which state;

- The Presidency of the United States for Garth when he was 35;

- Two sections (1280 acres) of land in Texas for her university;

- Five million dollars to jump-start the American Atheist "Centre";

- Herself as head of the O'Hair Plan, and whatever staff she wanted;

- No religious people involved in the O'Hair Plan.

"I want to know that my family is in the reigns [sic] for the next 1,000 years in the United States. Now — Garry DeYoung...get me two days with Rockefeller. You can come along."

Like the atheist compound in Kansas, the O'Hair Plan died a quiet death after Madalyn wrote Rockefeller that the plan would help him in his presidential campaign, allow complete dominance by the political group using it, and direct the United States' path for the next millennium. It would cost $5–8 million to get the training done by the 1976 elections, but that was "a paltry sum for political control of the nation." He was unable to find the time to meet with her.

Madalyn managed to organize her first convention in Florida, and spent the last week of January 1974 there, booking a venue at Horne's and cultivating wealthy Floridians.

DeYoung and his daughter Katrina flew down early to travel with her. Richard, who was to be the keynote speaker, refused to go. The official reason was illness —

Madalyn later said from "disabilities stemming from [the] seven purple hearts" he'd earned in the war (he spent the war stateside). But Richard was jealous of DeYoung, and Madalyn complained that he was lazy, drunk, and unkempt.

Katrina, a sweet, pretty girl, arrived two weeks before her father. The DeYoungs had raised their children by their own ideals of self-sufficiency and critical thinking, and they had turned out confident and independent, despite the suffering they endured — being spit on at school, shunned, and vilified — from their parents' activism.

Katrina knew why she was there. "It was thought that Garth and I might *get along?* — you know? — although that would be a *real leap.*" Garth spit when he talked, which "I found incredibly repulsive, [and] they were very crude. Vulgar and crude...they used dirty language all the time and thought in a vulgar way."

Garth was an English major at UT, busy and "smart, studious, with a dry sense of humor. [He] was very uptight. His room was neat, orderly...he was extremely modest...a very closed person, very self-controlled. But he was interesting, and he had ideas. He was well read."

The family loved animals. Arturo, the myna bird, "knew lots of bad words" and would fly to different parts of the house and call the two schnauzers, George and Martha. The dogs dashed here and there in confusion until the bird tired of the game.

Madalyn "was a very large figure in our lives growing up...despite her manipulating, conniving, using-people side. She was *so* smart. I went into her office; there were all these books, interesting books about everything. She told me to help myself. She was such an intelligent woman, a wonderful role model, really." She invited Katrina into the kitchen when she cooked, and showed her little homey tricks, like how to season a cast-iron skillet, and to rub cut garlic into the wooden salad bowl. "I felt a great domesticity from her." When she'd spoken at Garry's convention, she had brought Mary DeYoung and all five of her daughters gifts of Jean Naté perfume and powder. "We were very poor," said Katrina. "This was so — feminine."

She and her kids were "very very devoted to each other...Madalyn *loved* those kids — that was really clear, she'd do anything for them." Bill was estranged from them again; Madalyn had promised to put four DeYoungs and four O'Hairs on her library board, but she couldn't trust Bill any more, she told Garry, because he was reunited with his wife. "His fucking means more to him than the cause," she said bitterly. But she still spoke of him with pride, and the family was proud of him, how handsome he was.

"But I don't know that she had any real friends...outside of the children, I don't know that she had any real love in her life."

In April, the O'Hairs and DeYoungs, along with some of Madalyn's volunteers, left in a jolly caravan for the convention in Florida. It ran April 12 and 13 in Orlando, on Madalyn's 55th birthday, and featured cryogenics research. Madalyn declared that she planned to be frozen when she died. She gave several speeches to packed audiences after the convention, and made sure the kids got to visit Disney World, Marineland, Ripley's, and the French Quarter driving back home. In Alabama, they took a picture of Madalyn shooting the finger at a battleship shrine that featured a statue of Jesus; when the film was developed, someone put a thumb over the obscene gesture and blurred it.

Back in Austin, the DeYoungs rented a small apartment, and Garry started an assessment of the Stevens Library. He was considering joining forces with Madalyn, and subsuming his efforts under hers. Unfortunately, he inquired about records, funding, and an envelope he'd seen addressed to Richard from Grace Calvary Church.

Within days, he was locked out of the library, and a letter was slipped under his door expelling him as Vice President of SOS. His offense: having "stated publicly" at some point that he had the largest and best-organized atheist organization in the world.

He was stunned; it took awhile to realize he was being jettisoned for probing the books. Madalyn brooked no inquiries about money. "She was constantly begging for money," said Katrina, "saying she was broke. But they had all these *things.*"

The expulsion was illegal; neither DeYoung nor other board members were notified of the "meeting" where he was supposedly voted off. He later found that one person listed as a board member didn't even know he'd been elected, and that Madalyn didn't know where he lived. DeYoung had also discovered that Madalyn was reporting one SOS board of directors to the IRS and a different one to the postal service. He'd also seen her take seven $100 bills from a conventioneer in Orlando; it was a gift to SOS but he could never find it deposited in the account.

He wrote the IRS and Texas Bar Association, and contacted the Minnesota secretary of state to wrest back the name American Atheist Church from Madalyn. He wrote the Texas attorney general that the O'Hairs were running a shell game with their tax-exempt organizations. He contacted some of the people Madalyn had called thieves and liars. One of them wrote back, "Your letter . . . is no surprise to me. She is simply poison."

The DeYoung family moved from Minnesota to Mercedes, Texas, on the Mexican border, and put the *Crucible* back in publication. When they got the local newspaper to run their column, "The Scientific Atheist" — something Madalyn had never been able to bring off in Austin — "Madalyn drove down in her Cadillac. What are you doing? she screamed."

Yet, strangely, she could not give DeYoung up, and continued to write, beseeching him to move to Austin. There was a world of trouble to be made there — the legislature, the city council, the state offices — and maybe she could hire Mary. Couldn't they try to control their egos, she begged, enough to get something done?

Chapter 27 ~ $3 and Half a Pack of Salems

COOKIE NELSON had lost touch with David Waters when he went to prison. So she only faintly registered the story that appeared in the papers in early 1974. Just after midnight on January 30, police got a 10–23 — code for a fight — at 702 North Monroe. Neighbors heard breaking glass and screaming in the two-story duplex where Betty Waters lived.

Officers Larry Wight and R. D. Lee ran inside to find Betty and her youngest, eight-year-old Larry Hunt, backed up against the wall. She was aiming a long kitchen knife at her second son, Stephen Plumley. Stevie was advancing on her with a red-handled claw hammer. He'd already hit his teenaged companion, who sat dazed and bleeding on the porch.

The police shouted to both of them to drop their weapons. Betty laid down the knife, but Stevie whirled and charged the officers, who backed up, yelling warnings. Then they both fired, hitting him five times. One of the bullets went through and hit Larry Hunt in the thigh.

In short order, the scene was swarming with police. Betty was screaming and crying hysterically. "I had to stop him, he was going to kill the baby!"

Stevie was high on drugs, "running around with faggots" and involved in some drugstore robberies. She had been planning to call the police about it. He was "shooting downers in his arms [and] was a complete degenerate any more"; she was kicking him out of the house for good.

As she sobbed out her story, Stevie lay just inside the front door, convulsing and making gurgling sounds.

"I don't blame them," said a distraught Betty as Stevie was carried away on a stretcher. "If I had a gun I would have shot him, and he's my son."

Stephen Plumley was pronounced dead on arrival at St. Francis Hospital. His blood contained substantial amounts of ethanol and barbiturates. He was staying with a 13-year-old runaway girl with needle tracks on her arms.

A coroner's inquest was called, as the shooting was unusual: five bullets in a suspect armed only with a hammer. It was true the 23-year-old was headed down a bad path. He'd been committed to the state hospital at 14, and his release heralded a series of arrests. Still, instead of aggravated battery and murder, like his brother's, Stevie's rap sheet meandered around drug arrests, curfew violations, soliciting prostitutes, thieving, fighting, and having the bad judgment to spit at an officer who caught him with cannabis. Even a pending armed robbery case was mild — he'd held up a taxi driver with his pocket knife and made away with $3 and half a pack of Salems. Until that night with the hammer, he was just a troubled addict, described by acquaintances as sweet and loving.

David was still in prison. Nobody even bothered to tell him Stevie was dead. "I can't remember if he said he read it in the paper, or if somebody notified him of it," said a friend, "but it wasn't his family."

Chapter 28 ~ Please Come Home

AFTER HER FALLING-OUT with Garry DeYoung, 1974 found Madalyn at her spurting worst, writing angry letters day after day. Her newsletter was a breathtakingly nasty assault on her readers and members. The once steadying hand of Richard was gone. She was "absolutely ashamed" of them all. Not for the first time, she excoriated them for letting a *woman* bear all the abuse and worry.

It was a theme that arose repeatedly in Madalyn's writings, throughout her life — she missed being cherished and protected just because she was a female. To be sure, she chose masculinity as her model, and was scornful of other women's cloying domesticity and slavishness to convention. Instead of a cozy sentiment, the framed needlepoint over her kitchen door said, "Home is where the booze is."

But it couldn't be ignored how regularly a wail would go up in her newsletter that the nation's atheists should be ashamed for letting a *woman* take all the risks and abuse she'd endured.

Self-pity, outrage, and indignation dripped from the pages. She had gone to jail eight times for them, she'd lost her home and family, she'd even lost her (now four) college degrees since she couldn't get a job. She went on talk shows to be insulted, maligned, abused, her life was threatened — all for *them*.

"How in the hell," she wrote, "do you think I am going to fight the oldest, most powerful, richest, most politicized group in the world — organized religion . . . ?" Why couldn't they give her what she needed — "constant, devoted, understanding support"?

She had failed to score with Fahnestock. She blamed Paul Kurtz for conspiring with Fahnestock's trusted gardener and attorney to push aside the atheists she claimed the old man wanted his estate to go to. Kurtz had also maneuvered, she said, to have her ejected from the American Humanist Association, to which some of Fahnestock's money went. And he had convinced the old man that his connections were more productive than Madalyn's, and his organization more likely to endure.

Along with Kurtz, she was angry at James Hervey Johnson, "Scurvy," as she called him, editor of *Truth Seeker* and head of its parent organization. He was misusing corporate money, she wrote a confidante, indulging himself in racist magazine diatribes and dabbling in real estate instead of investing in atheist causes. His publication was shoddy, cheap, and error-riddled. "As soon as I get some spare funds I will take Johnson into court . . . and make him account for all the money which Atheists have willed to him . . . these thieving bastards must be stopped."

In fact, she'd sent to New York a couple of years before for his corporation and probate papers. "He was functioning out of a trust fund [that] had apparently been instituted at the time of the inception of the *Truth Seeker* magazine," she wrote. "When [Charles] Smith died, Johnson permitted the corporate entity from New York to die and he set up a phony Truth Seeker Corporation in California." Her longtime interest in the Truth Seeker money would prove fateful.

Some ire was to be expected at being outflanked by Paul Kurtz, but Madalyn's rage was out of proportion. It was explained by friends years later as blood-sugar spikes from her increasingly troublesome diabetes.

In August, there was a nasty exchange of letters with Gordon Stein. She had not forgiven his scholarly challenge to her Arno Press bibliography several years back, and refused to let him visit her library to do research for a book on blasphemy trials. Tax-exempt libraries had to be open to legitimate scholars like Stein, but Madalyn was sure he simply wanted to spy on her for Paul Kurtz' camp. Like DeYoung, Stein was soon writing the Texas attorney general.

Strangely, in this year of unrelenting stress, failure, and illness — she was sick most of the summer with hypertension and creeping problems with diabetes, and was behind on publications, correspondence, suit-filing, everything — Madalyn never looked prettier. When her new book, *Freedom Under Siege: The Impact of Organized Religion on Your Liberty and Your Pocketbook*, finally came out at the end of 1974, she was pictured on the jacket, vibrant, white-haired, and laughing, along with Robin and 20-year-old Garth, with his fledgling mustache and unruly masculine eyebrows. She had lost weight for her author photo, and sported a stylish gamin haircut that flattered her round face.

It charmed her followers that Madalyn included her children in her author photo. She was strong on family, and made them feel like they belonged in hers. "The first thing I noticed about her was her inclusion of her family, always in all things," said a colleague, "long before 'family values' was . . . a catchphrase."

Freedom Under Siege described how churches' tax breaks allowed them to secretly control the economy through huge business and stock investments, especially the Roman Catholic Church. On her book tour, Madalyn spoke at the University of Toledo. This was Catholic country, as she well knew from her years in Rossford, and she enjoyed bringing gasps of shock even from the student audience. She called Jesus "the most despicable man in human history, including Hitler," and the Bible "an ugly, brutal, vicious book." She loved disturbing Catholics. The *Toledo Times* filled with angry letters to the editor.

It was "dawning on everyone," she said, "that religion is not relevant to life." The churches used tools like sexual guilt to get power over people. "The real Holy Trinity," she said, was "anxiety, fear, and guilt." Indeed, around this time, two polls, Gallup and National Opinion Research Center, indicated a decline in church attendance. In 1957, Gallup had found that 81% of Americans believed religion's influence was growing. But during the 1960s, that belief plummeted — reaching a low of 14% by 1970. The most skeptical were people under 30 and those with college educations.

It was useful to Madalyn that 23% of readers of *Psychology Today* said they were atheist, agnostic, or had no belief (though the same affluent and educated readers replied yes when asked if they'd "ever felt in close contact with something holy or sacred," or wanted to).

But even as she spoke, an article in *Playboy* noted "a small but growing spiritual renaissance in Washington," with political prayer groups springing up all over the city, and pressure to be seen at the right ones. The patriot-piety axis was good politics even with the waning of Communism. In fact, in pardoning Richard Nixon after he had resigned in the wake of the Watergate scandal, President Ford said he acted "not as President but as a humble servant of God." The Jesus Movement, comprised of ex-hippies disenchanted with the slack, indulgent trajectory of the aging youth movement, was making news. This cult of "street Christians" had fled the offal of the Sixties — drugs, promiscuity, and alienation — but kept some of its counterculture forms. Jesus communes sprouted all over the country, taking in addicts, outcasts, and runaways and attempting to practice Christian principles of love and compassion in an anti-establishment, anti-materialist context. The movement surfaced, the *New York Times* noted, in a boom in religious geegaws, from Jesus posters, mugs, T-shirts, buttons, decals, and jewelry to bumper stickers: Honk if you love Jesus. Things go better with Christ. America: Handle With Prayer.

Madalyn's book redeemed a bad year. But at Christmas, she sat brooding with a glass of expensive liquor.

"I have baked enough cookies for 20 people, bought fresh fruit for over that score and whiskey, cognac, rum, Southern Comfort and turkey and cranberries," she wrote in her diary. "The house is beautiful. I will cook a meal to remember. Christmas music floods the air."

Under the tree were "chocolates and good things and nonsense toys and surprises and pretty ribbons and tinsel. In all kinds of sizes and shapes. All of it says, somebody, everybody, please come home. Bill's family or Dick's sons, or Garth, a wife and kids, anybody, please share our Christmas. Anybody, anybody, anybody . . ."

She missed Bill. "Every night now for some time, I have been sitting here and writing in this book as if by some magic I can bring Bill home." She hadn't seen him for nearly a year.

Slowly letting go of Richard, she wrote that she still loved him and wanted him around. She didn't like it that he was gone all the time now, even overnight. She was sure he was having an affair. She had put back on the weight she lost, and felt fat and unattractive.

She recalled one of their more endearing marital battles. She had cooked supper one night, and Richard bellowed, "Woman, where are the potatoes!" The next night, she served potato soup, mashed potatoes, fried potatoes, and scalloped potatoes. He roared with laughter.

It was sad, the ending of their intense ride together. He'd encouraged and comforted and guided her, and immersed himself in the Cause. And he'd taken in Robin, allowing the little girl a tiny entrée into his child-callous heart. She was entitled to his government pension now. His daughter Vicki later said, "Richard wasn't there for me, he wasn't there for my brother, he wasn't there for my two half brothers.

But he *was* there for Robin... And I'm not trying to say Richard was a good guy! But he atoned for some of his sins, through Robin."

On Christmas Eve, Madalyn was crushed when Richard didn't come home. He knew how important it was to her. He was probably with his lover, and it was probably someone whose salary Madalyn paid.

After Robin and Garth were in bed, she sat down and coded her hurt into a codicil to her and Richard's "contract-will," which stipulated that all their property would pass to their tax-exempt organizations. The assumption was that Garth would take them over. Now she wrote that if she died first, and Richard tried to unseat Garth, all bets were off — she wanted all her property to go to Garth alone. Garth was charged with caring for Robin and putting her through college.

"I give my husband Richard F. O'Hair nothing since this will will only be operative if he tries to fuck Garth out of his rightful place as succeeding director of SOS and CESAALA, Inc.," she wrote.

"I give my son William J. Murray   nothing — not even a dollar."

She signed and dated it and put it in an envelope addressed to Garth. Then she penned a note to Lester Buttram, saying there were damn few good Christians in the U.S., but "in twelve years, you probably are the one I found to head the list! Fondly, Madalyn." She sent him a copy of her book, with a note asking if he might have an 18-year-old daughter for Garth.

And suddenly, as if he had radar, Bill called, just after New Year's. He'd divorced Julie. He was sorry for their estrangement. He loved them all. His call was an immense relief to Madalyn.

Chapter 29 — The American Atheist

MADALYN WAS SURPRISED and delighted when Bill called again in the spring and said he would come to the 1975 convention in Hollywood, to see Robin. She immediately offered him $100 a week to work for her, but he declined. He had started a printing business in California with his 19-year-old secretary, Valerie Guillermo.

He later said he was just curious about the convention, and described the attendees as "An astonishing collection of tramps and nuts" and only a handful of "normal" people. He recalled an inventor who had a lot of money and gave Madalyn at least $10,000. "He had an invention that was revolutionary, that would totally change things. It was a series of zippers," to make cuffs and collars that zipped off so you only had to wash them and not the whole shirt. He felt his work was suppressed by the clothing and detergent manufacturers.

It was true that some of her followers bore a certain look, the kind of thing that was indulged if you were a famous scholar or scientist. At her conventions, you might see colored suspenders, long gray beards, polka dots, heavy makeup, bow ties. It was the look of eccentricity, or the isolation of people who lived inside their own heads. Garth still had his speech impediment, and a vow Madalyn had made to dress up in public had never translated into action. The attendees came across as timid, lonely folk, grateful to be there but fearful of their names in the papers. But who could blame them? All you had to do was look at a little of Madalyn's hate mail to see that it took courage to even be seen at an atheist convention.

Madalyn "is like a beacon for me," said Lloyd Thoren, Indiana member who opened an atheist museum on his property. "Without her aggressive publicity, I would never have known about atheism. That is the wonderful feeling of being free from the shackles of religion."

Thoren later recalled how Indiana Bell had disconnected his Dial-an-Atheist line, deeming it "profane." Another man told *Playboy* that his business was boycotted when he let his atheism be known; he'd had his head shaved and was run out of his small town. Another spoke of people refusing to work for him, and others of the persecution suffered by their children. One member became an atheist at a Christian youth camp when he realized that certain standards the minister laid down would doom his beloved grandmother to hell. "I decided I'd rather go to hell with her."

Madalyn understood all of it, sympathized with all of it. The bottom line was, religion made you hate yourself, she said. It terrorized you with threats of eternity spent all alone with your self-loathing, flesh-tearing flames burning your raw body without end.

Over the years of her conventions, reporters repeatedly saw that Madalyn's followers were in awe of her. She was "big-boned, aggressive . . . talks fast, loud, and abrasively," one wrote, but she had a wonderful grandmotherly smile and honest demeanor. Conventioneers got to see slides of her home, her pets, the kids, the office. They got to see photos of themselves in the newsletter and magazine. When she got *American Atheist* magazine back on its feet in the 1970s, activist members appeared on the cover as heroes.

About her first convention, said a member, "I *loved* it! Everybody was so happy. And Madalyn was a *great* orator — she could inspire you."

Jane Conrad, an activist with her own newsletter who would later become a bitter enemy, remembered her first convention. "Madalyn was in one of her best moods — pleasant, humorous, and a jolly companion. We [went] to a Greek restaurant . . . and had an informal evening of pleasant discussion . . . I suddenly became aware that I was not the only non-believer in all the world. There were many others besides me."

The 1975 convention was a gratifying success, but Madalyn returned home at 3 a.m. to find Richard gone. Suspicious, she drove to the home of Mary H_____, one of her employees. Richard's car was parked in front. Needless to say, the next day, Mary H_____ found herself unemployed. Richard promised to stay away from her.

With Richard's withdrawal, the office equipment was neglected, the ink hardening on the press, belts cracked, gears corroded, and parrot dung over everything. Madalyn had only one part-time employee on the newsletter, which was gotten out sporadically by a local printer. Publications were the lifeblood of cash flow, and though Madalyn had received several large bequests between 1972 and 1975, she hadn't published *American Atheist* in years.

She needed Bill. She tracked him down in Colorado and offered to pay all his relocation costs, and a handsome salary to him and Valerie, his new girlfriend. They could take whatever outside printing contracts they wished. She had $5,000 "seed money" to have AA Press reprint "old Atheist classics," and transcriptions of the American Atheist Radio Series. She also had a grant from the Norman Thomas Foundation, and a bequest from the estate of Floridian Simon Kaplan had paid for the third house at 4203 Medical Parkway which now housed CESAALA.

Bill agreed to come, he said, out of "some compassion as a son." (His mother claimed privately that he was on the run from creditors.) Garth, 20, graduated from UT in English, and immediately plunged full time into the AA "Centre" — they were using the English spelling for cachet.   :

With her sons in harness and bequests coming in, Madalyn was euphoric. *American Atheist* magazine would soon be on newsstands; it would carry ads. The AA radio series would be expanded, with cassettes and transcripts available. There would be a new push for television coverage. There would be book reviews, AA logo bumper stickers. Book orders and newsletters would now be on time, and membership would be tripled. Instead of just one law firm, they'd have specialty firms for all the different needs. They'd reorganize the library, start a long-promised Atheist Credit Union. The atheist university, retirement home, and summer camp were still in the wings.

In July 1975, *American Atheist* was back in print for the first time in a decade. The newsletter was mailed on time, looking much more professional, and subscriptions and donations increased.

"For the first time in ten years," Bill wrote later, SOS "was earning income from sources other than corpses, and Mother had more money than she knew what to do with."

Under his influence, she spent $83,000 on another property. Bill negotiated a complicated bargain on one of the oldest buildings in north Austin, a three-unit complex on Medical Parkway, with two-foot-thick interior walls made of native limestone. It sat on a triangular lot where Burnet Road ended, and was only minutes from Madalyn's home. There was a small upstairs apartment that could be used for visitors.

They moved to the new building in September. It was a busy summer and fall; American Atheist chapters were forming all over the country: southern California, San Francisco, Oregon, Indiana, Michigan, Dallas, San Antonio, Massachusetts, Ohio, Illinois, New Jersey, New York, Florida.

Madalyn had the members sending her clippings on church-state separation matters. The chapters would be breeding grounds for the lawsuits she needed to keep members invested. But she tried to get members to do as much of the legwork and financing as possible.

In the fall, Madalyn announced she was going to sue to revoke the tax exemptions of Allandale Baptist Church, up the street from her house, and other churches that spoke out in an October referendum against extending public drinking hours to 2 a.m. That was politicking, Madalyn said, and it provided an opening to go after their tax exemptions.

Chapter 30 ~ "Somebody, somewhere, love me"

ROBIN WAS PLAYING VIOLA in the 6th grade orchestra at Lucy Read Elementary. She and Val Guillermo, Bill's girlfriend, hit it off, and Val became concerned with the child's environment. She was lonely, dragged to atheist affairs to spend all her time around adults.

Val also pointed out to Bill the amount of alcohol Robin was consuming, as she had the job of making the nightly martinis. Richard began at sunrise with gin, and spent each day at his favorite bar, Montana Mining Company, shooting the breeze over beer, switching to bourbon at home in the late afternoon. His and Madalyn's exchanges now consisted mostly of nasty arguments, and she was again planning divorce. Several times, Bill reported, the quarrels got so violent that Robin slipped out to a neighbor's and called police.

Bill recorded extreme mood swings in his mother during this time. She would sit in her office crying for hours over her men. Richard wasn't attracted to her, and she was sure it was because she was fat. Bill chafed under her ego, sometimes encouraging rebellion in Garth. As she and Bill struggled, "My brother became her hope, and she began to refer to him as the future president of the United States — in front of me, of course." On a large number of the letters Bill wrote to his mother during the 1970s, he signed his name drolly, "Bill Murray, your *other* son" or "the other one" or "the first one."

"In her defense, there is a great possibility that my mother was either bipolar or manic-depressive...Nothing else can account for some of the things — the day she left the house smiling, and then 30 minutes later I get a call and her Cadillac is stopped in the middle of the street, with the door open, and she's gone, sitting in the park crying...Manic-depression would explain the *total*...separation from reality."

Bill called it his mother's fantasy world, where reality was tortured to fit the landscape inside her head. He had terrible toothaches in the army, and the military dentist had put in many fillings. "Then in 1975 when I went back to Austin,

[Mother] says, 'Oh, what beautiful teeth you have, I'm so glad I took such good care of your teeth when you were little!'" But she had never taught him dental hygiene. "Once I even thought I'd broken my tooth because a big piece of plaque broke off."

"Our life growing up was all fantasy. She would tell me all these stories about my father, how wealthy and great he was, how fine his family was. Everything had to be grandiose, had to be the best or the most or the biggest." Or the worst and most persecuted; in one newsletter, Madalyn's account of her suffering metastasized to being jailed 10 times, Bill being jailed seven times, Garth being jailed at the age of six, and "on five different occasions [her family being] on the streets, no money, stripped of all belongings down to just the clothes on their back." She told a cheering UT audience that she had five degrees, including a PhD in religion.

In another newsletter, she wrote that, as a child, she wore ermine and traveled in a chauffeured Rolls-Royce. "We always had servants... I grew up in Cadillac cars, with linen damask tablecloths and heavy silver and oriental rugs and a concert grand Steinway piano. I had fur coats and diamond rings and designer dresses." Her grandfathers were transformed into real estate magnates and captains of industry. Their chauffeur, "Nigger Leftridge," carried Madalyn on his shoulders, and purchased her mud pies.

"In 1975 when I picked up the production of the magazine," said Bill, "the volume number went on just as if it had been published consecutively! They just faked it — there *was* no February 1970 issue or whatever — But if you look at the volume numbers, it looks consecutive." Another interesting fake was her secretary's initials — "M.M.O'H.: e.i.s." at the bottom of her letters, wills, and other documents. From the very beginning of her public life, this mysterious "e.i.s." had typed her correspondence. She finally confided that it was the "ego, id, and superego" of Madalyn herself.

Bill's stint at American Atheists was cut short. "I had never been so unhappy ... within six months I was over the line of being a moderate drinker to being an alcoholic... I had forgotten the... self-centeredness that goes along with people involved in these types of organizations."

Madalyn was intolerable, he said. Nothing was enough for her; his coup on the purchase of larger quarters on extremely reasonable terms was dismissed — it still wasn't big enough. She drove off one of his best customers in the print shop. Lonely and without a mate, she unloaded on him intimate personal problems he had no desire to hear. "It was because of that fantasy world. You can't have any *real* friendships because real friendship would interfere with the fantasy."

After Christmas, Bill announced he was running as a Republican for the U.S. House of Representatives, 10th congressional district, held by Democrat Jake Pickle. It was an attempt "to feel better about myself and to prove to the community that I was more normal than my mother," but it caused such an uproar of "warfare" and derision from Madalyn that he took Val and fled.

"I abandoned my house — everything," including his printing equipment. He continued to campaign for the May primary from Houston, and astonished himself by getting 46% of the vote. Madalyn would later tell members he left because he just wasn't making enough money, but she was paying the couple $1,800 a month, plus free housing at Sinclair, free gas, and use of a vehicle.

Soon after Bill left, Mike W_____ got a call from Garth, asking him to sign an affidavit attesting to Garth's moral character. He needed it to become a security officer, to be Madalyn's official bodyguard.

Garth confided that it was because of Bill. His drinking problem had led to some terrible fights. In mid-January 1976, returning from a trip, Garth and Madalyn drove to Sinclair and found Bill drunk, loading the van with his packed bags and some items from the house. A screaming and shoving match ensued, and Madalyn fell off the edge of the porch. When Garth ran to her, Bill jumped in the van and drove off. His mother said she was afraid of him, but also feared for his sanity.

Madalyn was in for more pain. She had again caught Richard with that "skinny, ignorant woman," as she called Mary H_____. She was stunned and upset. Softhearted Mike felt terrible for her. "It hurt her deeply."

She was also afraid Richard would try to run off with the assets of SOS. She was sure the neighbors were spying on her for him. She issued a press release that they were separated, and set about trying to wrest from him any grip he might have on their properties. She was now tasting the unpleasant side of Texas' liberal community property laws.

In jettisoning Richard from the board and stripping him of the presidency of SOS, Madalyn announced a new constitution and by-laws. From now on, only members, not mere magazine subscribers, would get the newsletter; its name was changing to AA *"Insider" Newsletter.* Anyone who didn't average at least a dollar a month in extra donations would be dropped from membership.

And she reiterated that she wanted to be addressed as Dr. O'Hair from now on.

Her troubles were mitigated by two legitimizing developments: the *New York Times Magazine* asked to cover her 1976 convention in New York, and the White House granted her an interview with a special assistant to President Ford, to discuss the new interest group she represented, Atheists in America. She was also given the remnants of Walter Kennon's United Secularists of America, which had long ceased to publish *Progressive World.* In Washington, she debated Dr. Cynthia Waddell of Voice of America, over VOA's religious content, and spoke at Georgetown and American Universities. It was a highly rewarding visit, with elite doors inching open — she even stayed in the same Howard Johnson where the Watergate burglars had their headquarters four years before.

But her crumbling family relationships produced an anxious distortion of these gains. Bill picked the time of her White House invitation to tell the papers he'd disassociated himself from her. Richard claimed he was due 11 years of back salary from SOS, and ownership of its house on Sinclair. Judge Thomas Blackwell granted him temporary possession, so angering Madalyn that she called out, as the judge left the bench, that she would not obey his order. Then she went home and freed Richard's longtime pet birds. She hired an expensive law firm, Kammerman, Yeakel, Hineman and Trickey.

She was sure Judge Blackwell was taking revenge for insulting things she'd said about him earlier when resisting jury duty. Whenever she got a summons, she would hold a press conference and refuse to report, declaring the juror oath unconstitutional. Article 1, Section 4 of the Texas Constitution required that public officials acknowledge a Supreme Being even to hold office. She hoped for a contempt charge or fine, so she could mount a constitutional challenge, but the authorities thwarted her with indifference.

"No one really cares if she shows up or not," Sheriff Raymond Frank said once when she publicly set fire to a summons.

Even though Judge Blackwell's ruling was overturned in March and Richard was ordered out of Sinclair, the acting-out of stress on Madalyn was going beyond "Grandma having a few tantrums." She penned a breathtakingly crude note to an Ohioan who had volunteered in Austin. "You wore such tight pants that . . . I could see the outline of your penis and scrotum," she scolded. His hair and fingernails were dirty, and she didn't like the way he ordered his "woman" around. "We are in the most severe test for respectability," she admonished, and he was not presentable. It was a pointless, ugly undertaking that availed her nothing; he wrote back pointing out her own filthy language and slovenly appearance, and became a vocal enemy.

She also lambasted the UT atheists for sloth. They wouldn't come around and do any of the dirty work. "I don't want to teach," she said about her spurned bid for atheist courses. "Young people are too dumb." (The students repaid her in a few months with a scalding open letter detailing the hundreds of hours they'd put in sorting mail, collating, mowing AA's grass, and doing other volunteer work.)

Her personal troubles were broadcast in other freethought magazines. In her own newsletter, she presented all the juicy details of Richard's infidelity. Sex was such a powerful thing, she said — it could break up the only atheist organization in the country. She was bitter, not at Richard for betraying her, nor at Mary H_____, but at *them*, her members. If they'd supported her properly, she would not have had to go out on the road to make money and leave Richard and Mary without supervision. Either you want this organization or you don't, she accused. You have made me beg and badger and cajole.

"Sometimes I think they would take better care of their house pets than me," she told a local reporter. That she expected to be first in her members' affections before their beloved family pets — that she openly expected to be "taken care of" — showed how skewed her idea of leadership had become. Though she called Richard a traitor and vilified him in the newsletter as greedy and venal, privately she wrote that she still loved him, and pined in her diary, "Please: somebody, somewhere, love me . . . Please: someone else, somewhere, share a dream with me . . ."

At her convention, Madalyn glowed in the support she got from her gang. They were sympathetic about her troubles with Richard. There was a spirit of excitement; she planned a suit to make the U.S. Census Bureau gather information about people's religion, and about the properties owned by each church. She was fundraising for a suit to demand that federal money be withdrawn from schools that allowed even voluntary prayer, meditation, Christmas vacation, Easter vacation, baccalaureate services, football-game prayer, or anything else that smelled like religion. She wanted to force the U.S. Treasury to cut states out of any kind of revenue-sharing that gave any aid whatsoever to parochial schools, whether vouchers, busing, books, or services. She was following up on the Tax Reform Act of 1969, which she thought was supposed to make the churches start paying tax on income from non-church-related activities.

After the convention, she reported that the attendees had voted her President for Life of SOS.

Chapter 31 ~ Signs of Distress

DURING THE NEXT SEVERAL YEARS, a hardening occurred in which all but the most stalwart of Madalyn's fans were burned off. Whether it was due to the emotional crises with Richard and Bill, manic-depression, insulin resistance, unrelenting stress, or frustrated ambition, Madalyn would fly out of control and excoriate anyone who questioned her, even old friends, longtime supporters, and people she needed and treasured. She trusted no one, and increasingly found that the only way to deal with members who lusted for her position, and enemies who infiltrated her chapters, was secrecy, control, and "excommunication."

She proposed "censure" and "repudiation" of any atheist or agnostic who in any way supported the Unitarian Churches of America, though they had helped her both in Hawaii and Texas. It was hypocritical to let churchgoers into AA, she said, and decreed that no chapter could even meet in a church.

When member John Lauritsen upbraided her for anti-gay comments she'd made in New York, Madalyn wrote him a shocking rebuke that was copied and widely distributed: "I would expect this kind of literature to issue from a misogomist [sic]. I am a *female* head of an American Atheist group. You are a cock-sucker. You like men and boys. You don't like women. We don't have cocks for you to suck."

With another activist member, Saul Jakel, she got into an escalating exchange over Israel. "I am so gawd-damn fed up on Jews covering their continuing adherence to the…Jewish religion with the cry of anti-Semite that I could…very easily turn into an anti-Semite," she wrote Jakel. And P.S. — she was dropping him from membership for being a Zionist.

There were further signs of distress; New Jerseyites Jo and Charline Kotula were old friends who had volunteered for Madalyn since 1968. Jo, a successful commercial artist, had pitched in with excellent cover art for AA magazine when Bill resurrected it in 1975. He traveled to Austin in 1976 to establish a newsstand-grade layout and donate designs for stationery, Solstice cards, and convention brochures.

One day Madalyn and the Kotulas were in the car when the subject came up of a prominent member who was sensitive about not having gone to college. Madalyn's advice was to just say she'd graduated from some school in Europe — no one would bother to look it up.

From the back seat, 11-year-old Robin said quietly, "Liar, liar — Grandma has lied so much, she doesn't know when she's telling the truth."

Her life was filled with 18-hour days of woe — the printer broke down, she had no paste-up person, she was backed up with six months of correspondence and Garth backed up researching and writing the radio series, weeds were growing and toilets overflowing at the Centre, she got "walking pneumonia," the new printer turned out to be a drunk, Richard was dragging them into court, she had to fire her asinine lawyers, make grueling appearances, and deal daily with tedium and exhaustion. But the way she reported these, instead of broken promises, there was awe that somehow, she did it all, day in and day out.

With all these troubles, in July 1976 Madalyn suddenly announced her candidacy for governor of Texas in 1978. She didn't expect to win, she said, she just wanted to see how many atheist voters were staying anonymous to keep their jobs. Privately, she confided her real view of the electorate: "thug blades, flower children, cocksuckers, food stamp leeches, longhair freaks, filthy bodies, alcoholics, Jesus freaks."

For six weeks in the fall of 1976, Madalyn closed the Atheist Centre, took Robin out of school, and went to Europe. She wrote members that the trip was to forge international ties and plan a second World Atheist Meet since the first one, in India, had fallen through.

They visited Avro Manhattan in London. Madalyn displayed $6,000 in travelers' checks, ostrich shoes she told him cost $250, and "rare leather" handbags she bought in Madrid and Florence. "Madalyn must come from a family of millionaires," Manhattan innocently wrote Garry DeYoung. "Perhaps one day she will donate . . . money to the SOS or American Atheists?" DeYoung laughed at that, but it was sad when Manhattan wrote, "After all, I have seen with my own eyes letters from one or two war veterans, sending her one dollar . . . saying they could not afford any more."

Doubtless influenced by Manhattan's accusations of secret agreements between the Vatican and the Kremlin to keep Communism viable in Europe, Madalyn felt her eyes were opened. Europe was saturated with religion; "There is little for a tourist to see anywhere but religious monuments," and yet "Communism, Socialism, Marxism, is . . . taking over in every country in Europe. Portugal is gone. So is Italy.

Spain is going. France is almost there. Germany is highly socialist. England is almost totally so."

The Vatican was insinuating itself into the back rooms of the materialist ideology power structure. The RCC was nothing if not a survivor, she said. Now it had corrupted the greatest hope for mankind, Communism.

On their return, Madalyn reported that she and Garth had become president and secretary of a group called United World Atheists. Reparations were big that year, and UWA demanded that the Vatican pay $100 million for the atrocities committed by the Catholics against atheists, surrender to UWA the papal crown, the "instruments of torture by which it stifled dissent," and all its financial records, and stay out of politics and "not concern itself with the wombs of women."

Chapter 32 ~ "Mama, you need to be dead"

I N AUGUST OF 1976, David Waters was paroled after less than 12 years behind bars. He was 29. He'd missed so many things led by his generation — the Sexual Revolution, the Summer of Love, flower children, wandering mendicant longhairs, Earth Day, war protests, and the peace songs — Crystal Blue Persuasion, Let There Be Peace On Earth. He set about making up for lost time.

He reveled in small things — rolling in the grass with the family Rottweilers and Dobermans, drinking beer, driving a car, buying all the smokes he wanted. He reentered the world of apartments, trailers, backyards, and living rooms, and met the velour sofas and orange shag carpets and avocado green appliances of the 1970s.

He was muscled from lifting weights in prison, had grown a mustache. He was soon decked out in the hip bell-bottoms and paisley polyester of the day. He wore his shirt unbuttoned well down the front to display his buffed-up pectorals, and his neck and wrists were adorned with jewelry.

"David was the disco guy," said one of his girlfriends, Carolyn Bruce. "Not that he could dance, but the disco shirt and the jewelry, and the tight pants."

He took up with old friends, including Robert Taylor and Carl Welchman, his 1964 codefendants. "Bobby got out of prison maybe a month before David," said Cookie Nelson. Taylor had taken to dressing all in white; they hung out at the Gaslight, a tavern on Main Street. David met a biker there named Gerald Osborne, nicknamed Chico — a big, husky guy with baby-blue eyes, the obligatory facial hair of the seventies, and a pony tail. "We got off to a shaky start," David said later, but they stayed tight right through the end of the millennium, through all the trouble to come.

As usual, he had no trouble attracting women, especially a tall brunette beauty with sparkling eyes that Bobby Taylor was dating — Cookie's "sister," Marti Budde.

Cookie was "adopted" as an infant by a neighbor who caught her stepfather trying to smother her. He simply plucked her from the crib and walked away, adding her to his large brood. So when, at 12, Cookie brought home a little waif named Marti Budde, it was no big deal. Marti was exactly one year and two hours younger than Cookie. They were closer than sisters, the pretty 5'7" brunette and the even taller Cookie, frequenting the Colonial Cove and other hangouts like Little Velvet Freeze and Avanti's. "She was always trying to keep me out of trouble," said Cookie.

In Marti Budde's short life, she would never find a more loyal friend than Cookie. Cookie bore scars on her hands from her friend's sharp nails, digging in during childbirth when both girls were teenagers in 1968. "They let me hold [the baby] for awhile" before it went to the adoption agency, Cookie said later. "It was beautiful, with long black hair and a turned up nose. I'll never forget that night."

They launched careers as go-go dancers, traveling to clubs all over the state. Marti soon became a masseuse, which led to a life of prostitution and reckless excess. She drew a year's probation in 1973 for battery, waving a gun, and resisting arrest in a tavern brawl, and was soon arrested again in a similar incident.

Cookie was going through a divorce and tending bar in Peoria. She didn't even know David Waters was back in circulation. One night at work, she turned around and there was a familiar face.

"I know you from somewhere," he said. Yeah, she said, you look familiar, too. Then he said, "Well, I've got someone here I want you to meet," and pulled Marti up from where she was crouching under the bar. They all had a big laugh.

Marti was in love. "It was goodbye, Bobby," said Cookie. For David, "Marti was everything I had ever dreamed of in a woman," he wrote years later, "beautiful, intelligent, passionate, independent, courageous, and loyal...I have never before, or since, felt so wonderfully alive...so intensely alive as when Marti was an integral part of my life. Three years, five months, and two weeks. This was the brief period of time during which I was privileged to know her."

That was how long Marti had left to live — until Valentine's Day, 1980.

David moved in with Marti and her Afghan dogs in a little A-frame between Peoria and Chillicothe. At first, he didn't seem to care how she made her living; he even made her feel good about it, proud of bringing in the money.

They went on little road trips, a handsome couple in sunglasses, Marti in floppy hats and sexy halter tops. She had velvety skin, model's facial bones, and coifed big hair. She was like a happier, classier version of Betty — without kids.

Betty, 46, didn't see much of her son during his first 16 months of freedom. He'd come over once to visit a girl who lived with her. They'd eaten together once at Nashville North with a friend. Once, she was invited to dinner at Jeff's, and David barged in drunk. He "ripped my coat half apart...told [Jeff] he didn't want nothing to do with me."

So they weren't on that good a footing on December 6, 1977, when the police got a call at 8 p.m. to go to 507 East Pennsylvania Avenue, where Betty now lived.

Larry Hunt came running up to the police prowler and said his brother had been beating up his mother in the upstairs apartment.

A frantic Betty met them downstairs. She said David had tricked her to get inside. Upstairs, they found the living room a mess — a burnt wig on the floor, the TV and furniture overturned. Pieces of a broom lay broken on the floor.

She told them her 30-year-old son came in with Marti, went to the icebox and threw food all over the house, and then started beating her with the broom. He said she was no fuckin' good, and he was going to kill her. He knocked her down and started kicking her and beating her with the broom. She had bruises on her face and both legs, and her right wrist looked broken.

Photos were taken. She had a warrant issued.

Ten days later, David turned himself in. She would not drop the charges.

Trial was set for February 27, 1978. It lasted six days, and TV cameras rolled during most of them.

Betty said he was "ranting and raving like a madman, going back and forth... talking about Kessler whiskey and... [saying] he was going to have some fun." Marti got him some Pabst tallboys from the icebox, and he took a few swallows from each one, and poured the rest over Betty's head as she huddled on the sofa.

"He broke [the broom] over my knees and said he was going to break my legs... trying to beat my face, but I had my hands up... so he was hitting my hand." He jabbed her in the ribs with the broken broom. Does that hurt? Does that hurt?

He took two plaques off the wall and cracked them on her head. He got eggs from the icebox and hurled them down the hallway. Some hit the urn containing Stevie's ashes. Marti started to move it, and he screamed at her to get away from it! — and crying, started to wipe it off with his glove.

He went into the bedroom and got his mother's workaday wig, set it on the floor in front of her and lit it on fire, including its Styrofoam mount. The room filled with poisonous black smoke. "He sat there and watched it burning, laughed like a maniac." He urinated on the television, then in her face. He called her a degenerate, garbage, said all women were garbage.

Crying, he went over and closed the window. He was through with games now, he said, he was going to kill her. He picked up Stevie's urn, and accused her of killing Stevie. He said she was a whore, a dirty, rotten, filthy, bitch slut. "Mama," he cried, "you need to be dead and put under!"

Betty leapt up and bolted out the front door. Marti was blocking it, and Betty grabbed the girl by the hair. Both women went over the stair rail and crashed to the foyer below. The downstairs neighbor, Jim, jerked his door open, and Betty scrambled inside.

Soon there were police and photographers all over the place. When Betty ventured back upstairs, the back door was open, and Stevie's urn was gone.

Jim took her to the hospital. They watched her all night. She looked at the bruises on her legs and hands, but she would not look in the mirror.

Marti testified for the defense. David didn't trick his mother, she said. Betty invited them in and offered them beer.

The conversation got tense because David brought up Grandma Hayes and Stevie, Marti said. Stevie's ashes had been sitting around nearly four years, and she'd never even gotten a headstone for Grandma Hayes' grave. Why? It was disrespectful. He was still in great pain about Stevie's death, and how no one had even bothered to tell him about it in prison.

David got more and more agitated, and started crying. He went into the kitchen, got a carton of eggs and started throwing them at the wall. Betty got mad and threw one of the plaques at him, screaming that she knew he hated her, knew he blamed her for Stevie.

Stevie wouldn't have died, he screamed back, if she'd been home for them instead of out on the streets. And then she started yelling, kill me! Just kill me, kill me! and dropped to the couch and curled up and started pulling her hair. Her wig was in the living room, and David did set it on fire with his lighter.

Marti opened the front door and the next thing she knew Betty had rammed into her, grabbed her hair, and they fell. She scrambled up and she and David left, taking the urn.

As the jury listened, the trial turned from David's actions to character assassination of the two women.

Why on earth, David's lawyer asked Betty, would your son call you a whore?

The judge shut him down, but he scored his point when the lead police detective got on the stand. Had he been back to visit Betty since the incident? Yes. How many times? A few. Did he interview David? No. Marti? No. Larry or his friends? Jim? Any other witnesses or neighbors? No. Just Betty. Several interviews with   just Betty.

The prosecutor did the same with Marti. Was she still working at Belinda's Massage Parlor? It was Belinda's *Body Shop,* she corrected. Massage parlor all the same though, wasn't it? Wasn't any *workout* equipment in there, was there? The judge shut him up, too, but both lawyers had made their points against the women, while David sat at the defense table in a beige varsity sweater and slacks, looking about as menacing as a librarian.

Betty, who, it was established, used Valium and Librax, was testimony to the rough start he'd had in life. She wore, said a trial observer later, "about four pounds of makeup" to court for the television cameras. Her good son Jeff defended it as a middle-aged crisis; she feared she was no longer attractive.

But the police report, the photos of her injuries, and the broken broom made it clear David had done terrible violence to his mother. The only alternatives the jury could consider were aggravated assault, attempted murder, or exoneration. The first two brought serious jail time, and the last wasn't likely, so the judge threw David a life preserver. He added a milder count — assault — and the jury seized it.

On April 13, 1978, David was sentenced to 364 days in prison, minus time served. Immediately after the sentencing, he and Marti went into the judge's chambers. Before a few witnesses, they were joined in matrimony. David was photographed happily embracing his pretty bride, his shirt rakishly half-buttoned, before he had to change into prison clothes and go to his cell.

Stevie's ashes were returned to Betty, and ended up for awhile with Jeff. Many years later, David would say bitterly, "Now the urn's disappeared. It's as if Stevie never existed."

Chapter 33 ~ Living on Memories

O N JANUARY 1, 1977, American Atheists was officially incorporated, and the AA "Centre" became the plain old "Center" again. They had eight people now, counting Madalyn and Garth, and stayed open 12 hours a day, seven days a week. Madalyn was looking for a librarian, chapter coordinator, computer operator, convention planner, and secretary.

As before, Bill had not really cut his ties with her, and she talked him into taking the job of general manager of AA, Inc. He and Val started talking marriage. Madalyn didn't know it, but they also had the idea of making a more normal home for Robin, 12.

Robin was an unwilling loner at Lamar Junior High, and a precocious poet. At 11, she wrote:

> I am living on memories, memories alone
> Of a time that never was
> Of a love that was never felt,
> Of acts never consummated,
> Of enemies never hated. I have carefully built
> myself a past
> With which to avoid my present
> And ignore my future.

"She was cute and had a good sense of humor considering what all she had to put up with," said a classmate. "They gave her a hard time about her beliefs...I never understood why people picked on her so much."

Madalyn was fiercely protective of her.

For years in the hopeful Christian community, rumors had drifted that Bill or Garth or Madalyn had come to Christ. Much was made of Garth attending a Christian businessmen's prayer breakfast in January of 1974 with Mike W_____, but his real mission was to get a look at Lester Buttram's daughters and try to wangle a free archeological tour of the Holy Land on the Christians' nickel.

In late 1976, Buttram published in one of his brochures that Bill had "broken from [Madalyn] and has denied any ties with atheism." (He hadn't; he had simply told Buttram nearly five years before that he didn't go along with a lot of Madalyn's ideas.)

Bill shocked Buttram by suing him for a million dollars. He'd "severely damaged" Bill's ability to raise money for the atheist cause in his new capacity as AA's general manager. Buttram had told a deliberate lie calculated to raise money for the Gospel Tract Society (Madalyn assumed Buttram raised money on the crisis — she certainly did).

There were those who said the suit had Madalyn's fingerprints, since she knew Buttram's financial status. But he fought it, and, to her dismay, the case was dismissed for being filed in the wrong jurisdiction. Madalyn wrote him, "You are an ugly, mean, vicious, vindictive, offense [sic] son-of-a-bitch without one redeeming feature... I detest you, your false posturings, your despicable motivations, your lies and your hate. *Drop dead!*"

Buttram's family stated years later that the suit cost him around $70,000, but the minister would consider it money well spent, for Buttram did eventually help get Bill into the fold. Madalyn would hold this theft of her son bitterly in her bosom the rest of her life.

Right after the dismissal of the Buttram suit, Irv, 60, came back into his sister's life. She hadn't seen him for 11 years. Living in San Francisco, he suddenly started writing to her and to several AA chapters. He was out of a job and virtually unemployable, he said, and instead of helping, his sister had declared war on him, back when he was trying to cope with their mother's cancer.

Though Madalyn had depicted Irv to members and correspondents as an "alcoholic bum," she had reason to keep him quiet. Her mother had been well-liked. Madalyn's fight over Winford when Lena was sick and destitute was unknown to most of the membership. It would put her in a bad light if anyone wanted to bring it all back up. She sent for Irv, demanding in return all the documentation on his attempted coup a decade before.

He arrived December 14, 1976, and was greeted at the airport by Garth. He'd last seen his nephew half Garth's life ago, but the two recognized each other at once. "You're burned out," Garth commented. Irv didn't argue, and they rode in silence to the Center in an orange Cadillac.

Irv hadn't changed much; he had a thin mustache, wavy hair, and the same towering, beefy body his sister had — the Mays build, where all the weight went to the trunk while the arms and legs stayed slender. He looked out of the same slitted eyes, through horn-rimmed glasses.

At the office, he was taken inside and told to wait.

Shortly, Madalyn's beige Cadillac pulled up. His sister, he wrote, had "a 1960 style duck's ass haircut, a dress that fell around her body like a floursack and a waistline that would have put St. Nick to shame." He claimed she fixed him with an icy stare, told him, "I hate your rotten guts," and said he was only there because Garth had insisted she rescue him from poverty. His paycheck would be $3 an hour. He could live at Sinclair.

He was put to work emptying the trash in the morning, and handling book orders and convention registrations; Madalyn planned to have him place AA magazine on the newsstands when she got distribution off the ground. He was also assigned to open the mail, and track cash and checks.

"He was a grumpy old man and everybody disliked him," wrote Richard Bozarth, a member who would soon become a columnist for the magazine, and later, AA's printer.

"Irv was horrible, a bad example of the male gender," said a volunteer. "He'd openly call women pussies, and any man who knew how to type, he'd call a faggot."

Irv would sit at the table in a restaurant and bellow, said one of Madalyn's lawyers. If a fat person walked by, he'd thunder, "*Jesus Christ!* Look at that fat pig!" He was over six feet, 280 pounds, and he never lowered his voice.

By Irv's account, one of his first assignments was combing through records of the organization's seven-year relationship with the Pitney-Bowes Corporation, looking for "discrepancies which would justify...litigation." Madalyn was unhappy with the company and didn't want to pay her bill. Irv failed to come up with anything egregious, and Madalyn called him "boneheaded turkey," a fat-ass, and a leech.

Irv would stay with Madalyn for over four years, during which employees and volunteers complained unceasingly that he stole cash from the mail. His and Madalyn's relationship was one of those snarls that characterized most of her close bonds, both personal and professional. She gave Irv free room and board, and tolerated his pilfering, so why should she pay him more than starvation wages? And what did she owe him anyway, considering he had teamed up with Bill, Lena, and Kerpelman to steal her church tax lawsuit, and sell Winford?

But he *had* taken care of their sick mother, and kept the organization going in Hawaii when Madalyn fled to Mexico, and he'd only tried to snatch it from her because Bill had come in as boss. Now she berated and abused him in front of the employees, and cursed him privately for the pilfering, while he did his job plus running every conceivable errand for her regarding Richard, Garth, and Robin, and he kept her illegal secrets from members, fellow employees, and nosy tax snoops, and she wouldn't pay a living wage for all this — so why shouldn't he pilfer?

Nevertheless, that Christmas was one of Madalyn's happiest. She had come out of the last divorce hearing the winner, on grounds of adultery. She retained all the property — buildings, cars, furniture, equipment, and even the now-ruined fishing boat Richard had bought long ago with hopes of getting her out of the office.

And she soon found a treasure, Missoula Shelby — Zula — who came to work as a daily housekeeper and stayed 15 years. A thousand times over those years, Madalyn would fall into bed exhausted, soothed by the tidy, clean-scrubbed house, fresh sheets, and sparkling floors. Zula got there in the morning and made their breakfast, ran their errands, took care of the dogs, did the laundry, cleaned, straightened, filed, and sometimes even house-sat during their vacations.

On December 21, 1976, Madalyn gave her first public Solstice party, inviting local atheists and the media. She catered enough food for hundreds, and the house on Shoal Creek was beautifully decorated, with pine cones and stockings strung with ribbons and holly along the wall above the groaning board. It was heaped with finger sandwiches, cold cuts, and hors d'oeuvres around a huge golden-crisp ham. Liquor flowed like a river. Beethoven's Ninth Symphony boomed through the house. Two Christmas trees dripped with ornaments and shiny icicles. The piano held candles and poinsettias.

Madalyn was proud to show off her family. Irv was decked out in a proper woolen suit provided by his sister, and Robin was everything her grandmother wanted, poised and gracious beyond her years, looking like a junior debutante in her lace-sleeved gown and glossy red mane. Bill and Val looked gorgeous too, and Madalyn, in red lipstick and a long-sleeved shift with a stained-glass pattern, was supremely pleased. This was what she loved above everything: family and friends, high spirits and goodwill, good food, and festivity well deserved after a year of hard work. Her home was perfect now, with the drapes and leather furniture she wanted. She loved the table overflowing with bounty, loved the cute, clean dogs excitedly scooting among the guests. *Gemütlich,* her mother would have called it.

Happiest of all was Garth, decked out in a velvet dinner jacket. He had acquired a girlfriend, Marilyn Hauk, a rancher's daughter who was AA's layout artist. It was something Madalyn constantly yearned for in her diary — a woman for Garth. She wanted more grandchildren, a big family, and that Christmas, it seemed within reach.

The guests counted down to the arrival of solstice — 11:36 a.m. — as Madalyn again explained how, before the Christians had stolen this pagan celebration "[it] used to be a fine time. People sang and drank and fornicated."

Only three atheists showed up; it was Tuesday morning, a work day. However, 40 hungry reporters came, ready to drink before noon, and rewarded her with ample coverage.

Privately, she preferred their company anyway.

NINETEEN SEVENTY-SEVEN was a turning point in Madalyn's life. On January 25, Bill and Val were married, joined by Madalyn herself. In a few weeks, Val revealed that she was pregnant. And, in the January newsletter, Madalyn happily announced the engagement of Jon Garth, 22 — always called "Jon" to the members — to Marilyn Hauk. Madalyn's dynasty seemed to be in the pipeline.

But it was not to be. Bill arrived at work in January 1977 to find Madalyn moving herself and Robin into the small upstairs guest apartment, so Garth could move his "tramp" into the house. A few days later, Hauk's parents arrived to meet Garth's family. Madalyn locked herself in her office and refused to come out. Even the newsletter seemed to be in on it: of the many pictures of the Solstice party, there was only one of Marilyn, and her face was obscured.

"She does not want to join the family," Madalyn wrote. "She wants to split Garth off from it — a lumpen proletariat value, not a ruling class value." A few months later, Marilyn left American Atheists.

"My sons, my black one and my blond one," Madalyn mourned to her diary. "They both need an intellectual woman. I panic with them. So desperately do I want something to turn out right..."

As always when Bill was in her life, Madalyn's ambitions started multiplying in a dead-heat race with his. It was like the last time he'd come back, in summer of 1975 — schemes started proliferating, and more things were set in motion than could be managed. Eight books had to be published, three lawsuits, double the membership and subscriptions by summer, and then double that by Christmas, get caught up on 18 months of correspondence, form more chapters, start a television show and ship dubs to the chapters, print and mail 5,000 extra copies of the magazine to legislators, get the magazine into libraries.

Her plan to run for governor was still on, and she added to it an impulsive second run for the Austin City Council in April. Bill was her campaign manager, and steered her away from a rant on sex in massage parlors to her milder church-state issues, like Christmas music on the intercom in government buildings, "attend the church of your choice" signs on public property, and religious books in military libraries. It turned out most voters considered these harmless — and probably constitutional — comforts, and she got only five percent of the vote. However, as was her wont, she turned the loss around and raised money on it.

In the middle of her city council campaign, she met with Richard to finalize their divorce, and found him "walking with a cane and in physical distress." His girlfriend had left him. Madalyn took him to the VA hospital in Houston, where they found cancer in his lymph nodes. She told Irv to make room, Richard was coming back to Sinclair. The divorce went on hold.

Her enemies said she only reconciled with him to get a government widow's pension for herself and Robin. They later said she neglected Richard, railroading him into the hospital so she wouldn't have to deal with him, when he just wanted to die in peace at home.

Her reported callousness was refuted by others who were there and by her anguish for his suffering recorded in her diary. It was just a sad and difficult situation, and by most accounts Madalyn handled it with grace and generosity, even if she spouted outrageous things sometimes (once she said at work, "He's living to spite me so I don't get the...benefits!").

She took him in at Sinclair, and paid to have someone keep it clean. She sent Garth to bring him to the Center so he could work on the rare stamp collections donated to the Cause, and have a little usefulness and dignity in his last days. He was soon wheelchair-bound, and struggled mightily to dress, undress, and answer the call of nature. He never complained, and Madalyn watched how he accepted, one by one, the betrayals of his body, the collapsing knees, the diarrhea, the wracking cough. "It is a silent bravery," she wrote. She hoped she faced death with as much.

She wrote to a select group of close followers. Even though Richard had caused immeasurable damage in the past year, could they drop him a card or some flowers at the VA hospital?

She brought him home to Shoal Creek sometimes, and it was she who traveled almost daily to his VA hospitals in Temple and Houston, Garth at the wheel and her painfully swollen legs and gouty feet elevated. She had a ramp built at Sinclair for his wheelchair. She bought his medicine, made him soup, sat up with him. "So I'll do the death watch," she wrote, "I'll try to see that he is comfortable and has the best of care." As for his pension, "He can have a heyday for the balance of his life." She didn't ask for a penny of the $1,000 a month he received as a disabled veteran.

It was another thing his daughter Vicki admired about Madalyn.

"When Madalyn hooked up with Richard, I do believe he was the kept husband. 'Cause he didn't have a job. All he had was this little pension... She created jobs for him... That's why I'm thinking, 'and you left her for another woman!?... Boy, are YOU dumb!'"

Chapter 34 ~ "Shut your mouth, woman!"

EVEN WITH BILL'S DRINKING — he made daily visits to a bar across from CE-SAALA called the Common Interest, and had seriously injured himself falling down some stairs drunk at the 1977 convention — the magazine was getting out on time and looking professional. The "oldster" members were asked to make SOS a beneficiary on their insurance, as wills could be broken by hostile relatives. Some members wrote books and paid to have them vanity-press published; why not let AA Press do that, if they were going to spend $5,000 anyway? Bill also had AA buying $100 worth of blue-chip stocks per month.

And, just as he'd found the complex at Medical Parkway, he was moving the property investments up again. Bill had a genius for leveraging, and he traded some of the smaller properties for a much bigger headquarters on Hancock Drive, only a few blocks away and in a good neighborhood.

"I got a fantastic deal, got that property for 50 cents on the dollar," he recalled. It was an enormous space, only three years old, with plenty of parking, and convenient to everything. It had a large conference room, media room, print shop, library, file and mail rooms, kitchen, and smaller offices for legal research, book orders, writing, and editing. He negotiated extremely favorable financing, and was irritated that Madalyn was glum over the $146,000 mortgage.

She hated mortgages, but that wasn't what was really bothering her. Bill was moving too fast, running roughshod; he had no respect for how hard-won the money was, or how fickle its flow. He'd maxed out the business credit cards. She was paying him and Val $1,500 a month. He drank, was surly, could dish out criticism but not take it. And he was always screwing up, she felt — like putting out a "moving fund" appeal to get AA and CESAALA into the new building on Hancock, but not checking with her before reporting that CESAALA owned 15,000 books. She preferred to say 50,000 books and 100,000 total documents. You had to exaggerate to get donations, image was everything.

She had promised to take his advice when he became her business manager, but his spending decisions were destabilizing her emotionally. With Richard's cancer and no one to discuss financial matters with, the abrupt cancellation of Jon Garth's engagement, her poor showing in politics, and her mood swings, Madalyn began to make frantic, irrational grabs for some kind of control over something.

The rest of 1977 was a disaster that started on a Tuesday night in May.

Robin was playing viola in a concert at Lamar Junior High that evening. When PTA president Barbara Murchison began the invocation, Madalyn strode to the podium and interrupted, attempting to seize the microphone. Mrs. Murchison was not one to be bullied, and a bit of shoving ensued.

Of course, it made the papers, and humiliated Robin terribly. At school, people were "running up trying to save me, grabbing my clothes...they called me 'devil woman,' 'devil's mistress,'" Robin said later, "and several times the word 'bitch' was written on my locker."

Madalyn pledged to sue Murchison and principal Floyd Odom, for making "a common spectacle" of her and "degrading me in the public eye." The principal had "contributed to the delinquency of minors [by giving students] free will to abuse my granddaughter," she charged incoherently. "I will sue everybody from here to President Carter." She immediately started looking at boarding schools, to get Robin away from the humiliation she herself had caused.

She turned to Garry DeYoung again in Mercedes, offering him a job. She apologized for having neglected Mary in the years of their association, calling her lapse "male chauvinism."

Her compensation over the Robin incident bled into delusional inflations of her achievements in the June newsletter: "Dr. O'Hair has degrees in History, Political Science, Psychiatric Social Work, Law, and Philosophy," she wrote. She had "35 years of experience in government as a lawyer, as a supervisor of psychiatric social workers, as a probation officer and as an administrator." Bill's years of job-hopping and wild-oat sowing were transmogrified into a degree in Business Administration, a career as a commissioned officer in the military, and ten years as "personnel supervisor" at Braniff. He was barely 31.

(It was curious how few followers ever seemed to question Madalyn's claims. Repeatedly, she said she'd spent 17 years as a psychiatric social worker, but apparently neither reporters, employees, lawyers, volunteers, nor subscribers ever said to her, "Madalyn, your last job ended in 1962. Seventeen years of social work before that would put you in 1945. You were in the army. You had no college degree. You spent years in school and in various jobs, you went to France, you spent a year on unemployment." And if her members ever huddled among themselves at the conventions and totted up her lies, they didn't care. So grateful were they for her leadership.)

Perhaps she shouldn't have made such a decision when she was so upset about Robin, but she began negotiating for a series of debates with the flamboyant Reverend Bob Harrington, the self-styled "Chaplain of Bourbon Street," with whom she was often paired on the *Phil Donahue Show*. Harrington was the classic Southern preacher-man, handsome, florid, with thick, wavy hair, a booming laugh, red bow ties, and fancy boots. He was another one that liked white suits.

When *Freedom Under Siege* came out, they both saw what could be done when an atheist debated a fundamentalist. Publicizing her book, Madalyn had engaged in a television debate with a prominent Baptist minister, Dr. W. A. Criswell, another classic Southern-Colonel type with craggy, handsome features and a mane of silver hair. His First Baptist Church of Dallas had 20,000 members, the enemy Billy Graham among them, and he was a former president of the 13-million-member Southern Baptist Convention. Madalyn's membership wasn't a tenth of his weekly church attendance; though she was the one with brains and charisma, the masses preferred his silver tongue to her sharp one.

They despised each other. She put Criswell in her crosshairs when he pressed on two very tender spots. First, when he thought of "atheist," he drawled, he pretty much thought of "Russian red Communism." And second, speaking of PhDs whoever heard of that *Minnesota Institute of Philosophy*?

"You're no Princeton, you know!" she hissed. "You're no Yale!" (His doctorate in theology was from the Southwestern Baptist Theological Seminary.) She bullied him, pressing him over and over to respond to her points, and when he tried, she interrupted. Exasperated, he finally shouted, "Shut your mouth, woman!" and barked at the host, "Who's running this show, you or her?" When he said he loved her but hated what she stood for, she called him schizophrenic. These Christians were always hiding behind declarations of "love" when they clearly hated her guts.

"What Criswell was gonna do," said Bob Harrington, "was work her over, you know, expose her? And *she* worked *Criswell* over! I had to come in and replace him the second day. 'Cause she shot him outta the saddle *immediately* . . . all he [could] say bad about her was that she mus' be Commanist."

But their three hours of fireworks were covered in every paper in the region and picked up by the wires, spiking book sales and donations for both sides. She and Bob Harrington got along well, and Harrington called Bill.

"We should make a circuit out there of debates, and I'll pick out cities and underwrite all the expenses, and you jus' have Mama show up." They agreed that most of the paying attendees would be Harrington's followers, though "devil" Madalyn was the attraction. She'd get 44% of the take after expenses, with a $1,000-a-night minimum. They planned to keep the show going for a year.

They would start in August, on the wave of publicity from the grand opening of Madalyn's new headquarters on Hancock Drive. The move was an almost welcome distraction from her guilt over Robin, and the 10,000-square-foot building was a balm on her public shame. It "created a fine first impression," said an employee, and lifted everyone's morale.

The opening was well covered, including by NBC and the *New York Times*. Madalyn announced two highly inflammatory lawsuits, one to remove the motto from money in time to stop the minting of the new Susan B. Anthony coin, and the other a third attempt to remove "under God" from the Pledge of Allegiance. The suits would be the raison d'être for the debates with Bob Harrington; Madalyn told members that the $15,000 retainer to hire attorney Broadus Spivey was provided by an anonymous donor. (It was Harrington, and he likely got it directly from pornographer Larry Flynt, publisher of *Hustler* magazine, who was reportedly behind the debates.)

She broke it to the members. Think of the money, she said, and see if you can do as much.

At this slippery and stressful time, Madalyn probably shouldn't have invited a local reporter, Jane Daugherty, to follow her around for three months for a long feature story. But to her regret, she did.

Chapter 35 ~ The Demon-Directed Damsel

THE HARRINGTON DEBATES started on Pup's birthday, August 5, 1977. Just before she left for the tour, she took Garth and Robin to Acapulco. From there they traveled to Tucson to visit the boarding school Robin would attend in the fall.

Built on an old Hohokam site in the foothills, Fenster School had been started in 1941 by a couple fleeing New York City. In addition to prep-school academics, it offered clean air, solitude, and archeological field trips into the Sonoran desert. Each student had to care for a horse and learn to ride.

It wasn't East Coast elite, but Madalyn ticked off the positives for Robin: regular hours, balanced meals, kids her own age instead of wandering around the office, "lonely as a cloud, all day, among us adults." But without Robin, home was going to have a kind of loneliness that no triumph of the Cause could banish. "Grandma" was dreading the day her darling left.

She'd put aside one special day with her, the Fourth of July. They ate watermelon under "the beautiful blue blue summer sky," and attended fireworks and an outdoor symphony at Zilker Park. It reminded Madalyn of her last summer of girlhood, and was a rare interlude of peace before the stress and insanity resumed.

Forty-five hundred people showed up at the first Harrington debate in Chattanooga, and the next ones were just as crowded. People stood and waved their Bibles and tried to shout Madalyn down. They rushed to the stage, knelt, and prayed as she spoke. They hissed and booed, and she called them fools and ignorant idiots.

Harrington spat scripture at her and bellowed that this "Demon-Directed Damsel" had to be stopped. If she wasn't, he warned, the churches were goin' to have to pay income tax! They were goin' to have to start sellin' things and forget about givin' their resources to the Kingdom of God! She wanted to ram things down our throats! He gave ten reasons she had to be stopped and ten ways to do it, and cited the Ten Commandments of Atheism — "thou shalt not" do things like love, believe, pray, have hope, give.

Not much headway was made in debate over the Motto and Pledge suits, but Madalyn netted $5,000 the first weekend, was invited to be on *Good Morning America,* and was the subject of magazine and newspaper features. Donations rolled in.

Harrington remembered the debates vividly. There was usually a band, with a midget singer, paid for by Harrington, that played "Old Time Religion" or "God Bless America" before Madalyn strode onstage. "I came out one side of the stage, she came out the other. One or the other of us would start it off. And then she'd reach and get the Bible out of my hands and tear the pages out, and she'd throw it at the people. And I'd say, 'Look at her! Spreadin' the Word!'"

They had other gimmicks to rile the crowd and make them put more money in the collection plate: Harrington would lead the Pledge, and when the "under God" part came, Madalyn would start yelling. Or she would stomp on the Bible. The angrier she made the Christians, the more money they gave. They had no idea it was being split backstage.

Madalyn genuinely struggled at first with what to say to these fundamentalists, how to get her principles across. But her well-prepared list of statistics and facts and quotes was soon scrapped, as people shouted her down or chanted, "Jesus, Jesus, Jesus."

Harrington said someone would always ask, " 'F'you don't bleeve in God, where did *jew* come from?!' and she'd say 'my momma and daddy wuh fuckin' in th' bed one night, and nine months later I dropped out.' You'd see those people, they'd go gaspin' f'breath — they'd go into shock.

"Ever' *time,* somebody would ask her that!"

She was frightened in the Southern states, feeling terrible hostility. In Alabama, she was treated to shouts of "Communist!" as Harrington tongue-lashed her as a fraud that gave off a stink that needed to be eradicated. In North Carolina, the crowd booed, hissed, and called her "Satan's whore." She "worked them into a frenzy," wrote a reporter, "by calling Jesus a homosexual . . . [and God] a bloodthirsty destroyer . . . " But even in New York, she and her entourage had to flee one debate, with an AA chapter head "help[ing] with the getaway and changing of cars to fool the angry crowd," according to member Jane Conrad.

Madalyn also got energy from the crowds, and the danger. Bill went along a few times, and mingled, trying to ascertain how dangerous they were. Garth would stay backstage, ready to hustle her out. They had security guards around and on the stage.

Each debate drew from 2,000 to 6,000 attendees. In Peoria, Ingersoll's home, they had to turn people away. Harrington carried a trunk and stuffed his money in it, and Madalyn wrote of arriving home with paper bags full of $1 bills.

She bought a travel trailer so she could save on hotels and planes. It was top-of-the-line, with shower, television, and a CB radio (their handle was Yankee Clipper). But it was a $30,000 lemon; within weeks the generator, brakes, and steering had gone out, the toilet was leaking and stinking, and everything went bad in the refrigerator. It got nine miles to the gallon. Seven weeks into their purchase, it had to be hauled home.

Harrington traveled in a $155,000 custom vehicle provided by Larry Flynt.

It made Madalyn extremely nervous to turn her earnings over to Bill. He always had some huge, impatient list of things he wanted to buy or change. They fought constantly over money, and he angered her by demanding accountings the minute she set foot back in Austin — as if *he* had been the one out there facing bomb threats and psychos.

The stress of 1977 was probably responsible for the Kotulas' flying the coop. Jo painted a beautiful portrait of Thomas Jefferson for the new Center. Charline Kotula, a talented seamstress, made several outfits that smoothed Madalyn's bulky figure for television appearances. Madalyn resented the implication that something so superficial might be important, calling the clothes "those god-damned rags," but she wore them. She respected the Kotulas.

But she gave some kind of offense so severe the Kotulas couldn't forgive it. "Why don't we kiss and make up?" Madalyn begged them in August. It was the pressure, she wrote, that had caused her meltdown, and in the rarest of gestures, she pleaded, "I apologize. I apologize." They remained silent.

Another staunch supporter for years, Dr. Rodger Buck of Indiana, sat down and penned a long letter of dismay to some of his fellow AA chapter heads, and sent a copy to Madalyn. Why did she keep alienating people with her crude, nasty letters?

She had lost thousands and thousands of dollars simply by not answering correspondence — it was disrespectful. They claimed not to have the staff — nonsense, he wrote, they couldn't afford *not* to hire the staff for this — and why such a turnover at the AA Center? Atheism was not presented with dignity, but rather with emotional, hostile diatribes.

SOS's bylaws on electing the board were suspiciously vague (SOS, AA, and CESAALA now each had its own board). Buck was especially concerned about a cult-like letter she'd sent to chapter heads saying not to share certain information with the members at large, because they couldn't be trusted with it, were "not made of the sturdy stuff of which you are made."

And Madalyn's aggressive "outing" of members by identifying mailings as atheist literature was brutish and callous; it was literally not safe for some of these people. Had she forgotten her own persecution? People lost their jobs. Religious spouses found out and divorced them. Church types hounded them for conversion; their businesses were boycotted into bankruptcy; family relations were destroyed. They suffered violence and vandalism she was well acquainted with. Not everyone was cut out for martyrdom.

Many of them had tried for years to convince her to delegate responsibility, to tolerate leadership instead of seeing it as rivalry. Buck now thought she was incapable of changing.

The rejections stung her. What it all came down to, she felt, was stingy atheists sitting on their asses while she got out there and drummed up circus money to defend *their* rights. She was sick of it. She expelled Rodger Buck from her organization, along with a member who'd suggested she tone down her profanity. She wrote the Kotulas a cold letter of dismissal.

Her only pleasure that fall   and it was bittersweet — was going to Sears with Robin to buy the things she needed for boarding school. Robin was getting excited about school, while her grandmother's heart was breaking. "Home?" Madalyn grieved. "Where is home? The one that Robin makes."

Sipping whiskey and putting together the last of Robin's school supplies, she listened to Elvis singing "Love Me Tender" on the radio, and listed her male "darlings" — Garth, Bill, and even Richard — with whom she clashed and fumed, but whom she loved, and always would. And she loved her parents too, she wrote, when all was said and done. She didn't mention Irv, even at her most sentimentally drunk.

After they got Robin ensconced at Fenster, Madalyn and Garth wrote her faithfully. Several times a week for the entire semester, she got cards and mail from "Garf" and "G'ma." No matter where they were on the road, or how stressed from overwork and fights with Bill, they managed to keep a touching flood of affection directed toward Tucson. "I love you, Redhead!" was the way Grandma often signed her letters.

Her motto suit, *O'Hair v. Blumenthal* (secretary of the Treasury), was filed in September. Madalyn offered to put on the suit the name of anyone who contributed $100.

To critics who said she should concentrate on something more important, like a church tax suit, Madalyn made a measured and calm argument: symbolic lawsuits were much cheaper and laid the groundwork for the blockbuster suits. For little money, a symbolic suit could stir up huge religious opposition and raise the nation's consciousness, on the Christians' nickel. But others argued that her repeated defeats set crippling legal precedents.

Time would prove Madalyn the winner of that argument. As it turned out, law was more likely to be influenced by public consciousness than the other way around. Even Bill agreed years later that nuisance suits were shrewd.

To help keep them coming, Madalyn engaged Ralph Shirley, a reclusive retiree who began volunteering in 1976 and turned out to be an enduring asset to her. He'd practiced law in Washington and was now living off of real estate investments. He doubled as printer, editor, columnist, proofreader, notary — even roofer and carpenter. Madalyn came to trust him with everything. She saved money by having him help with legal research; then she would write the briefs, and he would vet them. The work would be mostly done by the time they hired a licensed attorney to file.

The money was rolling in from the Harrington debates, but the publicity was starting to backfire. Christian bookstores removed Harrington's materials from their shelves. In Arkansas, Southern Baptists took out ads against the show, decimating the turnout there. The midget band leader dropped out, saying it was unsavory. Harrington separated from his wife of 30 years.

The death blow was probably Harrington's connection with Larry Flynt. ("I'm the friend of sinners," he explained.) On September 9, 1977, Flynt was arrested in Atlanta for distributing *Hustler* and *Chic*, his two pornographic publications, setting the stage for the First Amendment fight he wanted to wage against Atlanta's obscenity laws.

Those able to put together Harrington's expensive travel trailer from Flynt, the $15,000 to file Madalyn's Motto and Pledge suits, and the guaranteed income for Madalyn, suspected Flynt was behind the entire show, using it to stir up publicity for his suit.

In mid-October, Madalyn walked off for good in Bryan, Texas. She'd come on-stage riding a broom, then tried to knock the flag out of Harrington's hand, and told him and the audience to go to hell. It was finally dawning on her, she wrote her members, that he was using the Pledge to impugn her patriotism and raise the specter of Communism.

Her explanation to the members was filled with exclamation points. Could you believe it? A midget! Dr. O'Hair had to downgrade her material to fifth grade level!

She'd given up selling books and literature because Harrington told her his followers were too dumb to read. That was why he sold record albums.

At least she got *Good Morning America, Donahue, Sixty Minutes, Playboy, Playgirl, Esquire,* and *Newsweek* out of it, good publicity for her upcoming suits. And the attention of Senator Strom Thurmond, who wrote Harrington on his Judiciary Committee letterhead that he would strongly oppose the Motto suit.

She portrayed herself as befuddled at having been swept up in this Harrington thing, but she couldn't hide the photos of herself onstage with him that peppered the newspapers wherever they went. Photos of her belly-laughing almost to tears between catcalls and death threats. Harrington was warm, hugely likable, and absolutely sure of himself. She couldn't stay mad at him for his stunts. She had a weakness for these evangelists, and the charming, funny, handsome, and outrageous Bob Harrington made her laugh.

They visited each other's homes, and traded war stories. "She always liked me...she said, 'you'd be good at anything you do.' She enjoyed being on the stage with me."

But atheism, he said, "is a non-happy religion. You have to look a long time to find a happy atheist." Robin "had the saddest-lookin' face. An empty-lookin' face. I never got to see her smile much. Because I think she thought I was an enemy to her granmotha, y'know. An' I was attempting to hurt her granmotha some way.

"Garth, 'course he loved his motha, and he was gonna be heir apparent to the atheist movement. And he was just there takin' care of Mama, bein' her helpa."

Back home, Madalyn got in another horrific fight with Bill, his "face full of fury and hate, outsize cursing, yelling and accusations [until] the veins stood out in his neck." Garth jumped in and defended her.

Bill had taken it on himself to buy an $8,000 memory typewriter, put in a new phone system, and hire a new staff member while Madalyn was on the road. She insisted he return all the equipment and fire the employee.

She was certain that most of his anger was because she wouldn't let him control the Harrington money. She noticed that Val did whatever he said, like a whipped cur, she wrote, like the German people in World War II, and the people who came to the Harrington debates — cowards all, who wouldn't take responsibility for their condition. Bill said his mother was constantly nasty to Val.

Years later, he remembered bits of that calamitous time. He used to keep a gun in his desk drawer because of all the weirdos who came into the Center. One morning at home, he and Val looked out the window and saw a woman on the street with "obviously everything she owned in several huge mesh bags, dressed straight out of the hippies at Haight-Ashbury."

He turned to his wife and joked, "She'll show up at the Atheist Center before sundown. Sure enough!" They went to the Center later and there she was.

He remembered sitting at breakfast in his mother's home once with a visiting atheist couple who were "swingers." It was a jolly morning, with the couple competing over how many sex partners they'd had the night before. "These people felt validated when they trotted out their nutty behavior in front of someone 'famous' and she didn't condemn them," said Bill.

On another occasion, in a restaurant, Madalyn "was going on and on about how people used to worship women because they didn't know where babies came from, and thought women had this mysterious power and so on, and how it was only in the 1880s or something that the Japanese discovered the ovum when they were doing an abortion or something.

"And Jon was going, 'Yeah? Yeah?' and I said, 'Mother — people didn't practice husbandry? They didn't notice where all those animals came from, those cows, those rabbits?' And she started yelling, '*Shut up! Shut up!*'" That was only one of several Austin eateries they were banned from, he said.

The day of their last fight, she screamed that she *was* the organization, she would decide what was best, and he should take Val and get out. He booted over a fish tank on his way out the door.

Naturally, she regretted it, but the Murrays refused to take her calls, even when, on October 11, 1977, Val gave birth to Jade Amber Murray, a green-eyed beauty who would have Bill's blond hair. Bill hung up on his mother, and she slumped into a gloom not even the latest cash from the Harrington tour could erase.

"Bill Bill Bill," she wrote drunkenly in her diary, "I understand, I understand why, I understand why not..."

Chapter 36 ~ "I'm going to take a two-by-four and hit Austin between the eyes"

IT WAS HARD TO SAY what set Madalyn off that day in late October 1977, shortly after the debates collapsed. One could tot up the suspects. The poisonous Harrington tour had damaged her credibility; invited to Florida for a debate on her Motto and Pledge suits, she found herself paired onstage with a 10-year-old who had been called into the ministry at age two. There was the censure from her old friends, Bill's latest defection, Garth's aborted engagement, the new baby (Bill later accused Madalyn of telling relatives that Jade was a "deformed idiot with one eye"). Topping the list was Robin, and the gaping loneliness left by her absence.

The catalyst was an employee named Susan Strobel, who had left after an argument over pay. Madalyn got word on the road that Strobel had stolen the Center's master tape containing all the computer programs and the mailing list. She brooded impotently, impatient to be home instead of out taunting Christian bumpkins.

Once home, she started a rampage. In one day, she visited the police, county attorney, and district attorney, and accused Susan Strobel of stealing the master computer tapes, effectively putting her out of business. (She was careful to declare the tapes' value at $11,000 — enough for a felony.) Then she formally charged Barbara Murchison, the PTA president at Lamar Junior High, with assault. That evening, she went to a San Jose Catholic church, where a bingo game was in progress, and turned over the tables. With her was Sam Miller, a longtime volunteer and sometime employee; he had found an anti-gaming provision in the Texas Constitution.

"She came charging in like a Brahma bull," accused a player, "throwing bingo cards and game chips...pushing and shoving people," and Sam Miller threw a punch at a man who shoved him for shoving the man's wife. Police were called.

The next day, Jane Daugherty, the reporter who had been following Madalyn around since June, ran a big story. Instead of the Jesus-and-the-money-changers stunt, she chose to showcase the charges against Susan Strobel.

Madalyn was upset; perhaps seeing her accusations in print made her realize she had no evidence against Strobel. The day of the firing had been one of shouting and threats, and after Strobel left, it was noticed that the tapes were missing. That's all she had.

After filing charges against two police officers who refused to "come to my rescue" at the bingo fracas, Madalyn spent an hour at the *Austin American-Statesman* complaining that Daugherty's story was premature.

Then she visited each of her banks and withdrew all her money.

That afternoon, Bill had called a press conference to defend Strobel, humiliating his mother. The tapes were never missing, he said; they were just mislabeled. He had hired the same attorney as Strobel, former Austin Mayor Jeff Friedman, saying he was still an officer in SOS and wanted to be severed from its corporate actions.

As her out-of-control day smoked the headlines, Madalyn told reporters she was going to "clean up this city...I'm fed up with [Austin]...Every week I'm going to find something wrong in this city." She had, a few years before, called Austin a "quite charming city...we have not had one iota of rancor or hatred..." Now, she said, "I'm going to take a two-by-four and hit Austin between the eyes."

She would sue the school district for allowing prayers in school, get its federal revenues revoked. She was going to disrupt invocations at city council and school board meetings, raid more bingo games until she got arrested, and "put a stop to every single religious thing" in town. "I will demand that there be no Christmas, no Easter in these schools."

It was about church-state separation, she insisted, but then said, "Austin, Texas, ran a little 12-year-old girl out of town."

"My life is so empty," she told Jane Daugherty, her eyes filling with tears. "I don't have any little Robin to take care of...There's no Robin to make supper for." No Robin to sew for, to set out milk and cookies for. She wiped her eyes angrily.

How she would come to hate Jeff Friedman over the next decade, as the Strobel affair mushroomed obscenely and siphoned thousands of man-hours and hundreds of thousands of dollars from AA's coffers. But she refused to blame Bill. "No matter what Bill Murray does," she said publicly, "I love him."

Indeed, the night before her rampage, she had written in her diary, "Bill. I love you. And you worry me and upset me," and said she suddenly understood why Bill wouldn't let her buy him a car: "He *must* make it on his own and there is the heartbreak, for . . . *he can't make it on his own.* Not too many people can. I can . . . for myself . . . for my family, for society."

At Fenster, Robin was doing 12th-grade work, chafing at classes that were too easy. Like her grandmother, she'd started a diary, and she copied Madalyn's handwriting, down to the little flourish over her signature.

"Let me tell you about all my friendships and how popular I am. All the 8th-graders dislike me . . . a lot of the kids hate me simply because I like *classical* music. They have nicknamed me 'Beethoven.'" She pined for a friend, Derek Keller, from Lamar. "I could talk to [him] about music, philosophy, religion, politics, anything," she wrote sadly. He "saved my sanity . . . when all the kids in school hated me."

But at the Halloween dance, a boy named Andy told her she was the only classy girl at Fenster, and her hair was beautiful. Two other boys made overtures, too. She was to be double-promoted into ninth grade (annoying Madalyn, who thought she should go into tenth).

Madalyn didn't know Robin had been excitedly awaiting the birth of her sister. From Tucson, she had called her father in Texas and got the news of Jade's birth.

"I knew it was going to be a girl!" she wrote. "I wanted a girl."

After leaving AA, Bill had made another tepid stab at capturing Madalyn's audience with a new atheist organization, Second Foundation. But he soon gave up and disappeared, surfacing in Tucson. His brief atheist-leader venture was replaced by WVJ (William, Val, Jade) Books, a shop that sold rare atheist and freethought publications. He also reportedly invested in a turquoise mine.

Madalyn didn't know where he was, or that Robin was secretly seeing her father and stepmother. Val told her how Madalyn had been kicking up trouble in Austin, using Robin as the excuse.

"Are both sides making this up, trying to gain my favoritism — or are both using me?" the girl fretted in her journal. But she had wonderful Saturdays with Bill and Val and Jade, playing miniature golf, going to swap meets, shopping at the mall, having ice cream, dinner-and-a-movie. She adored the baby. "There was such love around," she wrote one day. "Boy, is Jade cute!"

She was glad they were settling in Tucson, and looking forward to weekend trips away from campus. They wanted a new start, a family, and they wanted her to be part of it. She loved the baby, and Bill made a point of chauffeuring her to and from the airport on her trips home. But they didn't want her to tell Madalyn they were there.

"However, Gram insists on asking me if I've heard from Val, where are they, etc. ...I feel funny lying to Gram. Gram and Garth want me in their family...however, they want me totally."

Madalyn made good on her promise. As the November 3 city council meeting was called to order with the invocation, she called out, "I'm sorry it is necessary for me to interrupt this...You know that prayers in a government establishment are unconstitutional."

The mayor, Carole McClellan, said she'd checked on that, and felt it was quite legal, so please be quiet. Madalyn replied that she was an attorney sworn to uphold the Constitution and could not allow it. She was hauled out by constables in front of two wide-eyed groups of third-graders there for a civics lesson. The minister then asked prayers for those in our community who were disgruntled, and would disturb the peace.

That was the first blow of the two-by-four. She filed O'Hair v. Cooke, asking for a ban on prayer in public meetings, before year's end. Next, she filed a $9 million damage suit against the governor and attorney general for okaying a crèche in the Capitol rotunda during Christmas, O'Hair v. Clements. (New Jersey and Wisconsin had similar suits. The giant rotunda Christmas tree was okay because it was pagan.) She promised to disrupt the traditional hour of Christmas carols sung by state employees in the Capitol on December 20. And she pledged to go after a seven-foot Ten Commandments tablet at the Capitol.

She sued to fire the police chief, city manager, and district attorney, for failing to shut down church bingo games, asking $1 million in punitive damages. Next, she would sue to keep churches from being used for polling places. ("Dr. O'Hair and I have to vote in a Lutheran church," explained Jon Garth.) Prayers at sports events were going to go, and a group of teachers at McCallum High who prayed in the library were going to stop it, and a small room at the Capitol would cease doubling as a chapel, and the dispensing of alcohol at church socials without a license would cease — and she would get the money for these suits "Even if I have to put a red light in front of the American Atheist Center and get lambs to accommodate the customers."

Letters flooded into Governor Dolph Briscoe's office. Why is a heathen like this even allowed in our capitol building? Next she'll want to put the devil's picture on our coins.

She should be deported, put on a ship to roam the earth. Just look at her face — isn't the evil obvious? She's done more harm to our young people than marijuana. I am just a housewife in Midland, Texas, but I have rights too.

The days of the week and months of the year are named after gods — why isn't she trying to keep the government from using those? She's not an atheist, she's simply anti-Christian.

I wonder why the pagan Christmas tree is fine with her? Pagans worshipped too, in groves. Woe to any branch of government that depicts stars or planets, because they've been *worshipped* before. How long are we going to pander to her pseudo-intellectualism?

Please don't use my name, or she will be suing me, too.

Can't we send her to Siberia, or to the moon, maybe? Someone is going to *zap* her! Christians are the majority — why should we change to please her? We are behind you 100% here in Mineral Wells, Governor Briscoe. Isn't there some way of getting her out of the U.S. forever? The police, the capitol people, should make her get out of Texas.

"She wants the three wise men removed from the rotunda?" asked local humorist Cactus Pryor. "Madalyn, honey, there ain't been three wise men in that Capitol building for a long, long time."

In Tucson shortly before the 1977 Christmas holiday, Robin looked at the previous entries in her diary. How trivial they seemed, she wrote, compared to what she had to deal with now. Madalyn had just found out that Bill and Val were living in Tucson.

"And because I'm in contact with Val, she thinks I'm stabbing her in the back, helping them to ruin her organization."

What really upset her "is that my own grandmother doesn't trust me. All I ask is to lead my own life — by that I mean to have the liberty to think for myself — uninfluenced. Without being chastised and punished for doing it."

They were going on vacation to Hawaii over Christmas, and "I'm going to have a perfectly horrid time. Trapped with my grandmother and uncle, who all during vacation will be treating me as a traitor to Atheism and the family."

"How I long for the days of my youth," wrote the 12-year-old. "But as I think about [it], my youth wasn't that nice."

In Hawaii, they visited Lena's grave for the first time. How long ago it seemed, Madalyn reflected, that she'd fled to Mexico, leaving Garth and Robin in her mother's care! Lena had virtually raised her boys. Madalyn had written in her diary back in 1953 that she owed her mother an unpayable debt for her devotion to Bill, freeing Madalyn to pursue her own interests.

"The home would be nothing without her," she wrote back then. She had turned Bill into a "beautiful and well behaved [child], charming, intelligent, courteous..."

Through the screaming fights with Pup, and the moves in the middle of the night, and the ostracism from the lawsuits, and her daughter's flights to Hawaii and Mexico and Texas, Lena had tended the hearth fires. She'd stood on the Supreme Court steps with Madalyn to be photographed, braving hatred herself. From her, Madalyn had learned most everything she knew about making a home. "She changed your diapers and took care of you for the first year of your life," she told Robin.

Madalyn had called her mother a "dumb broad" in her first book, and said on film that she hated her guts — something she was ashamed of when she saw it aired. Standing at Lena's grave, she remembered the *fact* of loving her mother. But she was unable to call up any of the emotion. She had had to twist herself bloodily out of the matrix of family to become who she was.

She had her way in *Current Biography Yearbook* that year. Her version of Madalyn Evalyn Mays Roths Murray O'Hair prevailed: wealthy childhood, happy and secure, beautiful mother, grandmother who sewed her lovely dresses with matching bloomers, father who "was a knight in shining armor," Rolls-Royce, chauffeur, they were pillars of the church. She'd married William Murray, and had two children by him. She saw combat in the war and came away with five battle stars.

She also had her way with Robin. The 12-year-old came back from Christmas vacation with a resolution. "I have decided to disassociate myself from Bill and Val. I love Gram more than them."

Chapter 37 ~ Bloody Sunday

A S MADALYN EXPECTED, Federal District Judge Jack Roberts threw her nativity case out, and by early January 1978, it was on appeal in the U.S. Fifth Circuit Court in New Orleans. It did its job; members of Congress were asking for copies of the pleadings and news clippings about the case.

The Motto suit was also in front of Judge Roberts, who, Madalyn told a reporter, "simply hates my guts." It would fail there and go to New Orleans too, she said. "The atheist community sits on its collective ass … [while] the religious zanies have just absolutely flooded the Treasury Department with letters in support of the national motto."

It wasn't just that the crèches and slogans were offensive to her as an atheist. Religion genuinely oppressed people, and should be stamped out for political reasons.

"This invidious thought system," she wrote, "penetrates everywhere, controls, sucks money, time and effort, energy, promising everything and giving nothing. By now we could have conquered all disease with the money that goes to this sick philosophy. Slums could be cleared, unemployment solved, wars stopped … "

Since last fall, the New Jersey AA chapter had been rumbling about Madalyn's dictatorial ways, Bill's defection, the negative image of atheists, and Madalyn's brouhahas in Austin. They resolved to confront her, but worried that it would jeopardize AA's participation in the lawsuit that chapter head Paul Marsa was planning against the Metuchen, New Jersey Borough Council for opening with prayers.

A volatile situation had arisen over Garth. When Bill left, Paul Marsa had sent a girlfriend to Austin to pinch-hit. Soon, she was "intriguing my Garth," Madalyn wrote, wide awake one 3 a.m. because he was off with "New Jersey Barbara."

His loneliness was acutely painful to Madalyn. He wanted a woman so badly, but he was still a virgin, she was certain. She worried he might never function as a man, because he had an undescended testicle. (Indeed, the mustache he'd started in his twenties would stay sparse on one side and normal on the other. His doctor noted his acromegalic appearance, the enlargement of the bones of the hands, feet, and face, from an overactive pituitary. Madalyn and Irv had a similar appearance.)

Garth fell very hard for the woman, but the liaison fell apart after a few weeks, and she went back to New Jersey. Madalyn watched helplessly his misery, the dark, puffy bags under his eyes — even though it was, in fact, she who had blown the whistle after spotting Barbara using a pay phone near the Center. She was sneaking a call to her boyfriend, Madalyn told Garth; she was a spy. If it was an innocent call, she'd have made it from the office.

Madalyn agonized. Garth was such a faithful worker — didn't he deserve a woman? She bought him a new car, sent him shopping for a Rolex, and worried how to pay for it all.

When Marsa's group wrote of their concerns about American Atheists, Garth responded with a sulfrous letter to Marsa returning a donation. "I don't like hypocrites, liers [sic] or Jews, all of which you qualify for." Marsa just wanted to overthrow "National" — the Austin headquarters.

It was awkward for Marsa; there was a long article praising him in the upcoming issue of AA magazine. His picture was on the cover, and Madalyn was organizing a defense fund for his suit. But he felt he had to demand an apology. "No way," Madalyn replied. "Garth . . . has the right to his opinions." She removed Marsa as chapter head, saying he'd shown poor leadership.

Privately, Madalyn wrote Marsa that it was just a dispute over a woman and shouldn't have escalated, and she valued him in the organization. But to the chapter, she licked Garth's wounds: Marsa had "provok[ed] deep animosity with a member of the national staff," causing that person to write a heated letter.

By the end of January, Garth was hospitalized with stomach trouble and put on Valium, and Madalyn got word that the New Jersey chapter had set an emergency meeting to discuss his anti-Semitism. "What!" she wrote a member; "Garth made no 'anti-Semitic slur' . . . He called a Jew, a Jew. Is that slander?"

It was Lemoin Cree all over again — now that she had momentum, funding, and visibility, they were full of plans for her organization. Jane Conrad in Colorado and Anne Gaylor in Wisconsin were once trusted allies who wrote for the magazine and appeared on its cover. Now, aligned with the New Jerseyites, they were vultures, hoping to nudge her into retirement. And they actually thought they could by-pass Garth and seize National.

These never-ending waves of usurpers had no idea how much work went into just the magazine and newsletter, not to mention the lawsuits, bookselling and writing, radio show conventions, publicity, supervising employees, and unrelenting fundraising. They thought it all just magically appeared. They were "fleas on the dog" — a favorite expression. She described them: closet atheists, Zionists, woman-haters, Marxists, messianic types, hijackers who would capture the atheist movement for their own agendas — abortion like Anne Gaylor, gay rights like John Lauritsen. "We will deal with such detractors ruthlessly," she wrote. "We will permit no divisions."

And could any of them ever hope to attract the attention she did? She'd already done interviews this year, though it was barely 1978, and the *New York Times* was planning an article. Yes, she made mistakes, and she took her lumps for them. She had let Bill try out his own ideas, and he spent her hard-earned money like water. And despite the relative chaos at the Center, a huge amount of work did get done. She might be foulmouthed and impatient, but she could also be generous, charming, and tolerant.

She tried to give her employees appreciation and incentives to excel. The women got flowers and candy on Valentine's Day, and people were helped with transportation, medical and child care, and even loans.

On Sunday, February 12, the New Jersey rebels arrived at their special meeting to find Madalyn, Garth, Ralph Shirley, and private security police waiting for them. Madalyn thrust letters of expulsion at each of them, and then began reading a position paper explaining that anyone who claimed to be a Jew could not be an atheist — Judaism was a religion, not a race.

Someone who tried to tape the proceedings was removed by the hired guns. Everyone who tried to address the chair was expelled. When a member named Florence Fox tried to confront Madalyn, she hissed, "Why don't you go to the gas chambers . . . it's people like you who provoke the need for them!"

The episode was dubbed Bloody Sunday, and distressed the members to whom Madalyn was still an icon. One described himself as a whipped pet, unsure what it had done. In California, Richard Bozarth, an idealistic young Vietnam vet who had become a regular writer for AA magazine, received a letter from Anne Gaylor. He had been looking forward to seeing her at the American Atheist convention in April. She wouldn't be coming, she wrote. She'd been kicked out. Madalyn had a captivating and wise side, she said, but a dark one, too.

But "I was not prepared to receive any type of truth about Madalyn," wrote Bozarth later. "I had an image of her so gleaming and glorious that it blinded me."

Three days after Bloody Sunday, Madalyn opened the newspaper to find that she'd been sued for $50,000 for slandering Susan Strobel. She bitterly regretted going after Strobel, she admitted privately, and girded for battle.

Death was inching up on Richard, and Madalyn and Garth visited him almost daily. He couldn't sit erect, and was hallucinating, but his moments of clarity were full of wit and humor. He called Madalyn "Grandma." Garth patiently sat listening to his ravings and telling him he was going to get better, was going to come home and sit on the patio. Madalyn sent his burial suit to the cleaners. She didn't feel any emotion. She didn't care any more.

On Sunday, March 12, 1978, he died. "That is that," Madalyn told her diary.

She got the money and connections together to have him buried at Arlington National Cemetery. She had found among his possessions bitter complaints about Garth, whom he clearly hated, and plans to prove Madalyn was an alcoholic, and attempts to get some of the chapter mailing lists. But she gave him a hero's burial in print.

His sister and his sons from his two previous marriages were dry-eyed through the ceremony. Afterward, they went through Sinclair like locusts, taking his things.

"I hope I have lived my life in such a manner that when I die, some one cares," she wrote in her diary. "I think I want some human being, somewhere, to weep for me."

But after Richard died, a peculiar anxiety set in. Garry DeYoung had picked up and moved to Iowa, far away. Even though someone sent her a hurtful letter he'd written to the *Houston Post*, she sorrowed at his leaving. Stripped of all the uncontrollable men she'd bonded with, she felt cut adrift.

She was now certain that Bill had engineered the theft of the master mailing list and donor tape she had accused Strobel of stealing. She believed Val had hidden it for him to retrieve later and copy, so he could start his Second Foundation.

She couldn't sleep; night after night her brain filled with schemes and worries, crawling like maggots. The Cause seemed a slowly growing illness that allowed her no peace, no center of detachment, and no refuge from the savage monkeys swinging from tree to tree in her mind, picking at every scab of fear and failure, screaming for attention.

Her only respite came from the outside world, and was dependent on how it behaved. She felt love as long as the kids didn't take flight and the employees obeyed. She felt comforted by food and drink. She felt rich, buying some luxurious item, and cared for when the house was cleaned by Zula, and when one of the dogs jumped up on the bed and interrupted the flow of sewage and diamonds in her diary. She always felt the problem was not enough time, not enough money.

Chapter 38 ~ "Some human dignity, some grace in living"

THE 1978 CONVENTION in San Francisco showed the strain of Bloody Sunday, but for newcomers like Richard Bozarth, it was heady wine to be in Madalyn's suite at the BYOBs each night. Madalyn was "smooth and effective" for the TV cameras, and Bozarth was exhilarated to hear her say "70,000 families" when asked about AA membership.

He had been contributing articles to the magazine, and was tremendously flat-tered when editor Ed Bojarski had asked him in December to write a regular column. Circulation was listed in *Writer's Market* as 52,000. It would be more than a year before he found out that the figure was a 2000% exaggeration.

He remembered his first glimpse of Madalyn. "At first sight [she] looks like just another ugly, fat, gray-haired old woman." But up close, she had "what the military calls command presence, which is to radiate leadership like the sun radiates light." He literally felt as though he were meeting someone like Thomas Jefferson.

After the convention, the dissenters from New Jersey issued a press release an-nouncing an "Atheist Reformation." Bloody Sunday had spawned a rival group calling itself the Freedom From Religion Foundation (FFRF). Headed by Anne Gay-lor, AA's former chapter leader from Wisconsin, the group targeted AA members who disliked Madalyn's despotic ways.

The wires had picked up the story, and extensively quoted Madalyn's "ex-communicants" as to her personal shortcomings. "A cause organization has no business owning Cadillacs," they said, and detailed her rudeness, megalomania, nepotism, and secrecy about finances. The schism was covered by the *New York Times*, where Madalyn was pictured with bags under her eyes, insisting she'd simply purged the organization of a handful of Marxists and Zionists. But the article again spoke damning words: anti-Semitism, trivial lawsuits, enemy son, Harrington circus.

On April 17, U.S. District Court Judge Jack Roberts threw Madalyn's Motto suit out of court. She hadn't persuaded him that the phrase was anything but a patriotic slogan.

"The man is almost hysterical when it comes to anything I bring into his court," she responded. She would simply do what she always did — march it to the Fifth Circuit Court of Appeals in New Orleans.

Two days later, she was hit with another $50,000 lawsuit, this one for mali-cious prosecution, filed by PTA president Barbara Murchison. Like Susan Strobel, Murchison was represented by Jeff Friedman. Again, Madalyn regretted her actions.

She and Garth left on an organizing tour in late April. She had let Garth have his head, planning this junket. They'd worked 18-hour days for two weeks to prepare, though still exhausted from the convention, and left even more exhausted. Within days, they were sitting by the side of the road near Harrisburg, Pennsylvania, in the broken-down RV, her stomach churning.

A week later they jetted home, Madalyn fuming about the money wasted — hotels, taxis, restaurants, air fares in the high season, meeting rooms, security, not to mention the repair, loan, and insurance payments they were still hemorrhaging for the RV. They reached Austin to find work piled up, employees unable to proceed without them, and more 16-hour days just to minimally catch up. Their cars broke down, along with the new photocopier. The roof leaked into the AA Center kitchen.

Whether it was overtly stated, it was clear Garth's *pas de deux* with leadership was a failure. Even though he had run himself into the ground with details Madalyn hated, putting office matters to bed before they left, setting up meetings and booking appearances, driving the RV, making reservations, planning and organizing everything from picking the typeface for magazine ads to negotiating cut-rate prices on paper stock, to packing Madalyn's insulin, to buying groceries for the RV, he couldn't fill his mother's shoes.

Within days of their return, he was deathly ill, with a fever of 103 degrees.

He still wanted to go to India. Backpacking around the world, hitchhiking across the country, finding a guru — he'd missed all that. He'd hardly had a youth. This time, Madalyn would move heaven and earth to get him there.

Robin was feeling lucky in life. "I can afford to be in a boarding school, I'm smart, witty, fairly pretty, I have friends. And best of all I have a loving Grandma and Uncle."

She'd been researching other boarding schools, as Grandma had nothing but contempt for Fenster. She had picked a small, exclusive school in St. Louis, Thomas Jefferson High. Madalyn agreed — grudgingly, for her real dream had been to get Robin into prestigious Phillips Exeter, and she was upset when Exeter turned her down. She wrote them citing a recent Supreme Court decision barring discrimination because of creed. That included snubbing atheists. "Your last letter to me had a certain tone... I'm certain you really do not want to leave this impression." She was resubmitting Robin's application next year.

When Robin got home for the summer, she was put to work at the Center, working 20-hour days to help get things tied down so they could leave for India on July 3. The 13-year-old was an immense help with everything from working the receptionist's "cage" to organizing the library, helping with the mailings, and editing the magazine.

At the beginning of summer, Val called. She and Bill wanted to come back to work. Madalyn said no. Didn't she want to see Jade? *No*, Madalyn replied. She'd heard through Irv that Bill was in financial trouble and drinking heavily. She was not going to let him come back and stomp around and then throw a fit and bail out. Besides, she suspected they just wanted Jade on the gravy train like Robin.

Shortly after Val's call, Madalyn's bingo suit was thrown out of court. She hadn't shown how she suffered personal harm by a bunch of Catholics raising money, said Judge Jack Roberts. She had no standing to sue the county and district attorneys and police; a citizen can't do that unless they've been threatened or persecuted by their policies. She despised Roberts.

Both Strobel and Murchison had proposed settlements, of $8,000 and $3,000 respectively. Madalyn took this as evidence of weakness, and rejected the offers — a decision that would cost her many thousands more.

The night before they left for India, Madalyn stayed up all night, her legs swollen and aching, doing laundry and writing in her diary. As the alarm clocks went off and Robin and Garth rooted sleepily in their bathrooms at dawn, she reflected that the only significant thing atheists had accomplished in 100 years was her 1963 lawsuit. They needed to change their attitude, to organize.

The trick was to "wrest" the "system" out of the hands of those in power and fix it. "Our culture is sick," she brooded; "Ideas are wrong. Something must be done." It was up to her. She would have to do it.

Madalyn's plan for an annual World Atheist Meet had been in place at least since the early 1970s, when GORA's son, Niyanta, visited her at Shoal Creek. GORA died in 1975, and his Atheist Centre was taken over by his sons.

In New Delhi, they were met by Sanal Edamaruku, whose father Joseph was active in the Indian atheist movement. He took them to Madras, Bombay, Calcutta, and to GORA's Atheist Centre in Vijayawada.

Madalyn and the kids endeared themselves to the Edamarukus. Their home was new, "without any furniture and with no washbasins fixed," said Sanal. "Madalyn did not bother about the lack of comfort . . . Sleeping on mattresses on the floor and sharing bravely our hot Indian food . . . This was the beginning of a great friendship." They talked into the wee hours about their work and dreams. Madalyn invited Joseph to be speaker at the next AA convention, and arranged for the family to spend a month with her in Austin beforehand.

Privately, she found India a place of "insects and filth and swarming humanity." They were assaulted by stench, heat, and "the din of howled prayers." They took in the squalor, the beggars, and the attacks of mosquitoes and microbes, "buttocks covered with sores . . . diarrhea, upset stomachs, fever." Their skin was clammy, their fingernails black, their hair oily. "The toilets stink, baths are impossible . . . We tower over everyone."

Madalyn spoke at meetings, schools, and homes, to the newspapers. At the Atheist Centre in Vijayawada, she saw religion still underpinning form and action, and the outcome was the same: "[the] human animal [is] lower than the ape."

And she found the same problems as among the atheists at home: "leeches, spinoffs" and a few brave people who came out from behind the Rationalist label, but little help from the educated who knew the truth but cherished their jobs more.

Oddly, she awakened six times a night to give Garth his diarrhea medicine, as if he were a child. Robin fared better, wearing a new short haircut and rotating among a dozen stylish sundresses. She had a cute, shapely figure and would keep it until years of overwork drove her to obesity like her equally overworked grandmother and uncle. It was Robin who always read up on everything, got brochures, and made the trips interesting.

On the way back, they visited Iran, Turkey, Hungary, Germany, England. Madalyn loved clean, orderly Germany, her mother's ancestral homeland. They watched an old American movie on TV in their hotel, and Madalyn reflected that she had grown up in "an age of innocence in the U.S. . . . there were so many times in our home when life was beautiful. I have tried so hard to give that to my children: some human dignity, some grace in living, a quiet and glowingly beautiful home."

While they were traveling, Pope Paul VI died, on August 6, 1978. "This fanatical cretin," Madalyn wrote, "who gave the edict of humanae vitae which charged women with unrelenting pregnancy, is being eulogized even by the communist world in a sick abasement of the human intellect. I only wish I could spit on his corpse for the world to see that some of us consider this trust misplaced."

In September 1978, Robin, 13, was off to tenth grade at Thomas Jefferson High, which Madalyn immediately began demeaning. She wrote the Head of School that Jefferson was "a cultural throw-back...We wanted biology, astronomy, chemistry, Spanish, Russian, Chinese...not the obscurantism of the ancient world." They had tried to talk their darling out of Jefferson, Madalyn told the dean, but "our stubborn little red-head has a mind of her own." They were only going to leave her there one year, then she would be off to Exeter.

Madalyn wrote Robin the same day, a manipulative letter about adult matters calculated to unsettle, frighten, and make her feel guilty.

First, her "failure father" was claiming he'd found God, so "please call me." He was speaking at churches for $100 a night — disgusting, he should be getting $1,000 a night as the son of Madalyn Murray O'Hair. "Please call me." Bill was so unstable they were afraid of him; "We could be the target of a machine gun which he carried as he tried to be a soldier of the lord."

"Please call me."

She kept repeating "Please call me," as if only Robin — under pressures of adolescence, a new school, extraordinary academic rigors, and pressure to get into Exeter next year — could guide Grandma through this crisis.

And Grandma was carrying impossible burdens, she confided to Robin. The Center was in chaos, and she and Garth worked until 2 a.m. every day. Money was so tight they couldn't buy groceries. Garth had written a hot check for Robin's trunk. The lawyer wanted to be paid even after "fucking up our cases," and the New York chapter was threatening to bolt. She wanted to know "what kind of freaks they have in that school...Please call me."

Madalyn had gotten a large poster saying "Fuck Authority" for her office, she wrote her granddaughter, and they were shopping for a new home. There was in her letters a confusing mishmash of how destitute they were, and how extravagant. Shopping for a big new house and bouncing $12 checks. Buying a $2,000 painting and raiding Robin's $2 bill collection for Fish 'N' Chips.

Madalyn complained that Jefferson — TJS in their letters — subjected Robin to "barbarian" tactics such as testing and memorization. "Well," she wrote Robin, "you only have eight months to suffer up there."

Between letters excoriating TJS that fall, Madalyn flew to Albuquerque to provide interrogatories for a $7 million damage case against *Screw* magazine, for a spoof that she said defamed her. She had slim hope of getting any money, but she could use it as a free-speech issue.

However, a magazine that did have deep pockets, *Hustler*, was courting her. In December 1977, she'd met Larry Flynt's brother, Jimmy, at an Ohio Civil Liberties Union mixer. He'd told her his brother was going to expose Christians in *Hustler*, and asked for an interview. A few weeks after that, Larry Flynt underwent a religious conversion through the efforts of Ruth Carter Stapleton, the evangelist sister of the President, and resigned as publisher.

Then, on March 6, 1978, Flynt was shot by a sniper as he entered a courthouse in Lawrenceville, Georgia. He was paralyzed from the waist down. His religious conviction went on hold.

Now Althea Flynt — Mrs. Larry — personally asked Madalyn for an interview again. If AA members thought the Harrington debates were sleazy, there would be little doubt of their position on *Hustler*. But, Madalyn wrote, she could "rationalize it with the fight that the Atheists put up for human sexuality."

Chapter 39 ~ Circle the Wagons

ON THE DAY THE STROBEL TRIAL STARTED, October 23, 1978, Madalyn filed a *Schowgurow*-esque suit she hoped would throw a monkey wrench at Jeff Friedman. It was against 14 state and Travis County officials, including the treasurer, secretary of state, numerous judges before whom she had cases pending, county attorneys and commissioners, and Attorney General John Hill.

The suit, *O'Hair v. Hill*, said her civil liberties were violated by Article 1, Section 4 of the Texas Constitution, which mandated that judges, juries, and anyone who wanted to hold office had to acknowledge a supreme being. That cut atheists out of getting a jury of their peers or serving on one.

She asked the Strobel case judge, District Court Judge Hume Cofer, to recuse himself because he had appeared prejudiced against her a month ago when, called for jury duty in Cofer's court, she had refused to take the oath, and offered a brief on why it was unconstitutional. He had had the bailiff remove her from the courtroom.

Cofer denied her motion.

Strobel's side was armed with a spate of news stories about Bloody Sunday. They showed that Madalyn systematically harmed people with malice and slander when it suited her.

During the week-long trial, Madalyn's staff and inner-circle volunteers held loyally together, ready to go to jail rather than produce records, as they believed Madalyn was absolutely correct about the unconstitutionality of the Texas oath law. Records were taken to Galveston and hidden in the camper of Gerald Tholen, director of the Galveston-Houston AA chapter.

Strobel won an $80,000 judgment — $20,000 of actual damages and $60,000 in punitive.

Madalyn writhed at the verdict. First, Irv showed up in court in embarrassing, mismatched clothing, and came across poorly on the stand. Friedman and Judge Cofer were fellow Jews who conspired to ruin her because she was anti-Zionist. Cofer allowed an illegal jury to be impaneled — poor, biased, ignorant, in over their heads, and malicious. Madalyn began sleeping poorly, jerking awake in the wee hours and running down the list of items swirling in the drain: their home, the Cause, Robin's tuition, the Center, the cars, their furniture, the dogs, Zula — all because, she said, of a weak son and a "nutty Jew" who both hated her.

She would appeal, of course, and she filed against the *Austin American-Statesman*, too, for jumping the gun on the original story.

Richard Bozarth, the new writer whose column was called the Laughing Atheist, arrived to work at the AA Center in the teeth of the Strobel crisis. The staff raced over to paint and repair Sinclair so it could be sold to satisfy the $45,000 needed for bond during the appeal. Two volunteers forked over $1,000 each. They worked all night to get out a "Circle the Wagons" emergency mailing to raise the bond.

That was when Bozarth discovered how paltry an audience he was writing to — instead of the 52,000 subscribers advertised in *Writer's Market*, the entire bundle — members plus subscribers — came to only 3,200. He confronted Garth, who guffawed that he'd been taken in.

It was a blow to Bozarth, but it didn't dim his admiration for Madalyn. You had to exaggerate to the media to get momentum.

Madalyn fired her attorney and hired her old divorce lawyer to fight the two judgments. She paid a $3,500 combined retainer, but told the staff and volunteers, who had come through magnificently with round-the-clock labor, loans, and donations, that it was $11,500.

It was an ill wind that blew no good, and Madalyn was rather enjoying the headlines, seeing her punchy quotes about the Austin religious and judicial establishments. There were always articles about her, almost daily, somewhere. She was right — none of the pretenders to the throne could command the media coverage she drew.

"**R**obin will be all right," Madalyn wrote in her diary. "She can absolutely make her own way. My stubborn, sensitive, warm, humor-filled wonderful Robin." Her darling was talented and intelligent, she wrote, "charming, feminine and beautiful and I love her with all my heart."

Madalyn addressed her letters to "Robin Bobbin," "Rob Bob" and "Redhead." When Robin got sick, she wrote, "You are a little Hawaiian flower and not meant for the cold climate ... " And she didn't want Robin bicycling on that busy road — "because you don't know what a beautiful and precious young lady you are."

But it also comforted her to vent to Robin, and she shared confidences that most parents wouldn't.

"That kike Judge," she wrote the girl in December, "I want to knee-cap him like the radicals do in Italy, shoot him in the knees, . . . and say to him then, 'there you son-of-a-bitch, that is your brand of justice.' "

And Garth, she complained, simply subsisted on gloom. "He had nothing to moan about" when more money than he'd hoped for came in the November mail. He was almost happy that the IRS announced an audit of his 1977 return — apparently because Bill had given "the Jew Friedman" a canceled AA check they'd used to pay Robin's tuition at Fenster — to show they were using donations illegally.

She wrote Robin about a "dumb bitch" who made computer errors, and how a couple at the Center had "oral genital sex . . . that makes my flesh crawl." Garth had told her about it; he called it "gobbling the goo." Robin wasn't yet 14. She also reported that a contractor repairing Sinclair had taken a whore in there. So Robin should know that, "Instead of fighting for the Constitution . . . we are bogged down in a morass of whores, nitwits, drunks . . . Robin, all we can trust is you and Garth and me. The rest of the world are enlarged pains in the ass and incapable of decent living."

She genuinely felt that way. Because of Bill's role in the Strobel matter, her little universe of trusted souls had shrunk to this. She felt she'd been betrayed by love.

A week before Christmas 1978, Madalyn, Garth, and Robin sat after dinner, listening to old records Irv had discarded, Nelson Eddy and Jeanette MacDonald and Judy Garland. Sipping Crown Royale, Madalyn gazed at her granddaughter. How beautiful Robin was, in her pink housecoat trimmed with lace and ribbon. Her burnished hair shone. And handsome Garth, in his manly striped robe, drinking Cutty Sark.

She and the kids traveled to Detroit for a Solstice fundraising party. As she expected, it was covered by print, TV, and radio, because she filed an injunction to stop the minting of the Susan B. Anthony dollar while her Motto suit was on appeal at the Fifth Circuit. The family returned to Austin and long days at the AA Center, and mailbags fat with donations. Madalyn had $50,000 in the bank, though she told the staff they were still $11,000 short of their $45,000 goal for the Strobel bond.

She was establishing that she didn't own anything, so she wouldn't be worth suing, and had put everything in Garth's and Robin's names. (Indeed, her attorney eventually convinced the judge that only Madalyn, not SOS or AA or CESAALA, could be sued for the PTA scuffle, and the Murchison case faded away.)

On Christmas Eve, after another long day of work, the trio stayed up late and followed what had become a tradition: watching *White Christmas* on TV. Later, alone and drinking, Madalyn picked up her diary, which she called "the half-assed story of my life at home," and excoriated herself for writing about trivia instead of intellectual and philosophical and social matters.

It was frightening to imagine under what lash she labored, that she could put in 18 hours seven days a week, and still expect to be writing noble thoughts in her diary at 1 a.m. It was a glimpse into the churning need that drove her without mercy. Alcohol — she had a "diet of bourbon and popcorn," said one employee, and another remembered her job interview, during which Madalyn pulled out a bottle of vodka and drank straight from it — helped explain her semi-diabetic spurts of rage and weight gain, but also how she got through her punishing days.

The next day, she treated Richard Bozarth and two other employees to dinner. Bozarth watched Robin. She was, he thought, "more lonely than any child should have to be."

Chapter 40 ~ The We of Us

AFTER CHRISTMAS, Garth drove with Richard Bozarth to California to get his furniture. Madalyn was angry about it, with so much work at the office, and Garth had to make up a story about wanting to visit some chapters on business. She wasn't fooled, but she let it go. They had been screaming at each other all during Christmas week.

As they drove and talked, Bozarth realized how badly Garth needed to get away from Madalyn and the Center, and just chatter endlessly. He didn't seem much interested in ideas; he talked about minutiae or parroted Madalyn's politics. He simply wanted to be heard.

Bozarth was moved at how trapped Garth was. When they got back to Austin, Madalyn lit into him for not calling frequently enough, making her worry about whether he was dead on the roadside in some bloody wreck.

"I could see the blows hit Garth," said Bozarth, though he tried to shrug off his mother's hostility and guilt-making.

But Garth would get even in ways that upset both Madalyn and the flow of work at the Center. Madalyn had him writing monthly editorials, but he would either refuse to write his column or be late. Often Madalyn had to write it herself or farm it out to the editor. It caused unbearable tension near deadline.

And his gloom-and-doom side set Madalyn's teeth on edge. She seldom allowed anyone to see it, lest a disaster ensue, like the time a wealthy supporter stopped by with his wife, who appeared drunk. For some reason, this made Garth feel he could open his heart to them, and he confessed that he and Madalyn were stealing from SOS. They had big cars that they didn't need or deserve. Madalyn paid their personal maid, Zula, out of corporate funds. They had ripped off the money for India — it was a vacation, not a working trip at all.

"I could have shit," Madalyn wrote Robin. "You know how Garth does…his black moods and his 'mea culpa.'" Garth did this periodically, and it infuriated Madalyn. "I feel that I earn every gawd-damn thing that I get," she told Robin.

He had no compunction about screaming at his mother, calling her a fucking idiot and other names; the mildest term he used for her was "Fat Madalyn."

Once, when he publicized an organizing trip to Salt Lake City, the Mormon church responded with a statement that America was intended to be a religious nation. Garth couldn't wait to tear them apart, and started working on a press release. But Madalyn got one out first. Garth, enraged, said he was going to reissue it, and Madalyn flew into a fury. "Fuck you!" she yelled at her son, and accused him of being too stupid or lazy to do anything right.

A few weeks after the trip with Bozarth, Garth went to the Houston Astrodome for a nighttime football game — a six-hour round trip — and Madalyn called the highway patrol when he wasn't home by 11:30. Working late while he recreated, she expected him to tear back to Austin the instant the game was over.

"The poor bastard owes everything to his mother," wrote Bozarth in 1989, " . . . his job, his celebrity, even his major ideas. I've never known anyone else as completely dominated by another person as Garth is by his mother."

She was even more controlling of Robin. In early 1979, she wrote TJS that she didn't want Robin taking taxis to her music lessons or the airport, because "any intemperate minority" might rape or rob her. "I don't want Robin alone in a cab with a lumpen proletariat black, for instance," she wrote.

She received a dry note assuring her that 100% of cabdriver crime in St. Louis was the drivers getting robbed.

She also wrote that she disapproved of TJS's "bizarre grading systems which are not in accord with those of other schools." They graded hard and didn't use a curve, and she was afraid Exeter wouldn't know that.

The Phillips Academies were well aware of Jefferson's grading standards, the school replied. Robin had, in fact, already been given an excellent recommendation, *on her own merit.*

Madalyn had embarrassed the girl by sending a blistering registered letter to Exeter, with several misspelled words — including one she used frequently and considered erudite, "Weltanschauung" (world view) — accusing them of ignoring Robin's application. She finally found out she'd sent it to the wrong Phillips Academy, Andover instead of Exeter. You understand, she explained, "I blow up more easily where she is concerned."

Her instructions to Robin on what to wear to the Exeter interview revealed how close a study she'd made of the East Coast dream that had had her in its grip since childhood: "solid brown brogans, good wool skirt of earth colors, tailored blouse with four buttons of matching neutral color like creme, good wool sweater, bulky coat — don't wear the cashmere — and don't wear any jewelry."

Before the 1979 convention, though, Robin got "the thin letter" from Exeter, as opposed to the fat acceptance packet stuffed with enrollment forms. Madalyn was devastated. She felt personally rejected. It didn't occur to her that her own actions might have had something to do with it. It was beyond her to envision the admissions committee passing around her letters virtually threatening a lawsuit if

Robin didn't get an interview, and debating, what happens if we let Robin in, and she gets an F?

She promised to "grind their noses" in it.

Madalyn's need for loyalty from employees and members tightened, too. When an ex-employee joined Anne Gaylor's rival Freedom From Religion Foundation, Madalyn hinted she'd fire anyone who stayed friendly with him. In January 1979, the media coordinator was sacked for refusing to witness an insurance declaration that listed two of the O'Hairs' dogs as employees.

"We must restaff the office again," Madalyn wrote glumly in her diary when the editor quit. "We try to hold it together with baling wire, wax and chewing gum. We get . . . flotsam and jetsam, pimps, whores, cunt lappers and nigger fuckers, hopheads, queers, weirdos, pinkos, drunks, glue sniffers and freaks. I'm absolutely totally fed up with all of them. I am tired of the crisis and tired of hunting for money . . . "

Foul and forbidden language was ever a release for her. Madalyn frequently referred to members as "her people," and she had a sobriquet for herself, Garth and Robin: "the we of us."

In early 1979, the Fifth Circuit Court of Appeals rejected the Motto suit, but admitted there was an issue. Madalyn, now headed for the Supreme Court, told reporters that when you put that kind of slogan on money, you have a theocracy. To her diary, she said, "I must bring down the religious establishment, must sever its hold on the heart of America."

On the wave of publicity, Garth scheduled talks, debates, and chapter organizing in Florida, Kentucky, Tennessee, Minnesota, Kansas, Pittsburgh, and Dallas. They took off in the RV again. Despite their screaming fights, which were quickly forgotten, Madalyn loved the intellectual camaraderie she had with Garth, his dry wit and self-sacrifice. Pasty and paunchy from his 16-hour days in harness, he enjoyed the road; driving and chatting.

Along the way, in every city, she kept hearing rumors of Bill being born-again, but nothing came of it.

She had almost decided to work with Larry Flynt and be interviewed by *Hustler*, and maybe write for him. She hated it, she told Robin, but she needed the money. In April, she and Garth were flying to see Flynt in Los Angeles; in the meantime, Madalyn sent "Rob Bob," barely 14, a copy of *Hustler* at school. Read it, she said. Help Grandma make a final decision whether to get involved.

But she didn't really care what Robin thought; she returned from Los Angeles with her mind made up. She was impressed with Flynt. First, he was valiant about his disability. The bottom half of his body was withered, and yet 35 people depended on this half-man for a job. His office was tastefully furnished, and he seemed genuinely interested in social reform. And he wasn't really legitimizing pornography, she rationalized. He was legitimizing sex. He took pictures of sexual organs of people willing to display them, and sold them to people who wanted to look at them, that's all.

By the end of spring 1979, she had lost or had remanded three of her four church-state separation suits, *O'Hair v. Blumenthal* (the Motto suit), *O'Hair v. Clements* (nativities on government sites in Texas), and *Hunter v. Dallas Independent School District*. Dallas teacher and AA member Bruce Hunter was deemed justifiably fired after years of atheist activism; the motto "In God We Trust" was ruled ceremonial, not religious; and the nativity was ruled a symbol of the nuclear family.

O'Hair v. Hill was a far more serious case. Madalyn loved legal research, it fit her mind, and she rather enjoyed the virtual all-nighters she was pulling in early May for her cases. *O'Hair v. Hill* was eminently respectable compared to the bingo and nativity suits, and not frivolous. With it, she could hold Jeff Friedman at bay for a long time.

She had three cases in the Fifth Circuit, one headed for the Supreme Court, one in U.S. Federal District Court, one in the Court of Appeals of Texas, two in Travis County District Court, one in the Court of Appeals in New Jersey, one in Ohio, and another case perhaps coming up in California — to do with the *Truth Seeker*, which had been gnawing at her for years.

She was also dealing with IRS audit deadlines, and filing deadlines for the various appeals. And trying to find money to send Robin to Europe for six weeks, and sewing summer dresses for her. There were freak torrential rains, and the roofs were leaking both at the Center and home; she and Garth had dug trenches in the downpour. She had house guests left over from the convention, magazine and newsletter mailing deadlines, phone interviews.

She sent Robin, who was in the middle of finals, two long legal briefs and asked her to take an evening off to read them. She trusted the 14-year-old's judgment more than the attorney's. She had already sent Robin a Supreme Court brief, and after these two, was going to send her two more. Robin was on the Center's mailing list and was expected to critique magazine articles and give feedback on problems at the Center. In fact, Robin would soon have her own office at the Center, furnished with her father's old desk.

Late into the wee hours at the end of May, sewing and listening to maudlin music, Madalyn reflected that she and Garth were just waiting for Robin to grow up so she could pitch in full time, and that meant two years of high school, four of college, and three of law school. She sighed. It was too long to wait.

She was worried about Robin getting enough math in "that stupid-assed school." She nixed summer school, she told Robin, as it was too long and was held at "Austin High School Niggersville." But she could get Bruce Hunter "to come down here and give you the first year of Algebra over one weekend if you can hack it."

It was preposterous — and aggressive. The underlying message was, you must prove you could've gotten into Exeter. Hunter was "a weasel," Grandma added, and repulsive, but it would only be for that one weekend.

One day, Val called. Bill had been sober six months, she said. Madalyn knew through Irv that they'd moved back to Houston, in what she described as a shack, with only Val's Volkswagen to drive.

Madalyn was still drowning in the Strobel mess they'd brought on her. How can you have the nerve to call, she asked Val, after what you did to me? Oh, she'd forgotten all about that stuff, said Val, that was in the past.

"How convenient for you!" Madalyn said, and slammed the phone down. They'd do it again if they had the chance, she told Robin, they would. Privately, she wrote that the whole thing broke her heart.

Then she got devastating news. On July 11, 1979, police answering a domestic disturbance call arrived at the Murrays' apartment to find Bill holed up with the baby, a rifle, and an empty scotch bottle.

He'd stayed up all night breaking his sober streak, and shoved Val out the door. When she returned with the police and tried to enter, he blasted a shot through the door. He surrendered after an hour.

At first, it rocked Madalyn, and once again, she had to explain her son to the members and staff. This time, she drew a hard line.

Yes, he was personable, handsome, intelligent, and all that, but he was an alcoholic, the bad kind. "Everyone in the family [has had] physical encounters with him, including his wives"; he raised money for Second Foundation and then drank it up; he raised money for his Tucson book store. Drank it up. Sold her mailing list to a bunch of racists (she was sure he'd peddled it to "Scurvy" Johnson). Drank that up. Garth and Robin were persecuted, too, and they didn't become alcoholics or abandon the Cause.

Underneath the comparison to Garth was a deep anguish that those close to Madalyn knew: Bill, a traitor, had women to burn, while good, solid, loyal, hardworking Garth had not even the whisper of one.

Madalyn never spoke to Bill again. Val kept in touch with Irv, and with Madalyn's trusted confidante in South Texas, Gerald Tholen, so she got news of his now daily visits to Alcoholics Anonymous. "That won't help him," she snorted.

Ironically, the meetings of this second "AA" in Bill's life always ended with the Lord's Prayer that had started the whole merry-go-round back in 1960.

Chapter 41 ~ The Anti-Christer

IN MID-SEPTEMBER 1979, Madalyn filed a high-profile suit to prevent the new pope, John Paul II, from holding an October mass on the Washington Mall. She asked for $10,001 in damages for deprivation of atheists' civil rights. This was unconstitutional entanglement of religion with government. Why the Mall, why land owned by the federal government? "If the Pope wants to say a Mass, he has places to do it." The Catholics were up to their ears in land, $162 billion worth.

There were three more masses, in Boston, Philadelphia, and Chicago; in Boston alone, the city council had voted $750,000. And the costs weren't just platforms and security and porta-potties. In Chicago, they were paying for stress tests to see if the roof of an underground parking garage near Grant Park would hold up under the 1.5 million people expected at the mass there. Totaled, the costs could reach $10 million, Madalyn estimated. There was no secular purpose here.

In fact, the visit was a show of solidarity over aid to parochial schools, and a constitutional amendment against abortion. It was the advancement of religious agendas on government property, comparable to the fundamentalist theocracy of Iran's Ayatollah Khomeini.

She helped spark protests in Boston and Philadelphia. The ACLU sued over Philadelphia's spending, and the city's archdiocese promised to repay the city $168,000 if it lost the case, which would be heard a week after the pope's visit. An old cohort of Madalyn's, Boston abortion activist Bill Baird, vowed a restraining order against that city's expenditure.

But the ACLU angered her by filing an *amicus* brief on the government's side (she sued the Interior Department, which oversaw the Mall), saying the DC Mall should be available for people to exercise their free speech rights. The First Amendment barred support for religion but also interference with it.

The religious establishment argued that the pope's visit was political, not religious. The church didn't get up and protest when the government spent thousands to protect and entertain visiting heads of Communist states. You didn't need to change the Constitution, for crying out loud.

But Madalyn's opponents never seemed to effectively nail how slippery the slope was to ordinary people. Editorials tried to use reason and logic, but in neighborhoods and small sanctuaries and prayer groups across the nation, ordinary people were asking, would this eventually mean you couldn't pray on sidewalks because they were paid for by tax dollars? Or have an Easter parade — wouldn't the street be public property? What if you got in a wreck and prayed on the side of the highway — wasn't that public right of way? What happened if someone walking through a public park heard a hymn coming out of a church? What if you *overheard* an astronaut praying in space in a broadcast? And even if you didn't overhear them, were they breaking the law if they prayed privately in their tax-funded space capsule?

Didn't the city impose building codes on the churches? Was that separation of church and state? It was okay for the city to do stress tests on a sports stadium for sports, but not for any other gathering? What about the people who just saw the Pope as entertainment, like a ball game or a parade? Entertainment was secular, right? So if the Pope was banned, then the secular entertainees' civil rights were denied, right?

What if you could prove that most people went to church to meet the opposite sex, or hear the music, not the sermon? Was that entertainment, or religion?

So what *was* it okay to do on the Mall, or the park? Something secular, maybe soccer? Well, what if it was a Christian soccer game? What if they prayed before they started?

Jane Conrad wrote Gordon Stein that Madalyn was highly intelligent and knew the Bible, but she had an "inability to reason why religion has evolved...and does answer questions for some people." (Unknown to Madalyn, Conrad and Stein were collaborating on an exposé about her.)

Why was it that humans persisted in the God-belief, why did they insist there was "something out there" to reach for, something everyone at the moment called God, but earlier had split up into Zeus and Athena and so on? Why was it that humans had done this throughout recorded history? And perhaps throughout their evolution? In order for humans to evolve, in fact, wasn't there that same reaching for something "out there," or something that "could be"? Like upright postures, and thumbs, for example — how did those come about, if not from some idea, some "vision"?

Could religion and spirituality — faith, if you will — be related to the same kind of "reaching" that produced changes in the genotype throughout evolution?

This insistence on something bigger, a "Higher Power," as Bill would come to call it in Alcoholics Anonymous before he called it God, this insistence — might it have a highly functioning place in human evolution? After all, everything around Madalyn that was a human invention, things produced by the science in which she had such limitless faith, had all just been ideas at one time. And by something very akin to faith, they had been made real, and given three-dimensional life.

So why did she so unreflectively draw the line at a God, or an afterlife? Humans were infinitely creative. If they could imagine, and then create, a rocket to the moon, why not a life after death? It seemed to boil down to the religious admitting they didn't know the limits of human creative consciousness, and the atheists declaring that they did.

At home in Texas, they said, well, first she tried to kick the baby Jesus out of the rotunda, and now this. That *woman!*

On October 1, her petition to stop the papal mass was denied, and two days later, Federal District Court Judge Oliver Gasch, who had already dismissed Madalyn's suit against the Pope himself — he was head of a foreign state and outside the jurisdiction of U.S. courts — also dismissed her suit against the National Park Service, clearing the way for the DC mass.

But the attention triggered a storm of activity at the Atheist Center, 12-hour days doing membership drives while the publicity was there, and funding appeals, different letters to different mailing lists. Madalyn was dieting for the TV appearances, plowing through piles of unanswered mail, vowing to finish two books before year's end. She was writing grants to fund the library, planning to hold not just a

national convention, but one for each chapter, plus an annual Summer Solstice picnic. She still wanted to get an atheist TV series up and running, and hold a World
Atheist Meet in December 1980 in India. She wanted each of the 33 chapters to
have its own abortion clinic to finance itself and "National."

On October 5, 1979, the Pope, a Pole, visited "the most Polish of American
cities," he called Chicago. He spoke strongly against birth control for the country's
49 million Catholics, 80% of whom practiced it anyway. The crowd was estimated
at over a million.

From across the street, 75 or so American Atheists protested the church's position
on abortion and gay rights and accused it of censorship, racism, and repression.
Their chirps were dwarfed by the 123 loudspeakers with 8,000 watts of audio, the
16-foot-high altar, the skyscrapers and parking lots crammed with gawkers, people
standing five hours because they were too tightly packed to sit down.

Tears were streaming down faces, people were crossing themselves. There was
three minutes of "long live the Pope!"

On January 23, 1980, the Third District Court of Civil Appeals returned the
Strobel case to the District Court for a new trial, saying Madalyn was right: Judge
Hume Cofer should have asked another judge to rule on her motion that he recuse
himself.

At the AA staff meeting, there was rejoicing. Madalyn felt sure Friedman would
lose interest now, even though he hated her guts. Usually a case like this would be
dropped from the docket in a year or two. She put Strobel out of her mind.

Two weeks later, in a summary judgment, U.S. District Court Judge Jack Roberts
affirmed Texas' right to have religious scenes and celebrations in the Capitol
rotunda. A plastic Jesus and a couple of camels did not amount to excessive entanglement. There had been a Jewish Festival of Lights program in the rotunda for
years as well.

Madalyn said she would schlep it to the Fifth Circuit in New Orleans as usual.
And she *had* managed to lay a chill on the festivities — there was less caroling in
the Capitol, she said, and a smaller Christmas tree last year.

Her in-house attorney, Paul Funderburk, had been making noises that he wanted
some of the money coming from the returned Strobel bond. Madalyn scalded him
at a staff meeting, detailing his incompetence and assuring him he'd get none of
the money.

Two weeks later, he was sacked in a fiery parting where police arrived at the
Center to find his framed certificates hurled into the parking lot, and Madalyn
screaming from inside, "I want that skinny, goggle-eyed son-of-a-bitch out of my
office!"

He filed assault charges, accusing her of threatening him with a club she called
a "Christian beater."

Chapter 42 ~ A Double Murder

DAVID WATERS never cared much for jobs. He preferred to scheme, to get money using his brains. "He thinks Manual Labor is the president of Mexico," laughed Cookie Nelson.

Immediately after David's release from jail in August 1978 for the beating of his mother, Marti was arrested at Belinda's Body Shop for violating Peoria's massage parlor ordinance — code for giving the wrong kind of massage. It seemed to come home to David that he'd married a working girl like his mother. Betty Ann Waters, Marti Ann Waters. Both tall, slender brunette prostitutes.

"He liked Marti going out there on the street and bringing in the money," said a friend, "but he blamed her for being a prostitute."

He and Marti had a stormy year after his release from prison. In February 1979, he started an affair with Carolyn Bruce, an educated, professional woman with a good job and a nice car who wrote poetry. "He said to me, 'this is your walk on the wild side. You've been a pampered, coddled person all your life...that's why you like me.' And there was something to that. There's nothing a woman likes better than a dangerous man." But he was also "one of the most intelligent men, had a great sense of humor, quick wit, very intellectual."

He told her he was the ringleader in the Gibbs murder. "It had nothing to do with...drugs or any of those things. It had to do with, that David felt, if he wanted to see what it was like to take a life, that he had the right to do that...He had no conscience when it came to taking another human life...His thing, just like he did to his mother, was torture. Once the actual killing started, that was the time when any of his victims would have been relieved."

He told her "he had a can opener and he popped [Gibbs'] eyeball out while he was alive, long before he was dead, he was disfiguring him, while he was unable to defend himself."

Marti was deeply hurt and jealous over Carolyn and other infidelities, and Cookie commiserated, hugged her, and drove her past Carolyn's house to throw rocks. She calmed Marti after her screaming matches with David. She saw him hit Marti some, and once he threw a chair at her, but then Marti could really dish it out. Once, during a drunken fight in the street at midnight, she hurled her purse at her husband and then pulled a gun. Cookie ran over and pushed her arm down, saying, "Don't shoot David, now calm down." She picked up the purse and scattered items and got the combatants inside.

David used Marti's profession against her: if it didn't bother her to sleep with other men, he argued, how could she think it meant anything to him to have other women? She violently rejected that; it wasn't the same. He was doing it for pleasure, for her it was a job. She made the ultimate statement on David's 32nd birthday in March of 1979. Knowing he was deathly afraid of spiders, she presented him with a prettily wrapped box containing a live tarantula. By the fall of 1979, she had moved in with a girlfriend, 32-year-old Cheryl Jo Block, who had a trailer in Danville.

On Wednesday, February 13, 1980, Marti and Cheryl headed for a male strip club to catch Sexy Rexy and Go-Go Gordie. After the show, they split up. Cheryl needed to have a discussion with her boyfriend, to whom she was giving the boot.

In the wee hours of Valentine's Day, two men driving home from a card game found Cheryl on the edge of a rural soybean field, beaten and stabbed to death. By 5:30 a.m., officers were at her trailer. Inside, they found 29-year-old Marti Waters dead on the kitchen floor.

Cookie was devastated; she and Marti had had a spat, and hadn't made up yet.

Cheryl's boyfriend, Charles Silagy, 29, was arrested in Louisville and charged with two counts of murder. They said he stabbed Cheryl over the breakup, and then went to the trailer, where Marti arrived to find him washing up. She demanded to know where Cheryl was, and when he was evasive, she picked up the phone to dial the police. He beat her with the phone and then stabbed her to death with a kitchen knife.

At Marti's funeral, David was "a mess," all broken up, said a friend. For some reason, he ordered an open casket, even though she was savagely stabbed. So many times, said Cookie, and "her face was all bruised, they had to put a lot of makeup on her. She was slashed down the side of her neck. She put up one hell of a fight."

The mourners gathered for a wake at Big 500, a bar across the street from the Peoria Police Department. "You never saw so many bikers bawling," said an observer. One of them, hulking Chico Osborne, was "crying harder than anyone."

One of David's acquaintances from before the Gibbs murder had become a born-again Christian, and tried unsuccessfully to convert him. Waters had no belief in God, afterlife, ghosts, or anything supernatural, but something happened the day of Marti's funeral that always made him wonder. He came back to his apartment, and was standing with another woman in the living room. All of a sudden, one of the casement windows burst violently open of its own accord. He'd never seen anything like that.

Cookie had no such limitations. She was sure the friend she'd always called "sister" would be there to meet her when she died.

Chapter 43 ~ In Vino Veritas

ON HER BIRTHDAY IN 1980, Robin wrote in her diary, "Here I am, 15 years of age and in 11th grade. And lonely. But I'm always lonely. I want to do everything. I want to be an Atheist leader, research biologist, doctor, lawyer, poetic, chef extraordinaire, mathematician, chemist, electrician, writer, and actress. Oh well, stick to the first and foremost. I'll be an Atheist leader."

She had a short haircut, and looked cute in her oversized glasses. Madalyn had gotten a similar cut, short and fluffy, that softened her jowls and gave a whiff of impishness.

Robin also wrote that she'd met the man of her dreams, a fellow student, Alexander Stevens — Lex. "Our minds fit together like two parts of a puzzle," she wrote. "I would not marry at all but I want to leave [children] to carry on the work of Atheism."

It wasn't long before her grandmother and uncle found out. "Garth said you've absolutely no spine [regarding Lex]," Madalyn scolded, "since you have been so dumb that you have entertained him night and day rather than do your school work ... Boy! I didn't let Richard pull shit like that. You are in training to be walked over by your final man that you marry ... *Yuk!*"

Robin began suffering "severe depression ... massive depression ... because I do not think that I will be able to be a half-decent Atheist leader ... I have a fear that I will go up to almost graduation from law school and then suddenly quit and fuck the entire thing up."

Indeed, she had taken up smoking, resigned as junior class representative, and dropped out of the honors track. Her teachers were mad at her, but she didn't care. "I mean, what does it matter? Who cares?" She had also stopped writing poetry, feeling she was no good at it. She skipped school, with Lex and a bottle of bourbon.

"Why do I refuse the things I want most? I am incredibly self-destructive and self-hating."

She reflected it was because "when I was young we were poor, but occasionally Gram would snatch a little money to get something for me. I would spurn the gift because it meant that the entire family had sacrificed something. The second thing is that I was always hated for being an Atheist, and therefore I developed a self-defense mechanism of pretending to hate what I always wanted — friendship."

During Robin's visits home, Madalyn and Garth noticed she got a slew of letters from friends at Jefferson. Curious — they couldn't go even two weeks without contact, Madalyn frowned. And there were letters from old classmates at the officially hated Fenster; what did that mean? Robin was assumed to have made no friends there.

But Robin was making friends, and slipping away. Madalyn would have been furious if she'd known that her granddaughter was spinning a long-distance love affair with an AA member she'd met at the last convention who was twice her age. He was keenly aware of what Madalyn would think of him courting her "lovely dumpling" — he only contacted Robin at school.

Madalyn's spirits were always lifted by her beloved kids, who were cooking together during Robin's spring break: mousse, mushrooms flambeau, meat dishes, soups. Not only was it delicious, but their "planning and doing together ... makes the house a snug harbor ... everything turns to magic. I come home and the lights are on and music is drumming and good smells come out of the kitchen. The house is occupied. The puppies run and bark and show their teeth," and her kids were gorgeous.

She wondered where Bill was. He had been charged with attempted murder in the shooting incident, but the charge was reduced to assault because the police officer hadn't identified himself. All she ever wanted for her kids was a life of reflection and critical thinking, education, a nice home, music, good cars and clothing, nice beds, a piano.

Madalyn gained weight during the convention that year, and felt ill. They weathered a tornado driving home, and arrived to find a summons to appear in Judge Brock Jones' court for disrupting the city council in 1977.

She hadn't been able to get this suit dismissed with *O'Hair v. Hill*, and just before the convention, the U.S. Supreme Court had rejected her request for a federal trial. Now it would be useful in forcing the issue of a required God-belief into court. One of the county attorneys even said publicly that the issue was going to have to be confronted sooner or later. And she still had a suit before the Fifth Circuit to determine whether the council's prayer was legally part of a public meeting.

Back home after the AA convention, Madalyn got a letter from Bill. Struggling with profound changes in his life, he'd sat down to write after reading about some raucous events at the convention. Madalyn had read Bible passages she said were pornographic and set forth a sample Easter dinner gleaned from Leviticus: "And ye shall eat the flesh of your sons and the flesh of your daughters." At the convention banquet, the speaker was a stand-up comedian with a routine so crude that the stone-faced hotel waiters refused to bring in the rest of the food until he was done. Madalyn strode up, seized the mike and declared, "As far as I'm concerned, they can take their fucking food and shove it up their ass!" and stalked out with a group of diners to order take out.

"A sudden rush of sorrow and pity filled me," Bill wrote, "because I understood. I understand the hatred and self-pity you feel. Sometimes I still have those faults." He forgave her, he said, "for the heritage you have given me and your grandchildren ... [that] does not leave time for love, meditation and happiness. I am sorry for any harm I did to you while fighting to live a somewhat normal life." He could no longer use the bottle to escape; he'd found that others came from much worse situations, and overcame or accepted it. And that's what he was going to do.

Since the shooting incident, he had held to his 12-step program while his marriage dissolved. Then, on the night of January 24, 1980, he had a nightmare that ended with a great Winged Victory pointing his sword-tip at an open Bible; its hilt bore the words "In Hoc Signo Vince" — By This Sign, Conquer. Bill went out and bought a Bible.

Over the next weeks, he humbly confessed his sins and asked forgiveness in Jesus' name. His hatred for his mother melted. He wanted to apologize to his wives and children for failing them.

And to his country: a month after writing Madalyn, he mailed letters of apology to the cities of Baltimore and Austin for his role in removing prayer from schools, and in setting the Atheist Center on its feet and helping his mother build her "personal empire." Thirty-three years of his life had been wasted. He hoped he could spend the rest correcting some of the wrongs he had helped create, that set his country on a path of deadening secularism.

Atheism was negative; given the choice of tearing something down or building something positive, atheists chose the former every time. If religious groups ever stopped charitable works, he concluded, atheists would not fill the void.

When he was finally brought to his knees, his craving for alcohol and cigarettes vanished, and the simple miracles of gratitude and peace replaced them. He overcame violent and suicidal thoughts. He forgave the Christians who had taunted and bullied him back in Baltimore. He didn't hate his mother; he pitied her.

The apology letters were published just in time for Mother's Day. Every major media outlet carried them — it was all over the country. Madalyn called a staff meeting and passed out a statement to read if the media waylaid any of them. It said jauntily that atheists across the globe were happy to see Bill get "some of that religious scam money" and that Madalyn was looking forward to tithes from him, since it was his attacks on her generating the income.

That night, it started pouring rain. Despite her public bravado, Madalyn sat at home alone — Garth was on another organizing road trip — devastated and confused.

"What a Mother's Day present from my son," she mourned in her diary. A day or two later, Garth called from Chicago and told her Bill was to be on Tom Snyder that night.

"With what trepidation I turned the TV on," she wrote, " . . . what mixed feelings I have about Bill. There he sat, a treacherous dog . . . he saw himself as a person who had changed the culture of America. He used the prestige Garth and Robin and I have slaved for."

He wore a threadbare suit, she wrote, and stammered. Her pulse raced as she watched. But "I can't get emotionally involved any more. I can't take it."

He would disappoint her in every one of the ways she'd feared. Soon he would rip away the veil over his and Garth's illegitimacy, and reveal that she'd never been married to either father. There were no hooks in him any more.

The storming, lightning, and hard-blowing rain continued for a week, while the media conducted interview after interview with him. Madalyn was thrown into nostalgic reveries about the Hayesville farm, the morning Bill was born, Baltimore, Kerpelman, Pup — and the phone rang off the hook.

In the massive publicity that followed Bill's conversion, Representative Phillip Crane of Illinois gathered with some 30 conservative legislators and a group of preachers. They held a planning meeting to override the 1963 prayer decision by removing school prayer from the courts' jurisdiction. It was another of scores of such attempts since June 17, 1963.

Bill spoke at the meeting, describing his spiritual journey of the past year. At the press conference next day, the group applauded and flashbulbs went off as he stood under a large "In God We Trust" sign. He would soon launch the William J. Murray Faith Foundation, aimed at rebuilding the faith component of secular life through education.

The atheist community thought he was lying. Dr. Frank Zindler, an AA insider who taught biology and geology, and translated scientific patents and scholarly articles in dozens of languages, said it started with the shooting incident.

"Bill drew one of these judges who, if he had a young person in there, he'd make them go to church — you know. And now somehow Bill is doing the Good Work instead of going to jail." The religious conversion "came a suspiciously short time after the arraignment . . . three weeks later Bill Murray was in Washington, being introduced to a Senate committee by Jesse Helms."

It wasn't three weeks from the shooting incident to the public apology; it was almost a year. But that didn't rule out a conspiracy, and some of Madalyn's loyalists wondered — had he even perhaps been a mole in her organization, for the government? How did he suddenly get all those big-time connections — Strom Thurmond, Jesse Helms? As his autobiography would soon make clear, he seemed at home in the world of double-dealing and intrigue.

It was a good year for apologies and conversions, the *Washington Post* noted. Everyone from Nixon henchmen to Stalin's daughter was saying they were sorry for their role in some immoral debacle. Bill himself had received tons of letters and two book offers. He had been on television nonstop. He finally resigned his job as an aviation consultant to handle all the interview and speaking requests.

But he denied any born-again sensationalism. "My eyes did not turn glassy and I didn't pick up a Bible and run into the streets to convert others," he said — it was gradual, organic, and painful. He had to look at his life, had to admit he'd been born into strife and negativity. He had to get his own identity.

Bill wrote Robin a long letter, apologizing, he said, "for ever dropping her off at that house." Neither it nor the steady stream of letters and cards he sent over the years to follow was ever answered. Sometimes they were mailed back to him torn into pieces.

He got a letter from Lester Buttram, saying he'd always wanted to be friends, he'd always prayed for Bill and his family, even while Bill was suing him. He was getting a lot of calls about whether Bill was sincere. Could they talk? Just to touch base before he got behind Bill with his people. (He did get behind Bill with his people; his son ended up on Bill's board of directors.)

Madalyn used the publicity to file a suit she'd been contemplating, to rid taxpayers of the chaplains whose prayers we were forced to buy for Congress. She would have Garth do it. On June 12, 1980, *Murray v. Buchanan* was filed. Garth sued the

U.S.A., the Congress, House Speaker Tip O'Neill, Vice President Walter Mondale, and the House and Senate chaplains. The chaplains got free cars, Social Security and retirement benefits, franking privileges, $90,000 salaries — if this wasn't government benefiting religion, what was it?

Madalyn found that all she had to do was pick up the phone, and the media would respond. Right after her chaplain suit was filed, someone shot at Garth's car. She called the police, and it immediately hit the wires.

Chapter 44 ~ Greystone Sanctuary

ROBIN MADE IT UP to her grandmother for her scholarly lapses born of love, depression, and sloth. By the time her bleak report card reached Austin, she was back on track. She was offered a full ROTC scholarship. Several universities had written because of her astronomical PSAT and SAT scores. "The teachers are convinced that I should go to Harvard," she wrote in her diary. She had already been accepted to Brown University.

That should have put Madalyn on cloud nine, considering the whipping she felt she'd personally taken over the Exeter rejection. But as the day of Robin's freedom drew near, she made an abrupt about-face. Suddenly, UT looked just fine. She didn't tell Robin yet. Consciously or unconsciously, she knew that Robin going off to Harvard or Brown would be the death of "the we of us."

Robin worked at the Center all summer, the way Madalyn and Garth did, 12 and 15 hour days. She updated the computer, organized the library, worked on magazine layout, did research. She cooked, wrote poetry, and kept up a blizzard of letters with her friends from school.

Garth was having little success on his organizing tours, calling home with black, bilious, disillusioned reports. Madalyn knew it wouldn't work. She'd told him that.

She was planning a media tour herself, traveling to Atlanta and Los Angeles, being interviewed in Cleveland, and by the BBC in Washington. She'd hand-carried a motion to the Supreme Court asking them to enjoin the Fifth Circuit in New Orleans from opening with a prayer when it heard *O'Hair v. Hill* on July 16. They declined to hear her motion.

At home, she found that the Audi Robin was supposed to have for school had been stolen, the Center's signs vandalized, and one of the Cadillacs shot at. One night, vandals sprayed the Center with paint and blew BBs into some windows. Fed up, Madalyn erected a chain link fence with barbed wire along the top.

"I am so fucking sick and tired of this that I could take a sub-machine gun and kill hundreds and hundreds of the chicken fuckers," she wrote. Austin was no longer the sweet, safe haven she'd found in 1965.

She was immensely frustrated at not getting to travel or write her books, like McCabe and Ingersoll and Elizabeth Cady Stanton and Susan B. Anthony got to do. She loved research, and the words and ideas poured out when she was able to snatch a little time, but most of it was spent raising nickels and dimes and doing menial chores.

She was in despair about the Center's lack of a plan, a vision, but there was simply no time. She had vision to burn, but she was stuck typing, doing data entry, just coping from crisis to crisis.

She uncorked a spurt of venom at her employees: "We have *no one* to work in that office," she wrote, "but scums, chicken fuckers, fags, masturbators, dumb niggers, spicks, witless cunts, derelicts, lumpen proletariat and transvestites..."

In truth, even with the turnover, she consistently attracted well-educated, intelligent, willing, skilled staff who were tolerant of her outbursts, even if they had some eccentricities and came to work covered with cat hair. The problem was not the quality of the help, but her inability to relinquish authority.

She was hopelessly behind on correspondence, and now the half-hour television show she was finally ready to launch would be another huge drain of her time. She decided Garth would have to do it. It started on community access cable in July 1980 as *American Atheist News,* and later became *American Atheist Forum.* She hoped it would double membership by the end of the year, but it didn't work out that way.

As Madalyn's cases entered the pipeline of appeals and the interviews tapered off, she, Garth, and Robin spent the rest of the summer quietly, working at the Center, and house-hunting. They prepared their old properties for sale, moving Irv from Sinclair into an apartment.

Robin would be sorely missed when she went back to Jefferson for senior year. Everything seemed to go better when she was home. Madalyn realized she actually couldn't get along without Robin now. The girl could handle anything at the Center—besides cooking gourmet meals and taking care of the dogs.

Before Robin left for school, they found the perfect house, and Madalyn signed loan papers in mid-September. It was on Greystone Drive, in an upscale area of north Austin.

To Madalyn, it was the epitome of class: fireplace, wood paneling, formal dining room with a brass-and-crystal chandelier, large kitchen with double sinks, stylish yellow formica, and tons of mahogany cabinets. It suited her public image, and if she died tomorrow, the kids would be set up. She filled it with her ideals of the good life: leather sofas, Tiffany-style lamps, canopy beds with matching spreads and curtains, brass fireplace tools, heavy brocade drapes with swags, and a model ship on the mantel.

She and Garth spent October hanging paintings and mirrors, stocking the kitchen, planting flowers. They shopped together in the most domestic way, buying sheets, towels, crystal stemware, candles to match the rugs. By Thanksgiving, it was snug and orderly for Robin's break.

At Jefferson, Robin was acing her National Merit Scholar essay, getting honors in calculus and history, and writing of her confusion about Lex. She documented their agonizing courting dance, the acts of revenge, torment, and jealousy they threw at each other. She felt a jumble of protective affection, intellectual companionship, jealousy, sexual feelings — and was always in agony over whether to "go back" to him or not.

She'd been propositioned for a sexual liaison by another boy. "I don't love him — but what the hell, sex is sex."

She was doodling names for her children: "Eva Alice Murray-O'Hair, Justin Alexandre Murray-O'Hair, Alexandra Maxine Murray-O'Hair," but there was no hint of a father's surname.

The perfect lover, she wrote, would be someone "who doesn't particularly need me and whom I don't particularly need...there would be no encroachments on personal territory...The right to say 'Get lost!' and still be loved." It was an echo of Madalyn's 1965 *Playboy* interview.

Madalyn closed the Center for 10 days in December, and the family spent it visiting old sites in Pennsylvania, Ohio, and Maryland to do genealogy research — she was in a fever to get into DAR, Daughters of the American Revolution.

Here's what she'd uncovered, she wrote a cousin: the first colonist to set foot on U.S. soil was a Mays, there was a Mays on every boat that came to colonize the New World, most as "either the captain or the first mate or the second mate," the first minister to set foot on U.S. soil was a Mays, one of the Mayflower wives was maiden-named Mays, plus there were Mayses at Jamestown.

"I am absolutely delighted...a Mays was at the Battle of San Jacinto which established Texas as a nation." She was going to publish a book about this illustrious history and make sure it was in every library: *The Mays* [sic] — *First Family of America.*

They loved coming back to their splendid home. They spent the rest of Robin's Christmas vacation painting, waxing floors, picking out dishes and furniture. Madalyn felt guilty about neglecting the Center, and considered abandoning the Cause and shutting it down. But deep down, she knew the flow of stress and work was what held "the we of us" together.

On February 1, 1981, the Fifth Circuit ruled against Madalyn in the suit to ban prayers at public meetings, *O'Hair v. Cooke,* and she announced she would appeal to the Supreme Court. She had also lost the nativity suit to ban crèches in the Capitol rotunda in the Fifth Circuit. But on *O'Hair v. Hill* — the Texas constitution's supreme being matter, the court wasn't ready to rule. The outcome could affect her charge on disrupting the city council meeting, the Strobel case, and any others filed against her. (On April 2, the court ruled against Madalyn, and then recalled its decision a month later. It wanted to reconsider.)

During this time, something happened to drive a final wedge between Irv and Madalyn. None of the employees could ever understand why she defended him. He seemed to hate his sister and tried to sabotage her work. They concluded that she wanted him around as a pipeline to Bill, who was working on a *Mommie Dearest* book; the scuttlebutt was that Irv had plenty of dirt to contribute. The exact nature of his grip on her was never revealed, but when he mentioned retirement, "Garth blew up like a pressure cooker and . . . Madalyn accused me of attempting to extort money." Garth called him an "old cocksucker" and said, "We've been paying you hush money ever since your arrival."

The next day, he found a letter from his sister suspending him for three months. If he wished to return after May 31, it would be at the lowest level. He would have no special family status at the Center.

Irv went home to his apartment to find his utilities cut off. He called Bill, who came and took him back to Houston.

Privately, Madalyn had such a severe anxiety attack over it that she felt compelled to explain in the newsletter, without elaborating, that she'd jettisoned Irv because of some "unspeakable" things he'd gotten involved in. She said she foisted him off on Bill, who was making a fortune as a born-again Christian. So he wasn't out on the street.

The spring of 1981 brought several large donations for computers, over $40,000. Madalyn bought bookcases, filing cabinets, half a steer for the deep freeze, tickets to Greece and Egypt to celebrate Robin's upcoming graduation.

Impulsively, she bought an outdoor grill and new patio furniture. They seemed like an investment in some deathless dream of getting out from under the crush of work at the Center, of erasing the black puffy bags under Garth's eyes, his ulcers, indigestion, discouragement, and exhaustion.

Chapter 45 ~ High Hopes for Mankind

O NE OF MADALYN'S MAGAZINE CONTRIBUTORS and a Virginia chapter organizer, ex-Mormon David Kent, had written an exposé on Mormonism called "Joseph's Myth" for AA magazine. When he offered to work for Madalyn in late April, she gushed, "Mygawd! . . . If you are as good as you sound . . . if you are not a one-eyed, spaced-out, long-haired, dirty, freakish, ill-clad and smelly, delirium tremens possessed jerk, you may be our man." He could write, proofread, typeset, do calligraphy, design, layout. He was a serious amateur astronomer and professional genealogist to help with her DAR application; he also worked as a tax examiner for the IRS. He had delivered each of his several children in home births. He was a walking library, and devoted to spreading the message of atheism.

Kent exemplified the kind of love-hate relationship Madalyn had with the competent people she attracted. She needed their skills, but was uncomfortable with people as smart as she. Employees like Kent were the type to notice things like outgoing mail addressed to a Swiss bank. Nor did they need the comradeship of profanity and vulgarity the Founders and certain employees enjoyed. Madalyn liked to test people that way, and shortly after Kent's arrival, announced at a staff meeting that she would, as he delicately put it, "personally perform a sexual act" on any atheist who would donate $1,000.

"She'd say these provocative things and a lot of people didn't know how to respond," he remembered. "If you agreed with her, she'd likely fire you the next day."

But she needed Kent; the newsletter pickings were getting slimmer and the type larger, and every issue complained about too much work and too little money. The Center and its publications, and all Madalyn's schemes, were in gridlock. There were too many half-baked ideas kicked into gear, too many projects dropped in the middle to go handle something else. They were over their heads and far behind in transferring IBM records to their expensive new CADO computer system.

They also badly needed Robin. Madalyn aimed for her to finish college by age 19.

"Garth and Gram," wrote Robin hotly in her diary before graduation, "have flatly forbid me to go to any other college than the University of Texas. I have decided to ignore them and go to any college I damn well want to. Garth accused me of loving neither my family nor Atheism."

After a three-week family vacation in Greece, she started summer school at UT the first week in July 1981, as her friends jetted off to Brown, Princeton, Tufts, Swarthmore, Yale. She was getting chatty letters about trips abroad, museums in the great cities, Lex seen all about in his new silver Mustang, the Met, Shakespeare in Central Park, guess who I ran into in Boston. These were the bastions Madalyn had taught her to storm, and she'd earned it, but now she was trapped in Austin to grind out course credits ASAP and work in the sweltering Center.

Grandma bought her a Rolex watch.

Madalyn wrote incessantly about how to disentangle from the Cause, but she had Garth at the Center, doing electrical work, laying tile in four rooms, painting, and making files. At home he was slated to paint the house trim, do lawn work, and clean out the gutters, but Madalyn had to ask Sam Miller; Garth couldn't fit it in with his regular duties of paying bills, budgeting, ordering, installing, making appointments, arranging contractors, making repairs, coordinating, chauffeuring, organizing, fund-raising, audio and video taping, computering, giving Madalyn her insulin shots, trip research and ticket buying, getting the cars fixed and washed. Every time Garth left for a trip, Madalyn wished he'd hurry up and come home.

That year on his birthday, Garth had to stamp his foot and demand some presents and a cake, or be ignored as in the past. Robin and Madalyn, contrite, rushed to accommodate with dinner, flowers, and champagne. One gift was a dog they suggested he name Dudley; he named it Ginger.

Madalyn really did appreciate Garth, when she stopped long enough to notice he was sick, or when he was gone and her honey-do list swelled. She loved him deeply; unlike her husbands, father, and Bill, faithful Garth delivered. He never tried to take over, never abandoned her, emotionally or physically. He went shopping with her for things like dish towels and garbage cans. No man, husband or firstborn, could hope to compete with Garth. And yet she didn't respect him.

All she wanted was for "my kids . . . to live, get educated, love, reproduce and continue the cycle while they try to ameliorate the condition of mankind." "We have . . . high flown hopes for the nation, for all people — for mankind" — but mankind just turned a deaf ear.

In October 1981, James Hervey Johnson had an arson fire in one of his buildings in California, and reportedly most of the records of the Truth Seeker Corporation went up in smoke.

"So, there goes all that atheist money," Madalyn mourned. She wrote, addressing him as "Hervey" like his friends did. How tragic, what could you say? It was just "terribly upsetting and unnerving." How about turning the Truth Seeker Corporation over to her? "There is no one or nothing but . . . me" that could handle it.

He cordially declined, saying the Truth Seeker was solvent and would continue as before. The rebuff angered Madalyn, but it would be a year and a half before she showed it.

O'Hair v. Hill had been reheard in September in the Fifth Circuit, and Madalyn was pleased to see AA picketers protesting the opening prayer. Twenty-four judges from the circuit listened to arguments, and Madalyn thanked her supporters for wearing suits and showing "dignity and decorum." She planned to file identical cases in Pennsylvania and Tennessee, which had similar statutes requiring belief in a supreme being to hold office.

In mid-November 1981, the Supreme Court declined to review Paul Marsa's case on prayers at a New Jersey town's council meetings. Marsa bitterly addressed the next council session: they no longer needed to meet, he said, they could just pray for what they wanted.

A few days later, reminiscent of Marsa's situation on Bloody Sunday, the Los Angeles chapter of AA disintegrated because of an abusive letter from Jon Garth.

He'd written Dick James, the director, that the Founders were coming out to attend the chapter Solstice party and fix what they considered James' botched job on a nativity case in Santa Monica, and they needed a place to stay and some transportation. James, reportedly wealthy from a mail-order business that included sex toys, asked if he should get publicity.

"No, Bozo," wrote Garth, "we will just sit and play with a rubber doll out of your catalog. Of course you should, and *now.*" He berated James for also botching a chore he'd requested, and suggested he take lessons from an Arizona chapter head Garth liked; "... we should go to Tucson's party where we can meet some real Atheists and not a bunch of sniveling humanists or rationalists or libertarians (or Gen. Hershey Bars)."

The LA chapter leaders all resigned. Los Angeles was the largest of AA's 47 chapters, with 800 members. But far from reining Garth in, Madalyn wrote a long letter of "personal outrage," characterizing the soreheads as wannabes who, trailing the stench of pornography, had insinuated themselves into a dignified operation to seek legitimacy.

David Kent, the Center's office manager, laughed at the pornography smear. It wasn't that. Madalyn and Garth feared a coup from James' growing coterie. "Up to then, Madalyn thought [his livelihood] was a terrific joke." And indeed, soon after, Madalyn began working seriously with Larry Flynt.

Despite the signs of deterioration in the organization, Thanksgiving 1981 was good for Madalyn, with friends over and her kids cooking happily together, filling the house with delicious smells. She would watch Garth and Robin, and think how much she loved them, how delightful and witty and honest and good they were. She liked watching them ahead of her in the movie line, she wrote, or getting their coats to head off to the store together. Just looking at them made her happy.

And sad, because actually, they were a perfect couple. Seeing the perfection and knowing it was her handiwork always brought home to her that they had no mates, no life outside "the we of us."

Chapter 46 ~ Mommie Dearest

I N THE EARLY SPRING OF 1982, letters flew in the freethought community about Bill Murray's upcoming autobiography, *My Life Without God*. Madalyn warned her readers that it would be full of lies, and she would be pictured as "a drug-ridden drunken, money-grabbing, insensitive, ego-manic, abusive, sluttish, whore."

Jane Conrad, Gordon Stein, Walter Hoops, Jacques Musy (a Florida retiree who had been stiffed in 1964 on a loan to Madalyn's bail fund), Roy Torcaso, who had competed with Madalyn in the early years, Jo Kotula, and other old-timers were writing back and forth, documenting their experiences with Madalyn over the years. Stein, editor of the *American Rationalist*, had become the clearinghouse for contributions from Madalyn's exes. Richard Bozarth had self-published a diary of his years at the AA Center, and was working with Stein to distill it into an exposé to be called "A Mouth That Roars."

A plan was afoot to help get Jane Conrad's small volume, *Mad Madalyn*, out by the time Bill published. Stein also got a letter from Irv, saying, "I am the one who, in collaboration with a good free lance writer, could really bust Madalyn's gut."

Bill's publisher, Thomas Nelson, had hired a ghost writer from California, but when Bill read the first sunlit, soft-focus chapters about Baltimore, he called the editor.

"This won't work," he said. "You don't get it — I had a horrible, dysfunctional family." He sat down and wrote the book himself.

His first four chapters made them so nervous they hired a private detective to check out his story, and flew Irv in from Dallas for a video deposition. Irv confirmed everything. "He told us some things *you* didn't know," the editor told Bill.

Madalyn heard Irv was involved, and she wrote a threatening letter to Thomas Nelson. She was working on her own book, *Jesus Christ, Super Fraud,* preparing for a showdown with Bill. In the meantime, she sent a summary to her attorney about Bill, setting forth his every wart, character flaw, failure, cruelty, weakness, and treachery.

A *Third Coast* magazine writer showed up to do a story on the Center. It was buzzing and orderly, a computer spitting out membership labels in one room, the typesetting equipment occupied in another; neat stacks of books, magazines, flyers and pamphlets in the book room; the law room with texts lining the walls, the financial room, the TV and radio rooms, and the Stevens Library full of atheist and freethought books, pamphlets, old newspapers, picket signs and slogans, the memorabilia of Madalyn's lectures and appearances, historic family photos, letters, cartoons, and paintings. Madalyn had five books ready for printing and binding.

Her office was filled with paintings of animals. Her desk was enormous, stacked with piles of papers and books. She was writing "the definitive work on intellectual freedom...the Magna Carta for the future of Atheists," she told the magazine reporter.

Garth was interviewed too, with his speech impediment and expensive casual clothes. For the media, he was Jon. At first he gave the routine party line, but then relaxed and began to enjoy the interview. He loved to ramble, and he leaned back, stretched out his legs, and became expansive and funny, unveiling his dry humor.

The more he chuckled and opined, the more Madalyn found it necessary to come lumbering down the hall to poke her head into the room, urging him to hurry up. They needed to go together to buy a wedding gift, and they needed to do it pretty much exactly during the time Jon was enjoying being in his own skin.

The reporter asked him about Madalyn, what about her human side? He struggled with the concept. "Being an atheist is first," he finally said. It ruled how they saw movies, where they dined, what they read. Their lifestyle was "an asocietal existence."

The previous fall, arguments had taken place in the U.S. Court of Appeals in DC, on *Murray v. Buchanan,* the chaplain case. The lower court had said Congress managed its own internal workings and taxpayers didn't have standing to challenge them. Madalyn countered that they did when Congress used public money to violate the First Amendment. Now, on March 9, 1982, the Court of Appeals agreed, and reinstated the case.

Ruth Bader Ginsburg wrote the opinion — that Congress was not immune from judicial review when its actions concerned constitutional issues. The case went back to the trial judge, Louis Oberdorfer, in U.S. District Court.

The decision got lots of attention; legal commentators thought it would expose Congress' every item of legislative housekeeping to scrutiny as long as some constitutional issue could be raised. And the dissenting judge, George MacKinnon, said an "incidental expenditure" of $80,000 should not have been sufficient for the atheists to get into federal court.

On May 12, the Fifth Circuit, the full panel, issued a decision in *O'Hair v. Hill*. It reversed the earlier courts and ordered a trial on Madalyn's contention that it was illegal for the Texas Constitution to make public officials acknowledge a supreme being — and on her contention that her council disruption suit and four other civil suits should be dismissed.

It was almost unanimous, a huge win for Madalyn.

(The three dissenters said her complaint "rambled on" about likes and dislikes, and demanded over $5 million for injured feelings, but she never brought forth one atheist who had been barred from office or denied jury service.)

She was elated, and even said "hallelujah" to the press — "praise the Lord" in Hebrew. The sweetest thing was besting U.S. District Court Judge Jack Roberts, who'd thrown the case out in 1978. Intensely annoying was that Roy Torcaso's 1961 Supreme Court victory in an almost identical Maryland precedent was constantly trotted back out for comparison, and Madalyn felt it made hers look derivative.

She was emboldened to expand her chaplain suit from Congress to the armed services. Bill was on a book tour all summer, constantly in the headlines, and she and Garth raised money for these activities in his slipstream.

Bill said misguided bureaucrats had taken the 1963 decision and turned it into a tool of religious persecution. Bibles were taken out of school libraries; why? Christmas pageants were gone; in Lubbock, Texas, a group of school kids was suspended for praying on the lawn. This was not what the high court intended, he said.

Just as religion's tendrils in school had fattened on students getting religious instruction in Vashti McCollum's time, so the 1963 decision had, conversely, metastasized to absurdities like threatening to expel a junior high kid who prayed at the bus stop. High schools in Virginia and Maryland, Bill claimed, allowed student newspapers to advocate abortion and homosexuality, but no Christian rebuttal. Kids were free to form school clubs to "discuss the violent overthrow of our government, but a group of Baptists can't use the rooms at all." Teachers couldn't wear jewelry in the shape of a cross or star of David.

The Communist Party and KKK were legally entitled to meet in public buildings — but not the Baptist Fellowship. Madalyn's Denver chapter, Bill reported, was trying to block the conversion of two empty federal warehouses into homeless shelters, simply because they'd be run by the Catholic archdiocese.

Freedom of speech, press, and assembly were being threatened by this bigotry; it seemed the secular humanists and atheists were just as vociferous about claiming the hearts and minds of the young as the religionists they'd unseated.

His book, selling well, was often described as a vendetta against his mother. It seemed too much to believe that Madalyn had actually asked Bill to kill his grandfather, or that she'd lured Susan Abramovitz into her son's bedroom. It was unseemly that he told about his mother's crazy moods, tantrums, promiscuity, and boozing, that he thought of her and Garth as "two fat pigs waiting for the spike" after he'd stormed out of their life. Wasn't this a bit harsh?

"I have told the truth," he replied.

He wasn't trying to ruin Madalyn, he said, just explain, and deliver hope to others that they weren't alone. "I don't know whether it's anger I feel about my mother, or whether it's sorrow. I guess it's a feeling of pity . . . I want my mother to find salvation."

Madalyn now always referred to Bill in her diary as a loser or son-of-a-bitch. There was no more sentimentality about him, even when she was drunk.

Something — perhaps Bill's arguments were hitting home, or he was getting too much attention — brought out a terrible agitation in Madalyn. It was much worse than when he announced he'd found God.

Politics had always been her love, and since Bill's book had come out, more political articles had been creeping into AA magazine — nuclear arms, foreign policy, Congress — alongside the traditional pieces on church-state separation, freethought history, and the pagan roots of Easter. Usually her diary was about daily life, but during Bill's season in the sun, she wrote incessant tirades against the nation's leaders, full-scale toxic geysers, spewing immense rage, negativity, exaggerations, and self-pity.

It was disturbing to see Bill circling around the centers of power in Washington. He had been photographed with President Reagan two years ago, and she wrote that it hurt to see laurels heaped on him while she got her face shoved in "shit." She wrote scornfully, over and over, what a fool he was to let himself be used by the fundamentalists. She depicted him as an idiot with his feet stuck in flypaper, who thought he was James Bond.

It was astounding how, at the end of a 15-hour workday, she could sit down and pump out page after page of violent, spurting acid that seemed to bring no relief, just more burning and poison. Her culture "stunk," as did the common people, the whole society. She blasted corporate failure, the economy, Reagan, the "world situation," inflation, banks, Israel, South America, the budget, the Soviet Union, defense policy, the stock market. "Reagan is quite mad," she would write frequently; banking policy was "quite insane." Our leaders "spew shit."

She was so bitterly enraged at Reagan that if the government had seen her diary, she would have been put on a watch list. In fact, during a 1982 visit to New Zealand, she attacked Reagan so venomously on a radio appearance that the American embassy called to say it was monitoring the station.

Reagan's economic policies were a disaster, Nancy was a Marie Antoinette with no feeling for the masses, Caspar Weinberger and Alexander Haig were worms and nuts, Reagan wanted to kill everyone with neutron bombs and MX missiles, he was a union buster who would unleash the horrors of running-wild industry, he and his appointees were madmen, he was ramming his brand of capitalism down our throats. Her life and those of her children literally hung in the balance while psychopaths ran the country.

"[I] want to maneuver politically," she confessed. The way the nation and world were run caused so much human suffering — she had "a desire to do something to counter it all . . . the entire world . . . unemployment, nuclear posturing . . . starvation, uneven distribution . . . what am I doing to change it?"

She always saw the barriers as time and money, basically money. How could she and Garth see what mistakes they were making when they were so immersed in the minutiae of running the Center? They couldn't be decision makers, leaders, visionaries. They were too busy being clerks, mail handlers, typists. The details were killing them.

And yet there was money from a will coming in this year. In fact, several wills were coming to fruition, but the more money that came in, the harder she and Garth and Robin worked, and the farther behind they fell.

How did other people build an empire? She couldn't imagine. Musing about General Motors after a grueling day, and looking around at the piles of unfinished work, she reflected that the problems must be "staggering . . . non-manageable." And yet those huge companies did manage. She always concluded it was about money, and then flitted to another thought without reflecting.

Her cure for money-lust was usually to launch a new scheme or distract herself with a new project. The bequests due in soon were already burning a hole in her pocket. She wanted a new building. She laid plans for a new dating service, Lonely Atheists. To keep relevant with Bill, she started a project to screen school textbooks for religious indoctrination.

Meanwhile, the carnage in the AA chapters was spreading; the New York and Pittsburgh groups collapsed, and the newly appointed codirector of the Los Angeles group, Ralph Ennis, resigned after only a few weeks, citing doubts about Garth's leadership, Madalyn's connection with Larry Flynt, and her "disgusting and vitriolic language" in public.

A couple of days later, Madalyn herself drove a spike into the heart of the Dallas chapter, disbanding it and demanding its treasury and Dial-An-Atheist phone equipment. "Gawd, what turkeys you are!" she wrote its dismissed officers. How could they be so dumb, lazy, and impotent?

On the Fourth of July, she was a guest on a prominent DC radio call-in show when her enemy Roy Torcaso called. Madalyn knew he was in the Jane Conrad-Gordon Stein camp, and Garth had caught him trying to register for the AA convention.

She spat that Torcaso was "one of the most despicable persons who has ever lived or breathed," and overtalked him until the segment ran out.

She went home to an excruciating gout episode, with her considerate kids hovering, Garth chauffeuring her to the doctor, lab, drugstore, bed.

On Thanksgiving, Madalyn sat in the living room watching the fire Garth had built, recalling every house she'd ever lived in. The kids had cooked a wonderful meal, but she felt a great unquiet.

She got out pen and paper and wrote her cousin Leona Lacy, Homer's wife, with whom Garth had bunked on a recent organizing tour. Leona had shown him a picture of her daughter from her first marriage, Brenda, an architecture student. Studying the photo of the brown-eyed beauty, Garth said, "I don't have time to court, I don't have time to date, but I need a wife." After he returned to Austin, he sent Brenda roses and proposed by letter, though he'd never met her.

Now, Madalyn wrote to Leona, here was the deal: Garth had a very heavy schedule for 1982 December, arriving at Dulles on the 16th, booked solid until the Solstice party; the next day back-to-back interviews and appearances, then supervise the picketing of Jerry Falwell's church, then meet the chapter directors, and catch a flight to Boston and Connecticut, then back to Austin —

"So I have this figured out this way — if you'all can come to the Solstice Party with your daughter, Garth and she could get married the next morning." They could maybe plan a honeymoon when they got back to Austin.

And — send her transcript, they needed to get her registered at UT for the spring semester. And send a map immediately, so Garth could come collect Brenda. Or she could drive. "Garth is coming 3,000 miles," she wrote; surely Brenda could travel 350.

"We think he is damn near perfect ... kind, considerate, understanding, warm, humorous, love-filled ... works hard ... is a good provider ... does not smoke, drug up or booze ... is very aware of women's lib."

The bride would get to move in with Garth's family, and in two years they were going to build a "manor house" on 100 acres, with room for four individual families, with their own dens, libraries, etc. Just like the Kennedys and Rockefellers and Mellons, Madalyn wrote.

Robin read the letter and corrected typos before Grandma sent it. Brenda politely declined.

Robin had been slow to take root at home, Madalyn noted, becoming inseparable with Lex when he transferred to UT in the fall of 1982. In the spring of 1983, Madalyn gave him a job. She immediately let Robin know that he couldn't read, write, or spell, didn't know what a sentence was, and was hopeless in the law library.

"I don't like my friends, Garth's friends or her friends," Madalyn wrote grumpily. Robin "has these strong strong ties to this insufferable stodgy ineffectual school. I want her to have those kind of ties to her home and her family." By the end of summer, Lex was history (though the next year he was hired back for several months during an emergency).

After he was fired, Robin got seriously interested in gourmet cooking. She and Garth went shopping to outfit the kitchen. They formed a bond Madalyn couldn't penetrate; she found incomprehensible their interest in a TV show called *Dr. No*, and a series of books about "little people with hairy feet." It was the only life they had apart from the Cause.

Chapter 47 ~ Enemies

ANOTHER WILL CAME IN, and by December 1982 SOS had $150,000 in its trust fund and $100,000 to buy property. The Center was worth $500,000, and only carried a $113,000 note.

The pleasure of Christmas — splurging on silk and velour tops for Robin and clothes for herself and Garth, this year watching *A Christmas Carol* in black and white, mellowing with spiked eggnog before the twinkling tree lights — all soon gave way to work, and worries about Bill's book.

Her enemies in the atheist and freethought camps were using Bill to try to unseat her and siphon off members. She knew Bozarth's treatise was about to appear in the *American Rationalist*; the *Truth Seeker* announced it, and another freethought magazine was running a piece on her and Bill.

An *American Rationalist* piece in early 1983 quoted her describing certain ex-AA Jews as "gray-skinned, blue-lipped freaks with all the faults Hitler found in them." Blacks smelled bad, and were too lazy to better themselves. Gays made her sick, the article said.

A letter she'd recently written to a longtime colleague with whom she was feuding was widely circulated: "I keep getting letters ... that you want to kiss and make up," she wrote, "But that you want me to apologize for something. OK. I am sorry — that you are such an asshole."

Shortly after the 1983 convention, seeing criticism of herself in the *Truth Seeker*, Madalyn sat down and wrote James Hervey Johnson. His refusal to turn the Truth Seeker Corporation over to her meant he was a woman-hater, she wrote. His "publications are cheap and meaningless ... you should be now making arrangements to turn everything over to American Atheists ... [you are] a dying, defunct, discredited old man who will grow moldy in an unmarked grave ... you have nothing. You are nothing."

Johnson told a friend he didn't finish reading it. The religionists liked to see atheist infighting, he said — Bill was raking in the dough proving that.

A few days later, Jane Conrad, who had just self-published *Mad Madalyn*, also got a letter, at her Colorado home. "I think," wrote Madalyn, "that if I had been born with dwarf features such as you have, I would have 'turned against god' for that too. It must be horrible to go through life with a deformity of body, with the deformity of mind which accompanies that."

When Madalyn heard that one of her contributing magazine authors had bought a copy of Conrad's book, his membership was terminated. She repeatedly wrote that she couldn't figure out why she was so hated.

It was particularly vexing, because the 20th anniversary of *Murray v. Curlett* and *Abington Township, Pennsylvania v. Schempp* was coming up, and stories had started simmering in the media; UPI had already called. She knew there was going to be pressure to counter these charges, and talk about Bill, which she refused to do. She was cut from several shows for it.

Madalyn and Garth did a blizzard of television and radio appearances in the six weeks after the 1983 convention, helped by an April Supreme Court decision to hear a nativity case from Rhode Island. That, and several other cases before the court — tax exemptions for religious segregated schools (North Carolina); prayer in a state congress (Nebraska); tuition tax credits (Minnesota) — might determine the fate of the First Amendment, she said.

Ironically, given that Bill had exposed her 1960 defection attempt, Madalyn, the kids, and a handful of their inner circle left for the Soviet Union a few days after the 20th anniversary celebration.

As she finally entered the country of her Marxist dreams, Bill held a press conference on Capitol Hill. He said the Communist party had a role in Madalyn's suit, hoping it would collapse the free enterprise system by knocking out one of its props — the church. But that hated system worked in mysterious ways. Enough people sent her money, he said, that it became too profitable to be a revolutionary. That was why she moved away from Communism.

Her trip was billed as a World Atheist Meet. In Kiev, the Ukraine, Leningrad, and Moscow, Madalyn and her group visited the Atheist Museum, the Atheist Institute. She was astonished at the poverty and agrarianism in the USSR. The Soviets were slobs, she wrote; everything was in disrepair, littered, and nobody cared. Huge, ugly, unkempt buildings were going up willy-nilly; cranes littered the skyline, and exposed rebar stuck up from dormant projects. At first, she thought it was a failure of government, but decided it was ignorance.

When the family returned, they traveled to Peoria for Madalyn to speak at a three-day festival celebrating the sesquicentennial of Robert Green Ingersoll. At the festival, she singled out an elderly black AA member named John Glover Jackson. He had been a lecturer on African history at the Ingersoll Forum in New York for years, and in universities in the Northeast. He had authored numerous books, and

Madalyn arranged for some to be reprinted by American Atheist Press. She wanted him to write for her magazine. She wanted to commission another book from him.

She wasn't just trolling for authors; she had other plans for Jackson.

Chapter 48 ~ Hustler

LARRY FLYNT AND MADALYN finally hatched a deal in the summer of 1983. He would run membership pitches in his magazines, and distribute AA Magazine on newsstands along with *Hustler*, in return for her writing articles and position statements for his political endeavors. Besides his free-speech, anti-war, anti-cigarette and other projects, he was planning to run for President in 1984 as a Republican against Ronald Reagan.

Robin, 18, was now editor-in-chief of the magazine, though still a full-time student. (One of her first assignments was to return Paul Kurtz's subscription check. Madalyn had thoroughly demonized Kurtz for his Fahnestock end run and various other times he'd trumped her for grants and money, for his close association with her arch enemy, Gordon Stein, for his two successful magazines, which were always out on time, and his thriving publishing enterprise, Prometheus Books. Her CESAALA was in direct competition with Kurtz' Center for Inquiry Libraries in the Buffalo area.) Robin had spent all summer indexing the magazine collection, and by August knew the article inventory better than anyone. She set about designing a more presentable product for distribution in Flynt's network. By fall, she had turned out 500 sample copies.

The September AA board meeting, held in St. Louis, brought the expected opposition to Flynt, but Madalyn won them over; the magazine would get distribution for the first time, and Flynt might finance another big suit.

The Founders were flown out to the coast every few weeks during late 1983. At a party near Halloween, Madalyn met Dick Gregory, Terry Southern, Dennis Hopper, Timothy Leary, Gordon Liddy, and Jack Nicholson.

But she had come into Flynt's life at the front end of a tailspin. In the first three weeks of November, he was arrested for contempt (for defying a court order to surrender an audio tape involving automaker John DeLorean and a drug deal); he was forcibly removed from a Supreme Court session in a libel case after he screamed obscenities at the nine justices; he shouted at the U.S. District Court Judge in the DeLorean suit; he announced he would test First Amendment protection by running presidential campaign ads showing explicit sexual acts; he was arrested on charges of desecrating an American flag when he arrived in U.S. District Court wearing one as a diaper, and he paid his daily $10,000 contempt fine in garbage bags full of wadded-up $1 bills. He ran a satirical ad in *Hustler* depicting Jerry Falwell as having had sex with his mother in an outhouse (Falwell filed a $45 million libel suit which became a landmark free-speech case that Flynt won).

If he'd stuck to stunts like the full-page blank newspaper ad he'd taken out for his presidential campaign, it probably would have been okay, but this kind of publicity made AA members cringe. Donations dropped by 41%. Moreover, in December, Madalyn got the advance copy of the February 1984 *Hustler* containing an ad that showed a sultry, strapless girl sporting an AA-logo necklace. You could wear one "whether you're an American Anarchist, American Atheist, American Agnostic, or just a good ol' American Asshole." She quickly did a special mailing telling the members this ad had gone forward without her permission.

She and Garth and Robin flew to Los Angeles in December, when Flynt was imprisoned after the mêlée over the DeLorean matter. She decided he was too unstable to count on. Instead, she put out a funding appeal entitled "Continuing Attacks on Madalyn Murray O'Hair."

In January 1984, with money on her mind, she wrote James Hervey Johnson a measured, normal missive, as if nothing had happened. How about a merger! Instead of him just turning everything over? She listed AA's accomplishments, and assured him that it was destined to "capture the culture." He wrote a polite reply. The Truth Seeker Corporation was fine, thanks, and did not need to merge with anyone.

By the end of the month, she suspected Larry Flynt was in trouble too deep to renegotiate distribution of AA magazine after the January and February issues. She and the kids flew to Los Angeles and watched him draw a 15-month federal jail sentence for contempt.

They followed him to Butner, North Carolina, to the federal "psycho prison," as Madalyn called it, where he signed a power of attorney allowing her to transfer all the assets of his publishing empire — about $300 million — to American Atheists.

"I never saw her more jubilant than the day she thought she had a lock on Larry Flynt's financial empire," David Kent told a correspondent later. "She said, 'Never again will I have to depend on these piss-ant atheists with their pathetic "fortunes." To hell with those sons of a bitch. Gawd, I always hated them!'"

But Flynt's brother Jimmy blocked the power of attorney and filed a petition for conservatorship of Flynt Publications in Los Angeles Superior Court. His brother was incompetent to manage his affairs. (Indeed, at this time, Larry told CNN from jail that he had issued a contract to kill President Reagan.) Madalyn was trying to take advantage of him, Jimmy said, and was causing panic among the employees. He won, holding her power of attorney at bay for at least a month.

One of Jimmy Flynt's winning arguments cut deep: one proof of his brother's incompetence was the fact that he picked Madalyn, who had had many years to prove she could run a publishing empire and little to show for it.

On March 27, 1984, she gave up. "Pornography thrives [because] Christianity has perverted human sexuality," she said in a public statement. "We fight the cause.

Mr. Flynt gains from the effect. We decline to profit from that gain." Privately, she blamed the failure on greed, lying, double crossing, drugs, and dirty money.

Madalyn was being sought for serious interviews during the Flynt debacle, because of President Reagan's proposed constitutional amendment to allow prayer back into schools. Bill was at a strategy session Reagan had just addressed. He was photographed laughing with the President's special assistant, and standing outside Reagan's office, a Marine guard signifying that the leader of the free world was sitting inside only yards away. It was an irresistible contrast with Madalyn — Bill trusted in the corridors of power, while his mother's profile was raised because of her association with Larry Flynt.

She dreaded the 1984 convention because of it. Held in April in Lexington, it featured Bob Harrington as speaker, pinch-hitting for Flynt.

Usually Madalyn relished the attention of the media, but this year the *Wall Street Journal* gave a scathing assessment: her "domineering manner has driven away all but the freest of the nation's free-thinkers ... [she] attracts sideshows ... her followers are well outside the mainstream of atheism."

One of the most disturbing "sideshows" for the reporter was a home movie of an atheist burial in the Shenandoah Mountains. It was presented by Arnold Via, a retired merchant seaman and staunchly loyal, generous, tireless director of American Atheists in Virginia. A longtime ally of Madalyn's, he sported a lengthy gray beard and showed up at AA events covered head to toe with buttons bearing atheist slogans. He sometimes house-sat when the family was on vacation.

His movie showed the corpse of a murderer, Frederick Lonnie Conway, who had died in prison after being converted to atheism through Via's prison outreach. Via, bare-chested in cutoff jeans, was shown pulling the nude, plastic-wrapped corpse off the back of his pickup, digging a shallow grave, and nudging the body in with his foot. A newly minted penny was placed on its chest, to mark the year of burial, and dirt thrown in.

Then Via read to the conventioneers some of the hate mail he'd gotten when the burial made the local news. "You and that slut bitch O'Hair have put this nation in chaos"; "you bastard rat prick son-of-bitch"; "*You* are a bizarre creature from hell —! You and your kind are the scum of the earth"; "you are the scourge of the earth, a stinking maggot."

He didn't read the worst ones, that made him sleep with a gun: "Putting a bullet between your eyes would be to [sic] good of a death to a cock sucker like you. Nobody in this community wants faggots like you living around so why don't you get the fuck out and take your crybaby-dicksucking atheism half baked bullshit with you ... you dick sucking fucking prick ... you fuck face faggot motherfucker ... you'll probably die from AIDS if you don't get them dicks out of your mouth & ass ... eat shit and die. P.S. Go to hell."

After he finished, Madalyn took the podium and declared she didn't want Via burying *her*. But laughter was thin; the entire spectacle was disturbing.

Robin manned the book booth while her father preached not far away at South-land Christian Church. His picketers came to the hotel offering to "dialogue" with the atheists.

On July 27, 1984, Texas state officials agreed that the requirement of a God-belief violated the U.S. Constitution, and they would change it. Madalyn had won *O'Hair v. Hill.*

But it didn't make her happy. It had warded off Strobel, but had cost $35,000, taken nearly seven years, and not gotten her to the Supreme Court. And public officials would still be allowed to take an *oath* if they wanted.

The rest of the summer was filled with overwhelming work, nonstop visitors and house guests, and black gloom that no triumph could banish. It was grounded in small things. Jack Massen, a generous San Francisco benefactor, had donated a building, but he had the vexing habit of checking to see if his money was going for the things Madalyn had solicited it for. A sauna given them for the back yard looked shoddy, and cost too much to install. They went to see *Search for Spock,* and Madalyn emerged furious; it was just religion warmed over, she was sick of being beat over the head with it. She watched *Sophie's Choice* and wrote that the endless anti-German films about the Holocaust were turning her into a monster; irrationally, it offended her on behalf of her despised mother, whose terms she still used in her writing: *nur ein pfennig, wunderbar, und so wieder, mein kindern.*

She watched her *kindern* slave hand over fist every day. Robin had graduated from UT just after her 19th birthday — with a psychology degree Madalyn scorned — and was simply swallowed into the unrelenting maw of the Center without a breather. Garth worked himself to death on the tsunami of chores small and large, and all Madalyn could think when she saw the dark circles under his eyes, his mouth ulcers, inflamed gums, disturbed digestion, hemorrhoids, and the terrible trapped look he carried was, poor bastard.

Yes, he was trapped at the Center, but that was because there wasn't enough money. If there were more money, Garth wouldn't be trapped.

Member Shirley Moll remembered putting Garth up for a night in her Minnesota home, and they stayed up talking until 4 a.m. "He never really wanted to run an atheist organization. He simply wanted to be a writer."

In September, they traveled to China, but put in the same 16-hour days, visiting silk mills, planned-worker communities, pottery factories, jade-carving shops, the opera, tombs, the Great Wall — and falling into bed exhausted just as at home.

The rest of the year, Madalyn was very little in the news, the only article about her since the *O'Hair v. Hill* win a shopworn piece about Solstice.

Just before they left for China, Robin got a new black cocker puppy she named Gallagher. A year later, she got another cocker, Shannon. Both dogs would outlive her.

Madalyn's power was waning, her irritability increasing, and her enemies massing on the ridge. The media now often treated Madalyn as a joke, referring to her by her first name, tabloid-style. Columnist Cal Thomas cracked that any retirement of Madalyn, "perhaps the most famous three-named person since John Wilkes Booth," would be the worst news for conservative fund-raisers since Ted Kennedy declined to run for president.

She fired employees *en masse* and hired new ones. She dismissed an Illinois member, a generous monthly donor to the Trust Fund, for "willful acts," and another Outstanding Chapter Worker for mentioning Paul Kurtz' Prometheus Books in a chapter newsletter. Jeff Frankel, AA magazine's "Angry Young Atheist" columnist, resigned and wrote every chapter in the country, detailing Madalyn's tirades, despotism, vulgarity, anti-Semitism, waste, mismanagement, and ingratitude.

Madalyn's staunch friend, the erudite and forgiving Dr. Frank Zindler, reflected on her self-destructive behavior. She was increasingly upset and plagued with dizziness, as one after another of Robin's well-planned family diets fell to pieces under the pressure of work. They had irregular meals and often didn't have dinner until 11 or 12 at night.

"Madalyn was a brittle diabetic," said Zindler, "she rarely if ever had real control of her blood sugar. She was always either overdosing or underdosing on her insulin . . . it could result in a *wild* flare-up of temper."

Her supposed anti-Semitism, he said, was really anti-Zionism misidentified. True, "she used words like bombs [but] the dirty language was kind of anarchistic, defiant of social customs." She also expected others to work as hard as she did. "Well, nobody is going to work like Madalyn, Robin, or Jon. And to Madalyn, these people are just shirking their duties! They were just goldbricking. I don't think she ever could understand the difference."

But she also had "great sympathy for some of the staff when they were sick and so on, as long as she could believe it was true. Then she would be sending flowers and doing whatever was needed to help."

"And they would squabble all the time . . . When you're working under such pressure for such a long period of time, you have to have a lightning rod to drain the charge. They would holler and scream at each other and an hour later, 'well, are we gonna go get some supper?'"

"One starts out with a dream," Madalyn wrote in her diary, "and treats everyone else as themselves and then slowly is driven to tighten up, to become more rigid, to retreat into the safety net of one's self until one becomes dictatorial."

She was definitely on the decline, but, just as she had not emerged gradually into the limelight, her fate was not to fade gradually out — although it seemed that way for awhile.

Bill Murray and daughter Robin, ca. 1977, shortly before Robin was pressured to cut her father out of her life. Photo: Jimmy Nassour Archive

Madalyn at home in 1989, six years before she disappeared. Photo: Jimmy Nassour Archive

The inseparable Founders of American Atheists on vacation, ca. 1990. They ate, traveled, vacationed, and worked together 24 hours a day, seven days a week. Madalyn always looked happy in their vacation photos; Robin and Jon Garth often did not.
Photo: Jimmy Nassour Archive

Madalyn during her rise to notoriety, ca. 1966. She married Richard O'Hair in late 1965, and was struggling to regain control of her organization, which had gone through two takeover attempts. She built it into a multi-million dollar empire in Austin, Texas. Photo: Jimmy Nassour Archive

Jon Garth and Robin on vacation, ca. 1991. Though Garth was being groomed to take over American Atheists, it was Robin who kept the organization going – despite the increasing chaos generated by the Founders themselves. Credit: Jimmy Nassour Archive

Madalyn with her lifelong protector, son Jon Garth, ca. 1990. He lived with her his entire life and followed her to a shallow grave five years after this photo was taken. Neither he nor Robin ever married. Credit: Jimmy Nassour Archive

Madalyn on the Johnny Carson Show ca. 1972. A blunt and colorful outlaw, she was a guaranteed high-ratings guest. Photo: Courtesy of Vicki O'Hair Reed

David Waters, left, with his mother, brothers, and stepfather, ca. 1954. Stevie, who David tried to protect, is at far right. He was killed by police in 1974 while threatening his mother with a hammer.
Photo: Courtesy Cookie Wilkerson

David Waters and Marti Budde, the love of his life, on their wedding day, Madalyn's birthday in 1978 – the same day David was sent back to prison for the beating of his mother. Less than two years later, Marti was murdered. Credit: Courtesy Cookie Wilkerson

David Waters and lifelong friend Chico Osborne in 1994 after David's theft of $54,000 from American Atheists. Though Osborne rented the storage unit where the O'Hairs' bodies were stashed, he was never charged with any crime linked to the O'Hairs. Credit: Government exhibit

David Waters in the photo that snared him in 1999 as he was on the verge of slipping out of authorities' grasp. As a felon, Waters was not supposed to have guns or ammunition. The photo was supplied to prosecutors in time to keep him behind bars while the case against him and Gary Karr was built.
Photo: Government exhibit

Gary Karr on his release from prison in 1995, only weeks before he became involved in David Waters' kidnapping/extortion scheme. He drew a life sentence for his role in the O'Hair case. Photo: Illinois Department of Corrections

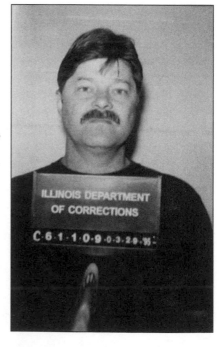

Danny Fry had only minor infractions on his record when he agreed to participate in Waters' abduction scheme. He bonded with the women during their captivity, listening in awe to Madalyn's accomplishments and chatting by the pool with Robin. Sickened by the murders, he knew he was held in contempt by Waters and Karr. He wrote his brother, "If you're reading this, I'm probably dead." He soon was. Photo: Dallas County Sheriff's Department

IRS Special Agent Ed Martin and FBI agent Donna Cowling spent countless hours running Waters and Karr to earth after the work of two men – *San Antonio Express-News* reporter John MacCormack and private investigator Tim Young – alerted them to the four murders. Assistant U.S. Attorney Jerry Carruth, right, proved his case with no witnesses or murder weapon, and none of the O'Hairs' bodies. Credit: Ed Martin

San Antonio Express-News reporter John MacCormack, right, filed more than 80 stories on the missing O'Hairs. His work and that of private investigator Tim Young, left, finally pressured the authorities to investigate David Waters. Here they were photographed tracking down a false lead in Michigan. Credit: Tim Young

Bill Murray and President George W. Bush in 2002. Murray's Washington-based Religious Freedom Coalition sponsors conservative causes, one being the return of school prayer, banished with the help of his and Madalyn's 1963 Supreme Court suit, *Murray v. Curlett*. Photo: William J. Murray

Chapter 49 ~ The Honor Farm

IN 1987, DAVID WATERS was being released from prison again in Illinois. After his wife's murder in 1980, he'd managed to stay free until the middle of 1985. Shortly after Marti's murder, he and his biker friend Chico Osborne went to Corpus Christi, Texas, for a job with an oil outfitter, Weatherby Engineering.

It had been gotten for him by Carolyn Bruce, the girlfriend he began seeing while he was still married to Marti. One of the last times she'd seen Marti was when she and David were sitting in a bar. Marti entered, marched up to Carolyn, and put a gun to her head. Coolly, Carolyn pointed to David. "Your problem is with him, not me," she said. Later, David slapped her, saying she'd been disrespectful to Marti.

By the time Marti was murdered, Carolyn was three months pregnant.

"It was a miserable time, many of the bars in the area putting out collection jars for Marti's funeral costs, and the weather was snowy and bitter cold, and we had to drive around picking up the jars," Carolyn remembered. They had to find Marti's father out on the streets, and get him cleaned up. "The undertaker had said pick something out of her clothes that goes all the way up her neck, because [of] the . . . stab wounds."

She never knew what happened to the money they collected. She came home from work one day to find pictures of Marti everywhere, and Marti's things in place of hers. Another day, she came home to find another woman in the apartment with David.

The stress and unhappiness made her go into labor three months early, and she gave birth in May 1980 to a son. When David threatened physical harm to her and the baby, she moved to Corpus Christi. For some reason, she relented and got him the job at Weatherby in 1981. But it was short-lived; according to a prosecutor later, he "got a little close to [someone's] wife," and fled in Chico Osborne's car, stranding Chico.

A few years later, he persuaded Carolyn to join him in Florida. He'd changed. He now wanted to take care of her and little David. "Like an idiot," she said, she packed a U-Haul and went. She immediately felt something wrong, felt she had been enticed there to be robbed or maybe even killed. He put her in a motel, and immediately left. He came and went over a couple of days, never saying what he was up to, and insisting she should put the U-Haul out of sight. She packed up and fled the third day while he was out. He tracked her down in Illinois and threatened to kill her.

"He was *twisted*, and yet I don't think I've ever laughed as hard, during the good times, I don't think I've ever had as good a time with anyone as I had with David. And I don't think I've ever had as bad a time, or been as afraid, as when I was with David."

Murder "was always on his mind. He used to tell me, murder is the easiest crime to commit. And he loved Texas, he said you could hide a body out here in Texas, nobody'd *ever* find it."

He told her he would never pull another job with anyone, because the guys he picked always screwed up. "But he did, he always felt he could throw his lot in with men because of the power he had, the fact that *all* men feared him. That was one thing he always said in Texas, 'I miss being in Peoria, because nobody down here knows . . . that they should be afraid of me.'"

One thing Carolyn Bruce concluded unequivocally: "He *hated* women."

After the job in Corpus Christi, he came home and got involved with a bubbly teenager, who bore him a red-haired daughter near the end of 1981. "He could be just the warmest, lovingest guy," she said. "Or he . . . could just be the devil, just hateful, and hell on earth." But they kept in touch for many years, and she regularly sent photos of the child. He was always reaching out to his past.

By the end of 1982, at age 35, he'd moved on to a serene-looking 21-year-old blonde named Lori G_____. They lived in the Peoria area, and for a time, he worked for G&H Tie Beams as a carpenter, while she did restaurant work. But a straight job and domesticity were never for him. He and Lori went to Naples, Florida, not long after the bullet-riddled body of a 36-year-old ex-con named Billy King was found stuffed under the seat of a locked van. It had been sitting across the street from a Peoria bar called the Owl's Nest for about a week. King had been shot numerous times at close range. His cash was missing. The last person known to have seen him alive was David Waters.

In August 1985, some Peoria chickens came home to roost in Florida. David had been convicted of a 1983 battery of two friends, both oddly named Joyce Carpenter, during a traffic dispute, and bonded out, but now a forgery caught up with him — he'd stolen an elderly Peoria man's account number and withdrawn $5,000 from his savings. All probation was revoked, and he went to jail for the two crimes, transferring in the fall of 1986 to the men's minimum-security "Honor Farm" at Vienna, Illinois. There, he made the acquaintance of a kidnapper and armed robber named Gary Paul Karr.

The Honor Farm was considered one of the model rehabilitation prisons in the nation. It was unfenced, and inmates had freedom to recreate, socialize, and dine together. Karr, a year younger than Waters, had been behind bars since 1975.

Karr was "mentally abused," by his father, according to his ex-wife Charlene Karr. His path was similar to David Waters'; by age 11, he was sent to juvy.

"Juvenile detention was supposed to teach him a lesson," Charlene said, but "it just made him a crook." The next seven years were a patchwork of destructiveness, theft, and rebellion, with repeated attempts by his father to discipline him.

Karr later said, "My father was a good man. He just didn't know how to cope with children." He was a good provider, working long hours as a painting contractor. As far as abuse — maybe, but that was by today's standards. "When I was growing up, it was normal to get spanked with belts, boards, etc. I have nothing bad to say about him, nor do I blame anyone other than myself for the choices I made."

He spent three months at David Waters' alma mater, the dreaded St. Charles Training School for Boys, the year Waters helped beat David Gibbs to death.

Just after his 18th birthday, he was charged with indecent liberties with a child. In June of 1966, he had taken a 14-year-old girl into a basement and "had sexual intercourse with [her] against her will." He was given one to three years.

That was a turning point, he later said. The judge had told his father he hadn't done anything worth going to prison for, and he'd set bond, but his father thought it would teach him a lesson to go to prison. He regretted that decision until he died, Karr said — the same way Dean Hunt regretted *not* letting David go to jail. Karr said he ended up resenting authority, and still had a problem with it.

Karr was released on New Year's Day, 1969. In 1971, at age 23, he went on a robbery spree with a partner. Over a 10-day period, they robbed three Chicago drug stores, binding the owners with surgical tape and draining the cash registers and supplies of Nembutal, Demerol, Seconal, and other drugs. Karr drew two years.

He was discharged in May 1973, just after his 25th birthday.

Charlene didn't even know he existed, though she hung around his house in the Chicago area. Her brothers — she had 10 siblings — played cards with Gary's brothers. She was also close to their sister, Sidney Karr, and their mother, Joyce. But Gary was off in prison, and no one mentioned him.

One day in 1973, she was driving somewhere. "This *cute* guy was in a car next to me." He was tanned and athletic, slender, with blue eyes, thick, luxuriant hair, and such a nice smile. She made eye contact.

"I honked my horn — I've never done that in my life! I'm so shy! He was wearing a southwestern shirt, you know, with the V's and the pearl buttons, peaches pink?"

The cute guy turned out to be Joyce's secret son.

She remembered their first date, at a nice restaurant, and so romantic. "They came by our table and played guitars...I was madly in love. [He was] giving, caring, loving, sensitive, understanding...I'd die for him."

Gary asked her father for Charlene's hand in marriage. Her father got her alone. "If you marry that man, you will be left alone, and you will be left with a child," he warned. He refused to give his blessing.

The 20-year-old didn't listen to her father. By early 1974, she was married and pregnant with a daughter, Chrystal, even though her beloved had recently been caught with burglary tools and a suspicious license plate.

The new husband began a downhill slide. During 1974, he went on a binge that included several counties in Illinois and Wisconsin. He and another man robbed a woman at gunpoint and raped her, the charge against him said. A few days later, they were accused of kidnapping, robbing, and raping a judge's daughter, subduing her with a sawed-off 20-gauge shotgun. Less than a week later, the two robbed a woman of $600 at gunpoint.

He was arrested in October 1974, and convicted of aggravated kidnapping and armed robbery. He was given 30–50 years. Chrystal was 18 days old when he went to prison.

After two or three years, Charlene divorced him, but continued to visit, and made sure he stayed in contact with Chrystal over the next 20 years. She never remarried.

"All my life," said Chrystal, "my mom told me he was a good guy . . . He used the time he was locked up to study — paramedics, fire fighting, and psychology. He's a smart man that made a bad decision to make bad friends again."

In June 1987, David Waters bade Karr and the Honor Farm goodbye. In eight years, they would see each other again under very different circumstances.

Waters, 40, was still good-looking, with hair still black and thick, styled with modified sideburns. He had a well-groomed mustache. He was again buffed up from working out in prison, and had the swagger and confidence of a man taller than his 5'10", 180 pounds. His two-year prison stint hadn't dulled the teasing smile or easy laugh. He still got along with all kinds of people.

His hands showed no signs of hard labor — he had good jobs in prison, and he'd worked seriously on his education this time. From MacMurray College in Jacksonville, Illinois, he'd earned As in computer programming, political science, writing, and other subjects. He excelled at history, and in the spring of 1987, he made the dean's list at Southeastern Illinois College. He attended seminars in College Orientation and Career Planning.

He still had the bad-boy demeanor that was so attractive to certain women. He immediately set about to reenter the world of sports cars, hard liquor, and black leather. He bought a diamond "Gent's" ring. He headed back to the place he'd liked before he got caught last time — Naples, Florida.

Chapter 50 ~ Where There's a Will

ALL DURING 1985, wills and bequests to Madalyn ripened. Thoren, Stimson, Hall, Bevan, Tirmenstein, Horner, Berkowitz, Smith, Bell, Reinhold. Florida, California, New Jersey, Indiana, Mississippi, Ohio, New York — aged atheists were seeing to it that she personally, or SOS, or AA were specified. By the end of the year, she expected to have upwards of $2 million. She felt 1985 would be the last bad year they'd ever have.

People streamed into Austin days early for the convention at the Wyndham Hotel that year, annoying the Murray-O'Hairs. They were not ready for the event, much less visitors and guests wanting attention. The offices were dirty, the ceiling not patched from the chronic leaks it sprouted. As always, Madalyn wondered if the conventions were worth the money. And as always, she came away feeling they were.

This year's speaker was Jack Jones, of the Free Thinkers Society based in Auckland. After the convention, Garth returned to New Zealand with him to look the place over. An idea was taking shape in Madalyn's exhausted mind.

"Madalyn and I," Garth wrote, "are desirous of depositing some funds, on a regular basis, in some financial institution outside of the United States...Should it become necessary for us to flee this country...an escape fund." Madalyn handwrote at the end, "This is absolutely confidential, between *only you and our family.*"

Jones set about finding a financial agent for them. He cautioned that accounts should be in all three names so any one of them could get the money should one die. The odds that something would happen to all three of them at once were so astronomically small they weren't even considered.

By January 1986, Madalyn had $1.5 million in cash. Another $33,000 came in two weeks. But she never really would tell the members straight out how much had come in bequests; it was done in such a way as to make it virtually impossible to analyze the contradictory, confusing, and incomplete information in the *Insider's Newsletter.*

But to Leona Lacy, now divorced from cousin Homer, Madalyn was able to exult about the money in a way she couldn't to anyone else, even Garth and Robin.

"I am *filthy* rich," she wrote Leona, "I have millions." She bought Garth and herself Mercedeses and Robin a Porsche. Since they'd just bought an expensive home, there was no need to get another one just yet. They went to China for a month, she bought Robin a diamond necklace, they were going to Europe this year, last year it was Egypt, a cruise down the Nile "in a luxury boat you wouldn't believe," a safari in Kenya, the Serengeti, Kilimanjaro, "and every gawd-damn fabulous place we could go. One hotel had gold-plated walls." She bought yards of raw silk, they shot 45 rolls of film.

"Jesus Christ it is wonderful to be rich."

She wanted some oriental rugs, so the kids simply went out and got two. "Robin wanted some imported cotton blouses, so Garth bought her a dozen...at $150 each." She bought a big carved giraffe in Africa and air-freighted it home. She bought all the books she wanted. She spent $350 a month on dog food.

"Leona," she wrote, "there is nothing can beat being filthy rich."

But even though they were now millionaires, there was no letup in the flow of work and trouble. The dogs dug up the yard, tore up door screens, and clawed the paint, Madalyn was behind on her mending, the yard was full of weeds and dead flowers, the carpets were dirty, she hadn't done her taxes, they still rushed to the office every day and worked 15 hours and came home and fell into bed. Her attorney was an idiot, a judge was out to get her, equipment and vehicles and appliances were breaking down, the nation was full of ripoff artists, one of her benefactors killed himself and it would be a hassle getting his money.

The more she fretted about the grinding work and parasitical employees at the Center, the more she felt they lived in a reactionary, fascist military state and degenerate culture. The political situation was destabilized by a greedy few who wanted to rape the many through the system — raving, generic shibboleths from her youth with no specificity, no solutions, that had become a poisonous, crooning lullaby.

She was immensely, unceasingly jealous and angry at President Reagan — he was a murderer, out to blow up the world, his spokesman was a cuckold, Poindexter and Meese should be in strait jackets. She totted up his outrages — Iran, Nicaragua, Israel, Grenada, Libya — and fumed at his inexplicable popularity. It must be the news media, she concluded, and that Congress was lousy with Catholics. "Why isn't the man unseated by now? I *must* change all this."

The family even had a will specifying that since Reagan's airline deregulation would result in incompetent air controllers, when they were shot out of the sky by terrorists, the organizations were to get everything, including the proceeds from the wrongful death suit against the airline. Neither Bill nor his spawn were to get anything. *Nur ein pfennig.*

A couple of days of sleet and snow in January 1986 kept the family at home cocooning, and Madalyn set some goals for all the new money. They needed better routines, more efficiency.

Incredibly, on her list for all of them in the coming year was "work harder."

She wanted a 72-page magazine now instead of 40. She wanted to publish 12 atheist books a year instead of the two they'd gotten out in 1985. And not a single one of the small things could be jettisoned or delegated — they still had to write briefs to challenge Gideon Bibles, travel to California to force AA magazine into a library, get Alcoholics Anonymous and its "higher power" out of the Austin State Hospital. The more Madalyn's ambition and hubris grew, the more Robin's and Garth's lives dwindled, and the fatter they all got. In fact, the Africa trip was the last time Robin was slender and pretty. Soon, even her glorious, fiery mane seemed to grow lifeless.

Despite Madalyn's letter to Leona Lacy, being a millionaire didn't really change anything. They worked harder than before, and had far more help, but the publications were still behind and payroll still a crisis. Madalyn saw the end of a month as another twelfth of the year shot to hell.

While she had a rather sophisticated understanding of economics, she reflected little on the nature of money. "Money makes the world go round," she was fond of telling her members, but she couldn't see that it expressed and magnified what was already there; she thought the trick was to get enough of it. Even ten million, she wrote, wasn't that much. She didn't have a clue about the principle of the work expanding to fit the resources.

Somehow, Madalyn had managed to snatch defeat from the jaws of victory, creating a money crisis within six months of coming into more than a million and a half dollars. She concluded that before, they just hadn't really understood how insidiously powerful religion was, how big the job was. That must be it.

In an unguarded moment, she finally put on paper an end to the Nigger Leftridge fantasy. She did not grow up rich, she wrote. "I only knew what I missed because I was poor."

On New Year's Eve 1986, the Founders worked almost until midnight. One of Madalyn's last diary entries of that overworked, million-dollar year was, "...I do wish we could get the financing we need. So much needs to be done."

For Christmas, Garth threw out all his clothes and bought new ones, and, with unintentional irony, bought the family a treadmill.

Chapter 51 ~ Two Fateful Things

I N 1987, two fateful things set in motion a scramble for balance that would last the short rest of the Founders' lives. First, the nine-year-old Strobel case came lurching back to life like a Frankenstein monster. In March, Jeff Friedman amended the original 1978 petition to ask $250,000 in actual and $1 million in exemplary damages. If he got a judgment, Madalyn would have to post a cash bond to appeal. She was worried; in April, the Supreme Court ruled in a similar California case that the Church of Scientology had to do exactly that. Her rage at Friedman was boundless. She realized someone had been sending him the *Insider's Newsletter,* as the money he requested was pointedly close to that reported in it. An urgent appeal went to members just like the original urgent Strobel appeal in 1978, only this time, instead of $80,000 to circle the wagons, she needed $1.25 million.

She began sending Jack Jones in New Zealand "eyes only" letters detailing the danger they were in — but not from the Strobel suit; it would be suicide to admit the entire operation was in jeopardy because of some hotheaded mess created by hormonal surges 10 years ago. No, it was because of the government, the theocracy just on the horizon. "The USA only subsidizes the military and religion now," she wrote Jones. She might need to move money quickly.

Madalyn asked members to loan money to SOS, and when Friedman asked that any money be jointly and severally awarded from both Madalyn and SOS, she set about creating corporations to receive assets so she and SOS would own nothing. By May 1987, she had six 501(c)(3) entities, and in a complicated scheme to dodge a Strobel judgment, she had to publicly get rid of the AA Center on Hancock. She set Garth quietly looking for another building to soak up money.

He found one quickly, at 7125 Cameron Road, in an area called Cameron Hill, and without looking too closely, they traded the Hancock property plus half a million cash for it, for a total of $1.7 million. It would become the newly hatched, but unmarked, American Atheist General Headquarters, Inc. — AAGHQ. Then

Madalyn announced that the Atheist Center was closing down, knowing the papers would cover it but hoping the members wouldn't bolt while she made the transfer.

The new building was a purchase they would come to regret. They had paid cash they would never get back out, and given up the safe, centrally located Hancock address captured for them by Bill. Though impressive-looking and enormous, the new building was in a blighted neighborhood, with trash blowing around the parking lot and vagrants urinating into the landscaping. Vandalism and burglaries were so common in the area that the employees came to call their Cameron Hill workplace Crime-on-the-Hill.

Madalyn fired her media coordinator, Brian Lynch, who was also SOS's treasurer, when he balked at signing the tax return. A former director of the Massachusetts chapter, he'd been on the job a year and a half, and like much of the talent she attracted, wore many hats. He wrote a column for the magazine, notarized, helped write legal documents. At some point he began quietly probing the finances, and felt the 990 form was full of lies. He went to SOS's board, concerned they were all vulnerable if the Founders were committing fraud.

Then Jack Massen called from San Francisco, asking why the $30,000 he'd donated had not been spent on computers as designated. Madalyn heatedly told him it was none of his business. She didn't want to have to explain the complexities of administration to donors; she needed room to maneuver.

She planned to stall the Strobel case with an ace-in-the-hole suit similar to *O'Hair v. Hill* , challenging the requirement of an oath to serve on a jury. Garth was now head of the organizations, so *Murray v. Travis County District Court* bore his name. She moved to file a third-party suit against Cox Texas Publications, which owned the *Austin American-Statesman*, which had run Jane Daugherty's first Strobel article back in October 1977. Judge Harley Clark granted her motion.

The second fateful event of 1987 was Madalyn's move to unseat James Hervey Johnson from the Truth Seeker Corporation. It had been gnawing at her for years, and with the danger from Strobel, its assets beckoned anew.

Johnson was a thin, sour man of 86 who took certain things very seriously: money, liberals, minorities, and homeopathic medicine. He was as anti-Zionist as Madalyn ("The Israelis have found that the American taxpayer is a fat sucker, easily exploited through the political parasites.") and his hate list included alcohol, modern medicine, Communists, and people on welfare. He was pathologically thrifty (afflicted with skin cancer that dissolved his left ear, he simply stuck a paper towel in the hole to catch drainage until it became severely infected), but a crafty investor who had amassed $17 million for the Truth Seeker — money Madalyn felt should come AA's way.

She had certain rationalizations for that. She was positive that Bill had peddled a bootleg AA mailing list to "Scurvy" back in 1977 when he'd thrown that Molotov cocktail called Strobel. It wasn't much of a stretch to rationalize that if she'd had the income from whatever use Johnson made of that list, she'd have some of that $17 million.

And it was simple to extrapolate that to all the atheists betrayed by Johnson's disgraceful "newsletter" that did almost nothing for church-state separation. The money he'd been investing all those years initially came from atheists, for atheist causes. And instead of filing lawsuits, or even putting out a dignified journal with well-researched information worthy of library collections, he'd typed up a shotloose bunch of drivel from his own head and not even bothered to correct the typos or get the Xeroxed and stapled product into the mail regularly. He'd become obsessed with race issues: " . . . if intelligence instead of religious superstition ruled the world, [South African blacks] would be grateful for [a] . . . government operated by superior thinkers," and "The Negro-breeding do-gooder does not understand geometrical increase of human beings."

Madalyn recruited the president of the San Diego AA chapter, Stephen Thorne. Thorne was an energetic activist who worked to get AA magazine into the Escondido Public Library and headed American Atheist Veterans. He and two members insinuated themselves into the Truth Seeker Corporation (TSC) to find out all they could about it, Johnson, and the American Association for the Advancement of Atheism and National Liberal League, both closely related to TSC for many years. Madalyn supplied a telephone card for reports and an American Express for expenses.

Between March and July 1987, they filched copies of Johnson's mailing list and recent will, secretly videotaped his home office, and discovered he was dying of cancer. The will, Madalyn accused later, left everything to Johnson's Christian banker in an open-ended trust that didn't provide for upkeep and publication of Truth Seeker materials.

Madalyn directed Ralph Shirley to find out if TSC, AAAA, and NLL were still legally registered in New York as chartered corporations. She began calling around the country to people she thought might be stockholders in TSC, or members of the other two organizations. She gathered information on how elderly the members were, and how unhappy with James Hervey Johnson. But she wasn't seriously looking for ex-*Truth Seeker* readers, her future accusers would say. She already had the one she wanted: 80-year-old John G. Jackson of Chicago, whom she'd singled out at the Ingersoll Festival in 1983.

Jackson had met Charles Smith, associate editor of the *Truth Seeker*, in 1928, and begun writing for the magazine in 1930. He continued for 25 years until, in about 1955, the wealthy Rogers Peet clothier family bequeathed $250,000 to Smith to run articles many considered racist, fascist, and anti-Semitic. Jackson quit. But before he did, Smith promised him five shares of Truth Seeker Corporation stock for his faithful contributions.

And, said Madalyn, he'd done the same for her. Promised her five shares after she won her big 1963 case.

She called Jackson. Would he become a plaintiff in a lawsuit? As a shareholder? He wouldn't have to do anything but lend his name. No expenses, attorney fees, or costs.

He agreed, and in her suite at the Denver Radisson for the 1987 convention, a select group — the Murray-O'Hairs, Stephen Thorne and co-infiltrator Robin Shelley, Arnold Via, and Jackson — planned a TSC "shareholders" meeting as soon as possible after the convention.

Madalyn's attorney, John Vinson, was promised a 10% return on whatever they pried out of James Hervey Johnson. If they got the whole thing, he'd get more than $1.6 million, plus his salary.

In June 1987, they held the first board meeting in Austin. There, in a move that echoed those against her by Lemoin Cree, Irv, and Bill, they voted Johnson out, and elected a new slate of Truth Seeker Corporation officers. Madalyn was president.

She created a TSC corporate record book to reflect the ten shares owned by herself and John Jackson, and then printed stock certificates bearing the TSC name and logo. She notified the New York Secretary of State Corporate Filings Division that the Truth Seeker had moved its headquarters to 7215 Cameron Road, Austin, Texas, and please direct all future communications to TSC's new agent, Stephen Thorne, in Escondido, California. This would later be called a violation of 18 USC 1341, or mail fraud.

Madalyn told members she was attempting to rescue several venerable old atheist organizations from a greedy usurper. She said the new board had "no idea what the assets may be," though she knew very well what they were.

At the end of September 1987, she launched a nightmare, filing suit against James Hervey Johnson on behalf of John G. Jackson, all other shareholders in the Truth Seeker Corporation, and all the members of AAAA and NLL.

Johnson was accused of "mulcting" the three organizations since 1965, of neglecting to call regular board meetings, or hold elections, and breaching his fiduciary duty. He'd commingled their funds with his personal money and played the stock market with it, all for his own selfish advantage. He'd sold off TSC books and pocketed the money. He'd become rich by misappropriating the organizations' money, and they wanted it back.

Along with John Jackson and Madalyn, Arnold Via filed an affidavit saying he was a life member of TSC and had also received a promise of shares for his activism on behalf of atheism.

Shortly after her suit was filed, Madalyn made a settlement offer that put her in charge and allowed Johnson to keep 15% of the $17 million. Laced with embarrassing language about Madalyn and the Austin Group being "exceptionally big names" in "the mainstream Atheist community," her offer was answered with a Cease and Desist notice to stop usurping TSC's name, mailing list, and trademark. She was warned that she was violating the Lanham Act by doing this in interstate commerce.

Madalyn ignored it.

There was one problem of which she was unaware. The late Charles Smith *had* signed share certificates, and they still existed. And her name wasn't on any of them, nor was Mr. Jackson's nor Arnold Via's — only that of James Hervey Johnson.

Chapter 52 ~ *Forever Proletariat*

NINETEEN-EIGHTY-SEVEN marked Jon Garth's last attempt to get a woman. He became engaged to a "young Madalyn," said a member, named June. June had given notice at her job in Ohio, and was moving to Austin to take over one of the jobs of the indispensable Gerald Tholen, who had just passed away.

She came at the worst possible time, with the press poking around about the closing of the American Atheist Center, the clandestine move to Cameron Hill during nonstop rainstorms, Madalyn's moves and countermoves in the Truth Seeker and Strobel cases, learning a complicated new computerized typesetting system called the Epic, the ever-tardy magazine and newsletter production, and a terrific flea infestation at Greystone, where Garth was making room for her clothes in his closet.

She pitched in, so busy she didn't even get to speak to Madalyn for several days. Madalyn had yearned nonstop for a woman for Garth, any woman, but all she wrote now was, "We'll see."

Madalyn slept poorly on June's first night in Garth's bed. She was up early the next morning, annoyed that the exhausted couple was still asleep; June's car was blocking hers, and she wanted to go to the office immediately. She paced until she heard Garth's alarm. Ordinarily she wouldn't have had such a hunger for work this early on a Saturday, nor begrudged Garth his sleep. The long-awaited "woman for Garth" was already rubbing her the wrong way.

Within two weeks, she was wondering when the girl would leave. They'd tried to make her welcome; Robin was especially kind. Madalyn couldn't figure out why it didn't seem to be working out. Years later, Arnold Via summed it up: "Jon got a little horny and got a girlfriend and let her move into the home.... Madalyn locked horns with her fast, and that was the end of that love affair."

One day in mid-July, June stalked out and didn't come home that night or the next. She left Austin. At the end of the month, Jon Garth wrote his ex in Ohio, "I'm very disappointed in you." She'd left them in the lurch, and Robin frantically interviewing replacements. "I enjoyed the sex and I have not come down with anything yet so I guess that part worked out," he wrote, but she had foolishly walked out on a fantastic opportunity to rise above her station.

"I personally don't think that you had the guts to make the transition from working class to managerial class. You will now remain forever proletariat," he scolded.

At Christmas, Madalyn was in the middle of a diary tirade about how Christmas had been wonderful when she was a child, but now it was venal and repulsive, when the phone rang. She was told that Irv, 71, had had a massive heart attack.

He died four days later, and Madalyn wrote that she didn't care. He was a leech, and she had "*not one* fond memory of [him] at all."

"He died a virgin," Bill said later, because of the hold that the women in his family needed to have over the men.

Madalyn spent Easter Sunday 1988 in nostalgia about the Easter baskets she used to make, the excitement of Halloween and Christmas, the innocence of her childhood, the parades and impromptu speeches. That was all dead now, people didn't decorate or put up lights like they used to at Christmas. The secular world she'd fought for gave her no happiness.

They were back in business in the new building on Cameron Road, and Madalyn held a grand opening of the new AA General Headquarters — GHQ — on June 17, 1988, 25th anniversary of *Murray v. Curlett* and *Abington Township v. Schempp.* There was a ribbon-cutting and a photograph of the three Founders with a tiered cake. That photo would be circulated around the globe later, when they went missing.

Madalyn was very proud of Robin, who a few months before had reported for jury duty and refused to take the oath. Judge Guy Herman said she didn't have to mention God, just swear to be truthful. She refused — even the act of swearing implied a God. She would say only that she understood the penalty for perjury. She drew three days in the slammer for contempt, much to Madalyn's excitement and pride. She served about six hours before being sprung, and Madalyn pronounced her "another one with true grit."

In the 25th anniversary issue of AA magazine, Madalyn also wrote a heartfelt paean to Jon Garth. It evoked the loneliness of his fatherless path, and unwittingly documented the colonizing of every Jon Garth cell for the slobbering maw of the needy, holy Cause.

He went silently to jail at 10, was sent away to Ohio so Mother could claw briefly at the flaming chigger-bites of lust on her lonely existence. Garth took over the role of father at age 15 while Mother stampeded across the land on speaking tours, trumpeting and snorting, sucking up coins and feebly flapping bills with her sensitive trunk and trotting bulkily back home to shower him and their shiny, laughing baby-elephant with dust, straw, money, fame, trinkets, gratitude, and love, such love.

In rendering the 25 years of light in which they'd basked, she depicted Garth as head of the household during most of them. Protector of her and Robin, "the single male authority . . . behind which the two Murray-O'Hair women have been able to work in the male-dominated society of the U.S."

There it was again, the yearning. She *would* have a husband, despite those four Catholics who let her down. She *would* have a man to protect her while she spun and spun her important world. She would have a work-horse honey-do who could handle anything, make a respectable bottom line on his 1040 (she was paying Garth upwards of $57,000 now), talk with her into the wee hours, be a wonderful traveling companion, plan and scheme with her, and never, ever leave her. Even if she had to spend a lifetime hammering out such a man herself.

A few months later, she finally broke her silence about Bill. He was totally dependent on her name, that was his only identity, his only drawing card, she said.

But her listing of some cases that set her against Bill made atheists sound like free-speech enemies. High school valedictorian forbidden to mention Christ in her address; pro-lifers forbidden to picket abortion clinics; math teacher forbidden to read her Bible while on monitor duty; people arrested for handing out religious tracts on city property and at city events; a school district forbidding teachers to mention religion, even among themselves; a public library reading room forbidding patrons to read the Bible in it.

In fact, the country was still awash in confusion and controversy over créches, crosses, menorahs, vouchers, the Pledge, and prayers at graduation and games. Church-state separation was proving slippery ground. Could a Christian landlord offended by fornication refuse to rent to an unmarried couple? Could a school board make a teacher remove sex-explicit classics like *Lysistrata* from her reading list? Could a dental hygienist talk about Jesus to her trapped patient? Christian Scientists were denying their children medical care, evangelists were channeling money to Republicans, Christian student clubs weren't allowed to use school facilities, but Communist and homosexual ones were.

Could we tax parsonages? Was a mural of Solomon in a courtroom constitutional? Should the sculpture of Moses and the Ten Commandments be sandblasted off the Supreme Court building? Could a church be made to quiet its ringing bells? The town of Pensacola passed an ordinance banning *Last Temptation* screenings; was that constitutional? A witch sued the Salvation Army after she was fired for Wiccan activities at work. A pro-choice Catholic was refused communion, a couple who donated 110 acres for a public park were forbidden to erect a statue of St. Francis there, the Los Angeles mayor flew the flag at half-mast when a prominent cardinal died. Conservative legislators attacked funding for the arts after federal grants were awarded for works like *Piss Christ* (a crucifix with a figure of Jesus immersed in the artist's urine) and a collection of sado-masochistic homosexual photographs.

Did private Christian schools and day care centers have to meet public school health and safety standards? Remove asbestos at their own cost? Refrain from corporal punishment though Proverbs 23:13–14 was a Christian duty? A public school wouldn't allow John Lennon's "Imagine" played at graduation. An atheist drunk driver was sent to Alcoholics Anonymous, arousing the ACLU. Creationist taxpayers opposed explanations of evolution at the St. Louis Zoo monkey section. A court found that opening prayers at public meetings had a secular purpose: to bring the meeting to order. A long tradition of Easter sunrise services at a California park ended. Some Iowa schools didn't assign Wednesday homework because so many students went to church that night. Licenses, degrees, and other documents issued by tax-funded entities often said, "In the year of our Lord." Was that constitutional?

If forces like American Atheists and the ACLU had their way, Bill said, you'd be arrested for uttering "God" in public. And indeed, a couple of years later, American Atheists recommended workplace reforms to the Equal Employment Opportunity Commission that smacked of that: besides no prayers or religious holiday themes except the AA-approved seasonal observations, there should be no mottoes, poems, crucifixes, pictures, calendars, jewelry, head scarves, yarmulkes, ornaments, brochures, or Bibles, no notices on shared bulletin boards, no humming, whistling, or singing of religious tunes, no "overt meditations," and no religious conversations. AA also planned to push for a new First Amendment whose language would, Madalyn promised members, make atheist cases easier to litigate.

Around this time, Arnold Via, their volunteer house-sitter, surprised the Founders with a new deck in the backyard. Madalyn loved it; it was soon covered with clay pots and hanging baskets full of flowers. But two days after Thanksgiving 1988, she slipped on it and smashed her left hip. Garth and Robin rushed her to Brackenridge Hospital, where an artificial stainless-steel hip was put in on November 28.

She was in bed a month. Don Sanders, a Houston AA member who had formed American Gay Atheists in 1983, drove up to Austin and filled in for her on American Atheist Forum.

The O'Hairs grew close to the capable, vivacious Sanders. Insiders thought he and Madalyn were cut from the same cloth; one said they were matching sociopaths who needed chaos and estrangement. It was rumored that Sanders enjoyed calling televangelist prayer lines pretending to be a repentant prostitute, and gradually increasing the vulgarity of his confessions until he'd upset the volunteer counselor.

Chapter 53 ~ Racketeering

OVER 1988, the Truth Seeker matter heated up. Madalyn wrote the TSC members in the U.S., Canada, and abroad about the new board and new headquarters in Austin. Most believed the takeover to be real. This would shortly be called mail fraud.

In April 1988, James Hervey Johnson produced all the share certificates, signed by Charles Smith, proving he'd been given them on October 15, 1963. If Smith had intended Madalyn to have five of them, surely that would have been the year to give them to her.

It was a blow, but Madalyn soldiered on. Ignoring last November's Cease and Desist notice, she put out her own *Truth Seeker* in June, using the TSC logo. It contained her version of how the organizations got so outrageously corrupted in the hands of Hervey Johnson. She said the burning of Johnson's "condemned slum" building in 1981 netted him an enormous insurance settlement, and that Lawrence True, Johnson's longtime *Christian* banker, now controlled and spent the assets when he wasn't going to church — and he wanted $80,000 a year to continue. And TSC Secretary Bonnie Lange was wanting $36,000 a year to be president. And the attorneys and accountants were lining up to keep all this out of the hands of the Austin group.

Truth Seeker attorney Roy Withers filed a countercomplaint for "Conversion, Trademark Infringement, Lanham Act Violations, and Violations under Racketeer Influenced and Corrupt Organizations" — the dreaded RICO statute usually associated with organized crime. He named Madalyn, Jon, Robin, Steve Thorne, John Jackson, Arnold Via, Robin Shelley, and all Madalyn's corporations — every conceivable one — outright on the caption page. That should defeat her shell game with assets, and expose her attempt to hide behind the elderly Jackson, he said.

The RICO statute allowed triple damages, along with punitive damages limited only by the loser's wealth. That was why Withers named all the corporations. The Founders *were* the corporations, and the boards their alter egos; insiders had joked for years that "When the three of them drove to work every morning, it was a board meeting." Withers was confining the punitive damage request to $1 million.

Madalyn fired back in August, placing a temporary conservatorship on Johnson's estate because he was mentally incompetent to care for it and himself. But in a great *faux pas*, Madalyn's conservatorship petition made no mention of Johnson's personal well-being, only his assets. It was immediately lifted.

Three days later, on August 6, 1988, Bonnie Lange found Johnson dead in his bathtub.

His will showed $1.75 million of real estate, $600,000 in cash, and $15 million in stocks. His estate was split into the Truth Seeker Trust and the Charitable Education Trust; the probate court appointed Lawrence True trustee of both. Madalyn challenged the appointment.

Despite the RICO action against her for trademark infringement, Madalyn put out a second *Truth Seeker*, an anxious, shrill rehashing of what a thief Johnson was, how Christers had taken over a legitimate atheist enterprise. Again, it used terms like "fine old atheist organization" and "group of mainline atheist leaders" to will into existence a large, established, comfortable, American Atheist tradition that loved its pipe and brandy in the paneled drawing room after a fine dinner served by Nigger Leftridge.

At the end of 1988, the ailing John Glover Jackson gave a deposition. He was "puzzled" why Madalyn was so interested in his writing. "For some strange reason," he said, she'd taken a liking to him. Had it ever occurred to him that Madalyn was using him in this lawsuit? "Maybe O'Hair used her charms on me," he replied, but "I've been used so many times."

In late March 1989, the 19th annual AA Convention was held in San Diego, on enemy turf at the Marriott, a Mormon chain. With input from a hipper, younger group including Steve Thorne and Arizonan Conrad Goeringer, it was rowdy and fun. There were 400 attendees at lectures like "Bimbos for Satan," and a skit where the pope visited to bring birthday greetings to Madalyn. There were T-shirts that said, "Jesus — Just Say No."

But the week before, an anti-Madalyn press release was issued by a group of local ex-AA members, headed by one named Frank Mortyn. She was Jerry Falwell's best friend, the release said, sending piles of money and converts his way.

Johnson's crude *Truth Seeker* newsletter was transformed by publisher Bonnie Lange into 36 glossy pages with articles on the greenhouse effect and Gaia. The politically incorrect Johnson diatribes disappeared. A month after the convention, Madalyn's contest of Johnson's will was dismissed by probate judge Peter Riddle. She was fined $3,120 for refusing to respond to deposition questions. After appealing a summary judgment granted to Lawrence True, and protesting his and TSC attorneys' commissions, Madalyn was fined another $11,625 for wasting the court's time.

Roy Withers later recalled the first time he deposed Madalyn. He was expecting to breeze through it. "I spent about an hour with her and asked for a recess. I went in the bathroom and stared in the mirror and asked myself what was wrong. And it hit me. 'This old gal is beating you up.'"

In later years, a video clip of one of those depositions would be widely shown in the search for the missing O'Hairs: a white-haired, slit-eyed Madalyn leaning across the conference table, elbows spread, hissing into Withers' face through clenched teeth, "*Don't fuck with me!*" Even though she was rolled in in a wheelchair, dizzy and sick with diabetes and high blood pressure.

But the work of Frank Mortyn, Gordon Stein, and others was beginning to sting, and Madalyn recklessly continued to make damaging enemies. After the convention, Fred Woodworth of Tucson became one. Woodworth was one of her best writers for AA magazine. He published not only a tight, punchy anarchist magazine called *The Match!*, but the chapter newsletter, *Arizona Atheist.* Madalyn wanted him in Austin; he knew everything about printing and production, and his writing was magnetic and often brilliant — though he could cut to ribbons anyone who became his target.

When he declined to relocate, Madalyn attacked him personally. He'd screwed up a love affair. He was scared of change. He *wanted* to be poor, *wanted* to fail. He hated himself. As a veteran psychiatric social worker, she said, she'd ascertained all this from reading his novel, *Dream World.* She called him a piss-ant.

She yanked *Arizona Atheist* away, and notified Tucson postal authorities that he was illegally using SOS's mailing permit and box. She appointed his longtime friend, Conrad Goeringer, as the new chapter head. Goeringer doggedly defended Madalyn, trying to explain that her feelings were hurt because Fred wouldn't move to Austin, and that was why she accused him of felony mail fraud.

That ended Woodworth's long friendship with Goeringer.

As usual, the gratification Madalyn got from this attack was massively expensive. Woodworth set to work on a booklet, *The Atheist Cult*, exposing yet-unknown things about Madalyn in colorful, powerful images. It would be devastating. Everyone in the atheist and freethought community had a copy.

Chapter 54 ~ Falling Apart

BY AUGUST 1989, *American Atheist* magazine was five months late, the newsletters were late, and the Founders were engulfed by unemployment compensation payments because of all the firings. They couldn't meet payroll for the workers who did manage to hang on.

In July, the U.S. District Court dismissed Jon Garth's suit charging that he'd been excluded from all jury service because he refused to say an oath. The court said there was no constitutional right to serve on a jury. Madalyn took it to the Fifth Circuit on appeal. The Founders wanted their specific language substituted, simply that the juror understands the penalties of perjury. No, said the New Orleans court; it upheld the district court. Madalyn publicly called the judges idiots.

During the summer of 1989, Brian Lynch, like Frank Mortyn in San Diego and Gordon Stein in Buffalo and others around the country, was sending out letters to AA chapter heads about the mess in Austin. He gathered "Madalyn" stories from all over, starting with the O'Hairs' conflict of interest in controlling all the boards of the corporations. Any board member who questioned them was thrown off. How long could she get away with this, before the feds clamped down? Board members might be personally liable for Madalyn's corporate actions. In fact, anyone who'd taken a tax deduction for a donation might find the IRS knocking on their door if Madalyn's tax status were revoked. Speaking of which, the library was no longer open to the public as required by the IRS.

Sure enough, in the fall, the IRS started an audit of Robin, and a few days later, Jon Garth. Then SOS and CESAALA. Madalyn suspected it was Lynch's work, but others were either dialing the IRS' number or soon would be. Lots of members were outraged by the life appointments of the Founders to the boards of the six or seven AA corporations, and somehow, without anyone knowing exactly how, Jon Garth had become "President for Life" of American Atheists. Once, when the IRS sent Madalyn a request for itemized records, she sent it back with a two-word reply: "Fuck you." In 1990, she sued personally the agents who had been auditing them, for $50,000 each. She sued the IRS, Treasury Department, United States of America, and Brian Lynch for conspiracy, harassment, violation of her civil rights, and racketeering.

This prompted Garth to write Jack Jones in New Zealand that their IRS troubles might blow up in as little as 60 days, and they'd need to get out of the country. Madalyn was 72 and in ill health. "I don't want to see her die in a prison on trumped-up charges."

"We are continuing all of our activity as if nothing really is the matter," Madalyn wrote Jones. They were planning conventions and filing lawsuits, "doing everything we can to pretend nothing is happening." She hoped they could drag things out over two years to give themselves time to get their money to New Zealand. The IRS was saying Jon and Robin were each personally on the hook for $750,000, and the organizations for ruinous amounts, too. Property values were dropping, so they couldn't get back the cash they'd put into Crime-on-the-Hill. Still, they were thinking of just cutting their losses, and would keep Jones posted.

For Jones, it was the start of a tiresome drain. Their requests were endless — how much of their stuff could they ship? How about the Mercedes? Do you guys have unleaded gas there? Would our office equipment work on your electric current? Could you locate a 20,000-square-foot building for CESAALA? Would it have to be commercial property, or was there some other category?

Could Jones look into Albania? Madalyn thought it was the only atheist country in the world. But weren't Muslims now gliding in, those "throat-cutting bastards"? Could he find out about an account for international drafts right away, in case they needed to get out of the country fast?

Could foreign citizens live there, or did they have to apply for citizenship? Could Madalyn continue to get her VA and Social Security payments? Could they get a 35,000-square-foot home, with acreage? What was the quarantine period for five dogs?

Jones did a prodigious amount of research for the family, on refugee versus "commercial immigrant" status, on tax and legal and banking resources. He looked into "charitable status" for CESAALA.

The *Encyclopedia of Associations* for 1989 reported that American Atheists had become inactive. Madalyn's actual suits at the time included challenging the Austin city seal, which had a cross in it, another nativity suit in California, some Florida school board members praying in the wrong place, the Concerned Women of America "trading on" Madalyn's fame, a $12 million suit filed against Travis County and various court officials for the six hours Robin had spent in the pokey two years ago (dismissed as frivolous), Zion, Illinois displaying religious insignia on too many public properties, a big cross on a California hillside, and a new "In God We Trust" suit. The more significant cases — a church tax effort in Texas, *Murray v. Travis County*, the jury oath — had to compete for funds with ferocious battles over the right to scribble out "God" on folding money and a congressional proclamation forbidding elected officials to deride citizens' beliefs.

Before fall 1989, $75,000 came in from the estate of longtime supporter Fletcher Pence, and Madalyn was expecting bequests from others — Lipe, Bennett, Holste,

Alt, Latta, Reitmeister, Kemp, Phillips, Rega, Marthaler, Mueller, Hanson, God-
win — even a man named Murray, no relation, who had created a trust for SOS.
Some were for money, others library collections, insurance, stocks, or real estate.
Lynch felt the Founders were hanging around the U.S. only long enough to collect
on a few more large estates, totaling about $6 million. The family was rumored to
have a number of overseas bank accounts opened with the social security numbers
of dead relatives. After she'd alienated the members and shrunk their number below 500 or something, Lynch reasoned, Madalyn would sell GHQ, liquidate all the
accounts, and leave. That explained why she had a skeleton crew at GHQ these
days, some with "pasts," so she could fire them easily and control them — and avoid
unemployment payments.

He, and later others, recounted the deteriorating conditions at GHQ: Jon Garth
exhibited symptoms of posttraumatic stress disorder, unable to focus even on short-
term goals, exploding over a box of paper clips left in the wrong place. The O'Hair
"troika" had lost all restraint, screaming at employees and never offering praise for
a job well done. The dogs roamed through the building, relieving themselves where
they pleased, for employees to clean up. Desperate for grandchildren, Madalyn
approached prospects with offers of money to carry Jon's child or impregnate Robin,
Lynch reported.

Lynch said he'd had queries from members whether there was incest going on
between niece and uncle. He didn't know — all he could testify to was the utter
absence of any normal social relationships for them.

"A couple of times they were embracing like they were making up after a fight,"
said a long-time volunteer who had seen Robin sitting in Garth's lap. People noticed
that they fought and made up like a married couple. Jokes flew that they should get
hitched and have the perfect atheist child. Secretary Cloe Madsen said Robin was
jealous of other women with Jon Garth; if their bond was turning physical, she felt
Madalyn would have shrugged. "So what? There's no God."

Staff artist Wendy Davis said the incest rumor was "bullshit. They were just
asexual types."

Ray Fleming remembered when he first volunteered on the television forum.
"You're not married, are you?" Madalyn said on their first meeting. "I can tell,
because your shirts aren't ironed."

"I wouldn't marry someone who thought they had to iron my shirts," he retorted,
and the next time she saw him, she nudged the 31-year-old physicist toward Robin.
"I tried a few times to engage Robin in conversation about other things" than AA,
he said, "but there was no depth. There was just no time." During his several years
volunteering, Madalyn periodically "ranted and raved about Jon and Robin being
virgins, in front of them. Jon would...tell her to shut up, but Robin would hide.
You'd see her slip away when Madalyn started."

Robin "was by far the brightest of the three," said Derek Nalls, who had known
her for nearly a decade. Nalls had volunteered steadily during that time, becoming

a paid employee in 1990. "I was real disappointed that Robin never left the house, and . . . let herself get ridiculously fat."

Most people found much to like about Robin, especially her sense of humor. She was a generous donor to KMFA, the local listener-supported classical music radio station, and the Humane Society. It was Robin who took care of the dogs and all the stray cats behind GHQ. She tried to cook healthy meals to reverse Madalyn's diabetes, bought nice gifts for departing employees, and fed the laborers who came to put in lawn plugs or prune the trees. When David Kent was in a financial crunch, Robin got the family to cosign a mortgage, though he didn't end up needing it.

Robin was the one who really understood the computers and the benefits of desktop publishing. She was the one who kept up the garden and planted flowers and put beautiful hanging baskets around the patio. She made sure the women at GHQ got flowers and chocolate on Valentine's Day. She had started organizing the library when she was a teenager, and she knew it inside out.

But Madalyn discouraged any friendships. When Robin was hospitalized with viral pneumonia, Wendy Davis took up a collection for flowers. "Well, Mrs. O'Hair said that we were *absolutely* not to buy Robin any flowers . . . they knew we didn't really like them, and . . . it was a completely insincere gesture." Wendy was a cheerful soul, and when Madalyn would hear guffawing around her, she'd sneer, "Well, aren't *you* just a little ray of sunshine!"

Wendy remembered an incident in Robin's office one day. Madalyn came in, feeling chatty, and told another version of an old whopper about bribing a Swiss Guard and getting into the Vatican papal apartments during the war. Her first story had her comrades breaking into the glass coronation case and crowning her the "first woman Pope." This time, it was the Pope's underpants, "made of fine linen and trimmed with handmade lace," that she tried on.

"All the time she was telling this story," said Davis, "Robin was gazing at her intently, with a look of such love."

After a year on the job, Derek Nalls lost respect for the people he'd once admired, even Robin. "They viewed themselves as far too important historical figures. They didn't even seem to think they were capable of [mistakes]. They didn't grow or change at all . . . it was a closed universe." Once, he made too many copies of something because of sloppy instructions by Jon. "You *stupid fucking idiot!*" Jon Garth screamed at him, while those in earshot fumed. Editorial assistant David Travis, a Vietnam vet, later heard Jon screaming, "*stupid goddamned employees!*" in another room. "I pushed my chair back and got up. I was going to go in there and whip his ass." He regained control and returned to his desk with no bloodshed.

The Founders also fought each other. "Jon would call Madalyn a fat, stupid bitch," said an employee. "She called him a *re*-tard. And then she would get on the phone and ask for money with her silky voice."

Madalyn would interrupt the work flow with "drop everything" projects for the staff without telling Jon or Robin. When the latter found out routine had been put aside, all three of them would attack the employees, Madalyn bellowing, "you know you're not to accept assignments from me, only from Jon or Robin!"

After David Kent labored over a CESAALA grant proposal to the National Endowment for the Humanities, Madalyn rejected it as too polite: "We must demand money *as a right* — not ask, or plead for it as a favor!"

They kept a death-grip on small expenditures, and meddled in the minutiae of production instead of leaving it to the experts they'd hired. Jon would buy cut-rate ink, dry mount, or paper for the artist and printer, and then explode when the product didn't look as slick as he expected.

The AA product was crumbling and declining on every front. The TV forum was an embarrassment, amateurish and boring. On the show's tenth anniversary in May 1990, Jon Garth sent out a "funding appeal" that could only be called a cry for help. The family was just working itself to death, he wrote, red eyes, bags under them, no life. "I want to start a family," he pleaded. "I want to see my sister be able to find a mate . . ." They were all so fatigued, so pitifully tired of fighting all alone.

But they were doomed, no matter Garth's cry. There was no move to cut back, or let the small stuff go. The magazine had to be between 48 and 72 pages. They poured massive resources and plotting-time into getting even with Brian Lynch, suing an ex-member for opining that they'd erred with the Strobel case, launching half-baked ventures like a time-consuming column called "Ask the Founders" and a short-lived something called Poor Richard & Company. They squandered time writing crash-courses in saddle stitching and postal routing, to explain to the members why the magazine was months late — did the pinch-penny members not *understand* what it took to put out a huge magazine like this? They launched an annual summer solstice picnic billed as "Madalyn's Money Day," on which every AA family was urged to send $200 "until the sun becomes a nova." By now, such spirits of fun were eclipsed by gloom, and quickly flopped.

Oddly, the die-hard members never seemed to tire of hearing about their leaders being under assault by the disgruntled, religious, jealous, incompetent, hostile, biased, greedy, corrupt, or crazy. Lynch speculated that many of them came from harsh or fanatical backgrounds that predisposed them to cults.

The Truth Seeker raid was a massive drain — on January 8, 1990, Judge Judith Keep ruled that Mr. Jackson was not a shareholder, and dismissed the case, leaving Madalyn to face TSC's deep-pockets retaliation.

Whether the report of stud and brood services for Garth and Robin was true, Lynch was right about Madalyn hiring people with "pasts." More than one person had heard Jon scream at a certain employee to go back to prison where he came from. But instead of giving Madalyn the control she craved, that practice led to murder.

Part Three

The End

Chapter 55 ~ Colleen

COLLEEN KAY SMITH* came to Texas in late 1991 at the age of 32. One of four siblings, she was bright, with an air Texas men liked — earthy, quick with a comeback. And smart, but she didn't throw it up to you. She was pretty, with long, tanned legs, thick chestnut hair, brown eyes, and an aquiline nose with a little Cherokee bump.

"Ever'body was in love with her" at the smoke-filled Poodle Dog Lounge on Burnet Road in Austin, where she worked while finishing her degree at the University of Texas. "She was a classy gal. The way she handled herself in the joint, ever'body liked her," said a regular, Jerry Basey.

She recalled the day the owner hired her. "Are you sure?" he said. "Do you know what kind of place this is?" She looked around at the Formica tables on their wobbly pedestals, the stackable chairs, the broken horoscope machine, pool tables, overflowing ashtrays, and assured him she'd be fine. She liked that rough edge. In a week or two she fit right in, and the regulars told her that at first they'd thought she was a narc.

Why? she asked.

"You have all your teeth."

She enjoyed shooting the breeze as they argued politics and played shuffleboard. Country music flowed like syrup from the jukebox, punctuated by the clack of pool cues. The dress ranged from boots and cowboy hats to flip-flops and Hawaiian shirts — it was Austin.

She never minded the dirty work. In the women's restroom, mildewed duct tape was slathered around the base of the toilet, but it worked fine. Bare pipes stuck out, and the toilet paper roll sat on a one-by-four nailed to the wall. The sink knobs were rusted and the trash can was a five-gallon pickle bucket, but the ashtray was kept emptied and the facilities clean.

Colleen liked the hunched patrons, listened respectfully to their stories, and joked with them until the stack of Styrofoam go-cups on the bar started dwindling at closing time. But she took no guff from the rough trade that frequented the Poodle Dog.

"A old boy came in here one day and they got in a little argument," said a regular. "She went to take his beer, and he went to keep it — she knocked him outta his chair!"

She had started working right out of high school, back in Peoria. At 22, she took a job at a popular restaurant near the Bradley University campus, Avanti's, and after 10 years, was supervising 40 people. In 1989, restless and bored, she cut her hours and registered at Bradley.

---

*"Colleen Kay Smith" is a pseudonym.

By the end of 1990 she was also bored with her long-time sweetheart — blue-eyed, blond, chin-dimpled Jeff Hunt, a.k.a. Ron Waters, third son of Betty Hunt, a.k.a. Betty Plumley, a.k.a. Betty Waters. Brother of David Waters.

"He is a ... *wonderful* person," Colleen said sorrowfully a decade after she left Jeff. " ... so smart, so much talent." He was a natural comedian, full of one-liners. "His mind worked a million miles a minute." He was a warm, kind soul, opening his pocketbook and his little house on North Douglas Street to Betty when she needed it, to brother David when he was broke or in trouble, to Dean Hunt, the only father he'd known.

"He was so selfless toward them," Colleen said. "But he didn't provide anything for *him*." Eventually, his pleasures dwindled to starvation rations — work, music, beer, a few indulgences.

Then Betty moved in, sleeping in the tiny living room. "The tension just grew and grew, and ... you can't really say, 'you know, you're being an idiot because you're being a selfless son,' because it's a good thing to be that way." But his increasing depression made her wonder. "You think to yourself ... is it you? Are you bringing them down?"

That was when David came back from Florida.

He'd been in Naples since his summer 1987 parole on the forgery conviction. He had actually gotten a conventional job down there, thanks to his new college credentials, at Parker Seal, the automobile sealing-ring division of a large manufacturer. He did clerical work — manning the phones, typing, getting vendor bids. He drove to a plain, one-story building with a treeless parking lot. He made some surprisingly conventional moves, getting a driver's license — with his own name and photo — and his own apartment. He took out a loan on a new Camaro. He earned achievement awards at work. He even joined Sam's Wholesale Club.

One day, a beautiful immigrant from the Dominican Republic, Euridania Tabar, walked into Parker Seal looking for work. She'd been in Florida a week, and could barely communicate in English. He managed to wangle her an assembly line position.

He was touched by her determination. She learned English, and during the time they were together, earned a Licensed Vocational Nurse degree. Then an RN, and her citizenship, and, only a decade after arriving in the U.S., she bought her first house, in New Jersey. She was the only person he could think of that he admired, except for the counselor in juvy who had tried to get him into a private school.

And she never forgot him. "If I got any courage today, it's because-a Dave," she said in 2003, in the accent that had charmed him while she studied English. "I was *so* naive ... I was believin' ever'body and ever'thing. And he would tell me Dania, don't be that way. In order for you to get up in life you hafta kick a few butts."

But Dania knew something was wrong. First, her brother's wife had disliked David from the beginning, and hired a detective. "And when she find out his *life!*...I couldn' believe what I was drawn into...I said 'what else did you do?'

"...and he goes — [pause, sigh] 'I don' know. This is for you to fine out.' I said well, I never gonna fine out if you don' tell me. And he said well, just leave it there."

She did. "You get to a point where...If I get anything more, I prolly gonna drop dead." He hid his criminal side until Parker Seal closed down and he lost his job. But it turned out he had helped drive the company into bankruptcy.

"He was definitely embezzling," said Beth Campbell, whom he was also dating at the time. "He might not have put them under singlehandedly, [but] he was paying himself as if he were a supplier." He loved a certain bank in Coastland Mall, Campbell said, "because they allowed him to open an account without verifying proper IDs and addresses. 'Nice people,' he called them."

His attractive, accomplished boss at Parker Seal was two years his elder, and he was seeing her, along with Beth, Dania, the brief rapprochement with Carolyn Bruce, and a married woman named Tina who lived in the Everglades. By late 1989, his boss was listing David's address as hers, and taking out an equity loan on her home.

What she didn't know was that he planned to get on the title to her house, and then get rid of her — an acquaintance said he planned to kill her — so he could marry Dania and move her in. Their affair reportedly ended with a beating for her and anger management classes for David. But he kept risqué photos of her and pasted them over newspaper articles about her that he kept in a scrapbook.

Beth Campbell found out about one of his trysts and broke up with him. One day in early 1988, he appeared at her apartment with one of his codefendants in the 1964 Gibbs murder. "He kept making me repeat to him that I was *his* F'ing woman." He forced her to have sex while the other man watched, she said. She gave birth in November 1988 to a daughter with "his eyes and his ugly feet," and made a dutiful attempt to bond them. But David refused to even hold the child, saying newborns were ugly. She shut him out of her life and went off to raise her daughter alone.

He was still courting Dania Tabar at the time Parker Seal went bankrupt, and that was when he started drifting, getting into trouble. "He wouldn' go to work...he used to talk about those big cars? He would see himself drivin' those cars. He just liked the good life. And I used to tell him, 'how you gonna get the good life if you don' work?'" By the end of 1989, he was running around with another transplant from Illinois, Danny Fry, a good-looking, gregarious alcoholic with a weakness for financial shortcuts.

Dania knew they were up to something. She laid down the law. "I used to tell him, please don' do anything wrong when I wit' you. Please don't," or she'd leave. When she found out they were pulling credit card frauds, "I tol' him, this is it. And he said it wasn't him, it was [Danny Fry] that did it." She didn't buy it. She moved out and left him at the end of 1990.

Broken-hearted, he returned to Peoria — just when Colleen was breaking up with his brother.

"He said 'let's go to Texas,' and for me, that was *it,*" said Colleen. "I was terminally bored."

"One feature I will always credit David with was his fearlessness . . . you come across someone who is willing to take a chance, willing to make choices by the seat of the pants, willing to ride upon the fates, and let the wave take you, and make your situation once you've landed . . . For me, that was the main attractant."

She gave notice at Avanti's, dropped out of Bradley University, and packed. Jeff watched her go. "I just wasn't enough of an adventure for her," he said.

But first, a car. The repo man was after the 1989 Camaro David had bought in Florida, so he had a plan. The couple went — with his old 1964 codefendant, Carl Welchman — to a car dealership on Memorial and University, where Waters test-drove another 1989 Camaro. Its key looked like his, and after returning, he switched the keys, came back that night, and stole the car. In Texas, he changed the VIN and registered it under his name.

His boldness was like ice water in Colleen's face — bracing.

They arrived in San Antonio in September, and found it charming — the shady River Walk, with paddle boats full of tourists, margaritas and mariachis on the sidewalks, the Alamo at sunset, the old King William Historic District and Spanish Governor's Palace, the famous zoo sprawling over cottonwood-shaded Brackenridge Park.

They set up housekeeping at the Warren Inn on Magic Drive and Fredericksburg Road, in northwest San Antonio. It was a cheap, rambling "residential motel" complex, two-story buildings scattered among groves of beautiful live oaks, with two swimming pools.

Fredericksburg Road was at the edge of the Balcones Fault, the ancient rift that divides the Edwards Plateau and the Gulf Coastal Plain. All along the fault, from Waco to San Antonio and into Mexico, the underground is riddled with treasure-caves of vertebrate fossils, mingled from the limestone of the plateau and the coastal shale. From a section called Balcones Heights atop the fault, you could look down on Fredericksburg Road. With its lovely old groves of hill country oaks, Balcones Heights was strikingly like the Greystone area where the O'Hairs lived, which also sat atop the Balcones Fault, some 100 miles north.

They lived there a year, with Colleen working and David staying home, laying plans.

"He just always thought he had to steal, or manipulate, or scheme to get money," she said. "If he'd put a fraction of that energy into just getting up and going to work, he could have had a brilliant career." She figured it was because of the genius IQ both Betty and Jeff had told her about — he'd just get bored.

Chapter 56 ~ Downward Spiral

FOR THE O'HAIRS and American Atheists, 1991 and 1992 were a continuation of their downward spiral. The thriving San Francisco chapter, in the capable hands of Jack Massen, atomized when Madalyn sued him and his wife for allegedly using her mailing list to start a rogue group. The equally vital Miami chapter dissolved in anger after Garth drained its $6,200 account, and the Houston chapter broke up over Don Sanders' "commissar" behavior. "National" didn't mourn; Madalyn planned to close all the chapters anyway.

KPFT radio in Houston dropped American Atheist Hour, the only live atheist radio show in the U.S., because of "irreconcilable differences" with Austin. Florida's Ed Golly, still on the CESAALA board, listened to the Founders' dilemma over whether to tell the general membership they were using the trust fund for operating expenses. Golly told them point-blank it was illegal. You might try living within your means, he suggested, cut back instead of hurling invective at the members for not sending more money. The magazine didn't have to be 72 pages. The operation didn't have to be housed in a huge, money-sucking GHQ. Golly knew he was crafting the overture to his own "excommunication," and it wasn't long in coming.

The only candle still flickering at AA was the newsletter, often full of good ideas and good writing about the gust of religious controversy that was sweeping the country and the world. Madalyn fretted often about Islam; in 1992, after the murder of a translator of Salman Rushdie's 1988 *Satanic Verses*, she wrote that the world was eventually going to have to deal with the planet's fastest-growing religion. The Muslims weren't going to stop at a few authors, she warned. It was going to be culture against culture.

National magazines like *Time* and *Newsweek* had more cover stories on religion than ever before. The past five or six years had brought a spate of controversial religion-themed movies. *The Last Temptation of Christ* created a firestorm; the 1991 remake of *Cape Fear* featured a psychotic Pentecostal murderer; *The Rapture* showed a mother killing her child to bring about a Bible prophecy; in *Agnes of God,* a nun murdered her newborn.

In 1991, the Boy Scouts were sued when three atheist kids were denied membership; the next year, presidential candidates Bush and Clinton traded accusations of religious bigotry. The Jesus Seminar was formed to comb the record for clues to the historical Christ.

In November 1991, the Supreme Court reached a decision in an important church-state separation case, *Lee v. Weisman.* Mr. Weisman had sued when a rabbi thanked God for a couple of things at a Rhode Island high school graduation ceremony. Weisman won in the lower courts, but the Bush administration appealed the case to the Supreme Court.

The court waited until summer vacation to release its ruling: prayers at public school graduations were unconstitutional.

Of all the chipping away at school traditions — Christmas and Easter pageants, posting of the Ten Commandments, moments of silence — the *Weisman* case banning even the smallest blessing on children at graduation seemed to stick in America's craw. There was an insidious kind of decay, said even liberal churchmen, when you have to surgically remove every shred of religion from public life. The country was gagging on its "values-neutral" educational system, said angry opponents. Factions parsed what a value actually was. School districts feared lawsuits if a teacher or administrator took a position on anything — punishment, sexuality, patriotism, history. There was no neutrality. The new value that rushed into the vacuum was diversity. That was the diabolical thing about this rampant litigation; in addition to running up everyone's costs and robbing institutions of their authority with threats of lawsuits, lawyers attacked the foundation of our sanity, the meaning coded into words and language. An unambiguous ruling of "pay your debt" could be blurred with a perfectly rational argument over the definition of "debt," and an irrational result got. The legal ground shifted instead of clarifying.

From schools to town hall meetings, Madalyn's life's work was blooming in the culture wars, the diversity craze, the political correctness movement. She had had a noteworthy part in the direction her culture was headed, but she felt angry and marginalized. Everything she'd striven for was hers; she was a success by her lights, but it was as if she couldn't admit it.

Bill was flourishing. He would soon leave Dallas behind for Washington, DC. He had his mother's organizing and communication skills, and he was sticking close to the political side of his new mission. In the mid-1980s, he formed Freedom's Friends to help the Nicaraguan Contras, living in their camps in Honduras to oversee distribution of medical supplies, Spanish-language Bibles, and Christmas gift boxes for children.

For years he'd been involved in smuggling Bibles to the Soviet Union before it collapsed. Now he was spearheading expeditions to bring "born-again capitalism" and religious free enterprise to the old Evil Empire. At the end of 1991, he was photographed handing out Bibles in Red Square.

He opened an office in Fredericksburg, Virginia, and founded the Religious Freedom Coalition and a political action committee called Government Is Not God.

His upstairs office at RFC was large and pleasant, filled with windows and bookcases. Madalyn's son was tall and fit, with blondish hair going gray, and large, shapely hands like his mother's. Shelves and walls held photos of him with Ronald Reagan, Phil Gramm, both George Bushes, Newt Gingrich, Tom DeLay, Dick Armey, Colin Powell, John Ashcroft, and of his younger daughters, pretty as prom queens. Framed certificates told of his contributions to the Republican Party, to the preservation of America's heritage. He was comfortable testifying before state and federal congressional committees. He had another office in Washington.

Restoring school prayer was part of his agenda, but it annoyed Murray that the media focused only on that irresistible irony, when RFC was also pushing for curricula about the Founding Fathers, supplying reprints of the Declaration of Independence and Constitution. It attacked the liberal education that had helped the public schools degenerate into a cesspool of drug-sniffing dogs, metal detectors, and plunging scores, while a blizzard of pathetic edicts from school boards across the country threatened grave consequences should "God Bless America" be heard in the hallways.

The one thing Madalyn didn't change yet was the yearly convention. They were important for appearances and continuity until the lawsuits were stable enough for the move to New Zealand.

The 1991 convention was held at a beautiful resort in Scottsdale, Arizona, with spas and tennis courts and heated pools. It included seminars, costumed actors, a Western dance, and a Grand Canyon tour. AA was honored with a special commemorative postage stamp cancellation, a first for any atheist group.

But Madalyn's keynote speech was "the most bizarre demonstration I've ever seen," wrote Steve Thorne later, after he defected to the Truth Seeker camp. "She called for the castration of stock and bond holders of companies which pollute the environment. She said that a major environmental problem was disposing of the urine of three billion people . . ."

A reporter inquiring about her new environmental concern reaped an incoherent geyser of the frustration that was jerking Madalyn through life like a runaway train.

"We simply have to change the system. It's crying out to be changed . . . I love my country. I love the world. I love the people . . . We are taking our whole ecosystem down with us . . . the human community needs to be wiped out. What a pity we can't have a nuclear war."

Garth had bailed on his speech at the members' dinner, said Thorne, so Madalyn pinch-hit, "commenting on the size of her son's testicles . . . because someone said he had no balls!"

At the convention, she took Thorne aside. Robin had seen him take something out of his briefcase and hand it to another member. What was it?

He'd only given his colleague an article on tax-exempt hospitals, but it was none of Madalyn's business, and he told her so. She called him a "fucking coward" and a "fucking traitor," accused him of "seditious" actions, and threatened to have him arrested if he didn't leave the hotel.

Her paranoia was breathtaking, but Ed Golly did believe there were AA factions trying to dethrone Austin to get their hands on the assets, especially the sustaining trust fund. But Madalyn was running it all into the ground anyway with the Truth Seeker and Strobel suits, and her vendettas against Travis County, Brian Lynch, and the IRS examiners.

On April 11, 1991, a few days after Thorne had been jettisoned, TSC sued Madalyn, her corporations and their boards, and all the players in the RICO suit against
her — plus her attorney, John Vinson — for malicious prosecution and conspiracy
to raid its assets. She had damaged reputations and cost TSC huge sums defending itself. Two million should be enough compensation. The RICO charges against
Thorne were dropped in return for his cooperation, and Vinson quickly extricated
himself, ultimately testifying against her. That fall, the Founders were sanctioned
nearly $10,000 for stonewalling in deposition proceedings again.

Garth invited Jack Jones to speak at AA's final convention in Sacramento next
year, after which the O'Hairs hoped to accompany him back to New Zealand for
good. Garth reckoned it would take six months to close out operations in the U.S.,
sell the house, GHQ, and office equipment, and ship the library. Jones didn't know
about the Truth Seeker succubus that had drained so much of AA's money, though
he'd been told about the $16,000 recently spent for the IRS attorney, and the
$32,000 for accountants.

Don Sanders was now in the family's total confidence. Jon sent him copies of
the New Zealand communications, and kept him apprised of the escape plans. The
family had built their social life around Sanders and his partner, Mark Franceschini,
visiting them in Houston, celebrating birthdays, and giving Sanders more and more
responsibility in the corporations. He was an officer in all of them, and appeared
regularly with Madalyn and Garth on *American Atheist Forum*.

In August 1992, Mark Franceschini died. Sanders' relationship with the Founders
was watched with some cynicism by insiders who noted that Sanders, HIV-positive,
was eminently trustworthy with secrets.

In May 1992, Madalyn and the TSC attorneys reached a settlement in the magistrate court of Judge Leo S. Papas. She was to publish a retraction of all claims of
ownership or control of TSC, along with "certain disparaging remarks" she'd made
about Lawrence True. She had to surrender all stationery, seals, stamps, printing
plates, etc. bearing the Truth Seeker name or logo. And never disparage Lawrence
True again, and never sue him. In return, TSC would dismiss the RICO suit.

She agreed. But all fall, drafts of the retraction letter went back and forth between
her and Roy Withers, with exasperation mounting until Judge Papas finally drafted
a retraction himself and sent it to Madalyn.

She had lost thousands and thousands of dollars and man-hours on the Truth
Seeker case. All she had to do was sign, and the hemorrhage would be stanched.

Instead, she sat on it for over two months — until the last possible moment before
the judge's deadline. When she finally sent it back, it came with an addendum saying
that neither she nor any of her organizations had "ever claimed any interest in the
Truth Seeker Company...there is really nothing that any of them can retract —
not even one word." She'd actually printed it on her outlawed TSC letterhead.

Withers was furious, and even the curiously patient magistrate was done with her. He took the settlement off the table. The trial was back on, joined with the malicious prosecution action, and on the docket for September 1993. She was ordered to pay $10,000 of the other side's attorney fees. She'd wasted everyone's time and demeaned the court.

Chapter 57 ~ Just Do Your Job and Leave

IN NOVEMBER 1992, during the retraction letter war, Colleen and David left San Antonio and moved to Austin, setting up housekeeping in the Central Park Apartments on North Lamar Boulevard — still called the Dallas Highway by old-timers. The complex was plain, with hackberry trees around the perimeter. In summer, the tenants' Fords, Chevies, and vans roasted in the parking lot. But there was a shady, well-groomed little swimming pool area with flower beds of red sage and japonica.

Colleen got a job with Self-Chem, a pool service with several retail locations. She planned to enroll in UT, and encouraged David to find something that would challenge his mind and use the education he'd gotten in prison.

On January 31, 1993, he saw American Atheists' ad for a typesetter. It required good grammar, spelling, and typing. He knew who Madalyn was. He had visions of lively intellectual debate and camaraderie.

On February 2, he drove to Crime-on-the-Hill. The building had a locked front door and no sign. Robin greeted his knock. The lobby was "elegantly furnished," he wrote later, with a big oil portrait of Madalyn and a bust of her on a pedestal. When she came out to meet him, he had a blur of impressions: commanding, fat but with skinny legs, greasy gray hair, no makeup, swollen hands, barking orders at Robin about someone she was feuding with.

He remembered a chaotic interview, a tour of the 17,500-square-foot building, outfitted for printing, direct mail, and sales, the now off-limits library worth $3 million, the handful of employees, rattling in the big place like seeds in a dried gourd. He remembered being seated across from Madalyn and Robin and wondering, why would people in the public eye dress like that?

The job paid $7 an hour. He started February 8, and joined American Atheists the same day. And signed an agreement to not reveal anything about AA or its affiliates to anyone, ever.

He did get to experience Madalyn's legendary charm, and the insider humor that kept people bound to the Cause. One of their funniest projects was designing a Shroud of Turin tablecloth, purportedly to add to their direct-mail items. He found the O'Hairs rational and polite when pointing out his errors, and their hospitality at holiday season was well known.

But the camaraderie he'd expected was poisoned with tension. Not long after he started, an employee came out of Madalyn's office and announced loudly, "The old cow just fired me!" Madalyn stepped out into the hall, shaking with rage. "What did you just say!?"

"I *said the old cow just fired me!*" the woman yelled on her way out the door.

There was a cloak-and-dagger atmosphere in the executive suite, and a "just do your job and leave" feeling. No one was allowed to even cut through the library. Waters became friends with the office manager, Denise Cushman. She told him she'd been ordered to deny ever seeing certain Truth Seeker documents if she was summoned to California to testify. Certain TSC and financial files were headed for the shredder, and she'd been asked to spirit out checkbooks and cash if the constables showed up. She could no longer unlock the Financial Room to collect book orders, lest she see a fax that would cause her legal difficulty later. By the way, Madalyn had asked, would Denise and her husband consider relocating to New Zealand? If the husband balked, Madalyn would make it worth her while to leave him.

Waters soon saw that it was Robin who really did all the work, and knew how things operated and what the problems were. When she got sick, Garth took over, and it was a disaster.

David saw Madalyn's manipulativeness, how she kept people off balance. Once, she asked him to have a talk with a temp who kept sleeping at her desk. He tactfully told the employee it was okay to do personal work or read during down time, but sleeping was off limits. He dutifully reported this to Madalyn.

A few days later, Madalyn went to the girl and started a friendly conversation. The temp confided that she was fatigued. Madalyn said, "Well, why don't you just take a nap? Feel free, if you get tired."

Waters got along with everyone, said Derek Nalls, men and women alike, and they respected him. He was warm, likable, even had charisma. He seemed a little streetwise, but that was expected when you grow up anywhere near Chicago, Nalls thought.

Shortly after he was hired, Waters said later, he was called into Madalyn's office. The Founders braced him about being an ex-con. But before he could reply, Madalyn said all they cared about was the work. He'd paid his debt to society, she said. As long as he kept his mouth shut, he'd have a job.

He decided later that they'd been pondering his possible usefulness to them in their getaway to New Zealand.

Garth wanted to skip the country before the next Truth Seeker trial started in September 1993. He wrote Jack Jones that he was secretly moving the library to Houston for loading onto a ship container. David Waters and Conrad Goeringer were quietly packing it. Photos of the Founders' paintings and textiles were with

Houston art dealers; the piano and grandfather clock were out on consignment, and he had a buyer for one Mercedes. He was looking for a buyer for Robin's Porsche.

Robin was unhappy. She didn't want to go to New Zealand at all, and she did not want to give up her red-brown Porsche. At 28, she'd had no life of her own. She wanted to stay in Austin, rent an apartment, and "do something for atheism." She put up a fight, and Madalyn pressed Jack Jones so hard to get her a visiting professorship in New Zealand that he became angry — it was absurd; she wasn't qualified for anything like that. He was just being used. Madalyn hastily apologized and withdrew her request.

It was Robin's last attempt to do what her father had done, and escape.

Garth had transferred a $400,000 T-bill to New Zealand the previous summer, and another $350,000 six months later. He wired another $100,000 in July, telling Jones they'd buy round-trip tickets for October; even though they wouldn't use the return ones, it "would look better to arriving immigration officials if we could show a return ticket out of the country . . ."

Rapid-fire, letters arrived in Auckland, bureaucratic missives that showed Garth's ever-worsening stress. One letter asked Jones for two simple things: meet me at the airport, and book a hotel. This took a full page, detailing how far in advance he'd have to buy his ticket, where he'd have layovers, the original date he'd wanted to leave, but his One Pass points weren't flexible enough, and so on.

Similarly, a plan to telephone Jones took half a page: Let's see, you're 17 hours ahead, Austin is on Central Time, and the best time to reach you would probably be on a weekday evening, but that's 1 a.m. here and I'll be too tired, so if I called you at 9 p.m., our time, on Friday night, that would be Saturday your time, about 2 p.m. and it would be a weekend day, in the afternoon . . .

They wanted to bring their furniture — would they have to pay taxes on it? How about the animal paintings that had hung at GHQ? Should those be shipped as the organization's property, or personal property? Their file folders were 15⅛" from rod to rod and 8¼" deep — would they fit New Zealand file cabinets?

And so it went, stultifying details of library packing, the days of the week they packed, how long the round trip to Houston took, which weekends they were doing it, how many people were driving, the furniture shipping bids, the things they still had to decide whether to auction or not, and they just had a telephone conference with their attorneys, not the ones in Austin or California, but the IRS ones in Washington, who represented both them personally and also the corporations, whereas with the attorneys in California they had to have one set for the corporations and one for personal, those Washington attorneys said that there is no way to negotiate out of the IRS charges, people at the highest levels of government had pledged to destroy atheism in this country, and the IRS was the chosen vehicle for that, and —

Jones had stopped writing back his thorough replies, and started scribbling notes on their originals and mailing them back. Garth offered to buy him a fax machine. He declined, lest the hail of errands become a blizzard.

Jon Garth's speech impediment was worsening, employees noticed. His face had taken on a subtle contortion. Once rather attractive, he now had a twisted look. His inability to prioritize would have surprised no one who saw his checkbook register alone: in addition to running GHQ and keeping up appearances with the newsletter (the magazine was virtually defunct), dealing with the IRS audits, preparing Truth Seeker defenses, planning board meetings and vacation trips, finding pay phones and blind faxes to hide the library, and planning the complex flight to New Zealand, he was picking up the dogs at the vet, buying liquor for meetings and parties, shopping for groceries, picking up Madalyn's medicine, getting the properties fumigated, paying for cable, gas, electricity, picking up the cleaning, taking the cars to be washed, buying computer parts, pet supplies, landscaping plants...

Later, volunteer Sharon Summers remembered sadly what a kind, self-sacrificing guy Jon Garth could be. One Thanksgiving at Greystone, he came home at 3 p.m. to a houseful of guests after putting in seven hours at GHQ, and cooked the entire feast himself, while doing loads of family laundry. He could be a very effective speaker when Madalyn wasn't there. He would give a fine talk at a rally or convention, "and then the next day you'd see him with his shirt off... fixing the air conditioner."

Chapter 58 ~ Firings and Thefts

I N AUGUST 1993, Derek Nalls, the all-round glue for GHQ's many cracks and fissures, was fired for refusing to volunteer on the TV forum. He immediately got a commiserating letter from Brian Lynch.

Video coordinator James Steamer was fired earlier that year, ostensibly over a $45 typewriter repair bill that set Robin screaming, but later attributed to Madalyn's suspicion that he had also been consorting with Lynch. GHQ was down to three or four employees and some volunteers. By summer's end, the bulk of the library was packed, a fact that found its way to both the IRS and Truth Seeker lawyers.

And the Founders were not going to escape in September 1993 after all. New Zealand had discovered the FBI's surveillance of Madalyn, and now required more documentation about her. They'd have to face the Truth Seeker action after all, reset for November 2, 1993, though the outcome hardly mattered. Garth wrote Don Sanders, now sick and dizzy with AIDS, that they'd be shipping by mid-November.

John Glover Jackson died October 13. Not counting all the appeals and maneuvering, he had been catalyst for four suits. Madalyn had lost her two and was now on the defensive. But *Truth Seeker* ex-editor James Prescott believed Madalyn really had been sincere about her concern for the TSC books and the magazine. If she was a vulture, Roy Withers and Lawrence True were simply better-equipped ones, using the corporation to line their pockets, Prescott said.

Withers was asking $5.5 million in attorney fees and damages, and one of Madalyn's biggest assets was the library. The idea of turning CESAALA over to True was unthinkable. Alerted by Derek Nalls that it was being packed, Judge Judith Keep demanded to know where it was. Madalyn would only say it was in the Houston area. The judge sent the case to the jury, and sent the litigants home to await the verdict. She issued an order forbidding Madalyn or any of her minions to dispose of any assets, including the library and Crime-on-the-Hill.

The Founders went home and promptly put the latter up for sale.

It was a few days after their return from the Truth Seeker trial that Robin noticed the library's computer was missing. It had the only copy of the library catalogue, she fretted to police, who quickly decided it was an inside job, probably through the rear door at night. The O'Hairs listed Derek Nalls as their suspect, but only Denise Cushman had the keys or knew the security code, and she was a very unlikely thief or accomplice.

It never occurred to any of them that someone might have been bold enough to just carry the computer out the door in broad daylight. But that was what happened.

Cushman was so stressed that she resigned, and David Waters was promoted to office manager. (David Travis had thought he might get the job; he'd been there longer, was a fellow vet, and was dependable and devoted to the Cause. But Madalyn had a frequent criticism of Travis: "You're too nice.")

December brought a surprise: the Truth Seeker jury hung. Nobody expected that. Judge Keep declared a mistrial, and set a new trial for February 1, 1994.

How they'd dodged the bullet, no one could say. All but one juror had voted to convict. The evidence against Madalyn was overwhelming, the others told Roy Withers. The holdout was a mystery.

Jon Garth began moving the library again. He had a Michigan loyalist named Henry Schmuck — Uncle Henry, they called the bespectacled "Madalynoid" — looking for storage units in the Detroit/Toledo area, and Conrad Goeringer in Little Rock and Kansas City. It was cloak-and-dagger stuff — Don Sanders was to hire the trucks from different rental companies, using cash or his late lover's credit card, to destroy things after reading them, and to use pay phones, as Withers had subpoenaed the records from both GHQ and Greystone.

Besides Don Sanders, New Jerseyite Ellen Johnson was one of the few insiders the Founders trusted, along with Goeringer, Frank Zindler, Arnold Via, and a handful of others. Johnson was now on several boards, and responsible for keeping the storage bills paid on the nomad library.

Johnson had first admired Madalyn on television in 1979. When Bloody Sunday left a power vacuum in her state, Ellen began cultivating "National." She made her mark with the Founders by helping bring off the 1986 New Jersey convention, and with her communiqués about Bill's doings, church-state separation infractions, and scuttlebutt about plots to unseat Jon Garth. She sent a leather love seat and wingback chair for AAGHQ.

Garth had developed a permanent crush on the attractive blonde, whose husband remained far in the background of her activism. She was slender and pretty, with brown eyes, fluffy blond hair, and shapely legs. At convention parties she liked to go strapless in silk or taffeta.

Garth sometimes sent her flowers, found reasons to confer with her, or gave her special awards, according to employees who watched during the years. Madalyn knew of the gossip, and put this spin on it: "Ellen is so much in love with Jon that he, being the gentleman he is, won't even be [alone] in the same room with her."

Johnson was ambitious, and after a few years getting her sea-legs, turned out to be a competent spokesman for American Atheists, and far more telegenic than Madalyn. Or, as Bill Murray put it, "She's just as much of a [conniver] as my mother, but when she does it, she smiles and shows cleavage. She shows leg."

In January 1994, the O'Hairs discovered that 12 bearer bonds worth over $60,000 had been stolen from the safe in Jon's office. They weren't sure when the theft occurred, and Madalyn called Denise Cushman, probing for a reaction. Doubts about Denise lingered from the computer theft last November.

Madalyn told David Travis that one bond had been left on the floor. Had she had it checked for fingerprints? No, she said, the police technician told her that would destroy it. Travis had experience with fingerprinting, and didn't believe it. He wondered if she'd set the theft up. He reflected that the stolen computer had the only record of the hidden library's holdings. And the hard drive couldn't be backed up for some mysterious reason, according to Robin.

On January 28, 1994, Madalyn, very frustrated, wrote Jack Jones. New Zealand wanted still more ridiculous documentation. "I thought that we could just ship ourselves and our furniture down there (after putting all that moola into NZ)," she fumed. "USA [United Secularists of America] has over $1 million NZ there and Jon has sent down almost $200,000 for himself... I suppose if we were bare-assed bloody coons, we would have received warm letters of welcome by now." But no — the lawyers wanted proctoscopic documentation of their heritage — "as if we were slopes trying to pass as Caucasians."

Jones would be stunned, she promised, when they finally did arrive, and she sat him down to tell the "rotten, rotten, rotten" things the IRS was doing to them. "I simply want to get the hell out of the United States *now*... I am so fed up."

The Truth Seeker case had been postponed to March 28, 1994, and had been transferred from Judge Keep to the court of U.S. District Court Judge Manuel Real in Los Angeles. The O'Hairs were leaving Friday, March 25. They left unsigned checks for David Travis to pay bills in their absence.

After the near-miss in the first trial, everyone was bracing for a loss, but a strange twist was curling in the courtroom of Judge Real. Real was a highly controversial life appointee with no love for lawyers. A criminal defense attorney said of him, "Off the bench he is one of the most considerate, kindest persons I know. Then he takes the bench and he becomes rude, intolerant and abusive." He was frequently reversed by the Ninth Circuit Court of Appeals.

Against Roy Withers' wishes, Real chucked the jury; he alone would be the trier of fact. During the trial, whenever Withers made an objection, "Real would roll his eyes and say 'shut up and sit down,'" said John Vinson, Madalyn's attorney. And he should have held Madalyn in contempt for her constant *sotto voce* defamations of Withers.

Real took seriously Madalyn's story of having been promised Truth Seeker shares. He appeared unconvinced that James Hervey Johnson had any more right to the TSC fortune than Madalyn. He didn't seem to think TSC had been damaged, and appeared disgusted by the fees Withers had raked in.

On Thursday, March 31, Robin called David Waters with the surprising news that the trial was going really well. It would probably be over tomorrow, and if so, they were going to take a little break at Caesar's Palace in Vegas. They'd be back April 8.

On Saturday, April 9, 1994, Robin got to the office late in the morning. Within a couple of hours, police were swarming over GHQ.

The first thing she'd found was a voice message from David Waters, resigning — he couldn't tolerate the "mystique" of GHQ any more. She checked the time cards, postage meter, and mail room. No mail had gone out for over a week. No one had come to work except Waters.

David Travis told them Waters had laid everyone off. The bill-paying checks they'd left were gone. Calling the automated bank number, Garth found they had been cashed, for a total of $54,415.

Travis was underwhelmed by the police's ardor. They asked *him* to track down Waters' license plate number. He preserved a used Fresca can — Waters was the only one who drank Fresca — in a plastic bag and took it to the station. "Why don't you run his prints?" he suggested, "To see if he's someone you're looking for?"

"The cops were just not interested...they never even ran his license" until one of Madalyn's fans in Peoria did some research and found Waters' criminal record. They were given all the particulars, said Travis, "bank records, canceled checks, there was no doubt whatsoever who had written and cashed all those checks...and they didn't even bother to pick him up."

David Waters was driving to Manteca, California, the home of Cookie Nelson Wilkerson, with whom he'd stayed on good terms since Marti's murder. He was traveling with a wad of cash stuffed into a sock. He'd never been to California.

He posed with Cookie in front of Alcatraz, bounced her cute granddaughter on his knee. He told her he'd gotten a big bonus from Madalyn. He bought a used

Jaguar in San Francisco. Then he headed for Las Vegas, where Colleen joined him at the MGM Grand. David bought himself a $700 leather jacket with a roulette wheel on it, some Italian shirts, and some leather vests, and a Stevie Ray Vaughan style black cowboy hat. In Arizona, driving home, he bought Colleen an authentic concho belt she coveted, made by a Navajo named Yellow Horse. He paid $1,000.

"Now I wonder if she guffaws, or just snickers a little when she polishes her shiny silver conchos," he said bitterly seven years later.

The police had been leaving messages on his voice mail, and on April 29, 1994, he turned himself in. He had a story for them, and it had nothing to do with theft.

Jon Garth had taken him aside just before the second Truth Seeker trial, he said, and asked him to discreetly drain the accounts while they were in California. There should be about $100,000. He was to leave enough in each account to keep the Truth Seeker lawyers from getting suspicious, and put the rest in the safe in Jon's office. He could take a 15% commission, since it was unlikely he'd have a job for long.

He'd gotten up to $54,000, nervous that he was being observed by the other employees, when Jon's daily calls from California suddenly stopped. He feared the feds would show up, and he'd be headed back to prison for conspiracy to violate Judge Keep's order not to liquidate any assets.

He took his $15,000 commission, put the rest in the safe, and split.

The O'Hairs were angry that he'd taken the whole commission but only done half the job. They turned him in, counting on his criminal record to sink him, and not only get their $15,000 back, but milk another $39,000 out of him by fraud.

To the ex-GHQ community, and even to loyal David Travis, this sounded exactly like something the Founders would do. That draining the accounts was criminal contempt of court would be of no consequence to Madalyn. She had been walking that edge her whole life, since before that stop-payment trick with Pup's hospital bill back during the war. She had nothing but contempt for the authorities' backbone to carry out their threats. They had been bending over frontwards and backwards since she'd picked the judicial system as the arena for the drama of her life. She had never found anyone except Pup, Bill, and Richard O'Hair who would stand up to her.

Waters paid a $2,500 retainer to attorney Andrew Forsythe, and was allowed to post personal bond of $10,000. He was to provide a list of people who would vouch for him. That wouldn't be hard, with Madalyn's list of excommunicants.

Madalyn was discouraged about New Zealand. In addition to the never-ending documentation, Jack Jones resigned from the Rationalist Association because of "nitpicking rules," ending her needed link with a bona fide organization. In fact, Jones was now talking about piggybacking a breakaway group on one of Madalyn's organizations.

Then there was the money. Madalyn and Garth couldn't even figure out how much USA Inc. had in its accounts. Bank statements were incomprehensible and late. They were supposed to be getting more than twice the interest rate the U.S. was paying — at least 6% — and yet USA's interest income seemed to be half what it would have been if the money had stayed in the U.S. Madalyn asked Jones to find out what the hell was going on. New Zealand was talking about a General Services tax on the library. They couldn't afford that, especially if USA Inc. was making only 1.5%.

The Truth Seeker case seemed threatening with the encouraging rulings of Judge Real, and the DC tax lawyer, Craig Etter, was making progress with the IRS. It looked promising enough that Madalyn was having Robin research other states in the U.S. Maybe Madalyn could take CESAALA someplace and retire among her books. If she simply left town, the mired-down Strobel case might die, too.

Robin's meticulous research — on home and land prices, economic development, taxes, schools, libraries, and weather for 19 states — was settling on the place where it all began: Pittsburgh.

They were asking $880,000 for GHQ, about half what they'd paid in 1987. But it was unlikely they'd get even that. The neighborhood was blighted with crime, decaying retail, and ugly architecture. Nearby Reagan High School looked like a prison, its curious slogan, "Not Without Honor" painted on the side in huge letters. As David Kent put it in a letter, "There's a taco stand on one side, a former nudist colony on the other, and constant break-ins across the street. *Nobody* would want it."

Shortly after David Waters turned himself in, his attorney had him take a private polygraph, which he passed. Madalyn's enemies and exes believed him, and were eager to supply information to his attorney. When the grand jury heard about his priors and recommended $50,000 be added to his bond, the DA declined. Madalyn wrote him an angry letter. Even in Texas, she fumed, the DAs couldn't be stupid enough to believe a story like Waters'. He was probably on the Truth Seeker payroll, she said, and had stolen the library computer at their behest. The DA's office did contact the Truth Seeker attorney, but it didn't result in pressure on Waters. By October 1994, his trial had been postponed four times.

The O'Hairs said they were being stonewalled because they were atheists. Their enemies said the whole theft was just another headline-grabbing stunt to raise money; Madalyn had pulled it many, many times. Waters was granted repeated continuances — 13 in all, as the Founders wrote, called, and demanded a trial.

On November 16, 1994, Garth's 40th and last birthday, Judge Manuel Real released his opinion in the Truth Seeker case. And a generous birthday gift it was.

Roy Withers had done nothing right for his millions in fees, it seemed. His request for a jury trial wasn't timely or proper; he didn't prove the AA corporations were alter egos of Madalyn, nor that any of the Founders authorized a takeover attempt; he didn't prove that any reader of the *Truth Seeker* was confused by the two magazines issued from different places, both claiming to be the One True *Truth Seeker*; he didn't prove fraud, or that the defendants ever profited from what they did, or that they acted with ill will toward TSC, or that TSC was damaged by Madalyn's conduct. Real said Madalyn and Jackson *did* have probable cause to bring the underlying suit, and that mooted the malicious prosecution case.

What seemed to anger Real more than anything was Withers' attorney fees. TSC appealed.

Late that year, Conrad Goeringer closed down his well-known Tucson bookstore, Good Books, and left town so abruptly it made the local papers. He told Fred Woodworth he'd been offered a position with American Atheists in New Jersey, working with Ellen Johnson. Spike Tyson, Goeringer's "lieutenant," in Woodworth's view, also left, to work at GHQ. Woodworth wondered why both men would suddenly pull up stakes after decades in Tucson. It was suggestive of a plan, and he joined the camp that believed the Founders were planning to flee.

One day, Robin carelessly left some unscreened mail in David Travis' box. Among the letters he opened was a bank statement showing $1.25 million in a New Zealand account. He was stunned. He and the skeletal staff were working for peanuts — Madalyn and Jon Garth had said there simply wasn't enough money to pay full-time salaries.

He kept remembering a faithful supporter who sent a $10 bill every month along with his donation, and a note: "Buy your employees a beer." They'd never had one of those beers.

In May 1995, David Waters finally got to trial, more than a year after he'd turned himself in. His new lawyer, Patrick Ganne, asked for a 14th continuance, but the judge turned off the tap that day. Trial would be at 1 p.m.

Ganne, Waters said later, had not interviewed any of the witnesses he'd lined up, among them Jim Steamer, Derek Nalls, and the Truth Seeker's private detective. Moreover, Waters had taken out a little insurance, copying dozens of faxes, letters, and other documents — communications with Don Sanders about hiding the library, and Jack Jones about fleeing to New Zealand, letters between the O'Hairs and their New Zealand bankers; he even found a letter to Sanders noting that the library computer would be brought to Houston as soon as the packing was finished. All proved they were planning to leave the country, and had probably stolen their own computer. He was eager to present his findings.

But the DA made what Ganne considered a very good offer — deferred adjudication. Waters would plead guilty, repay the $54,000 over 10 years, and remain free. It would certainly beat a trial, which would be costly, and his criminal record was a huge liability. He faced up to 99 years if he lost. It also turned out Madalyn wasn't that eager for a jury trial. Perhaps she despaired of a fair trial, or didn't want her affairs probed to unearth information the IRS, Truth Seeker, or Strobel attorneys could use. The DA's office reported she wanted to settle.

Waters didn't want to go back to jail. He had a memory he couldn't shake, of a terrible morning when he was still married to Marti. He was lying in bed before daybreak, slowly waking up from a dream, but he didn't want to open his eyes. He was sure he'd been caught for something, and was going to open them to prison bars. He kept them shut for a long time, until some sound confirmed he was at home.

He took the deal.

Madalyn and Garth asked for a restraining order. Madalyn started working on an account of Waters' past for the *Insider's Newsletter,* dwelling on the Gibbs murder and the sordid beating of his mother, especially the part where he urinated on her.

Robin begged her not to publish it. They already had a judgment — what would be gained? But Madalyn had raised money on far weaker outrages.

Chapter 59 — "I have lived a long, long time"

THE MONTH OF THE WATERS SETTLEMENT, Don Sanders died of AIDS, with the O'Hairs at his hospital bed. A few weeks later, Madalyn made what turned out to be her last public appearance, in Houston at her alma mater, the South Texas College of Law. Too lame to stand, she spoke sitting at a conference table, Garth beside her. She wore a diamond ring, and both mother and son wore Rolexes, clearly visible on a video someone made of the talk.

Madalyn's contempt, braggadocio, and spurting vigor were undiminished, though she was a white-haired old woman, fragile from diabetes and heart failure, with her walker nearby.

She issued a long, bloated litany of heroics, including that it was she who persuaded President Truman to condemn the McCarran Act. She knew she was a folk hero, she said, and they were supposed to have rough pasts, but she didn't

"My mother was not a slut, did not use cocaine, was not a lesbian. My father neither beat nor abused me, and I was not raped when I was three months old...I was not porking my boss...I was not porking any radicals...I have never been...into sado-masochistic relationships, dominance, slavery or bondage, oral or anal sex, dual masturbation..." The clean-cut students recoiled as she went on and on about sex.

When it was his turn, Garth began an interesting rundown of encroachments into secular government — the Pledge, the Motto, the national days of prayer proclaimed by recent presidents. His speech impediment started out strong, with its "fweedom of wewidgeon" and "That man we ewected pwesident" — but he soon warmed up, and was endearing himself to the audience with an anecdote about a math teacher, when Madalyn started flopping her hands on the table and shifting in her chair.

Glancing over, he quickly gave her the floor, and she bellowed how she was lied about, maligned, in the early days; she was *not* involved with the Fair Play For Cuba Committee!

"The hell with Thomas Jefferson! I didn't give a *damn* what Madison thought! They had slaves! They wouldn't give women the right to vote!" She illustrated her points by citing premature ejaculation and climax.

Watching her, it seemed impossible that she could ever have just died quietly in her bed.

The O'Hairs set out for a vacation trip to colonial Williamsburg in early August. Before they left, Jon Garth notified the organizations' officers of the fall board meetings planned at "Pope Picket '95" in New York on October 3.

As always on vacation, Madalyn left her cares completely behind. The strung-out process of getting some of their money back from New Zealand, the still unresolved Strobel, IRS, and Truth Seeker threats, the hopeless work at the Center, all burned off in the late-summer heat of escape.

They visited Arnold Via in the Shenandoah Mountains, and Madalyn reveled in the unbridled nature of the place — hemlock, red spruce, locust, poplar, the woodland sounds of the tanagers and warblers. Berry vines tangled over the ground, and lichens, Virginia creeper, and columbine clung to the rocks and trees.

Via took photos of the family relaxing and laughing on his shade-dappled porch and in the swing, enjoying the quiet of his family acreage at the end of a country road.

Also on their itinerary was Pup's 1893 birthplace, New Millport, Pennsylvania. Madalyn was repelled by the tiny village, "pig-poor, a slum," she called it, split by a skinny road with a one-lane bridge. She hated the isolation and poverty she felt vibrating there, the *Deliverance* feel of the hilly, deep-wooded place. It was dead quiet, except for the urgent calling of birds, hammering away at their mating and territories, the mad trilling of frogs in brush-hidden streams, and the wind in the trees. Small, narrow houses sat silently back from the road, and any strange car brought squinty-eyed stares from the windows.

There were Mayses in the roadside cemetery, and other names from Madalyn's DAR folder — Bloom, High, McCracken — the ones that didn't get out.

She was happy to head back to Virginia, to wonderful seafood restaurants, shopping, and the comfortable Princess Anne Motel in Williamsburg. She was, in fact, not far from where Bill lived. "The miracles!" she wrote. "I am ever aware of air conditioned rooms and automobiles, hot water and clean sheets. I have lived a long, long time."

They were home by mid-month. On Saturday, August 26, Garth took the cars for washing and fuel. That evening, he stopped at the market near Greystone and bought two Snapples, a loaf of bread, some shredded wheat, and a muffin.

He sat down to write Jack Jones about the money still sitting in the Bank of New Zealand. He was sending a power of attorney to expedite its transfer back home.

On Sunday, August 27, 1995, the O'Hairs went to work as usual. It was hot. A volunteer came to groom the foliage, but when he rang the bell to get inside for a drink, no one answered. He left.

Spike Tyson and other employees arrived Monday morning to find a mysterious message from Jon taped to the door of AAGHQ. The family had been called out of town on an emergency. They hoped it would take no more than two weeks. Paychecks through August 31 had been mailed to employees' homes.

Spike went to Greystone and saw two dogs in the backyard. The garage was empty. He left a note saying he'd keep an eye on the house and dogs.

It looked very strange.

The next day, August 29, Gretchen Clapp at Griffith Small Animal Hospital on Northland Drive answered the phone. It was one of their best customers, Robin O'Hair, sounding very upset. They'd had a family emergency and left town. Could someone pick the dogs up and board them until September 8 if she didn't get them before then?

Gallagher, 11, and Shannon, 10, were picked up that day. Gannon, who had cataracts, was in the house, and it was arranged for the housecleaning service (Zula Shelby had left in 1993) to bring him to the clinic. When Spike Tyson checked the house that afternoon, his note and the dogs were gone. He had no idea who had taken them. He continued to drive by and check the house every day.

People tried to contact the O'Hairs. Phil Donahue was retiring, and wanted Madalyn on his last show, as she'd been his first guest. In New Jersey, Conrad Goeringer was editing AANews, the fledgling on-line newsletter, and was hard on his deadline. Everything had to be cleared through Robin, but his calls, faxes, and emails went unanswered. Finally he remembered they had a cell phone.

A man answered, and gave the phone to Garth.

What gives? Goeringer asked. Garth was noncommittal, said they were in San Antonio on business and would be done soon. Uneasy, Goeringer asked, well, what's going on? Is Madalyn okay?

In the background, Madalyn's voice said loudly, "I'm okay, Goeringer."

But when he asked for Robin, he found her upset, and trying to convey that something was terribly wrong. He asked if she was being held. If so, she answered, how could she tell him? Then Garth took the phone. Should he come to Texas? asked Goeringer, and Garth said no, and he didn't know why Robin was so upset. He wouldn't say more.

Goeringer hung up and called Ellen Johnson. She coolly told him it was a big business deal that took all three of them to put together. Spike Tyson called her as well; to all who asked, she gave the same answer.

On September 11, Tyson got a package from Garth postmarked San Antonio, enclosing a paycheck and instructions to get the mail, pay bills, clean dried ink off the press rollers, edit, dub, and ship the TV forum tapes, and so on, and *don't* let anyone into the building until he returned.

Curious, Tyson went to Greystone, pulled down the attic ladder in the garage, walked through the attic, and came down the inside ladder in the hall, bypassing the alarm. He found Madalyn's insulin and heart medication, some dirty dishes. Garth's bed was messy, and there were dog droppings in Robin's room — unheard of. Madalyn's walker was gone.

Ellen Johnson fielded more than two dozen calls to and from San Antonio in September 1995. She was a good soldier, doing what was asked, but suspicious enough to at first refuse one of Garth's requests — that she send him blank corporation checks. "I have no idea if there's a gun to your head or not," she scolded, but he got her to relent. But he was being very mysterious. She'd talked to Robin, too, and found her extremely upset and trying to speak in code. "I know you'll do the right thing," was her last trembling attempt.

On September 27, the family's tax attorney, Craig Etter, called the cell phone. He needed one more piece of information. The outcome with the IRS was looking good. He spoke with Jon, who "was very agitated, did not want to talk to me ... he would have Madalyn call me the next day." But he didn't.

In late September, the first rumors appeared in the media. Where were the O'Hairs? They hadn't been seen in public in weeks. Jon's mysterious note had made its way to the wires. One source said Madalyn had probably died, and her kids were keeping it under wraps, so no Christers would find out and pray for her or create a circus.

Her 1986 publication, *Plotting Atheist Funerals*, was scrutinized: she wanted cremation, and no funeral parlors, mortuaries, or flowers. "I don't want a bunch of numbnuts listening to my favorite music ... I would prefer that blathering idiots not attempt to encapsulate my life."

No cremation permits had been applied for in Austin, San Antonio, or Houston.

Bill, citing his mother's one-time interest in cryogenics, said, "I wouldn't be surprised if she was sitting frozen in the back of a van somewhere."

USA Today, the *New York Post,* and other papers ran stories on September 29 about the mysterious disappearance. That was the last day Jon's cell phone worked. His last call was to GHQ at 12:24 p.m., and lasted seven minutes, and then the phone went dead.

October 3, 1995, was the day the Founders were due at Lyden House in Manhattan for American Atheists' "Pope Picket '95" and several board meetings. The O'Hairs hadn't shown up yet.

Frank Zindler was worried. Madalyn had not told her closest friends where she was. Those who spoke to the trio during September had urged her to speak in code, "use a certain word as a signal if she were being held against her will," but she didn't. She gave no sign of duress. Zindler was puzzled; she had definitely wanted to leave Austin, but there was no reason to be secretive about it at this point.

Details surfaced in the press: unfinished breakfast on the table, dogs unattended, insulin and heart medication left behind. The guesses were: foul play, absconding with AA funds, Madalyn going off to die. She was 76. Jon Garth was 40, Robin 30.

Spike said he was going to chew her out for making them worry like this.

But David Travis was thinking about the things he'd seen, the money in New Zealand when the Founders were crying poverty, the cutbacks.

He decided they had fled the country as long predicted. He asked the Austin Police Department to reopen its investigations of the thefts. Like so many before him, he called the IRS.

What really decided him was a recent conversation with the beleaguered David Waters. Waters was still unhappy having to pay back $54,000 when he'd only gotten $15,000, and his story dovetailed with everything that had happened. After years of loyalty, Travis believed the Murray-O'Hairs were corrupt. They had stolen their own computer, bonds, and cash to hide assets.

But one thing nagged at him: the papers had all mentioned the "half-eaten breakfast" at Greystone. That didn't fit with the note on the door, and the paychecks in the mail. The latter showed planning, the former, haste.

In the leadership vacuum at the Pope Picket, Ellen Johnson glided into place. She had the final plans for the picket, so it was natural for her to direct things. She went room to room in the hotel, urging that someone had to do something, and reportedly, all nodded their assent that it be her.

Arnold Via, vice president of at least one of the corporations, was actually next in line to take charge, but he wasn't in New York to protect his interests, and he soon heard that he'd been nudged out.

Ellen Johnson took the reins, traveling to Austin to look for clues to her bosses' whereabouts. At Greystone, she found their passports. Tyson had received the cell phone bill, and called the numbers on it. He took photos of Madalyn and Jon to hospitals and hotels in the area in San Antonio where some of the calls were made. He couldn't find anyone who recognized them.

On October 14, a registered letter came for Robin. The dogs were now considered abandoned, and would be destroyed in 12 days. Tyson retrieved them.

Two months into the family's disappearance, Ellen Johnson was still assuring reporters that Madalyn was alive and off on a business trip. She was "just fine . . . this has nothing to do with her health." No money was missing. But by early November, all the GHQ employees had left except Tyson, who went to the office every day with the dogs.

A late-1995 CBS news story on the vanished atheists quoted Craig Etter: the back taxes the IRS was seeking would be only a fraction of the original huge tab. The O'Hairs weren't hiding from the IRS.

But almost as he spoke, Gannon and Shannon disappeared from the fenced area in back of GHQ while Tyson was out on errands. The fence was six feet high, topped with razor wire, and padlocked. No one had broken the locks. Had the beloved dogs been delivered to their masters at a secret location? From Washington, Bill vividly remembered how their chaotic 1964 flight to Hawaii had to include the dogs.

Another disappearance was reported in late 1995. A Florida man called the Austin police and filed a missing persons report for his brother, Danny Fry. The report was filed away and forgotten.

Six months later, a teenaged girl filed a missing persons report in Naples, Florida. It was her dad, Danny Fry. Five-ten, 170 pounds, green eyes, light brown hair, in sales, last seen Austin Texas, 9–30–95. The Naples police entered all the data in the Federal Citizen Information Center/National Crime Information Center database that day. But it was all removed three weeks later because the missing man didn't meet the criteria for an endangered adult.

In May 1996, the third dog disappeared from GHQ.

Chapter 60 ~ A Lot of Reason to Kill Someone

S an Antonio Express-News State Editor Fred Bonavita pulled aside one of his veteran reporters, John MacCormack. "Hey, why don't you go do a one-year anniversary story on the Madalyn Murray O'Hair disappearance?"

"She's missing?" asked MacCormack. He knew who she was, and respected her convictions, but he hadn't kept up. It was late summer, 1996. He drove to Austin with little to go on.

Tall, with a long, businesslike stride and sharp blue eyes that didn't miss much, MacCormack was a courtly, intense professional. A New Jerseyite like Ellen Johnson, he had been two decades in journalism, working mostly in Oregon, New York, Miami, and Texas. His freelance stories appeared in the New York Times, Dallas Morning News, and other venues. After a stint at the Miami Herald, he settled in San Antonio, covering South Texas first for the Dallas Times-Herald and then the San Antonio Express-News, winning awards and becoming fluent in Spanish along the way. A few years before, he'd garnered a Nieman Fellowship at Harvard.

When he was assigned the O'Hair story, he never dreamed he would become such a big part of it. But in a way, his life experience was perfect for it. One of the seven children of a scientist and college instructor father and "the loving, forgiving, intelligent mother we all wish we had," he grew up indifferent to church. But as an Eagle Scout, he was influenced by a godly, straight-arrow mentor, and enrolled in a strict Christian college in Houghton, New York. "We were surrounded by dairy cows, and you could barely get into trouble."

A year there ended his experiment with religion, and after graduating in English Literature, he bolted for the West Coast in an old bread van — his sometime home for a few wanderjahre. But his years among his religious fellows, and the friendship that led him there, had given him empathy. "I wasn't one of them, but I recognize that humanity has a very specific spiritual component." He gradually became "a total atheist... [but] not an enemy of religion."

AAGHQ had reopened in June 1996. He interviewed Spike Tyson and others, gathering information about the organizations. His first story, published in August, reported a mysterious item: Jon Garth Murray had placed an ad in the *San Antonio Express-News* around the time the family disappeared. He'd put his beloved Mercedes 300 SEL up for sale — at $5,000 under book value. It was snapped up by a real estate agent named Mark Sparrow. Shown a photo, Sparrow said the 6'2" burly Jon was definitely not the man who sold him the car. The seller was sandy-haired, in his 40s, 5'9" or so. No speech impediment, mentioned a daughter.

A couple of days later, Robin's Porsche was found at the Austin airport. Nothing suspicious was found in or on it by Austin police.

That was when MacCormack "got some friendly advice [to] check [United Secularists of America's] 990 forms." They were filed in November 1996. Sure enough, USA reported to the IRS that $612,000 was missing, and believed to be with Jon Garth Murray, whereabouts unknown.

Why hadn't Ellen Johnson reported this apparent theft to the police? Well, she said, "Everything seemed to be normal at that time and there was no reason to think he shouldn't have that money."

But was it still normal a year later, when the forms were being prepared and the O'Hairs still hadn't been heard from? MacCormack called Johnson repeatedly, asking to talk to her about USA's 990s, but she ignored him. Nor would she comment when, in November 1996, CESAALA's and SOS's tax exemptions were revoked. The IRS would say only that they were operated for private benefit and not for a tax-exempt purpose.

MacCormack called Arnold Via, who was filing a criminal complaint with the Texas attorney general, contending Ellen Johnson's presidency was illegal and the current board was withholding financial information.

Hearing about the $612,000 was a personal blow to Via. These were people whose cause he'd championed, and contributed to generously, and with whom he'd shared meals, troubles, and laughter over many years. He told MacCormack how they'd talked of New Zealand; he told him about Jack Jones. But he'd always thought they meant moving the organization there, not scooping up its assets for themselves.

"If they misled us," he said, "they are criminals... they are crooks."

MacCormack's article about the missing money appeared the first week in December, 1996. Besides the $612,000, there was another $15,500 missing from American Atheists, also believed to be with Jon, and another $259,013 squirreled away in New Zealand under USA's name. And another $800,000 had been liquidated from unnamed investments. Adding in Jon's reconnaissance trips to New Zealand, the possibility of flight grew stronger.

CNN and *Time*, *NBC Nightly News*, and other major media were covering the story, calling the detective assigned to the case, Steve Baker. The missing O'Hairs were just another case, he said — he had 20 in line ahead of them. "It's not against the law in Texas to be missing," explained an Austin Police Department spokesman.

But Spike Tyson, now director of GHQ, made a dark comment to MacCormack: "Six hundred thousand dollars is a lot of reason to kill someone."

If APD wasn't stirred by MacCormack's story, 29-year-old Tim Young was. The lanky, brown-eyed Texan, brimming with confidence and blessed with a talent for mimicry that came in handy in his trade, had started his career early. The son of a police officer, he'd left his native Beeville, Texas in his teens to work as a skip-tracer. In 1986, he started his own company, Pathfinder Services, in Phoenix.

"I *loved* finding people but *hated* collecting the money." Even before he read MacCormack's story, he was hooked on the O'Hair mystery. Fresh off a high-profile triumph (he found a computer executive who had run off with his partner's $3 million and eluded authorities), "I was just as cocky as could be. I thought, just gimme a couple weeks, I can find this woman." Young was without peer at getting people in banks, phone companies, utility companies, hotels, hospitals, and military offices to cough up records.

He called MacCormack and offered his services. All the newspaper had to do was pay his expenses and credit him if his work led to finding the family.

They were in business before Christmas. MacCormack opened his files to Young. "We just started checking out the leads" — names and phone numbers, major players, and all the trailing ends.

Mark Sparrow had viewed Jon Garth's Mercedes in the parking lot of a residential motel — the Warren Inn. The car was immaculate, with only 24,000 miles. Sparrow met the seller the next day at Bonnie Jean's Cocktails, across from the motel. They headed for the bank, traded keys and money, and the Sparrows saw him squeeze into a brown 1960s-vintage Chevy pickup driven by a white man, with a fat white woman in front.

By Christmas 1996, someone else had gotten intrigued by MacCormack's article about the missing money — the IRS's Criminal Investigation Division (CID). In particular, Special Agent Edmond Martin.

A fit man of 50 with deep-set eyes and an affable grin behind a professional poker face, Martin spoke in the accents of his native New Orleans, where he had run high school track and worked summers in the oil fields. He didn't really know why he ended up majoring in accounting — he'd always liked chemistry. And he was restless, not the type to sit at a desk and audit tax returns. His accounting professor noticed. "I don't think you're going to like being a CPA. I think you'd rather be an agent."

Martin did become an IRS special agent in 1969, after graduating from Southeastern Louisiana College in Hammond. Working first in New Orleans and then

Austin, he tried the private sector in 1984. But he returned seven years later, when the IRS started doing money laundering probes. He liked "investigating what's happening at the time the crime is committed, instead of waiting for a tax return." The big financial and narcotics investigations brought people to justice who wouldn't have been caught any other way.

He knew who Madalyn was; the year he turned 12 was when "In God We Trust" was first printed on folding money. He remembered looking at the bills given to him at his confirmation in the Catholic Church, and thinking, wow, that's new — then she had sued to remove the motto. He was in the Rotary Club when she spoke there, only a few years ago. She launched into language so foul Martin stood up and said, "I don't have to put up with this." Half-a-dozen others got up and left with him. He was a Grand Knight of the Knights of Columbus in 1995 when the Pope Picket was scheduled.

He had no idea that, for the next several years, his life would be utterly consumed by the players behind that six hundred grand, and all the things that happened during the month of September, 1995.

American Atheists had never filed a missing persons report, claiming only a family member could do that. Bill Murray said they'd call him "a money-grubbing grave robber" if he did, but something had to be done.

He filed a request to locate them in September 1996, and, not long before Christmas, petitioned for guardianship of their estates — drawing the howling accusations he expected. The last thing the new AA *jefes* wanted was Bill Murray rooting around in their books, he knew.

But an accounting was definitely needed, Bill said. Johnson and the current AA regime had repeatedly said no money was missing, when they knew they were $627,500 light. And where was the $3 million library? And on whose authority had Spike Tyson been living at Greystone since February 1996? He, the donors who paid for all this, and the media deserved answers.

Indeed, AA was on the spot. Ellen Johnson had said the corporations' officers had done "everything conceivable" to find the missing family. Had they hired a detective? No, because there was no evidence of foul play. Had they requested police help? No, for the same reason. Yet she had asked Jon if there was a gun to his head. She and Zindler and Goeringer had all told the O'Hairs to speak in code if they were being held. She told *Time* magazine that during the month of cell calls, "They were being very cagey...You couldn't get a straight answer. They were lying about a lot of things, that was obvious. I was screaming, 'What the hell is going on, are you OK.'...Everything was not OK. Robin was totally disturbed...something terrible had happened."

That was all certainly evidence of foul play, wasn't it? So why had she continued to say they were okay for over a year? And to say no money was missing? She tried to explain: she didn't want to publicize that they were out there with $627,500, and sic some nut or murderer on them. She was operating on best information, and forced to make decisions based on very few clues.

But the unpleasant questions drove Johnson into silence, and she stopped returning calls about the O'Hairs. She did admit in the AA newsletter late that year that she knew the money was missing early on, but kept hoping the O'Hairs would turn up. But that made it sound like the new bosses had been helping the Founders embezzle money and go into hiding. Said David Travis, "I can't imagine anybody inheriting the presidency of an organization because the previous president absconded with $630,000, and not filling out a police report."

Bill Murray agreed: "If you were missing $600,000, would you just put it on your income tax return? Or would you report it to the authorities?" He said his guardianship petition was the best way to flush out the Founders if they were alive. "I think my mother would step forward in the face of anything to keep me from taking control of her estate."

But by early 1997, the courts, and the IRS Collection Division (different from Ed Martin's Criminal Investigation Division) were tangled in such a Gordian knot of lawyers and bureaucracy that Bill quit in disgust.

Judge Guy Herman, Madalyn's old nemesis who had sentenced Robin to three days in jail, made a standard move of appointing an attorney to represent the trio. The attorney felt his clients needed a guardian ad litem, so Sam Houston Clinton, Madalyn's long-ago champion in the Maryland extradition fight, came on board. Then the judge allowed the hiring of a private detective; they couldn't be declared legally dead for at least five more years, but depending on what was found, they could be declared incapacitated.

Then, halfway into January 1997, the IRS filed a lien against Greystone for unpaid income taxes. The private detective couldn't find the trio, and they were declared incapacitated by Judge Herman. That meant a receiver had to be appointed for each of them. Each receiver immediately hired a bankruptcy attorney to fend off the IRS. To this snarl of estate-draining appointees, Bill was asked to add a large bond to be guardian. He withdrew his petition.

In mid-February 1997, IRS vans pulled up to Greystone to suck out the family's earthly possessions and catalogue them for auction. Bill tried to stop them. He hadn't been notified of the seizure, nor had the family's guardian.

"There were pictures, notebooks, everything from my childhood in that house ... I didn't even get the only existing photo I had of my father. He was with his crew in front of his bomber." He got no memorabilia from the home. He was surprised to learn that a large portrait of him still hung over the piano.

But the family's three receivers gave a hard yank on the IRS's reins. They each filed bankruptcy for their clients, and the auction was halted for the time being.

Murray was also disgusted with the Austin Police Department. The detective handling the case, he said, told him he only knew what he read in the papers. Murray read the papers too, and asked APD who was using Robin's credit card, and who was cashing Madalyn's VA and Social Security checks — all reported in the newspapers. There were plenty of signs of foul play, but the police said only that they had no new information, and that American Atheists wasn't cooperating.

Finally, under pressure from the national media, APD issued an anemic press release. They'd interviewed the Sparrows and decided there was nothing illegal about Mark Sparrow buying Jon Garth's car, even though the seller was not Jon. (An observer said the APD artist kept producing a face that looked like his own, rather than the Sparrows' description of the seller.) The upshot was, there was no foul play and the missing $627,500 was IRS's business — APD didn't consider it a lead.

That left insiders scratching their heads as to what APD did consider a lead. A Mercedes seller who didn't resemble the missing owner; a Porsche abandoned at the airport for over a year, its owner also missing, a hasty departure leaving behind clothes, passports, dogs, and vital medication, over half a million dollars vanished and millions in assets left moldering, and a camera-hungry old woman eschewing 18 months of national and international attention?

"We're at a dead end," said Bill Murray, "unless the press finds them."

If those weren't leads to APD, they were to Tim Young and John MacCormack. They believed Jon and Robin, at least, were alive. Young had canvassed the O'Hairs' old neighbors on Shoal Creek; MacCormack was probing disaffected ex-Madalynites. They checked insurance companies, pharmacies, New Zealand immigration and property records, the American Diabetes Association. There was a rumor that placed the family on remote land in Arizona, owned or obtained for them by Conrad Goeringer. Insiders said they might have impersonated dead relatives, or used fake Social Security numbers. "We checked out specific leads in Hawaii, Mexico, Germany, Canada, New Zealand, Australia, and India," MacCormack said later.

But they had to have an accomplice, Young told MacCormack, and it had to be someone whose name they had already run across.

The Holy Grail was Jon Garth's cell phone records. Everything important had happened during the month of September 1995, and it was coded into those records. The IRS had a death-grip on them; even the estates' lawyers couldn't get them. Young called Detective Baker. Not only did he not have them, he didn't know the phone number itself.

Young was exasperated with the lack of police work. It was time to call on some of his unique talents. Before long, he had the records. How he did it remained his secret.

There were calls to jewelry stores, travel agencies, drug stores in San Antonio and Austin. To Continental Airlines, to an accounting firm, to Griffith Animal Hospital. Intriguingly, they found "46 calls to long distance service connectors — a necessary step to making international [cell] calls," wrote MacCormack later. And dozens to banks and credit card companies the O'Hairs had never done business with before.

"There were many . . . calls to Ellen Johnson," said Young. "They'd make a call, and then a minute later they'd call Ellen."

Ed Martin traveled to DC to meet Johnson and Craig Etter. He was trying to get Johnson to say whether Jon had the money illegally.

"If Jon took the money and spent it on himself, then that's money laundering and interstate transportation of stolen goods. *Bam.* I got 'im. But I needed 'em pissed off at Jon . . . [they] had to say 'he stole the money' to make it a criminal act."

But "Ellen thought the O'Hairs *had* absconded, and she wasn't going to do anything to help me." She'd cherry-picked Greystone and GHQ, he said; "She had the passports, the diaries, the bank records . . . I never got access to the contents of the house."

Martin did get one lead from Johnson, however. The money had traveled from New Zealand to a United Secularists of America account in New Jersey near Ellen Johnson's home. It then went to Frost Bank in San Antonio.

It was enough for a grand jury subpoena. Martin called Assistant U.S. Attorney Gerald Carruth in Austin. He wanted to know: where had the money come from in New Zealand? And where had it gone after Frost Bank?

Everything Martin unearthed about the O'Hairs showed them to be frugal, conservative investors. He was working with Gordon McNutt, Jon's receiver, a banking veteran who was busy locating assets. Using the letters between Jon Garth and Jack Jones, McNutt found five separate accounts in New Zealand. The $600,000 had to come from one of them.

Working separately, John MacCormack also contacted McNutt, particularly about one of Jon's cell calls. It had led to a shop on Fredericksburg Road called Cory's Fine Jewelry. MacCormack and Young approached the owner, Cory Ticknor. When the name O'Hair came up, "He immediately whipped out his attorney's card," said Young. "MacCormack and I looked at each other like, 'what the heck did we just hit here?'"

MacCormack got an evasive story from Ticknor's attorney about gold being purchased from his client by the O'Hairs, and an IRS agent working the case. That was when he and Young first ran across Ed Martin.

Ticknor was sitting on $100,000 worth of Canadian Maple Leaf coins for the O'Hairs. He'd had them for over two years. It was the tail-end of a big order, over $600,000 worth, placed in September 1995 by Jon.

The coins started coming into Cory's on September 21, and he had $500,000 worth by Friday, September 29. On that day, in the early afternoon, Jon — the real one — met Ticknor in a secure room at Frost Bank. "He kind of didn't smell very good, like he'd been out in the heat for a while and hadn't showered," said Ticknor. He had "kind of a scraggly beard" and a wrinkled shirt. A moonlighting policeman was present for security, but Jon gave no sign of distress. He opened several boxes of the Krugerrands, American Eagles, and Canadian Maple Leaves, checked them, showed identification, signed the paperwork, loaded the 100 pounds of coins into a suitcase, and put them into the trunk of a blue Lincoln Town Car.

That was a Friday. The last batch of Jon's order would arrive Monday, October 2. See you then, Ticknor waved, and that was the last he saw of Jon. On Monday, no one answered the cell phone. He tried for two more weeks, and then gave up.

Ed Martin promptly seized the coins. Eventually, they were turned over to American Atheists. Later, Martin was asked in court why he hadn't kept them, to pay off the O'Hairs' tax liabilities? He didn't think the IRS was entitled to them, he replied. That attitude — that he was a public servant, not government muscle, and his dogged work for years on the O'Hair case, earned Martin high praise from everyone he encountered.

Chapter 61 ~ "It was a kidnapping"

J OHN MACCORMACK was preparing a story about the IRS's money-laundering probe. A few days before it ran, Tim Young sent him a letter. He no longer believed the disappearance was planned. "Something overwhelmed them," he wrote MacCormack. "Maybe their lives were threatened? Maybe they found a government tap on their phone. I don't know, but something happened...."

It was normal right up until the day they left, Young wrote. They taped the cable TV shows, paid bills. They'd bought $242 worth of groceries a few days before. Those weren't things people did when they were planning to flee.

As early as the spring of 1996, Roy Withers had decided Madalyn was dead, and that Robin and Jon were living in Mexico. He had petitioned for a rehearing on Manuel Real's ruling, still seeking $6 million in damages from the American Atheist organizations. But Real's decision was upheld in California in the Ninth Circuit, and on December 1, 1997, the U.S. Supreme Court denied Withers' petition for review.

It was safe to bring CESAALA out of mothballs, and in January 1998, the library was finally moved back into AAGHQ.

The year dragged into summer, with new developments at a trickle. Life went on in Austin — the droning of cicadas, the heat, the Mexican freetail bats clouding out from under the Congress Street bridge at dusk, and the cowboys, hippies, yuppies, and cholos of Austin fogging into the music dens and watering holes on Sixth Street.

Young and MacCormack were treading the same ground as Ed Martin that summer of 1998; Young was pressing the family's receivers for medical records, diaries, and credit card purchases — anything, even pet-care and auto repair statements

One record got their attention. A travel agency showed that Jon and someone named Conrad Johnson had flown from San Antonio to New Jersey on September 21, 1995, and returned the next day.

MacCormack called Spike Tyson and Fred Woodworth about the curious name. The conflation of Ellen Johnson and Conrad Goeringer was the first thing to occur, he told Woodworth, "but it seems too silly to contemplate."

Spike Tyson had been in constant contact with both namesakes, and there was never a hint that Jon was flying to New Jersey with some strange guy. Ellen was surprised to learn he'd been in town.

MacCormack tried the Federal Aviation Administration; it had been requiring photo IDs since the guilty verdict against Sheik Rahman in the 1993 World Trade Center bombing. But in a near miss, the FAA's rule was put in place October 1, 1995 — nine days after Jon and "Conrad Johnson" flew.

All summer, the investigators ran down leads and fished dry holes. Letters from psychics occasionally came to their desks, especially after ABC's *Nightline* ran a big TV special on the disappearances in June. "I see news in the future," allowed one visionary to MacCormack. Another wrote Assistant U.S. Attorney Jerry Carruth that the O'Hairs were "near water," and please send the reward money to the following address . . .

In Florida, a man watched the ABC special. At the end of the show, he saw MacCormack's number. He called it June 20, 1998.

Generally, a caller had about 30 seconds to get MacCormack's interest. This one succeeded.

"It was a kidnapping," the man said. "I was told by a third party who was involved. That person has disappeared . . . They held the O'Hairs hostage at a place called the Warren Apartments in San Antonio. The motive was money." The third party was a man named Danny Fry.

"David Waters . . . Walters? — he's the one who masterminded it."

MacCormack sat up. He had, of course, come across David Waters' name in his research because of the $54,000 judgment in May 1995, but it was just another in an ocean of names of people Madalyn had crossed — Strobel, Murchison, Lynch, Massen, Stein, Nalls, Kurtz . . . suddenly, all the characters — the Spike Tysons and Ellen Johnsons and Jack Joneses and Truth Seekers — dropped off MacCormack's radar.

He remembered something. Back when the missing $600,000 was made public, Waters had used it to convince a judge that he'd been telling the truth about the bribery. He'd gotten his restitution lowered from $54,000 to $15,000. The O'Hairs weren't around to object.

MacCormack's caller didn't want to give his name at first, but he soon relented. He was Bob Fry, Danny's brother. He knew something had happened to Danny, and he just couldn't live with it any more. David Waters had flown him from Florida to Texas to participate in some big-money deal. And he went missing right when the O'Hairs did. He had last talked to Danny September 30, 1995. "His daughter had a birthday on that date; he said he was on his way back. That was the last contact anyone had with him."

Danny used to be a siding salesman; he had a big drinking problem. He was one of eight siblings, very charming and vivacious, liked people.

"If he was in a bar," said Bob, "and somebody's giving mouth or something, he would turn it into a joke…get it off of violence. He'd have everybody singing a song together before you knew it." Danny had quit high school when he found he could sell ice to Eskimos. He was often into some off-color business deal, but nothing more criminal on his record than DUI.

He had met David Waters in 1989. He was doing construction cleaning, and selling oil products for a Naples company called Slick Willie, whose owner skipped town under the shadow of an arrest warrant. It was the kind of thing Danny got into — he was weak where easy money was concerned, but he'd give you the shirt off his back.

In January 1990, they were in a wreck on Airport Road in Naples. David was drunk, but Danny covered for him. That planted a fateful seed, said Ed Martin. "'Cause that's the big thing with these guys, standup. If you don't snitch me off, you're a standup guy, so the next time I'm planning a crime, I'll call ya."

In 1995, Danny started telling his brother about a big score of some kind with Waters in Texas. He went there in July.

MacCormack and Young started looking at David Waters. It was a rather fascinating coincidence: four people all disappeared at the same time, and they all knew Mr. Waters.

Tim Young quickly established trust with Bob Fry, and obtained his brother's 1995 phone bills. "That's when we quit sleeping for a couple of weeks." The bills showed a blizzard of calls linking the Warren Inn, David Waters' apartment, and the Florida phones of Bob Fry and someone named Charlene Karr — who led to a Gary P. Karr.

MacCormack contacted Danny's daughter, Lisa, to whom he was very close. He'd raised her. He'd called all the time during August, his vivacious self. He mailed her a sweet letter. She was a "great daughter" and they were going to celebrate her 16th birthday, just the two of them. He just had to finish this one last job. "Love, Dad."

But in September, he got shorter and shorter with his daughter and fiancée. A couple of times he sent money, around $5,000 in all. Gradually, he became more secretive, curt, and nervous. His last call was September 30, Lisa's 16th birthday. He was sorry he didn't make it, but he'd be home in a couple of days.

He failed to show up. Lisa called David Waters, and he gave her cruel news: her father went off with a guy named C. J., gambling and drinking. (He told Bob Fry that Danny had gone to Kansas City. Another time, he said Danny had a girlfriend in San Antonio.)

Then Bob Fry told MacCormack that, in late September 1995, Danny had sent a letter marked something like "Do not open until October 3." Bob immediately

opened it. "If you're reading this, I'm probably dead. Take this letter to the FBI."
It said they were at the Warren Inn, waiting to get money, which was coming in
slowly. Danny's job was to guard the O'Hairs, who thought they were going to be
released. So did Danny. Now he was just terribly sorry he'd gotten involved. The
FBI would have no trouble connecting the crime to David Waters.

Danny called shortly after that, and Bob told him he was coming to Texas. No,
said Danny, don't. He didn't want anyone in his family involved — "These people
are animals." He said to destroy the letter; it would be over soon and he'd be home.

Bob destroyed the letter, but when Danny didn't show up and Waters gave
different stories about his whereabouts, Bob ran a little test.

He told Waters about the "do not open until" letter. Should he open it?

There was a long silence on the other end of the phone. "It was the first time
he didn't have a quick answer," said Bob later.

Then Waters said no, Danny would probably show up soon; in fact he'd called
last night from Dallas, drunk — and *don't open that letter.* Two days later, there was
a knock on Bob's door. Waters and another man stood on the porch.

"We were sent here to get that letter."

The men came inside and made sure Bob was alone. Bob said he'd burned the
letter back when Danny told him to; he had lied to see if it jarred loose any news
about Danny's whereabouts. David questioned him closely. "The people that sent
us are worse than the Mafia," he warned. They'd have no qualms about getting the
letter by whatever means it took.

"Your brother has a bad drinking problem, doesn't he?" Waters asked. Bob said,
well, he does like to drink. "And he talks a lot when he's drinking," nodded Waters.

"That keeps haunting me," Fry told MacCormack. "He said, 'your brother's . . . got
a big mouth.' "

The two men left, but Fry kept in touch with Waters, pretending to believe
Danny was alive, because Waters was his only link to his brother. "The Austin
police . . . didn't seem very concerned about anything," he told MacCormack. They
never called him back, even though he gave them David Waters' name.

MacCormack dug, and found Waters' criminal records. He now had a September
1995 connection among Waters, Danny Fry, Gary Karr, and the Warren Inn. But
no direct link to the O'Hairs.

In August, Tim Young sent MacCormack 10 pages of ownership history of David
Waters' cars. Two car-buying splurges for Waters and Colleen Kay Smith coincided
with the O'Hairs being separated from big chunks of money — in May 1994 and
September 1995. One was a white 1990 Cadillac Eldorado David bought on September 16, 1995, in San Antonio. The couple who sold it were wide-eyed at the
stack of bills — $13,000 cash.

Young was now certain they were looking at four homicides. He wanted to go
to the authorities. But MacCormack wanted to do his story. The Austin cops had
never shown an interest in this case, he argued, nor had the Austin paper been

working on it. No one was putting pressure on Waters. Young argued that Waters might bolt if MacCormack exposed his connection to Danny Fry. He wanted to go to Detective Baker.

"MacCormack said, 'We don't understand, why are you doing this?'" Young recalled later, "and I said, 'No, I don't understand, why are you going to print it?'...MacCormack thought I was nuts. He said, 'Don't you know I *write* for a living?'"

On August 11, 1998, their arrangement ended. Bob Fry sided with Young. He held onto his phone records, which MacCormack badly wanted.

Young faxed a three-page letter to Detective Steve Baker. He provided names, phone numbers, dates, addresses, Social Security numbers, and, in detail, his and MacCormack's activities of the past year and a half. He laid it out: the link of four missing people to Waters, Waters' large cash purchases when he had no job, Colleen's name — and proof she also had bought a nearly new vehicle in October 1995, a truck — the name of the new guy, Gary P. Karr, and the Warren Inn. He also warned that MacCormack was about to blow the lid off, and Waters and Karr might disappear.

"I thought within an hour my phone would be ringing off the hook from APD."

Instead, the day ended and he went to bed. He waited most of the next day, then finally called Baker. He got the impression Baker hadn't even read his fax all the way through. APD already had a backlog of cases less circumstantial than this one, he said.

Disgusted, Young called the FBI and left a message that he had information about a kidnapping and possible multiple murders. There was no response. He tried again, and then called someone he knew would respond — Ed Martin.

Chapter 62 ~ Dallas County Detectives and the FBI

O N AUGUST 14, MacCormack felt ready to run his story about Danny Fry being missing and feared dead. He had one more call to make — his first one to David Waters.

Waters' deep smoker's voice answered the phone. MacCormack introduced himself and plunged in.

"I'm looking into a story about a person who disappeared a couple years ago here in San Antonio? You may have known him. Danny Fry?"

He could feel the shock wave through the phone. After a short silence, Waters recovered himself and warily said he'd known Danny in Florida, and heard he'd "touched base with some people" in Austin. Pressed, he admitted Danny had stayed with him awhile. As he realized how much MacCormack knew, he became cool, even bantering. Even when MacCormack's questions revealed that he knew that

Danny and Waters were in San Antonio at the same time, that he'd bought a Cadillac down there, that he had a shady past with the O'Hairs, Waters was animated and mockingly helpful.

He knew nothing about Danny, he said, but he had a *very* good idea what happened to the O'Hairs. He referred MacCormack to a March 1997 *Vanity Fair* magazine story on the disappearance. He'd supplied the author with his stash of faxes and documents about New Zealand, offshore accounts, and library packing. In fact, he'd signed with Harry Preston, a Dallas screenwriter, to ghost a book he was calling *Good Gawd, Madalyn!*

Well, said MacCormack, their phone records showed they were in San Antonio all of September. And they stopped calling on the 29th, about the same time Danny Fry made his last call.

Hell of a coincidence, said Waters.

"Well, let me ask you straight out."

"Yeah?"

"Did you have anything to do with the disappearance of Danny Fry and the O'Hairs?"

Waters replied with a gravelly laugh.

"I mean, convince me," said MacCormack. "You're a guy with a rough past, and. . . ."

The laughter stopped.

"I'm a guy with a rough past. How do you figure that?"

MacCormack went through the litany — murder, battery, theft, forgery.

Waters said he'd made some mistakes when he was 17, got in with some bad people, and that was a long time ago.

MacCormack, unable to shake any more fruit from the tree, thanked him, and asked him to call if he came up with anything else.

"If *you* come up with anything, *you* give *me* a call," Waters threw back.

"If I come up with anything, it'll be in the paper."

Three days later, on August 16, 1998, it was in the paper. Danny Fry was missing, feared murdered, and it was directly linked with the O'Hairs' disappearance, David Waters, $500,000 in missing gold coins, Jon's impersonator selling his Mercedes, Waters buying a Cadillac with a stack of bills — all of it, just as Tim Young had feared. MacCormack recounted Waters' criminal convictions, and his contention that the Murray-O'Hairs were "kicked back somewhere, very comfortable and having chuckles."

But Waters didn't bolt. He was still holed up in his apartment, working on his book. "Brass balls, that guy," MacCormack commented to Tim Young, who had continued to work the case on his own. He was totally convinced Waters was their man. "He was cool as a cucumber and lied with facility." Young ended up giving

MacCormack several new leads, as the cops "will probably take a couple of years to follow [them] up."

America's Most Wanted was featuring the O'Hair case in late September. Still fearing Waters might bolt after seeing it, Young sent him a telephone card with several hours of free calls. As he expected, Waters assumed it was a promotion from his phone service. Every time Waters used the card, Young got a page, so he knew immediately where Waters was calling to and from. During the *America's Most Wanted* airing, he called Gary Karr, the name that had come up on several phone bills, from someplace near Dallas.

"What was he doing in Dallas? Who's this guy he was staying with?" Young wondered. The name Chico Osborne was about to emerge.

When Ed Martin saw the article about Danny Fry, he knew his money-laundering case was almost surely a kidnapping and multiple homicide. He now had all of Young's research, plus whatever else Young was spading up. Madalyn's list of drugs bought in San Antonio was "just enough to keep her alive for a month," said Young. He'd also run down collect calls to Waters from the prison where Gary Karr was incarcerated, and from ex-wife Charlene Karr's house in Florida after Gary was released. The *piece de resistance* was a collect call from the Newark airport on the day Jon and "Conrad Johnson" flew there. It was to Charlene Karr. Conrad Johnson was almost surely Gary Karr.

Martin took it all to Assistant U.S. Attorney Jerry Carruth, along with information he'd gotten through subpoenas — the $90,000 in cash the family had withdrawn from bank accounts and credit cards that September, for example.

Martin and Carruth presented the information to the FBI, who joined the investigation.

Martin started a timeline, taping pieces of paper on the wall of the war room at Jerry Carruth's offices, and scribbling new information into date boxes as it came in. The coincidences started piling up.

A huge one was about to arise, but it wouldn't be Martin or the FBI that saw it. It would be John MacCormack.

Anniversaries were fodder for story ideas, and on October 2, 1998, MacCormack routinely scanned the wires. One story caught his eye. It said that around 2:30 p.m. on October 2, 1995, a nude male corpse had been found on the bank of the East Fork of the Trinity River in an unincorporated area of Dallas County. It was missing the head and hands. It had never been identified, because there were no fingerprints or dental records. No clothing or other items were found at the scene.

The date struck MacCormack: a couple of days after the O'Hairs' disappearance. And the description: white male, perhaps in his 40s, average height. Waters had told several people that Danny Fry had "gone to Dallas."

MacCormack called the sheriff's office and got the detective who had been haunted by the headless, handless corpse for three years, Robert Bjorklund.

The way the body was laid out on its back, he told MacCormack, near the water, "it was almost where they were kind of daring us to discover this thing. Why didn't they dump it in the water? These people were cocky."

The man's undigested stomach contents were pinto beans, and some greens like salad. There was no alcohol or cannabis in him, only antihistamine; his lungs were congested. The body was at least 12 hours dead.

The autopsy reported a waist-up tan, numerous ant bites, fly eggs in the bloody meat of the neck and wrists. On his chest were a couple of scratches, and abrasions near the left collarbone. A one-inch bruise on the right arm.

There was a Florsheim shoe print in the soft earth near the body, tire tracks where someone had backed in and stepped on the brake, maybe opened the trunk, and pulled out the heavy body. Or not; opinions differed as to whether he was killed there or somewhere else.

Bjorklund — "B. J." — had worked the case every day for the first two months, following every lead, and checking the National Crime Information Center, but had come up dry. Finally, tissue samples were taken and the body given a pauper's burial.

With the description of the corpse, MacCormack made some calls to Danny's relatives, and within days, he was sitting in a tiny room with six Dallas County detectives, who sat riveted as he opened his briefcase and took out photos of Danny and David Waters, and copies of his August story about Danny.

The detectives took him out to Malloy Bridge Road, where the body was found. The site was near the gritty village of Seagoville, which housed a federal prison. It had become a dumping ground — mattresses, garbage, and the collectible aluminum cans that accounted for the early discovery of the corpse.

They agreed to request DNA from the Fry family. Processing could take months; all MacCormack asked was that they keep quiet about it until he could publish the results.

After MacCormack left, B. J. called the Austin Police Department. He found that after Bob Fry's 1995 call, Danny's name was never entered into the NCIC computer. Well, they got hundreds of these calls, B. J. was told, they didn't put 'em all in the computer. They'd tried to contact Bob but couldn't get him, so they closed the case.

In a few weeks, Detective Baker was replaced on the case.

Bob Fry now finally sent the phone records MacCormack had wanted for months. They showed Danny was with Waters up until the last minute he was heard from — proof Waters was lying. MacCormack couldn't wait to see the DNA results.

He was also on the trail of Gary Karr. He soon had his criminal record from the Illinois state police, detailing the nonstop "bad decisions" as his daughter later called them, that had kept Karr behind bars most of his adult life.

On October 15, 1998, American Atheists announced it was striking the tent in Austin. It was selling AAGHQ — for less than half what Madalyn had paid — and moving to New Jersey. MacCormack had to hurry to catch Spike Tyson. He wanted his take on that $54,000 theft, or bribe, or whatever it was.

Tyson recounted how upset Jon had been at finding the accounts empty. Waters' bribery story wasn't holding up.

Across town, FBI Special Agent Donna Cowling was meeting with Ed Martin, Jerry Carruth, and APD officers. The O'Hair disappearance had become a joint case now, though they didn't know anything about Dallas County or the DNA test yet.

Cowling, attractive and blond, had started with the FBI in 1991, a refugee from public school teaching and coaching. She had the unflinching blue eyes of a coach, someone who could size a person up on the spot.

"I got disillusioned. I was having a hard time, with so many children who come from such terrible home lives, and nobody wanted to do anything about it. I did lots of volunteer work with underprivileged kids... a lot of [them] had way, way too much drug knowledge for a nine or ten year old. I thought, 'how do you win this?'"

She decided to try attacking it from the drug side. She applied to both the FBI and law school, and took the LSAT. She was quickly accepted at the FBI Academy, and in June 1991, left law school behind for Quantico. She started out in drug investigations and domestic terrorism.

The O'Hair case was all circumstantial — no bodies, no weapon, no witnesses — and her boss gave her two months to find one piece of hard evidence. But Ed Martin was skilled at building circumstantial cases to prove tax evasion, and the two of them headed for the Warren Inn with a subpoena and Tim Young's information.

"We started digging through a big box of receipts," said Ed Martin; he had the impression they were about to throw them away. Finally, Cowling pulled out a lease agreement. It had David Waters' driver's license photo. He'd taken Room 11 in the Warren Inn Village for a month, starting August 28, 1995.

Gary Karr was also listed on the agreement with his driver's license photo.

They were jubilant. "Tim was right on point," said Cowling. "... and that's when I thought, 'you know, these people probably really *are* dead.'"

Chapter 63 ~ Prose and Cons

DAVID WATERS had a rough summer, and fall of 1998 was looking worse. He'd stiffed ghost writer Harry Preston on the second half of his $5,000 fee, and Preston was sending angry faxes, letters, and emails, all ignored.

The truth was, he thought Preston's work was dry and boring, and he realized he could write better than the man he'd hired. His association with *Vanity Fair* had boosted his confidence, and yielded a list of agents and publishers. He wanted to do more interviews and write a more salable account. He'd worked on the book most of 1997, spicing the dull parts with renderings of the O'Hairs' flatulence, body odor, screaming tantrums, racism, and small daily cruelties. He claimed to have witnessed a torrid sexual encounter between Jon and Robin. He worked diligently at totting up the evidence for flight, mixing his purloined letters and faxes with his own recollections and statements from others about the shredding of files, the secrecy, the requests to lie if they were subpoenaed.

It wasn't just literary ambition; a splashy book might get his debt completely discharged. Over 1997, and so far in 1998, he'd spent hours in online forums, collecting Stein/Lynch/Massen-type material, and found a lot of support for his contention that the O'Hairs were in hiding.

But the book was stalled, even though neighbors said he mostly stayed inside at the computer. If they could have peeked in, they'd have seen it wasn't *Good Gawd, Madalyn!* keeping him in his chair — it was pornography. He spent up to 20 hours a day online, mixing business with pleasure.

The business part was finding the physical addresses of the porn sites he visited. Pornographers usually had a lot of cash, and were perfect targets for home invasion robberies because they were reluctant to report them to police.

Just that summer of 1998, in fact, a young man in Indianapolis answered his door to two floral-delivery men. They forced him inside, handcuffed him, and ransacked the house, making off with a small safe, cash, a pearl necklace, a diamond tennis bracelet, a Ruger, a Tech 9, and a Lorcin .380.

A few weeks later, David presented Colleen with a diamond tennis bracelet. She later saw him cleaning a Tech 9, and, Gary Karr gave a pearl necklace to his daughter, Chrystal.

Waters also had a little sideline. He'd open Yahoo! or Hotmail accounts using a woman's name, sometimes Colleen's. He'd solicit men to the site using naked photos of women he claimed to be, and engage them in correspondence. They thought they were flirting with a pretty, sensitive college student who needed help with tuition. It was surprising how often money came in the mail. He also seduced women over the Internet, looking for lonely, needy females with property, or the potential for a big divorce settlement.

But his relationship with Colleen was falling apart. As usual, she was support-ing them. Since March 1997 she'd worked at the Austin Resource Center for Independent Living, ARCIL, a service for disabled people. He had a couple of minimum-wage, sometime jobs, and was falling so far behind on his restitution that they were talking about putting him in the Travis County Jail work-release program.

There was a hearing about it in August 1998, and though Colleen came to court with him to show support, she was throwing him out.

He left on a road trip the second half of July, and while he was gone, a new resident moved in next door, DeWayne Chavez, a San Antonio gang member fresh out of rehab. Stay away from women, his counselor had warned, urging him to concentrate on his job at a steel construction firm.

The first thing that caught his eye was Colleen, sitting by the pool. Fourteen years his elder, she was sexy, he said later, a "flashy chick with a lot of money" and what he thought was a Rolex watch.

It was immediate electricity. Chavez went through David's porno collection and his expensive clothes — a dozen pairs of fancy boots, Florsheim shoes, designer suits, leather. Waters always dressed snappy, smelled like perfume. His stuff was all packed in one room; Colleen was trying to get him out. They hadn't slept together in a long time, but she didn't know how to end it; she kept hoping he'd move after the book was finished, or after he got back from wherever, or got caught up, or did this, or that.

She confided to Chavez that she'd started hating David "that time when he shot that cat in the head. He offered it a piece of salami, and it swiped at his finger and scratched it? And he shot it in the head." Chavez, who was heavy-set and tough, with lots of biker friends, felt she was afraid of Waters.

By late August, she'd nudged David to go to Peoria to see about moving in with Jeff. Once he got there, she told him there was someone else. He rushed back, but only for the ugly parting. Chavez confronted him and was suddenly looking at a gun. "I kept telling him, 'Shoot me, motherfucker!'" Colleen came out of the house and Chavez scooped her up, sending friends back to get her things.

Waters "dropped 30 pounds like that," said Chavez later. "He used to be tough, big, all buffed up. Now he's just a skinny old man."

In a way, Colleen felt terrible about leaving him. "He was an anvil around my neck...[but] I didn't just want to say 'Get the fuck away from me,' because he was vulnerable. Because it *would* expose his weakness, and his leechiness — and I didn't want anybody to see that," she said years later. Plus, "*it was my stuff!*...And you know, he never had any money, nothing. He probably felt protected being around me."

But he soon set out to prove her wrong. In September 1998, a few days after she left with Chavez, David wrote her a cool letter and copied it to his lawyer and probation officer. He wished their relationship could have ended on a more positive note, but he'd been threatened physically by Chavez; therefore, would she please get all her stuff out of *his* apartment by Friday?

He'd turned the tables; she was the one getting the boot. She had the utilities cut off; he had them back on the same day. He even got her jealous, denying a rumor he was seeing someone else. "50-year-old men don't get laid quite as often as 40-year-old women with large breasts," he wrote the 39-year-old, and assured her that the past eight years were full of cherished memories.

"Since we both know that it's highly unlikely your current relationship will stand the test of time" — Chavez was 25 — he wished her luck with whoever she ended up with. And if she ever needed a shoulder to cry on, call him.

It was hardly the gutted, fragile victim she'd pictured. In fact, he was more like the David who used to tell her sometimes, after the O'Hairs disappeared, that if he went down, he was taking her with him. "You're my weak link," he'd say.

At another hearing in October over his unpaid restitution, he fended off jail by getting Chico Osborne to supply a fake payroll check. But he was still behind. You better get current, the court scolded. Your cable bill, for example, those movie channels? That's half your payment!

On October 12, 1998, said DeWayne Chavez, he and Colleen were driving around, giddy, with a marriage license. "It's now or never," he said to her.

She was so sweet, so different. She was brilliant, he said, very peaceful, into health food, and was always trying to get him to do something good for himself. He'd get up for work at 4:30, and Colleen would get up too, and make him a big breakfast and an "energy drink." She'd walk him to the car, kiss him good-bye.

Every evening when he came home, she'd have him read something about current events, and explain what he thought it meant, and how things might have been different. She would run his bath. She always had dinner ready.

"We went to the judge . . . I was so nervous . . . the judge said, 'aren't you gonna put your arm around this little lady like you're gonna get married?' He had to tell [me] everything to do, like you can kiss the bride, *look* at the bride." At one point during the nuptials, DeWayne looked at his shirt front. "It was covered with McRibs." He didn't remember how or when.

The day after the wedding, David found two old love notes from Colleen. He broke down and cried. "Chavez and [Colleen] must have had some really good laughs at my expense," he grieved.

A week later, the newlyweds had a big bash at the Poodle Dog Lounge, with all their friends and the regulars. Jerry Basey, a fixture at "the Dog," lent his barbecue grill. They cooked brisket, boiled crawfish, and Mexican rice.

It rained hard that day; the Poodle Dog flooded, and escaped crawfish were spidering across the parking lot toward Burnet Road. But it didn't dampen the party. When the couple was poised to cut the wedding cake, someone came over and put two live crawfish on top. Then a drunken guest lurched up and cut it before the newlyweds had a chance. Fond memories, beamed DeWayne several years later.

On the day of the party, however, Colleen wrote David a brooding email. David had kept all the nice things they bought, mostly with her money. The table, the bed, the artwork.

"I paid and paid and paid," she wrote, and she was still paying. "You never loved me." That was what hurt most, she accused.

He sat down and wrote a long, arch reply — "at the risk of impeding your progress toward martyrdom." She couldn't possibly believe he hadn't loved her. She was the one who walked out. Snidely, he allowed that her judgment might have been impaired by "young love," and said she could have some of her stuff back.

The last time she saw him outside of a courtroom was just before Christmas. Marti's Christmas stocking had mistakenly ended up in her possession, and she knew he had a strange attachment to it, taking it with him on trips. She asked Chavez to return it, and he left it on David's porch, stuffed with nudie pictures.

David called her at work. *"Very fucking funny!"* She was scared, and called her husband. Chavez caught Waters outside ARCIL, and beat him up as Colleen watched. It upset her terribly. "I didn't want to see him staggering backward into the bushes with blood on his mouth — that's not what I wanted."

Chapter 64 ~ For Sale to the Highest Bidder

IT WAS NEAR CHRISTMAS 1998, and MacCormack was antsy. The DNA results were still not in, and Bob Fry still wouldn't go on record about the "do not open" letter. But Waters seemed to be showing the strain, MacCormack told Fry. "I think he realizes he may be in for some very serious trouble."

Also by Christmas 1998, the IRS had resurrected its move on Greystone, and there was no stopping it this time. The receivers extracted what papers and photos might be important to the ongoing investigation, and her government, which Madalyn had urged that people trust instead of God, filled hundreds of cardboard boxes and black garbage bags with clothes, dishes, cookware, appliances, bedding, pet toys — the stuff of daily life. They hauled off mattresses and box springs and drapes.

Madalyn's diaries were in a bank vault, to be auctioned separately. Bankruptcy trustee Ron Ingalls allowed reporters and writers to quote from them and take notes to generate interest — though American Atheists had plucked the critical tomes, covering the Supreme Court years and the Truth Seeker/IRS years, and declined to share them.

Much was made of the entry saying "Somebody, somewhere, love me." Bill commented that his mother felt unloved because people not involved in the sort of higher compassion of a God didn't understand love. She thought it meant blind obedience to her will. He predicted the IRS wouldn't get much for the diaries. They only showed a "very troubled and disturbed woman."

Another interesting item, which the *Baltimore Sun's* Dan Fesperman had noticed in the IRS's earlier auction attempt, was a large dollhouse in Madalyn's bedroom, furnished strikingly like Greystone. Arnold Via said that playing with it was her "therapy." The irresistible association was her playing God; but underneath was a pathology everyone close to her had seen: a need for control so profound it was barely comprehensible to a normal person.

There were over 100 boxes of their everyday possessions, and hundreds of books from home, holding the ideas that bound their minds together. It was somehow obscene that the intimate emblems of their extraordinary bond were heaped into these mounds, to be picked over and even made fun of. Madalyn's needlepoint, the auctioneer joked — when she wasn't prayin', she was knittin', and that left her a lot of time for knittin'. How much?

Who at the auction would lift Robin's viola from its case and remember when she played Mozart at a Solstice party? — it was snatched up by some stranger for a pittance. The Christmas decorations caused much wry comment and brought $30. It was doubtful that the leather wingback chairs, grandfather clock, silver, and Waterford crystal that were, for Madalyn, the definitive emblems of wealth and status, could bring anyone else such immense comfort and validation as they had her. And her prized genealogy folder — who would end up with that? Who would care now if she ever got into DAR?

Robin's red-brown 1985 Porsche, one of the few sparks of sexuality and independent spirit she'd ever been allowed, went to a Baptist for $2,750, still a cherry though it had mysteriously acquired another 8,000 miles on its odometer since being found at the airport.

The bargain hunters spent about $20,000 all told.

What the receivers had kept from the IRS's clutches were stored in boxes — records, letters, photos. Thousands of photos. The lives of Madalyn and her two captive children were coded into snapshots — of the yearly conventions that cemented their bond with admirers, and of the sacred vacations that were their only relief from the crushing pressures of the Cause.

There were rows of atheists at desks, atheists listening to a speaker, atheists standing around talking, atheists drinking coffee. Atheists at the banquet table in the 1970s, with their sideburns, bouffant hair, polyester, and wide ties. Atheists lecturing at the podium. And among the hip and educated, the fat, intense, gotch-eyed, humorless, and lonely ones that Bill once felt made up the bulk. All basking in the wonderful camaraderie of the parties thrown for them by Madalyn and Garth.

And then their vacations: temples, tugboats, giant Buddhas, bronze statues, castles, fountains, ruins, children in cobbled streets, Robin on a merry-go-round, Robin feeding a baby pig. Seashores, circus tents, Madalyn lifting a sunburned arm to shade her eyes, taking in monuments, onion domes, and windmills.

Garth beaming at the Pyramids, the Great Wall, the Houses of Parliament, the Taj Mahal. The Founders smiling in Red Square. Aquariums, icebergs, skylines, bridges, pagodas, waterfalls, a sad-faced Robin at Auschwitz. Niagara Falls, Sea World, rain forests, yachts, Pirates of the Caribbean, redwoods, the Angelus Temple at 1100 Glendale Boulevard, Los Angeles.

As the years rolled by in shutter-click instants, their faces and bodies got rounder, and the kids' expressions sadder. But Madalyn was always so very happy on vacation, belly-laughing, pointing, or mugging.

When they took those thousands upon thousands of photographs, they probably thought that one day they'd all sit down together and reminisce. Maybe when Madalyn was done with her high blood pressure, 80 pounds of fat, and diabetes. Or when Robin had children, or when Jon Garth got a woman. There were many new photo albums, still in their wrappers.

Some 400 people showed up at the auction that January 23, 1999, in Pflugerville, Texas. Among them was David Waters. Nervy, thought MacCormack.

It was the first time Ed Martin laid eyes on him up close. "He was a cold, calculation' guy. Like an owl. He has this head thing, his head rises up, and his eyes move. Like he's scannin' for prey."

MacCormack went over to chat, and got Waters' usual drill: everything pointed to New Zealand, Sanders was the perfect trusty as he was dying, he was probably making them fake IDs.

MacCormack had a big story ready, just waiting for the DNA. After the auction, he dropped by to talk to Jimmy Nassour, the Catholic lawyer who had paid $2,000 for a Bible found in Madalyn's belongings, and who would end up high bidder — $12,000 — on Madalyn's diaries (American Atheists made a token bid under $3,000). Nassour told him Waters had come by with a copy of *Mein Kampf* signed by Madalyn.

"It had some really interesting sex underlined. He wanted $2,000. I paid him $100." His impression of Waters: "Likable, smooth, broke."

On January 27, MacCormack's phone rang. It was B. J. The DNA results were in. The probability that their unidentified corpse was Danny Fry was 99.99%.

MacCormack called Waters.

He always answered the phone, "Yell-o!"

Couple of quick questions, Mr. Waters, said MacCormack. Had he gone to Florida and threatened Bob Fry? Over a letter Danny wrote, saying that if he disappeared

"I have *no idea* what you're talkin' about!" Waters stormed. "I don't know where you come up with this strange shit!"

"Okay, Mr. Waters, just about done. A guy named Gary P. Karr showed up in San Antonio in September '95, then Austin. And I think you two are acquainted? From the Vienna correctional facility?"

No. He'd never heard of Gary P. Karr.

"Okey-doke. That's it."

They hung up.

When Bob Fry got the DNA news from MacCormack, even though he thought he was prepared for it, he was overwhelmed with rage and grief. A Vietnam vet with 25 combat missions as a helicopter crew chief and gunner, and numerous medals, he suffered from posttraumatic stress disorder and survivor's guilt, especially about his brother. He'd been having a recurring nightmare. It started as a real memory of pulling dead bodies into the helicopter. Something rolled past his foot. He thought it was a helmet, and picked it up. It was a severed head. In his dreams, it was Danny's.

"That's the thing," he told MacCormack. "To cut someone up like that . . . I wish I could just watch him sweat."

"He'll be sweating on Sunday," MacCormack assured him, when the article came out. Waters had no idea Danny had been identified. He only knew there was buzz that Danny may have been murdered or whatever — stuff he could deal with. Even the name Gary Karr hadn't fazed him. But it would be a different story when he read that they actually had Danny's body.

Bob agreed to go on the record now about Waters' threatening visit. When the Sunday paper came out, maybe he'd better arrange not to be around for awhile, MacCormack suggested. Bob agreed. He'd already been locking himself in with a gun.

Chapter 65 ~ What Colleen Saw

MacCormack's story identifying the headless, handless corpse ran on Sunday, January 31, 1999. It was a gratifying coup for the reporter, whose work on the O'Hair case drew a nomination for the Pulitzer Prize in journalism.

The story was laid out along the bread crumb trail left by the O'Hairs' cell phone. MacCormack showed how the family's last month eddied around the Warren Inn area. They had ordered Tex-Mex from across the road, rented videos from the nearby Blockbuster. Cory Ticknor's shop was a few blocks north. MacCormack connected the dots among the O'Hairs, David Waters, and the man from Florida. Once he became Danny Fry through the blood of his relatives, the fuse was lit, not just under his murder, but under the entire O'Hair case which, MacCormack dryly wrote, had stagnated "despite the dogged efforts of private investigators and reporters." Law enforcement was pointedly left out.

The article brought up a third man, an ex-con who now lived in Michigan, and wouldn't return MacCormack's calls. He'd been in the Vienna, Illinois Correctional Center at the same time as Waters. He'd come to Texas less than four months after being paroled. His crimes included kidnapping and rape. His name was still mum publicly, but Gary Karr wouldn't have any trouble recognizing himself in MacCormack's story.

When Donna Cowling saw the story, she called the Dallas County Sheriff. "I need to talk to your detectives." She was not happy that MacCormack hadn't shared his scoop with the FBI.

On the day the story appeared, Colleen Kay Smith Chavez "freaked out in the living room," said her husband. Earlier, they'd been at the Poodle Dog and gotten into a big argument. Upset, she'd run off in the car. When he got home about two hours later, she was crying, and tried to slap and hit him; she was sobbing about the O'Hairs. He left the house, went to a phone, and called APD.

This time, the report was passed on to the FBI. The next day, Donna Cowling called Chavez. His wife needed to come clean, she said.

Donna Cowling, Colleen said later, was the *only* person who could have gotten her to come forward and tell what she knew.

"It was a Tuesday evening," said Cowling. "She was absolutely terrified. She didn't know what to expect from us — and she didn't trust us."

And why would she? Colleen reflected later that she'd watched as David convinced the court to reduce his restitution, and as various publications printed his side of the $54,000 theft and the O'Hairs' disappearance. She saw how seriously the police took the disappearance — and she'd spent the subsequent four years as David's "weak link."

"He is a most incredibly patient planner. David has the vengeful memory of an elephant . . . he seems always to nurture a seed of resentment and hate for those who have wronged him."

Surely the law saw her as an accomplice. She knew Waters had done something to the O'Hairs, and had kept silent. She'd taken money she knew was theirs. She felt guilty and afraid, and at one point had gone to a counselor, planning to tell everything. But the things she had to say were so far outside anything in her nice family counseling specialist's experience. The other people in the waiting room had problems, but not like hers. Not headless corpses, stacks of cash, bloody clothes.

But Donna Cowling was nice. Blond, blue-eyed, pretty, and normal, she looked like a soccer mom from affluent Cat Mountain. You'd never know her life's work was confronting all kinds of terrible darkness in her fellow humans. By her 30s, she'd developed an eye for good and evil, and it was hard to fool her.

"That night, she told us bits and pieces," said Cowling.

It was a closed-mouth rendering, and over the next few days, Cowling coaxed her. "I know you're not telling us everything," she said, and Colleen replied that she was scared for her life, and for her family. Cowling got busy on an immunity letter, and Colleen got a lawyer. By Friday, she had "use immunity" — "As long as I tell everything, no matter how awful, and I tell the truth, that it can't be used against me because I didn't do anything to those people. I might have accepted money, and [I] did some really stupid things, but I didn't kill anybody or participate in the planning of it . . . but if I killed Danny, it would not protect me from that."

Prosecutor Jerry Carruth clarified: "She does not have immunity from prosecution. She has immunity from the *use* of her testimony against her in prosecution."

It was enough. Little by little, over a series of interviews, it all came out.

During July, August, September, and October 1995, this was what Colleen saw and heard. Gary Karr and David had been in touch all summer by phone. Karr got out of the "honor farm" in April after serving 21 years, and made a beeline for his ex, Charlene, in Florida. Finding that reconciliation would take money, he took David up on an offer of a big-money deal, and arrived in Austin in August. He told Charlene it was a high-stakes poker game.

Danny Fry arrived in July. He got along with everyone — "super bubbly," Colleen called him, and crazy about his kids. He was talking marriage with his girlfriend, Lisa Jones. He needed money for that, and decided to work for David. He told Jones it was to bring some construction outfit to Florida with backers from Texas. He swore he'd be home for his daughter's Sweet Sixteen party on September 30.

The three men hung around the apartment and played video games most of August. None of them had jobs. Someone faxed David the July *Insider's Newsletter* that featured him urinating on his mother. He became obsessed with hurting Madalyn. "He said often that he'd like to torture her, to take a pair of pliers and pull her toes off... He was truly furious... he had a sense of vengeance... a calm came over him about Madalyn."

On Sunday, August 27, 1995, the men "left as though they were just, you know, going down the street to the store or whatever, but they didn't come back." That night, Colleen went out listening to jazz and got drunk. She was arrested for public intoxication. Bailed out in the wee hours by a friend, she was afraid David would be angry when she got home. But relief: he wasn't there. All of them were gone.

David called the next day to say he'd be back, but not when. For the next 30 days, he came back a few times, sometimes alone, sometimes with Gary. Colleen was working days at the Poodle Dog, taking a class at Austin Community College.

Once during that month, David mailed her $5,000 in cash. Another time, she came home to find an envelope next to the bed with $11,000 in it. She asked him where it all came from.

"He said laughingly, to let me know that it was tongue in cheek, that he was 'gambling.'"

With his permission, she bought a 1985 GMC Sierra shortbed pickup — a stick shift, which David had never mastered.

She noticed that two pairs of handcuffs he'd bought in 1994 were missing, along with a Browning 9 millimeter he'd purchased from a police officer.

He'd gotten the handcuffs when he stole the $54,000 from the O'Hairs. Yes, he'd stolen it outright. There was no bribery, and of course he'd passed the polygraph — he paid for it, and he was supplying the questions, rather than the police.

While working at GHQ, he'd stolen numerous rare books and some of the special cancellation stamps from the 1991 convention. During his Internet obsession, they turned up on Ebay.

He'd stolen the library computer, too, calling Colleen at work one day when the O'Hairs were in San Diego. Come to GHQ over the noon hour, he said, and park at the side door. He came out with a sports bag, put it in the car, and bade her good-bye. At home, he tried to break into the library catalogue, but couldn't get past Robin's encryption code. He made backups, and they went downtown, where

Shoal Creek emptied into the Colorado River by the city power plant. Colleen threw the hard drive into the water. Back home, he tossed the computer and monitor in the dumpster. And he'd stolen those bearer bonds out of the GHQ safe. The two of them had destroyed them sitting in the car behind the Filling Station Restaurant on Barton Springs Road.

During the second Truth Seeker trial, he'd gone over to await the O'Hairs' return, with handcuffs, rope, and duct tape. He told Colleen the $54,000 was nothing to the millions they had. He knew about the money in the New Zealand accounts. He had been prowling GHQ, copying the faxes and documents he later used to bolster his bribery story.

That day he lay in wait, he gave Colleen strict orders not to call GHQ or come by. But knowing what he was planning, she couldn't work. "I sat in great isolation, thinking to myself that...the unthinkable might be happening and...it would be my responsibility because I knew about it." She went outside and sat in a field of bluebonnets. Then she went back in and called GHQ and begged him to just leave, get out of there. He did, but he was furious, told her she had no guts at all, and was no better than his dead whore ex-wife. It was the only time anyone ever reported him speaking ill of Marti.

What made him turn against the O'Hairs so?

He'd admired Madalyn at first. "He considered her to be true intelligentsia." But after awhile, "he felt like she was, like, a televangelist and would get people to send her money, that all of her money...wasn't earned. It was just taken from people." In fact, he'd told David Travis that people who gave their money to frauds like Jimmy Swaggart deserved what they got. Most people, he said, were marks, "just waiting to be had."

His scorn for his bosses had hardened into hatred by Christmas 1993. Colleen was never sure what the pivotal event was, but it was focused on Madalyn.

"Whatever it was, it wouldn't have had to be anything enormous." David's temper could be tripped by the tiniest things. It happened after he was made office manager. "There was a distinct while when he was part of the team. Yes, he talked about, oh, their *greed*, but it was more with a twinkle. He was definitely part of the team, and then *something* happened."

Perhaps it was when Madalyn cold-shouldered him after overhearing him sharply shut down one of Jon's 30-minute answers to a simple question. For a week, she snubbed him. He'd be standing right there, and she'd tell Robin, "When you see Waters, tell him..."

And it just flipped a switch. It was like when he killed the cat. That was how he was — he could just *turn*, and after that, he had no conscience. When Colleen remembered his daydreams about torturing the O'Hairs, she pictured him doing it to her.

He'd taken sharp notice of the dynamics among the family members, and jotted some down, including a character trait of Jon's that Madalyn, he said, abhorred:

"Jon did not have Mother's killer instinct." And he agreed. He disliked Jon for being weak and easily manipulated.

"Before his big obsession with [Madalyn]," Colleen said, "he was interested in living, setting goals, even though he [worried] people would find out about his past." But even if the blood hadn't already been in the water from the Truth Seeker and IRS, he would probably have reverted to his old ways.

"Dave, in spite of getting good jobs, and in spite of being sharp, and having lots of potential, would always revert to his criminality," said a family member.

One day during his September in San Antonio, he came home in a white Cadillac. He asked Colleen to put it in her name, and got mad when she balked. This time she didn't ask how he got it, or what he and the other two were doing. He didn't want her to know, anyway. "He thought I was a coward when it came to crime," and the less information a coward had, the better.

She thought maybe he was involved in some check scam — he was always talking about how easy that was.

Toward the end of September, a number of things happened. David came home exhausted one night and fell asleep fully dressed, though he seemed wired. He asked her to rent a small unit at Burnet Road Self Storage, across from the Poodle Dog Lounge, and buy a lock. She did, and gave the keys to him.

Shortly after that, he and Karr showed up and borrowed her truck for a full day. David told her not to go out to the parking lot. He also told her he was going to put half a million dollars in gold coins in the storage unit she'd rented. She could see Karr motioning him to shut up.

David asked her to find out if there was "anyplace like where he could get away, you know, a place way far away from everything. And I said, well, you know, how about a hunting lease?"

She asked Jerry Basey. They stood at the end of the Poodle Dog bar and Basey drew her a map of the hunting camp he leased on a large ranch, 100 miles southwest of San Antonio. He gave her the gate lock combination into the pasture.

He was happy to help; she deserved a little vacation. "Go down't the deer lease," he urged. "Go swimmin' in the river." It was perfect for the dog days of summer.

On September 25, David gave her an envelope with $700 in it, and said Chico Osborne was coming for it in the morning. He did, and returned later to drop off another one. It contained keys to a second storage unit — one big enough to drive a truck into — that he'd rented at David's request.

On Saturday, September 30, David, Gary, and Danny returned. They all seemed worn out. David had thousands of dollars, a Raymond Weil watch, and bags of clothing from Saks Fifth Avenue. Hugo Boss, Zania, Hermes. Gary Karr had a Raymond Weil watch, too, and Donna Karan clothes.

Danny lay down on the futon sofa. It was unusual for him to be so subdued. He wasn't drinking, and Colleen wondered if he had been drying out in the month he'd been gone.

She covered him with a blanket "and he closed his eyes and he just kind of smiled." He asked her to pack his clothes, and tear some women's phone numbers out of his address book, as he was returning to Florida. She packed, and then ran an errand. When she returned, all three men were gone.

She had a horrible feeling. She went into the bedroom where they had piled their stuff. Danny's things were unpacked. His suitcase was sitting there empty. There was a garbage bag with some of his stuff in it. A souvenir mug for his daughter Lisa was on a bookshelf.

At least one night and part of another day passed, and then Waters and Karr came back alone. They were laughing. Karr was teasing Waters about not being able to read a map.

She asked where Danny was, and David said he left with some guy.

"I handed him his empty suitcase, and I said, 'What's this?'" She thrust the souvenir cup at Gary and screamed, "Is this yours? Is this yours?" He said no, and she screamed, "Get this stuff out of here!"

That night — October 1, she thought — she noticed a Randall's Supermarket bag sitting in the tile foyer of their apartment. There was a certain washcloth lying on top, a keepsake from her dead father. She picked it up, and David shouted at her to leave that bag alone and never look in it again. She started to cry. "My Dad's washcloth," she stammered, and he yanked it away, took it to the sink and washed blood out of it, and thrust it at her angrily.

After awhile, he left, and she looked inside the bag. She saw bloody tennis shoes, three pairs, with smears, splatters. "Chunks of blood," she said, "like they were standing in a puddle of blood." Shortly, the bag disappeared.

Over the next few days, David badmouthed Danny. He talked too much, he was a low life, a drunk.

On October 3, David and Gary had planned a romantic evening at the Four Seasons Hotel downtown on the river. Gary was flying Charlene in from Florida.

Colleen was in the shower when the phone rang. It was David, frantic, calling from the Poodle Dog. Someone had broken into the storage unit across the street and stolen the suitcase full of gold. She dressed and sped over, afraid he'd think it was her, that she'd kept a spare key.

She talked to the storage facility manager. He had no idea why the door was ajar and the lock missing.

Before she could report back, David "disappeared for several hours and didn't call me back and say, what did you find out? or anything that you would think would be reasonable."

When he finally called her, he was nonchalant, and said something like, "Oh, well. It's gone." He said Karr wasn't particularly upset, either. He thought either Fry or Fry's son, who had lived awhile in Austin, stole the coins. Or that the coin dealer had put a tracking device in the suitcase.

They checked into the Four Seasons that afternoon with the Karrs, but both couples stayed in their rooms and ordered in. Colleen had a massage, paraffin treatment, and salt rub. Looking into David's bag while he showered, she saw a lock like the one she'd bought for the storage unit.

The next day, walking along Town Lake, Colleen saw him reach into his pocket and throw something into the water. He did this five or six times. She didn't see any of the items, or ask what they were.

He told her to tell Jerry Basey that they'd never used the hunting lease because it rained.

After the evening at the Four Seasons, Colleen saw David clean his glasses with a scrap of torn-up T-shirt. Danny Fry had been wearing it when she last saw him. Danny's daughter and girlfriend and brother were calling, wanting to know where he was. Colleen made David deal with them.

On about October 7, David asked her if she wanted to take a drive to Florida and visit the Karrs, even though they'd just bade them goodbye a few days before. They jumped in the white Cadillac and took off, driving straight through. When they got there, David took his Browning, and the men disappeared the whole day.

Then they headed back to Austin, after only a two-day visit. When they got back, David had her drive him in her truck to the large storage unit Chico had rented. He had a three-gallon spray bottle from Self-Chem in the back. He told her to pull ahead of the garage door, and stay in the truck. He was in there five or ten minutes, and she could smell bleach.

Gary Karr came and went during the rest of 1995, and she described David's scorn when he'd go running back to Charlene.

"That infuriated David because he never thought that you should give out to a woman...he said...there was $100,000 just waiting, just sitting there, and...we can't take care of business." By Christmas 1995, however, Gary and Charlene had split up, and Gary moved back to Illinois.

David would go out to 7–11 and buy the papers and tabloids, looking for something about the O'Hairs. He collected every article that came out. A *Time* magazine article said a white van was seen at the family's house when they disappeared. Colleen remembered a phone message that had come for Karr during that September, to return a van he'd rented.

At some point, David had her box up a knife and the two sets of handcuffs, and send them to her mother's house.

She told how truly black was that edge she'd found so attractive in David. Even before they left for Texas back in 1991, he punched her during a spat, bloodying her nose. When they lived at the Warren Inn that fall, she went for a drink one day after work. She could tell he was angry when she walked in the door, even before he jumped up out of his chair, knocked her to the floor, and kicked her. Then he picked up a barbell and sat on top of her. He was going to smash her head in, he said.

Another night at the Warren Inn, they were both drunk. All Colleen could remember was eating spaghetti, and then sitting on the bedroom floor, hearing a dripping sound on the carpet. It was blood from her chest where he'd stabbed her with a kitchen knife. She began screaming, but pulled herself together and got into the shower. Her arm was slashed, too.

Frantic himself, he dropped her at the hospital and drove away, fearful of police. The doctors called them, but Colleen wouldn't tell them what happened. The truth was, she couldn't remember. He didn't return to get her, and she hitchhiked home, in the middle of the night, and beat on the door. He wouldn't let her in until he was sure she wasn't towing any cops. He was always sorry, so sorry he'd hurt her.

There was no violence for some time, but then in October 1996, Karr was staying with them, as he did periodically. Colleen went out after work, and got a taxi home because she was drunk. David was angry when she walked in.

"Where's the truck?" he demanded. Why, she asked, do you need to use it? That was a jab; he'd never learned to use a stick shift. Gary stared at the television as the tension built.

David got very calm. "I'm going to show you what pain is," he said. Karr slipped into the bedroom and closed the door. David and Colleen circled the furniture in the living room. He slid the couch over in front of the door. "This time," she thought, "he is going to really, really, really hurt me."

There was her Ruger in the bedroom. She bolted for it, but he reached it first. She called him a scum bag, and he smashed her in the mouth with the gun, breaking her teeth. "Do whatever," she moaned, much as Betty had done in the 1978 attack. "Do whatever."

As she spat blood and enamel, he sank to the floor against the wall, quiet. "Is this what happened to the Os?" she screamed. Had he beat and killed them because they pissed him off?

He stood up and told her never to say those words again. She fled, but came back, unable to find a place to spend the night. Next morning, Waters left early, and Karr sat her down. Don't ever bring up the O'Hairs again, he warned.

At the end of 1996, Colleen got her degree from UT Austin in English Literature. Karr continued to visit periodically. When David would be gone, and then come home with money or a car, she wondered. But she didn't want to know. She later remembered once when Karr was visiting with his girlfriend, Kelly. The two men came rushing home in a panic. Karr shaved his beard and had Kelly dye his hair, saying they were going to get caught by police. Colleen never knew what it was about.

In spring 1998, Waters returned from one of his trips to Illinois driving a red Ford Bronco; he said the owner wanted to report it stolen. He pressured her to register it in her name, but she refused.

She spent eight years with Waters, doing his bidding and knowing he was into dark, lawless activities, probably kidnapping and murder. She wired money on his orders, lied to Danny's relatives, bought a truck and didn't ask where the money came from. She pawned a man's gold-and-stainless Rolex watch band on David's orders, accepted a gold coin from him and pawned it, she rode in the Cadillac and spent the money he brought in, rented a place to store the coins, and found a remote ranch site for David to use for something. She kept in touch with him by pager during his month in San Antonio, mailed weapons to her family members, and kept silent about bloody shoes and cash that showed up in her home. She got the undercarriage of his Camaro cleaned of a certain kind of mud caked there, and the inside scoured, after Danny disappeared. Once, when David came back in September 1995, she saw a shovel and bow saw in the trunk of his new Cadillac. Another person might have thought, "Oh, the previous owner forgot his tools," but the items filled Colleen with dread, and she wondered if they had "any evidence" on them. She must have known he was deeply involved in something bad. He was a criminal, and she had known it for years. But she just kept working at her jobs, and chipping away at her degree, and having normal friends outside of home.

Asked later about the double life she'd led, she said, "I guess I just held it all inside."

Chapter 66 ~ Happy Birthday

COWLING, MARTIN, and the Dallas County team went into high gear, checking out Colleen's mesmerizing story. They obtained subpoenas for Doc Holliday's Pawn Shop, the storage units, the Four Seasons Hotel, and Capp's Van and Car Rental. Some APD detectives were added to the team.

The records from Capps showed three van rentals by Karr, in August, September, and October 1995. One tested positive for blood.

At the Warren Inn, a maintenance man recognized Madalyn from a photo. She'd had to be helped on the stairs. She used a walker. Two men helped her. He couldn't identify them.

The Sparrows each separately picked Danny Fry out of a photo lineup as the man who had sold them Jon's Mercedes.

On February 10, 1999, most of the investigators were at Public Storage on North Lamar, watching Luminol be sprayed in unit 52 to check for blood. Manager Dale Coryell remembered renting it to Chico Osborne on September 26, 1995; he'd said he was going to store furniture. A few days later, he saw Chico there with two other men. There were two pickups and three blue barrels, 55 gallons or larger. Coryell noticed because the drums might contain illegal toxic chemicals. He made a mental note to keep an eye on unit 52.

The detectives knew bleach degraded DNA. Waters must have known it, too, because the Luminol showed bleach, just as Colleen had described. Then Martin and B. J. took out the angle iron on the floor along the wall. Under it was something else that reacted to the Luminol. It turned out to be blood.

A few weeks later, Colleen and DeWayne Chavez went into the federal witness protection program.

David Waters was riding a bike to his $6-an-hour job at Tomlinson's Feed. He was about to be evicted. He had a March appointment to get on welfare to help with his rent. Why would someone with $500,000 in gold have to do that, he asked a reporter who was probing his relationship with the O'Hairs. He was embarrassed by all this attention, he said.

March 17, 1999, was first time Donna Cowling saw him in the flesh. She was watching from across the street as he pawned an exercise bike at Doc Holliday's. A couple of days later, he opened a birthday card from his mother. "Happy Birthday to a son who has something in common with all great professional athletes!" It opened on a football player with a hand that popped up: "Can I have some more money?"

"Just kidding," Betty wrote. "Love you, Mom." There was a check inside. They seemed to have put the past behind them.

Wednesday, March 24, 1999, was David's 52nd birthday. He was due in court at 9 a.m. with $350 in restitution money to fend off jail. As he got ready, there was a knock on the door. On his porch were about 12 agents from the FBI, IRS, Alcohol Tobacco and Firearms, APD, and the Dallas County Sheriff's Department. They had a warrant to go through his apartment and car.

Waters stood, smoking, as the agents combed through his every possession.

"They took out boxes and boxes of stuff, for the media's benefit," he said later. "So people watching it would say, 'whoaa, look what they got on *him*!' They took papers, books, that didn't have anything to do with anything. They took the refrigerator magnets!"

Their work took eight hours. The warrant was sealed, so reporters didn't know what the authorities were looking for. But the warrant, said its author, Ed Martin, later, "was written right off [Colleen's] story." It had all checked out, and led to mountains of circumstantial evidence.

They quickly found something to hold Waters on — 119 rounds of ammunition. He was a felon; possessing it brought up to ten years in prison. And it wasn't manufactured in Texas, which violated interstate commerce laws. It was Colleen's, he said. She'd left it behind.

They took him out the back way, cop-grip on his neck and shoulder. The neighbors said he was just the nicest guy, model tenant.

Among his possessions were pages from the criminal code, dealing with parole revocation and habitual criminal charges, and how to appeal deferred adjudication.

There was a wallet with snapshots of his most important women, starting with Marti and ending with lovely Colleen, with her lush auburn hair and red lips. He had a copy of her marriage license to Chavez. There were hundreds of floppy disks and videotapes containing pornography.

Donna Cowling, Ed Martin, and Jerry Carruth — the "team" who would spend two more years immersed in David Waters' and Gary Karr's lives — found some items of great interest to them: two pairs of men's Florsheim footwear, two switch-blades, two large, sharp butchering knives with fancy handles, two pairs of handcuffs, pieces of torn T-shirt, duct tape, rope, padlocks, false IDs — including one with Jeff Hunt's name but David's photo, and Jeff's Social Security card. They found books with titles like *New ID in America* — *How to Create a Foolproof Identity*, and instruc-tions on how to get people's Social Security numbers, send untraceable emails, dig up dirt on people, find out if you were being investigated.

Before sundown, a grand jury was considering a two-count indictment: a felon possessing firearms and transporting weapons across state lines.

Held without bail, Waters appeared in state court in Austin, where the commu-nity supervisors who had been responsible for him the past five years decided he was probably a danger. He should be refound guilty of stealing all 54,000 of the dollars taken from the O'Hairs in 1994.

The 1994 polygraph that had helped him get deferred adjudication now seemed a skillful tapestry of lies and deflections that rang true because they drew on truth. His argument was similar to the way Madalyn framed some of hers. It was the Big Lie strategy: the premise is false, but is brought off by a set of plausible scenarios, often bolstered by witnesses with some sort of tangential interest in the Big Lie. In the end, it's believable to the outsider who can't verify the facts.

The DA could have verified the facts in 1994, though. It wouldn't have been all that hard to prove Waters spent far more than the $15,000 he said he'd taken. But Madalyn had established herself as a twister of truth, and Waters was able to play that against her. No one but Colleen really knew how much he hated her.

D AVID'S 52ND BIRTHDAY was busy elsewhere, too. Cowling and Martin had sent out four coordinated teams armed with warrants. Besides Austin, there was Weatherford, Texas, Novi, Michigan, and Chicago.

In Chicago, Cowling knocked on the door of Sidney Karr, Gary's sister. She had bought a Rolex from her brother — either Robin's or Madalyn's — and it was a critical piece of hard evidence. Rolexes had registration numbers. She was livid, and denied having any Rolex. But they found mention of it in her will, receipts for an appraisal of it, and a picture of her wearing it.

While Cowling dealt with her, Ed Martin was ringing Karr's doorbell in Novi, and the team in Weatherford was interviewing Chico Osborne. With all the targets being questioned at once, they couldn't call and warn each other.

Chico was surprised. He asked his wife and stepdaughter to help jog his memory. He'd never heard of Seagoville, Texas, hadn't seen David Waters since last September. And when he rented that unit back in 1995, he had no idea David had pled guilty to stealing that $54,000. In fact, when Waters had asked him to rent it, he said, "Why can't *you* do it?" Bad credit, Waters replied, something wrong with his ID, he was out of town, etc.—he'd pay Chico $200. So Chico did it.

They found five rounds of .357 caliber bullets. Like Waters, Chico was a felon in possession of ammunition. When they arrested him, his stepdaughter screamed at them. He'd been her daddy since she was just a little thing. He was a family man.

At Novi, "the wind was blowing hard," remembered Ed Martin. "It was *cold* and I was underdressed." He, B. J., two FBI agents, and a detective from Michigan's Oakland County stood on the porch as Gary Karr opened his door.

On the plane to Detroit, Martin had gone over the ways he could appeal to Karr: David Waters was the bad guy, he dragged you in over your head before you knew it. You thought it was just going to be a kidnapping/extortion, you had no idea murder would be involved. A lot of people fell under Waters' spell.

Rapport was one of Martin's skills. He was low-key, warm, and could look people in the eye without intimidating them.

Karr let them in, and Martin seated himself at the coffee table. Karr sank into the sofa and lit a cigarette. Martin read him his Miranda rights in an offhand way.

To his intense annoyance, before he could ease into his drill, one of the FBI agents spoke up. They were investigating the O'Hair disappearance and Danny Fry murder, he told Karr, and they had documents putting him at the center of it all. Karr clammed up.

Martin drew him back out, talking about David Waters, and Karr said he was pissed at him, shouldn't have taken up with him right out of prison, because now Waters had got him in so deep he was worried about his own safety and his family's.

Then FBI agent William O'Leary did a sweep of the house. He found two loaded guns, a revolver and a semiautomatic pistol.

"You're under arrest," he told Karr. Ed Martin groaned inwardly. Couldn't this wait? Once again, Karr clammed up.

Martin got him talking about his parrot, Jo-Jo. They talked computers, and pretty soon Karr was telling Ed Martin about four killings in Texas, that he helped get rid of the victims' property, and rented some vehicles.

Martin didn't take notes, so as to not curb the flow, and it went on for hours as he siphoned out a cache of tidbits large and small. At noontime, they ordered Karr two cheeseburgers and a chocolate malt, and he smoked the Winstons someone had fetched for him, while Martin pulled out his laptop and crafted a statement.

Mentally, he was holding his breath; it looked like Karr might actually sign it voluntarily. Martin wanted to get it while the getting was good, but he had to phrase it to meet the needs of the FBI, IRS, and Dallas County, plus what he'd need for a detention hearing the next day — and he had to print it out and get Karr to actually put his name on it.

"I had a little bubble jet printer that took about ten minutes to print out a page. I asked Karr and he let me use his laser printer. I took my disk, popped it into his computer, and printed out his statement on his own printer."

It was eight pages. After three alterations, Karr signed. He was handcuffed and taken to jail in Pontiac. He was allowed to release Jo-Jo before he left.

Karr's statement was a tale of him passively renting vehicles and handing over the keys and waiting for orders, of sitting in cars while David Waters jumped out and did things with gold and money and bodies. A "gullible, out-of-touch errand boy," MacCormack wrote later.

But the bland statement was a gold mine, because it finally linked the Warren Inn, Waters, and the O'Hairs. He knew they were dead. He knew about the gold. He described the day of the kidnapping, the ditching of Robin's Porsche. He was "Conrad Johnson." He confirmed all the things Tim Young and John MacCormack and the authorities and Bob Fry and Colleen had laid out.

He minimized his role: the O'Hairs wanted help with an illegal flight from the IRS. Waters offered Karr the job of guarding them while he helped them finalize their business. They went voluntarily, and moved about freely, except that Danny Fry was always present for "security." Karr didn't say why they needed security or guards if they went voluntarily.

He saw Waters throwing around a lot of cash. He saw him with two guns he heard Colleen had bought. He rented some vans for Waters. Waters asked him if he'd be willing to do something illegal for $70,000. He said no. Waters gave him three Rolex watches — a man's and two women's. He said the O'Hairs didn't want them any more.

He corroborated Bob Fry's story of the threatening visit in early October 1995. Waters wanted to kill Bob, but Karr threatened to walk out.

Later that month, Waters called him to come to Texas: it had been flooding, and he was concerned the bodies might wash up. He wanted help moving them. Karr drove straight through. He and David went out into the country after dark. David got out and looked around with a flashlight, got back in, and they left.

Karr said he'd never heard of Gerald "Chico" Osborne.

Ed Martin saw Karr one last time, just before he was whisked off to his arraignment by the FBI. Martin thought he could have gotten more out of Karr, but he was never allowed access to him again. He knew his gentlemanly interview technique was fingernails-on-the-blackboard to the Bureau men, but as it turned out, what he pried out of Karr would be the only thing any Fed ever got. He often wondered how things would have turned out if he'd been allowed to keep talking to Karr.

He did get another piece of information at that last meeting. Karr drew a detailed map of where the O'Hairs were buried. It was on a ranch near Camp Wood, Texas. He remembered they'd had to go through three gates. There was a fork in the road, some sheds off to the side. There was a dirt pile; he remembered a bridge.

Chapter 67 ~ No Bodies

O N Friday, Saturday, and Easter Sunday, April 2, 3, and 4, 1999, a large crowd gathered at the Cooksey ranch in Real County near Camp Wood. Armed with Karr's map, they began at 7:45 a.m. on Friday. There were several score of FBI and law enforcement agents, Texas Rangers, cadaver dogs and their handlers, Real County sheriff's deputies, FBI forensics experts, emergency technicians, air-ground radar, search experts. They brought in a back hoe, a helicopter with infrared capability, and the O'Hairs' dental records. Their search warrant covered 1,000 acres.

Ed Martin's search warrant was still sealed, and the Feds wouldn't say whether they were looking for gold or bodies, but a rumor had leaked that the O'Hairs had been dismembered and put into 55-gallon barrels. But old-timers clucked: you couldn't bury a barrel out there — 12 inches and you hit rock.

The searchers also had to factor in the 1995 flood that Karr said had panicked David Waters, made him worry that hands were sticking up out of the ground. "There *was* a helluva flood" in October 1995, remembered Jerry Basey. "It completely changed the course of the Nueces River." If they'd washed out, the remains could have been scattered by the goats, sheep, and cattle that grazed the land. Feral hogs also migrated through, running in groups of 25 to 50. They killed livestock, said a trial expert later, ate and "destroy[ed] everything, flesh, hair, bones, feathers, everything"

But they wouldn't eat the stainless-steel hip-replacement joint Madalyn acquired in 1988. Besides bodies, Jerry Carruth wanted to find that more than anything. Like her Rolex, it had a registration number that led straight to her.

American Atheists, planning a dedication of its New Jersey headquarters on Easter Sunday, was upstaged by the noisy clamor at Camp Wood. But the searchers decamped that afternoon with nothing but three broken padlocks and nine soil samples, leaving in their wake a residue of curiosity seekers — and a small nocturnal army of trespassers with metal detectors looking for gold coins.

John MacCormack quipped that reporters the world over had lost "the headline of a lifetime: 'Atheist Rises from Grave on Easter.'" Another brief visit to the ranch a few days later yielded nothing.

The Austin detective who had taken over from Steve Baker wrote MacCormack a note of praise. MacCormack appreciated it, but when he called and asked if the department was now persuaded that some crimes might have occurred? — and had it reviewed its handling of the O'Hair case? — he got back a stiff, defensive letter saying they had never uncovered any foul play in Austin — all the action was in San Antonio. But the trail started in Austin (and federal investigators would soon turn up its bloody presence there again), and it sounded like criminals could rest easy if they were careful to do their business on the other side of the Austin City Limits sign. After enduring a number of scathing articles, APD finally admitted that the O'Hair case wasn't its finest hour.

And the DA's office hung its head that Waters had taken them in, both in 1995 when he got spanked with deferred adjudication instead of being jailed as a habitual criminal, and later, when he got his restitution reduced based on an ingenious lie he'd retrofitted to cover up a terrible crime.

With authorities finally pursuing the leads he'd helped develop, Tim Young felt he could close the case that had obsessed him for two-and-a-half years. But for a long time, he still did a double-take whenever he saw a white-haired old lady.

Just after the fruitless search at Camp Wood, Waters was indicted by a federal grand jury for being a felon in possession of ammunition. He had sent a gun to his brother Jeff, so he was also charged with transporting weapons across state lines. He wasn't charged with any crimes naming the O'Hairs — nor was Karr — but the newspapers spoke of little else.

Soon Karr was indicted in Michigan on similar counts, one for each of his guns. His public defender, Richard Helfrick, said his client was shocked at the ingratitude of the Feds after he gave them 10 hours of information pointing at a murderer — David Waters.

But if Karr's revelations to Ed Martin were supposed to intimidate Waters, they didn't. Waters wasn't talking or trying to make any kind of deal.

He and Karr were both set for summer trials, and both men's attorneys planned to attack the searches of their apartments as unlawful. But a little surprise awaited Waters at his hearing in late May 1999.

"They've got 30 pictures of him," said Patrick Ganne glumly.

They were taken outdoors in beautiful, balmy weather, showing a pudgy, relaxed Waters, holding and firing a gun at a shooting range. Felons weren't supposed to do that. "Without the pictures, we had a chance," mourned Ganne.

Jerry Carruth had brought Jeff Hunt down from Peoria to testify that his brother had shipped him four guns at different times. He didn't have to get on the stand. Waters admitted it.

Waters pled guilty in the court of U.S. District Court Judge Sam Sparks. Sparks then unsealed Ed Martin's search warrant. Now, the world — and Ganne, who leafed through the warrant, white-faced, finally got a look at what the Feds had to go on. It was 36 packed pages, and said publicly for the first time that the O'Hairs were kidnapped and killed for money and revenge. It named Chico Osborne as the fourth suspect in a scenario that included butchering the O'Hairs, storing them in three blue barrels, and killing and butchering Danny Fry. It pointed the finger at Waters as the mastermind.

Ganne snorted that the search warrant, with its twists, turns, and double crosses, sprinkled with cut-up bodies, stolen gold, and bloody tennis shoes, looked like "a script for Oliver Stone's next movie," and reminded reporters that it was speculation, not direct evidence.

Besides Colleen, it relied on another unnamed source — Charlene Karr. She remembered hearing the men whispering in her kitchen in October 1995, and Waters mentioning the name O'Hair. She confronted her ex-husband when they were alone. What was really going on here? He stuck to his high-stakes card game story, but said Waters killed the four players after the game and buried them in a field. Karr only rented the van to get the bodies to the grave.

"He told me about Madalyn O'Hair, that she took the prayer out of school, and that David Waters hated her." Karr told her the men had won a lot of money but someone stole most of it from a storage unit. Actually, he suspected David. But for some reason he wasn't mad at him.

Near Christmas 1995, David was in Florida, and he and Gary stumbled upon Charlene with another man. Waters was ready to kill her anyway because Karr had told her so much, and Karr's rage was the perfect nudge.

The two men hid behind a tree in front of her house, but for some reason, Gary couldn't do it. But later he told her, "I came *this close* to pulling the trigger . . . You came this close to dying."

"David Waters is very powerful," said Charlene. "It's like a, what do you call it, a cult. Gary was . . . just a weak person, he got caught up with the wrong people."

Chapter 68 ~ Hell Hath No Fury

A HIGHLY CIRCUMSTANTIAL CASE was the kind of challenge Jerry Carruth rather enjoyed. Carruth was aggressive, a risk-taker, but not the crap-shooting kind. He came to court exquisitely prepared, and kept a tight grip on his cases. A 1971 graduate of UT Law School, he'd put in half-a-dozen years as a policeman and public school teacher, and six more as counsel for the state police, which oversaw the Texas Rangers. He was licensed to practice in Texas, before the U.S. Supreme Court, all the U.S. District courts, and all the U.S. Courts of Appeal. He was assistant attorney general of Texas for two years.

He was the kind of gentlemanly Texan Madalyn had written about with affection when she first arrived in Austin, courteous to the point of chivalry. Blue-eyed, bald, and rotund, with an air of merriment outside court, Carruth was little troubled by moral ambiguity; he knew right from wrong, and he knew the law. When it came to criminals, he had the empathy of a snapping turtle.

With no bodies, witnesses, or weapons, he wasn't planning murder charges. But Carruth saw enough in the way of Rolexes, diamond rings, gold coins, van rentals, and hints of mutilated corpses to create an echo of murder around Gary Karr. And he could put David Waters' name so profusely throughout the record that he'd have one foot in the stirrup when Waters' trial came around.

His work was cut out for him, though. He had to make every scrap from Martin and Cowling count, and lead the jury, by reason, to the place beyond reasonable doubt.

As Karr's gun charges played out in Michigan during the spring and summer of 1999, the team built most of its case. Carruth subpoenaed Madalyn's papers and photographs from the receivers. The team wanted pictures showing the O'Hairs wearing their Rolexes, and certain jewelry that had passed through the hands of Colleen and Charlene.

They waded into Shoal Creek where Colleen said she'd thrown the CESAALA computer's hard drive. "We dug in there, never found it," said Carruth. But they found a passel of guns.

After a summer *ABC News Special*, there was a spike in O'Hair sightings, mostly at fundamentalist churches and Mexican food restaurants. One caller said they need look no further than tiny Yarnell, Arizona, where Robin was working for the government and walking around in a stupor.

The team got an anonymous tip on Memorial Day weekend, 1999, that led to a stunning, but enigmatic, revelation. A Joey Cortez had stolen some gold coins in 1995, and his friends had been selling them in San Antonio. Cowling and Martin found massive coin sales in jewelry and coin stores, made by fences but all going back to the same three people — Joey Cortez, Jaime Valdes, and Joey Cardenas.

After negotiating immunity, the three twentysomethings told a crazy story. Cortez had been given a Master Lock key from an acquaintance named Larry Soto. It was supposed to open a certain kind of Master brand lock, the silver kind. He and Valdes had already done a number of burglaries with it in San Antonio.

On October 3, 1995, the three drove to Austin to try the key there. They remembered the date because it was when O. J. Simpson was acquitted. They stopped at the first storage place they saw, and were able to open a locker. They stole a TV but couldn't pawn it. They then went to Burnet Road Self Storage across from the Poodle Dog Lounge, and tried unit 1640. The key fit.

Inside was a black suitcase, so heavy it took two of them to lift it into the car. Stopping for hamburgers, they looked into the case, and found box upon box of gold coins, rolled in paper tubes. They returned to San Antonio and divided them up. They were worth $300 to $400 apiece. The thieves spent the money on luxury items and parties they couldn't remember much about.

The fate of the gold coins had always been one of the biggest mysteries of the O'Hair case. No one believed they were stolen in a random burglary. However, by mid-July, when the FBI finally went public with the story, Cowling and Martin had tracked down $420,000 of the original half-million through receipts and fences. They asked for the public's help in tracing the other $80,000.

They found no link between the burglars and any of the players in the O'Hair case. "We believe they discovered the coins by accident," said FBI spokesman Roderick Beverly. It was just dumb luck.

Really? MacCormack wondered. Three hooligans drove 100 miles up Interstate 35 to Austin, looking for storage units to burgle — though there must have been plenty in San Antonio and the towns in between — happened to find out-of-the-way Burnet Road in Austin, happened on Burnet Road Self-Storage, happened on unit 1640, and the key also happened to fit the lock Colleen had bought (plus an earlier unit), and there happened to be a suitcase full of gold inside. And all in broad daylight, before lunch, without getting caught by the security people or the perpetrators, who also went to the unit that morning. And they happened to be from San Antonio, where David and Colleen had lived for a year, and where David had just spent a month. FBI spokesman Rene Salinas told MacCormack there were "just some parts of this we cannot reveal."

For that matter, MacCormack wondered if it was really a straightforward abduction. Why was Jon allowed to travel to New Jersey, rent a car, and be away from his supposed captors for hours at a time?

For MacCormack, that was the other big mystery besides the gold: if it was a kidnapping, how had Waters convinced them, especially Madalyn, to be so docile? Karr had stated that they all played cards at night, and video games, they seemed to get along. They were not your ordinary kidnapees. They obviously thought they were going to live. Maybe they *were* crafting an embezzlement with David's help.

Bill Murray had a grim answer: Jon "was cooperating with them *at the direction of* his mother. There is no other explanation... Jon wanted to please my mother. I think Waters knew that. There's no better psychologist than a criminal mind."

In mid-August, Waters was in county court to be sentenced for violating parole. The hearing was routine at first. Donna Cowling testified about the guns he'd sent to his brother, and the photos at the shooting range.

After closing statements, Judge Wilford Flowers looked around the courtroom. Was there anything else before he passed sentence?

Well, said the county prosecutor, we do have one more little witness, your honor, very brief. And into the courtroom walked Colleen Kay Smith Chavez, surprising everyone. She got on the stand and faced her lover of eight years. She told how he threatened her with a barbell, smashed her mouth with a gun, stabbed her in the arm and chest. She told about his guns, handcuffs, duct tape, rope, thefts from GHQ of the computer, bonds, and money. She cried. She spat bitterness.

Patrick Ganne tried to unsettle her with questions about her mental health and drug use, but she wouldn't rattle. Asked what "benefits" the government was providing in return for ratting out David and Gary, she replied sarcastically, "You know what I thought would be a *benefit*? I thought it would be a *benefit* to no longer be involved in a situation where a man was decapitated and his hands cut off!"

Ganne felt sandbagged. It was clear, he told Judge Flowers, by the presence in the courtroom of Jerry Carruth, "[and] all his FBI agents sitting there like vultures in a row...what they are trying to get you to do is punish someone for a crime that may or may not have been committed, that they have no evidence of." The question before the court was, did Waters violate his parole. "I beg of you not to succumb" to Colleen's inflammatory testimony.

No one knew how Judge Flowers would have sentenced Waters without Colleen's testimony, but he got 60 years for second degree felony theft. As he was led off, stoic in handcuffs, Waters drawled to clamoring reporters, "Hell hath no fury like a woman scorned."

A few days later, Judge Sam Sparks sentenced him to eight years for having the ammunition. It was to be served consecutively with the 60 years, not concurrently.

But Texas prisons were near capacity, and there was talk of new guidelines short-tracking people in for nonviolent crimes like Waters' theft. Even with the 60-year sentence, he was eligible for parole in 2006. It could happen much sooner if there were new guidelines. He'd have to serve his eight-year federal term for possessing ammunition, but that would still put him back on the streets by 2014 at the latest.

Before Christmas, Gary Karr was ordered to stand trial in Texas for conspiring to kidnap, rob, and extort the Murray-O'Hairs, for transporting stolen property across state lines, and for using interstate communication systems to "commit an act of violence," five counts in all. He was 51.

His attorney, Tom Mills of Dallas, had volunteered. After a visit, Karr enthusiastically told a cellmate that he had a high-powered, top-notch lawyer who was taking his case for the high profile.

And indeed, Tom Mills was dapper, confident, and every inch the good-looking tall Texan, with humorous brown eyes, and going gray at the temples. He'd run with the bulls in Pamplona in the 1970s, and was fit and athletic. He liked risk. But he gave the impression that he didn't take anything on earth that seriously.

The Houston native had grown up listening to his father's criminal defense attorney friends' shoptalk, and migrated toward criminal law. He prepared himself with a psychology degree from Southern Methodist University before graduating from UT Law School in 1972. He learned the ropes in the criminal system, but his cosmopolitan office suite in one of Dallas' glass towers, with landscaping and fountains, was the farthest thing from a public defender's cubicle.

His prosperity came not from the unpopular causes he liked — "I was active in a lot of ACLU causes when I was young, until I discovered that was considered a Communist thing to do in Dallas, Texas" — but from defending businesses and conservative Republicans.

Nevertheless, "the plight of the underdog" remained his passion, and he made room for as many such cases as the budget would allow — from representing elderly people put in mental institutions so their estates could pass down, to defending separatist Richard McLaren, whose plans for a sovereign Republic of Texas ended in an armed standoff near Fort Davis in 1997.

Mills had the same questions as MacCormack: if they were kidnapped and held hostage, why was Jon free to come and go? Why were they telling their colleagues they were fine, and bypassing a lot of chances to get help? And if Karr wasn't telling the truth, why did he open up to Ed Martin? He let all those agents into his home. That was odd for someone who did what they said he did.

And there were no bodies. The indictment said Karr's actions resulted in the deaths of the O'Hairs, but didn't charge murder. And it named only Karr and no other conspirators. A conspiracy indictment that names only one person? "How odd is that?" asked Mills.

"Draw your own conclusions," Carruth told reporters. Karr had drawn a map of a burial site. If that didn't imply bodies . . .

Mills argued that the government shouldn't be allowed to use its DNA evidence from the large storage unit unless it proved the O'Hairs were dead. He offered the many sightings of them around the world.

Lots of sightings of Elvis, too, replied Carruth.

On February 28, 2000, Detroit Judge Paul Borman threw out the FBI's gun case, saying Karr hadn't given permission to search his house. Mills and Carruth failed to reach a deal in return for Karr testifying against David Waters.

Trial was set for May 2000 in Sam Sparks' court, known for its no-nonsense "rocket docket." If convicted, Karr faced life without parole. The trial was a squeeze play, Mills said, to "threaten him . . . hoping he'll tell them something that helps their case" against David Waters.

In Fort Worth, Chico Osborne pled guilty to possessing firearms and drew two years' probation. But the team wasn't through with him yet. They thought he knew a lot more than he was telling.

Chapter 69 ~ *Star Witness*

J UDGE SAM SPARKS had no tolerance for lawyer shenanigans. If one did something that seemed frivolous or like a fishing expedition, he stared through his coke-bottle glasses and yanked the attorney to some statute or case law. And he knew the law. If they couldn't jump through his hoop, it was "*Siddown*, counselor." Or, "Ov'ruled. P'ceed."

Karr's prison pallor lay like a caul over his expressionless face and small mouth. He had heavy bags under his eyes. He sat at the defense table like a trapped possum, a contrast to his trim lawyer with his mustache and wire-rimmed glasses, who carried himself erect as a military officer. Mills' co-counsel was Christie Williams, pretty, sharp, smartly dressed, and able to switch from wisecracking to professional blankness in an instant on the words "All rise."

Mills handled most of the questioning. He liked to pace as he probed witnesses in a magnificent drawl. He liked the press, even though he called them "buzzards" and complained that they didn't report enough of his side. Early on, he announced that the Founders were thought to be either in northern England or Romania.

Across the courtroom was the prosecution team — Carruth, an associate, and the two who had run down and strung together so many little facts, names, and slips of paper, Donna Cowling and Ed Martin. Cowling's cool style and blue-eyed good looks clashed with the hideous affairs that would be spread before the jury. On the stand, she was solid; Mills didn't even try to rattle her.

Carruth went from an engaging jokester during breaks to a poisonous lizard when court was in session, turning heavy-lidded, cold blue eyes on the insects at the defense table. He moved his portly frame with surprising speed and grace around the courtroom, intimidating his foes. Once, Tom Mills complained that Carruth wouldn't stop "staring" at his client with his "beady eyes." He and Carruth were as different as a chipping wedge and a ball-peen hammer, even though both wore cowboy boots.

Brown-eyed Ellen Johnson was the first witness, in a hot-pink suit with a short skirt that showed off her perfect legs, and matching sling-back stilettos. Everyone commented on how good-looking she was as she sat on the stand like a cloud of cotton candy in the courtroom full of dark suits.

Her job was to establish that the corporations had lost money because of the O'Hairs' disappearance, and that they were engaged in interstate commerce. The O'Hairs were, she told Mills, "honest people, truthful people." They never hid assets, "not even a nickel." She cocked her head to the side and described efforts to find her missing bosses. She had spoken to "Dr. O'Hair" frequently during September 1995.

Mills asked her what Madalyn was doctor of, and she cited Madalyn's law degree. "So," said Mills, "that would be Dr. Carruth over there, and I'd be Dr. Mills?" Throughout the rest of the trial, the reporters called the attorneys Dr. Carruth, Dr. Mills, Dr. Williams.

Johnson was not pressured about why she had covered for the family so long, or why someone who had never hidden assets, not even a nickel, had spirited off the library and written all those "destroy after reading" letters to Jack Jones, or why AA never hounded the authorities about the missing Founders, or about how she'd come to power. Her job was to establish that a law had been broken.

Conrad Goeringer walked a razor's edge, testifying about the library; was it being hidden, or moved? Both he and Johnson circled the wagons, portraying the library and Truth Seeker matters as Madalyn would have wanted, and insisting that New Zealand was just a fantasy. The spectators snickered, learning that Jon's beeper number was 666 and some code for Goeringer was S-A-T-A-N.

Craig Etter said the IRS was no threat; Madalyn loved to fight them, their problems were about resolved, and running from anything was not in her character.

Denise Cushman testified about Jon's mama's-boy dependence, Robin's emotionality, how Jon's women would criticize him. Even if they were fleeing, she said, they would never have asked Waters for help. She described a diamond dinner ring Madalyn wore that was found in the possession of Charlene Karr. As with Spike Tyson's testimony, hers dealt extensively with David Waters.

Then Colleen, the star witness, took the stand, not looking at Karr except when she was asked to identify him. In a black suit, with light makeup and thick hair pulled into a bun, she looked like an attorney. She was well-spoken, but looked exhausted, and sighed repeatedly. Her deep, sultry voice was flat and depressed. It was odd, hearing her tell of blood and shovels and handcuffs, using words like "ebullient" and "paradigm."

She told her entire story in detail, adding that David had once beaten Jeff so badly that Jeff was still afraid of him. She identified pictures of herself, David, and Chico Osborne. She identified Karr and Danny Fry in a laughing group around the apartment pool before the kidnapping. There was a little boy of 6 or 7 splashing with Danny. He'd always loved kids.

She cried frequently, and would at times flinch as if in pain. When she said yes, she shook her head no, as if in habitual denial. She was on the stand for hours.

What struck observers was how many times she'd turned her head and ignored things like bloody rags and envelopes full of cash. And how she'd rent storage units, mail off guns, wire money, and buy or pawn things without question. When she and David "would see a movie where bodies were disposed of, David would be interested; he'd say, 'Oh, that would be easy. Just take them out to the desert and bury them, or just put them in a 55-gallon drum and pour acid over them.'"

She must have known. And yet "I didn't ask, I didn't want to know," she told Carruth. Why not? She sighed heavily. At first she couldn't imagine that whatever they were doing would involve murder. And when she did imagine that, she thought, "What are the police going to do? . . . I figured it was too late."

Why did she finally come forward? She started to cry. "When I saw it in black and white" in MacCormack's article identifying Danny. "All I had been trying to push away was true, right there. I tried to [push away] so much. And then John MacCormack changed my whole paradigm."

The court observers were fascinated. Why had she stayed with Waters? "Battered woman syndrome," said Ed Martin. But MacCormack suspected it was excitement. She was too smart not to know she was an accessory to murder and mayhem.

The prosecution was trying to make her out to be a codependent victim, but MacCormack thought she was a more willing accomplice than she let on.

"Let me give you some timing, okay?" he said outside the courtroom. "August 15 of '98, I write the story that says Mystery Man Disappears with O'Hair. She moved out on Waters and married Chavez... So do you see a woman who sees where things are heading?

"And then I write the other story [identifying Fry]... and suddenly... this was the scales falling off her eyes? And suddenly she put it all together?... that kind of stretches the imagination.

"There's a part of her mind that dovetails very neatly with David Waters' mind... They might be closer soul mates than we'll ever know."

A friend of Colleen's concurred. "[Colleen's] not dumb, she is in no way stupid. She had to know in advance about the kidnapping... I liked [her] a lot, I thought of her as a real good friend. But I knew she had a game going... she's not the type to sit on the sidelines — she'd step up and have a part to play. She was with David's brother for so many years... she had to know his past...

"I know she encouraged [David] in his fantasies of how to do in Madalyn, gave him... a few 'Murder, She Wrote' scenarios. And I heard her ask Jerry Basey for the deer lease, down there at the end of the bar. 'David and I just wanna go off and be by ourselves.'... There's two sides to her — we all have that walk-on-the wild-side danger thing going. [But] when she was in too deep and got scared and the money was gone, adios."

A year later, Chavez reflected. He and Colleen had separated soon after going into the witness protection program. "[Colleen] likes bad boys," he said. "She knew the shit was going to hit the fan." But he drew the line at accomplice. What she liked was that masculine edge, maybe danger or thrill — but not murder. "She never wanted it to be like this... she felt terrible about what happened to those people, so sad, so sad."

The other person who came to know Colleen intimately agreed. "She's a good person," Donna Cowling judged. She came forward even though she was terrified, and worried about culpability. She had no guarantee of her safety. She didn't know if she'd be believed. She didn't lie or make demands. She did the right thing.

The two women came to have great respect for one another. Colleen called Cowling a straight shooter, tough but compassionate, and nobody's fool. "She's absolutely the best, the best. Without her, I might have died or killed myself."

"I know [Colleen] was a good woman," said David's old true love from Florida, Dania Tabar. She had kept in touch, feeling always that she owed him, and the women talked intimately. Dania warned Waters to be good to Colleen; "I used to tell him all the time, you're never gonna find another person like this. And if you lose her, you're gonna get into trouble again.

"If she would have gone to the police? — and they would have done nothing about it? She would have been dead. He would have killed her."

Just as Jerry Carruth intended, Colleen's testimony tarred Gary Karr, even though she said little about him. Jeff, looking miserable, testified that his brother had deposited with him guns, handcuffs, switchblades, photos, and bullets, but also said little about Karr. Others testified extensively about Waters; in fact, wrote MacCormack, Karr "was little more than a figure in a gray suit on the sidelines" of a blizzard of testimony about David Waters. Tom Mills tried to capitalize on that, asking Colleen if she knew what Karr was doing "In the 27 days in September when you did *not* see him." But the juggernaut was in motion.

Charlene Karr was one of the few who testified more about Gary. She wore a green silk suit and stared at her ex-husband throughout her testimony, sloe-eyed and bitter. She smiled ruefully at the judge and attorneys, her dark hair piled high, with fluffy bangs teasing down into big, dark eyes. At the Four Seasons, she'd ordered lobster and wine.

She told of Gary's Armani suits, silk ties, leather jacket, motorcycle, computer, furniture. And she didn't believe he got the money from winning at cards.

The defense did its best; the government only had mitochondrial, not nuclear DNA from the large storage unit, but it was consistent with Madalyn, Garth, and Bill. Didn't one in four Caucasians have the same DNA sequences as the sample, though? Christie Williams asked the government's witness. Yes. "So statistically," she said, "the blood was just as likely from one of *them*, right?" She pointed to the four people at the prosecution table.

Bob Fry got on the stand, and the words from his last conversation with Danny rang in everyone's ears: "These people are animals. Crazy animals."

The trial had its light moments. The three gold thieves described their spending — titty bars, big-screen TVs, black-leather couches, trips to Vegas, cars, and guns. Asked what remained of their spree, Cortez and Cardenas said they had nothing. "Only a 3-year-old daughter," said Valdes, drawing laughter.

But three other prison informants hacked at Tom Mills' work. One said Karr told him he'd helped move bodies. Another said Karr told him, "All we got for this was a half-million dollars in gold and we expected a lot more." They said Karr told them his hair turned gray after the murders, and that he grew a beard after the Public Storage manager stared at him one day.

Most damaging was a bank robber named Jason Cross, who said Karr had told him he shot Fry, and he and Waters decapitated him and cut off his hands. And that he'd cut up the O'Hairs, put them in barrels, helped bury them, then helped move them. He got $30,000 for his work. He said the plan was always to kidnap the O'Hairs and get their money. He said nothing about bodyguarding. He said he, Waters, and Chico knew where the bodies were buried, and Chico got $5,000 for his work. Karr said Chico and Colleen set up the gold theft.

Mills pointed out that Cross could have seen most of this in the paper, when Ed Martin's search warrant was made public in May 1999. Moreover, it was common to lie in prison about how violent and mean you are, to keep people off your back.

And Cross was getting time sliced off his sentence for testifying, right? A tour through Cross' shady past prompted Carruth to invoke a timeworn but useful quote: "Conspiracies hatched in Hell aren't gonna have angels as witnesses."

One chilling thing was not followed up. Jerry Carruth asked Cross if Robin had been sexually assaulted. "David Waters," he answered.

What did Karr say about David Waters?

Cross glanced at the jury. "Do you want me to say that in here?"

"Yes, sir."

"He said that he was butt-fuckin' her . . . Sorry."

That was all that was said about the subject. There was no mention of any sexual assault in the papers or in Ed Martin's search warrant, so that information had to come straight from Gary Karr. It wouldn't come up again for a year.

Mills called a few defense witnesses, including a preacher who said he'd seen Madalyn eating pasta in Romania in 1997.

Karr's three van rentals were painstakingly laid out. They corresponded to the O'Hairs' disappearance date, the date they were last heard from, the date prosecutors said they were taken to Camp Wood, and entry and exit times at the big storage unit, where the bodies were cut up.

There were some gaps in the rental records, and Mills pounced on them, but from the receipts bearing Karr's name, you could easily picture the three large Founders being herded into a van at gunpoint, their dead bodies being heaped into a van in San Antonio, and a third van backed up to the bloody storage unit on North Lamar to remove them to Camp Wood.

And it was hard to imagine David Waters doing that all by himself.

The trial took 18 days. The prosecution put on 68 witnesses and Mills only four. He and Christie Williams told jurors the government simply hadn't proven its case. They had the right to expect more than a theory.

Carruth implored them to use their common sense. Certainly Karr was part of Waters' plot. Certainly the O'Hairs were gone, certainly they'd been robbed, and certainly Danny Fry didn't cut off his own head and hands. He ended by quoting Robin's last pleading words to Ellen Johnson: "I know you'll do the right thing."

On Tuesday, May 30, 2000, they left to deliberate, taking hundreds of exhibits and Ed Martin's timeline. They had a nice computerized copy of it; the real one was strung along a whole office wall a few blocks from the courthouse, three feet high, fluttering with a rainbow of colored sticky tabs.

The week marched on. Judge Sparks joked with the courtroom die-hards: half the jurors ordered roast beef for lunch and half ham — hung jury. Seriously, he said, he did take away their cell phones, nine of them.

Tom Mills showed reporters the typed oath that the clerk hands to all witnesses. For this trial, a line was drawn through "so help me God" — which some witnesses made a point of saying loudly anyway.

Jerry Carruth relived some of his more notorious cases, including the Kerrville Slave Ranch mass-murder trial, in which fabled defense attorney Richard "Race Horse" Haynes had hissed at him, "I'm not going to be intimidated by some potato-shaped prosecutor!" In a twist of fate, Carruth also worked on the Republic of Texas armed standoff case that Mills had been involved in.

By the third day of deliberations, the lawyers were joking that the jurors were in it for the lunches. Give 'em peanut butter sandwiches on stale bread and a carton of lukewarm milk. If we didn't get a verdict in 15 minutes, said Mills, lock the bathroom door.

Karr watched quietly as the adversarial snarling melted into collegiality. It was all just a play. Maybe no one was really in his corner. Once, his lawyers made wisecracks about the O'Hairs' Rolexes — evidence highly damning to his case — as if he weren't there.

Finally, on Friday afternoon, June 2, the jury came out. The courtroom filled, and the foreman read the first verdict, on the kidnapping count. Not guilty. Karr's eyes leapt with excitement. The next four counts were all guilty, and his happiness drained away. His face tightened with anger as Mills polled the jury.

The reason it took so long was that there were so many little pieces, and gaps in the evidence, and the information was five years old. But it was Jon's actions that caused the most delay. He didn't act like a kidnap victim, so they couldn't find Karr guilty of that. And if the O'Hairs weren't kidnapped, then the other charges were thrown into doubt. But once they agreed that stolen property had been taken across state lines, they were able to see the conspiracies to interfere with commerce through robbery, and barter of stolen property, and interstate travel in racketeering. It was the documents, more than the witnesses, that convinced them.

However, most of them thought the O'Hairs were still alive. None of them believed the bodies had been dismembered. And none of them was convinced that Karr was a violent person. In mid-August, when he was sentenced to two life terms and two ten-year terms, with no parole, five jurors who attended the hearing were astonished to learn the extent of Karr's "prior bad acts" that weren't admissible at trial. "He should be fried," exclaimed a juror who had wanted to go easy on him. She now believed him guilty of both kidnapping and murder.

Karr poured out his bitterness to Dave McLemore of the *Dallas Morning News*. The government had simply used him, to try their real case — against Waters. They'd never have gotten key details if not for his statement to Ed Martin. In it, he said Waters' name 75 times.

Waters himself was silent, except for a few maneuvers. He still hadn't been charged with anything regarding the O'Hairs' disappearance. The prosecutors would have a difficult time convicting him without Karr as a witness. He wrote Mills that the government had suppressed evidence — did Mills know about the faxes to Don Sanders, the fake IDs? By the way, did Bill Murray know his brother and daughter were "involved" with each other?

He wrote Harry Preston, who still hadn't been fully paid for his work on *Good Gawd, Madalyn!* to ask if all the publicity had generated a sale. And just for the record, that search warrant affidavit? It was "a self-serving document rife with false allegations. I abhor the egregious manipulation of the media by the federal authorities in what appears to be a concerted effort to destroy any semblance of impartiality," he wrote. These were the same people who engineered Ruby Ridge and Waco!

Chapter 70 ~ A Small Corner of the Outdoors

ON SEPTEMBER 19, 2000, David Waters was indicted on the same five counts as Karr had been. Chico Osborne was also indicted, for fraud in using a false Social Security number to rent the big storage unit. The prosecution team was certain he'd played more of a role than had surfaced. Jason Cross knew his name, and said Osborne knew where the bodies were buried and had been paid for something. Osborne said he never went back to the storage unit after renting it, but the manager saw him there with two other men, at least one pickup, and some barrels.

At Osborne's trial on January 2, 2001, Carruth, Cowling, and Martin seemed almost more tense than at Karr's trial. The stakes appeared minuscule in comparison, but they weren't; if Chico had a hand in any of the mayhem, he could be pressured to testify against David Waters.

Everything about Osborne was heavy, from his thick, curly ears and beefy fingers to his jowly face with bloodshot, pale blue eyes. He was barrel-chested, and you could imagine him heaving a loaded barrel into a van. Perhaps preemptively, his attorney established that he'd hurt his back some time ago, and couldn't work. He came into court leaning on a cane.

What the prosecutors knew was that he'd rented the storage unit, that Fry's body was found only 30 miles from his then-home, that he'd watched the 1998 *America's Most Wanted* with David Waters and taped it for him, that he'd received a handgun from Waters and mailed it to Jeff, and kept ammunition for the gun, that he'd sent a fake wage check when Waters needed proof of employment, and that witnesses said he'd do *anything* for David Waters. To rent that unit, he'd had to get up in the wee hours, because it was done before 10 a.m. And he had to drive over 200 miles and stop by Colleen's first, to get the money. What was the urgency?

The sad answer was about to come out, and it involved Robin.

As in the Karr trial, the featured attraction of this one was David Waters. On January 3, 2001, the jurors found Chico Osborne guilty. He seemed stunned, and in his moment of disorientation, Carruth stepped over to the defense table and handed him a subpoena to testify at David Waters' trial.

Gary Karr was subpoenaed to testify too, but let it be known he'd take the Fifth. He seemed more afraid of Waters than of prison.

Shortly before Waters' January 29, 2001 trial date, Donna Cowling sat him down and told him about some new, devastating information they had on him. She never revealed what it was, or who came forward. "[Waters] realized his lips were not as tight as he thought they were," was all Ed Martin would say.

Within a short time, Waters' attorneys, William Gates and Tracy Spoor, were crafting a plea bargain for their client. He had to tell everything he knew, including where the bodies were.

On January 24, 2001, in a hearing sealed off from agitated reporters and the public, David Waters' trial was canceled. He pled guilty to the second count of the indictment, Conspiracy to Interfere with Commerce by Robbery and Extortion. The other four counts were dropped. He got 20 years, all in a federal prison, instead of the Texas "rathole," as Cowling called it, that he was in now.

For that day and the next, he was grilled on every detail of the O'Hairs' disappearance and deaths. Maddeningly for reporters and the public, part of his plea bargain was that his entire confession be kept secret.

An FBI agent telephoned forensic anthropologist Dr. David M. Glassman at Southwest Texas State University in San Marcos. One of only two such specialists in Texas, he was called upon a dozen times a year to help identify skeletal remains. Glassman and the government gathered what they needed for another search of the ranch in Camp Wood.

Only this time, they had David Waters along.

The caliche soil was moist; it had been raining, and the sky was overcast much of Saturday and Sunday, January 27 and 28. The dog handler explained to Jerry Carruth that moisture in the soil enhanced the cadaver dogs' ability to smell. Scent travels up plant roots, and in a moist year, there is more growth to carry the smell to the surface. The searches in 1999 were done during a drought.

"Where Waters pointed and where the dogs hit were a foot apart," said Carruth. "We probably walked right over the original site the first time." Glassman did some digging, and the two dogs, Grace and Mercy, went crazy. Glassman ordered two four-square grids set up.

The first bone they found was a femur, sawed off above the knee. It lay in the soft tan soil like a stick of firewood, large, blackish on one end, nestled in the youngest roots of the plants its flesh had nourished. It was Jon Garth's. Glassman and two assistants lifted the dirt away. They found him jackknifed on his back, his head twisted to the side, and a rotted plastic bag wrapped tightly around it. Pieces of the bag fluttered in the breeze, stuck in the dirt. His belt was still there; it looked like he'd been wearing jeans.

Madalyn was found on her back, legs apart, her chrome hip replacement, with its traceable serial number, glinting in the winter sun "like a trailer hitch," said Jerry Carruth. That was when he felt closure. Pieces of her dress — as always, the broken-glass-like fragmentation she was drawn to, of aqua, orange, and black — lay up around her hips. One of her arms was sticking up, found only a few inches under the dirt, and Ed Martin remembered Waters' worry of "hands sticking up out of the ground."

Nestled under her right arm was Robin's skull, with her beautiful red mane still in a neat braid down her back. "I love you, redhead!" It was the way Madalyn had so often signed her letters to Robin at boarding school.

Danny Fry's skull was near Robin's, his watch lying between the two women's skulls.

Miscellaneous hand and finger bones were recovered. Some of the material in the grave was charred. The O'Hairs' legs were cut off at mid-thigh, and thrown on top. No toes were obviously snipped, though some of Madalyn's toe and hand bones appeared to be missing.

The excavation took 21 hours. They worked until 10 p.m. Saturday under lights and tarp shelters. On Sunday evening, they hurriedly packed the grave items for transport to Glassman's lab, as lightning dashed impatiently across the sky, and thunder rolled closer. Just as they finished taking the last item out of the grave, the sky split open. Rain bucketed down. "The grave filled right up, immediately," said Donna Cowling.

After he got home, Glassman's temperature shot up to 104. He'd contracted tick fever, and was in bed for over a month. His findings were finally presented to the Real County Justice of the Peace on March 5, 2001. The bodies were indeed Madalyn, Jon Garth, and Robin. The fourth skull awaited dental records. There was a bullet hole in it.

Bill wanted to give his family a quiet burial, but American Atheists wanted the remains. Texas law allowed them to go to next of kin, but Bill had been disowned. Ellen Johnson recruited a cousin of Madalyn's to help lay AA's claim, and prepared to file a restraining order.

"This was a man who lived his life publicly despising her and making money off her," Johnson protested.

"Ellen wants to use their dead bodies to raise money," retorted Bill bluntly, noting that AA's 2001 convention was coming up Easter Sunday.

Arnold Via asked if they could go into his cemetery, presumably alongside Frederick Lonnie Conway, with a newly minted penny for each.

As it turned out, Bill was quietly given the bodies, and a tiny group gathered secretly early on the morning of March 23, 2001, to lay them to rest — Bill, Carruth and Martin, Cowling and FBI victim coordinator Cathy West, a minister friend of Bill's, and Madalyn's biographer. Bill didn't want reporters or news trucks, and he wanted the location kept secret.

"My mother's life was a circus. The events and the trials around her death were a circus. It's time for somebody to just put a *stop* to this, just bang! right now!" Ellen Johnson had hired an Austin lawyer and was flying in that day. They'd be buried before she touched down.   .

In *Plotting Atheist Funerals*, Madalyn had written, "William J. Murray III has been a traitor... Under no circumstances, for no reasons whatsoever, do I care to have him in attendance for any activities related to my death, [or] to the disposal of my body."

And yet it was Bill, her firstborn, handsome, productive, dressed respectfully in a black coat and tie, who laid her to rest, the day before David Waters' 54th birthday.

It had been drizzling since sunrise, but by the time the group gathered, it was sweet-smelling, overcast and balmy — a perfect Austin spring day.

It was a little tree-sprinkled burial ground, deserted at that time of morning. The remains were together in a vault, in five boxes. They had lived and died together. It seemed arbitrary and even cruel to separate them now.

At the head was the boxed urn with Madalyn's ashes. Dr. Glassman's forensics report said the cause of her death was unknown. Next was a large box marked, "J. Murray — skull." Glassman's description said Garth had only three fillings in his teeth. He had a "very robust skull... large mastoids, a square chin." His skull had fractures on the left and right occipital and left temporal bones, indicating blunt-force trauma as a possible cause of death. His bones were in adjoining boxes.

At the Camp Wood excavation, Ed Martin said, "I felt I knew who these people were as they came out of the ground. You could tell Jon — he was just *big*." A piece of plastic ligature was found associated with his hands.

Mirroring Jon's boxes were two more, labeled "R. M. O'Hair — bones; R. M. O'Hair — skull." As with Madalyn, there was no clue to the cause of Robin's death.

Scattered among the boxes were ten brown-paper sacks of varying size, containing clothing, hair, and other materials from their shallow grave.

The group stared down at the boxes and sacks representing the terrible end of Madalyn, Jon Garth, and Robin. Madalyn had written that she wanted them to throw her carcass in the van and drive to San Antonio where there was a crematorium. She never dreamed how closely she was describing what would actually happen.

What did she want on her tombstone? Madalyn had been asked this many times since the 1960s, and had never wavered in her answer: "Woman, Atheist, Anarchist."

"But," she always amended, "I expect there will be no tombstone."

And there was none. Bill wanted the grave unmarked for at least a year. He didn't want the site to become a cult attraction, like Jesse James' grave, strewn with beer cans and stinking of urine. Only a casket spray marked the place.

He said a few words about the ending of this story, and how we'd never know whether they accepted the grace of the gospel before they died. The group walked to another part of the cemetery, and the minister offered a prayer for Bill, for closure, for the end of destructive beliefs for Madalyn's bloodline and all its descendants, for healing of others that still needed it, and for the work still remaining to bring about justice. Gary Karr was already crafting an appeal.

Returning to the vault, Bill stared into it one last time.

"I always believed that nature would take its course, that my mother would die, and then after awhile of being on their own, Jon and Robin would come to the light — if not the light of Christ, just the light, the truth," he said. "But Robin and Jon did not have lives, they lived for my mother. If anyone was cheated out of life, it was those two."

As the heavy lid was placed, Bill remarked that there were 1,000 Christian schools when Madalyn filed her suit, and now there were 27,000. He had recently published a fundraising manual for private schools to encourage the trend.

The vault was lowered into the black, fresh-smelling earth.

"I want a little place," wrote Madalyn in *Plotting Atheist Funerals*, "... a small corner of the outdoors... where the sun will filter through the trees and lay its gentle, warm hand upon one's face."

That was exactly what she got. As the group moved over to the cars to leave, Bill looked around. "It's a pleasant little peaceful place," he said, and gave a deep sigh.

Several people went for coffee after the burial. Inevitably, talk turned to why Jon Garth was so docile during that month in San Antonio. Why didn't he try to get help? When he picked up the gold, there was a cop right there, and no one was watching him. Why was he so compliant?

Bill recalled how Garth was cowed by Madalyn. "My brother would do everything he could to please her, and there would be these *digs*." He remembered when Garth bought his first computer system. "My mother *had* to put in the newsletter that Jon had bought a 'bastard system.'" He recalled telling his brother once, "'Garth, they're gonna put Mom in jail. If the IRS catches her, she's going to jail.' And he said, 'That won't happen. I'll go to jail for her.'"

"All his life, she had talked down to him, and made fun of him, and now, in his mind, he would show her his worth by single-handedly rescuing her."

She seemed always to be looking for a man stronger than she was to balance her, but whenever she found one, she was compelled to fight him with all her strength. Bill believed Madalyn was contemptuous of Garth's failure to be stronger than she was, and showed it by making him her errand boy and then leading them all to the grave.

"And I think my mother *knew* how it was going to end. And this was the ultimate control — she knew they were all going to be killed, and she was exercising the ultimate control over my brother, calling the shots."

It was a harsh view, and Martin softened it by mentioning that Garth had an electronic listening device attached to him for awhile whenever he went out — though it didn't work and was eventually abandoned.

Searching for clues to his family dynamics, Bill had studied cults, power seekers, and serial killers, and found that power was at the heart of these pathologies. "In almost every single case of a serial killer, there was a domineering mother or female in the home." When the notorious 1979 "orange socks" murder occurred — it was thought to be the work of the I-35 serial killer who picked victims off the highway through Austin — he thought of Garth, and the pressure cooker he was in. "He perfectly fit the profile of a serial killer."

That was harsh, too, but Bill was onto something. At some level, Madalyn had to know Waters was capable of murder. She wrote in detail about him urinating on his mother — an act so defiling and degrading that in some ways it was worse than murder — and it showed he was psychologically prepared to murder. Madalyn, who ranked motherhood above all other satisfactions in her life, must have registered that. In a way, he did kill his mother. Deep down somewhere, she must have known they weren't going to get out alive.

As it turned out, Bill was closer to the truth. But it wasn't Madalyn that Garth trusted and obeyed in San Antonio. It was David Waters.

Chapter 71 ~ Unanswered Questions

DAVID WAS FORMALLY SENTENCED on January 24, 2001. "And Mr. Waters, I hope I never see you again," said Judge Sparks. The courtroom observers rose to leave.

"Butcher! You stinking ghoul!"

Waters' head jerked around. "He's an *animal*!" an older man was yelling. "Why don't they execute him! He murdered a *wonderful woman*! He tortured her! He tortured an old woman in a wheelchair!"

The guards hurried Waters out, and reporters clustered around the man. It turned out to be Samuel Miller, 68, the member who had burst into the Catholic bingo game with Madalyn in 1977. He was outraged at what seemed like a light sentence — 20 years, for apparently four murders.

Jerry Carruth explained: a trial would have cost a million dollars, and we still wouldn't know where the O'Hairs and Danny Fry were. And Waters got a virtual life sentence anyway — he was 54, facing 20 unparoled years, plus eight more unparoled, plus 60 state years, served consecutively.

"You do the math," said Carruth. He didn't mention Waters' hepatitis C.

And Waters' trial wouldn't have been any cakewalk. They had a much weaker documentary case — no van or storage rentals, no plane tickets or Rolex sales. And neither Chico nor Gary could be pressured to go against him. One of his co-counsels, Tracy Spoor, was a tough former prosecutor. "*She's* got a bag of tricks," said one attorney who'd seen her work.

So David Waters went off in chains, leaving a host of unanswered questions.

Why had the O'Hairs cooperated with Waters?

How were they killed, and where, exactly? Jon had a bag over his head but also a fractured skull, and wrist ligatures. How were the women killed? Had Robin been raped?

Why did they bring them to Austin — why didn't they just take them to Camp Wood from San Antonio? When did they bury them?

Who killed Danny? How did they get him to Dallas? Was he killed on the riverbank or somewhere else?

What happened to the barrels? What was Chico's role? Did Waters even confess to murder at all? Or did he blame Karr? Chico?

And — what really happened with the gold? The idea that it was a random theft was too much to believe. Even Ron Sievert, Jerry Carruth's boss, said, "It just doesn't make sense. The real big gap was, where's the money?"

But Waters' plea bargain made these matters secret.

Waters arrived at the federal prison in Leavenworth, Kansas, on May 24, 2001. By then, Chico had been sentenced to three years' probation, and Gary Karr's appeal was slated for the beautiful courtroom in the Fifth Circuit Court in New Orleans, where Madalyn had spent so much time, and where the first words of the day were still, "God save the United States and this honorable court!"

It was easy to see in Colleen Kay Smith the "good person" Donna Cowling saw. She didn't try to spin her story. She spoke of her painful failings with humility. She admitted some responsibility, and she would be forever haunted by guilt. Whatever her character flaws, as Cowling pointed out, she came forward and did the right thing.

Yet she did have a dark and curiously stubborn bond with Waters. Her friends had told her to just boot him out, but she couldn't. He would come into the Poodle Dog and "exude this aura of mystery, where people would actually say, 'Is he connected? Does he, like, work for the mob?' His dignity was built on what he could project to others. I considered him extremely fragile . . . I felt sorry for him . . . when push came to shove, I guess basically I couldn't expose him to ridicule. Being shown to be utterly unable to support himself.

"There's that pop song, she's a brick, and I'm drowning slowly. That's always the way I felt about him, like . . . I'm just drowning slowly . . . I was angry at him most of the time . . . and at the same time I felt really sorry."

And there was her own stubbornness. "You rode a stallion and it bucked you off and kicked you in the face. Well, what do you do when you get thrown off? Well, you get back on. You don't just allow something to defeat you . . .

"I didn't want to leave Texas. I didn't want to just run home to my family, I was broke, living check to check, because there was absolutely no help from him . . . and it was *my stuff*. It was my life!

" . . . and it's not like I came home every day and, uh-oh, he's swinging his fist. You know, we had moments of actual fury, but . . . it's not like you think to yourself, this is *obviously* a bad situation."

That September of 1995, "I honestly had no idea what he was doing. At first I thought well, okay, he's stealing cars. Just any number of things go through your mind, because you know, he's got two buddies with him." She thought they might be doing credit card fraud; David had done it before, and it was clear he was siphoning money out of the O'Hairs as he'd done in 1994.

When the O'Hairs were reported missing, she felt it was too late. She got fatalistic.

"What's the next step, what do you do? You can't go to the police. What do you do? There's no proof of anything. What most people see is things like . . . evidence lists, or this is what . . . the FBI put together after years . . . of course it's obvious. But it's not obvious like that at the time."

And as the Austin police continued to say things like, it wasn't against the law to go missing, she had little hope of being taken seriously, and none of being protected.

"I think it used to annoy the authorities that I gave [David] so much credit. Well . . . he fooled the police; he fooled the prosecutors and judge . . . The DA believed him. [*Vanity Fair*] believed him. He's extremely convincing. He's a consummate liar."

But then came the identification of Danny. "I can't emphasize it enough, when I read about Danny in the paper, I melted down. I was extremely upset . . . they found him dead in Dallas. That's *real.*"

It was real. The prosecution team had the photos of Danny. First the laughing, green-eyed charmer who went for the easy money but was generous to a fault when he had it, who loved his children "with all his heart," said the women closest to him, and who "liked to make other people happy."

Then the Danny with leaf-litter all over him, dirt caked on the severed stumps of his neck and wrists, lying on his back in dappled sun among the jimsonweed and vines, robbed of all dignity and even his identity, with strangers staring at him. Someone needed to do right by him.

Chapter 72 ~ Father Prison

LEAVENWORTH WAS a turn-of-the-century fortress, huge and rambling, with 42 steps up to its metallic dome. The largest maximum security prison in the country, it housed 2,000 inmates — including at one time Machine Gun Kelly, Bugs Moran, Manuel Noriega, and Leonard Peltier. Robert Stroud, the Bird Man of Alcatraz, actually did his avian work during his 28 years in Leavenworth, before his transfer to the Rock.

The visitors' room was a long, shotgun affair accessed through several heavy, clanging gates with chipped paint showing many layers and many bland, government-issue colors. It had a line of vending machines along one wall and a line of plastic chairs along the other. Guards were posted at either end. A little plastic table sat in front of each visitor chair, and the inmate's chair was pulled up facing it. The interior lights were fluorescent, and all the windows were spray-painted, so the inhabitants lived in that strange, artificial twilight of hospitals, movie theaters, and casinos. Time stretched, vaporized, and started to mean nothing.

They brought David Waters through a door at the far end of the room, and he stood with his chin up, looking around coldly with what Ed Martin had called his owl look. He was an attractive man, with a well-shaped head, thick, short black hair mottled with gray, and a neatly trimmed goatee. His smile was warm, teasing, and his teeth were straight and white. (Caps, Colleen said; he'd had them for years.) He laughed a lot, sparkled, and engaged easily in conversation. The hands that had killed were shapely and sensitive, but something about his body seemed off, as if it had expected to come into this world taller. His right hand and wrist were swollen, like he'd smashed his fist into something.

He was the kind of person who sized up every situation and assessed what was in it for him. If there was nothing, he might get on the roller coaster and ride anyway.

"He relished living on that edge," Colleen said. Back when MacCormack was closing in on him, "The closer he got to the horrifying, being-caught part . . . he was chuckling, he was like well, guess it's time to get out the Chivas and the Xanax! I mean, he was just ready to ride the storm."

He had made a close study of victimhood, which he practiced smoothly. He was critical of his country and all its systems — prison, government, legal, educational — that had shafted him. It was oddly reminiscent of Madalyn's diary tirades.

He was well read, and could hold his own even when he didn't know much about the subject. He was interested and eager for every topic that came up. Like Madalyn, he was a history buff. He talked of religion, of whether the mind dies when the body does, of the law of thermodynamics, the reptilian brain. He worked in the print shop, doing quality control on prison publications. He listened to NPR on his little radio.

He seemed almost cheerful about prison, comfortable, but that was misleading. He had a sophisticated understanding of the legal system, and a plan to try and unravel the intermingling nets that had caught him. As Colleen commented after the plea bargain, "I'm sure David's still trying to outthink the competition." And he was. Like his deceased brother Stevie, he had an extremely logical mind, and it was as if he were patiently taking his prison bars apart atom by atom, starting with a paralegal course to craft an appeal of his 60-year state sentence he hoped would unravel Jerry Carruth's work.

He had contempt for prison's rehabilitative claims. "My case worker asked me, 'where do you want to be in five years?' — he wanted a Five Year Plan! If I said, 'In five years I plan to have you kiss my ass,' they might put me in the hole for a few weeks, and then what're they gonna do? Five Year Plan!"

He was reluctant to acknowledge that he was a threat to society, but he couldn't resist lively discussion about anything. On first mention of the O'Hairs, a kaleidoscope flicked past in his eyes — shame, defiance, cunning, challenge, and rapid-fire telepathies: "you're not getting a thing out of me" and "I'm a piece of shit, I'm dirt" and "what's in this for me" and "prison is where I belong" and finally, "someone tell my story."

That was the thing, Colleen said, "It was always his dream to have some sort of notoriety. To have some sort of fame, whether negative or positive. That seemed to be behind everything. His drive was to not be mediocre. And I always believed he . . . aimed to 'please' Father Prison, so he would be welcomed back home. Where the guards and bosses learn to respect him . . . where he's given the best jobs, where he can run his own team. Where he isn't made to work in order to feed himself. He'll be taken care of, back in the womb. Poor child, really, poor child!"

He fought back tears when he spoke of his grandmother's grave not even having a headstone — one of the things he was raging about the night he beat his mother. Grandma Hayes prayed for him often with a friend. She worked for years at Laidlaw Plastic and Wire, a self-sacrificing woman who loved cooking and gardening, and in return for many kindnesses, had reaped "a drunk for a husband, a wayward daughter . . . and a grandson prone to delinquent behavior."

He missed Austin terribly, missed the combination of small-town community and city amenities. It had the best of both worlds, he said. He used to raise birds and dogs, and missed animals in his life. He missed barbecue and Tex-Mex and steaks at the Hofbrau, and a certain pot roast he used to make. He wanted his photo albums back from the FBI, full of pictures of the women he'd loved, clothed and unclothed, dozens of them. Pictures of dogs he'd loved, cars he'd loved, prison buddies he'd loved. Pictures of himself and Stevie as children, of Grandmother Hayes, and of Betty as a young spitfire. Through his tumultuous life, through all his moves and prison stays, he held onto those photo albums. They were thumbed ragged.

He spoke worshipfully of Marti, and clouded over when he remembered the songs that took him painfully back to that time — Heat Wave's "Always and Forever," Queen's "You're My Best Friend," and the Commodores' "Three Times A Lady."

He said matters of the heart were his "Achilles heel . . . I act much too viscerally." Colleen called him a "mush-ball" because he got emotional over certain music — especially George Jones' "He Stopped Loving Her Today" and Mario Lanza. He still cried when he thought about Stevie. If he could keep his emotions in check, he could take any kind of pain. He had a twisted but sincere view of the moral high ground: "I firmly believe in . . . retaliation, revenge, and pre-emptive strikes . . . but I am not cruel. I may be a hard man in some ways, but . . . I do not delight in the pain of others."

He wished he'd never gotten Chico involved in the O'Hair matter; like Cookie and most of his women, Chico was someone he wanted to protect from the consequences of being his friend. And Colleen — there was a real story *there*. Don't believe her if she says she doesn't care for expensive luxury items! And she'd change into a harridan when she drank. Oddly, there was something almost good-natured about the way he dismissed Chavez, like he was a good loser, it was all a game anyway, where women were concerned.

Colleen running off with Chavez just showed cowardice and weakness, but her testimony against him in the revocation hearing had come as a genuine surprise. That was the worst, he said, "discovering you can't believe a person you care for and really want to believe."

He had called her on the day of MacCormack's devastating article identifying Danny Fry. Would she back him up? he asked, verify that Danny had left on September 30, 1995, with some guy? She had promised to. That was before Donna Cowling came along. He genuinely expected her to be "standup" for him.

Colleen remembered that call. He was nervous but almost cheerful. Kind of excited. Oh, sure, that'd be fine, she said. "I mean, what was I going to say?" Now, she was scared of his reach from prison, learning he'd asked an old acquaintance to look up a certain address in a certain city — the one where she was living, in the witness protection program.

He laughed cynically at the FBI's gold theft story, but indicated it was in some way true, except not exactly as told. He left the impression that a theft had been set up, but bungled — it took place on the wrong day or time of day, or the wrong people had the key, or got bad instructions — and he indicated he was protecting someone he'd dragged in over their head, or whose innocence he wanted to preserve. As Donna Cowling had once asserted, he truly didn't seem to care much about the gold.

(However, the theft was almost certainly set up, and some of the gold routed back to David. When he and Karr went to Florida in October 1995 to threaten Bob Fry, Charlene Karr recalled that the two men drove to Clearwater for a big shopping spree. Then, around Christmas, David approached a Poodle Dog patron, Karl Kinser, and offered to sell him some gold coins. When Kinser declined, he asked if Kinser could fence them, or knew someone who would. Sometime before the end of 1997, Kinser saw nine gold coins at David and Colleen's apartment. In 1998, David bought a new Gateway computer and printer, was able to afford an Internet connection, movie channels, and other amenities with no job. At the end of 1998, he bought a $5,000 painting from Austin artist Warren Cullar, and made payments until his arrest three months later. The painting was inspired by a pile of bones Cullar saw in a gully in New Mexico.)

He had no signs of illness from his hepatitis C, but, he said, "my quality of life has diminished to a point where death would almost be a non-event . . . [it's] disheartening to be too introspective these days."

Then, suddenly, he was gone. It wasn't hepatitis C. It was lung cancer, and it blazed up around Christmas 2002. He died January 27, 2003, at the Federal Medical Center in Butner, North Carolina, where Madalyn had visited Larry Flynt and briefly held the key to his empire. It was exactly two years to the day after Waters had lifted his manacled hands on the Cooksey ranch and pointed to where she was buried.

Betty was with him during his last days. He told his mother he wanted to be cremated, and his ashes scattered over Marti's grave. The last anyone heard, he was still in an urn in her living room.

Chapter 73 ~ "That smell stayed on me for a long time"

DAVID WATERS no longer had an expectation of privacy regarding his secret confession, and Donna Cowling and Agent Kevin Clendenning bent over backward to get the confession tapes transcribed and through the FBI's painfully slow Freedom of Information process in record time. By summer, the 321-page document was released.

It consisted of four interviews. The first took place on January 24, 2001, and described the kidnapping.

Fry and Karr had posed as delivery men that Sunday afternoon, August 27, 1995, while David hid in the rented van. Jon answered the door, and they pulled guns, backing him inside. Fry came out and got David. They restrained Madalyn and Jon. Robin soon arrived from home, and was taken, too.

David had Jon prepare the payroll checks and the letter to tape on the front door. They drove their captives in the van and Mercedes to Greystone to wait for dark, and later moved Robin's Porsche to the airport. At Greystone, David said, "began the entrance into the bizarro world."

It was bizarre partly because of the collegiality. Everyone was polite, they made sandwiches and ordered pizza. Then Karr wanted to go through the house for valuables, and made Robin go with him. They were gone a long time, and David sent Danny to see what was going on. He came back and said Karr was forcing himself on Robin. Waters put a stop to it, pulled Karr aside and laid down the law. "Because everything was predicated on ... that they would be treated well." He couldn't believe sex was the first thing on Karr's agenda.

Robin was amazingly composed, he said.

After dark, they drove in the van and Mercedes to Buda, to the Interstate Inn just south of Austin — Robin said Madalyn needed to rest. The family got the beds, and the kidnappers dozed on chairs or sat on the floor. The next day, Karr and Waters drove to San Antonio and rented a two-bedroom apartment, at the Warren

Inn, while Danny guarded the captives in Buda. They again waited until night to travel.

At the Warren Inn, Waters sat the family down in the living room. "Okay folks...this is what it's gonna take to get you home safe and sound." When he told them he knew how much was in New Zealand, he saw a look pass between Jon and Madalyn. He later pulled Jon aside, and found out they were in the process of repatriating the money. It was already on the way.

He persuaded Jon and Madalyn that it was best to just go along, because no one would ever believe they had been kidnapped and robbed. In fact, if she tried to float that story, she'd never be able to raise money again. "She's gonna go tell somebody that she was snatched by David Waters and two unknown people, kept in a motel for a month...? Wasn't anybody gonna buy that." Karr and Fry were using fake names.

Moreover, he told the family, a fourth kidnapper was involved, a silent partner "affiliated with law enforcement," so the cops wouldn't believe any kidnapping story. That was buttressed by what had happened with the $54,000 — the 13 trial delays, the DA refusing to increase Waters' bond.

So it became a waiting game. While the New Zealand money trickled in, Waters had Jon drain all the credit card and bank accounts of cash, and sell his Mercedes. He used it to buy them food and clothes, to rent video games, movies, and a car.

The O'Hairs had one bedroom and Waters and Fry the other. Karr slept on the sofa. The family's bedroom door had to stay open at night, but other than that, they had the run of the house. "Believe it or not, it was almost a family situation." Danny was in awe of Madalyn, and sat at her feet. He also bonded with Robin; they chatted in deck chairs by the pool until David found out and nixed it.

"During the course of the month, Jon and I bonded...Jon and I were like working together. He was like, responsible for his group and I was responsible for controlling my group."

Karr clashed with everyone. "Karr would get mad at what he considered Madalyn's arrogant attitude...he would fly off the handle and I would get on his ass and he'd get mad at me. He'd get mad at Danny Fry 'cause Danny was kinda absentminded...Next thing I know, he's ready to kill Danny. He's ready to kill Madalyn. I gotta make sure he doesn't get Robin off by herself."

Madalyn amused herself by baiting Karr into debates, and then humiliating and infuriating him, as she had the Reverend Dr. W. A. Criswell and so many others. He would say, "shut up and speak when you're spoken to," and tell her she wasn't running anything. That just made her worse. She would complain loudly about all kinds of little things and make demands, noting that it angered Karr, and turning up the heat just to see him fume.

"I don't mean to make light of this," Waters said, "but there were times that it was just like having to put up with four whiny kids.

"So I had to talk to Jon. 'Jon, please talk to Madalyn. You see, I'm dealing with this guy, he's not wrapped real tight,' and I says, 'She keeps poking him with a stick. He's like a mad dog. He's gonna try to bite her.'"

Karr didn't understand why the money was taking so long, or why they were spending so much on the O'Hairs. With the cash from the bank cards and the sale of the Mercedes, Waters kept the larder stocked with plenty of food, five or six hundred dollars a week worth, which drove Karr mad. Waters rented a Lincoln for Jon to drive, a car he liked. "There was nothing denied them...I saw no reason for it...I wanted to keep everybody happy." It wasn't just to keep the friction down. "If these three people just come out of the blue and tried to tell authorities there's never been any harm done to 'em, they've lived well for a month. Nobody's gonna buy that."

Karr did not understand the subtlety, and Waters had to keep reminding him that a huge stash was coming in, please try to keep his eye on the prize instead of brooding over Madalyn's arrogance and lusting after Robin. But he never gave Karr or Fry the whole picture. They never knew exactly how much was coming in, how much was gotten from the credit cards, or how much they were going to get when it was all over. He kept them happy by giving them cash and taking them shopping for clothes. Danny got them all playing card games.

Waters and Jon would go out shopping for clothes for the women. They'd go across the street to La Fonda to pick up Mexican food, and have margaritas. They shared pizza and beer. Waters bought a video game console, and Jon got hooked.

"He and I would sit in the living room, playing video games. Robin became his cheerleader...This pissed Madalyn off. He was having fun. You know, something he probably has not ever been allowed to do in his 40-some years. He was actually having fun...Madalyn didn't like this, she didn't like this."

David decided on gold coins because they weren't traceable. He didn't want a problem down the line with serial numbers. He sent Jon to New Jersey, where the New Zealand money was coming into a United Secularists of America account. Jon had to sign in person for such a large transfer to Cory Ticknor's Frost Bank account.

Karr went along as Conrad Johnson, ostensibly to keep Jon from going for help, but it wasn't necessary. The whole month, Jon never tried to get help. It wasn't because of Karr, or the fourth kidnapper, or the electronic listening device. "This is hard to explain," said Waters, "I know this sounds bizarre, but I trusted Jon. Jon trusted me. I believed him. I didn't think he would break his word to me. He did not believe that I would break my word to him. It's as simple as that."

The month wore on, the money inched in, and finally they put in their order. On Monday, September 25, Ticknor ordered the coins from his broker in Dallas.

That night, David and Jon went out for drinks. "Soon as we walked in, I just knew something was terribly wrong. It was quiet. I could see Madalyn was in her bedroom. She was reading. Danny was sitting in the kitchen. He wouldn't...look at me. And Karr was in the bedroom. He looked like he was mad at somebody. So I sent Jon into [the O'Hairs'] bedroom and told him to close the door."

"I asked, 'Where's Robin?' and [Fry] says, she's in the bedroom . . . I headed to the bedroom and Karr got up and followed in behind me. She was dead."

Karr had strangled her. Waters said he had no idea if she'd been raped; Karr was "beyond explaining anything."

"I believe I almost passed out. The reality of everything come tumbling down." Once he digested what had happened, he started thinking. "I had to come up with a reason why Robin would no longer be part of the trio."

He told Madalyn that, because the gold was due in any minute, he was going to keep them all three at different locations to be sure there were no "trip ups." He said his fourth man from Austin had arrived and quietly taken Robin while Jon and Madalyn were shut off in their room. As soon as the gold was safely in his possession, he'd tell them each where the others were. "[Madalyn] didn't like that at all." He pretended to let her talk him out of separating her and Jon.

He then made an urgent call to Chico to rent a big storage unit to stash Robin's body. That night, Robin was wrapped in a blanket. It was a massive struggle to get her body down the apartment stairs and into the trunk of the Lincoln. The next day, September 26, Waters and Karr drove her to Austin. They tailgated into Public Storage behind someone else, and put Robin in unit 52.

Karr was calmer now, but Danny was traumatized. They all realized that "with this event, Jon and Madalyn were gonna have to go. There was just no two ways about that." And when they were alone, Karr told Waters Danny had to go, too, He was just too upset — he was going to tell someone.

On the 27th, Karr rented another van. He and Danny went out and found three barrels.

On the 29th, most of the gold was finally in, $500,000 worth, and Jon went alone in the Lincoln to pick it up. Danny rented two back-to-back rooms with a connecting door at the La Quinta Motel on Loop 410, under his false name. After the struggle with Robin's body, they needed a ground floor.

Jon delivered the gold, and Danny was sent out of the motel room on a fake errand. His real job was to call the room pretending to be the fourth man holding Robin, so that David could pretend in front of Jon and Madalyn to arrange her release. It would be at 9 p.m., at an undisclosed place.

When the hour arrived, they bound Jon and Madalyn with flex cuffs they'd bought at Home Depot. Madalyn resisted, but Jon was cooperative, and told her to just "go along with the program, that things would be all right, it's no big deal." He was going on the trust bond he and Waters had, and the fact that they'd been treated so well.

Madalyn was taken into the second bedroom, and then, "the three of us strangled Jon." He fought like mad, and his head crashed into the night stand, fracturing his skull. When blood started running out of his nose, they put a plastic bag over his head to keep it off the motel carpet, and dragged him into the bathroom.

Then David went in and strangled Madalyn.

He and Danny went over to clean up the Warren Inn, leaving Karr with the bodies. When they returned, Karr was furious at Danny. He'd let Madalyn have a pencil and paper, and Karr found some notes she'd made, describing him, the fact that he had no earlobes.

They returned the rented Lincoln, put the bodies in the van, and again tailgated into the Public Storage unit to leave them. They locked the gold in the other unit, across from the Poodle Dog.

David was unclear on where they spent that night; he was so sleep-deprived by then that the days and nights swam together. Karr said he'd been taken to a Super 8 Motel. Waters remembered that they all went to the apartment. Colleen said they didn't. It was five years ago. He couldn't remember every detail of the timeline.

The next morning, Saturday, September 30, they went to the big storage unit. The smell was awful. It stunk so badly that David and Danny each offered Karr $25,000 to do their share of the dismembering and putting the bodies into the barrels. He agreed.

They spread plastic sheeting over the floor and up the sides of the walls. Karr used a big chef's knife — a "French knife," he called it — to cut them up. They left the door open about halfway for light and air. That was when the property manager drove by and glimpsed the barrels. Contrary to what he said, there was no pickup there, said David, only the van. No Chico.

Karr called Danny in to help him put the cut-up bodies and all the plastic into the barrels. Then they closed the storage unit and left. They dropped all the O'Hairs' new clothes at Goodwill.

It was unclear exactly when things happened during the rest of Saturday and Sunday. They returned the rental van and Colleen packed Danny's belongings. David was certain they killed Danny Saturday night, but the forensics indicated Sunday night, or the wee hours of Monday morning.

Whether it was Saturday or Sunday, the three men drove toward Dallas in David's Camaro to look for a spot to dispose of the O'Hairs' bodies. At least that's what they told Danny. It was a lie; David already had Camp Wood arranged.

They checked out a field and rejected it. When they got out of the car at Malloy Bridge Road, it was night. Karr came up behind Danny and shot him in the head with David's 9mm. They drove off, then came back in about half an hour and cut off his head and hands with the French knife, took off his clothes and Florsheim shoes, and put them all in a garbage bag in the trunk.

On the way back to Austin, they had a flat, and had to move the grisly cargo to the back floorboard to get the spare out.

On Sunday, October 1, as David remembered it, they dropped off Danny's possessions at Goodwill. On Monday, Karr rented a third van. They loaded the barrels and Danny's head and hands in it and drove to Camp Wood. Colleen had provided Jerry Basey's map drawn on a cocktail napkin. Before he left, David gave her the key to the small storage unit. He told her "[if] the next time she heard from me was over a television news blurb, be advised that there's half a million dollars over here. Half of it's yours, half of it's [Charlene's]." He gave her an American Eagle coin.

At the ranch, they dug the mass grave with a pick and shovel from Home Depot; it took a couple of hours. They dumped in the bodies, doused them with gasoline, and set them afire. After it burned down, they replaced the dirt. By then, it was about 4 a.m. on October 3. The job was done, but "that smell stayed on me for, for a long time," Waters said.

They loaded the empty barrels in the van and drove back through the soft, beautiful hill country as the dawn inched up. They went the back way, on little country roads, dumping various items at picnic rest stops and in creeks along the way, including the digging tools and French knife. They pulled into a self-service car wash in Oak Hill, on Austin's far south side. They rinsed out the barrels and left them there with some other barrels. In a few days, they were gone.

The last thing they disposed of was Madalyn's cane, in the dumpster at the HEB market on Burnet Road and Koenig Lane, where the Founders had bought so many groceries. It was near her first sweet home on Shoal Creek. Then they went to the Genie Car Wash on Burnet and had the van washed.

David rented a motel room near Highland Mall. He was going to bring the gold there to divide it up. But when he got to the storage unit, it was gone. He was sure Colleen had taken it. She denied it, and he started worrying about how to tell Karr about the theft, how to protect Colleen from him.

They all went to the Four Seasons, and there he told Karr the gold was gone. "He didn't go off." He told Karr Colleen wasn't involved, and Karr accepted it all.

Was Colleen involved? During the month in San Antonio, he had instructed her to call his beeper at prearranged times to give the O'Hairs the impression that their fourth "silent partner" in law enforcement was checking in with information on what kind of heat was on them. He said the beeper was Colleen's idea, and that she knew the overall scheme — to get money — but not the details. She wanted him to call her every few days to keep her informed.

He said Colleen surely figured out that things had gone wrong when he asked her to help him find a secluded spot. But he said she knew nothing about the situation with Robin.

Especially not that. "She'd have freaked...I mean, I almost freaked, and I'm a tad more callous than she is...it's not something that you would go home and tell your spouse, darling, there's been a change in plans...No, she was not aware of the homicides."

On January 25, 2001, the second interview with David Waters began. All of a sudden, he got cocky. He'd be flippant about terrible things, like their flat tire after they killed Danny — a trooper might just wanna have a look-see in that bag, he grinned, and that would be awfully embarrassing. He chuckled often. One inquiry was rambling, and he said curtly, "So what is your question?" He allowed as how one query reminded him of an old Rory Calhoun movie. He would answer "Yep" or "Nope."

He started backpedaling; he didn't hit Colleen with the gun that night, she basically crashed into it while they were struggling, didn't even break the skin. Cowling had seen the dental records. One tooth was broken off at the gum line.

There was no sack of bloody tennis shoes, he never took the bearer bonds, the rare books he sold over the Internet were given to him. He never took the library computer. He was bribed and double-crossed in 1994. He had not lain in wait for the O'Hairs back then, as Colleen said. He bought the handcuffs for sex, he snickered, the bow saw to trim the base of the Christmas tree. Even the details of some home invasion robberies and car thefts he'd admitted to were retooled.

By the time they got to Billy King, Donna Cowling was losing her temper. He said he didn't know anything about Billy King's murder. Cowling told him she thought he was lying. And lying that he'd planned to let the O'Hairs go. If he had, why did he and Karr register at the Warren Inn under their own names? First, Waters said, he didn't believe Jon would pursue him — they had a deal. And if he did, so what? He and Karr were at the Warren Inn. Didn't prove the O'Hairs were.

"You're gonna sit there and you're gonna tell me that . . . you did not intend on killing the O'Hairs the whole time."

That's right, said Waters, until Robin died, he didn't think it was necessary.

After more exchanges, Cowling threatened to pull the plea bargain off the table. "I'm not gonna have my chain yanked by you, 'cause you . . . tell me what you wanna tell me when you want to tell me." If he didn't come clean with all of it right now, he could rot in state prison and forget about a federal incarceration.

He didn't want that. He went over his story again. This time, he changed three things: He *had* stolen the computer, bonds, books, and $54,000. He had planned to kill them from the start; they were all three killed at the La Quinta, and he'd lied about Robin's early death. And he, not Karr, shot Danny.

A few details changed — on September 29, they left the bodies in the van all night, not the storage unit; he asked Colleen for a place in the country, she didn't volunteer it. He wanted to move the bodies because Colleen surely knew they were there, and he wanted her out of the loop. He was still excruciatingly careful to avoid implicating Chico Osborne.

It was never clear why David suddenly started lying about small things and getting sarcastic that second day. Perhaps it was a reflex; "when [criminals] get away with a crime," said a veteran reporter, "they think it was because they were smart, not because the cops were lazy or busy, which is almost always closer to the truth." Whatever it was, it convinced them he was lying about planning to let the family live, and about Robin's early death, and it seemed important to get him to admit that. So he did. But which story was the truth?

No one will ever know, unless Gary Karr decides to say more, but a mound of little facts indicates Waters was telling the truth the first time about Robin. Repeatedly during his four days of interviews, he reflexively dated things — like the urgent storage rental — from Robin's death, and repeatedly referred automatically only to "Jon and Madalyn" after her death. This continued even after he changed his story.

He volunteered details that implied memory, things about which there would be no reason to lie — that Jon and Madalyn didn't want to be separated, that Robin's body was put into the Lincoln, not the Cadillac, that she was wrapped in a blanket (and the Warren Inn's September 1995 inventory of Room 11 listed a missing bedspread). He volunteered the artifice of having Danny call the La Quinta pretending to be the fourth man, holding Robin — an inexplicable embellishment if Robin was there.

He repeatedly talked about the unbearable stench, how it stayed with him for weeks and weeks. If they were all killed on the night of the 29th and buried 72 hours later as in the second story, the smell could be starting to get bad. But if one of them had been dead a week, it would be unbearable.

It was around September 26 that Danny sent the "do not open" letter, and told his brother, "these people are animals." What had happened to make him do that? And was Danny's murder planned from the start? That seemed unlikely, given his freedom to call home, write, send money, and so on.

When David asked Colleen to find the deer lease, "I mentioned Karr had fucked things up." If Robin were alive, what had been "fucked up?"

The deer lease was one of a flurry of last-minute needs, along with the ground floor rooms at La Quinta, the urgent larger storage unit, the barrels. It showed lack of planning. Even a detail that came out of the Karr camp later indicated Robin had died early. It was never mentioned by Waters, apparently because he didn't know it: Robin had been smothered with a pillow, not strangled, during the sexual assault.

Most important, if the O'Hairs were all three alive on September 29, and there were only two more days until the last $100,000 came in, what made it so urgent to kill them and abandon one-sixth of the take?

Was there some reason Waters' questioners wanted to hear that the murders were premeditated? They were capital crimes no matter when they were conceived, said Jerry Carruth, so it wouldn't have changed his sentence.

Something eerie happened at Griffith Small Animal Hospital in 1995. Shannon, Robin's 10-year-old black cocker, had suddenly gone into a slump on September 25. She wouldn't eat or respond to anyone for days. A note was made on her chart: "seems depressed."

Along with his second version, David also formally confessed to the murder of Billy King in 1984, for coming on to David's woman at the time.

Chapter 74 ~ "God isn't a merciful God"

GARY KARR lost his appeal in the Fifth Circuit, and a second one claiming Tom Mills was ineffective counsel. He called Waters' confession "garbage." There was no kidnapping. The walls at the Warren Inn were so thin you could hear the neighbor's TV. If it had been a kidnapping, "we would have rented someplace out in the middle of nowhere." And how could anyone have raped Robin without being heard?

He spent much of that September in Florida, he said, returning to Texas only a couple of times. As for him dismembering bodies with a French knife, "I hope the French have a patent on this knife — it sounds like an amazing piece of cutlery."

And, he said, "How about this? I kidnap, extort, torture and kill all these people — for money. Then David says, 'Hey, all the money is gone, I don't know what happened to it.' I shrug my shoulders and say, 'don't worry about it, I'm OK with that'?"

The government just pressured David to say what went along with their search warrant. "Sure they accomplished an end — got David off the streets. But... at the expense of whom? I don't see myself as a meaningless, worthless piece of trash... I had a life. I was loved and had loved ones — daughters, family and grandchildren, friends."

He only hoped, he said, that those who made him out to be a monster didn't ever have to face the monsters they'd created.

"God isn't a merciful God."

Appendix

The Story Behind the Book

Madalyn Murray O'Hair's life was the polar opposite of my previous subject, television evangelist Jimmy Swaggart. But there were fetching similarities. In fact, Madalyn admired Swaggart's skill, and many of her own loyalists had backgrounds and psychological wounds similar to his.

She built her church-state separation movement in my home town, Austin, Texas. As soon as I started working on her biography, odd coincidences began presenting themselves.

My brother had filled many florist orders for the O'Hairs over the years; one of my sisters served them at their favorite restaurant; a friend groomed their dogs. One of Madalyn's enemies worked at my dad's old veterinary hospital. An old friend worked for American Atheists (AA) in the 1970s, another turned out to be the daughter-in-law of Madalyn's famous predecessor Vashti McCollum. My literary agent had been an in-law of Madalyn's co-plaintiffs in her landmark lawsuit. The O'Hairs' last home on Greystone Drive, from which they were taken as kidnappees in 1995, had once been a neighboring pasture where I rode horses. The apartments where David Waters, the criminal who masterminded the kidnap-murders of the O'Hairs and the theft of close to a million dollars, lived with his girlfriend, were next door to Dad's old animal clinic on North Lamar.

One night, interviewing one of Madalyn's ex-employees, I saw a beautiful, familiar-looking tapestry on the wall. During our conversation, I mentioned that my late uncle had lived in the apartments across from the AA headquarters. When she heard his name, she gasped. She had lived there too, had been fast friends with my uncle, and had been his nurse during his last days 11 years before. He had given her the tapestry. She even produced a photo album containing pictures of him.

A close friend, Austin singer-songwriter Kim Miller, introduced me to Wendy Davis, who had not only worked at AA alongside David Waters, she had kept diaries, a priceless insider glimpse of how the decaying organization became the setting for murder. Wendy introduced me to many sources and even gave me lodging in her house close to the courthouse where I covered the May 2000 criminal trial of Gary Karr (one of Waters' recruits in the kidnap-murders).

At the banquet in 2000 where I accepted the Best Nonfiction award from the Texas Institute of Letters for my Swaggart biography, I met John MacCormack, who had given *Swaggart* a wonderful review in the *San Antonio Express-News*. Only a few months after the banquet, MacCormack decided to put his voluminous files on the crime story at my disposal.

On the road doing research into Madalyn's and Waters' pasts, I was given amazing access — to boxes in people's attics, collections, private papers, letters, photos, birth, medical, phone, and criminal records, legal pleadings, diaries, video and audio transcripts, libraries, files, and news archives. I found the atheist community helpful and open (though American Atheists declined to assist). Madalyn's favorite cousin gave me wonderful recollections and story confirmations only months before he died. In Florida to interview some of Madalyn's relatives and ex-AA members, I impulsively knocked on the door of Charlene Karr, the ex-wife of Gary Karr and a key witness against both him and Waters. I knew she had turned down all interview requests, but for some reason, she invited me in. We talked for hours, along with the Karrs' daughter, Chrystal.

Miraculously, Madalyn's next-door neighbor in Baltimore during her tumultuous, headline-grabbing activity of the 1960s was still there, sharp of memory and tongue. And the day I stood gazing at Room 11 of the Warren Inn in San Antonio, where the doomed O'Hairs spent their last weeks believing they were going to get out of their nightmare alive, the door suddenly opened. The current tenant allowed me in for a tour.

These breaks happened so frequently I lost track of them, but the most astounding was the fluke that opened to me the story of David Waters and "Colleen Kay Smith."

In fear of her life after testifying against Waters, Colleen had gone into the federal witness protection program with her new husband, DeWayne Chavez. She was intelligent and articulate, and Donna Cowling, the much-respected FBI agent who persuaded her to come forward, thought highly of her. But, though Cowling courteously conveyed my interview requests, they were ignored.

In the spring of 2001, I set off to do research in the Midwest. My husband, Gary, a professor at the University of Southern California, joined me on the road during his break. Late one night we pulled into a motel in a small town. The next morning, Gary went to look for bookstores. He was soon back with an unbelievable piece of news. He hustled me into the car and we headed for the outskirts of town.

In a rundown, isolated building on old Route 66, with a sign that said, "Pabst Blue Ribbon – Books," was a bookstore that doubled as a biker bar. Taking a nap in a back room was DeWayne Chavez, now estranged from Colleen.

Chavez told me how to contact her. After she came to believe my purpose was to give the principals in the story their rightful human dimension, we took up a fascinating correspondence, and were even able to meet face to face. When I was finally able to start visiting David Waters in Leavenworth federal prison, I had some valuable insights about him.

I admit to being one of the people who felt a certain relief when Waters passed away suddenly from cancer in the spring of 2003.

Acknowledgments

Every biographer has a long list of people to thank, and space never permits a proper appreciation of the trust, cooperation, generosity, expertise, and even risk these people undertake to help the writer. In that last category are several who did not wish to be named. These include family members and acquaintances who felt they would suffer in their communities from any connection with Madalyn; certain associates of Richard O'Hair; and people who have participated in crimes or been close to those who have.

It also includes "Colleen Kay Smith," David Waters' longtime girlfriend whose testimony put him and Gary Karr behind bars. After she began helping with the book, she started receiving ominous telephone messages even at her location in the federal witness protection program. I am most grateful for her willingness to help even under those circumstances, and I have respected her desire to use a pseudonym.

Of the names below, many resulted in friendships which will outlast this work, but some must be singled out. Mary and Garry DeYoung and their daughter Katrina generously shared their time and memories of their years with Madalyn, along with hundreds of personal communications with her and 50 boxes of freethought and atheist archives.

Bill and Marion Young not only extended gracious hospitality at their Cedar Springs Library in Auberry, California, but loaned me an almost unbroken run of AA magazines and newsletters from the 1970s through the 1990s.

John Rush, an ex-AA member, tirelessly forwarded information and documents and tracked down informants. June Sauter sent numerous letters and documents concerning Madalyn and Bob Harrington. Leona Goedde gave personal letters and valuable insights into the family, plus warm hospitality, as did Abigail Martin, who turned over to me the archive of the late Jacques Musy. Ed Golly dug up his old files and trusted me with them for more than two years.

Private investigator Tim Young, a man with talents in every direction, shared his archive of detective work and videotapes, plus a glimpse into a P.I.'s ever-changing bag of tricks. The receivers for Madalyn, Jon Garth, and Robin — Don Carnes, Gordon McNutt, and Walker Arenson — were generous and helpful beyond measure in giving me access to the family's papers.

"The Team" — Agent Donna Cowling of the FBI, Special Agent Ed Martin of IRS Criminal Investigation Division, and Assistant U.S. Attorney Jerry Carruth — bent over backward to extend every possible courtesy. They were all unfailingly responsive and helpful.

337

Last, three large debts are owed.

Madalyn's surviving son Bill Murray gave me hours of articulate, intelligent, honest memories and perspectives, despite his hectic schedule. He took the trouble to have me present at his family's burial near Austin. He trusted me with their story.

Jimmy Nassour, the Austin attorney who purchased Madalyn's diaries and other papers from her bankruptcy trustee, has been a careful steward, concerned that the materials become part of a serious work. I am honored that, of all the people who approached him, he chose to share these historic documents with me.

Immeasurable thanks are due all the reporters whose work laid thirty-five years' foundation for this book, but none more than John MacCormack of the *San Antonio Express-News*. He cracked the case when the Austin police dropped the ball, and handed the FBI two-thirds of their case. Even though his work was not finished when I began my book, MacCormack introduced me to everyone he knew who could help with both the crime story and Madalyn's life. He filed more than 80 stories on the missing family. When he decided not to write his own book, he gave me full access to the six years of research and labor that landed him a Pulitzer nomination. His words still ring in my ears: "Just write another book I want to read."

I hope I have done that.

The following people are owed a great debt for their help, whether it be inside information, special expertise, sharing of documents, insights, and hospitality, or all of the above.

Andrea Ball, Mrs. Grace Bamberger, Jerry Basey, Joshua Benton, Timothy Binga, the Biographers' Group of Los Angeles, Martha Bloom, G. Richard Bozarth, Catherine Braslavsky, Jack Brimeyer, Byron Bromley, Donna Brooks, Clarence Brown, Ellen Kuniyuki Brown, Carolyn Bruce, Robert Bryce, Shannon Burke, Anne Bushel, David Buttram, David Paul Buttram, Tom Buttram, Richard Cardillo, Beth Campbell, Marie Castle, Dr. Thomas L. Charlton, DeWayne Chavez, Tom Clarkson, Hazel Clinton, Lindsay Clinton, Kevin Clendenning, Maudine Cox, Warren Cullar, Wendy Davis, Judy Dean, Bill DeWolfe, Marshall Dinowitz, M. Neven Du Mont, Doug Duncan, Charles Duricek, Jim and Irene Durst, Robert Elkins, Roberta Eley, Susan Fisher, Walter Fix, Ray Fleming, Rodney Florence, Larry Flynt, Noonie Fortin, Arnold Frautschi, Jr., James Freudiger, Freytag's Florist (David Wupperman), Bob Fry, Christopher Gabel, Siobhan Gambito, William Gates, Jane Genthe, Dr. David Glassman, Al Goldstein, Dr. George Green, Christine Hafner, Martha Hammer, David Haney, Katrina Harper, Rev. Bob Harrington, Mary Holder, Jeff Hunt, John Johnson, Julia Jones, Charlene Karr, Chrystal Karr, Gary Paul Karr, Cynthia Keith, David Kent, Leonard Kerpelman, Cam King, Kenneth L. King, Karl Kinser, Robert Knight, Paul Kurtz, the late Homer Lacy, Mary Lampkin, Jean Lane, Bob Lawrence, Joyce Lawrence, Artist Elizabeth Jane Liggett, Marilyn Jill Lunderville, Kevin Lyons, Mary Mackzum, Cathy Marable, Darren Martin, Jack Massen, Maury

Maverick, Dannel and Jeanette McCollum, Wayne Meissner, John Mercadante, Susan Mignatti, Kim Miller, Tom Mills, Mike Milom, Mary Mura, Francis Mortyn, the late Jacques Musy, Bill and Nancy Murray, Derek Nalls, Brenda Nelson, Bobbie Jane Nelson, Stephen Nordlinger, Bruce Nygren, Richard O'Hair (grandson), Frank Oveis (my editor), Ruth Brooks Palmer, Peoria Police Department, Kim Sue Lia Perkes, Pepi Plowman, Julie Popkin (my agent), Harry Preston, Dick Reavis, Vicki O'Hair Reed, David Richards, Kevin Rische, Mindy Rosewitz, Don Rossmoore, Joseph Rowe, Donna Saunders, Benton and Jane Sauter, Carolyn Sawyer, Louetta Sayne, Bill Schultze, Rochelle Sears, Ralph Shirley, Ronald J. Sievert, Dr. Audrey Slate, Marty Smith, Cloe Sofikitis, Sharon Summers, Dania Tabar, Lonn Taylor, David Travis, Naomi Twining, Arnold Via, Joe Wase, the late David Roland Waters, Mary Cervenek Watson, Cookie Wilkerson, Christi Williams, Bennett Wilson, Eddie Wilson, Fred Woodworth, Liz Wupperman, Frank and Ann Zindler.

Notes

Because Madalyn shuffled money, staff, and agendas among her many organizations and publishing entities, it was not always clear when someone was representing, working for, suing, borrowing from, loaning to, or applying for grants for any one of them. For example, during her divorce action from Richard O'Hair, all property owned by American Atheists was deeded to the Society of Separationists and the Stevens Library to keep it from her husband, and later deeded somewhere else. This juggling happened frequently when judgments or other crises loomed; I have done my best to be accurate about which attorneys, assets, volunteers, lawsuits, etc. were associated with which organization at any given time.

Similarly, before American Atheists and *American Atheist* magazine became stabilized in the mid-1970s, a hodgepodge of organizations and publications emerged. These are described in one of the footnotes to Chapter 10. I hope I've located them all.

Thousands of documents, including passports, medical records, resumes, bank statements, tax returns, police reports, warrants, news articles, indictments, legal pleadings, diaries, handwritten notes, birth records, adoption papers, phone records, trial transcripts, speeches, personal letters, video and audio transcripts, press releases, receipts, and other materials, down to grocery lists and auto repair records, were used to compile this story. In handling so much material, mistakes are inevitable, and I apologize for any egregious oversights, errors, or omissions.

Space does not permit sourcing each bit of information. Rather, the overall sources consulted for each chapter are listed at the beginning of the notes for that chapter. In general, only quotes from published materials are sourced. Quotes from Madalyn's diaries and oral history at Baylor University are not sourced.

The private archives listed below were used extensively for each chapter. Rather than repeating the archives' names in each chapter source list, suffice to say that, in general, the most heavily consulted were DeYoung, Rush, Stein, Golly, Cedar Springs Library, and the Toledo Blade for AA publications and Madalyn's public life; Baylor, Nassour, DeYoung, Stein, Kent, Mills, the Gospel Tract Society, and the three O'Hairs' papers held by their receivers for personal aspects of Madalyn's story; and the Durst, MacCormack, Young, Mills, and Waters papers, plus items I was able to view in the Evidence Room, for the crime story.

The FBI provided hundreds of documents through the Freedom of Information Act. Among them were news articles whose city of origin was not given (for example, "Times News," "Evening Star," "State Journal"). Such names are included in the master list of periodicals but no further information about them is available.

Police and FBI reports are identified only by date and office. Madalyn's published writings are identified in the Notes by title rather than surname.

Last, the chapters in this book rely on hundreds of interviews. Some sources wished to remain anonymous altogether, many wanted anonymity regarding their information, and many provided access to letters and private papers. Therefore, the list of interviewees who consented to be named appears only here in the Acknowledgments section, not in the chapter source lists.

ARCHIVAL RESOURCES

Private Archives, Collections, and Papers

Cedar Springs Library, Auberry, California
Wendy Hale Davis Papers
Garry and Mary DeYoung Archive
Quentin "Jim" Durst Papers
Robert Elkins Archive
Evidence room, U.S. Attorney General's office
Leona Goedde Papers

Ed Golly Archive
The Gospel Tract Society Archive
Katrina DeYoung Harper Papers
Bob Harrington Archive
David L. Kent Papers
Dannel and Jeanette McCollum Papers
John X. MacCormack Papers
Walter Martin Religious Infonet Archive
Tom Mills Archive
Frank Mortyn Papers
Jon Garth Murray Papers (Gordon McNutt, receiver)
Jacques Musy/Abigail Martin Archive
Bill Murray Archive
Jimmy Nassour Archive
Madalyn Murray O'Hair Papers (Don Carnes, receiver. Includes papers under the names Madalyn Mays,
    Madalyn Roths, Madalyn Murray, and Madalyn Murray O'Hair)
Robin Murray-O'Hair Papers (Walker Arenson, receiver)
Peoria Journal-Star Library
Kim Sue Lia Perkes Papers
Vicki O'Hair Reed Papers
John Rush Archive
Benton and Jane Sauter Papers
The Gordon Stein Papers at the Center For Inquiry Libraries, Amherst, NY
Trinity Foundation, Dallas
The *Toledo Blade* Library, Toledo, OH
Arnold Via Papers
David Roland Waters Papers
Eddie Wilson Archive
Fred Woodworth Archive (*The Match!*)
Tim Young Papers

Libraries, Historical Societies, Public Records

Allegany County records, Cumberland, MD
Altoona Public Library, Altoona, PA
Ashland County Public Library, Ashland, OH
Austin History Center, Austin, TX
Austin Public Library, Austin, TX
Azusa Public Library, Azusa, CA
Leonard H. Axe Library, Pittsburg State University, Pittsburg, KS
Baltimore County Public Library, Towson, MD
Carnegie Free Library, Pittsburgh, PA
Case Western Reserve University, Cleveland, OH
Center for American History, University of Texas at Austin
Center for Inquiry Libraries, Amherst, NY
Community Library of Allegheny Valley, Tarentum, PA
Curwensville, PA Public Library
Dallas Public Library, Dallas, TX
Doheny Memorial Library, University of Southern California, Los Angeles
Erie Public Library, Erie, PA
Erie, PA Historical Society
Georgetown University Library Special Collection, Washington, D.C.
Hawaii State Library, Honolulu
Illinois Supreme Court Library
Indiana Co., PA Historical Society
Labadie Collection, Special Collections Library, University of Michigan, Ann Arbor
Madison Public Library, Madison, OH
Mansfield Public Library, Mansfield, OH
Maryland Historical Society, Baltimore, MD

McCollum Archive, University of Illinois Historical Survey Library
Morley Library, Painesville, OH
National Archives and Records Administration
National Personnel Records Center
Ohio Historical Society, Columbus
Ohio Northern University
Painesville, OH Public Library
Pasadena Public Library, Pasadena, CA
Peoria County Records, Peoria, IL
Peoria Police Department, Peoria, IL
Peoria Public Library, Peoria, IL
Enoch Pratt Library, Baltimore, MD
Purdy Library, Wayne State University, Detroit, MI
Harry Ransom Humanities Research Center, University of Texas at Austin
Rossford Public Library, Rossford, OH
Joseph and Elizabeth Shaw Public Library, Clearfield, PA
South Texas College of Law
Special Collections, Larringer Library, Georgetown University, Washington, DC
Special Collections, Michigan State University
Special Collections, University of Maryland, Baltimore County Library, Catonsville
Stanford University Libraries, Academic Information Resources, Religious Studies Collections
The Texas Collection, Baylor University, Waco, TX
Texas State Historical Association
Texas State Library
Toledo-Lucas County. OH Public Library
University of Maryland Library at Catonsville
U.S. Bureau of Prisons
U.S. Department of Justice
Vermont Historical Society, Montpelier
Vertical File, Dolph Briscoe Collection, Center for American History, University of Texas at Austin
Wabash, IN Carnegie Public Library
Wayne State University, Reuther Library of Labor and Urban Affairs
Western Historical Manuscript Collection, University of Missouri-St. Louis
Western Reserve Historical Society, Akron and Mentor, OH
Western Reserve Historical Society and Archives, Cleveland, OH

GLOSSARY OF ABBREVIATIONS USED IN THE NOTES

AA	American Atheist
AA Mag	*American Atheist Magazine*
AA News	*American Atheist News* (online)
AA Vets	American Atheist Veterans
AAC	*American Atheist Center*
AAIN	*American Atheists Insider's Newsletter*
AAS	*Austin American-Statesman*
AC	*Austin Citizen*
AP	Associated Press
APD	Austin Police Department
AR Mag	*American Rationalist* Magazine
ARS	Ann Rowe Seaman
Aus Chron	*Austin Chronicle*
Baylor	The Texas Collection, Baylor University, Waco, Texas, Madalyn Murray O'Hair oral history interviews
BBB	*Bill Murray, the Bible, and the Baltimore Board of Education*
Blade	*Toledo Blade*
BM	Bill Murray
CAMMO	*A Case Against Madalyn Murray O'Hair*
Chi Trib	*Chicago Tribune*
CKS	"Colleen Kay Smith"

Dallas Life	*Dallas Life* Magazine
DFP	*Detroit Free Press*
DMN	*Dallas Morning News*
DOJ	Department of Justice
DRW	David Roland Waters
DT	*Daily Texan* Newspaper
EBMM	Ex-communicated by Mad Madalyn, unpublished manuscript
Eve. Star	Undesignated publication acquired through Freedom of Information
Eve. Sun	*Baltimore Evening Sun*
FWST	*Fort Worth Star-Telegram*
GDY	Garry DeYoung
GGM	*Good Gawd, Madalyn!* unpublished manuscript
HP	*Houston Post*
HSB	*Honolulu Star-Bulletin*
IRS CID	Internal Revenue Service Criminal Investigation Division
Irv	Irvin Mays
JGM	Jon Garth Murray
LAT	*Los Angeles Times*
Life	*Life* Magazine
ltr	Letter
MFY	*My Four Years with Madalyn Murray O'Hair, My Sister,* unpublished manuscript by Irv Mays
MLWG	*My Life without God*
MM&BAB	Mad Madalyn and Born-Again Bill, unpublished manuscript
MMO	Madalyn Murray O'Hair (including the surnames Mays, Roths, Murray, and O'Hair)
MMO:AMTR	*Madalyn Murray O'Hair: A Mouse That Roars* unpublished manuscript
MMO TS	Madalyn's version of *Truth Seeker* magazine
NARA	National Archives and Records Administration
n.d.	not dated or date unknown
Newsweek	*Newsweek* Magazine
NPRC	National Personnel Records Center
NYT	*New York Times*
OA	Other Americans
PB	*Playboy* Magazine
Phila. EB	*Philadelphia Evening Bulletin*
PJS	*Peoria Journal-Star*
PPD	Peoria Police Department
PPG	*Pittsburgh Post-Gazette*
PRR	*Poor Richard's Reports*
PRRN	*Poor Richard's Reports Newsletter*
Realist	*The Realist* Magazine
Ripsaw	*Ripsaw* Magazine
RMOH	Robin Murray-O'Hair
ROH	Richard O'Hair
SAEN	*San Antonio Express-News*
SFChron	*San Francisco Chronicle*
SOS	Society of Separationists
SUN	*Baltimore Sun*
TJS	Thomas Jefferson School
TM	*Texas Monthly* Magazine
TS	*Truth Seeker* Magazine
UPI	United Press International
unk.	Unknown; refers also to correspondents who wish to remain anonymous
VF	*Vanity Fair* Magazine
WP	*Washington Post*
WTH	*Waco Tribune Herald*

Chapter 1 ~ Waterloo

Unpublished sources: Interviews; Karr Indictment 12-7-99; ltr Etter to JGM 10-3-95.

Published sources: Richmond Times-Dispatch 9-29-95; Life 6-19-64; Life 4-13-63; Schulz; AAS 12-9-99; Lawler; Hickey; Ramos; Handbook of Texas Online.

11   Waterloo - It is not known why the hamlet was called Waterloo, but almost from its beginning, the Texas Republic was recognized by the French government; King Louis Philippe signed a treaty of amity in 1839, and the French Legation still stands in Austin. Moreover, some of the aristocratic Prussian and German freethinkers who settled Texas in the 1840s had fought at the real Waterloo.
11   "Most Hated" - Life 6-19-64.
11   "groveling" - Life 4-13-64.
11   "stupid cows" - Life 6-19-64.
13   iconoclasts - These included the likes of Lucy Parsons of Waco and later the 1886 Chicago Hay-market Riot, Waco's James D. Shaw, publisher of *The Independent Pulpit* in 1883, William Cowper Brann, publisher of *The Iconoclast,* who was gunned down by a fundamentalist in the streets of Waco in 1898 (he managed to draw and kill his assailant before dying), Dallasite Wilford "Pitch-fork" Smith, whose monthly *Plain Talk* emerged in 1907, modeled on *The Iconoclast,* and William Sydney Porter, O. Henry, whose lampooning *Rolling Stone* appeared in Austin in 1894. The liberal, educated German Freethinkers who settled Central Texas in the late 1840s included the German Free School Association begun in Austin by the author's great-great grandfather, Wilhelm von Rosenberg.
13   university of the first class - UT Austin was the first major Southern university to admit blacks as undergraduates, and the city moved to integrate movie theaters, restaurants, and other public facilities. By 1968, African Americans had a school board seat, and by 1971 a city council seat.

Chapter 2 ~ Madalyn Evalyn

Unpublished sources: Interviews; FBI report 4-28-58; Pittsburgh Credit Bureau report 10-16-41; ltr MMO to BM 5-7-69.

Published sources: PPG 9-13-77; MLWG; Caldwell; Straw; 1900, 1910, and 1920 Census; city directories for Erie, Pittsburgh, Beechview, Tarentum, Crafton, and Creighton, PA, and for Madison and Mans-field, OH. Toledo Times 6-18-63; PB October 1965; unlabeled newsletter re August Scholle, ca. 1972; Pasadena Star-News 1-1-72; Pasadena Star-News 1-7-72.

19   "old Al" - Another of Madalyn's favorites was her aunt Jessie Wason, Pup's sister. In 1971 Jessie, 68, was living with a 53-year-old boyfriend, Herbie Jones, in a trailer in Arizona. Jessie's sister, Grace Kacy, rescued her from the abusive Herbie and brought her to California. On New Year's Eve 1971, Herbie burst into the apartment and fatally shot Grace and her daughter Patsy. A week later, police arrested Jones in Illinois, reportedly on his way to kill other family members. It was the kind of thing Madalyn hated about Pup's side of the family, with their "coarse raspiness of . . . speech and petty utterances."

Chapter 3 ~ Rossford, Ohio

Unpublished sources: Interviews; maps and historic photos of Rossford; FBI report 4-28-58; FBI memo 6-13-57; ltr MMO to Kent "Bastille Day" 1989; ltr MMO to Kent 8-4-89; ltr Kent to Massen June 2, 1993.

Published sources: Rossford and Toledo city directories; *Maroon N Gray*; *As I Recall*; Van West; Smithsonian June 1989; St. Petersburg Times 4-22-90.

Chapter 4 ~ Love and War

Unpublished sources: ltr MMO to RMOH 11-30-78; untitled ltr 5-18-44; FBI report 4-28-58, Pittsburgh Credit Bureau report 10-16-41; Allegany County records; Roths divorce decree 1–43; MMO passport application 10-29-64; ltr MMO to BM 5-7-69; NARA 4-12-02; FBI airtel 9-14-60; ltr Matt Murray to MMO 1-28-45; ltr Wm. Murray II to MMO 4-13-56; FBI report 11-26-62; FBI memo 6-13-57.

Published sources: Good Housekeeping November 1940; Blade 6-22-64; Toledo City Directory; American Atheists online (photos); MLWG; DT 5-3-74; unlabeled newsletter re August Scholle, ca. 1972; AA website photos ca. 1963 © 2000.

25 subcontracting business - Madalyn maintained that Pup's business, the Pittsburgh Steel Erection Company, lasted for years and paid her $200 a month as both an office manager and engineer. No record of such a company could be found other than a reference to "John I. Mays & Son" on an FBI report citing a 1946 credit application by John Mays.

Chapter 5 ~ Master William Mays

Unpublished sources: Interviews; NARA 4-12-02; NPRC; ltr MMO to BM 5-7-69; EBMM 8; FBI report 11-26-62; FBI report 4-28-58; Pittsburgh Credit Bureau report 10-16-41; PPD report 1-31-74; ltr CKS to ARS 5-29-01; ltr DRW to ARS 3-25-02; Separation Certificate, U.S. Army.

Published sources: MLWG; telephone and city directories for Mansfield, OH; Current Biography 1977; Blade 2-4-75; McCollum; TS October 1946; *McCollum v. Board of Education*, 333 U.S. 203 (1948); *Torcaso v. Watkins*, 367 U.S. 488 (1961); ltr Thomas Jefferson to Danbury Baptist Association 1-1-1802, cited in Library of Congress Information Bulletin January 1998; Blade 11-21-48; Blade 11-22-48; Blade 3-3-52; Blade 11-16-52; Blade 12-12-52; Life 7-23-56; Hamburger.

28 shipped home - Madalyn bore a Victory Medal, an ETO Ribbon with two battle stars, her WAAC Service Ribbon, and the American Theater Ribbon.
28 shortly before Madalyn returned - Her divorce proceedings had been frozen during her military service, and she was still legally Mrs. John Roths. According to Bill Murray, Roths valiantly offered to be a father to her child. But Madalyn refused. She'd been an officer. She was ambitious. Roths was a laborer and enlisted man.
30 "reduce juvenile delinquency" - TS October 1946 pp. 151-52.
30 "what is a child to understand" - TS October 1946 pp. 151–52.
31 "ban God from public life" - Blade 11-22-48.
31 "legalistic tyranny of the omnipotent state" - Blade 11-22-48.
31 "Christ must be the Master . . . projects" - Blade 11-21-48.
31 "We are a religious people . . . supreme being" - Blade 11-16-52.
32 "money, schemes, and weapons" - Blade 12-12-52.
32 "ennobling purpose" - Blade 12-12-52.

Chapter 6 ~ "I'm an outsider"

Unpublished sources: FBI airtel, 9-10-60; FBI memo 6-13-57; ltr Registrar, Ohio Northern Univ. to ARS 8-12-04; communication Registrar, South Texas College of Law to ARS 8-12-04; ltr Wm. Murray II to MMO 4-13-56; FBI letterhead memo, 9-12-60; Pittsburgh Credit Bureau report 10-16-41; FBI report 8-24-55; Stanford University Libraries/Academic Information Resources, Religious Studies Collections; FBI report 4-28-58; FBI report 11-16-55; FBI report 9-11-56; FBI memo 9-3-60; FBI memo 8-31-60; MMO ltr to Correspondence Publishing Co. in Detroit 8-21-61; Ryan.

Published sources: MLWG; Blade 2-4-75; Blade 9-29-95; Current Biography 1977; AAS 1-10-99; AAIN June 1983; An Atheist Looks at Women and Religion; Bilstein; SAEN 1-7-99; PB October 1965; Le Beau; McCabe; Life 6-27-55; Newsletter on the Murray Case 6-25-62; MCSCS Newsletter January 1963; The Realist September 1964; www.exlibris.org; Cannon; Melton; atheism.about.com; Columbia Electronic Encyclopedia.

35 "Life-hating puppets" - The Realist September 1964.
36 deeply ashamed - In August 1955, Madalyn reported to the FBI that an attorney (likely one for her paternity suits) was threatening to expose the illegitimacy of her children. The FBI decided it was a fee dispute, not extortion as Madalyn accused, but Madalyn had a real fear of losing her job if her bosses found out.
36 Jon Garth Murray - The name Garth was that of a dog they'd once owned, and also of a family acquaintance, according to Bill.
37 great American rationalist orator - Robert Ingersoll was only one of a long line of American reformers whose activism began under the influence of the freethought movement. It is beyond the scope of this biography to include a history of that movement, but it includes luminaries ranging from Giordano Bruno and Epicurus to Thomas Paine, George Bernard Shaw, the prolific Joseph McCabe — a vocal and aggressive advocate of church taxes and a world leader of atheism — to paleontologist Stephen J. Gould and entertainer Steve Allen, as well as women's rights activists Elizabeth Cady Stanton, Susan B. Anthony, Margaret Sanger, Theosophy founder H. P. Blavatsky, and hundreds of others.

39 leftist groups - The voluminous FBI files on Madalyn mention her attending a group called the Socialist Study Group of Baltimore, and one called the Maryland Committee for Democratic Rights, which she chaired from August 1961 to December 1962. She also was involved with a group called Student Committee for Travel to Cuba, and was associated by the FBI with the Citizens Committee for Constitutional Liberties, the Baltimore Freedom of the Press Committee (formed around 1949 by the Maryland Communist Party to support the East Coast Communist newspapers *The Worker* and *The Daily Worker*), the National Assembly for Democratic Rights (formed to combat the requirement that the Communist Party USA register with the Attorney General as a communist-action organization), and the Committee to Secure Justice for Morton Sobell (convicted and imprisoned for spying for the USSR with Julius and Ethel Rosenberg).

40 kicked out of Howard - This was Madalyn's account; she may have dropped out, but graduate schools almost never expel students except for cheating, theft, or some other serious infraction.

Chapter 7 ~ A Discreet Inquiry

Unpublished sources: Interviews; ltr Reznichenko to MMO 4-8-60 ; ltr MMO to Reznichenko 5-10-60; ltr MMO to USSR embassy 3-13-60 ; ltr MMO to USSR embassy 4-13-60; FBI memo 9-3-60; FBI memo 10-31-60; FBI memo 8-31-60; FBI airtel 9-19-60; FBI memo 2-7-61; FBI Summary report 6-18-62; FBI report 6-18-62; FBI airtel 9-10-60; FBI airtel 9-14-60; FBI memo 4-5-62; FBI report 2-4-65; FBI report 8-15-62 and an undated FBI report filed just after it; FBI report 2-1-65; Citizens Research Council of Michigan.

Published sources: MLWG; SAEN 1-7-99; NYT 1-25-99; Michigan CIO News 5-16-57; Lansing Labor News; NARA; Newsletter on the Murray Case 6-25-62; MCSCS Newsletter Jan. 1963; Blade 6-13-57; Blade 7-31-57; Blade 4-2-58; Blade 8-22-58; 1958 Congressional Record Senate, page 18645; Blade 12-17-59; The Liberal August 1960; Blade 5-18-60; BBB; Cannon; Churchill and Vander Wall; Tyson; Sun 10-27-60; Sun 10-28-60; Sun 1-25-61; unlabeled clip 4-15-62 FOIA; U.S. Department of the Treasury Fact Sheet; Vestal.

41 She already subscribed to *Soviet Life* - In 1961, Madalyn wrote a correspondent that she subscribed to the *Weekly People* (Socialist Labor Party), *The Militant* (Socialist Workers Party), *The Worker* (Communist Party), *Freedom* (Anarchist party in England), and the *IWW Weekly*.

43 Gus Scholle was now president - Scholle also had a suit in the U.S. Supreme Court challenging the senate apportionment provisions of Michigan's 1908 constitution, which he won. This was a great source of family pride, and inspiration to Madalyn.

43 "I quit the union" - Madalyn belonged to the American Federation of Government Employees.

43 "telling them exactly" - MLWG p. 50.

43 flew back to Baltimore - Madalyn's itinerary included England, France, Germany, Italy, Greece, Israel, and Russia, but she couldn't get visas to any of those countries. She told several people she considered Israel "a truly Socialist country" and wanted to live and work there.

43 "God is great" - Blade 7-31-57.

44 "Leave religion to the churches . . . atheistic humanism" - Blade 12-17-59.

45 "religious propaganda . . . supernatural revelations" - The Liberal August 1960.

45 "politics touches the altar . . . compromised" - Blade 5-18-60.

46 First and Fourteenth amendments - The Fourteenth Amendment's statement, "No state shall make or enforce any law which shall abridge the privileges or immunities of citizens of the United States," was construed by Madalyn to mean that if the First Amendment did erect a wall of separation, it had to be enforced in all the states.

46 "My son is not going to bow" - Sun 10-27-60.

47 open accusations that she was a Communist - Interviewed by the FBI on June 8, 1957, Madalyn said the U.S. was expendable and was the only thing blocking world Socialism; interviewed again in 1960 in connection with her defection attempt, she said she would do anything in her power to convert the U.S. government to Socialism.

Bill Murray recalled that his mother's denials about being a Communist started in earnest after Lee Harvey Oswald was revealed to be a member of the Fair Play for Cuba Committee. The family was glued to the TV news when the phone rang. Madalyn hung up, pale, and asked Bill to drive her to a house and drop her off. She returned in the wee hours. He later learned that the call was from Communist Party USA headquarters in New York, ordering Madalyn to find anything in the Baltimore Fair Play for Cuba chapter's files about Oswald or anyone who might be connected with him, and destroy it.

"I've always wondered if Madalyn was somehow connected with Oswald," said one of her colleagues years later. "There weren't that many Fair Play/defector types running around. It was a very small community, the people who wanted to defect."

The Fair Play For Cuba Committee was the pet target of J. Edgar Hoover's COINTELPRO. The Committee was founded in 1960 with help from American Socialists to support the revolution of Fidel Castro — a revolution that captured American youth. "Fidelismo" swept the U.S. (a toy manufacturer even produced Fidel action figures), attracting prominent intellectuals, journalists, and artists, including Norman Mailer, Allen Ginsberg, I. F. Stone, James Baldwin, and many others. It was the kind of company Madalyn yearned to keep.

The Eisenhower White House deemed Cuba not a fledgling democracy but a Communist beachhead (indeed, asked to define democracy, Castro understood it to be "a meeting of a group of men who know the road on which to take the people, that freely discuss the things they are going to do, having in their hands all the power of the State to do it."). The Fair Play committee was asked to register as a "Communist-action" organization; it refused. (Later, the FPCC's activities helped tip off Castro that Cuban exiles were plotting to unseat him with CIA help. The failure of that plot — the Bay of Pigs invasion in April 1961 — humiliated the CIA.)

Madalyn had a close connection with the FPCC through her friendship with Willie Mae Mallory, assistant to militant civil rights leader Robert Williams. A Marine veteran who had organized blacks in his native North Carolina to take up arms against the Ku Klux Klan, Williams was a major COINTELPRO target, and in 1961 he fled to Cuba, where Castro allowed him to broadcast "Radio Free Dixie" to the U.S. South. Madalyn and Mallory would remain friends for several years — and be watched by the FBI.

Chapter 8 ~ "Your petitioners are atheists"

Unpublished sources: Interviews, letters between Arthur Cromwell and Madalyn 12-3-60, 12-6-60, 12-10-60, 1-17-61, 1-25-61, 11-3-62, 11-3-62, and 12-14-63; letter MMO to Vashti McCollum 9-11-64; letter Cromwell to Hoops 11-3-62; letter Toby to Vashti McCollum 9-16-64; letters between MMO and Corliss Lamont 10-6-64 and 11-23-64; letter Alan Robinson, M.D. to Vashti McCollum 10-13-64; ltr Hialeah, FL teacher to MacCormack 9-4-96; MM&BAB; EBMM; ltr MMO to Hoops assumed 6-25-62; ltr MMO to Cromwell 12-3-60; ltr MMO to Hoops 1962, ca. mid-September; ltr MMO to members, 4-6-62; ltr Lewis to readers November 1962; ltr MMO to Rationalists 9-30-62.

Published sources: MLWG; Sun 10-28-60; Mills; Esquire October 1964; AA News June 2002; partial MCSCS Newsletter assumed December 1962; Sun 4-10-61; Sun 4-28-61; Ripsaw March 1961; TS April 1961; The Liberal October 1962; The Liberal July 1961; Sunday Oklahoman 8-18-63; Phila. EB 7-2-63; unlabeled clip dated 8-63; OA Newsletter April 1963; MCSCS Newsletter March 1963; Sunday Oklahoman 8-17-63; Newsletter on the Murray Case 6-25-62; AA Mag July 1964; *Engel et al v. Vitale et al,* 370 U.S. 421, June 25, 1962; Sun 4-6-62; Sun 7-20-61; American Atheist Heritage; MCSCS Newsletter November 1962; Progressive World August 1962; MCSCS Newsletter February 1963; MCSCS Newsletter January 1963; HA 12-4-65; MCSCS Newsletter June 1963; www.exlibris.org (Ranters); Sun 4-28-61.

49   "go fuck yourself!" - Mills pp. 185–86.
50   "Every misfit in America" - MLWG p. 75.
50   "good Christians . . . spat upon" - Ripsaw March 1961.
51   "Mrs. Murray . . . has battled on her own" - The Liberal October 1962; The Liberal July 1961.
51   "admitted nudist atheist" - Sunday Oklahoman 8-17-63.
52   "subordinate all pupils . . . objective is religious suppression" - Sun 4-28-61.
52   Maryland high court ruled against her - "Neither the 1st nor the 14th Amendment was intended to stifle all rapport between religion and government," said the majority opinion (Sun 4-6-62). It wasn't like they were teaching sectarian religion, and other states had held such practices valid. But it was a narrow vote, 4-3, and the dissenting opinion by Chief Judge Frederick C. Brune took the words out of Madalyn's mouth: the Bible and Lord's Prayer were nothing if not sectarian — they were "Christian religious exercises [that] seem plainly to favor one religion . . . against [others and] against non-believers." Since the "coercive power of the state" required attendance, the prayers were essentially coerced.
52   over 40 years - Lewis had published numerous freethought magazines, including *Bulletin of the Freethinkers of America, Common Sense, The Freethinker,* and *Age of Reason.* By his death in 1968, he had 4,000 readers. His Thomas Paine Institute and Freethinkers' University in New York failed for lack of funding.

53 "The more I see of atheists" - partial MCSCS Newsletter assumed December 1962.
53 "Madalyn and the boys" - MCSCS Newsletter February 1963.

Chapter 9 ~ A Huge Amount of Confusion

Unpublished sources: Interviews.

Published sources: Hall; MLWG; Blade 6-29-69; Blade 6-18-63; Blade 6-11-67; Blade 6-23-64; Blade 6-25-62; Blade 6-27-62; Freedom Writer Spring 2004; Blade 6-28-62#1 and #2; Blade 8-31-62; Blade 7-2-62; Blade 6-30-62 #1 and #2; Blade 7-4-62; Blade 7-8-62; Blade 9-6-62; MCSCS Newsletter January 1963; Philadelphia News 3-6-02; WTH 6-12-79; The Holy Bible; Gaustad; Davidson and Guiness; U. of MD Diamondback 11-8-63; MCSCS Newsletter February 1963; *Plessy v. Ferguson,* 163 U.S. 537 (1896); Blade 6-11-67; Blade editorial 6-18-63; Blade 8-23-64; *Yellin v. United States,* 374 U.S. 109 (1963); Horowitz; BBB; Baron and Friedman; Madison; Key; *Everson v. Board of Education,* 330 U.S. 1 (1947).

55 "one of the reasons that caused many of our early colonists" - Blade 6-25-62.
55 "in the presence of God" - Freedom Writer Spring 2004; *Everson.*
55 "the support and maintenance of public Protestant teachers of piety" - Baron and Friedman.
56 "with religious solemnity" - Madison.
56 "broke the hearts...Communism fear[ed]" - Blade 7-2-62.
56 "enter into thy closet" - Matthew 6:6, Holy Bible.
56 "Parents...can surely have a word of prayer" - Blade 6-30-62#2.
57 "the danger of encroachment" - Gaustad; Davidson and Guiness.
57 "and this be our Motto" - Key; MCSCS Newsletter January 1963.
57 The Warren court - For Madalyn's case, it was comprised of Earl Warren, Arthur Goldberg, Byron White, Hugo Black, Tom C. Clark, Potter Stewart, William O. Douglas, William Brennan, and John Marshall Harlan.

Chapter 10 ~ The Most Hated Woman in America

Unpublished sources: Interviews; FBI report 8-15-62; FBI report 8-15-62; FBI memo 8-22-61; Western Historical Manuscript Collection, University of Missouri-St. Louis; transcript of MMO speech, 8-25-62; ltr MMO to Hoops 5-30-62; ltr MMO to Hoops 1962, ca. mid-September; reconstructed ltr MMO to Hoops ca. March 1963; ltr MMO to Hoops assumed 6-25-62; ltr MMO to Hoops 7-31-62; ltr Cromwell to MMO 11-23-62.

Published sources: MLWG; Murray Newsletter ca. December 1963; The Liberal September 1962; Phila. EB 7-2-63; MCSCS Newsletter March 1963; AR Mag November 1964; Newsletter on the Murray Case 6-25-62; MCSCS January 1963; Life 6-19-64; Ripsaw August 1963; Blade 4-7-64; Anthony.

59 New Era Book Shop - according to the FBI, George Meyers, chairman of the Communist Party in Maryland, met with Madalyn in New York on June 25, 1962 to discuss her disclaimer from the Welfare Department. Meyers brought up the possibility of her running the New Era bookstore. She "reacted favorably and suggested it might be set up near Johns Hopkins University... [its] purpose was to sell Communist literature and serve as a place where new...party members might be recruited. The book shop is completely controlled and dominated by the CPUSA." The Party would put up $2,000 to start it and pay Madalyn $50 a week. Communist Party USA leader Gus Hall called the store a "blind" for the Party, and warned Meyers that Madalyn should not "control" it, and that its funding should be kept secret. Arrangements were made for Madalyn to meet some Communist publishers in New York to establish credit. Meyers stated that Madalyn's "$3 per month contribution to the CP...would continue...as long as she remained employed" by the bookstore. She would soon fall out with George Meyers over her views on the fight against the McCarran Act, among other things.
      Later, when Madalyn was denying any association with the Communist Party, she told the Baylor historians that it was Bill who pushed the book store, and found and rented the storefront himself.
59 a crazy quilt of organizations - Madalyn formed a hodgepodge of accompanying publications as well. Her first organization was the Skeptics of Maryland, formed on January 13, 1961 (Pup appeared from the dining room and announced loudly to an elderly visitor, "They are talking about overthrowing the government of the United States!"). Next, she formed the Maryland Committee for Separation of Church and State and its newsletter of the same name; then she put out the *Newsletter on the Murray Case* and the *Murray Newsletter;* she formed Other Americans, Inc. and a newsletter of the same

name; she took over the *Free Humanist* magazine from Lou Alt and soon launched *American Atheist* magazine. Alt turned over to her his Freethought Society of America to her (along with his library) in 1963, and she then formed a newsletter called *A Voice of Reason*. In 1964 she formed the International Freethought Society. *American Atheist* magazine was actually launched in the early 1960s as *The American Atheist - A Journal of Reason*, but didn't come out with any consistency until 1975. The organization American Atheists was founded in 1963 but not incorporated for more than a decade.

By the end of her life, Madalyn had founded the above organizations and publications plus the Gustav Broukal Press and the American Atheist Press, had inherited and incorporated the United Secularists of America, had helped form United World Atheists, and had launched and/or incorporated Poor Richard's Church of American Atheists, the American Atheist Centre, the American Atheist General Headquarters, Inc., the Society of Separationists, and the Charles E. Stevens American Atheist Library and Archives. Others, such as the Gay Atheist League and Prison Atheist League, were closely affiliated with American Atheists. The Maryland Committee for Separation of Church and State, Other Americans, the International Freethought Society, Poor Richard's Church of American Atheists, University Students for Atheism/University Student Atheists, Atheists In America, and United Atheist Women, had fallen by the wayside.

Her publications at the end had boiled down to *American Atheist* magazine and the *American Atheist Insider's Newsletter*, but along the way had formed, in addition to the above, *Tax-the-Church Newsletter*, *Society of Separationists Newsletter*, *Poor Richard's Reports*, *Poor Richard's Newsletter*, *American Atheists' Newsletter*, the *American Atheist Center Newsletter*, and others. During the 1980s *American Atheist* magazine for a time used the French revolutionary calendar, so some issues were labeled Prairial, Messidor, Thermidor, Fructidor, and so on, until the scheme was declared a disaster.

60 "offensive to our individual liberties and our freedom of conscience" - Blade 4-7-64.
60 wrote Walter Hoops - Madalyn wrote Hoops that she had 25 years' work experience, but actually her job history during the period of her lawsuit and Socialist activity was spotty. She was fired from the Social Security Administration in summer 1960. Her defection trip to France took place in August. She returned in September, and began drawing unemployment. The Woodbourne episode began then. She filed suit in December 1960. She became ill in April 1961 — about the time unemployment benefits ran out — and entered the VA hospital, telling a confidante later that you could get unemployment benefits extended up to six more months if you were sick. The illness stretched to six months, until September 1961. Shortly after her discharge, she got a job with the Baltimore Welfare Department. She was fired six months later, on May 16, 1962, shortly after she filed her appeal. She never held another job. Between 1960 and 1962, she reportedly authored a pornographic novel under the pseudonym Rey Anthony.
61 "the most hated woman in America...anathema to millions" - Life 6-19-64.

Chapter 11 ~ "You got your wish, Spider"

Unpublished sources: Interviews; MFY; FBI memo 2-7-61; ltr MMO to Scholl 1-14-63; ltr Scholl to Whitten 2-13-63; reconstructed ltr MMO to Hoops ca. March 63; reconstructed ltr Hoops to MMO, ca. May 1963; ltr MMO to Hoops 3-22-63.

Published sources: Eve. Sun 6-25-64; MLWG; MCSCS Newsletter November 1962; MCSCS Newsletter January 1963; PB October 1965; Ripsaw January 1963; Blade 10-8-62; MCSCS Newsletter March 1963; Life 3-15-63; MCSCS Newsletter February 1963; Sun 4-10-64; Blade 4-9-63; Blade 3-25-63; OA Newsletter March 1963; MCSCS Newsletter April 1963; OA Newsletter April 1963; Life 4-13-63; MCSCS Newsletter November 1962.

64 "You got your wish, Spider" - MLWG p. 8; MFY p. 13.
64 "Letters from Christians" - PB October 1965 p. 70.
66 "religious leaven" - Life 3-15-63.
66 "taking away the right of a free people" - Sun 4-10-64.
67 "fine real estate" - OA Newsletter April 1963.
67 "I cringe...all too human" - MCSCS Newsletter March 1963.
67 "find God to be sadistic, brutal" - Life 4-13-63.
67 "Mother's talent to infuriate" - MLWG p. 105.

Chapter 12 ~ June 17, 1963

Unpublished sources: Interviews; ltr Hamilton to Schruben 9-27-96; ltr Cope to Waller, 8-18-63.

Published sources: Blade 6-17-63; Toledo Times 6-18-63; Phila. EB 7-2-63; Sunday Oklahoman 8-17-63.

68 "when presented . . . neither aiding nor opposing" - Blade 6-17-63.
68 "turn every church into a hospital" - Toledo Times 6-18-63.
69 "advance the philosophy of materialism" - Phila. EB 7-2-63.
69 "ain't a dang thing anybody can do" - Sunday Oklahoman 8-17-63.

Chapter 13 ~ In Government We Trust

Unpublished sources: Interviews; open ltr Whitten to MMO 1-13-64 ; FBI Airtel 7-29-64; ltr Scholl to Whitten 2-13-63.

Published sources: The Liberal February 1964; Murray Newsletter n.d., ca. late 1963; MLWG; HA 7-9-64; The Realist September 1964; Baltimore American 11-3-63; Murray Newsletter December 1963; HA 6-1-66; HA 12-4-65; HA 3-22-67; Eve. Sun 6-20-66; Eve. Sun 4-6-64; Blade 4-7-64; WP 4-8-64; Blade 4-1-64; Blade 4-14-64. Focus on Asian Studies; www.historyplace.com; *War Against War*; Bexte.

70 *piece de resistance* tax suit - It was captioned *The Murray Family v. the State of Maryland* and the *Murray Family v. the Archdiocese of the Roman Catholic Church of Maryland.*
72 accused their government of infiltrating - And rightly; the government created secret files on thousands of Americans.
72 "Americans don't think of themselves as doing that" - *War Against War.*
73 "citizen instruction" -Blade 4-14-64.

Chapter 14 ~ Get That Bitch!

Unpublished sources: Interviews; MM&BAB 22; ltr MMO to Buttram 3-31-64; ltr Cree to members 7-14-64; MM&BAB; ltr GDY to Woodworth 1-12-90; EBMM.

Published sources: MLWG; The Realist September 1964; Ripsaw July 1964; AA Mag July 1964; unlabeled clip ca. May 1964; Blade 5-26-64; unlabeled clip, hand dated 6-2-64; unlabeled clip in AA Mag June 1964; Sun 7-23-64; unlabeled clip 6-22-64; Ripsaw August 1963; Ripsaw July 1964; The Volcano 9-24-68; News American 6-28-64; PB October 1965; Washington Daily News 6-24-64; Blade 6-21-64; Life 6-19-64; HSB 6-25-64; HA 6-25-64; Sun 6-24-64; Time 7-3-64; unlabeled clip, date of 6-27-64 extrapolated; Sun 6-27-64; HA 12-4-65; Eve. Star 7-5-64; Blade 7-2-64; HSB 7-20-64; Murray Newsletter 7-2-64; HA 9-15-64; News American 8-4-64; unlabeled clip 7-3-64; News American 7-2-64; WP 7-1-64; New York Post 7-3-64; Sun 10-3-64; Eve. Sun 8-1-64; OA Newsletter August 1964; CAMMO; AAS 1-27-85; Progressive World August 1964; IIA 7-9-64; HA 8-19-64; HA 8-18-64; News American 1-22-65; Eve. Sun 8-15-64; Blade 7-23-64; Eve. Sun 7-22-64; Negri.

76 complaint should have been filed in juvenile [court] - Madalyn was twisting the truth; the complaint was properly filed in criminal court because Madalyn refused to waive a jury trial.
77 the Fourteenth Amendment's equal protection clause - "No state shall make or enforce any law which shall abridge the privileges or immunities of citizens of the United States; nor shall any state deprive any person of life, liberty, or property, without due process of law; nor deny to any person within its jurisdiction the equal protection of the laws."
79 "You Christian, you Christian" - unlabeled clip 6-22-64.
80 "nice brick Colonial" - PB October 1965 p. 74.
80 "We are fleeing for our lives" - Sun 6-24-64.
80 "maybe they will begin to love Jesus" - HA 6-25-64.
80 "simply because we were who we were" - Bill specifically remembered a visit Madalyn received in Hawaii from Communist Party USA leader Gus Hall.
81 11-count indictment - Seven of the counts were for assault, though Madalyn would claim more in the years to come.
81 "[let them] go at it" - PB October 1965 p. 72.
82 "It's going to take a pretty big man" - PB October 1965 p. 70.
82 "splendid and brilliant" - AA Mag July 1964 p. 2.
83 "true friend" - Murray Newsletter 7-2-64.
83 "our members" - OA Newsletter August 1964.
83 "command presence" - CAMMO Vol. 1 p. 19; AAS 1-27-85 contains another observation of Madalyn's command presence.
84 the indictments - The extradition order now included two more counts to Madalyn's indictment, for a total of 13.
84 new passports - Madalyn applied under the name Madalyn Evalyn Murray-Mays.

Chapter 15 ~ Training School for Boys

Unpublished sources: Interviews; Peoria County records; ltr DRW to ARS 5-26-02; ltr DRW to ARS 3-25-02.

Published sources: Klein.

87 pretty, dark-haired girl - The child, a son born in the spring of 1965, was given up for adoption.

Chapter 16 ~ The Switzerland of Mexico

Unpublished sources: Interviews; ltr Lamont to MMO 11-23-64; FBI airtel 8-20-65; FBI airtel 9-14-65; MFY; ROH FBI file p. 28, 29, 31, 32, 14, 11; FBI urgent teletype 9-18-65; FBI urgent teletype 9-21-65; FBI airtel 9-24-65; ROH birth certificate; ROH death certificate; marriage certificate ROH and Helen Bisher Aug. 1953.

Published sources: Sun 9-15-64; MLWG; HA 10-22-64; AA Mag July 1964; Sun 10-3-64; unlabeled clip 10-3-64; HA 12-4-65; HA 10-15-65; HSB 10-6-64; WP 9-16-64; HA 9-15-64; The Realist September 1964; HA 8-18-65; WP 2-5-65; News American 1-22-65; HSB 7-23-65; Murray Newsletter ca. December 1963; The News, Mexico, D.F. 10-1-65; HA 6-1-66; SAEN 12-28-99; Chi Trib 2-26-52; Mexico City Times 9-24-65; FWST 6-24-78; North America Gazeteer n.d.; Sun 6-25-65; HSB 6-11-65; HSB 7-21-65; HA 9-2-65; Blade 8-30-66; unlabeled clip 8-21-65; Sun 8-25-65; Blade 9-27-65; HSB 9-24-65; Blade 9-22-65; The News, Mexico D.F. 9-27-65; Eve. Star 9-26-65; Mexico City Times 12-16-65; Blade 9-26-65; unlabeled clip 10-22-64.

88 "controlled experiments" - MLWG p. 143.
88 "muckraking" - unlabeled clip 10-22-64.
88 "any problems Bill has are caused by his mother" - HA 10-22-64.
89 "There's a real aloha spirit here" - HSB 10-6-64.
89 Fairness Doctrine - Madalyn also asked for the "preferential rates" afforded religious programs that paid.
89 "cage me like an animal" - HA 12-4-65.
90 "The Switzerland of Mexico" - Mexico City Times 9-24-65.
90 Otumba - The district was named after a battlefield near Mexico City where Cortez slew 20,000 Indians.
91 "He could tell good tales ... 13 years old" - FWST 6-24-78.
91 war wound - There is no evidence O'Hair saw action in any war. However, he liked the story, telling Bill later that he'd gotten wounded by a "Jap shell." (MLWG)
92 "the good FBI" - On O'Hair's marriage license, his occupation was an "adjuster in the electrical industry," but he had a investigative agency under his own name in a neighboring county.
93 continued offering information - Wilson Quarterly editor Stephen Bates cites a 1966 FBI memo saying O'Hair was never an employee; but he was an informant until the agency rejected him in 1962. The FBI got a call on June 24, 1965 from the Continental Hilton in Mexico City, saying that the Murrays were there and about to run out of money, that Madalyn had been granted asylum in Cuba, and was planning to leave soon, "balking slightly" at leaving Garth behind in Honolulu. So it seems likely that O'Hair had a contact who knew Madalyn was there.
93 freethought' wasn't controversial - The FCC deliberately "misunderstood," Madalyn felt. The issue was separation of church and state, not freethought. But her Freethought Society had filed the complaint, so she was stuck with their interpretation.
93 "[They] embarrassed me" - HA 9-2-65.
95 "They should be pinning medals on me" - HSB 9-24-65.
95 "I've found ... A man. I mean a real man." - Mexico City Times 9-24-65.
95 "John David" - Eve. Star 9-26-65.
95 "she left Blake college an empty shell" - The News, Mexico, D.F. 10-1-65.

Chapter 17 ~ Rebels without a Cause

Unpublished sources: Interviews; statement of Welchman 12-15-64; Woodford Co. Sheriff's Department offense report 12-14-64; statement of Frisby 12-16-64; statement of Hawkins 12-16-64; statement of Woods 12-16-64; combined statement of Litterly, Meador and Durst 12-15-64; statement of Frost 12-16-64; statement of Peddicord 12-14-64; arrest records Welchman, Waters, and Peddicord; Testimony before Woodford Co. Grand Jury 1-1-65; Illinois Bureau of Criminal ID and Investigation Crime Lab report 3-1-65; Coroner's autopsy report 12-14-64; Pleading in Woodford Co. Circuit Court 12-15-64; PPD complaint report 12-13-64; Evidence Room documents; Motion to Proceed with Adjudication of Guilt 4-1-99; note "Jerry" to Durst n.d.; date stamps on back of photos in DRW papers; ltr report by Durst 2-14-65; report Gay/ Rowland to Durst 2-17-65.

Published sources: PJS 3-26-65; PJS 1-8-65; Bloomington Pantagraph 12-16-64; PJS 1-25-65; PJS 2-12-65; PJS 2-27-65; PJS 2-18-65; PJS 3-22-65; unlabeled clip 3-26-65; Bloomington Pantagraph 3-26-65; unlabeled clip Decatur, IL 3-26-65; PJS 3-23-65; Bloomington Pantagraph, 3-23-65.

Chapter 18 ~ Extraordinary Freedom in Texas

Unpublished sources: Interviews; Lindsay Clinton paper 2-25-97; MM&BAB; TS letter to recipients 4-70; Mike W_____ affidavit 2-26-77; ltr Irv to Blois 12-15-65; ltr Blois to Hoops 1-8-66; letter Cree to members 7-14-64; Pleading 2-14-66.

Published sources: Fehrenbach; Schulz; Lawrence; Mexico City Times 12-16-65; MLWG; Blade 9-26-65; Blade 9-27-65; WP 9-27-65; HA 11-11-65; Twair; Clinton obituary AAS 10-7-04; HA 10-6-65; unlabeled clip 10-7-65; St. Louis Post-Dispatch 10-7-65; News American 10-23-65; Tax-the-Church Newsletter December 1965; Blade 10-27-65; National Guardian 11-13-65; unlabeled clip 11-11; unlabeled ltr 6-25-65; Blade 11-7-65; Eve. Sun 10-20-65; unlabeled clip 10-18-65; Toledo Times 10-19-65; PRRN November 1971; The News, Mexico, D.F. 9-30-65; FWST 6-24-78; AA press release 4-78; AAS 3-14-78; Mays-Murray Newsletter January 1966; Blade 10-20-65; HA 12-4-65; WP 12-5-65; Mays-Murray Newsletter December 1965; Tax-the-Church Newsletter January 1966; Blade 10-10-66; unlabeled clip 4-11-66; HA 12-12-66; Baltimore American 11-3-63; Murray Newsletter December 1963; Murray Newsletter April-May 1964; Sun 6-27-64; Murray Newsletter 7-2-64 (from Honolulu); Blade 7-2-64; AA Mag July 1964; HA 7-9-64; Eve. Sun 8-1-64; Blade 12-18-64; Blade 1-8-65, undated money appeal ca. March 1965; Toledo Times 7-29-65; HSB 9-24-65; Tax-the-Church Newsletter November 1965; unlabeled clip 4-11-66; WP 4-11-66; HA 6-1-66; Blade 8-30-66; Eve. Sun 6-12-66; Eve. Sun 6-20-66; Catholic Register 9-14-66; SOS Newsletter August/September 1966; Baltimore Evening News 10-10-66; Newsletter November 1968; Oklahoma City Times 11-1-68; PRR December 1968.

99   "one of the finest women I have ever known" - The News, Mexico, D.F. 9-30-65.

99   one of the first families of San Antonio - Maury Maverick's great-grandfather, Sam Maverick, gave the language a synonym for "nonconformist," as he refused to brand his longhorns, and any unbranded stray became a "maverick." Sam Maverick was a Yale graduate who helped draft Texas' constitution and signed its Declaration of Independence.

99   ministers of the gospel - Texas also barred banks from incorporating.

101   "Madalyn, will you keep quiet" - FWST 6-24-78.

103   plenty of her paychecks - The ownership of the Winford Road house was unclear. Madalyn insisted she helped pay the mortgage, but apparently she was not on the deed obtained for the Mayses by her cousin Homer Lacy.

104   another landmark lawsuit - The church tax suit was as snarled as Madalyn's other affairs. It had been dismissed in Baltimore's circuit court and gone to the Maryland appeals court in September 1965, with the Crees and the Freethought Society still on the caption page despite Madalyn's feud with them. A decision was expected in February 1966. The Crees lost a second church tax suit in July, *Cree v. U.S.* and *Machiz.* This suit, to make churches pay income tax on non-church related businesses, was filed with money from the Baltimore Freethought Society, but donations slipped and ownership of the building on Calvert Street became unclear because of Madalyn's attempts to regain control.

Chapter 19 ~ Mothers and Daughters

Unpublished sources: Pleading 2-14-66 in MEM, *Trustee, et al and Lemoin Cree, et al v. Comptroller of the Treasury, State of Maryland;* Pleading 4-26-66; Interviews; undated draft of Mad Madalyn; ltr ROH to RMOH 10-12-77; Mike W_____ affidavit 2-26-77.

Published sources: Tax-the-Church Newsletter January 1966; DT 2-11-66; Blade 10-10-66; unlabeled clip 4-11-66; WP 4-11-66; Eve. Sun 6-12-66; WP 4-6-66; unlabeled clip 6-23-64; SOS Newsletter August/September 1966; MLWG; HA 3-22-67; HA 6-1-66; Baltimore Evening News 10-10-66; HSB 4-7-67; PRRN November 1971.

104   oral arguments took place - Madalyn's attorneys in the church tax suit kept being replaced, fragmenting the strategy; that and her personal and family troubles weakened the suit. After Kerpelman

was fired and Greenstein quit, she hired a female attorney from Cleveland, probably recommended by Mae Mallory; several other firms also worked on the suit.

104 "As soon as I become...ensconced" - DT 2-11-66.
105 "register Negro voters" - WP 4-11-66.
106 "I don't want to live here as a deadbeat" - HA 6-1-66.
106 "I would rather see the house eaten up in legal costs" HA 6-1-66.
108 The adoption went through. Robin's name was legally changed to Robin Eileen Murray O'Hair. Later, when it became fashionable, she would hyphenate her two surnames.

Chapter 20 ~ Poor Richard and Devil O'Hair

Unpublished sources: Interviews; ltr MMO to Western Voice 8-1-66; ltr Buttram to MMO 9-6-66; ltr MMO to Buttram 5-30-67; ltr MMO to Buttram 2-10-69; Gospel Tract Society press release 3-19-77; ltr Buttram to MMO 6-8-67; ltr MMO to Buttram 11-3-67; two ltrs 3-29-67 between MMO and Buttram; ltr Freudiger to ARS 7-17-01; Walter Martin Religious Infonet debate with MMO n.d.

Published sources: PRR 3-68; Elkins; Donahue 11-6-67; unlabeled clip AAS ca. spring 1996; AAS 8-27-68; Newsletter November 1968; AAS 1-7-69; SOS Newsletter January 1971; unlabeled clip 11-19-74; SOS Newsletter June 1971; SOS Newsletter December 1969; SFChron 1-27-70; Houston Chronicle January 1970; Blade 1-26-70; Time 2-9-70; AAS 1-28-70; AAS 3-14-78; DMN 2-22-70; Poor Richard's Church of American Atheists brochure 1-27-70; AAS 6-18-71; Houston Chronicle 3-8-70; AA Mag June 1988; St. Paul Dispatch 5-19-75; Des Moines Sunday Register, n.d. 1967; TS April 1970.

110 another suit against the FCC - It was filed in U.S. District Court in Washington, DC.
110 "systematically denied [her] the use" - Des Moines Sunday Register, n.d. 1967.
110 equal time on all of them - If religious programs paid to be on a station, SOS would pay the same rate.
110 "non-stop unchallenged monologue" - SOS Newsletter June 1971.
110 "Come on, Madalyn" - unlabeled clip ca. 11-19-74.
111 "unique opportunity for giving" - SOS Newsletter December 1969.
111 "religion for atheists" - SFChron 1-27-70; Blade 1-26-70; Time 2-9-70.
112 "Devil O'Hair" - Madalyn's new entity received a variety of confusing monikers. Besides Poor Richard's Universal Life Church, Richard labeled the Sinclair house the National Headquarters of American Atheism, and the O'Hairs printed letterhead called it Poor Richard's Church of American Atheists. One news article called it the Centre for Atheism. (The actual name American Atheists, Inc. wasn't official until late 1976 or early 1977.) Madalyn later told with amusement a story that the inspiration for the church's name came when they'd called Richard's mother to tell her they were married, and the old lady wailed, "Oh, my God, poor Richard!"
112 "We've drawn from the Mormons" - SFChron 1-27-70.
112 From this seed would come the...atheist university - Richard O'Hair reported that support had come in for the university: an 82-year-old man in Chicago set up a $40,000 trust fund for SOS when he died. A man in Texas deposited $40,000 in a Swiss bank account which SOS would get when he died. An 83-year-old woman in Washington was deeding her $18,000 house to SOS. A man in Florida gave SOS $10,000 outright. But it was impossible to tell if the figures were true.
113 "Between appearances I managed to force her" - Newsletter November 1968.
113 "She would be ironing for the family" - Newsletter November 1968.
113 "it's something I manufacture inside" - Elkins.
114 "She'll be saying, just as sweet," - Houston Chronicle 3-8-70.

Chapter 21 ~ Houston, We've Got a Problem

Unpublished sources: ltr MMO to 4 recipients 8-16-71; ltr Buttram to MMO 11-21-68; ltr MMO to Buttram 11-3-67; ltr MMO to Sauter 2-17-68; ltr Buttram to MMO 12-30-68; ltr MMO to Buttram 2-2-69; ltr Buttram to MMO 2-7-69; ltr MMO to Buttram 2-2-69; ltr MMO to Buttram 2-10-69.

Published sources: Newsletter February 1969; Oklahoma City Times 11-1-68; PRR 12-68; Burgess; AAS 12-27-68; Blade 12-28-68; Newsletter February 1969; Dallas News 3-8-69; AAS 8-9-69; Blade 2-10-69; Gainesville Sun 2-8-69; AAS 8-7-69; DMN 8-7-69; Church/State News Service press release 19-23-69; AAS 9-11-69; Blade 9-17-69; AAS 11-29-69; PRRN, November 1971; SOS Newsletter February 1971; Words Magazine 1976.

116 "Why is she so afraid of prayer" - Blade 2-10-69.

116 "I've had my tit in the wringer since I was 14" - Gainesville Sun 2-8-69.
116 "historical first...publicly hugged" - Newsletter February 1969.
117 "directing or permitting religious activities" - AAS 8-9-69; DMN 8-7-69.
117 "a Christian, sectarian bias" - AAS 8-7-69.
117 irresistible irony - A hearing on NASA's motion to dismiss her suit was set for late November 1969 in Austin. Madalyn got her tribunal — two district judges and a Fifth Circuit Court of Appeals judge.
117 "What's the Matter With Prayer?" - PRRN, November 1971.

Chapter 22 ~ To Mother, with Love

Unpublished sources: Interviews; ltr MMO to BM 5-7-69; Mike W_____ affidavit 2-26-77; Complaint 1-30-71, Peoria Co. records; PPD report 1-31-74.

Published sources: MLWG; AAS 11-29-69; AAS 11-26-69; Blade 11-28-69; Houston Chronicle 3-8-70; DMN 2-22-70; St. Petersburg Times 3-7-70; TS April 1970.

118 Bill had married Julie Susan remarried in 1968 as well.
118 "I really wanted to kill her" - MLWG pp. 233–34.
118 pacifist group - Madalyn said this was called Quakers Underground, and that he'd organized another one called American Deserters Co-op.
118 "He's been through so much" - Houston Chronicle 3 8 70.
119 "Poor Richard is now out on a $300 bond" - DMN 2-22-70.
119 quoted a drunken paean - This happened in February 1970; after speaking on her radio show about Poor Richard's Church, Madalyn launched into an intimate tribute to Richard's "amber eyes," his "incredibly warm and soft [lips]...He, it was, who saw...my struggle...Patiently, he would sit there as I paced the room, back and forth, going over the assaults against human dignity...I raved and I wept. I stormed...But those big warm hands upon me as I fell, exhausted, on his shoulder, always gave me a renewal of energy." Alcohol was her reward, comfort, solace, distraction, recreation, and celebration, and compensation for the immense energy spun off in her customary 18-hour workdays.
119 "To her, every mountain is a battle...temper tantrums." - Houston Chronicle 3-8-70.
119 Betty Waters - Betty changed surnames frequently, toggling among Waters, Hunt, and, briefly, Plumley; one of her street names was Kris Ann Gray.
119 Hepatitis C - Even friends were skeptical of this story; by the time Waters told it, Hepatitis C was an epidemic in prison from dirty needles and sex.

Chapter 23 ~ Dr. O'Hair

Unpublished sources: Interviews; MM&BAB; ltr MMO to GDY 9-15-72; ltr Chastain to students 9-13-72; ltr MMO to GDY ca. January 1973; note MMO to recipients, attached to 8-3-76 ltr to IRS commissioner DC Alexander; ltr JGM to GDY 6-26-73; ltr MMO to GDY 6-27-73; attachment to ltr MMO to GDY 2-22-74; ltr GDY to "top level ministers" 8-23-71; American Atheist Church Articles of Incorporation ca. 6-11-71; AA Fall Classes ad 1972; ltr Stein to Arno 1-29-72; ltr Lewis to Stein 2-3-72; ltr Lewis to Stein 2-25-72; ltr Stein to Lewis 3-6-72; ltr Lewis to Stein 4-20-72; ltr Stein to MMO 6-6-68.

Published sources: BBB; Blade 9-24-70; SOS Newsletter October 1970; http://history.nasa.gov.; DT 11-15-74; CAMMO; Blade 3-8-71; AAS 2-9-71; SOS Newsletter June 1971; PRRN July 1971; MLWG; PRRN November 1971; DT 9-29-71; PRRN January 1972; AAIN January 1976; AAC Newsletter June 1977; DT 9-9-72; PRRN September 1971; AA Mag August 1975; Santa Barbara News-Press, 12-9-72; PRRN January 1973; Miami Herald 1-20-73; PRRN February 1973; Newsweek 5-22-72; Minneapolis Star 8-26-72; Austin Citizen 7-26-76; DT 8-1-76; St. Paul Pioneer Press 12-2-72; AR Mag May-June 1984.

121 "no ascertainable legal interest" - Blade 9-24-70.
122 "nothing but crude propaganda" - CAMMO Vol. I, p. 2.
122 "tersely dismissed" - Blade 3-8-71.
122 latest prayer bill - This was the Wylie Amendment to permit prayers in public schools.
122 traveled and spoke tirelessly - Sometimes Madalyn tripped herself up; in one interview she wanted The Pill at every bus stop, "issued free by the federal government," but later said about pro-lifers, "It is time American women told government...to get the hell out of our bedrooms."

123   she wrote the president - Though the teachers were paid privately, not by the university, Madalyn said the state was partly funding the program by printing the classes in the course schedule, violating the First Amendment.

123   Avro Manhattan - In 1972 Madalyn secured exclusive rights for SOS to publish Manhattan's 18 books in the U.S.

124   American Atheist Church - DeYoung's ordinees were "officers," not ministers, in an Army of Emancipation, similar to the Salvation Army. He'd given Madalyn the position of colonel. His church had 150 scattered members.

124   It was Gordon Stein - Stein was closely associated with Paul Kurtz as director of Kurtz' Center for Inquiry, and editor of *Free Inquiry* and *American Rationalist*.

124   *The Atheist Viewpoint* - Included in the bibliography were a sampling of atheist magazines, plus works by Annie Besant, Chapman Cohen, Ira Cardiff, Bertrand Russell, Joseph Lewis, Friedrich Nietzsche, Avro Manhattan, H. G. Wells and, of course, Madalyn herself. Stein would eventually edit the *American Rationalist*, *Free Inquiry*, and numerous encyclopedias of atheism, freethought, and unbelief.

Chapter 24 ~ Money and Power

Unpublished sources: ltr MMO to Whom This Concerns 7-15-72; ltr MMO to entities 6-24-72; ltr MMO to GDY 9-15-72; ltr MMO to Graham 9-22-72.

Published sources: PRRN April 1972; PRRN January 1972; PRRN March 1972; Valley Morning Star 1-11-99; PRRN February 1972; Smith and Jones; Minnesota Daily 10-23-72; Miami Herald 9-30-72; Texas Observer 10-20-72.

125   "Now, how-in-the-hell can you expect" - PRRN February 1972.

126   The board would consist of six people - One of these six was to be, she said, a "front" for DeYoung. It was unclear why he needed a "front"; possibly because of the bad press his Institute had received, or his lack of as viable a tax-exempt organization as CESAALA. She wanted DeYoung's help controlling the elderly Fahnestock, who was, she said, represented by a treacherous duo comprised of his attorney and his gardener.

126   get her union-scale fees - Madalyn wanted AFTRA rates.

127   "out and out liar" - Miami Herald 9-30-72.

127   "a fine art form" - Minnesota Daily 10-23-72.

127   "It is natural for women to hate God" and all the hate mail quotes - Texas Observer 10-20-72. The non-hate letter ("Do you ever listen to Billy Graham?") was included in this collection.

Chapter 25 ~ Give Me a Child the First Seven Years

Unpublished sources: Interviews; ltr MMO to GDY 1-5-73; ltr MMO to GDY 2-26-73; ltr MMO to GDY 7-1-72; ltr MMO to GDY 7-21-72; ltr MMO to GDY 3-25-74; ltr MMO to GDY 2-26-74; ltr MMO to GDY 11-25-72; MM&BAB; EBMM; ltr MMO to GDY 12-2-72.

Published sources: McCollum; MLWG; Atheist Heroes and Heroines; LAT 12-28-72; PRRN January 1973; Santa Barbara News-Press, 12-9-72; Miami Herald 1-20-73; PRRN February 1973; SF Chron 11-29-72; Yuma, AZ News 12-18-72; State Journal 12-10-72; Cincinnati Enquirer 2-2-73; PRRN March 1973; PRRN November 1971; Oldmeadow; Dallas News 9-20-70; DT 6-25-71; DT 9-9-72; SOS Newsletter August 1972; AAS 10-11-72; Le Beau; VF May 1991.

131   "civil religion...work or else" - Santa Barbara News-Press, 12-9-72.

131   "I asked for a sign" - SF Chron 11-29-72.

131   "when we took prayer out of the schools" - PRRN, November 1971.

133   World Atheist Conference - Richard disapproved and refused to go, and their visas were denied. To those who had signed on, Madalyn blamed the religious Nixon White House and Indian government, but her private writings indicted that both she and GORA had simply missed some bureaucratic deadlines with the Indian embassy.

133   "Nazarite oath" - Dallas News 9-20-70.

Chapter 26 ~ We Are The Leaders

Unpublished sources: Interviews; ltr MMO to GDY assumed January 1973; ltr MMO to GDY 1-5-73; ltr MMO to GDY 3-28-73; ltr MMO to GDY 1-22-74; ltr MMO to Rockefeller 2-23-74; ltr MMO to

Hinman 2-28-74; ltr MMO to GDY 2-1-74; ltr MMO to GDY 5-10-74; ltrs GDY to IRS 5-15-74; ltr GDY to Texas Bar 5-22-74; ltr GDY to Minnesota Secretary of State 5-29-74; ltr Rocca to GDY 6-18-74; ltr MMO to GDY 5-7-77.

Published sources: St. Paul Pioneer Press 12-2-72; PRRN January 1973; SOS press release 4-8-73; PRR February 1974; PRR April 1974; PRR n.d., vol 9 #8.

134   fired from his job - DeYoung worked as an information writer for the Minnesota Department of Highways.

Chapter 27 ~ $3 and Half a Pack of Salems

Unpublished sources: Interviews; Complaint 1-14-71 (assault); Complaint 7-21-71 (patronizing a prostitute); Complaint 5-1-72 (unlawful use of weapons); Complaint 6-18-73 (unlawful possession of cannabis); Complaint 6-25-73 (disorderly conduct); Complaint 6-27-73 (battery); Arrest 11-26-73 (armed robbery); Warrant 4-25-72 (Theft); PPD police reports 1-31-74 by officers Lee, Wight, Esslinger, Rigg, Krider, Daniels, Thode, Hunt, Lock, Hill, Graham, Walker, Singley, Poynter, King, Davis, Galloway, Wilson, Ganda, Gerontes, and Dailey; evidence sheet 3-7-74; Springfield Crime Lab report 2-28-74; Chicago Toxicology Lab report 2-11-74; evidence sheet 2-14-74; PPD Case Data Sheet 2-4-74; FBI record for Steven Hunt/Douglas/Plumley/Waters 6-26-73.

Published sources: PJS 2-2-74.

Chapter 28 ~ Please Come Home

Unpublished sources: Interviews; ltr MMO to GDY 8-15-72; ltr MMO to Whom This Concerns 7-15-72; A Message From the Most Famous Atheist, April 1989; ltr MMO to entities 6-24-72; ltr MMO to GDY 9-15-72; PRR June 1973; ltr MMO to GDY 7-8-73; PRR August 1973; ltr MMO to GDY 2-1-74; undated ltr MMO to GDY, ca. 1974; ltr MMO to Stein 8-5-74; ltr Stein to MMO 8-11-74; ltr MMO to Stein 8-15-74; ltr Hirsch to Marek 8-22-74; ltr Stein to MMO (refused) 8-31-74; ltr Dumont to ARS 8-17-03; contract-will 12-24-74; note MMO to Buttram 12-24-74.

Published sources: Freedom Under Siege; PRR January 1974; Austin People Today Magazine December 1975; PB October 1965; Texas Ranger February 1970; AA Mag June 1988; Blade 1-30-75; Blade 3-1-75; Pearl Magazine March 1975; Biography News January-February 1975; LAT 2-10-75; PB March 1975; NYT 2-13-73; PRR April 1973; SAEN 1-7-99; AAS 1-10-99; Free Inquiry winter 2000-2001.

140   "absolutely ashamed" - PRR January 1974.
140   "How in the hell" - PRR January 1974.
140   blamed Paul Kurtz - Kurtz, in fact, would become what Madalyn aspired to. Like her, he was a war veteran, though he'd ended up anti-Communist. He had a Ph.D. from Columbia University. He would soon join the faculty of the State University of New York at Buffalo, to remain for 25 years, teaching philosophy. He would found several magazines — *Free Inquiry*, the *Skeptical Inquirer*, the *Scientific Review of Alternative Medicine*, among others — and Prometheus Books, a successful publishing house. He authored numerous books and founded several organizations, among them the Council for Secular Humanism and the Campus Freethought Alliance. His Center for Inquiry in Amherst, New York became the umbrella organization for his many interests, all of which thrived over the years, including the Center's well-managed libraries. By the end of the twentieth century, his yearly budget was more than $11 million, and his organizations had branches over the world. His achievements were all precisely what Madalyn dreamed of in her letters and diaries. Though they were enemies, he wrote a tribute to her in *Free Inquiry*.
141   "dawning on everyone" - Pearl Magazine March 1975.
141   "The real Holy Trinity" - Biography News January-February 1975.
142   "not as President but as a humble servant" - PB March 1975.

Chapter 29 ~ The American Atheist

Unpublished sources: Interviews; ltr Thoren to recipients 10-5-76; MM&BAB; EBMM; transcript of MMO talk at American Rationalist Federation convention 8-25-62.

Published sources: MLWG; PB October 1977; AA Mag July 1964; NYT Mag 5-16-76; Eve Sun, 4-19-77; AAIN March 1976; AAIN November 1976; AAIN December 1976; AAS 5-11-80; AAS 1-7-69; SOS

May 1975 (no header); SOS "Letter" June 1975; PRRN September 1975; PRRN November 1975; notice of Detroit chapter formation 11-16-75; AAS 10-27-75.

143 "An astonishing collection of tramps and nuts" - MLWG p. 248.
145 the third house at 4203 Medical Parkway - Madalyn also paid off the Shoal Creek house, which gave her great satisfaction, but she told only her diary — not members or the IRS — that she'd used corporation money to pay for her home.
145 "For the first time in ten years" - MLWG pp. 258–59.

Chapter 30 ~ "Somebody, somewhere, love me"

Unpublished sources: Interviews; MM&BAB; ltr Kent to Massen 6-2-93; ltr MMO to Jones 6-29-93; Mike W_____ affidavit 2-26-77; EBMM; ltr NYT Mag to MMO 2-2-76, ltr White House to MMO 2-4-76; ltr MMO to McG_____ 2-8-75; ltr MMO to McG_____ 6-17-75; ltr McG_____ to MMO 2-16-75; ltr students to SOS chapters summer 1976; Divorce Petition 1-30-6.

Published sources: MLWG; AAIN September 1976; undated DT clip marked "early 1974" by CAH; AAIN June 1980; Houston Chronicle 5-21-80; two unlabeled clips dated 1-9-76 and 2-12-76; AAIN May 1976; AAIN January 1977; undated portion of Special Bulletin, ca. 11-9-76; AAIN January 1976; AAIN February 1976; WTH 2-12-76; AAIN April 1976; SAEN 3-14-76; DT 11-15-74; DT 3-31-76; TS March 1976; Le Beau; AAIN March 1976; *Walz v. Tax Commission of City of New York,* 397 U.S. 664 (1979); CRS Report on History of Federal Taxes for Congress, January 19, 2001; www.philanthropicadvisor.com; www.irs.gov; Eastland; Speech transcript from the 25th National Convention of American Atheists; Ryan.

147 "on five different occasions" - AAIN September 1976.
147 "We always had servants . . . Nigger Leftridge" - AAIN June 1980.
147 "I had never been so unhappy" - Houston Chronicle 5-21-80.
147 "to feel better about myself" - MLWG p. 264.
148 "I abandoned my house" - Houston Chronicle 5-21-80.
148 46% of the vote - In her diary, Madalyn recorded 43%. As it turned out, she persuaded Bill to slip quietly back to Austin and use her printing facilities for his campaign while running the magazine. It was one of many reconciliations between them.
148 she wanted to be addressed as Dr. O'Hair - In 1975, the South Texas College of Law changed its LLB degrees to JDs — Doctor of Jurisprudence. It was retroactive, so technically Madalyn could call herself "Dr." though few other attorneys did.
149 "No one really cares if she shows up" - DT 11-15-74.
149 "Sometimes I think they would take better care" - DT 3-31-76.
150 Tax Reform Act of 1969 - This act dealt with philanthropy and not specifically churches. In *Walz v. Tax Commission,* decided in 1970, the Supreme Court upheld the granting of tax exemptions "to religious organizations for religious property used for religious purposes." These exemptions specifically did not violate the First Amendment.

Chapter 31 ~ Signs of Distress

Unpublished sources: ltr MMO to Lauritsen 5-20-76; ltr MM to Jakel 7-5-76 ; ltr Kotula to MMO 4-26-76; "Account of Recent Changes in the New Jersey Chapter, ca. 2-12-78; MM&BAB; ltr Second Foundation to recipients 10-31-77; ltr Manhattan to GDY 10-25-76.

Published sources: AAIN April 1976; The Match! Summer 1990; AA Mag May 1977; AAIN May 1976; Austin Citizen 7-26-76; AAIN August 1976; AAIN September 1976; AAS 5-6-76; Austin Citizen 10-1-76; AAIN December 1976; AAIN November 1976.

152 "instruments of torture" - Austin Citizen 10-1-76.

Chapter 32 ~ "Mama, you need to be dead"

Unpublished sources: Interviews; DRW handwritten statement re Betty's prostitution; Dean Hunt ltr of recommendation for DRW; ltr DRW to ARS 4-29-02; ltr Wilkerson to ARS 8-28-02; ltr DRW to ARS 5-26-02; PPD police report 12-6-77; trial transcript ca. 3-1-78.

Published sources: PJS 1-28-78; PJS 2-1-78; PJS 2-28-78; PJS 3-2-78; PJS 4-14-78; PJS 2-15-80; SAEN 12-28-99.

Chapter 33 ~ Living on Memories

Unpublished sources: Interviews; Murray petition 1-20-77; ltr MMO to Buttram 11-26-77; MM&BAB; MFY; ltr MMO to Goedde 5-23-83; ltr MMO to "old friends" 5-15-77; EBMM; Divorce Petition 1-30-6; ltr Neal to MMO 3-1-77.

Published sources: AAIN December 1976; Austin Citizen 12-22-76; Houston Post 1-17-77; AAIN January 1977; Kansas City Star 3-19-77; Buttram press release 3-19-77; AAIN January 1977; others); Buttram press release 4-19-77; CAMMO; undated portion of Special Bulletin, ca. 11-9-76; Austin Citizen 12-22-76; AAS 12-22-76; MLWG; SAEN 1-7-99; Austin Citizen 7-26-76; Le Beau; undated appeal, O'Hair For Council Committee, ca. January 1977; AAS 2-8-77; DT 2-8-77; Austin Citizen 2-16-77; unlabeled clips 2-27-77 and 2-28-77; SOS Secretary's Report 1978; AAS 10-15-98; AAC Newsletter April 1977; Chi Trib 4-14-77.

157   "severely damaged" - Austin Citizen 12-22-76.
158   retained all the property - Madalyn silenced his claim on the Shoal Creek house as homestead by buying him out for $7,500, loaned interest-free by Indiana member Lloyd Thoren. This was kept from the members.
159   "[it] used to be a fine time" - Austin Citizen 12-22-76.
160   "tramp" MLWG p. 267. Madalyn's diary reflected no explanation of why she and Robin had to make the dramatic move out of their home into an apartment instead of simply giving the vacant apartment to Garth and Hauk.
160   Madalyn...refused to come out - This was Bill's account. Madalyn's diary says the lovers were having difficulty and that Hauk's mother was hostile.

Chapter 34 ~ "Shut your mouth, woman!"

Unpublished sources: Interviews; ltr BM to recipients 6-27-77; ltr MMO to GDY 5-7-77; ltr Buttram to MMO 2-5-75; ltr MMO to Golly 2-25-91.

Published sources: MLWG; Let Freedom Ring; AAC Newsletter May 1977; PB October 1977; AAC Newsletter March 1977; SOS Secretary's report 1978; AAC Newsletter July 1977; CAMMO; Austin Citizen 12-13-77; AAS 7-28-77; Pittsburgh Post-Gazette 9-13-77; Austin Citizen 5-5-77; AAC Newsletter June 1977; AAIN June 1977; NYT 7-28-77; unlabeled clip 6-3-77; DMN 2-2-75; FWST 2-2-75; Minneapolis Star 2-8-75; Blade 2-8-75; Chi Trib 2-8-75; Le Beau; Austin Sun 7-23-77; Fresno Bee 7-27-77; unlabeled clip 10-30-77; AAIN August 1977.

162   "running up trying to save me" - Pittsburgh Post-Gazette 9-13-77.
162   "a common spectacle" - Austin Citizen 5-5-77; AAS 7-28-77.
162   "Dr. O'Hair has degrees in..." - AAC Newsletter June 1977.
162   "35 years of experience in government" - AAIN June 1977.
163   "Russian red Communism" - DMN 2-2-75.
163   "You're no Princeton, you know!" - DMN 2-2-75.
163   "Shut your mouth, woman!" - Minneapolis Star 2-8-75.
163   "Who's running this show" - FWST 2-2-75.
164   a third attempt to remove "under God" from the Pledge of Allegiance - Madalyn filed pledge suits when she wanted a high-profile cause.

Chapter 35 ~ The Demon-Directed Damsel

Unpublished sources: Interviews; Fenster registration packet, 1977; MM&BAB; ltr MMO to Kotulas 8-22-77; ltr Buck to fellow atheists 8-7-77; ltr Buck to MMO 9-12-77; ltr Richards to AA chapters 2-9-78; ltr Thurmond to Harrington 9-22-77.

Published sources: Herndon; Harrington; MLWG; Bob Harrington Heartbeat (promo sheet) September 1977; Austin Citizen 10-26-77; unlabeled clip Sunday Express News 8-14-77; Meeting Satan Herself; unlabeled clip 10-30-77; CAMMO; SOS Secretary's Report 1978; Eve. Sun 9-2-77; Austin Citizen 9-2-77; Austin Citizen 9-1-77; Salmon River News 9-18-90; WP 9-10-77; New Orleans States-Item 10-25-77; AAIN September 1977; AAIN November 1977.

165   "Demon-directed damsel" - Fight to the Finish.
165   "Jesus, Jesus, Jesus" - unlabeled clip Sunday Express News 8-14-77.

165   "they'd go into shock" - An American Atheist member attending one performance, H. B. Dodd, became so incensed when she bellowed, "Fuck all of you goddamn Christians!" that he strode to the stage and burned his AA membership card.
166   "Satan's whore" - Meeting Satan Herself.
166   "worked them into a frenzy" - Meeting Satan Herself.

Chapter 36 ~ "I'm going to take a two-by-four and hit Austin between the eyes."

Unpublished sources: Interviews; ltr MMO to Golly 2-25-91; MM&BAB; ltr Second Foundation to recipients 10-31-77; ltr Second Foundation to recipients 11-18-77; WVJ ad 11-25-77; ltr MMO to RMOH 2-8-80.

Published sources: MLWG; AAIN November 1977; Austin Citizen 11-2-78; AAS 10-26-77; AAS 10-27-77; Austin Citizen 10-27-77; Austin Citizen 10-26-77; DT 10-27-77; AAS 1-19-69; AAS 10-30-77; Le Beau; CAMMO; WTH 11-4-77; Council minutes 11-3-77; Austin Citizen 11-3-77; DT 11-4-77; Houston Post 11-4-77; Austin Citizen 11-4-77; WTH 11-5-77; Austin Citizen 11-7-77; DMN 11-6-77; Austin Citizen 11-15-77; AAS 11-17-77; DT 11-21-77; Austin Citizen 11-16-77; FWST 11-16-77 (2 articles); Houston Chronicle 11-16-77; Austin Citizen 12-13-77; Austin Citizen 12-14-77; AAS 12-14-77; AAS labeled "late 1977" by CAH; Life 6-19-64; BBB; Elkins; Current Biography Yearbook 1977.

170   "deformed idiot with one eye" - MLWG p. 280.
171   "charging in like a Brahma bull" - Austin Citizen 10-27-77.
171   "clean up this city" - Austin Citizen 10-27-77.
171   "quite charming city" - AAS 1-19-69.
171   "I'm going to take a two-by-four" - AAS 10-30-77.
171   "put a stop to every single religious thing" - AAS 10-30-77.
171   "ran a little 12-year-old girl out of town" - Austin Citizen 10-27-77.
171   "My life is so empty" - Austin Citizen 10-27-77.
172   "No matter what Bill Murray does" - DT 10-27-77.
173   "I'm sorry it is necessary" - WTH 11-4-77.
173   $1 million in punitive damages - In March 1978, Madalyn filed suit in federal court, saying the officials were essentially providing financial aid to Catholics by shielding them from gambling laws.
173   "Dr. O'Hair and I have to vote" - Austin Citizen 12-13-77.
173   "Even if I have to put a red light" - Austin Citizen 12-13-77.
174   "She wants the three wise men removed" - unidentified clip labeled "late 1977" by Center for American History.
175   "knight in shining armor" - Current Biography Yearbook 1977.

Chapter 37 ~ Bloody Sunday

Unpublished sources: Interviews; Account of Recent Changes in the New Jersey Chapter ca. 2-12-78; Marsa Appeal Fund ca. 11-6-78; MM&BAB; ltr JGM to Marsa 1-4-78; ltr MMO to NJ chapter 2-8-78; ltr MMO to Marsa 1-21-78; ltr MMO to Marsa 2-8-78; "Constructive Criticism" list ca. 2-11-78; undated open ltr from Conrad; ltr MMO to Goldie 3-7-78; EBMM; ltr Schapiro to MMO 9-27-92; SOS Secretary's Report 1978; statement by Fox, 2-12-78.

Published sources: Houston Post 12-22-77; Austin Citizen 1-3-78; Austin Citizen 1-10-78; Austin Citizen 11-16-77; FWST 11-16-77 (2 articles); Houston Chronicle 11-16-77; Austin Citizen 12-13-77; Austin Citizen 12-14-77; AAS 12-14-77; DT 1-24-78; CAMMO; Metuchen Home News 11-13-78; AA Mag September 1977; AA Mag December 1977; AA Mag March 1978; AAIN March 1978; AAS 1-10-99; AA Mag April 1978; Detroit News 10-3-78; Austin Citizen 2-14-78; FWST 6-24-78; AAS 3-14-78; AAIN April 1978; Sunday Des Moines Register 5-8-80; Houston Post 10-23-77; Austin Citizen 10-27-78; Austin Citizen and AAS undated clips, assumed 10-25-78.

175   "simply hates my guts" - DT 1-24-78.
175   "sits on its collective ass" - DT 1-24-78.
177   "fleas on the dog" - AAIN March 1978; AAS 1-10-99.
177   "We will deal with such detractors ruthlessly" - AAIN March 1978.
177   Bloody Sunday - It was also called the New Jersey Massacre.
177   "I was not prepared" - CAMMO Vol. 1 p. 18.

178 "Houston Post" - DeYoung's letter said Madalyn was "held in contempt by the larger atheist community for her disgraceful and self-aggrandizing behavior." Houston Post 10-23-77.

Chapter 38 ~ "Some human dignity, some grace in living"

Unpublished sources: Interviews; ltr MMO to Fenster 10-27-78; application to Phillips Exeter 10-31-78; ltr MMO to Exeter 9-13-78; ltr MMO to GDY 7-1-72; ltr MMO to GDY 7-21-72; ltr MMO to GDY 9-15-72; ltr MMO to GDY 11-25-72; ltr MMO to TJS 9-13-78; ltr MMO to RMOH 9-13-78; ltr MMO to RMOH 9-21-78; ltr MMO to RMOH 9-25-78; ltr MMO to RMOH 9-24-78; ltr JGM to RMOH 9-18-78; ltr JGM to RMOH 9-14-78; ltr MMO to RMOH 9-14-78; ltr MMO to RMOH 9-18-78; ltr MMO to RMOH 9-26-78; ltr MMO to RMOH 10-1-78; ltr MMO to RMOH 10-5-78; ltr MMO to RMOH 10-4-78; ltr MMO to RMOH 10-19-78; ltr MMO to RMOH 11-14-78; ltr MMO to RMOH 12-2-78; ltr MMO to RMOH 9-27-78.

Published sources: CAMMO; SFChron 4-10-78; Freedom From Religion Foundation press release 4-12-78; NYT 5-17-78; Blade 5-6-78; WTH 5-6-78; Austin Citizen 4-18-78; Austin Citizen 4-20-78; DT 12-12-78; Austin Citizen 6-2-78, Austin Citizen 12-13-77, Austin Citizen 12-14-77, AAS 12-14-77; Austin Citizen 1-10-78; WTH 3-17-78; Austin Citizen 3-17-78; WTH 3-17-78; AAIN August 1978; AAIN September 1978; AA Mag May 1979; Edamaruku; SAEN 1-7-99; AAIN January 1978; WP 12-21-77; WP 3-9-78; Atlanta Journal-Constitution 5-8-02.

179 "At first sight [she] looks like just another ugly," - CAMMO Vol. 1 p. 19.
179 "A cause organization has no business" - Blade 5-6-78.
179 "The man is almost hysterical" - Austin Citizen 4-18-78.
179 this one for malicious prosecution - Madalyn had missed the deadline to produce witnesses for her assault suit against Murchison, so the charges were dropped. Since Murchison had witnesses who said there had been no assault, Madalyn's charges were malicious.
181 "without any furniture and with no washbasins" - Edamaruku.
182 a spoof that she said defamed her - The magazine centerfold showed a nude woman with her legs spread and a man's profile peering into the gap while he asks if this is where the daddy bee puts his pollen. The caption read, "Sex Education is an Atheist plot" and an arrow pointing to the woman's head said, "Madalyn Murray."

Chapter 39 ~ Circle the Wagons

Unpublished sources: Interviews; ltr AA to members 5-1-87; ltr MMO to RMOH 11-30-78; ltr MMO to RMOH 12-2-78; ltr MMO to RMOH 12-7-78; ltr MMO to RMOH 9-27-78; ltr MMO to Golly 2-25-91; ltr MMO to RMOH 2-2-79; ltr MMO to RMOH 11-16-78.

Published sources: CAMMO, Austin Citizen 10-31-78, DMN 1-24-00, AAS 10-25-78; Austin Citizen 3-17-78; Austin Citizen 10-27-78; Austin Citizen undated clip, assumed 10-25-78, Austin Citizen and AAS undated clips, assumed 10-5-78; AAS 10-25-78; Austin Citizen, 11-2-78; AAS 5-28-78; AAS 12-9-78; National Enquirer 10-30-79; Circle the Wagons appeal; AAIN January 1979; SAEN 1-7-99; DT 12-12-78; Austin Citizen 4-20-78; AAIN December 1978; Fresno Bee 12-17-78; WTH 12-17-78.

183 a jury of their peers - She requested that four proceedings against her, including her disruption of the City Council, be halted, and that state salaries be withheld from the judge and court personnel. When her request to halt the proceedings was denied, she asked for a federal jury trial, not being able to get a fair one in Texas. That request went to the Supreme Court.
183 Cofer denied her motion - He also denied a request that the matter of his recusal be put before the administrative judge of the judicial district.
183 hidden in the camper of Gerald Tholen - Tholen and his wife, Gloria, would be steadfast, ever-giving supports for Madalyn over the next decade, helping with everything from magazine writing and layout to organizing chapters to painting and building library shelves. They had pitched in when Bill left the last time, and were constantly driving to Austin to volunteer wherever they were needed.
185 had put everything in Garth's and Robin's names - Even the diamonds belonged to Robin, she wrote the girl — "remember that in case you are ever asked!!"

Chapter 40 ~ The We of Us

Unpublished sources: Interviews; ltr MMO to RMOH 4-20-79; MMO:AMTR ms.; ltr MMO to RMOH 1-27-79; ltr MMO to TJS 1-28-79; ltr TJS to MMO with grade report 2-7-79; ltr Exeter to RMOH 2-12-79; ltr MMO to Andover 1-30-79; ltr MMO to Andover 2-13-79; ltr MMO to RMOH 1-30-79; ltr MMO to RMOH 2-17-79; ltr MMO to RMOH 9-13-78; ltr MMO to RMOH 10-4-78; ltr MMO to RMOH 4-20-79; ltr MMO to RMOH 4-30-79; ltr MMO to RMOH 5-16-79; ltr JGM to subscribers 5-24-79; ltr MMO to RMOH 4-24-79; ltr MMO to RMOH 4-26-79; ltr MMO to RMOH 9-19-79; ltr MMO to RMOH 9-10-79; ltr MMO to RMOH 9-10-79#2.

Published sources: CAMMO; MLWG; SAEN 1-7-99; WTH 2-6-79; Blade 2-17-79; AA Mag May 1979; DT 4-19-79; FWST 6-9-79; Blade 6-12-79; Chi Trib 6-12-79; WTH 6-12-79; AAIN July 1979; AAIN June 1979; AAIN March 1979; Houston Chronicle 5-21-80; Denver Post 10-4-79; AAS 7-15-79; AAS 5-11-80; AAIN August 1979.

186   "I could see the blows hit Garth" - CAMMO Vol. 2 pp. 6–7.
187   "The poor bastard owes everything to his mother" - CAMMO Vol. 2 p. 7.
190   "Everyone in the family" - AAIN August 1979.

Chapter 41 ~ The Anti-Christer

Unpublished sources: ltr Conrad to Stein 7-19-80; ltr Conrad to Hoops 2-26-82; ltr Stein to Conrad 3-23-82; ltr Conrad to Stein 3-16-82; ltr Brown to Kent 3-29-82; ltr Kent to Brown 3-31-82; ltr Kotula to Torcaso 4-10-82; ltr Richards to Musy 4-12-82; ltr Stein to Nigel 5-24-82; ltr Scholl to Stein 6-15-82; ltr Conrad to unk., presumably Stein 6-16-82; ltr Chambers to Stein 2-1-83; ltr Irv to Stein ca. March 1983; ltr Viers to Stein 10-1-83; ltr Thorne to Musy 11-25-91; ltr MMO to RMOH 9-19-79; ltr AA to members 5-1-87; MFY 14-15.

Published sources: CAMMO; Eve. Sun 9-18-79; AA Mag December 1979; DMN 9-18-79; DT 9-18-79; Dallas Times Herald 9-18-79; DT 9-20-79; Winnipeg Free Press 9-25-79; DT 10-2-79; Austin Citizen 10-4-79; DT 10-4-79; WTH 10-4-79; Blade 10-6-79; AAIN October 1979; AAIN November 1979; Austin Sun Dec. 16, 1979; AR Mag May-June 1984; DT 2-7-80; AA Special Bulletin 9-24-79; DMN 1-24-80; DT 1-24-80; AAIN February 1980; AAS 2-25-80; DT 2-21-80; DT 2-28-80.

190   "October mass on the Washington mall" - Madalyn filed one suit against the Pope and another against Cecil Andrus, Secretary of the Interior, and William J. Whalen, director of the National Park Service under whose purview the mall fell. Though there were four masses, in Boston, Philadelphia, Chicago, and DC, the first three were in venues owned by cities, where "the Murray/O'Hair team" had no residence. The mass was on federal land. They merely protested the others.
191   "If the Pope wants to say a Mass" - CAMMO vol. 3 pp. 9, 11–12.
192   collaborating on an exposé about her - The collaboration grew out of a blizzard of letters concerning Madalyn. A few consulted are listed above.
193   Two weeks later, in a summary judgment - Shortly after Judge Roberts' ruling, the Supreme Court threw out Madalyn's bid to use the misdemeanor charge of disrupting the city council prayers to challenge the Texas Constitution. She had argued that her trial should be in a federal rather than a state court because of Texas' "supreme being" requirement. State court was "like an all-white court prosecuting a Negro," she said.
      Article 1, Section 4 of the Texas Constitution stated, "No religious test shall ever be required as a qualification to any office, or public trust in this state; nor shall anyone be excluded from holding office on account of his religious sentiments, provided he acknowledge the existence of a Supreme Being."
193   "that skinny, goggle-eyed son-of-a-bitch" - AAS 2-25-80.
193   "Christian beater" - AAS 2-25-80; DT 2-28-80.

Chapter 42 ~ A Double Murder

Unpublished sources: Interviews; GGM; ltr DRW to ARS 5-26-02; Search Warrant Affidavit 3-23-99; Pre-sentence investigation report 6-26-95.

Published sources: PJS 2-15-80; PJS 2-16-80; Official Detective February 1981; AAS 4-18-02.

194   disfiguring him - There was no report of Gibbs' eye being gouged out in the autopsy report; however, his eyes were horrifically swollen. Waters revealed to another woman that he persuaded some jail

buddies to torture another kid by tying him to his bare metal bunk and lighting a fire under it, and then putting him in the shower, but turning on hot water instead of cold.

Chapter 43 ~ *In Vino Veritas*

Unpublished sources: Interviews; ltr MMO to RMOH 2-7-80; ltr MMO to RMOH 10-11-79; report card and ltr TJS headmaster to MMO 4-28-80; MM&BAB; ltr BM to MMO 4-13-80; Karr trial notes; ltr BM to Buttram 10-1-80; ltr Buttram to BM 10-6-80; ltr Buttram to BM 7-31-80.

Published sources: MLWG; National Enquirer 10-30-79; Denver Post 10-4-79; DT 4-11-80; DT 2-26-80; FWST 2-26-80; Blade 2-26-80; DT 2-16-80; Rocky Mountain News 4-15-80; WTH 5-21-80; Atheists On Trial 11-79 (AA funding appeal); Austin Citizen 8-13-80; DT 1-21-81; DT 4-15-80; AA News bulletin Floreal 5-1980; AAIN May 1980; Dallas Life 3-13-83; Sun 3-2-97; DT 5-10-80; Texas Methodist 8-21-80; AAS 5-11-80; WTH 5-10-80; CAMMO; WP 5-21-80; WTH 7-26-80; Houston Chronicle 5-21-80; Moral Majority paper 6-18-80; TM October 1980; WTH 8-23-80; FWST 8-24-80; Life's Answer July 1980; DT 6-17-80; FWST 6-14-80.

197 "And ye shall eat the flesh" - AA News bulletin Floreal 5-1980; AAIN May 1980.
198 "Just in time for Mother's Day" - May 10, 1980.
198 "that religious scam money" - CAMMO Vol. 1 p. 9.
199 "My eyes did not turn glassy" - WP 5-21-80.
199 "for ever dropping her off" - Sun 3-2-97.

Chapter 44 ~ Greystone Sanctuary

Unpublished sources: ltr MMO to unk. 3-10-80; MFY; Interviews.

Published sources: AAIN May 1980; AAIN August 1980; WTH 7-17-80; Blade 1-20-81; Dallas Observer 2-24 to 3-4 -99; CAMMO; MLWG; Houston Chronicle 7-28-84; Blade 5-15-82; AAIN February 1981; DT 2-4-81; AAIN March 1981; AAIN December 1980.

202 DAR - Madalyn said she wanted into DAR so she could sue to remove their God-oath for membership (she planned a similar move on the Veterans of Foreign Wars), but it is likely that the legitimacy for which she'd always yearned was a stronger attractant.
202 ruled against Madalyn in...O'Hair v. Cooke - Not because the god-belief requirement wasn't substantive, but for other reasons, probably to do with her insistence on writing the briefs herself and guiding the attack. Before it reconsidered, the court said she lacked standing to claim her First Amendment rights had been violated. One of her questions was political, and "nonjusticiable." She wasn't entitled to stop the criminal and civil proceedings against her in Texas. She lacked standing to freeze any court officials' salaries. She'd suffered no monetary damages.
203 'unspeakable' things - These were never specified, but Irv later wrote Gordon Stein that, during a hysterical, screaming reminiscence of how Irv and "our no-good hag of a mother" had "connived to rob me of all my possessions in Baltimore," Madalyn had accused him of numerous outrageous acts, including having sexual relations with their mother. Madalyn's diary mentions reluctantly taking Irv in because he was destitute and still had three years before he could draw Social Security.

Chapter 45 ~ High Hopes for Mankind

Unpublished sources: Interviews; ltr MMO to Kent 4-28-81; ltr Kent to MMO 5-2-81; ltr Kent to Massen 4-21-93; ltr Kent to Massen 8-3-93; ltr Kent to ARS 10-27-00; ltr Kent to Massen 5-10-93; ltr Kent to ARS 10-27-00; ltr MMO to Kent 8-6-89; Kent affidavit for Steamer, n.d., ca. April 1993; MMO:AMTR; ltr MMO to Johnson 4-12-83; EBMM; ltr MMO and JGM to LA chapter 12-9-81; ltr JGM to James 11-9-81; ltr MMO to "friend" 12-9-81; ltr Kent to Sauter 10-6-84; ltr Ennis to MMO 2-22-82.

Published sources: AA Mag April 1981; AAIN January 1981; CAMMO; AAIN February 1981; AAIN March 1981; Setting the Record Straight; Houston Chronicle 7-28-84; Blade 5-15-82; AAS 5-13-82; AAIN October 1981; AAIN December 1981; AA Mag August 1981; Blade 1-13-80; AAIN January 1980; SFChron 12-14-81.

205 "no one or nothing but...me" - Setting the Record Straight.
205 "dignity and decorum" - AAIN October 1981.

Chapter 46 ~ Mommie Dearest

Unpublished sources: Interviews; ltr Irv to Stein 3-4-83; letter Stein to Irv 3-30-83; MFY; ltr Irv to Stein February-March 1983; MM&BAB; ltr Ennis to MMO 2-22-82; ltr MMO to Kirzner and Adams 3-3-82; ltr MMO to Goedde 12-3-82.

Published sources: AAIN September 1981; AR Mag January -February 1983; Third Coast April 1983; Blade 10-26-81; WP 3-10-82; Houston Chronicle 7-28-84; Blade 5-15-82; AAS 5-13-82; Chi Trib 6-26-82; Washington Times 11-15-82; Dallas Life 3-13-83; Corpus Christi Caller 11-15-82; Faith Bulletin April 1984; AAIN March 1983; Woodworth tract ca. 7-2-82.

206 The American Rationalist - Walter Hoops and Paul Kurtz were contributing editors.
207 "definitive work on intellectual freedom" - Third Coast April 1983.
207 "Being an atheist is first" - Third Coast April 1983.
208 "discuss the violent overthrow" - Faith Bulletin April 1984.
209 "two fat pigs waiting for the spike" - Washington Times 11-15-82.
209 "I have told the truth" - Corpus Christi Caller 11-15-82.
209 "I don't know whether it's anger" - Dallas Life 3-13-83.

Chapter 47 ~ Enemies

Unpublished sources: Interviews; ltr MMO to Scholten 2-3-83; ltr MMO to Johnson 4-12-83; ltr Johnson to Nelson 4-25-83; ltr Viers to Stein 10-1-83; ltr Rush to ARS 5-26-01; Re Jackson, et al, 12-16-88, case # 87-1441-K(IEG); ltr Richardson to MMO 8-18-83; ltr Frankel to chapters March 17, 1985; transcript, MMO speech, 8-13-83.

Published sources: AR Mag January-February 1983; Setting the Record Straight; TS February 1989; The Atheist Cult; Houston Post 3-16-83; Dallas Life 3-13-83; Atlanta Weekly 6-12-83; Tallahassee Sentinel 6-12-83; DMN 5-28-83; Washington Times 6-26-83; AA Mag June 1983; PJS 8-12-83 .

212 "gray-skinned, blue-lipped freaks" - AR Mag January-February 1983.
212 "publications are cheap and meaningless" - Setting the Record Straight.
213 blizzard of... appearances - The swell of news around Bill's book, and the 20th anniversary of *Murray v. Curlett*, had roused a perennial aggravation for the FCC — an old rumor that Madalyn Murray O'Hair had a petition to get religious broadcasting off the air waves. Desperate, the agency put out a news bulletin at the end of May: there was NO petition. Please stop sending letters and counter-petitions. (It had started in 1976 with a talk Madalyn gave at a Texas college; a magazine, *Texas Churchman*, covered the talk, and misreported that her NASA suit had mutated into a plan to "ban all mention of God on television and radio, including services of worship." That spread like wildfire through the religious community, and was an ever-yielding gold mine for preachers raising money. The FCC was still dealing with it into the 21st century, as the rumor flared anew via the Internet.)
213 John Glover Jackson - Jackson was a professor-lecturer at Newark College of Arts and Sciences, and a visiting professor at Northeastern Illinois University in Chicago.

Chapter 48 ~ Hustler

Unpublished sources: Interviews; ltr MMO to Viers 9-27-83; ltr RMOH to Kurtz 8-6-83; ltr MMO to Johnson 1-18-84; ltr Kent to Massen 1-9-94; Judgment July 27, 1984 in *O'Hair v. Hill*; ltr Moll to ARS 10-25-00; ltr MMO to Zaluba 2-23-84; ltr Frankel to chapters 3-17-85.

Published sources: Miami Herald 7-23-83; WP 9-10-77; WP 12-21-77; WP 3-9-78; Miami Herald 7-14-83; Miami Herald 9-20-83; WP 9-20-83; Miami Herald 10-23-83; Miami Herald 10-14-83 [2 articles]; Miami Herald 10-20-83; Miami Herald 10-21-83; Miami Herald 11-24-83; Miami Herald 8-8-86; Hustler November 1983; Houston Chronicle 10-28-88; Miami Herald 11-1-83; Miami Herald 11-2-83; Miami Herald 11-3-83; Miami Herald 11-6-83; Miami Herald 11-9-83; Miami Herald 11-16-83; Miami Herald 11-18-83; Miami Herald 11-24-83; Miami Herald 12-9-83; Miami Herald 12-10-83; WP 12-10-83; Miami Herald 2-9-84; Miami Herald 3-15-84; Miami Herald 3-19-84; WTH 4-2-84; Miami Herald 3-29-84; Miami Herald 1-3-84; Boston Globe 12-5-84; Boston Globe 12-6-84; Boston Globe 12-7-84; Boston Globe 12-13-84; ; Richmond Times-Dispatch 3-3-84; AAIN December 1983; Miami Herald 12-3-84; Time 2-10-97; Faith Bulletin March 1984; Hustler February 1984; Continuing Attacks on MMO n.d., ca. December 1983; 12-15-83 AA funding appeal; Setting the Record Straight; TS February 1989; Dallas News 3-16-84; Houston Chronicle 3-14-84; Wm. J. Murray Faith Ministries letter April 1984; AAIN:

September 1983; AAIN January 1984; AAIN March 1984; AA Mag June 1984; Wall Street Journal undated clip, ca. 4-84; Richmond Times-Dispatch 8-31-83; Blade 4-21-84; Houston Chronicle 7-28-84; Dallas Times Herald 12-16-84; Milwaukee Journal 4-27-86; AAS 1-10-99.

214 Flynt and Madalyn finally hatched a deal - Their deal was that 40% of American Atheists' 40,000 copies had to sell, and they were hovering at 38%.
215 "Pornography thrives" - WTH 4-2-84; Miami Herald 3-19-84.
216 trusted in the corridors of power - Bill was using his mandate to educate (he was urging people to read the Constitution and Bill of Rights to know what their rights were, and what school authorities could and couldn't do).
216 Harrington as speaker - Harrington was now an ex-preacher, director of something called the Institute for Balanced Living, and "official motivator" for a chiropractic association.
216 "domineering manner has driven away" - Wall Street Journal undated clip 4-84, Arnold Via papers.
218 "perhaps the most famous three-named person" - Milwaukee Journal 4-27-86.

Chapter 49 ~ The Honor Farm

Unpublished sources: Interviews; Government's Notice of Intent to Offer Rule 404(b) Evidence, 1-23-01; Motion to Proceed with Adjudication of Guilt 4-1-99; FBI report 2-8-99 through 2-11-99; DRW Statement re Billy King 4-24-01; DRW confession 1-24-01 through 2-2-01; PJS 4-17-02; Complaints for Reckless Conduct and Battery, Peoria County 8-4-83; Proposed Indictment DRW 9-24-85; FBI report 2-3-99; ltr Karr to ARS 12-9-00; Order of Detention 4-7-00, Gary Karr; Government's Response to Defendant's Motion to Quash Information and Notice of Enhancement under "Three Strikes" Law 8-16-00 re Gary Karr.

Published sources: SAEN 12-28-99; AAS 4-18-02; PJS 11-17-85; PJS 8-14-85.

219 She never knew what happened to the money - Twenty years after Marti's murder, when Cookie got up enough money to buy her friend a headstone, she was told David had never paid the funeral expenses.
220 The last person known to have seen him alive - On January 8, 1984, David had gone out drinking with Billy King and Carl Welchman. The next time anyone saw Billy King, he'd been dead about a week, shot in the body and head. David Waters was a prime suspect. But they could never pin it on him.
221 "had sexual intercourse with [her]" - Order of Detention 4-7-00.

Chapter 50 ~ Where There's a Will

Unpublished sources: ltr JGM to Jones 8-11-85; ltr Jones to JGM 8-26-85; ltr Massen to members May 1986; ltr MMO to Goedde 5-9-86; MMO Will August 13, 1986.

Published sources: AAIN October 1985.

223 never really would tell the members - For example, unaware of the flood of money, in May 1986 Jack Massen wrote an earnest appeal to fellow members to get behind Jon Garth and "stabilize" the AA Center. He had given another $10,000, plus pledging 48% of his household income.

Chapter 51 ~ Two Fateful Things

Unpublished sources: Interviews; ltr MMO to Jones 3-21-87; Bringing Down the American Atheist Center, funding appeal ca. April 1987; AA ltr to members 5-1-87; ltr MMO to Golly 2-25-91; Petition against Cox and AAS, n.d., ca. May 1987; ltr JGM to members ca. Summer 1987; ltr Kent to Massen 8-17-93; ltr Thorne to Musy 11-25-91; ltr Lynch to Nalls 9-29-93; MMO will August 13, 1986; Second Amended Counterclaim 12-2-89; ltr Thorne to Johnson 5-19-87; ltr Rush to Musy 8-15-93; ltr Kent to Rush 11-14-93; Complaint for Malicious Prosecution and Civil Conspiracy to File a Malicious Lawsuit 4-11-91; Re Jackson, et al, 12-16-88, case # 87-1441-K(IEG); Complaint 9-27-87; Proposed Settlement Agreement 12-15-88, with attached brief re Johnson's codicil; Johnson Will and codicil; Motion to Strike Exhibit A 2-22-88; Counter Complaint 7-14-8-88; Answer to the Counter Complaint and Affirmative Defenses 9-13-88; Order After Hearing 4-10-90; Order After Hearing Regarding Order to Show Cause, 6-9-93; Affidavit of MMO 7-1-87; Answer 11-30-87; Summary Legal Matters 12-3-91.

Published sources: AAIN September 1991; AAIN October 1991; AA Mag October 1985; AA Mag January 1986; DT 8-12-87; AAS 11-1-93; San Diego Reader 9-8-88, in MMO TS September 1988;

LAT 4-10-89; AAIN March 1987; Setting the Record Straight; MMO TS June 1988; LAT 2-1-90; Affidavit of Johnson 4-11-88, reprinted in TS February 1989.

225   six 501(c)(3) entities - Society of Separationists, American Atheists, Charles E. Stevens American Atheist Library and Archive (CESAALA), American Atheist General Headquarters (called AAGHQ or GHQ), United World Atheists (UWA), and United Secularists of America (USA). At some point, American Atheist Press was incorporated as well.
    It was Byzantine; reportedly, in forming the new corporations, Madalyn found an old promissory note that had never been paid, held by CESAALA against SOS for the Center's building on Hancock. So, through Jon, president of SOS, she had CESAALA foreclose the old note and — voila! — the vulnerable SOS owned nothing and CESAALA owned a building. It later turned out that SOS had loaned money as well as borrowing it; in 1980, Jon Garth had bought the Greystone house with a loan from SOS, and claimed to have paid SOS back. In February 1987, he sold his interest in Greystone to Robin for $10. After the 1987 convention, SOS held its regular board meeting. To dodge any Strobel judgment, they voted to shut down all activities and stop asking for contributions. That way, Madalyn wrote a confidante, Friedman, "whose main concern is simply to harass us, can get a judgment and then wipe his ass on it ... I intend to wind up with about six or eight corporations and any that can be sued will simply be 'shoestring' operations." Her secret plan was to allow the entire organization to die, by paring it down to only publications and the conventions, and retire somewhere with her kids.
    The members knew nothing of these maneuvers; all they knew was what they read in the papers — and they read that on April 30, 1987, Madalyn suddenly closed down the American Atheist Center. The media were swarming; it was reported across the country, including the New York Times, and Madalyn worried that the members would bolt. She couldn't give an explanation yet — the new AAGHQ purchase of the Cameron Road property wasn't complete. All she'd say was, "The American Atheist Center is dead." Out of business, up for sale. The Strobel judge granted SOS a 90-day continuance in May, which helped, and the massive move to Crime-on-the-Hill began.

226   committing fraud - Lynch later said it was possible that millions were being tucked into accounts in Texas, Ontario, Saskatchewan, and New Zealand; he thought will money had been deposited to Cayman Island banks and then moved to Switzerland.

226   "the American taxpayer is a fat sucker" - San Diego Reader 9-8-88.

227   "intelligence instead of religious superstition" - LAT 4-10-89.

227   both closely related to TSC - Subscribers to Truth Seeker magazine were automatic members of NLL.

227   gathered information - At the 1987 convention, Madalyn sent around a flyer asking that anyone who had ever subscribed to Truth Seeker, or been a member of AAAA or NLL, come to her suite. That was what she said later, when her activities at the convention would be called a violation of 18 USC Sections 1961(5) and 1962(b) — a "pattern of racketeering activity."

228   new slate of... officers - Madalyn later said Hervey Johnson had been notified of this meeting, but he denied it, and the letter of notice Madalyn produced had no verification or receipt proving it was ever sent.

228   settlement offer - Hervey Johnson wrote a codicil to his 1987 will. It deleted paragraph 7, which gave all Johnson's TSC stock to AAAA. Now, the stock would stay in his personal estate. Madalyn, informed of the codicil, made the settlement offer, which included voiding the codicil.

Chapter 52 ~ Forever Proletariat

Unpublished sources: Interviews; ltr JGM to JB 7-28-87; ltr AA to EEOC 4-29-94; Forensics report 3-5-01.

Published sources: Sun 3-2-97; WTH 6-18-88; DT 6-20-88; AAS 6-17-88; FWST 6-18-88; AA Mag June 1988; AAS 2-12-88; AAS 1-9-88; DT 1-13-88; AA Mag October 1988; Harte-Hanks Community Newspapers 7-1-93; AA press release 5-2-94; Chi Trib 12-17-88; UPI 4-18-89; UPI 5-26-89; WP 1-28-01; AAIN December 1988; AAIN September 1989; AAIN July 1990.

229   "Jon got a little horny" - Sun 3-2-97.

Chapter 53 ~ Racketeering

Unpublished sources: Interviews; Complaint for Malicious Prosecution and Civil Conspiracy to File a Malicious Lawsuit 4-11-91; Re Jackson, et al, 12-16-88, case # 87-1441-K(IEG); Complaint 9-27-87;

Proposed Settlement Agreement 12-15-88, with attached brief re Johnson's codicil; Motion to Strike Exhibit A 2-22-88; Johnson Will and codicil; Counter Complaint 7-14-8-88; Answer to Counter Complaint and Affirmative Defenses 9-13-88; Order After Hearing 4-10-90; Order After Hearing Regarding Order to Show Cause, 6-9-93; Affidavit of MMO 7-1-87; Answer 11-30-87; ltr Lynch to fellow atheists March 1989; ltr MMO to chapter directors 1-23-89; ltr Tidd to recipients 3-29-89; Musy open letter 6-7-89; ltr GDY to Woodworth 1-12-90; ltr Woodworth to GDY 1-1-90; ltr Rush to Sikos ca. March 1990; ltr Sikos to Woodworth 5-11-89; ltr JGM to Post Office 5-23-89; ltr MMO to Woodworth 5-24-89; ltr Woodworth and Martin to readers 6-19-89; MMO ltr to Post Office 5-23-89; ltr Woodworth to Bearden 4-4-90. A Message From the Most Famous Atheist.

Published sources: Houston Chronicle 12-29-96; MMO TS June 1988; LAT 2-1-90; MMO TS September 1989; TS February 1989; AAS 11-1-93; San Diego Reader 9-8-88; MMO TS March 1989; press release 3-17-89; AA Mag May 1989; San Diego Union 3-25-89; Freedom Writer March 1989; AA Vets Newsletter 4-18-91 [misdated 1990]; unlabeled memo "Update to Atheists, Freethinkers, Separationists, and Media People" 3-11-89; LAT 4-30-89; The Californian 5-6-89; WTH 7-21-90; Setting the Record Straight; American Justice 11-28-01 (video); AAIN April 1981; Woodworth.

233   RICO statute - Madalyn was accused of fraud for disseminating a fake TSC Newsletter; doing it via interstate commerce made it a RICO violation.

233   "when the three of them drove to work" - AAS 11-1-93.

233   His will showed - Johnson directed that administrator Lawrence True, whom he'd known for 25 years, use his estate to keep the Truth Seeker going, expose religion as against reason, and publicize his views on health. Johnson had shunned advice to establish a foundation to shelter assets; now Uncle Sam would get as much as $9 million, said True. And by the time the attorneys and accountants got through, there would probably only be about $5 million left. True quit his job at Security Pacific Bank to work full time on the Johnson estate, taking a one-time fee of $170,000 for his probate work.

Madalyn's challenge of True's appointment snarled the case; with appeals, it would be nearly two years before it was overruled for good.

233   "fine old atheist organization" - MMO TS March 1989.

233   Jackson gave a deposition - Jackson remembered that Charles Smith had given him physical Truth Seeker shares around 1957. He didn't think they were worth anything. They were just scraps of paper he put in a drawer and forgot about. He hadn't seen them since he left New York, many years back. Anyway, he had the impression TSC was bankrupt. He had no idea how many shares TSC was authorized to issue.

When James Hervey Johnson took over TSC, Jackson thought he was just some poor slob trying to keep the organization going. The magazine was sloppy and late and book orders were sometimes ignored. Jackson later came to believe that Johnson had invested whatever was left of the Peet money in the stock market. In fact, this was implied in Johnson's book "How to Make Money in the Stock Market."

Enter Madalyn in 1987, he said. She'd published one of Jackson's Ingersoll Forum lectures and told him it was a "bestseller." She paid him $1,000 a year in royalties. She said she had "an interest" in TSC. In mid-1988, she told him she'd gotten legal possession of TSC, and found Johnson had embezzled funds. She didn't show him any documents, though, or say how she'd gotten control. But since the magazine was a crude, typed sheet full of spelling and typesetting errors, it was clear no corporate money was being spent on it.

234   "This old gal is beating you up" - Houston Chronicle 12-29-96.

234   "Don't fuck with me!" - American Justice 11-28-01.

Chapter 54 ~ Falling Apart

Unpublished sources: Interviews; ltr Lynch to chapter directors 8-9-89; Karr trial transcript; *O'Hair v. Phillips, IRS et al, Cause #A90CA561*; ltr JGM to Jones 7-2-90; ltr JGM to Jones mid 1990; ltr Jones to JGM 7-20-90; ltr JGM to Jones 7-31-90; ltr JGM to Jones 12-11-90; ltr JGM to Jones 6-3-92; ltr JGM to Jones 5-21-93; ltr JGM to Jones 5-31-93; ltr MMO to Jones 6-8-93; ltr MMO to Jones 6-12-93; ltr JGM to Jones 6-18-93; ltr JGM to Jones 6-25-93; ltr RMOH to Jones 6-93; ltr Jones to MMO and JGM 6-15-93; ltr Jones to RMOH 6-93; ltr Jones to JGM 6-25-93; ltr MMO to Jones 6-29-93; ltr JGM to Jones 7-2-93; ltr Jones to JGM 9-6-93; ltr JGM to Jones 10-17-93; ltr JGM to Jones 7-10-94; ltr JGM to Jones ca. 12-93; ltr MMO to Jones 1-28-94; ltr Jones to O'Hairs 3-30-94; ltr Jones to JGM 5-25-94; ltr Jones to JGM 7-4-94; ltr Jones to JGM 7-20-94; untitled, unsigned incomplete missive from either JGM or MMO to members, 8-13-94; ltr unk. to Jones 8-13-94; ltr Jones to O'Hairs 5-4-95; ltr JGM to

Jones 8-26-95; ltr Travis to ARS 4-6-01; ltr Lynch to unk. 10-5-89; ltr Lynch to recipients 3-15-90; Kent affidavit for Steamer, n.d.; Order After Hearing 4-10-90; Complaint for Malicious Prosecution and Civil Conspiracy to File a Malicious Lawsuit 4-11-91; Order After Hearing Regarding Order to Show Cause, 6-9-93; open letter "The Real Truth About American Atheists (From an Ex-employee)" March 1991.

Published sources: UPI 3-1-90; DMN 12-16-87; AAIN July 1990; AAS 3-22-97; AA Vets Newsletter 4-18-91 [misdated 1990]; UPI 4-18-89; UPI 5-26-89; UPI 10-2-89; Dallas News 12-12-89; AAIN December 1990; AAS 11-16-89; AAIN November 1989; Chi Trib 3-20-91; Daily Herald 3-20-91; Chicago Sun-Times 3-21-91; AAS 8-30-91; Houston Chronicle 12-29-91; NYT 8-30-91; AA funding appeal May 1990; Ask the Founders July 1989; Setting the Record Straight; LAT 2-1-90.

Chapter 55 ~ Colleen

"Colleen Kay Smith" is a pseudonym.
   Unpublished sources: Interviews; GGM; Karr trial transcript; FBI report 8-13-99; ltr CKS to ARS 9-7-01; hearing transcript 8-11-99 on Motion to Proceed With Adjudication of Guilt; ltr CKS to ARS 5-17-02; Investigative report 8-19-99; Government's Notice of Intent to Offer Rule 404(b) Evidence, 1-23-01; Motion to Proceed with Adjudication of Guilt 4-1-99; Collier County, FL warrant for arrest of DRW for violating probation 4-30-91.

Published sources: www.lib.utexas.edu/geo.

245   risqué photos - Through countless moves, David clung to a dozen photo albums put together over the years since his incarceration for the Gibbs murder; several contained many pictures of his lovers when they were children and teenagers.

Chapter 56 ~ Downward Spiral

Unpublished sources: Interviews; Complaint for TRO, Misappropriation of Trade Secret 5-8-92 (re Massen); ltr Christos to South Florida AA chapter 10-18-91; ltr JGM to Golly 2-8-92; ltr Christos to JGM 9-3-92; ltr Divoky to Stein 6-28-91; Divoky to Stein 6-24-91; ltr JGM to Houston chapter members June 1991; ltr JGM to Christos 7-19-91; ltr Christos to JGM 7-21-91; ltr Golly to JGM 11-16-91; ltr JGM to Golly 3-5-92; ltr Golly to Musy 3-21-92; ltr Golly to JGM 6-24-92; AAS 8-23-92; AAS 9-4-92; *Lemon v. Kurtzman* 403 US 602 (1971); *Lee v. Weisman*, 505 U.S. 577 (1992); Complaint for Malicious Prosecution and Civil Conspiracy to File a Malicious Lawsuit 4-11-91; Answer to Counter Complaint and Affirmative Defenses 9-13-88; Answer of Vinson 6-27-91; ltr Kent to Massen 6-2-93; ltr JGM to Jones 6-3-92; ltr Sanders to former chapter heads February 1992; ltr JGM to Sanders 6-20-92; ltr JGM to Sanders 12-24-92; ltr Sanders to JGM 12-28-92; ltr JGM to Sanders 12-28-92; ltr Sanders to JGM 3-2-93; ltr JGM to Sanders 5-21-93; ltr JGM to Sanders 6-3-93; ltr JGM to Sanders 7-23-93; ltr JGM to Sanders 12-26-93; JGM's statement to police 4-13-94; ltr Sanders to Gay Atheists; Order After Hearing Regarding Order to Show Cause, 6-9-93; Declaration of Withers in Support of Opposition to Motion to Strike Jury Request 8-6-93.

Published sources: AAIN February 1992; AAIN January 1992; AAS 1-10-92; AA Mag March 1991; San Antonio Light 6-24-92; AAIN July 1992; Times News 5-6-93; Danville Register & Bee 5-7-93; unlabeled AP story 8-10-85; WTH 8-26-85; Dallas Life 12-15-91; AA Vets Newsletter 4-18-91 [misdated 1990]; AAIN April 1991; Arizona Republic 4-6-91; New Times 4-17-91 through 4-23-91; AAS 11-1-93; AAIN December 1990; Rappoport; Setting the Record Straight; AAIN July 1990; AAIN June 1995 Freethought Today December 1993.

247   using her mailing list - By the end of 1991, Garth and Madalyn were planning to sue heads of numerous defunct chapters they thought were using old mailing lists to compete with AA. In their crosshairs were San Diego, San Francisco, Los Angeles, Miami, and St. Petersburg.
247   *Lee v. Weisman* - This case was important because it challenged a three-part test the Supreme Court had been using since 1971 to decide church-state separation cases. That test, called the *Lemon v. Kurtzman* precedent, said that any government practice had to have a secular purpose, couldn't advance or inhibit religion, and couldn't foster excessive entanglement with religion. Numerous decisions since 1971 had applied the test, and *Lee v. Weisman* was challenging it as a standard.
248   handing out Bibles in Red Square - Bill had competition; as Russia's generations of Stalin-and-Lenin-engineered spiritual blank slates, now reincarnated through *perestroika*, hungered for the Word, Bill was challenged by the Muslims and Jews and Catholics and Hare Krishnas and Mormons and Buddhists and Pentecostals and Moonies who were also elbowing their way in.

249 "the most bizarre demonstration" - AA Vets Newsletter 4-18-91.

249 "We simply have to change the system" - New Times 4-17-91 through 4-23-91.

249 "commenting on the size of her son's testicles" - AA Vets Newsletter 4-18-91.

249 "fucking coward" - AA Vets Newsletter 4-18-91.

250 back to New Zealand for good - The O'Hairs weren't eager for Jack Jones to find out about the *Weisman* decision. They had been plying him with letters describing the vendetta aimed at them directly from the White House, and had predicted *Lee v. Weisman* would go against the Cause. Garth even implied it was an AA case, and said a negative ruling would moot six other AA cases headed for the Supreme Court. The positive ruling took some of the starch out of the portrait of extreme persecution they'd been painting for Jones.

250 "ever claimed any interest in the Truth Seeker" - Setting the Record Straight.

Chapter 57 ~ Just Do Your Job and Leave

Unpublished sources: Karr trial notes; Karr trial transcript; Interviews; GGM; FBI report 2-3-99; Motion to Proceed with Adjudication of Guilt 4-1-99; DRW Personal Bond; Notice to Appear 6-29-98; ltr JGM to Sanders 12-26-93; ltr Kent to Massen 10-14-93; ltr JGM to Jones 5-21-93; ltr MMO to Jones 6-8-93; ltr MMO to Jones 6-8-93; ltr JGM to Jones 6-3-92; ltr MMO to Jones 6-29-93.

Published sources: AAS 1-31-93; DT 3-6-00; AAS 10-15-98; Houston Chronicle 12-29-96.

Chapter 58 ~ Firings and Thefts

Unpublished sources: Interviews; GGM; ltr JGM to Nalls 9-16-93; ltr Nalls to Steamer 9-18-93; Nalls declaration ca. November 1993; ltr Lynch to Nalls 9-29-93; ltr Steamer to MMO 1-19-93; ltr JGM to Steamer 2-19-93; Steamer "Addition to Fact Finding Sheet" 2-22-93; statement from Steamer n.d., ca. February 1993; Karr trial notes; Karr trial transcript; affidavit DRW re polygraph, 5-2-94; ltr Travis to Watson 10-24-95; incomplete ltr MMO to Swan 8-13-94; Motion to Proceed with Adjudication of Guilt 4-1-99; APD fax to MacCormack 4-14-99; Government's Notice of Intent to Offer Rule 404(b) Evidence, 1-23-01; ltr Travis to O'Hairs 10-24-95; ltr JGM to Sanders 12-26-93; ltr Rush to Musy 6-10-91; ltr Kent to Massen 8-3-93; ltr Travis to Cushman 11-11-95; ltr MMO to Jones 1-28-94; JGM statement to APD 4-13-94; Motion to Prevent Transfer or Disposal of Assets; Notice to Appear 6-29-98; Opinion 11-16-94; FBI report 3-3-99; ltr DRW to ARS 5-26-02; Personal Bond of David Waters 4-28-94; ltr Kent to Steamer 5-12-94, attached to incomplete ltr Kent to Steamer 6-1-93; Affidavit for Warrant of Arrest and Detention 41-4-94; ltr Jones to JGM 7-4-94; ltr JGM to Jones 7-10-94; ltr Jones to JGM 7-20-94; ltr MMO to Taliaferro 8-10-94; ltr JGM to Etter 12-28-91; ltr Kent to Massen 5-10-94; ltr Kent to Massen 10-14-93; ltr JGM to Jones 7-10-94; ltr Kent to Massen 9-9-93; ltr Ferris to Forsythe 5-9-94; ltr JGM to Case, 7-27-94; ltr JGM to DA of Travis Co. 3-11-95; Forsythe Motion to Withdraw; ltr JGM to DA of Travis Co. 1-30-95; ltr JGM to DA of Travis Co. 3-8-95; Declaration of Schutzman 8-19-97; Declaration of Schutzman 7-24-97; ltr Travis to Cushman 11-11-95; ltr MMO to Etter 5-24-95.

Published sources: AAS 11-1-93; Setting the Record Straight; AAS 12-20-93; AA Mag July 1986; Action Magazine March 2001; NYT 10-4-00; AAIN March 1994; AAS 9-16-94; Rappoport; Dallas Observer 4-1-99; AAIN April 1994; AAIN July 1995; AAIN December 1994; Aus Chron 5-3-96; AAS 5-18-96; Detroit News 4-11-99; AAS 4-18-99; VF March 1997; AAS 4-18-99; Rashidi; Rappoport; Elias.

255 storage bills paid - The official story was that the library was being stored because GHQ was being sold, and that the secrecy surrounding its storage was because it was so valuable, AA shouldn't broadcast where it was.

257 "Off the bench he is one of the" - Elias.

257 "Why don't you run his prints?" - The police did send Waters' prints to the FBI and requested his history, but the FBI's files were not computerized yet. So, without all of his priors to undermine it, his story rang true.

259 USA had in its accounts - The accounts were at Bank of New Zealand and New Zealand Guardian Trust.

259 what the hell was going on - Jones had USA Inc.'s power of attorney.

259 Nobody would want it - Commercial broker Robert Knight was asked to list GHQ in 1994; the building looked good, but the neighborhood and in-your-face screeds on the walls were a liability.

"I looked around and then went back in and met Madalyn . . . I said they should mow, weed, and — take the posters down, because they wanted people to focus on the property, not the message on the walls." Madalyn said no, to hell with any ignorant fool who might be offended by them.

Knight observed, "It's interesting that you'd be so intolerant, you being a champion of the first amendment and all." Oh yeah? she said. "Well, tell you what—you're fired."

259 stolen the library computer at [Truth Seeker's] behest - Just when the computer disappeared, an ad appeared in a freethought publication describing a new facility-to-be in Buffalo—the J. H. Johnson Freethought and Humanist Library. It sounded exactly like CESAALA, and the Buffalo area was where Madalyn's old nemesis, Paul Kurtz, was building his research facility. So Withers and True, Madalyn surmised, were expecting to win, seize CESAALA, and make a deal with Kurtz. After the hung jury, the ad did not reappear.

Chapter 59 ~ "I have lived a long, long time."

Unpublished sources: Interviews; Karr trial transcript; ltr JGM to Sanders 7-23-93; ltr MMO to Etter 5-24-95; ltr MMO to Schmuck 8-18-95; ltr MMO to Etter 8-18-95; ltr Sanders to Gay Atheists, Sanders' Will; unlabeled clip 6-22-95; ltr Travis to ARS 4-6-01; Video of speech at South Texas College of Law, ca. July 1995; ltr JGM to Board 7-31-95; ltr JGM to Jones 8-26-95; ltr JGM to employees 8-27-95; FBI report 11-18-99; ltr JGM to Tyson 9-7-95; ltr Etter to JGM 10-3-95; Search Warrant Affidavit 3-23-99; ltr Travis to O'Hairs 10-24-95, attachment; ltr Travis to Watson 10-24-95; ltr Travis to Cushman 11-11-95; ltr Via to Tucker 6-20-97; ltr Griffith Small Animal Hospital to RMOH 10-14-95; APD Incident Report 11-2-95; Collier Co., FL Sheriff's Dept. Missing Person Report 5-4-96; Collier Co., FL Sheriff's Dept. Missing Person Report 5-31-96.

Published sources: AAIN June 1995 (insert); VF March 1997; Richmond Times-Dispatch 9-29-95; USA Today 9-29-95; New York Post 9-29-95; Plotting Atheist Funerals; WP 10-22-95; WP 10-22-95; Dallas News 10-3-95; Detroit News 4-11-99; Aus Chron 11-20-98; Houston Chronicle 12-29-96; Detroit News 10-27-95; SAEN 12-16-95; DMN 12-16-95; New Braunfels Herald-Zeitung 12-15-95; Aus Chron 5-3-96.

264 "I wouldn't be surprised" - WP 10-22-95.

265 "half-eaten breakfast" - It later turned out that this was a false detail planted by Spike Tyson to see who might come forward and refute it. The only person who did was David Waters. In a November 1998 Austin Chronicle interview, he said the O'Hairs "didn't rush out of here leaving breakfast on the table."

Chapter 60 ~ A Lot of Reason to Kill Someone

Unpublished sources: Interviews; Dallas Co. Sheriff report 3-3-99; United Secularists of America IRS Form 990, Statement 13, 11-15-96; Karr trial transcript; ltr MacCormack to Johnson 12-5-96; MacCormack-Young agreement document 12-6-96; Search Warrant Affidavit 3-23-99; O'Hair home inventory auction lists; APD press release 2-5-97; Note Young to MacCormack 4-14-97; ltr Young to McNutt 12-8-97; Notice of Coin Seizure, 1-26-98; Dallas Co. Sheriff report 2-14-99.

Published sources: Houston Chronicle 12-29-96; SAEN 8-11-96; SAEN 1-3-96; SAEN 10-2-96; WTH 10-3-96; Freethought Today December 1999; AA News 12-9-96; SAEN 12-8-96; AAS 10-3-96; Aus Chron 5-3-96; Houston Chronicle 2-5-97; AP 10-2-96; Chi Trib 10-3-96; San Diego Union-Tribune 10-5-96; AA News n.d.; AAS 1-4-97; AAS 1-22-97; WTH 1-23-97; AAS 1-17-97; AAS 2-1-97; Houston Chronicle 2-19-97; AAS 2-19-97; Sun 3-2-97; AAS 3-22-97; AP 3-22-97; AAS 3-21-97; Time 2-10-97; AAIN December 1996; AAS 1-24-97; SAEN n.d. ca. 1-28-97; SAEN 2-6-97; Houston Chronicle 2-5-97; WP 8-17-99; SAEN 2-1-98.

267 "got some friendly advice" - Freethought Today December 1999.

267 "If they misled us" - SAEN 12-8-96.

268 "It's not against the law in Texas" - AAS 10-3-96.

268 "a lot of reason to kill someone" - SAEN 12-8-96.

269 "money-grubbing grave robber" - Aus Chron 5-3-96.

269 rooting around in their books - The grueling IRS audits had made it clear that the family routinely mingled personal and corporate monies, so, as guardian, Bill would likely have been given access to all the records, not just personal ones.

269 "everything conceivable" - Houston Chronicle 12-29-96.

269 "They were being very cagey" - Time 2-10-97.

270 "I can't imagine anybody inheriting" - Time 2-10-97.

270 "I think my mother would step forward" - Houston Chronicle 12-29-96.

270 "There were pictures, notebooks" - Houston Chronicle 2-19-97.

270 auction was halted - The date was set for Saturday, March 22, 1997.

271 "We're at a dead end" - SAEN 2-6-97.
272 cherry-picked Greystone - Of Madalyn's diaries, begun in 1953, the years 1959 to 1972 and 1990 to August 1995 — the most significant periods of her life — ended up in Johnson's possession.

Chapter 61 ~ "It was a kidnapping."

Unpublished sources: Interviews; Karr trial transcript; ltr Young to MacCormack 1-27-98; Declaration of Schutzman 7-24-97; ltr Young to Arenson 6-7-98; Petry Travel document 6-8-98; ltr Young to McNutt 6-10-98; ltr Young to Tucker 6-8-98; Car Talk documents 8-4-98; Karr Voluntary Statement #1 3-24-99; IRS CID Memo 2-18-99; ltr Young to Baker 8-11-98.

Published sources: SAEN 8-16-98; SAEN 2-1-98; Aus Chron 5-3-96; UPI 12-1-97; Kansas City Star 10-3-95; Freethought Today 12-99; SAEN 5-17-00.

Chapter 62 ~ Dallas County Detectives and the FBI

Unpublished sources: Karr trial transcript; ltr Preston to ARS 2-10-00; SAEN 8-16-98; Interviews; DRW telephone records; ltr Young to Martin 8-17-98; list of Madalyn's drugs; JGM credit card receipts; Dallas County Sheriff's report 10-14-98; Autopsy Report (Danny Fry) 11-17-95; ltr MacCormack to Dallas Co. Medical Examiner 10-2-98; Dallas County Sheriff's report 10-5-98; Dallas County Sheriff's report 10-20-98; Motion to Proceed with Adjudication of Guilt 4-1-99; Testimony of Edmond Martin Before Grand Jury 1-12-7-99; Search Warrant Affidavit 3-23-99.

Published sources: VF March 1997; Aus Chron 11-20-98; AAS 12-23; Freethought Today December 1999; DFP 4-3-99; DFP 6-22-99; Dallas Observer 4-1-99; DMN 10-2-98; SAEN 1-31-99; AAS 10-15-98; SAEN 8-16-98.

278 "kicked back somewhere" - SAEN 8-16-98.
279 several hours of free calls - When the calling card's free hour dwindled, Young would pay for another hour.
280 "they were kind of daring us" - DMN 10-2-98.
281 headed for the Warren Inn - Tim Young later discovered that the Warren complex was actually three separate entities, with slightly different names. Poring through old electric company bills, he stumbled on the 1991 account of [Colleen Kay Smith], with a roommate — David Waters. It gave him chills to discover that Waters had lived at the Warren Inn before.

Chapter 63 ~ Prose and Cons

Unpublished sources: Karr trial transcript; GGM; Interviews; Motion to Proceed with Adjudication of Guilt 4-1-99; ltr Preston to DRW 2-23-97; ltr Preston to DRW 9-3-97; ltr Preston to Eakin 3-16-98; ltr Preston to DRW 4-1-98; email Waters to group 11-7-97; IRS CID Memo 4-7-99; IRS CID Memo 4-5-99; FBI report 2-8-99 through 2-11-99; Government's Notice of Intent to Offer Rule 404(b) Evidence, 1-23-01; Search Warrant Affidavit 3-23-99; FBI report 2-22-99; FBI report 8-17-99; FBI report 3-3-99; Goff Affidavit 5-10-00; Notice To Appear 6-29-98; FBI report 5-26-99; FBI report 5-27-99; FBI report 7-12-99; ltr CKS to ARS 5-20-02; FBI report 2-3-99.

Published sources: Houston Chronicle 1-31-97; SAEN 5-1-99; AAS 4-18-99; SAEN 8-16-98; Aus Chron 11-20-98.

282 behind on his restitution - Waters also paid community supervision fees every month.

Chapter 64 ~ For Sale to the Highest Bidder

Unpublished sources: Interviews; Karr trial notes; O'Hair home inventory auction lists; Dallas Co. Sheriff's Dept. report 1-27-99; Search Warrant Affidavit 3-23-99.

Published sources: SAEN 1-7-99; AAS 1-24-99; SAEN 1-24-99; NYT 1-25-99; Sun 3-2-97; SAEN 4-20-99; AP 5-5-99; Johnson.

285 "very troubled and disturbed woman" - Johnson.

Chapter 65 ~ What Colleen Saw

Unpublished sources: Karr trial transcript; Interviews; APD log of Chavez call 1:29 a.m. 2-2-99; Motion to Proceed with Adjudication of Guilt 4-1-99; FBI report 2-8-99 through 2-11-99; FBI report 2-3-99; FBI report 8-17-99; FBI report 2-4-99; Dallas Co. Sheriff's Dept. report 2-4-99; Search Warrant Affidavit 3-23-99; Dallas Co. Sheriff's Dept. report 2-8-99; FBI report 2-21-99; APD fax to MacCormack 4-14-99; Government's Notice of Intent to Offer Rule 404(b) Evidence, 1-23-01; email Waters to group 11-7-97; Travis' statement to police 4-9-94; GGM; ltr CKS to ARS 7-2-01; Dallas Co. Sheriff's Dept. report 2-2-99; FBI report 2-23-99; FBI report 3-3-99; FBI report 8-10-99; FBI report 2-22-99.

Published sources: SAEN 1-31-99; SAEN 5-19-00; DFP 4-3-99; SAEN 12-28-99; SAEN 8-12-99; SAEN 5-17-00; AAS 8-12-99; Los Angeles Daily Journal 8-12-99; AAS 5-18-96.

288 "despite the dogged efforts" - SAEN 1-31-99.
290 "He said often that he'd like to torture her" - SAEN 8-12-99.

Chapter 66 ~ Happy Birthday

Unpublished sources: Karr trial transcript; Interviews; Dallas Co. Sheriff's Dept. report 2-12-99; Dallas Co. Sheriff's Dept. report 2-16-99; Karr trial transcript; Dallas Co. Sheriff's Dept. report 2-14-99; Search Warrant Affidavit 3-23-99; Dallas Co. Sheriff's Dept. report 3-3-99; FBI report 2-12-99; FBI report 2-9-99; Motion to Proceed with Adjudication of Guilt 4-1-99; Return Inventory of DRW's items; DOJ press release 5-27-99; Waters Indictment 3-24-99; Dallas Co. Sheriff's Dept. report 3-25-99; Osborne trial notes; Dallas Co. Sheriff's Dept. report 3-31-99; Government's Combined Motion and Brief for Reconsideration of the Court's Suppression Order; O'Leary Affidavit 3-25-99; Criminal Complaint 3-25-99; Karr Voluntary Statement #1 3-24-99; Attachment to Motion to Reconsider Suppression Order; Supplemental Violation Report; affidavit DRW re polygraph, 5-2-94.

Published sources: unlabeled clip 3-2-00; AAS 4-28-00; AAS 5-24-00; NYT 3-25-99; DMN 3-11-99; AAS 12-9-99; DMN 12-8-99; Dallas Observer 4-1-99; SAEN 3-25-99; DFP 4-3-99; DFP 6-22-99; AP 4-5-99; SAEN 1-4-00.

300 eight pages - In early 2000, Karr's statement to Ed Martin was finally released to the media.
300 "gullible, out-of-touch errand boy" - SAEN 1-4-00.

Chapter 67 ~ No Bodies

Unpublished sources: Karr trial notes; Karr trial transcript; Interviews; Search Warrant Affidavit 3-23-99; FBI report 4-7-99; Dallas Co. Sheriff's Dept. report 4-7-99; O'Leary hearing transcript 3-26-99; Karr Indictment 4-21-99; DOJ press release 5-27-99; FBI report 2-22-99.

Published sources: AP 4-5-99; SAEN 4-5-99; DFP 4-3-99; AP 4-4-99; SAEN 4-10-99; Sun 4-8-99; Philadelphia Enquirer 4-18-99; USA Today 12-9-99; DMN 12-8-99; SAEN 5-6-99; AAS 4-30-99; SAEN 4-8-99; DFP 6-22-99; LAT 5-28-99; AAS 5-27-99; Dallas Observer 3-9-00; Aus Chron 6-4-99; AAS 8-12-99; SAEN 4-6-99; SAEN 5-23-00; Valley Morning Star, Harlingen, TX 5-24-00; SAEN 5-27-99; UPI 8-20-99; SAEN 4-2-99; SAEN 4-23-99; AAS 4-11-199; AP 5-27-99; AAS 12-9-99; LAT 5-28-99; DFP 5-28-99; AAS 5-28-99.

301 "the headline of a lifetime" - SAEN 4-10-99.
302 "They've got 30 pictures of him" - SAEN 5-27-99.
302 "Without the pictures, we had a chance" - SAEN 5-27-99.
302 Waters pled guilty - The plea was to being a convicted felon in possession of firearm ammunition and transporting weapons across state lines.
303 "a script for Oliver Stone's next movie" - LAT 5-28-99.

Chapter 68 ~ Hell Hath No Fury

Unpublished sources: Interviews; Karr trial transcript; Search Warrant Affidavit 3-23-99; Return Inventory of DRW's items; Motion to Proceed with Adjudication of Guilt 4-1-99; Government's Notice of Intent to Offer Rule 404(b) Evidence, 1-23-01; Dallas Co. Sheriff's Dept. report 3-25-99; Osborne trial notes; Dallas Co. Sheriff's Dept. report 3-31-99; Government's Combined Motion and Brief for Reconsideration of the Court's Suppression Order; O'Leary Affidavit 3-25-99; Criminal Complaint 3-25-99; Karr Voluntary Statement #1 3-24-99; AP 3-26-99; DFP 4-3-99; O'Leary hearing transcript 3-26-99;

Supplemental Violation Report; FBI report 4-7-99; Dallas Co. Sheriff's Dept. report 4-7-99; Dallas Co. Sheriff's Dept. report 4-12-99; fax APD to MacCormack 4-14-99; Karr Indictment 4-21-99; DOJ press release 5-27-99; ltr DRW to Preston 6-3-99; ltr DRW to Preston 6-16-99; Subpoena for diaries 4-6-99; ltr DA to Brown 6-30-99; DOJ press release 7-20-99; APD O'Hair sightings list; Government's Motion for Upward Departure and Imposition of Consecutive Sentence 8-18-99; Sentencing Before the Honorable Sam Sparks 8-20-99; DOJ press release 8-20-99; Karr Indictment 12-7-99.

Published sources: SAEN 6-2-99; AAS 12-9-99; Waters indictment 3-24-99; DMN 12-8-99; Dallas Observer 4-1-99; SAEN 3-25-99; UPI 8-20-99; DFP 4-3-99; NYT 3-25-99; DFP 6-22-99; AP 4-5-99; SAEN 4-2-99; SAEN 4-5-99; AP 4-4-99; SAEN 4-10-99; sun 4-8-99; Philadelphia Enquirer 4-18-99 ; SAEN 4-6-99; AAS 4-11-99; SAEN 5-6-99; SAEN 4-8-99; AAS 4-30-99; SAEN 4-20-99; AP 5-5-99; AAS 4-22-99; SAEN 5-3-99; Buffalo News 4-25-99; DMN 4-25-99; SAEN 4-23-99; SAEN 5-1-99; SAEN 5-26-99; AP 5-27-99; TM May 1999; SAEN 5-27-99; LAT 5-28-99; AAS 5-27-99; AAS 5-28-99; DFP 5-28-99; SAEN 6-2-99; SAEN 7-24-99; Aus Chron 6-4-99; AAS 8-12-99; SAEN 4-27-99; SAEN 6-21-99; AAS 7-20-99; Freethought Today December 1999; SAEN 11-7-99; AAS 4-22-99; SAEN 5-3-99; SAEN 7-20-99; AAS 7-21-99; Dallas Observer 7-29-99; *Vanished* transcript 7-22-99; Los Angeles Daily Journal 8-12-99; SAEN 8-12-99; SAEN 8-19-99; AAS 9-7-00; SAEN 3-15-00; AAS 12-9-99; AAS 12-8-99; USA Today 12-9-99; SAEN 12-8-99; SAEN 12-9-99; Dallas Observer 12-16-99; NYT 12-8-99; SAEN 3-29-00; AAS 3-30-00; SAEN 4-15-00; AAS 4-5-00; SAEN 3-2-00; SAEN 3-9-00; Dallas Observer 3-9-00; AAS 4-28-00; SAEN 5-23-00; AAS 5-24-00; SAEN 3-29-00; AAS 5-10-00; SAEN 5-15-00; SAEN 5-16-00; Valley Morning Star, Harlingen, TX 5-17-00; SAEN 5-17-00.

306 "Hell hath no fury like a woman scorned." - SAEN 8-12-99.
307 "How odd is that?" - Dallas Observer 12-16-99.
307 Mills and Carruth failed to reach a deal - Under something called the Bruton Rule, Carruth could only use Karr's confession if Karr testified against Waters. Carruth could have made such a deal with Karr from the beginning. But Karr had insisted he be let off the hook on any killings, and Carruth believed he had participated in them. With Colleen's testimony, Carruth wagered, he could get two killers. First put Karr away, then conduct the same trial against Waters.
307 "rocket docket" - SAEN 3-29-00.
307 "threaten him...hoping he'll tell" - SAEN 12-9-99.

Chapter 69 ~ Star Witness

Unpublished sources: Karr trial notes; Karr trial transcript; Interviews; ltr DRW to Mills 6-22-00; ltr DRW to Preston 6-3-99; ltr DRW to Preston 6-16-99.

Published sources: AAS 5-15-00; SAEN 5-17-00; AAS 5-24-00; SAEN 5-23-00; AAS 5-25-00; AAS 5-19-00; SAEN 5-19-00; AAS 5-23-00; WTH 5-24-00; Valley Morning Star, Harlingen, TX 5-24-00; SAEN 5-26-00, WTH 5-26-00; SAEN 5-30-00; SAEN 6-2-00; AAS 5-31-00; SAEN 6-3-00; AAS 6-1-00; WTH 6-6-00; AAS 7-2-00; Dallas Observer 6-15 through 6-21, 2000, Aus Chron 6-19-00; AAS 7-12-00; Secular Nation July-September 2000; SAEN 7-12-00; SAEN 8-18-00; DMN 8-18-00; DT 8-18-00; AP 8-17-00; SAEN 7-24-99.

308 "staring" at his client with his "beady eyes" - AAS 5-15-00.
311 "little more than a figure in a gray suit" - SAEN 5-17-00.
311 "the blood was just as likely from one of *them*" - AAS 5-24-00.
311 "Only a 3-year-old daughter" - SAEN 5-23-00.
311 three other prison informants - Aaron Morris, Brian Chase, and Jason Cross.
311 "All we got for this was a half million" - SAEN 5-25-00.
312 they left to deliberate - The charges were: Kidnapping, Conspiracy to Interfere With Commerce by Robbery, Interstate Travel in Aid of Racketeering Enterprise, Conspiracy to Engage in Monetary Transaction in Criminally Derived Property, and Interstate Transportation of Stolen Property.
313 two life terms - The convictions meant at least one mandatory life term. Judge Sparks was dismissive of the defense that Karr hadn't done anything violent enough to trigger the three-strikes law. Nonsense, he said; Karr got out on April Fool's day 1995 and four months later was deep into this crime. Mills said Karr would appeal, but it was another vise for him: under federal law, he had a year from his sentencing to cut his jail time by "substantially" helping prosecutors. Should he testify against Waters? Or go for the appeal, which would use up his year? He chose the latter, and lost.
313 "He should be fried" - SAEN 8-18-00.

Chapter 70 ~ A Small Corner of the Outdoors

Unpublished sources: Interviews; Osborne trial notes; DRW confession 1-24-01 through 2-2-01; ltr DRW to ARS 5-26-02; ltr DRW to ARS 4-29-02; ltr Rush to ARS 3-9-01; Judgment in A Criminal Case, 2-7-01; Glassman photos; Forensics report 3-5-01; DOJ press release 3-15-01.

Published sources: AAS 9-7-00; Daily Breeze 9-20-00; DMN 9-20-00; SAEN 9-20-00; SAEN 11-29-00; SAEN 12-20-00; AP 12-20-00; Aus Chron 12-29-00; AAS 9-20-00; AAS 1-4-01; SAEN 1-4-01; AAS 4-26-00; SAEN 1-23-01; AAS 1-24-01; AP undated clip ca. 1-25-01; AAS 1-25-01; SAEN 1-25-01; SAEN 1-30-01; SAEN 2-1-01; AAS 1-30-01; DMN 2-9-01; Daily Breeze 1-28-01; AAS 1-28-01; WP 1-28-01; SAEN 1-28-01; SAEN 1-29-01; AAS 1-29-01; Newsweek 2-2-01; People 2-12-01; SAEN 2-18-01; SAEN 3-17-01; Sun 3-16-01; AAS 3-16-01; unlabeled clip ca. 3-24-01, AP 3-24-01; Sun 3-24-01; SAEN 3-27-01; Plotting Atheist Funerals; AAS 8-8-00.

314 indicted, for fraud - Osborne used not only a false Social Security number to rent the large storage unit, but a false address and telephone number. His stepdaughter Jamie Sipes said he had used the false information to get her into a better high school and was simply still carrying it when he rented the unit.

315 more afraid of Waters than of prison - Unless Karr was let off on murder charges, he had little to gain by cooperating except to earn Waters' wrath. Carruth declined to let him off, gambling that he could convict Waters even without Karr's testimony.

315 never revealed...who came forward - Cowling said only that it was a male who had no role in the Karr trial, who had been incarcerated with Waters, and who came forward under Texas' Crimestoppers program, which worked only inside the prison system.

316 "man who lived his life publicly despising her" - AP 3-24-01.

316 "Ellen wants to use their dead bodies to raise money" - AP 3-24-01.

316 Madalyn's biographer - The author.

317 "William J. Murray III has been a traitor" - Plotting Atheist Funerals.

317 "very robust skull" - Forensics report 3-5-01.

317 "there will be no tombstone" AAS 3-16-01.

318 "I want a little place" - Plotting Atheist Funerals.

Chapter 71 ~ Unanswered Questions

Unpublished sources: Interviews; DOJ press release 3-30-01.

Published sources: AAS 1-30-01.

319 20 years - The prosecutors promised to ask Travis County and other jurisdictions not to charge Waters, but they couldn't force them not to, so in the unlikely event he outlived his sentence, a murder charge could be brought by Dallas or Bexar Counties. He was also to pay total restitution of $563,685.42 to United Secularists of America and the O'Hairs' receivers.

319 "You do the math" - AAS 1-30-01.

320 what really happened with the gold? - No one believed the thieves just happened onto the storage locker. A bartender at the Poodle Dog reported seeing "three Mexicans" during the fall of 1995, but she didn't think David set it up; "David would never trust a Mexican. He's done hard prison time. That is just something that you come out with." "I am wondering if maybe [Colleen] had a little plan going on and it back-fired," said a Poodle Dog regular. "Maybe she took money for [telling] them where the coins were or passed the info on through someone else." Speculation continues, though Colleen denies ever having but the one gold coin David gave her.

Chapter 72 ~ Father Prison

Unpublished sources: Interviews; ltr DRW to ARS 3-25-02; ltr DRW to ARS 4-29-02; ltr DRW to ARS 5-26-02; Government's Notice of Intent to Offer Rule 404(b) Evidence, 1-23-01.

Published sources: The Big House; AAS 2-4-03.

323 He spoke worshipfully of Marti - But court documents said he'd told a fellow inmate he was enraged when she left him, and he'd had her killed, and then somehow pinned it on Charles Silagy. He scoffed at that, but Colleen said, "That did cross my mind from time to time. That he might have [had Marti killed]. 'Cause he will keep a secret, you know."

Chapter 73 ~ "That smell stayed on me for a long time"

Unpublished sources: DRW confession 1-24-01 through 2-2-01 (this is the source of all quotes in this chapter); Griffith Small Animal Hospital medical record 8-29-95 to 10-2-95; DRW Statement 4-24-01.

Published sources: AAS 4-18-02; PJS 4-17-02; PJS 4-18-02.

332   smothered with a pillow - To fellow inmate Jason Cross, Karr pinned Robin's rape on David, but Karr was the one with rape in his past. Waters had never had that M.O. Under pressure to change his story, Waters said he'd made up the Robin story to get even with Karr, but given the evidence, that seemed unlikely.

332   they were capital crimes - Capital because they were committed during the commission of another felony. Of course, there was an obvious way for both of David's stories to be true: he *had* intended to kill the O'Hairs from the start, but was forced to speed things up with Robin's untimely death. However, he never volunteered that explanation, nor was it sought. And it would mean that Danny Fry's murder was planned, too. There was no evidence of this degree of advance planning.

Chapter 74 - "God isn't a merciful God"

Unpublished sources: ltr Karr to ARS 12-9-03; ltr Karr to ARS 7-22-03; ltr Karr to ARS 9-7-03; ltr Karr to ARS 9-24-03; ltr Karr to ARS 10-20-03.

Published sources: DMN 8-16-00.

Bibliography

Books and Cited Articles/Documents

Aiken, William Earl, *The Roots Grow Deep*. Cleveland, OH: Lezius-Hiles Co., 1957.

Anthony, Rey, *The Housewife's Handbook on Selective Promiscuity*. Tucson, AZ: Seymour Press, 1961.

Baron, Charles and Lawrence Friedman, *The Body Politic and the Social Contract*, citing the Massachusetts Constitution.

Barson, Michael, *Better Red Than Dead: A Nostalgic Look at the Golden Years of Russia Phobia, Red-baiting, and Other Commie Madness*. New York: Hyperion, 1992.

Bexte, Martina, "Background Information Relating to Southeast Asia and Vietnam" (3rd Revised Edition). Washington, D.C.: U.S. Government Printing Office July 1967. © Pagewise, Inc. 2002

Bilstein, Roger, *The American Aerospace Industry*. New York: Twayne Publishers, 1996.

Biography Index. New York: H. W. Wilson Co., 1977, 1980, 1983, 1984, 1986, 1993.

Biography News. Detroit. Gale Research, 1975.

Bozarth, Richard, *A Case Against Madalyn Murray O'Hair*. Austin, TX: self-published, 1987.

———. *Madalyn Murray O'Hair: A Mouth That Roars*. The American Rationalist, January-February 1983.

———. *Madalyn Murray O'Hair: A Mouse That Roars* unpublished manuscript.

Burgess, James E., Th.G., *America's Most Hated Woman*. Anderson, SC: self published booklet, ca. 1969.

Caldwell's Atlas of Clearfield County. Condit, OH: J. A. Caldwell, 1878.

Cannon, James P., *The Revolutionary Party: Its Role in the Struggle for Socialism*. New York: Pathfinder Press, 1975.

Carleton, Don E., *Red Scare*. Austin, TX: Texas Monthly Press, 1985.

Churchill, Ward and Jim Vander Wall, *The COINTELPRO Papers: Documents from the FBI's Secret Wars Against Dissent in the United States*. Cambridge, MA: South End Press 2002.

City of Rossford, Ohio, As I Recall. Rossford, OH: City of Rossford, 1999.

Clayton, James, *The Making of Justice*. New York: Dutton and Co., 1966.

Conrad, Jane, *Excommunicated by Mad Madalyn*. Unpublished manuscript, 1982.

———. *Mad Madalyn and Born-Again Bill*. Unpublished manuscript, 1982.

———. *Mad Madalyn: Madalyn Murray O'Hair, Her Family, Her Problems, the Truth and the Lies*. Brighton, CO: self-published, 1983.

———. *Pillars of Religion: Ignorance, Indoctrination, Inadequacy*. Brighton, CO: self-published, 1978.

CRS Report on History of Federal Taxes for Congress, January 19, 2001. www.philanthropicadvisor.com.

Current Biography Yearbook 1977. New York: H. W. Wilson Co., 1977

Davidson, James and Os Guiness, editors, *Articles of Faith, Articles of Peace: The Religious Liberty Clauses and the American Public Philosophy*. Washington, D.C.: Hunter, 1990.

"The Dust Bowl," *Smithsonian* June 1989 p. 46.

Eastland, Terry, *Religious Liberty in the Supreme Court: The Cases That Define the Debate over Church and State* (1993).

Edamaruku, Sanal, "Remembering Madalyn Murray O'Hair," *Rationalist International Bulletin* #70, April 13, 2001.

Elias, Paul, "Manual Real Profile." www.law.com, September 1999.

Elkins, Robert (see videotapes).

Fehrenbach, T. R., *Lone Star, A History of Texas and the Texans*. Avenel, NJ: Random House/Macmillan, 1968.

"Focus on Asian Studies," The Asia Society, Special Issue, No. 1, Fall 1983.

Gaustad, E. S., *Faith of Our Fathers: Religion and the New Nation*. New York: Harper & Row, 1987.

Gosse, Van, *Where the Boys are: Cuba, Cold War America and the Making of a New Left*. Verso Publishing, 1996

Hall, Kermit L., ed., *The Oxford Companion to the Supreme Court of the United States*. New York: Oxford University Press, 1992.

Hamburger, Philip, *Separation of Church and State*. Cambridge, MA: Harvard University Press 2002.

Harrington, Bob, *The Chaplain of Bourbon Street*. Old Tappan, NJ: Spire Books, 1971.
———. "Fight to the Finish" (see videotapes).
———. *Let Freedom Ring*. LP album, New Orleans, n.d.
Herndon, Bob, and Bill Faulkner, *Eight Days With Bob Harrington*. New Orleans: Bob Harrington, 1972.
Hickey, Dennis V., "The Complete Illustrated List of Vulcan Gas Company Posters and Handbills," on the web at www.faculty.smsu.edu/d/dvh804f/vulcan.htm.
The Holy Bible. London: The British and Foreign Bible Society, Oxford University Press, 1954.
Horowitz, Morton J., *The Warren Court and the Pursuit of Justice*. New York: Hill and Wang, 1998.
Jefferson, Thomas, *Letter to the Danbury Baptists*. Library of Congress Information Bulletin, June 1998.
Johnson, Olivia J., *Is Atheism Done?* www.worldnetdaily.com 1999.
Key, Francis Scott, *The Star Spangled Banner*. September 14,1814.
Klein, Jerry, *Peoria!* Peoria: Visual Communications, Inc., 1985.
Lawler, Kelly, *The Origins of Psychedelic Music in Austin, Texas, Part 5*. www.austindaze.com, 2000.
Lawrence, Don, *Freethinkers in Texas*. Compiled from the *Handbook of Texas Online*, Texas State Historical Association March 2003.
LeBeau, Brian, *The Atheist*. New York: New York University Press, 2003.
"Letter from Lhasa," *Vanity Fair*, May 1991.
Lewis, Joseph, *Ingersoll the Magnificent*. Austin, TX: American Atheist Press, 1983.
Long, Christopher, "Old Three-Hundred." *Handbook of Texas Online*, Texas State Historical Association December 2002.
Lowery, Charles D., John F. Marszalek, and Thomas A. Upchurch, *Encyclopedia of African-American Civil Rights*. Greenwood Publishing Group 2003.
Madison, James, *Annals of Congress*, Twelfth Congress part 2, 2224. A Proclamation. Messages and Papers of the Presidents, James Madison, vol. 1, p. 498, the 9th day of July, A.D. 1812.
Maverick, Maury, *Texas Iconoclast*. Ft. Worth, TX: Texas Christian University Press, 1997.
Mays, John I., *My Four Years With Madalyn Murray O'Hair, My Sister*. Unpublished manuscript, 1983.
McCabe, Joseph, *The Story Of Religious Controversy*. Boston: First Stratford, 1929.
McCollum, Vashti, *One Woman's Fight*. Boston: Beacon Press, 1952.
"Meeting Satan Herself," *I Was a Teenage Heretic*, www.CompleatHeretic.com/bio/atheist2.html#satan, 9-14-88.
Melton, J. Gordon, *Encyclopedia of American Religions*, 7th edition. Detroit: Gale Publishing, 2003.
Mills, Barbara, *And Justice For All*. Baltimore: American Literary Press, Inc., 2000.
Moehlman, Conrad H., *The Wall of Separation Between Church and State*. Boston: Beacon Press, 1951.
Murray, Jon G. and Madalyn Murray O'Hair, *All the Questions You Ever Wanted to Ask American Atheists: With All the Answers*, 2nd ed. Austin, TX: American Atheist Press, 1986.
———. *Essays on American Atheism Vols. I and 2*. Austin, TX: American Atheist Press, 1986.
———. Introduction, *The Bible Handbook*, revised edition. Austin: American Atheist Press, 1992.
Murray, William J., *My Life Without God*. Eugene, OR: Harvest House, 1992.
———. *The Church Is Not For Perfect People*. Eugene, OR: Harvest House, 1987.
———. *Let Us Pray: A Plea For Prayer in Our Schools*. New York: William Morrow and Co., 1995.
Negri, Vitali, "Freethought Leadership and the Paranoid Personality." *American Rationalist*, November 1964.
O'Hair, Madalyn Murray, *All About Atheists*. Austin, TX: American Atheist Press, 1988. [Radio series broadcasts July 13, 1970 to August 16, 1971.]
———, and Jon G. Murray, *All the Questions You Ever Wanted to Ask American Atheists: With All the Answers*, 2nd ed. Austin, TX: American Atheist Press, 1986.
———, Ed., introduction. *American Atheist Heritage: Joseph Lewis*. Austin, TX: American Atheist Press, 1981.
———. *The American Atheist Radio Series of Ingersoll the Magnificent*. Austin, TX: American Atheist Press, 1977.
———. *An Atheist Believes*. Austin, TX: American Atheist Press, 1971.
———. *An Atheist Epic: Bill Murray, the Bible, and the Baltimore Board of Education*. Austin, TX: American Atheist Press, 1970. [Reissued in 1989 as *An Atheist Epic: The Complete Unexpurgated Story of How the Bible and Prayers Were Removed From the Public Schools of the United States*.]
———. *An Atheist Looks at Women and Religion*, rev. ed. Austin, TX: American Atheist Press, 1994.
———. *An Atheist Primer*. Austin, TX: American Atheist Press, 1980.
———. *An Atheist Speaks*. Austin, TX: American Atheist Press, 1986. [Radio series broadcasts June 2, 1969 to July 6, 1970.]
———. *An Original Theory in Respect to the Origin of Religion*. Austin, TX: American Atheist Press, 1984.

————. "Atheism." *The American Rationalist*, September-October 1962.

————. *Atheist Heroes and Heroines*. Austin, TX: American Atheist Press, 1991. [Radio series broadcasts August 23, 1971 to August 26, 1972.]

————, Ed., *Atheist Magazines: A Sampling, 1927-1970*. New York: Arno Press and New York Times, 1972.

————. *Atheist Primer: Did You Know All the Gods Came From the Same Place?* (for children), Austin, TX: American Atheist Press, 1978.

————. *The Atheist World*. Austin: American Atheist Press, 1991. [Radio series broadcasts September 2, 1972 to September 1, 1973.]

————. *Atheists: the Last Minority*. Austin, TX: American Atheist Press, 1990.

———— (ed.) Charles C. Moore, *Behind the Bars*, 2nd edition. American Atheist Press, 1990.

————. *The Best of Dial-an-Atheist*. Austin, TX: American Atheist Press, 1982.

————. "Is Atheism the Religion of the Future?" *Progressive World*, July 1971.

————. Foreword, *The Bible Handbook*, revised edition. Austin: American Atheist Press, 1992.

————. *Everyday Atheism*. Austin, TX: American Atheist Press, 1975.

————. *Freedom Under Siege*. Los Angeles: J. P. Tarcher, Inc., 1974.

————. *James Licht American Atheist* Austin, TX: American Atheist Press, 1983.

————. *Jesus Christ: Super Fraud*. Austin, TX: American Atheist Press, 1984.

————. *Let Us Prey: An Atheist Looks at Church Wealth*. Austin, TX: American Atheist Press, 1970.

————. *Letters From Christians*. Austin, TX: American Atheist Press, 1973.

————. "Madalyn Murray For Miscreant," *The Realist*, September 1964.

————. *Nobody Has a Prayer*. Austin, TX: American Atheist Press, 1982.

————. *O'Hair on Prayer*. Austin, TX: American Atheist Press, 1980.

————. *Our Constitution: The Way It Was*. Austin, TX: American Atheist Press, 1988.

————. *Religious Factors in the War in Vietnam*. Austin, TX: American Atheist Press, 1975.

————, Ed., and introduction, *Robert G. Ingersoll, The Trial of C. B. Reynolds*. Austin, TX: American Atheist Press, 1986. (Also listed as *The Trial of C. B. Reynolds: Robert G. Ingersoll's Address to the Jury*.)

————. Introduction, *Sixty-Five Press Interviews With Robert G. Ingersoll*. Austin: American Atheist Press, 1983.

————. *Understanding Atheism*. Austin, TX: American Atheist Press, 1971.

————. *War in Viet Nam: The Religious Connection*, with introduction by Jon G. Murray. Austin, TX: American Atheist Press, 1982.

————. *What on Earth Is An Atheist!* Austin, TX: American Atheist Press, 1969. [Radio series broadcasts June 3, 1968 to May 26, 1969]

————. *Why I Am An Atheist*. Austin, TX: Society of Separationists, 1966. (Reissued in 1991 as *Why I Am An Atheist; Including, A History of Materialism*.)

————. *Women and Atheism: the Ultimate Liberation*. Austin, TX: American Atheist Press, 1979.

Oldmeadow, Harry, *The Western Quest for 'Secret Tibet.'* Esoterica Vol. III, 2001. Michigan State University.

Pahl, Larry, "Establishing the History of the Establishment Clause" Part Two Liberty Point Institute 2-5-1996.

"Plotting Atheist Funerals" *American Atheist* Magazine, November 1986.

Ramos, Mary G., *Texas Almanac 1998-1999*, © Dallas Morning News.

Ranters. www.exlibris.org/nonconform/engdis/ranters.html, © 1997-2003 ExLibris.org.

Rappoport, Jon, *Madalyn Murray O'Hair: the Amazing Disappearance and Possible Murder of the O'Hair Family*. San Diego, CA: Truth Seeker, 1998.

Rashidi, Runoko, *Professor John Glover Jackson (1907-1993): Humanist and Pioneer to the Past*. ©1998 Runoko Rashidi. All rights reserved. www.cwo.com/ lucumi/jackson

Ryan, William F., *Madalyn Murray O'Hair and the "Business" of Atheism*. Unpublished manuscript, 1977.

Maroon 'N Gray. Rossford, OH: 1934, 1935, 1936.

Schulz, Robert G., *The Germans: Geh Mit Ins Texas*. Self-published 2001. www.hal-pc.org/ dcrane/txgenweb/ gehmitinstexas.htm

"Setting the Record Straight." *Truth Seeker* April 1995.

"She's Fighting Our Battle." *Progressive World* August 1962

Smith, Martin R. and Ellen T. Jones, *Neophobia, Ontological Insecurity, and Existential Choice Following Trauma*. Journal of Humanistic Psychology, Newbury Park, CA: Sage Publications, 1993.

Stein, Gordon, editor, *Encyclopedia of Unbelief*. Buffalo, NY: Prometheus Books, 1985.

Straw, Albert Y., Compiler, *Some Genealogies and Family Records*. Clearfield, PA: Press of Clearfield Republican, 1931.

Sweet, William Warren, *The Story of Religion in America*. New York: Harper and Bros., 1930.
Twair, Pat McDonnell, "Maury Maverick, Jr.: A Fearless, Cantankerous, Free Thinker From Texas." *Washington Report on Middle Eastern Affairs* August-September 1997. © American Educational Trust1995-1999.
Tyson, Timothy, *Radio Free Dixie: Robert F. Williams and the Roots of Black Power*. Chapel Hill: 2001.
Van West, et al, *Tennessee Encyclopedia of History and Culture*. Nashville: Tennessee Historical Society, 1998.
Vestal, Theodore M., *The Eisenhower Court and Civil Liberties*. Westport, CT: Praeger Publishers 2002.
"War Against War," Minnesota Public Radio transcript 2000, americanradioworks.publicradio.org re vietnam.
Waters, David R., *Good Gawd, Madalyn*. Unpublished manuscript, n.d., ca. 1998.
Who's Who in America. 44th edition, 1986-1987. Wilmette, IL: Marquis Who's Who, 1988, 1982-83.
Who's Who in the World. 8th edition, 1987-1988. Wilmette, IL: Marquis Who's Who, 1989.
Who's Who of American Women. 15th edition, 1987-1988. Wilmette, IL: Marquis Who's Who, 1989.
Woodworth, Fred, *The Atheist Cult*. Tucson, AZ: The Match! Press, 1991.
World Almanac Biographical Dictionary. New York: World Almanac, 1990.
Wright, Lawrence, *Saints and Sinners*. New York: Knopf, 1993.

Websites

www.angelfire.com/pr/red/usswp/contents.htm (Communism)
www.atheism.about.com/library/glossary/© 2003 About, Inc. (Joseph Lewis)
www.ci.austin.tx.us/library/ahc/faq2.htm (Austin History Center)
The Columbia Electronic Encyclopedia, Columbia University Press.
www.exlibris.org (Ranters)
www.findlaw.com (Legal case list)
http://www.tsha.utexas.edu/handbook/online/. Handbook of Texas Online (Freethinkers in Texas)
http://history.nasa.gov. (NASA)
www.historyplace.com.
www.irs.gov (IRS)
www.law.com (Manuel Real)
www.lib.utexas.edu/geo. (Balcones Fault)
www.nps.gov/fowa/waac (WAACs)
www.philanthropicadvisor.com (History of Federal Taxes)
www.slp.org (Socialist Labor Party)
www.treas.gov/education/fact-sheets (In God We Trust)
www.va.gov/vso (Veterans' Affairs)
www.womensmemorial.org (Army)
www.law.com/regionals/ca/judges/usdistrict.

Videotapes

Atheists: Their Dilemma 4-10-93
The Atheists: What They Really Believe, Religious Freedom Coalition 1998
The Big House - Leavenworth, The History Channel © 1998.
The Disappearance of Madalyn Murray O'Hair, American Justice, A&E 11-28-01
The Disappearance of Madalyn Murray O'Hair, American Justice, A&E 10-24-02
Donahue 11-6-67
Empty Graves, City Confidential, A&E, 2001
Fight to the Finish, © Bob Harrington, ca. 1977
Let Us Pray, Gospel Films n.d.
Madalyn, Robert Elkins 1970
The Most Hated Woman in America, ABC News Nightline 8-1-98
PBS Late Night 1982 (Dennis Wholly)
Speech of Madalyn O'Hair and Jon Garth Murray at South Texas College of Law, ca. July 1995.
Vanished, ABC News 7-22-99
Without a Trace, Dateline NBC 2000

Cemeteries

New Millport Cemetery, New Millport, PA
_____ Cemetery, Austin Texas

Census Records

1900 Census, Allegheny County, PA
1910 Census, Allegheny County, PA
1920 Census, Allegheny County, PA

Index